EUROPEAN MERGER REMEDIES

As merger transactions become more complex, so do the remedies involved. This book seeks to identify and examine the most important aspects of merger remedies, which have emerged and evolved in the European Commission's policy and practice over the past 20-plus years. The in-depth analysis of applicable provisions and guidelines is structured in accordance with a typical 'remedies lifecycle': the negotiation, submission, assessment, adoption, implementation and enforcement of remedies. Furthermore, numerous conditional clearance decisions and judgments as well as studies and legal literature on the subject are described and put into a coherent analytical framework with the aim of providing as much nuance as possible in the evaluation of the Commission's past and present remedies policy and practice.

While the Commission indisputably has accomplished numerous successes in its remedies enforcement over the years, it has also encountered some significant obstacles and shortcomings along the way. To this effect, the final chapter in the book critically assesses whether the current framework, which has remained unchanged since 2008, continues to provide an adequate regulatory response to today's remedies issues and challenges. Where adjustments and improvements are deemed desirable or necessary, possible measures are considered.

**Volume 7 in the series Hart Studies in Competition Law**

**Hart Studies in Competition Law**

Volume 1: *Intellectual Property, Antitrust and Cumulative Innovation in the EU and the US*
Thorsten Käseberg

Volume 2: *State Aid and the European Economic Constitution*
Francesco de Cecco

Volume 3: *The Private Enforcement of Competition Law in Ireland*
David McFadden

Volume 4: *Cross-Border EU Competition Law Actions*
Edited by Mihail Danov, Florian Becker and Paul Beaumont

Volume 5: *Competition Laws, Globalization and Legal Plurism: China's Experience*
Qianlan Wu

Volume 6: *Joint Ventures and EU Competition Law*
Luis Silva Morais

# European Merger Remedies

## Law and Policy

Dorte Hoeg

·HART·
PUBLISHING
OXFORD AND PORTLAND, OREGON
2014

Published in the United Kingdom by Hart Publishing Ltd
16C Worcester Place, Oxford, OX1 2JW
Telephone: +44 (0)1865 517530
Fax: +44 (0)1865 510710
E-mail: mail@hartpub.co.uk
Website: http://www.hartpub.co.uk

Published in North America (US and Canada) by
Hart Publishing
c/o International Specialized Book Services
920 NE 58th Avenue, Suite 300
Portland, OR 97213-3786
USA
Tel: +1 503 287 3093 or toll-free: (1) 800 944 6190
Fax: +1 503 280 8832
E-mail: orders@isbs.com
Website: http://www.isbs.com



British Library Cataloguing in Publication Data
Data Available

ISBN: 978-1-84946-411-6

Typeset by Hope Services, Abingdon
Printed and bound in Great Britain by
TJ International Ltd, Padstow

# *Preface*

As merger transactions become more complex, so do the remedies involved. The purpose of this book is to provide a comprehensive account and analysis of the most important merger remedies aspects, which have emerged and evolved in the European Commission's policy and practice over the past 20-plus years. The description of applicable provisions and guidance is structured in accordance with a typical 'merger remedies lifecycle': the negotiation, submission, assessment, adoption, implementation and enforcement of remedies. Furthermore, relevant conditional clearance decisions and judgments as well as studies and literature on the subject are described and put into a coherent analytical framework with the aim of providing a nuanced evaluation of the Commission's past and present remedies policy and practice.

While the Commission indisputably has accomplished numerous successes in its remedies enforcement over the years, it has also encountered some significant obstacles and shortcomings along the way. To this effect, the final chapter in this book critically assesses whether the current framework, which has by and large remained unchanged since 2008, continues to provide an adequate response to today's remedies issues and challenges. Where adjustments and improvements are deemed desirable or necessary, possible measures are considered. As the topic of merger remedies embraces a wide range of comprehensive issues, the main focus in this book is on structural remedies as they continue to be the most frequently occurring and preferred solution in the Commission's decisional practice.

This book has been in the making for many years. My first professional encounter with merger remedies dates back to the mid 1990s when I worked as an official for the Danish Competition Authority and among other things participated in the consultations of the EU's Advisory Committee on Concentrations and had the opportunity to observe and be involved in the Commission's remedies work from the perspective of a Member State. When I later became a national expert and a case handler in DG Competition (then Merger Task Force) a substantial amount of my time and efforts were devoted to the day-to-day handling of merger remedies cases. Later I enjoyed the privilege of undertaking doctoral research in the very same field, which led to the award of a PhD by King's College London in 2012. Thus with the experience from a Member State, the Commission and academia, I have strived to write a balanced and comprehensive account of how the Commission's remedies policy and practice are perceived today and how they have evolved over the years.

Many people have helped, encouraged and inspired me along the way, including mentors, colleagues and friends. As this publication is a revised version of my PhD thesis, I would like to thank Richard Whish, Ariel Ezrachi and Philip Marsden for their helpful and constructive feedback. A special thanks is also extended to the staff at Hart Publishing for taking on this publication and for their patience in waiting for the completion of the manuscript and their help throughout the drafting and publication process. Finally, I wish to thank the people dear and close to me for allowing me to stubbornly pursue my ambition of writing this book, which I would like to dedicate to my three children, Sophie, Olivia and Sebastian.

During the writing and editing of this book I have been reminded how the topic of merger remedies continues to constantly evolve, requiring continuous attention and adaptation. Every endeavour has been made to include the very latest developments and sources as of 1 May 2013. As it is my hope that this book will be the beginning of an evolving process following future merger remedies developments, I would be grateful for comments and ideas on any aspects dealt with in this publication at merger.remedies@gmail.com.

Dorte Hoeg
Brussels, May 2013

# *Contents*


*Preface* v
*Abbreviations* xiii
*Table of Cases* xv
*Table of Legislation* xxv
*Table of Agreements* xxxv

1. The Commission's Remedies Policy 1
2. Negotiating, Submitting, Assessing and Adopting Remedies 35
3 Essential Features of Divestiture Remedies 79
4 Implementing and Enforcing Remedies 123
5 Building on Successes and Learning from Mistakes 186

Annex A: Remedies Statistics 215
Annex B: Table of Commission Remedies Decisions under the Merger Regulation 217
Annex C: Table of the EU Court's Judgments containing Remedies Aspects 231

*Bibliography* 233
*Index* 241

# *Detailed Contents*


*Preface* v
*Abbreviations* xiii
*Table of Cases* xv
*Table of Legislation* xxv
*Table of Agreements* xxxv

1. The Commission's Remedies Policy 1
1.1 Introduction 1
1.1.1 Merger Remedies 1
1.1.2 This Book 3
1.1.2.1 Objectives and Limitations 3
1.1.2.2 Structure 5
1.1.2.3 Citations 6
1.2 Chronological Overview 7
1.2.1 The Learning Phase 7
1.2.2 The Acceleration Phase 9
1.2.3 The Consolidation Phase 11
1.2.4 Forthcoming Re-evaluation Phase? 13
1.3 Remedies Guidance 16
1.3.1 Merger Regulation 16
1.3.2 Remedies Notice 17
1.3.3 Best Practice Remedies Guidelines 18
1.3.4 US Remedies Guidance 20
1.4 Remedies Reviews 21
1.4.1 The DG Competition Remedies Study 21
1.4.2 The DG Enterprise Econometric Remedies Study 22
1.4.3 The FTC Divestiture Study 22
1.4.4 Other Reviews 23
1.4.4.1 The OECD Remedies Studies 23
1.4.4.2 The ICN Remedies Review Project 25
1.4.4.3 Other Studies 26
1.5 Reflections on Remedies Enforcement Objectives 28

2. Negotiating, Submitting, Assessing and Adopting Remedies 35
2.1 General Principles 35
2.1.1 Step One: Identifying Competition Concerns 35
2.1.2 Step Two: Remedying Competition Concerns 38
2.1.2.1 Initiatives, Onus and Responsibilities 38
2.1.2.2 Pre-clearance Modifications 40

2.1.2.3 Commitments to Modify Post Clearance 42
2.1.2.4 Classifications of Remedies 43
2.2 Submitting Remedies 45
2.2.1 Requirements 45
2.2.2 Phase I 47
2.2.3 Phase II 50
2.2.3.1 Deadlines 50
2.2.3.2 'Exceptional Circumstances' 51
2.2.3.3 Post-Deadline Modifications 52
2.3 Assessing Remedies 54
2.3.1 Proportionality and Elimination of Competition Concerns 54
2.3.2 Certainty 57
2.3.3 Complexity and Monitoring 58
2.4 Consulting on Remedies 59
2.4.1 Market Test 59
2.4.2 Member States 64
2.4.3 Involvements of Other Authorities 68
2.5 Adopting Remedies 70
2.5.1 Imposing Conditions and Obligations 70
2.5.2 'Take Note Commitments' 73
2.5.3 Adoption and Publication 77

3 Essential Features of Divestiture Remedies 79
3.1 Ensuring Viability 79
3.2 Types of Structural Remedies 81
3.2.1 Stand-alone Business 81
3.2.2 Carve-outs 83
3.2.3 Selected Assets 84
3.2.4 Licence Arrangements 86
3.2.4.1 Technology 86
3.2.4.2 Re-branding 88
3.2.5 Severance of Links with Competitors 93
3.2.5.1 Introductory Remarks 93
3.2.5.2 Divestiture of Minority Shareholding 94
3.2.5.3 Waiving of Rights and Termination of Agreements 100
3.3 Purchaser Requirements 101
3.3.1 Introductory Remarks 101
3.3.2 Independence 102
3.3.3 Resources, Expertise and Incentives 103
3.3.4 No New Competition Concerns or Delays 106
3.4 'Ancillary' Viability Tools 108
3.4.1 Additional Assets 108
3.4.2 Up-front Buyers 109
3.4.3 Fix-it-first 113

3.4.4 Alternative Proposals: Crown Jewels 116

4 Implementing and Enforcing Remedies 123
4.1 Divestiture Periods 123
4.2 Role and Functions of Trustees 127
4.2.1 General Characteristics 127
4.2.1.1 Approval Procedure and Mandate 127
4.2.1.2 Independence 130
4.2.1.3 Qualifications and Specialist Advisors 135
4.2.1.4 Liaison between the Commission and Trustee 136
4.2.1.5 Remuneration 137
4.2.1.6 Replacement, Discharge and Reappointment 138
4.2.2 Monitoring Trustee's Tasks 139
4.2.3 Divestiture Trustee's Tasks 142
4.3 Interim Preservation 144
4.3.1 The Parties' Obligations 144
4.3.2 Preservation of Assets 145
4.3.3 Hold-separate Measures 146
4.3.3.1 Hold-separate Manager 146
4.3.3.2 Ring-fencing 147
4.4 Divestiture Process 149
4.4.1 Putting the Business up for Sale 149
4.4.2 Price Setting 151
4.4.3 Voluntary Addition of Assets 153
4.4.4 Modification of Remedies 154
4.4.4.1 Extending Divestiture Deadlines 155
4.4.4.2 Request for Waivers 157
4.4.4.3 Means of Communication 163
4.5 Completion of the Sale 164
4.5.1 Approval of Purchasers 164
4.5.2 Rejection of Purchasers 167
4.5.3 Transfer and Closing 169
4.6 Post-closure/'Aftermath' 170
4.6.1 On-sales Bans 170
4.6.2 Re-acquisition Prohibitions 173
4.6.3 Information Obligations 175
4.6.4 Breach of Remedies 176
4.6.5 Challenging Remedies 180
4.6.5.1 The Merging Parties 180
4.6.5.2 Third Parties 182

5 Building on Successes and Learning from Mistakes 186
5.1 The Overall Success Story 186
5.2 Viability Requirements: Is the Commission Realistic? 188

5.3 Are Remedies Procedures Sufficiently Transparent? 189
5.3.1 Pre-decision 190
5.3.2 Decision 191
5.3.3 Post-decision 193
5.4 Are Phase I Proceedings Suitable for Today's Remedies? 194
5.5 Policing Remedies: Does the Commission Do Enough? 199
5.6 Forms and Guidance: A Potential Straightjacket? 202
5.7 With Guidance come Responsibilities: Has the Commission Delivered? 204
5.8 International Cooperation: How Much Further Can the Commission Go? 206
5.9 Concluding Remarks 211
5.9.1 Impact of the Identified Shortcomings on the Remedies Policy 211
5.9.2 Impact of the Remedies Policy on Enforcement Outcomes 213

Annex A: Remedies Statistics 215
Annex B: Table of Commission Remedies Decisions under the Merger Regulation 217
Annex C: Table of the EU Court's Judgments containing Remedies Aspects 231

*Bibliography* 233
*Index* 241

# *Abbreviations*

| | |
|---|---|
| AAI | American Antitrust Institute |
| ABA | American Bar Association |
| AC Opinion | Opinion of the Advisory Committee on Concentrations |
| ACCC | Australian Competition & Consumer Commission |
| BIAC | Business and Industry Advisory Committee (OECD) |
| CCP | Centre for Competition Policy |
| Commission | EU Commission |
| Competition Report | Annual Report on Competition Policy by the EU Commission |
| DG Competition | Directorate General of the Commission for Competition Policy |
| DG Enterprise | Directorate General of Enterprise and Industry |
| DoJ | US Department of Justice (Antitrust Division) |
| ECR | European Court Reports |
| EU Court | European Court of Justice and European General Court |
| FMCGs | fast-moving consumer goods |
| FTC | US Federal Trade Commission (Bureau of Competition) |
| IBA | International Bar Association |
| ICN | International Competition Network |
| ICPAC | International Competition Policy Advisory Committee |
| IFLR | International Finance Law Review |
| IPRs | intellectual property rights |
| JV | joint venture |
| MFT | Merger Task Force (DG Competition) |
| MTDC | Model Text for Divestiture Commitments |
| MTTM | Model Text for Trustee Mandates |
| OECD | Organisation for Economic Co-operation and Development |
| OJ | Official Journal of the European Union |
| SIEC | Significant Impediment to Effective Competition |
| SO | Statement of Objections |
| SPA | sales and purchase agreement |
| TFEU | Treaty on the Functioning of the European Union |
| UK CC | UK Competition Commission |
| UK OFT | UK Office of Fair Trading |
| US SEC | US Securities and Exchange Commission |

# *Table of Cases*

**European Union**

***Commission Decisions***

*ABB/Daimler–Benz* (M.580 II 1995)...8, 72
*Abbott/Guidant* (M.4150 I 2006)...12, 96, 100
*Abbott/Solvay Pharmaceuticals* (M.5661 I 2010)...49
*ABF/GBI Business* (M.4980 II 2008)... 12, 36, 50, 67, 114, 116, 119–20
*Aerospatiale/Matra* (M.1309 I 1999)...74
*Aerospatiale–Alenia/de Havilland* (M.53 II 1991)...38
*Agfa–Gevaert/DuPont* (M.986 II 1998)...72
*Agilent/Varian* (M.5611 I 2010)...49, 110
*AIG/bmi* (M.6447 I 2012)...12
*Air France/KLM* (M.3280 I 2004)...12, 43, 178–79, 188
*Air France/Sabena* (M.157 I 1992)...7
*Air Liquide/BOC* (M.1630 II 2000)...53, 209
*Airtours/First Choice* (M.1524 II 1999)... 51–52
*Akzo Nobel/ICI* (M.4779 I 2007)...12, 89, 98
*Alcan/Alusuisse* (M.1663 II 2000)...67, 85
*Alcan/Pechiney (II)* (M.3225 I 2003)...105, 117
*Alcatel/Finmeccanica/Alcatel Alenia Space & Telespazio* (M.3680 I 2005)...55, 86
*Alcatel/Telettra* (M.42 II 1991)...71
*Alcoa/Reynolds* (M.1693 II 2000)...85, 135
*Allianz/AGF* (M.1082 I 1998)...93
*Allianz/Dresdner* (M.2431 I 2001)...93, 95–96, 127, 143
*Amcor/Alcan* (M.5599 I 2009)...82, 178
*American Home Products/Monsanto* (M.1229 I 1998)... 100–101
*Anglo American Corporation/Lonrho* (M.754 II 1997)... 8, 102, 117, 141, 165, 167
*AOL/Time Warner* (M.1845 II 2000)...9
*Apollo/Bakelite* (M.3593 I 2005)...12, 49, 55, 86
*Areva/Urenco/ETC JV* (M.3099 II 2004)...50, 98
*Arjowiggins/M–Real Zanders Reflex* (M.4513 II 2008)... 2, 15, 67, 84, 110–11, 124, 143
*ARM/Giesecke & Devrient/Gemalto/JV* (M.6564 I 2012)...11, 45, 88, 129
*Arsenal/DSP* (M.5153 II 2009)... 2, 15, 37, 63, 67, 191
*Astra/Zeneca* (M.1403 I 1999)...9, 22, 207
*Astra/Zeneca/Novartis* (M.1806 II 2000)...116, 119–20
*AXA/GRE* (M.1453 I 1999)...93, 95, 116, 118
*Axalto/Gemplus* (M.3998 I 2006)...88
*Bank Austria/Creditanstalt* (M.873 I 1997)...93, 98
*BASF/Ciba* (M.5355 I 2009)... 86–87, 110, 143, 162, 168
*BASF/Congis* (M.5927 I 2010)...108–109, 191

*BASF/INEOS/Styrene/JV* (M.6093 I 2011)....129, 192
*BAT/Skandinavisk Tobakskompagni* (M.5086 I 2008)....89
*Bayer/Aventis Crop Science* (M.2547 II 2002)....9, 62, 83, 117–18, 147, 207
*BHP Billiton/Rio Tinto* (M.4985 II 2008)....2, 15
*Bilfinger Berger/MCE* (M.5664 I 2009)....81
*Blackstone/Acetex* (M.3625 II 2005)....75
*BNP Paribas/Fortis* (M.5384 I 2008)....12–13, 93, 141
*Boeing/Hughes* (M.1879 II 2000)....74
*Boeing/McDonnell Douglas* (M.877 II 1997)....39, 66, 69, 72, 210
*Bombardier/Adtranz* (M.2139 II 2001)....160
*Bosch/Rexroth* (M.2060 II 2000).... 109–112
*BP/JV Dissolution* (M.1820 I 2000)....106
*BP Amoco/Atlantic Richfield* (M.1532 II 1999)....50, 66, 153, 174
*Bridgepoint/Dorna* (M.4357 I 2006)....102
*British Airways/TAT* (M.259 I 1992)....7
*British Telecom/MCI (II)* (M.856 II 1997)....127
*BT/AT&T* (JV.15 II 1999)....50
*BT/MCI* (34.857 1994)....174
*Buhrmann/Samas Office Supplies* (M.2286 I 2001)....108
*Campbell/ECBB (Unilever)* (M.2350 I 2001)....106, 152
*Carnival Corporation/P&O Princess* (M.2706 II 2002)....190
*Carrefour/Promodès* (M.1684 I 2000)....18, 95, 97, 155–56
*Cendant/Galileo* (M.2510 I 2001)....47
*Ciba–Geigy/Sandoz* (M.737 II 1996)....72, 87
*Cisco/Tandberg* (M.5669 I 2010).... 12, 41, 69, 123, 128–29, 194, 207–08
*Coca–Cola/Amalgamated Beverages GB* (M.794 II 1997)....74
*Colgate Palmolive/Sanex Business* (M.6221 I 2011)....106, 191
*Continental/Phoenix* (M.3436 I 2004)....98, 113–15
*Courtaulds/SNIA* (M.113 I 1991)....8
*Crown Cork & Seal/CarnaudMetalbox* (M.603 II 1995)....7, 83
*CVC/Lenzing* (M.2187 II 2001)....65
*CVC/SLEC* (M.4066 I 2006)....102
*CVC/Univar Europe/Eurochem* (M.5814 I 2010)....50
*DaimlerChrysler/Deutsche Telekom/JV* (M.2903 I 2003)....78, 185
*Danish Crown/Vestjyske Slagterier* (M.1313 II 1999)....53, 66, 93, 103, 128, 135, 149
*Danone/Numico* (M.4842 I 2007)....87, 89–92
*Degussa/Laporte* (M.2277 I 2001)....82, 104
*Delta/Northwest* (M.5181 I 2008)....35
*Deutsche Bahn/Arriva* (M.5855 I 2010)....106, 148, 174, 178
*Deutsche Bahn/EWS* (M.4746 I 2007)....49, 71
*Deutsche Börse/NYSE Euronext* (M.6166 II 2012)....2, 12, 58, 60, 63, 69, 77, 188, 191
*Deutsche Post/DHL* (M.1168 I 1998)....74
*DFDS/Norfolk* (M.5756 I 2010)....49
*DONG/Elsam/Energi E2* (M.3868 II 2006)....162
*Dow Chemical/Union Carbide* (M.1671 II 2000)....71, 113, 116, 120
*DSM/Roche Vitamins* (M.2972 II 2003)....36, 50, 86, 110
*DSV/Vesterhavet/DFDS* (M.5454 II 2009)....2

*DuPont/ICI* (M.214 II 1992)........8, 26
*E.ON/MOL* (M.3696 II 2005)........12, 51, 163, 181
*EDF/British Energy* (M.5224 I 2008)........12
*EDF/ENBW* (M.1853 II 2001)........9, 93
*EDF/Segebel* (M.5549 I 2009)........12, 126, 157
*EDP/ENI/GDP* (M.3440 II 2004)........52, 58
*ENBW/ENI/GVS* (M.2698 II 2002)........50
*ENI/EDP/GDP* (M.3440 II 2004)........12, 100
*Enso/Stora* (M.1225 II 1998)........74
*Ericsson/Nortel Group (MSS & Global Services)* (M.6095 I 2011)........40, 47
*Eurostar* (M.1305 I 1998)........40
*Evraz/Highveld* (M.4494 I 2007)........69, 93
*Exxon/Mobil* (M.1383 II 1999)........9, 82, 93, 106, 113
*Exxon/Shell* (M.1137 I 1998)........207
*Ferrovie Dello Stato/Cube Transport/Arrive Deutschland* (M.6124 I 2011)........106
*Fiat/Ford New Holland* (M.009 I 1991)........7
*Fortis/ABN Amro Assets* (M.4844 I 2007)........12–13, 15, 43, 83, 93, 110, 128, 146, 156, 198
*Framatome/Siemens/Cogéma/JV* (M.1940 II 2000)........40–41
*France Telecom/Orange* (M.2016 I 2000)........98, 106
*Friesland/Campina* (M.5046 II 2008)........12, 51, 67, 146, 178
*FrieslandCampina/Zijerveld & Veldhuyzen and Den Hollander* (M.6722 I 2013)........100
*Fujitsu/Siemens* (JV.22 I 1999)........127
*Galp Energia/Exxonmibil Iberia* (M.5005 I 2008)........93, 141
*Gaz de France/Suez* (M.4180 II 2006)........12, 51, 158, 163, 192
*GDF Suez/International Power* (M.5978 I 2011)........95, 97–99, 105, 124, 146, 148, 161, 174–75
*GE/AGFA NDT* (M.3136 I 2003)........113–15
*GE/Honeywell* (M.2220 II 2001)........57, 69
*GE/Instrumentarium* (M.3083 II 2003)........9, 192, 207
*Generali/INA* (M.1712 I 2000)........93, 192
*Glaxo/Wellcome* (M.555 I 1995)........8, 86, 117
*Glaxo Wellcome/SmithKline Beecham* (M.1846 I 2000)........22, 56, 87, 117, 120, 124, 137
*Glencore/Xstrata* (M.6541 I 2012)........12, 16, 45, 93, 128, 192, 198, 209
*Guinness/GrandMet* (M.938 II 1997)........102, 124, 128, 165, 169
*Halliburton/Dresser* (M.1140 I 1998)........41, 208
*Haniel/Cementbouw/JV(CVK)* (M.2650 II 2002)........9
*Heidelberger Zement/Scancem* (M.1562 I 1999)........106
*Hoechst/Rhone–Poulenc* (M.1378 I 1999)........9, 160–61, 178–79, 201
*Hoechst/Rhône–Poulenc* (M.1378 I 2004 – modified decision of 1999 clearance)........104
*Hoffmann–La Roche/Boehringer Mannheim* (M.950 II 1998)........22, 87, 118, 128, 155, 158, 163, 165, 204
*Hutchinson 3G Austria/Orange Austria* (M.6497 II 2012)........12, 50, 65, 68, 70, 107, 110
*Hutchison/RCPM/ECT* (JV.55 II 2001)........66
*IAG/BMI* (M.6447 I 2012)........33, 49, 128, 184
*Imetal/English China Clays* (M.1381 I 1999)........120
*INCO/Falconbridge* (M.4000 II 2006)........104, 113, 115
*Industri Kapital/Dyno* (M.1813 II 2000)........103, 116, 118–19, 125, 141, 165

*Industri Kapital/Perstorp (II)* (M.2396 I 2001) ....85
*Intel/McAfee* (M.5984 I 2011) .... 12–14, 45, 71, 88, 159, 192, 210
*Interbrew/Beck's* (M.2569 I 2001) ....40, 47
*IPIC/MAN Ferrostaal* (M.5406 I 2009) ....95–96, 141
*J&J/Pfizer Consumer Healthcare* (M.4314 I 2006) ....116, 206
*J&J/Synthes* (M.6266 II 2012) ....12, 208
*Johnson & Johnson/Guidant* (M.3687 II 2005) ....80, 82, 116
*Kali–Salz/MDT/Treuhand* (M.308 II 1993) ....74
*Kimberly–Clark/Scott* (M.623 II 1996) ....8, 22, 71
*Kinnevik/Billerud/Korsnäs* (M.6682 I 2012) ....56, 85
*KNP/Bührmann–Tetterode and VRG* (M.291 II 1993) ....175
*Konica/Minolta* (M.3091 I 2003) ....93, 97–98
*Kraft/Danone Biscuits* (M.4824 I 2007) ....89
*Kraft Foods/Cadbury* (M.5644 I 2010) ....82, 141, 146, 153
*Kronospan/Constantia* (M.4525 II 2007) ....36, 40, 50
*La Poste/Swiss Post/JV* (M.6503 I 2012) ....81
*Lagardère/Natexis/VUP* (M.2978 II 2004) ....12, 35, 83, 108, 132, 139, 167, 194, 231
*Linde/BOC* (M.4141 I 2006) ....99, 108–109, 198
*Lufthansa/Austrian Airlines* (M.5440 II 2009) ....12, 15, 35, 67, 71, 131, 152, 192
*Lufthansa/SN Airholding* (M.5335 II 2009) .... 12, 14, 67, 71, 192
*Lufthansa/Swiss* (M.3770 I 2005) ....12
*Lyonnaise des Eaux/Suez* (M.916 I 1997) .... 8–9
*Maersk/PONL* (M.3829 I 2005) ....100, 147
*Manitowoc/Enodis* (M.5180 I 2008) ....82, 127, 166, 208
*Mannesmann/Orange* (M.1760 I 1999) ....9
*Masterfoods/Royal Canin* (M.2544 I 2002) ....9, 85–86, 89, 91, 104, 109–10, 112, 143
*MCI WorldCom/Sprint* (M.1741 II 2000) ....58, 178
*Mercedes–Benz/Kässbohrer* (M.477 II 1995) ....74
*Metso/Aker Kvaerner* (M.4187 II 2006) .... 12, 36, 50, 86–87, 113–15, 128, 143
*Microsoft* (COMP/C–3/37.792 2004) ....136
*Mitsubishi Heavy Industries* (M.1634 II 2000) ....61
*Mitsui/CVRD/CAEMI* (M.2420 II 2001) ....36, 75
*Mobil/JV Dissolution* (M.1822 I 2000) ....106
*Monsanto/Pharmacia & Upjohn* (M.1835 I 2000) ....22, 137, 143, 171
*Neste/IVO* (M.931 I 1998) ....9, 174
*Nestlé/Novartis (Medical nutrition business)* (M.4540 I 2007) ....81–82, 89–91, 141, 151
*Nestlé/Perrier* (M.190 II 1992) .... 8, 26, 30, 167, 175
*Nestlé/Ralston Purina* (M.2337 I 2001) ....9, 89–91, 110–11, 116, 120, 143, 171, 173
*New Holland/Case* (M.1571 I 1999) ....116, 119–20
*News Corp/Premiere* (M.5121 I 2008) ....71
*Newscorp/Telepiu* (M.2876 II 2003) ....43, 75, 158–59
*Nordbanken/Postgirot* (M.2567 I 2001) ....9, 93, 95–97
*Novartis/Alcon* (M.5778 I 2010) .... 16, 49, 116, 120, 207, 209
*Olympic/Aegean Airlines* (M.5830 II 2011) ....2, 12, 181
*OMV/MOL* (M.4799 II 2008) ....2, 15
*Omya/Huber PCC* (M.3796 II 2006) ....12, 51, 60, 72, 105, 108, 110, 180
*Oracle/Sun Microsystems* (M.5529 II 2010) ....38, 41, 60, 69, 73–77, 182–83, 196, 208, 210

*Orkla/Chips* (M.3658 I 2005) ....................36, 100–01
*Orkla/Volvo* (M.582 II 1995) ....................128
*Otto/Primondo Assets* (M.5721 I 2010) ....................85
*Outokumpu/Inoxum* (M.6471 II 2012) .................... 12, 51, 126, 135, 192
*PAI+UGI/Elf Antargaz* (M.2375 I 2001) ....................106
*Panasonic/Sanyo* (M.5421 I 2009) ....................69, 117
*Pernod Ricard/V&S* (M.5114 I 2008) ....................89, 146
*Pernod Richard/Allied Domecq* (M.3779 I 2005)....................100
*Pernod Richard/Diageo/Seagram* (M.2268 I 2001) ....................167
*Pfizer/Pharmacia* (M.2922 I 2003) ....................9, 117, 119–20
*Pfizer/SP Assets* (M.5195 I 2008) ....................106
*Pfizer/Warner Lambert* (M.1878 I 2000) ....................113, 117
*Pfizer/Wyeth* (M.5476 I 2009)....................12, 16, 209
*Pirelli/BICC* (M.1882 II 2000)....................26
*Pirelli/Edizione/Olivetti/Telecom Italia* (M.2574 I 2001).................... 160, 163, 177, 201
*Polestar/Prisa/Inversiones Ibersuizas/JV* (M.3322 I 2003)....................192
*Posten AB/Post Danmark A/S* (M.5152 I 2009)....................12, 74, 85
*Procter & Gamble/Gillette* (M.3732 I 2005) ....................159
*Procter & Gamble/VP Schickedanz (II)* (M.430 II 1994) ......8, 41, 62, 135, 143, 148, 165, 177
*Raytheon/Thales/JV* (M.2079 I 2001)....................47
*RCA/MAN Cargo* (M.5096 I 2008) .................... 97–99
*Reckitt Benckiser/SSL* (M.5953 I 2010).................... 85, 89, 104, 111, 145, 148
*Repola/Kymmene* (M.646 I 1995)....................8, 85
*Reuters/Telerate* (M.3692 I 2005)....................113
*Rexam/American National Can* (M.1939 I 2000) ....................86, 106, 108, 174
*Rhodia/Donau Chemie/Albright & Wilson* (M.1517 I 1999) ....................161, 179, 201
*Rohm+Haas/Morton* (M.1467 I 1999) ....................127
*RWE/Essent* (M.5467 I 2009)....................68, 81, 141
*Ryanair/Aer Lingus* (M.4439 II 2007) ....................2, 12, 47, 61, 97, 110, 191, 196
*Ryanair/Aer Lingus II* (M.5434 I withdrawn in 2009)....................97
*Ryanair/Aer Lingus III* (M.6663 II 2013) .................... 2, 81, 97, 188, 197
*Sanitec/Sphinx* (M.1578 II 1999)....................56, 108–09, 164
*Sanofi/Synthélabo* (M.1397 I 1999) ....................3, 9, 22, 177
*Sanofi/Synthélabo* (M.1543 1999) (Art 14 proceedings) ....................177
*Sanofi–Avantis/Zentiva* (M.5253 I 2009) ....................39, 73, 198
*Sanofi–Synthélabo/Aventis* (M.3354 I 2004) ....................207
*SCA/Georgia–Pacific Europe* (M.6455 I 2012) ....................85, 89, 91–92, 104
*SCA/P&G (European Tissue Business)* (M.4533 I 2007)....................109
*SCA Packaging/Metsä Corrugated* (M.2032 I 2000)....................22, 135
*Schering–Plough/Organon Biosciences* (M.4691 I 2007)....................49, 106, 198
*Schmalbach–Lubeca/Rexam* (M.2542 I 2001) ....................106
*Schneider/Legrand* (M.2283 II 2001)....................53, 66, 91
*SCJ/Sara Lee* (M.5969 II 2011 withdrawn)....................2, 11, 56, 192
*SEB/Moulinex* (M.2621 I 2002)....................9, 89–92, 108
*SEB/Moulinex* (M.2621 II 2003)....................224
*SFR/Tele 2* (M.4504 II 2007)....................12
*Shell/BASF – Project Nicole* (M.1751 I 2000) ....................46, 85

*Shell/Enterprise Oil* (M.2745 I 2002)....47
*Shell/Montecatini* (M.260 II 1994 and 1996)....159, 173
*Siemens/Elektrowatt* (M.913 II 1997)....72
*Siemens/Italtel* (M.468 II 1995)....74
*Siemens/VA Tech* (M.3653 II 2005)....12, 81, 95–96, 100, 160
*Skanska/Scancem* (M.1157 II 1998)....106, 180, 196, 201
*SNCF/LCR/Eurostar* (M.5655 I 2010)....35, 49, 59, 71
*Sonoco/Ahlstrom* (M.3431 II 2004)....36, 50, 110
*Sony/Mubadala Development/EMI Music Publishing* (M.6459 I 2012)....13, 49, 104
*StatoilHydro/ConocoPhillips* (M.4919 II 2008)....36, 50, 67
*Südzucker/ED&F MAN* (M.6286 II 2012)....51, 93, 98, 128, 143
*Syngenta/Monsanto's Sunflower Seed Business* (M.5675 II 2010)....36, 50–51, 67, 70, 104–05, 146, 148, 174–75
*T–Mobile/Orange* (M.5650 I 2010)....12, 68, 129, 136, 192
*T–Mobile Austria/Tele.ring* (M.3916 II 2006)....59, 113–15
*Talanx/Gerling* (M.4055 I 2006)....93
*TCCC/Carlsberg* (M.938 II 1997)....102
*Teijin/Zeon/JV* (M.3235 I 2003)....39, 98, 141
*Telefónica/O2* (M.4035 I 2006)....38, 100
*Telia/Sonera* (M.2803 I 2002)....9
*Telia/Telenor* (M.1439 II 1999)....51, 117
*Tetra Laval/Sidel* (M.2416 II 2001)....47, 60–61
*Tetra Laval/Sidel* (M.2416 I 2003)....9
*Teva/Barr* (M.5295 I 2008)....39
*Teva/Cephalon* (M.6258 I 2011)....191
*Teva/Ratiopharm* (M.5865 I 2010)....116, 192
*The Post Office/TPG/SPPL* (M.1915 II 2001)....9, 71, 82, 110, 112, 125
*Thomson Corporation/Reuters Group* (M.4726 II 2008)....50, 56, 67, 69, 126, 185
*Thyssen/Krupp* (M.1080 I 1998)....100, 127
*Tokyo Gas/Siemens/Tessenderlo Chemie/International Power/GDF Suez/T–Power JV* (M.6422 I 2012)....95
*TotalFina/Elf Aquitaine* (M.1628 II 2000)....9, 51, 53, 85, 102, 104, 106, 165, 167–68
*TUI/CP Ships* (M.3863 I 2005)....100
*TUI/First Choice* (M.4600 I 2007)....81–82
*Tyco/Mallinckrodt* (M.2074 I 2000)....47
*Unilever/Amora–Maille* (M.1802 I 2000)....85, 108
*Unilever/Bestfoods* (M.1990 I 2000)....82, 85, 106, 108, 142, 152
*Unilever/Sara Lee Body Care* (M.5658 II 2010)....33, 37, 51, 67, 85, 89, 106, 191
*Unilever France/Ortiz Miko* (M.422 I 1994)....127
*Universal/BMG Music Publishing* (M.4404 II 2007)....36, 60, 62, 86, 108
*Universal Music Group/EMI Music* (M.6458 II 2012)....12–13, 16, 51, 104, 192, 208–09
*UPS/TNT Express* (M.6570 II 2013)....2, 14, 30, 40, 46, 107, 122, 188
*Usinor/Cockerill* (M.1329 I 1999)....85
*UTC/Goodrich* (M.6410 II 2012)....12, 16, 36, 50, 128, 192, 207–09
*Vattenfall/Nuon* (M.5496 I 2009)....84
*Veba/Degussa* (M.942 II 1997)....8
*VEBA/VIAG* (M.1673 II 2000)....62, 93, 96, 98-99, 116, 118, 141–43, 148, 156

*Verbund/Energie Allianz* (M.2947 II 2003) ... 9, 68, 75, 98, 110–11
*Vienna Insurance Group/EBV* (M.5075 I 2008) ... 93, 113, 115
*Vivendi/Canal+/Seagram* (M.2050 I 2000) ... 9, 95
*Vodafone/Vivendi/Canal Plus* (JV.48 I 2000) ... 127
*Vodafone Airtouch/Mannesmann* (M.1795 I 2000) ... 106, 158
*Volkswagen/Scania* (M.5157 I 2008) ... 98
*Volvo/Renault V.I.* (M.1980 I 2000) ... 97–98, 156, 163, 167, 196
*Volvo/Scania* (M.1672 II 2000) ... 35, 52, 58, 97, 196
*Western Digital Ireland/Viviti Technologies* (M.6203 II 2011) ... 12–13, 70, 72, 110, 127–29, 191–192, 207–09
*Wind/Blue* (M.2958 I 2002) ... 160
*WorldCom/MCI* (M.1069 II 1998) ... 9, 58, 109, 178, 201
*WPP/TNS* (M.5232 I 2008) ... 114, 116, 119–20
*Xstrata/Falconbridge* (M.4256 I 2006) ... 115
*Yara/Kemira Growhow* (M.4730 I 2007) ... 85, 93, 96, 98–99
*YLE/TDF/DIGITA/JV* (M.2300 I 2001) ... 143, 148

### *Court of Justice*

*Cementbouw Handel & Industrie v Commission* (C–202/06 P 2007) ... 36, 42, 54–55, 57, 71, 180
*Commission v Éditions Odile Jacob* (C–553/10 P 2012) ... 132–34, 164, 184, 194, 200
*Commission v Éditions Odile Jacob* (C–404/10 P 2012) ... 184
*Commission v Schneider Electric SA* (C–440/07 P 2009) ... 182
*Commission v Tetra Laval* (C–12/03 P 2005) ... 36, 44, 184
*Éditions Odile Jacob SAS v Commission, Lagardère SCA* (C–551/10 P 2012) ... 34, 132, 183
*France and Others v Commission* (C–68/94 and C–30/95 1998) ... 36, 74
*Lagardère v Éditions Odile Jacob* (C–554/10 P 2012) ... 132–34, 164–65, 184, 194, 200

### *General Court*

*Aer Lingus v Commission* (T–101/13 pending) ... 184
*Aeroporia Aigaiou Aeroporiki and Marfin Investment Group Symmetochon v Commission* (T–202/11 pending) ... 181
*Air France v Commission* (T–3/93 1994) ... 182–83
*Airtours v Commission* (T–342/99 2002) ... 10
*ARD v Commission* (T–158/00 2003) ... 34, 48, 62, 182–83
*BaByliss v Commission* (T–114/02 2003) ... 48, 62, 89, 91–92, 182–83, 205
*BASF v Commission* (T–105/10 withdrawn 2011) ... 162, 168, 181
*CCE Grandes Sources and others v Commission* (T–96/92 1995) ... 182
*CCE Vittel v Commission* (T–12/93 1993) ... 167, 182
*Cementbouw Handel & Industrie v Commission* (T–282/02 2006) ... 38, 54, 56, 71–72, 180
*Coca–Cola v Commission* (T–125/97 and 127/97 2000) ... 73, 76
*Communauté de communes de Lacq v Commission* (T–132/10 2011) ... 75, 184
*Deutsche Börse v Commission* (T–175/12 pending) ... 181
*E.ON Ruhrgas and E.ON Földgáz Trade v Commission* (T–57/07 2009) ... 15, 163, 181
*easyJet v Commission* (T–177/04 2006) ... 34, 43–44, 55–59, 108, 178–79, 182–83, 188
*EDF v Commission* (T–389/12 pending) ... 15, 126, 157, 181

*Éditions Odile Jacob SAS v Commission* (T–279/04 2010)........................34, 132–33, 167, 183
*Éditions Odile Jacob v Commission* (T–452/04 2010)............ 132, 137, 150, 164–65, 184, 194
*Éditions Odile Jacob v Commission* (T–237/05 2010) ..........................................................184
*Éditions Odile Jacob v Commission* (T–471/11 pending)............................................134, 184
*EDP v Commission* (T–87/05 2005) ............................................................ 39, 42, 52–53, 55, 58–59, 66, 71, 73, 88, 182
*Endemol v Commission* (T–221/95 1999)................................................................................42, 62
*Gencor v Commission* (T–102/96 1999) ...............................................................44, 182–183
*General Electric v Commission* (T–210/01 2005) ................................ 38, 55, 57, 71, 116, 182
*Kali & Salz* (T–88/94R 1994)........................................................................................................182
*Kaysersberg v Commission* (T–290/94 1997)................................... 34, 41, 61–62, 66, 182–83
*Lebard v Commission* (T–89/06 2009)...................................................................10, 179, 184
*MCI v Commission* (T–310/00 2004) ...........................................................................................180
*Microsoft v Commission* (T–201/04 2007)..................................................................136, 140
*Monty Program v Commission* (T–292/10 pending) .............................41–42, 73, 77, 182–84
*MyTravel* (T–212/03 2008) ...........................................................................................................182
*Niki Luftfahrt v Commission* (T–511/09 pending) .......................................................15, 152
*Niki Luftfahrt v Commission* (T–162/10 pending) .......................................................15, 182
*Omya v Commission II* (T–275/06 withdrawn 2008).........................................31, 56, 72, 180
*Petrolessence and SG2R v Commission* (T–342/00 2003)..............................165, 167–68, 184
*Qualcomm v Commission* (T–48/04 2009).............................................................78, 182–85
*Royal Philips Electronics v Commission* (T–119/02 2003)...................36, 48–49, 158–59, 205
*Ryanair v Commission* (T–342/07 2010).................................................. 47, 73, 110, 112, 182
*Scania v Commission* (T–163/03 withdrawn)................................................................................97
*Scania v Commission* (T–248/04 withdrawn)................................................................................98
*Schneider v Commission* (T–310/01 2002)...........................................................................10, 35
*Socratec v Commission* (T–269/03 2009)........................................................................................183
*SPAR Österreichische Warenhandel v Commission* (T–405/08 pending) ............................184
*Tetra Laval BV v Commission* (T–5/02 and T-80/02 2002) ......................................10, 44, 60
*Union Carbide v Commission* (T–322/94 R 1994) ........................................................................62
*vwd Vereinigte Wirtschaftsdienste v Commission* (T–353/08 withdrawn 2013) ..................185
*Virgin Atlantic Airways v Commission* (T–344/12 pending) ...................................................183
*Western Digital and Western Digital Ireland v Commission* (T–60/12 2012 withdrawn 2012) ......................................................................72, 181

### *European Ombudsman*

Decision 353/99/ME of 26 October 2000 (re *Skanska/Scancem* (M.1157 II 1998)............196
Decision 1115/2003/BB of 17 October 2003 (re *Volvo/Scania* (M.1672 II 2000) and *Volvo/Renault V.I.* (M.1980 I 2000).........................................................................196
Decision 1342/2007/FOR of 27 April 2009 (re *Ryanair/Aer Lingus* (M.4439 II 2007)........61

## United States of America

### *Department of Justice (Antitrust Division)*

*United States v Inco Limited and Falconbridge Limited*, Case No 1:06CV01151................115

*United States v The Manitowoc Company, Inc., Enodis plc, and Enocis Corporation,* Case No 1:2008CV01704, Final Judgment of 17 February 2009 ............ 127, 166, 208–209
*United States Of America v The Thomson Corporation And Reuters Group Plc,* Case No 1:08–cv–00262 ............ 126
*United States v UTC/Goodrich,* Case No 1:12–cv–01230–RC ............ 192

### *Federal Trade Commission*

*BP Amoco/Atlantic Richfield Company* (File No 991–0192, Docket No C–3938) ............ 128, 173–174
*Hoechst and Rhone–Poulent (Aventis)* (File No 991 0071, Docket No C–3919) ............ 118, 144, 160–161, 202
*Nestlé/Dreyer* (File No 021017, Docket No C–4082) ............ 84
*Nestlé/Ralston Purina* (File No 011 0083, Docket No C–4028) ............ 171–172
*Procter & Gamble/Gillette* (File No 051 0115, Docket No C–4151) ............ 128
*Roche Holding Ltd, Re* (File No 971 0103, Docket No C–3809) ............ 118
*Western Digital Corporation, Re* (File No 111 0122, Docket No C–4350) ............ 128, 207

## Denmark

### *Konkurrencerådet (Danish Competition Council)*

*Danish Crown/Steff-Houlberg (decision of 24 April 2002)* ............ *103*

# *Table of Legislation*

## Canada

### *Competition Bureau*

Information Bulletin on Merger Remedies, September 2006.............17
Outline Consent Agreement.............18

## European Union

Rules of Procedure of the Commission [2000] OJ L308/26 as amended by Commission decision of 15 November 2005 [2005] OJ L347/83
Art 1.............163
Art 3.............163
Arts 12–13.............77
Art 14.............77, 163
Treaty on the Functioning of the European Union (TFEU).............205
Art 101.............55, 191
Art 102 (ex 82).............55, 136, 191
Art 263.............180, 182
Arts 278–279.............182

### *Commission Notices and Guidelines*

Commission's Consolidated Jurisdictional Notice under Council Regulation (EC) No 139/2004 on the control of concentrations between undertakings [2008] OJ C95/1.............95
Commission Notice on remedies acceptable under Council Regulation (EEC) No 4064/89 and under Commission Regulation (EC) 447/98 [2001] OJ C68/3 (old Remedies Notice).............10, 17–19, 21, 38–39, 45, 48, 53, 74, 81, 115, 117–119, 124, 135, 139–140, 144, 165, 173, 205
para 6.............39
para 9.............45
para 12.............70, 74
para 17.............56
para 20.............109
para 21.............153
para 22.............116–117
para 23.............116
para 32.............58
para 35.............68
para 37.............48

para 43 .......... 52–53
para 49 .......... 101, 173
paras 50–51 .......... 144
para 52 .......... 140, 144, 146
para 55 .......... 130
para 57 .......... 139
para 58 .......... 165
paras 108–12 ..........
119, 144
Commission Notice on remedies acceptable under Council Regulation (EC) No 139/2004 and under Commission Regulation (EC) No 802/2004 [2008] OJ C267/1 (new Remedies Notice) .......... 3–4, 13, 17, 19, 21, 37, 39, 45, 48–53, 56, 60, 66, 68, 72, 75, 79, 83–84, 88, 92–93, 104, 107, 109, 113, 116, 124, 126, 128, 136, 139–141, 147, 154, 158–159, 165, 171, 173–175, 178, 186–187, 201–202, 204–205
para 1 .......... 54
para 5 .......... 40–41
para 6 .......... 38, 71–72, 108
para 7 .......... 46
para 8 .......... 39
para 9 .......... 43, 54–55
para 10 .......... 57, 173
para 11 .......... 57
para 12 .......... 54
para 13 .......... 45, 59, 75
para 14 .......... 58
para 15 .......... 44
para 16 .......... 43
para 17 .......... 45, 56
para 19 .......... 70, 129
para 20 .......... 70–71, 123, 173–174, 176
para 21 .......... 19, 47
para 22 .......... 45
para 23 .......... 45, 56, 79, 108, 153, 173
para 24 .......... 45, 79
para 25 .......... 45, 79–80
paras 26–27 .......... 45, 79
para 28 .......... 45, 79, 166
para 29 .......... 45, 79–80
para 30 .......... 45, 79–80, 119, 157, 166
para 31 .......... 45, 79–80, 166
para 32 .......... 45, 80–81
para 32 .......... 80
para 33 .......... 45, 80–81
para 34 .......... 45, 80, 82
para 35 .......... 45, 56, 80–81, 83
para 36 .......... 45, 56, 80, 83

para 37 ........ 45, 80, 84–85
para 38 ........ 45, 80, 86–87
paras 39–40 ........ 45, 89
para 41 ........ 45, 89–90
para 42 ........ 45, 89, 92
para 43 ........ 45, 70, 162, 173–175
para 44 ........ 45, 80, 116–117
para 45 ........ 45, 80, 116–117, 119
para 46 ........ 45, 80, 113, 117, 121
para 47 ........ 45, 80, 101
para 48 ........ 45, 101, 105, 107
para 49 ........ 45, 170
paras 50–51 ........ 45
para 52 ........ 45, 105
para 53 ........ 45, 80, 109
para 54 ........ 45, 80, 109, 113
para 55 ........ 45, 80, 109, 121
paras 56–57 ........ 45, 80, 109, 113
para 58 ........ 45, 93–94
paras 59–60 ........ 45, 94, 100
paras 61–64 ........ 45
para 65 ........ 45, 88
para 66 ........ 45, 68, 88
paras 67–68 ........ 45
para 69 ........ 45, 75
para 71 ........ 45, 154
para 72 ........ 45, 154, 155
para 73 ........ 45, 154, 157, 162, 173–174
para 74 ........ 45, 154, 157–158
para 75 ........ 45, 72, 154, 162
para 76 ........ 45, 154, 163, 178
para 78 ........ 46–47
para 79(b) ........ 47
para 79(d) ........ 46–47, 59–61
para 80 ........ 59–60, 68–69
para 83 ........ 49, 60
para 84 ........ 75
para 85 ........ 57, 71–72
para 88 ........ 50–51
para 89 ........ 50, 60
para 90 ........ 46, 50–51
para 91(b) ........ 47
para 91(d) ........ 46, 59–61
para 94 ........ 52–53, 60
para 97 ........ 124
para 98 ........ 123–124, 142, 169
paras 99–100 ........ 124

para 101 ... 164, 167
para 102 ... 105, 164
para 103 ... 103, 151
para 104 ... 102, 105, 107, 168
para 105 ... 151, 165–166
para 106 ... 165–167, 170
para 108 ... 144
para 110 ... 145–146
para 111 ... 141, 148
para 112 ... 146–147
paras 113–15 ... 83
para 116 ... 149, 151, 167, 169
para 118 ... 136, 140
para 119 ... 83, 137–139, 141, 151, 164, 167, 169
para 120 ... 135, 137, 140
para 121 ... 142, 152
para 122 ... 142
para 123 ... 127–129
para 124 ... 102, 127–128, 130, 138
para 125 ... 127, 130–132, 135, 138
para 126 ... 127–128, 130, 137
para 127 ... 127, 138–139
para 128 ... 175
para 129 ... 45
Commission Notice on the rules for access to the Commission file in cases pursuant to Arts 81 and 82 of the EC Treaty, Arts 53, 54 and 57 of the EEA Agreement and Council Regulation (EC) No 139/2004 [2005] OJ C325/7 (Notice on Access to the File)
para 26 ... 196
paras 35–38 ... 46
DG Commission's Best Practice Guidelines for divestiture commitments 2003 (Best Practice Remedies Guidelines) ... 3, 10, 18–19, 96, 128, 136, 146, 154, 156, 203
Explanatory Note
point 2 ... 19
point 4 ... 19
point 21 ... 140, 146
point 22 ... 96
point 25 ... 149
Model Text for Divestiture Commitments (MTDC) ... 4, 18–19, 109, 139, 147, 173, 202, 204
para 1 ... 109
para 2 ... 124, 169
para 3 ... 70, 162, 173–174
para 5 ... 145
para 5(b) ... 145
para 5(c) ... 146
para 6 ... 145
para 7 ... 140, 145, 147

para 8 ... 96, 141, 145
para 9 ... 148
para 11 ... 149
para 13 ... 149
para 14 ... 101
para 14(c) ... 107
para 15 ... 151, 165–166
para 16 ... 127–128
para 17 ... 127, 130, 137–138
para 18 ... 127–130
para 19 ... 127, 129–130
paras 20–21 ... 127, 129
para 22 ... 136
para 23 ... 139, 165
para 23(vi) ... 137
para 23(vii) ... 164
para 24 ... 142, 152
para 27 ... 165
para 30 ... 135
para 31 ... 138
para 33 ... 138
para 34 ... 154–155
Sections A–D ... 19
Section F ... 137
Model Text for Trustee Mandates (MTTM) ... 18–19, 130, 139, 202, 204
paras 1–3 ... 127
para 4 ... 127, 136
para 5 ... 127
para 6 ... 139
para 6(d) ... 96, 141
para 10 ... 151
para 11 ... 142, 152
para 13 ... 142
paras 14–16 ... 137
para 19 ... 135
para 20 ... 131
para 21 ... 132
para 22 ... 130, 132
para 23 ... 132
para 24 ... 130, 137
para 26 ... 130
para 28 ... 138
para 35 ... 130
Sections A–J ... 19
para 2 ... 203
para 4 ... 204
para 15 ... 124

para 41 ....................39
DG Competition's Best Practices on the conduct of EC merger proceedings 2003 (Best Practice Guidelines on Merger Proceedings) ....................11, 14
para 33(a) ....................37
para 38 ....................196
para 39 ....................63, 196
para 41 ....................46
paras 45–46 ....................196
Draft revised Commission Notice of 24 April 2007 on remedies acceptable under Council Regulation (EEC) No 139/2004 and under Commission Regulation (EC) No 802/2004 (draft new Remedies Notice) ....................13–14, 17, 46, 57, 68, 70, 87,100, 119, 129–131, 136–137, 140, 147, 156, 162, 165, 170, 173–175
para 19 ....................130
paras 118–21 ....................136
Guidelines on the assessment of horizontal mergers under the Council Regulation on the control of concentrations between undertakings [2004] OJ C31/5 (Horizontal Merger Guidelines) ....................29, 37
para 4 ....................37
para 8 ....................29
para 79 ....................29
Guidelines on the assessment of non-horizontal mergers under the Council Regulation on the control of concentrations between undertakings [2008] OJ C 265/ 6 (Non-Horizontal Merger Guidelines) ....................37
Manual of Procedures for the DG Competition ....................166

*Decisions*

Decision 2011/695 of the President of the European Commission of 13 October 2011 on the function and terms of reference of the hearing officer in certain competition proceedings [2011] OJ L275/29 (Terms of Reference of the Hearing Officer) ....................63, 195
Recital 8 ....................63
Art 1(2) ....................63
Art 3(5) ....................63, 195
Art 3(7) ....................63
Art 8(1)–(6) ....................64
Art 14 .................... 63–64
Art 14(1) ....................63
Art 15 ....................64
Arts 16–17 ....................63

*Regulations*

Council Regulation (EEC) No 4064/89 of 21 December 1989 on the control of concentrations between undertakings [1989] OJ L395/1; corrected version [1990] OJ L257/13; as last amended by Council Regulation (EC) No 1310/97 of 30 June 1997 [1997] OJ L180/1; corrigendum in [1998] OJ L40/17 (original Merger Regulation) .................... 1, 7, 9–10, 21, 37, 53, 124, 127, 136, 165, 167, 177, 194

Recitals 30–31 ... 9
Art 6(2) ... 9
Art 7(1) ... 109
Art 8(2) ... 7, 16
Art 10(1) ... 47
Implementing Regulation (EC) No 3384/94 of 21 December 1994 on notifications, time limits and hearings provided for in Council Regulation (EEC) No 4064/89 on the control of concentrations between undertakings [1994] OJ L377/1 (1994 Implementing Regulation) ... 51
Recital 14 ... 7
Art 18(1) ... 7
Council Regulation (EC) No 1310/97 of 30 June 1997 amending Regulation (EEC) No 4064/89 on the control of concentrations between undertakings [1997] OJ L180/1 ... 9
Recital 8 ... 17
Implementing Regulation (EC) No 447/98 of 1 March 1998 on notifications, time limits and hearings provided for in Council Regulation (EEC) No 4064/89 on the control of concentrations between undertakings [1998] OJ L6/1 (1998 Implementing Regulation) ... 9
Art 18(1) ... 48
Art 18(2) ... 53
Proposal for a Council Regulation on the control of concentrations between undertakings COM (2002) 711 final [2003] OJ C20/4 ... 10
Council Regulation (EC) No 139/2004 of 20 January 2004 on the control of concentrations between undertakings [2004] OJ L24/1 (Merger Regulation) ... 1, 3, 5, 11, 16–17, 28–29, 33, 37, 40–43, 52, 66, 95, 115, 121, 128, 169, 205, 217
Recitals 3–5 ... 28
Recital 30 ... 16–17, 43, 54
Recital 31 ... 176–177
Recital 42 ... 193
Art 2 ... 175
Art 2(1)(a)–(b) ... 35
Art 2(2) ... 35
Art 2(3) ... 28, 35
Art 3 ... 1, 173
Art 3(2) ... 95
Art 4 ... 59
Art 6(1) ... 176
Art 6(1)(c) ... 36–37, 50
Art 6(2) ... 16, 36, 43, 70, 72, 174, 177
Art 6(3)(a) ... 3, 177
Art 6(3)(b) ... 176, 178
Art 6(4) ... 176
Art 8 ... 52
Art 8(1) ... 176
Art 8(2) ... 16, 43, 70, 72, 176

Art 8(3) .... 1, 38, 176
Art 8(4) .... 38, 17, 180, 215
Art 8(4)(b) .... 176
Art 8(5) .... 177
Art 8(5)(b) .... 176
Art 8(6)(a) .... 76–77
Art 8(6)(b) .... 176
Art 8(7) .... 176
Art 8(7)(b) .... 176
Art 9 .... 12, 159, 215
Art 10 .... 17
Art 10(1) .... 47
Art 10(2) .... 31, 50
Art 10(3) .... 50–51
Art 10(4) .... 47
Art 11 .... 47, 59, 61
Art 13 .... 47
Art 14 .... 17, 163, 178
Art 14(2)(c) .... 177
Art 14(2)(d) .... 129, 177
Art 15 .... 17, 163, 178
Art 15(1)(c) .... 129, 177
Art 15(1)(d) .... 177
Art 18(1) .... 61
Art 18(3) .... 61
Art 18(4) .... 60, 62
Art 19(1)–(2) .... 64
Art 19(3) .... 64, 177
Art 19(4) .... 64
Art 19(5) .... 65–66
Art 19(7) .... 66
Art 20 .... 17, 77, 193
Art 22 .... 56
Art 23(1)(c) .... 17
Commission Regulation (EC) No 802/2004 of 21 April 2004 implementing Council Regulation (EC) No 139/2004 on the control of concentrations between undertakings [2004] OJ L133/1, as amended by Commission Regulation (EC) No 1033/2008 of 20 October 2008, [2008] OJ L279/3 (Implementing Regulation) .... 11, 13, 17–18, 136, 203
Recital 17 .... 49
Art 13(2) .... 37
Art 16(1) .... 60
Art 17(1) .... 61
Art 18(2) .... 61
Art 18(4) .... 192
Art 19 .... 17, 52
Art 19(1) .... 47

Art 19(2) ........ 50–51, 53
Art 20(1) ........ 46
Art 20(1a) ........ 46
Art 20(2) ........ 46
Art 20a ........ 136, 200
Annex IV (Form RM for divestiture commitments) ........ 13, 17, 19, 46–47, 186, 202–203
para 2 ........ 203
para 5.13 ........ 203
Section 3 ........ 19, 47

**Germany**

*Bundeskartellamt* model mandate form for monitoring trustees ........ 18
*Bundeskartellamt* model texts covering different types of divestitures ........ 18

**International**

***International Competition Network (ICN)***

ICN's Merger Notification and Procedures Implementation Handbook 2006 ........ 25
Ch 7 ........ 26
ICN's Recommended Practices for Merger Notification and Review Procedures (ICN Recommended Remedies Practice) ........ 25
Comment A.1 ........ 43
Comment 2 ........ 39
section XI ........ 25

**United Kingdom**

***UK Competition Commission***

'Application of Divestiture Remedies in Merger Inquiries' (2004) ........ 17
'Merger Remedies: Competition Commission Guidelines' (2008) ........ 17
1.26–1.27 ........ 38

**United States of America**

***Department of Justice***

'Antitrust Division Policy Guide to Merger Remedies' (old DoJ Merger Remedies Guide 2004) ........ 20
Pt IV.H ........ 117
Merger Remedies Guide 2011 ........ 20, 119
Pt I.A ........ 204

Pt II.A.2 ....................109
Pt IV.A.1 ....................115
Pt IV.A.2.a....................109, 111
Pt IV.A.2.b ....................117, 119
Pt IV.C.1 ....................151
Pt IV.C.2 .................... 170–171
Pt IV.C.3 .................... 103–104
Pt IV.E....................151
Pt IV.I....................140, 146–147
caveat 1 ....................143
Pt IV.I.3....................140
Pt V ....................199
Pt V.A ....................206

*Federal Trade Commission*

Guidelines for Negotiating Merger Remedies 2012 ....................20, 118
p 6....................85
p 7 ....................85, 109–110
p 8....................109
p 10 ....................149
p 11 ....................104, 151
pp 13–14....................105
p 16 ....................140, 204
p 21 ....................117
'Statement of the Federal Trade Commission's Bureau of Competition on Negotiating Merger Remedies', April 2003....................20

# *Table of Agreements*

Cooperation agreement between the EU and the US 1991 [1995] OJ L95/47 (1991 EU-US Cooperation Agreement)....68
Art VIII....207
EU/Canada cooperation agreement 1999 [1999] OJ L175/50....68
EU/Japan cooperation agreement 2003 [2003] OJ L183/12....68
EU/Republic of Korea cooperation agreement 2009 [2009] OJ L 202/36....68
US–EU Best Practices on Cooperation in Merger Investigations 2011.. 16, 69, 206–207, 210
paras 16–20....69

# 1

# The Commission's Remedies Policy

## 1.1 Introduction

### *1.1.1 Merger Remedies*

This book explores the policy and practice on merger remedies developed by the European Commission (the Commission) within the framework of Council Regulation (EC) No 139/2004 on the control of concentrations between undertakings (the Merger Regulation).[1] The Commission has enjoyed powers to remedy mergers since 1990[2] and over the past two decades its policy has undergone substantial changes from being virtually unregulated and characterised by an ad-hoc approach to arguably the most guided and regulated area in merger control enforcement.

The procedural mechanism behind remedies under the Merger Regulation is that the merging parties[3] propose, in response to competition problems raised by the Commission after an initial investigation, amendments to their notified concentration and, if deemed acceptable, the Commission makes such amendments enforceable by imposing them as conditions and obligations when approving the merger.[4] Such remedial measures are typically implemented post-clearance and are generally referred to as commitments, undertakings or remedies.[5]

The possibility of proposing and accepting remedies is paramount in merger proceedings where competition concerns have been identified, as it is the only way for the respective transaction to proceed.[6] Thus, remedies allow for a restructuring of the problematic and typically non-core part(s) of a proposed merger in order for the overall transaction to materialise. A restructuring may range from a 'traditional' divestiture of assets or businesses of one (or

[1] Council Regulation (EC) No 139/2004 of 20 January 2004, Official Journal (OJ) [2004] L24/1.

[2] See Council Regulation (EEC) No 4064/89 of 21 December 1989 on the control of concentrations between undertakings [1989] OJ L395/1; corrected version [1990] OJ L257/13; as last amended by Council Regulation (EC) No 1310/97 of 30 June 1997 [1997] OJ L180/1; corrigendum in [1998] OJ L40/17 (the original Merger Regulation).

[3] Such parties are understood as being the contractual parties to the respective merger agreement and in the present context they are referred to as the merging or notifying parties, the parties to the concentration or the transaction or merely the parties. The terms also refer to situations with only one notifying party.

[4] The terms merger, acquisition, joint venture, concentration and transaction will be used interchangeably and refer to certain changes of control on a lasting basis as defined in Art 3 of the Merger Regulation.

[5] In the present context the generic term 'remedies' covers 'commitments' submitted by the parties and the corresponding 'obligations' and 'conditions' imposed by the Commission in a conditional clearance decision in accordance with the Merger Regulation.

[6] It follows from Art 8(3) of the Merger Regulation that once the Commission has established that a concentration will significantly impede effective competition, it has no other choice than prohibiting it. Alternatively, the merging parties are of course free to abandon their transaction in order to prevent a formal prohibition decision but the outcome is in effect the same.

both) of the merging parties to more innovative transitional arrangements allowing for competitors to access capacity or infrastructure on certain conditions. In many cases remedies packages contain a combination of several remedial measures.

The 'art of remedies' is to find the right balance between, on the one hand, preserving competition in the best possible way through adequate remedies in the given problematic market and, on the other hand, retaining the overall commercial and financial incentives and benefits that facilitated the merger in the first place. If the remedies are inadequate, competition problems may not be (fully) addressed and that may cause substantial economic losses for competitors in the given market to the ultimate detriment of consumers. If the remedies are excessive, the parties may conclude that the anticipated benefits and synergies of the merger will be jeopardised with the result that they abandon their planned transaction altogether.[7] This scenario may not only be a case of 'missed commercial opportunities' for the companies involved but competition may also ultimately suffer if the overall benefits of the transaction could have promoted competition in core areas.[8]

Not surprisingly, several commentators have considered the remedial aspect of merger enforcement paramount in past practice.[9] Indeed, the nature and complexity of the negotiation, design, assessment, implementation and enforcement of remedies have posed many challenges to competition authorities over the years as experience has shown that numerous individual aspects of a remedy must be successful in order for the overall remedy to succeed. Also, what makes the topic of remedies particularly challenging and at times also slightly frustrating for all parties involved is that, while the negotiation, design and assessment are based on a prospective analysis, the ultimate success – or failure – of a remedy can be determined only several years post-clearance when the effects of the remedies are visible in the given market.[10]

Moreover, unless the Commission's decision is successfully challenged before the Court of Justice of the European Union (the EU Court),[11] either by the parties or third parties with standing, through an action for annulment, the Commission cannot reverse or unilaterally amend its conditional clearance decisions unless fraudulent circumstances, on which

[7] This has happened on several occasions. For pre-decision abandonments, see *SCJ/Sara Lee* (M.5969 II 2011) (withdrawn on 8 June 2011); *DSV/Vesterhavet/DFDS* (M.5454 II 2009) (withdrawn on 16 June 2009); *OMV/MOL* (M.4799 II 2008) (withdrawn on 6 August 2008); and *BHP Billiton/Rio Tinto* (M.4985 II 2008) (withdrawn on 26 November 2008). For post-decision abandonments, see *Arsenal/DSP* (M.5153 II 2009) and *Arjowiggins/M-real Zanders Reflex* (M.4513 II 2008). For a statistical overview of abandoned transactions (and hence withdrawn notifications), see Annex A.

[8] There are of course cases where a prohibition is the only regulatory solution, if the competition problems are so severe that they cannot be addressed satisfactory through remedies, see most recently *Ryanair/Aer Lingus III* (M.6663 II 2013), *UPS/TNT Express* (M.6570 II 2013), *Deutsche Börse/NYSE Euronext* (M.6166 II 2012), *Olympic/Aegean Airlines* (M.5830 II 2011), and *RyanAir/Aer Lingus* (M.4439 II 2007).

[9] In 2000 the then-Chairman of the US Federal Trade Commission (FTC) said 'I believe there is no more important set of policy questions facing the antitrust community than defining the nature and limits of appropriate restructuring in merger review', see Speech by Pitofsky (2000). Along the same lines, when the then FTC Chairman paid tribute in 2009 to the then-outgoing Director-General of DG Competition Philip Lowe he highlighted that '[a]mong Philip's most important achievements was his work on mergers and merger remedies guidelines', see Speech by Leibowitz (2009).

[10] As elaborated upon later, the preparation of ex-post studies is therefore crucial.

[11] The EU Court (formerly known as the Community Courts) includes the European Court of Justice (the Court of Justice) (formerly the Court of Justice of the European Communities) and the European General Court (the General Court) (formerly the Court of First Instance of the European Communities). For the sake of consistency and simplicity, the current terms will be applied also to the judiciary bodies and their judgments prior to 1 December 2009.

the decision was based, can be proven.[12] From a general policy point of view the Commission is thus faced with the dilemma of wishing to pursue a dynamic and flexible remedies policy while at the same time being aware that its approach must be sufficiently 'tried-and-tested' in order to minimise the risk of unforeseen regulatory misjudgements, as any unfortunate effects thereof cannot be subsequently impeached.

By way of introduction, the Commission's current policy and practice are based on the following remedies-specific measures and initiatives: (i) the Commission notice on remedies acceptable under the Merger Regulation (the Remedies Notice) from October 2008;[13] (ii) the Commission's Best Practice Guidelines for divestiture commitments (Best Practice Remedies Guidelines) from April 2003, consisting of two standard model texts relating to the submission of commitment proposals and trustee mandates together with an explanatory note;[14] and (iii) the Commission's in-house study of merger remedies (the Remedies Study) from October 2005.[15] This framework should be considered in the context of nearly 320 conditional clearance decisions adopted by the Commission over the past two decades[16] as well as jurisprudence from the EU Court. Also a considerable number of guidance and studies from other jurisdictions, international organisations, academia as well as other Commission bodies have influenced the Commission's evolving remedies policy and practice.[17]

### *1.1.2 This Book*

#### 1.1.2.1 Objectives and Limitations

This book seeks to identify and examine as many as possible of the most important and interesting merger remedies aspects, which have emerged and developed in the Commission's policy and practice over the past 20-plus years. Indeed, in order to fully understand and appreciate the current remedies framework it is necessary to draw on past experiences and initiatives where the Commission has gone through phases of learning, acceleration and consolidation of its remedies policy. Along the way, the Commission has accomplished

[12] To date, a conditional clearance decision has never been revoked under the Merger Regulation (in the past only one unconditional clearance decision has been revoked in accordance with Art 6(3)(a) based on misleading information, see *Sanofi/Synthélabo* (M.1397 I 1999)).

[13] Commission Notice on remedies acceptable under Council Regulation (EC) No 139/2004 and under Commission Regulation (EC) No 802/2004 [2008] OJ C267/1.

[14] The standard model texts and explanatory note are available at ec.europa.eu/comm/competition/mergers/legislation/best_practice.html and introduced in the Commission's press release IP/03/614 of 2 May 2003. For further details, see 1.3.3. The guidelines are not to be confused with the best practices on the conduct of EC merger proceedings, containing provisions on eg 'state-of-play' meetings which are also relevant for remedies, see n 54 below.

[15] Throughout this book references to the Remedies Study refer to the version of the study published on the DG Competition's website (not the book version subsequently published by the Commission in 2010), see ec.europa.eu/competition/mergers/legislation/remedies_study.pdf. See also Commission press release announcing the study, IP/05/1327 of 21 October 2005.

[16] Statistics relating to remedies cases under the Merger Regulation in the current context are sourced from the DG Competition's website at ec.europa.eu/competition/mergers/statistics.pdf. Furthermore, Annex A contains an annual breakdown of merger remedies statistics in phase I and phase II proceedings, respectively, and put in the context of the total number of clearance and prohibition decisions. As of 31 December 2012, the Commission had adopted 218 remedies decisions in phase I and 100 remedies decisions in phase II out of a total of nearly 4,900 clearance and prohibition decisions (ie disregarding referral decisions). Overall, remedies decisions accounted for around 6.5% of all such decisions.

[17] See section 1.4 below.

numerous successes but inevitably it has also faced some not insignificant obstacles and shortcomings in its enforcement.

The analysis in this book is structured in accordance with the 'remedies lifecycle': the negotiation, submission, assessment, adoption, implementation and enforcement of remedies. Throughout the examination a number of critical remedies issues will be highlighted and, on this basis, the overall objective is to verify whether the current remedies framework provides an adequate regulatory response to the raised issues. It will be argued that the current sophistication and complexity of enforcement may in some instances risk weakening and even potentially undermining some of the enforcement successes accomplished throughout the years if the Commission does not consider further improvements or adjustments to its current remedies regime within the foreseeable future. Such areas include the need for enhanced procedural safeguards particularly in phase I proceedings, additional post-decision transparency and monitoring measures as well as in periodic re-evaluation of submission forms, guidance and decisional practice. Where possible, specific measures aimed at improving the Commission's remedies policy will be suggested and considered.

Needless to say, in view of the substantial scope of the Commission's remedies policy and practice over the past 22 years, the analysis in this book has had to give priority to (and by the same token, exclude) certain areas. Among other things, the main focus is on structural remedies as they continue to be considered the most important and frequently used remedial solutions, partly due to the Commission's clear preference for such remedies[18] but also due to structural solutions being the most obvious and straightforward choice for the parties in many cases. Accordingly, non-structural remedies will be described only sporadically where appropriate in the context of main features of the Commission's remedies policy, especially in situations where such remedies may be more appropriate than structural solutions or where they are ancillary and supplementary to structural solutions.[19] However, it is worth stressing that this priority does not imply that non-structural solutions are insignificant in the Commission's policy and, indeed, some of the most recent developments indicate that such remedies may prove increasingly prominent in future policy but for the present purposes it has been necessary to focus on structural solutions in order to devote sufficient resources and space to this aspect.

Furthermore, several remedies topics could easily warrant a dedicated book in their own right due to their scope, nature and complexity. Such topics will be limited to what is essential in order to reflect on the overall remedies discussions and identify successes and/or failures in this respect. Arbitration is an example where such provisions in remedies cases could easily justify an in-depth analysis but where the topic in the current context has been strictly limited to what is necessary to assess the workability and impact of such clauses in a remedies package. Another example is the transatlantic cooperation in merger remedies cases where, although the policies of the Commission's US counterparts have proven highly relevant in EU contexts, such aspects will be mentioned only where they highlight particular similarities or differences in order to further enhance the understanding of the Commission's policy and practice.

[18] Commissioner Almunia continues to emphasise a clear preference for clear-cut, structural and immediately effective remedies and hence reinforces the past and current policy in this respect, see Speech by Almunia (2011e).

[19] This priority is in line with the attention non-structural solutions are given in the Remedies Study, Model Commitments Texts and Remedies Notice. Furthermore, as correctly pointed out by the Commission it is difficult to evaluate eg access remedies as they often do not have an obvious beneficiary, being offered unilaterally to the world at large or to an open ended category of beneficiaries that are not always known to the Commission, see Remedies Study, p 114 (point 4).

Finally, it is worth pointing out that while remedies are a direct response to competition problems, a description and analysis of the latter in this book will be limited to what is strictly necessary for the understanding and discussion of the corresponding remedies. This priority should in no way be seen as a statement that the evaluation of the competition problems is less important but merely as a means of focusing the analysis on the remedies aspects.

#### 1.1.2.2 Structure

This book is structured in the following way. The remainder of this chapter is devoted to an introduction to the Commission's past and present policy by providing a chronological overview of its remedies framework as developed over the past two decades. It will be explained how the Commission's policy has gone through the following three main phases: learning, acceleration and consolidation.[20] In addition, certain remedies aspects, which may justify a possible re-evaluation within the foreseeable future, will be introduced. Furthermore, as a basis for the analysis in the following chapters, an overview will be provided of the current remedies framework, consisting of relevant provisions in the Merger Regulation, guidelines and standard model texts as well as relevant remedies reviews and studies not only from the Commission but also from the US competition authorities, the Organisation for Economic Co-operation and Development (OECD) and the International Competition Network (ICN). Finally, some introductory considerations about remedies enforcement objectives will be submitted.

Chapter 2 contains a detailed analysis of the substantive and procedural provisions governing the Commission's remedies policy. The sources are not confined to the relevant legislative framework and guidance but include to a large extent the Commission's decisional practice as well as jurisprudence from the EU Court. First the general principles governing the identification of competition concerns as well as corresponding remedies proposals are explained, including reflections on initiatives, onus and responsibilities in this process. The remainder of the chapter is devoted to a detailed examination of the requirements for all parties concerned when negotiating, submitting, evaluating and adopting merger remedies.

Chapter 3 sets out essential features of divestiture remedies. The analysis is mainly based on the Commission's guidelines and decisional practice but references are also made to the findings in the Commission's Remedies Study and other reviews. The focus is on structural remedies in the form of stand-alone businesses, carve-outs, selected assets and licences in lieu of divestitures. Also purchaser requirements are discussed as well as newer provisions aimed at further enhancing the viability of the business to be divested, such as additional assets, up-front buyers, fix-it-firsts and crown jewels.

Chapter 4 examines the main post-decision features and modalities when the remedies are being implemented. While the analysis is based on guidance provisions and decisional practice, it also includes more speculative aspects as some of these implementing steps are based on sources, which are generally not publicly available. The chapter deals with 'traditional' implementation issues such as interim preservation, hold-separate provisions and the appointment and tasks of trustees but it also highlights newer and slightly more controversial issues like re-selling restrictions on the purchaser and re-acquisition prohibitions

[20] The three phases are briefly set out by De Souza and Brockhoff in Drauz and Jones (2012) paras 7.2–7.12.

on the merging parties. As part of the implementation phase the chapter furthermore examines cases where remedies have been reviewed and modified as well as the implications of non-compliance. Finally, the possibilities for the parties and third parties to subsequently challenge a conditional clearance decision are briefly explained.

Chapter 5 reviews, with the benefit of hindsight, a number of critical issues in the Commission's past and present remedies policy and practice. First the identified successes throughout the years are briefly summed up and then the remainder of the chapter is devoted to further reflections on identified shortcomings. It will inter alia be argued that some of the current standard provisions are in danger of imposing undue burdens on the parties in terms of disproportionate requirements and inflexible procedures. The lack of transparency, in particular throughout the implementation stage, will be highlighted and addressed. Concerns will be raised as to whether phase I proceedings are indeed suitable for today's often complex remedies cases, especially in view of the tight deadlines and the lack of additional 'phase II procedural safeguards'. Enforcement and monitoring issues will be highlighted as an area where there is scope for improvements and need for tightened policy. With respect to the currently used standard submission forms and models, it will be submitted that rigid information requirements and standardisation may result in some provisions being disproportionate and/or inflexible. Finally, the Commission's responsibility to update guidance and undertake ex-post studies will be examined.

The ultimate aim of the final chapter is to critically discuss and verify whether the identified shortcomings are of such a nature and extent that they may risk diminishing or even undermining some of the accomplished successes as well as to evaluate these shortcomings in the context of the overall objectives of the Commission's remedies enforcement. It will be concluded that there are valid reasons for arguing that the Commission should indeed reconsider some of its existing enforcement priorities and policies. Also, possible improvements to the Commission's current remedies policy are suggested.

#### 1.1.2.3 Citations

As the analysis throughout this book to a large extent is based on the Commission's vast decisional practice as well as relevant jurisprudence from the EU Court, it has been considered useful to make the case references as short as possible. By way of example, a reference to a Commission decision is made in the following way: *Hutchinson 3G Austria/Orange Austria* (M.6497 II 2012).[21] Likewise, reference to a judgment by the EU Court is made in the following way: *Éditions Jacob v Commission* (T-452/04 2010).[22] It is hoped that the short reference style will make the numerous references to decisional practice and jurisprudence less disruptive for the flow of the text in this book. Annex B contains a table of all remedies decisions adopted by the Commission, and Annex C contains a table of remedies-related judgments by the EU Court.

Similarly, when referring to and citing relevant literature, sources are referred to by way of citing the author's name and year of publication (for example Whish and Bailey (2012)).[23] All other relevant information is contained in the bibliography, which is divided into three

[21] The reference thus contains information on: the case name and number, and indication of whether the decision has been adopted in phase I or II, and the adoption year.

[22] The reference thus contains information on the name and number of the case as well as the year of the judgment by the EU Court.

[23] The reference is usually followed by an indication of the specific page or paragraph in question.

sections: books and journals; reports, studies and working papers; and speeches.[24] Furthermore, when referring to press reports, company statements and other relevant documents in the public domain, endeavour has been made to provide web-links whenever possible in order to ease access to such information.

Finally, it should be noted that a number of 'commentaries' have been inserted throughout the book. The purpose of these short statements is to single out and conclude upon particularly significant aspects and/or in some instances provide a more personal observation on the issues at hand.

## 1.2 Chronological Overview

### *1.2.1 The Learning Phase*

The original Merger Regulation contained few provisions on remedies, notably Article 8(2) according to which the Commission had powers to remedy phase II cases by attaching conditions and obligation. Although the Commission lacked express legal powers to remedy cases in phase I, it considered it justified to accept such commitments in clear-cut cases.[25] During the merger review in 1994 a 3-month deadline for submission of phase II remedies was introduced in response to an increasing number of cases where remedies were submitted (too) late during the administrative proceedings making proper assessment and consultation of the Member States (through the Advisory Committee on Concentrations (the Advisory Committee)) difficult, if not impossible.[26]

This period was obviously a time of learning and characterised by an ad-hoc, case-by-case approach to the design and implementation of remedies. The main source of remedies guidance was the Commission's own decisional practice and it meant that a few of the early-adopted detailed remedies decisions unofficially served as templates in other cases.[27] It is fair to say that during this period the Commission's analysis often lacked elaboration and sophistication and the remedies were often confined to traditional 'simple' divestitures

[24] Reports, studies and working papers are referred to in the following way: for example, 'Working Paper by Davies and Lyons (2008)', 'Study by Cosnita and Tropeano (2005)', and speeches are referred to as 'Speech by Almunia (2012a)' for example.

[25] See Report from the Commission to the Council on the implementation of the Merger Regulation, COM (93) 385 (1993 Commission Report to the Council) para 17. The Commission explained that it had accepted phase I commitments in cases where the competition concern was clear-cut, could easily be remedied and where compliance was easily monitored, see eg *Fiat/Ford New Holland* (M.009 I 1991) and *British Airways/TAT* (M.259 I 1992). In the report the Commission nevertheless acknowledged that its practice could raise questions with regard to procedure and especially transparency and the ability of the Commission to enforce post-merger commitments (para 17). Although third parties lodged complaints about possible breach of phase I remedies (*Air France/Sabena* (M.157 I 1992), cited in the Commission's annual report on competition policy (Competition Report) 1994, para 322), the Commission never publicly concluded breach of remedies and the EU Court never ruled on possible enforcement issues in this respect.

[26] The 3-month deadline was introduced by Recital 14 and Art 18(1) in the Implementing Regulation (EC) No 3384/94 of 21 December 1994 on notifications, time limits and hearings provided for in Council Regulation (EEC) No 4064/89 on the control of concentrations between undertakings [1994] OJ L377/1 (the 1994 Implementing Regulation).

[27] One of the first elaborate remedies decisions was *Crown Cork & Seal/CarnaudMetalbox* (M.603 II 1995) where the parties' commitments (reproduced in para 115 of the decision) contained many detailed provisions and therefore served as a template for notifying parties in subsequent cases.

of overlapping activities.[28] However, this approach seemed justified as many of the early remedies cases involved traditional industrial sectors with ample scope for consolidation and therefore the competition problems and the corresponding remedies were relatively straightforward.[29]

In terms of procedure, transparency in remedies cases was extremely limited at the beginning of this period: contents of proposed remedies were generally considered business secrets and third parties were not informed about or consulted on possible remedies proposals.[30] Thus, only once a formal conditional clearance decision had been adopted, would the existence of remedies become known to the outside world,[31] and even then would the contents of the remedies in these cases sometimes be omitted from the public version of the decision.[32] The Commission gradually became aware of these shortcomings and started to improve transparency by for example introducing consultation of involved third parties as a standard procedure[33] and being more rigorous in limiting what information was considered 'business secrets' to be withheld from the public domain.

Overall in this period, the Commission adopted a total of 37 remedies decisions, with the majority being phase II cases.[34] Remedies decisions accounted for around 6 per cent of all decisions in this period. On an annual basis, the Commission adopted between two and nine remedies decisions so practice developed at a relatively slow pace. Due to persistent criticism of the Commission's lack of formal powers to adopt phase I remedies decisions, the Commission kept such decisions to a minimum (less than four decisions per year).[35] By 1997 the Commission started to experience a sharp rise in the number of notifications as well as remedies decisions, indicating the beginning of a forthcoming merger wave which started to put pressure on the Commission's resources and necessitated improved remedies procedures.

[28] For a critique of the Commission's remedies policy in its very early days, see Neven, Nuttall and Seabright (1993) 117–31.

[29] Examples of typical cases for this period: *Lyonnaise des Eaux/Suez* (M.916 I 1997), *Anglo American Corporation/Lonrho* (M.754 II 1997), *Veba/Degussa* (M.942 II 1997), *Kimberly-Clark/Scott* (M.623 II 1996), *ABB/Daimler-Benz* (M.580 II 1995), *Glaxo/Wellcome* (M.555 I 1995), *Repola/Kymmene* (M.646 I 1995), *Procter & Gamble/Schickedanz* (M.430 II 1994), *Nestlé/Perrier* (M.190 II 1992), *DuPont/ICI* (M.214 II 1992) and *Courtaulds/SNIA* (M.113 I 1991).

[30] See 1993 Commission Report to the Council, paras 17–18 and Conclusion 4 (p 23). The practice of non-disclosure applied to phase I as well as phase II proceedings.

[31] Typically, the standard press release announcing the adoption of the decision would merely mention the nature of the remedy in very general terms. Further details would be known only once the decision was formally published, either by the DG Competition (phase I cases) or in the OJ (phase II cases). The delays in publication were often considerable, typically ranging from three to nine months.

[32] The lack of transparency was especially pronounced in phase I decisions, see eg *Repola/Kymmene* (M.646 I 1995) where every fact relating to the remedies was considered a business secret, see para 67.

[33] In its Competition Report 1993 the Commission acknowledged that 'other competitors and undertakings do not enjoy an opportunity to comment on the adequacy of the commitments offered' and suggested that 'transparency can be improved by the prior publication of proposed commitments' (para 73). Although the Commission subsequently refrained from publishing commitment proposals, it did start consulting on an individual basis interested third parties on remedies proposals, see Competition Report 1994, para 236. It also initiated voluntarily consultation of the Member States on such proposals. However, this new procedure created unexpected problems as it was difficult for the Commission to allow enough time for consultations to take place during a phase I procedure which then lasted one month.

[34] The Commission adopted 14 phase I remedies decisions and 23 phase II remedies decisions.

[35] For a critique of the Commission's lack of powers to adopt and enforce phase I remedies prior to 1998, see Broberg (1997), in particular pp 852–66.

### *1.2.2 The Acceleration Phase*

In 1998 the Commission finally received explicit legal powers to remedy phase I cases[36] and, at the same time, a three-week deadline for the submission of phase I commitments was introduced and the total duration of phase I remedies proceedings was extended to six weeks.[37] Thus, the procedure in phase I cases now mirrored phase II cases, albeit with shorter deadlines. The new explicit provision to accept phase I remedies resulted in an explosive increase in phase I remedies cases rising from merely 2 decisions in 1997 to 12, 16 and 26 decisions respectively in the following 3 years.[38] Although the overall share of remedies decisions rose only slightly to 8 per cent of all clearance and prohibition decisions being adopted during this period, the Commission adopted each year significantly more phase I remedies decisions than phase II remedies decisions.[39] The total number of remedies decisions in this period reached a staggering 129 (compared to 37 decisions in the previous period) and, on a yearly basis, the total number of remedies decisions ranged from 15 to 38.

Understandably, during the first half of this period the Commission's resources were stretched to their limits, not only due to the substantial increase in notifications and decisions as a result of the merger wave in the late 1990s and early 2000s but also due to the increased scope and complexity of the transactions.[40] The sectors involved were less traditional than previously and more complex (such as hi-tech)[41] as well as more consolidated as a result of the intense merger activity and deregulation of certain sectors (such as telecoms and energy).[42] It was also during this period that the Commission adopted some of its more questionable and borderline remedies decisions, some of which were subsequently challenged before the EU Court.[43] It was therefore crucial for the Commission to respond

[36] By then the Commission had settled 15 cases in phase I, the last being *Lyonnaise des Eaux/Suez* (M.916 I 1997).

[37] The changes to the original Merger Regulation were made by the adoption of Council Regulation (EC) No 1310/97 amending Regulation (EEC) No 4064/89 on the control of concentrations between undertakings of 30 June 1997 [1997] OJ L180/1. The changes entered into force in March 1998. With respect to remedies the most important changes were stipulated in the new Recitals 30 and 31 as well as Art 6(2). The new procedural rules (on deadlines for submission of remedies and the total duration of remedies proceedings) were laid down in Implementing Regulation (EC) No 447/98 of 1 March 1998 on notifications, time limits and hearings provided for in Council Regulation (EEC) No 4064/89 on the control of concentrations between undertakings [1998] OJ L6/1 (the 1998 Implementing Regulation).

[38] Although the increase in phase I remedies decisions followed the general development of notifications and decisions being on the rise due to the merger wave, the number of phase II remedies decisions did not increase at the same rate. By comparison, from 1997 to 1998 the number of phase II remedies decisions fell from 7 to 4, and during the following 2 years the number would be 7 and 12, respectively.

[39] Phase I remedies decisions accounted for of all remedies decisions.

[40] The term 'mega-merger deal' was used when eg AOL and Time Warner merged in 2000 (*AOL/Time Warner* (M.1845 II 2000)), creating one of the largest transactions in value and signalling the start of the 'dot com' era. As it happened, the deal was subsequently undone in 2009 when AOL was separated from Time Warner through a spin-off.

[41] For a review of specifically hi-tech remedies, see Jenny in Lévêque and Shelanski (2003) 160–71.

[42] Examples of typical cases in the period: *Tetra Laval/Sidel* (M.2416 I 2003), *Pfizer/Pharmacia* (M.2922 I 2003), *Verbund/Energie Allianz* (M.2947 II 2003), *GE/Instrumentarium* (M.3083 II 2003), *SEB/Moulinex* (M.2621 I 2002), *Masterfoods/Royal Canin* (M.2544 I 2002), *Telia/Sonera* (M.2803 I 2002), *Bayer/Aventis Crop Science* (M.2547 II 2002), *Haniel/Cementbouw/JV(CVK)* (M.2650 II 2002), *Nordbanken/Postgirot* (M.2567 I 2001), *Nestlé/Ralston Purina* (M.2337 I 2001), *EDF/ENBW* (M.1853 II 2001), *The Post Office/TPG/SPPL* (M.1915 II 2001), *Vivendi/Canal+/Seagram* (M.2050 I 2000), *TotalFina/Elf Aquitaine* (M.1628 II 2000), *Astra/Zeneca* (M.1403 I 1999), *Sanofi/Synthelabo* (M.1397 I 1999), *Mannesmann/Orange* (M.1760 I 1999), *Exxon/Mobil* (M.1383 II 1999), *Neste/IVO* (M.931 I 1998), and *Worldcom/MCI* (M.1069 II 1998).

[43] One of the more memorable decisions from this period is *Hoechst/Rhone-Poulenc* (M.1378 I 1999) where few would dispute with the benefit of hindsight that many aspects, including the remedies, were questionable. Among other things, the implementation of the remedies lasted an unacceptably long time with the result that two of the

quickly to the need for new approaches and flexibility as well as increased transparency and consistency in its remedies policy.

To this effect, the Commission initiated the following measures: (i) the adoption of its first guidance notice on remedies in 2001;[44] (ii) the establishment of an Enforcement Unit within the DG Competition in 2001 dedicated to ensuring a consistent application and development of the Commission's merger remedies policy;[45] (iii) the publication of the Best Practice Remedies Guidelines, including the standard model texts, in 2003;[46] and (iv) the initiation in 2002 of a comprehensive internal review of the Commission's remedies policy and practice (between 1996 and 2000) which continued for several years and which would eventually result in the Remedies Study.[47] Also, this period was characterised by a wide-ranging discussion on the reform of the Merger Regulation launched in December 2001, including the need for greater flexibility in the timetable in remedies cases.[48]

By the end of this period, other institutional changes were made within the DG Competition, which would prove important for the execution of its future remedies policy. Most importantly, as part of a large reorganisation of the DG Competition in 2003 the long-standing Merger Task Force (MTF) was abandoned and so was the short-lived Enforcement Unit.[49] From now on the handling of merger cases, including remedies, would be decentralised to sector-dedicated units while overall remedies policy would be placed in a general merger policy unit within the DG Competition.[50] Also, some other significant institutional changes were made in order to improve the quality of the Commission's decision-making process in merger cases,[51] including: (i) the launch of a peer review panel in all in-depth investigations with the task of scrutinising the preliminary conclusions with a 'fresh pair of

remedies had to be modified and swapped with other remedies and the original conditional clearance decision was eventually challenged by a former chairman in an affected company in 2006, claiming that the remedies had not been properly implemented and that the Commission had refused to review this aspect (see *Lebard v Commission* (T-89/06 2009)). The former chairman, Mr Lebard, went on to publish a book on the issue, see Lebard and Ottenheimer (2008), and there were attempts by members of the European Parliament to instigate an inquiry into the Commission's handling of the case claiming that the remedies swap had 'tarnished the Commission's reputation for a rigorous approach to remedies, see further section 4.4.4.2 below.

[44] See Commission Notice on remedies acceptable under Council Regulation (EEC) No 4064/89 and under Commission Regulation (EC) 447/98 [2001] OJ C68/3 (the old Remedies Notice). As a supplement, the Commission drew up internal staff guidelines on workings methods in remedies cases and established an electronic monitoring system of the parties' compliance with remedies, see further Competition Report 2000, para 500.

[45] The Enforcement Unit was inspired by the FTC's Compliance Division. For an overview of the main tasks of the Enforcement Unit, see Competition Report 2001, para 290.

[46] See sections 1.1.1 above and 1.3.3 below.

[47] In parallel, an external study on merger remedies was commissioned by the Commission's Directorate General of Enterprise and Industry (DG Enterprise), see further section 1.4.2 below.

[48] See Green Paper on the Review of Council Regulation (EEC) No 4064/89, COM (2001) 745/6 (the 2001 Green Paper) and the Commission's press release IP/01/1795 of 11 December 2001, as well as Proposal for a Council Regulation on the control of concentrations between undertakings COM (2002) 711 final [2003] OJ C20/4.

[49] For an overview of the reorganisation, see IP/02/1856 of 11 December 2002. The changes were partly initiated in response to a number of severe judicial defeats that the Commission experienced as a result of the judgments in *Airtours v Commission* (T-342/99 2002), *Schneider v Commission* (T-310/01 2002) and *Tetra Laval BV v Commission* (T-5/02 2002).

[50] The unit still exists and is called A/2 Merger Case Support and Policy. It is believed that the remedies work of this unit includes the management of a so-called Merger Remedies Network consisting of representatives from the sector-specific merger units.

[51] See n 49 above.

eyes';[52] (ii) the appointment of a Chief Competition Economist with the task of providing independent economic advice in individual cases as well as on policy issues;[53] and (iii) the introduction of a number of so-called 'state-of-play' meetings between the Commission and the parties at decisive points of the merger procedure, including negotiations of remedies.[54]

All in all, the Commission's remedies policy in the late 1990s and early 2000s was characterised by the pressure of coping with the overwhelming number of cases caused by the merger wave and, once the workload had peaked, the reflection on the lessons learnt and the formulation of its policy while putting into place a number of measures in order to mitigate repetition of past administrative mistakes and shortcomings.

### *1.2.3 The Consolidation Phase*

From 2004 and in the following years consolidation was undertaken in several ways. Firstly, the new Merger Regulation entered into force in May 2004, providing for greater flexibility in the timeframe available to consider remedies in phase II cases, extension of the Commission's enforcement powers vis-à-vis remedies compliance, and it gave the Commission power to adopt implementing provisions regarding the procedure and time limits, not only for the submission of commitments, but also for their implementation.[55]

Secondly, the number of remedies cases followed a more steady and predictable pattern, as opposed to the rather frantic cycle in the previous period. On an annual basis, I and II remedies decisions ranged from 16 to 24 decisions from 2004 to 2010 and accounted for around 6 per cent of the total number of clearance and prohibition decisions in each year which was more or less the same as in the previous periods. The only major deviation was in 2011 where the total number of remedies decisions dropped sharply to an unprecedented total of 6 decisions, being the lowest figure since 1996. While this dramatic fall may be explained by the accumulation of a number of circumstances, it should be observed that although the number of notifications rose in 2011 for the first time since the recession and economic downturn commenced in 2008, larger transactions (being the ones most likely to cause competition concerns) were generally put on the backburner due to continuing volatility around the Eurozone and uncertainty about the direction of the global economy.[56] While financial uncertainties generally continued to dominate merger and

[52] See also Competition Report 2003, Foreword by Mario Monti. It should be stressed that the peer review panels (consisting of DG Competition officials) are part of the Commission's internal procedure and therefore their findings and meetings are confidential and thus add little to transparency in the administrative proceedings.

[53] See IP/03/1027 of 16 July 2003 and Competition Report 2003, paras 14–18. For a detailed description of the role, function and resources of the Chief Competition Economist, see Röller and Buigues (2005).

[54] See the DG Competition's Best Practices on the conduct of EC merger proceedings (Best Practice Guidelines on Merger Proceedings), available at ec.europa.eu/comm/competition/mergers/legislation/proceedings.pdf.

[55] See Commission Regulation (EC) No 802/2004 of 21 April 2004 implementing Council Regulation (EC) No 139/2004 on the control of concentrations between undertakings [2004] OJ L133/1, as amended by Commission Regulation (EC) No 1033/2008 of 20 October 2008, [2008] OJ L279/3 (the Implementing Regulation).

[56] See eg article by Anousha Sakoui, 'Deal Cash On Tap: But Will It Flow?' *Financial Times* (28 March 2012). Furthermore, it may be noted that the number of notification withdrawals in 2011 were relative high and thus potentially problematic transactions may have been withdrawn in response to preliminary concerns voiced by the Commission. *SCJ/SaraLee* (M.5969 II 2011) was one of the high-profile withdrawals in 2011. Other withdrawn notifications were later re-notify and conditionally cleared, see recently *ARM/Giesecke & Devrient/Gemalto/JV* (M.6564 I 2012).

acquisition (M&A) activities in 2012,[57] the total number of adopted remedies decisions rose to 15 that year.[58]

Another interesting statistical development for most of this period was that the share of phase I remedies decisions compared to phase II remedies decisions continued to grow at an unprecedented speed. By way of illustration, from 2004 to 2011 remedies decisions were adopted roughly four times more often in phase I than in phase II.[59] However, in 2012 this long-standing trend was brought to an abrupt end as the Commission adopted nine phase I remedies decisions and rather surprisingly a staggering six phase II remedies decisions that year.[60] The Commission has not publicly explained this sudden change of direction and it is thus yet unknown if the latest development signals a change in policy or a one-off rise in this particular year due to individual circumstances of each of the respective cases.[61] Another observation for this period was that the Commission adopted only four prohibitions (in 2004, 2007, 2011 and 2012), the lowest figure ever in any period.[62] This development could indicate that more remedies negotiations were successful in terms of finding an acceptable solution for all parties concerned during the administrative proceedings.

Thirdly, it should be observed that the remedies cases during this period covered a variety of sectors.[63] Consolidation in previously regulated sectors, such as energy and postal services, continued. Pharmaceutical companies and airlines consolidated on a large scale whereas more traditional industries like chemicals, paper and dairy underwent further consolidation. Mid-period the banking sector saw its first victims from the financial crisis,

[57] Global M&A activity in 2012 reached similar levels as in 2011 despite the first nine months being 20% lower than the same period in 2011 but overall deal volume caught up on value by the end of the year due to a few large end-of-year deals (notably *Glencore/Xstrata* (M.6541 I 2012)), see data from www.mergermarket.com, press release 'Mergermarket Releases Global M&A Round-up for Legal Advisers for Year End 2012' (14 January 2013).

[58] Thus the ratio between remedies decisions and overall decisions in 2012 resembled 2010 levels.

[59] The actual figures for phase I and II decisions in this period were: 12/4 (2004), 15/3 (2005), 13/6 (2006), 18/4 (2007), 19/5 (2008), 13/3 (2009), 14/2 (2010), and 5/1 (2011). Thus, the only exception to the rule in this period was the year 2006 where the Commission adopted 'only' twice as many remedies decisions in phase I than in phase II.

[60] To put this 2012 figure into the context of overall remedies statistics, not since 2001 have phase II decisions represented such a high proportion of overall remedies decisions adopted by the Commission in one year.

[61] As the texts of most of these 2012 decisions are not yet publicly available, it is currently difficult to identify any specific data points or circumstances that warranted in-depth investigations in these cases. As preliminary observations, it may be noted that some of these cases concerned further consolidation in already concentrated markets (*J&J/Synthes* (M.6266 II 2012) and *Outokumpu/Inoxum* (M.6471 II 2012)) while others involved international cooperation (*Universal Music Group/EMI Music* (M.6458 II 2012) and *UTC/Goodrich* (M.6410 II 2012)) or Art 9 referral requests (*Hutchinson 3G Austria/Orange Austria* (M.6497 II 2012)).

[62] See *Deutsche Börse/NYSE Euronext* (M.6166 II 2012), *Olympic/Aegean Airlines* (M.5830 II 2011), *Ryanair/Aer Lingus* (M.4439 II 2007), and *ENI/EDP/GDP* (M.3440 II 2004). In all cases the parties submitted substantial remedies packages, which were deemed unsuitable and insufficient by the Commission. By way of comparison, the Commission adopted a total of eight prohibitions from 1990 to 1997 and a total of 10 prohibitions from 1998 to 2003.

[63] Examples of typical cases in the period: *Glencore/Xstrata* (M.6541 I 2012), *AIG/bmi* (M.6447 I 2012), *Western Digital Ireland/Viviti Technologies* (M.6203 II 2011), *Intel/McAfee* (M.5984 I 2011), *T-Mobile/Orange* (M.5650 I 2010), *Cisco/Tandberg* (M.5669 I 2010), *Pfizer/Wyeth* (M.5476 I 2009), *Posten AB/Post Danmark A/S* (M.5152 I 2009), *Lufthansa/SN Airholding* (M.5335 II 2009), *Lufthansa/Austrian Airlines* (M.5440 II 2009), *EDF/Segebel* (M.5549 I 2009), *ABF/GBI Business* (M.4980 II 2008), *BNP Paribas/Fortis* (M.5384 I 2008), *Friesland/Campina* (M.5046 II 2008), *EDF/British Energy* (M.5224 I 2008), *Fortis/ABN Amro Assets* (M.4844 I 2007), *SFR/Tele 2* (M.4504 II 2007), *Akzo Nobel/ICI* (M.4779 I 2007), *Abbott/Guidant* (M.4150 I 2006), *OMYA/J.Huber PCC* (M.3796 II 2006), *Gaz de France/Suez* (M.4180 II 2006), *Metso/Aker Kvaerner* (M.4187 II 2006), *Apollo/Bakelite* (M.3593 I 2005), *Lufthansa/Swiss* (M.3770 I 2005), *Siemens/VA Tech* (M.3653 II 2005), *E.ON/MOL* (M.3696 II 2005), *Air France/KLM* (M.3280 I 2004) and *Lagardere/Natexis/VUP* (M.2978 II 2004).

which led to restructurings being notified.[64] The telecoms and media sectors experienced less activity in the beginning of the period but 2011 and 2012 saw some important emerging consolidations in the technology and (online) music sectors in particular.[65] All in all, the remedies throughout the period were significantly more sophisticated and experimental compared to the previous period and provisions like up-front buyers, crown jewels and fix-it-first remedies continued to gain acceptance.

Fourthly, during the first half of this period the Commission devoted time and resources to further build on its remedies experience and issued the following – and to date most important – remedies publications:[66] (i) the Remedies Study in October 2005; (ii) public consultation of the Commission's draft new Remedies Notice in April 2007; (iii) the publication of an external remedies study commissioned by DG Enterprise; (iv) the so-called 'remedies reform' in October 2008 consisting of a revised Remedies Notice and some changes to the 2004 Implementing Regulation relating to the appointment and role of trustees as well as the introduction of a Form RM for divestiture commitments.[67] With respect to the latter it should be emphasised that this 'remedies reform' was primarily an endorsement and clarification of past and current practice rather than the introduction of new radical thinking and therefore it is considered that the reform constituted the ultimate consolidation of this period rather than the beginning of a new period.

Finally, by the end of this period the Commission pioneered a new kind of ex-post assessments as it started to calculate observable customer benefits derived from its so-called 'corrective' horizontal merger decisions (consisting of prohibitions and conditional clearance decisions) adopted in 2010 and onwards.[68] Thus, this newly introduced methodology indicated an increasing awareness of the need for further ex-post reflections. Towards the end of the period the Commission's decisional practice continued to be very much in line with previous decisions and guidance and hence no significant new measures or change of line of assessment were introduced through practice.

### *1.2.4 Forthcoming Re-evaluation Phase?*

As of 31 December 2012, the Commission had adopted 318 remedies decisions, accounting for around 6.5 per cent of all clearance and prohibition decisions since 1990.[69] Roughly two-thirds of the remedies decisions were taken in phase I and one-third in phase II.[70] Prohibition decisions accounted for less than 0.5 per cent of all decisions since 1990 and

[64] See notably *BNP Paribas/Fortis* (M.5384 I 2008) and *Fortis/ABN Amro Assets* (M.4844 I 2007) (in the latter case the Dutch State's acquisition of Fortis Bank Nederland in 2008 meant that the state assumed responsibility for the implementation of the remedies).

[65] See *Universal Music Group/EMI Music* (M.6458 II 2012), *Sony/Mubadala Development/EMI Music Publishing* (M.6459 I 2012), *Intel/MacAfee* (M.5984 I 2011) and *Western Digital Ireland/Viviti Technologies* (M.6203 II 2011).

[66] For references and details, see sections 1.1.1 above as well as 1.3 and 1.4 below.

[67] See Competition Report 2008, paras 58–62. It is worth mentioning that the initiatives during this period were influenced by similar international work, see further sections 1.4.3 and 1.4.4.

[68] For latest data, see the DG Competition Management Plan 2013 (p 31), available at ec.europa.eu/atwork/synthesis/amp/doc/comp_mp_en.pdf. Accordingly, the Commission estimated that the observable customer benefits derived from its merger interventions amounted to EUR 4.0–5.8 billion in 2011 (p 30). For further details on estimates the two previous years, see further ch 5 n 15 below.

[69] During this period the Commission issued a total of 4,895 clearance and prohibition decisions.

[70] To be precise, 218 remedies decision were adopted in phase I and 100 remedies decisions were adopted in phase II.

thus the overall share of interventions amounted to roughly 7 per cent. Although the Commission has made no announcements as to forthcoming remedies-specific legislative initiatives or changes,[71] there are indications that 2013/2014 may see the initiation of some kind of re-evaluation of the existing merger remedies policy. While these issues will be elaborated upon throughout the book, the following introductory comments serve to illustrate which remedies aspects could prompt a forthcoming re-evaluation.

First, a number of long-running remedies issues were not included or addressed in the Commission's so-called '2008 remedies package'. For example, the Commission has yet to update its Best Practice Guidelines from 2003, including the important standard model texts.[72] Furthermore, during the review in 2008 it was generally expected that the Commission would have further elaborated on increasingly occurring issues in decisional practice like arbitration clauses[73] and/or various modalities in correction with behavioural solutions.[74]

Along the same lines, new market developments have emerged after the 2008 review, which could prompt the Commission to re-evaluate or further reflect on its current policy. For example, during the implementation of remedies it has occasionally proven difficult for the Commission to find suitable purchasers for the assets to be divested; either because certain sectors get increasingly consolidated with the result that interested purchasers do not fulfil the purchaser criteria[75] or because markets participants are reluctant or simply not interested in taking over the assets in question.[76] The risk of the latter situation occurring may be even more pronounced in the foreseeable future given the continuing unfavourable financial climate. Furthermore, another implication of the recent economic slowdown is that some remedies cases now involve parallel state aid proceedings, which, apart from further complicating the proceedings, raise new issues to be taken into account

[71] In the DG Competition's management plans for 2013 there is no mentioning of specific merger remedies initiatives plan for that year, see the DG Competition Management Plan 2013, n 68 above. By the end of 2012 Commissioner Almunia confirmed that the DG Competition was currently working on reforming certain aspects of its merger control (simplifying referral procedures and looking into a possible enforcement gap for the acquisition of non-controlling minority stakes) but no explicit references were made to any planned merger remedies measures, see Speech by Almunia (2012a).

[72] Upon publication of the 2008 remedies reform package the Commission gave no explanations or details as to why the Best Practice Guidelines had not been revised or indeed if/when a revision could be expected.

[73] During the public consultation of the draft revised Remedies Notice in 2007, a number of respondents proposed the publication of arbitration model texts to aid further clearance and guidance on this aspects of remedies negotiations and drafting.

[74] While structural remedies firmly remain the Commission's favoured solution, it is increasingly being recognised that there are situations where the Commission cannot ignore that certain behavioural remedies are indeed more appropriate and effective, such as in innovation-heavy markets (see eg *Intel/McAfee* (M.5984 I 2011)).

[75] Director General Italianer has highlighted this issue in respect of oligopolistic markets where significant competitors of the merging parties are unlikely to be accepted as suitable purchasers, see Speech by Italianer (2012).

[76] By way of illustration, in *Lufthansa/SN Airholding* (M.5335 II 2009) it is believed that the Commission initiated phase II proceedings, despite a comprehensive remedies package being offered in phase I, due to third parties' lack of interest in taking up slots on the respective routes, see MLex, 'Comment: More Innovative Remedies Could be Needed in Airline Merger Reviews' (5 February 2009), www.mlex.com/EU/Content.aspx?ID=41007. Also, in *UPS/TNT Express* (M.6570 II 2013) the remedies discussion came to a halt (and the transaction was prohibited) because only very few potentially suitable purchasers existed: the obvious purchaser (FedEx) was not interested in acquiring the assets to be divested, another market player (DHL) would have created competition concerns and the merging parties were unable to conclude an agreement in a timely manner with the only other potentially acceptable market player (La Poste/DPD), see Commission press release IP/13/68 and MEMO/13/48 of 30 January 2013 (public decision not yet available) as well as MLex, 'Comment: EC's Veto of UPS, TNT Reveals Pressure on Up-front Buyer Solution' (30 January 2013), www.mlex.com/EU/Content.aspx?ID=314061.

in the competitive assessment, including the modalities and execution of remedies.[77] It remains to be seen whether such coinciding state aid proceedings have implications that need to be accommodated for in merger remedies proceedings.

Secondly and in terms of procedures, in recent years a number of transactions have been abandoned by the parties either pre-decision or post-decision, claiming that the remedies were excessive and undermined the economic rationale behind the merger.[78] Thus, while it is entirely up to the parties to decide whether they wish to propose remedies, there may be a need for further reflections on the reasons behind these cancellations – which may not necessarily be in the interest of competition – and if/how they could or should have been avoided.[79] Also, the EU Court continues to receive appeals on a variety of remedies-related issues,[80] some of which may prompt adjustments to the Commission's administrative proceedings.[81]

Thirdly and as part of enforcement reflections, the Commission may feel compelled to repeat – in one form or the other – an ex-post evaluation of past remedies cases similar to the one carried out in its Remedies Study in 2005 as the cases analysed in that study dated back to 1996 to 2000.[82] It could be a general ex-post evaluation of remedies across sectors, like the previous one, or a narrower evaluation of a certain sector that has undergone noteworthy consolidation or changes in recent years (such as energy, airlines or pharmaceuticals).[83]

Fourthly, there is an unresolved issue which no competition authorities or organisations have yet managed to fully address in their remedies policies: international cooperation in multi-jurisdictional or cross-border remedies cases. In the past various initiatives have been launched in order to discuss and explore the issue further but, for a number of legal, administrative and political reasons, an enhanced cooperation has not yet materialised. However, as an increasing number of markets become worldwide, there is a growing need for enhanced cooperation and coordination when large international market players consolidate.[84] Recently

[77] In *Lufthansa/Austrian Airlines* (M.5440 II 2009) parallel state aid proceedings were undertaken (see IP/09/1256 of 28 August 2009 and decision published in [2010] OJ L59/1) in order to assess whether the negative price paid by Lufthansa for Austrian Airlines to the Austrian State amounted to illegal state aid (this was not the case). The state aid decision and the competition (conditional clearance) decision were adopted on the same day, 28 August 2009, as the cases were intertwined (Lufthansa would not have bought Austrian Airlines if the respective aid scheme had not been cleared). Both decisions have been appealed by a competitor and it remains to be seen whether the appeals will have implications on the conditional clearance decision, see *Niki Luftfahrt v Commission* (T-511/09 pending) and *Niki Luftfahrt v Commission* (T-162/10 pending), respectively. Another example of interdependent remedies and state aid proceedings triggered by the financial crisis can be found in *Fortis/ABN Amro Assets* (M.4844 I 2007), see further ch 4 n 243 below.

[78] For examples of cancellations pre-decision, see *OMV/MOL* (M.4799 II 2008) and *BHP Billiton/Rio Tinto* (M.4985 II 2008). For examples of cancellations post-decision, see *Arsenal/DSP* (M.5153 II 2009) and *Arjowiggins/M-Real Zanders Reflex* (M.4513 II 2008).

[79] Similarly, in some proceedings before the EU Court the parties have claimed that (excessive) remedies were forced upon them and 'imposed' by the Commission. Although the Court has yet to rule on this issue, the Commission may wish to re-evaluate its negotiating process (tactics) in this respect, see section 2.1.2.3 below.

[80] See section 4.6.5 below.

[81] By way of illustration, as a new kind of remedies-related appeal, merging parties have referred disagreements with the Commission about the interpretation of certain obligations in remedies to the EU Court, see eg *E.ON Ruhrgas and E.On Földgáz Trade v Commission* (T-57/07 2009). Also, a Commission refusal to extend a divestiture deadline has recently been appealed, see *EDF v Commission* (T-389/12 pending).

[82] For details on the study, see section 1.4.1 below. Indeed, several commentators have emphasised the need for the Commission to undertake a new evaluation of more recent remedies cases, see further section 5.7 below.

[83] Recent sector inquiries undertaken by the DG Competition have focused on anti-trust issues, such as the reports into pharmaceuticals in 2009 (IP/09/1098 of 8 July 2009), retail banking in 2007 (IP/07/114 of 31 January 2007) and energy in 2007 (IP/07/26 of 10 January 2007). To this effect, see also the 2012 food report published by the European Competition Network (ECN) (IP/12/502 of 24 May 2012).

[84] With respect to the worldwide consolidation of the pharmaceutical sector, see eg Competition Report 2010, paras 291–93.

there have been indications of renewed focus on such a need and it is thus expected that the Commission will devote additional time and resources in this matter, including enhanced cooperation with the US Department of Justice (DoJ) and the FTC, which was recently reinforced by the adoption of a new set of best practices in merger cooperation cases (the US–EU Best Practices on Cooperation in Merger Investigations).[85] Moreover, as more transactions are reviewed by an increasing number of jurisdictions around the world, additional international initiatives are called for.[86]

All in all, despite no formal indications from the Commission that it intends to revise its current remedies guidance and framework within the foreseeable future, the constantly evolving decisional practice and dynamic market conditions surrounding merger remedies cases suggest that it may soon be appropriate for the Commission to pause and reflect on its past achievements and its future goals which may then see the start of a new phase in the Commission's remedies enforcement. However, for now the existing merger remedies framework will be outlined below.

## 1.3 Remedies Guidance

### *1.3.1 Merger Regulation*

The core substantive provisions governing remedies are found in Articles 6(2) and 8(2) of the Merger Regulation according to which the Commission may declare a concentration compatible with the common market if, following modification by the undertakings concerned, it no longer raises serious doubts (phase I) or no longer significantly impedes effective competition in the common market or a substantial part of it, in particular as a result of the creation or strengthening of a dominant position (phase II). To this effect, the Commission may attach to its clearance decision conditions and obligations intended to ensure that the undertakings concerned comply with the commitments they have entered into vis-à-vis the Commission with a view to rendering the concentration compatible with the internal market.[87] These two provisions form the foundation of the Commission's remedies policy and they have by and large remained unchanged since their introduction.[88]

In addition, Recital 30 of the Merger Regulation stipulates some important and basic requirements relating to the nature of acceptable remedies, in particular in phase I (competition problems must be readily identifiable and easily remedied) and emphasises the import-

[85] See press release IP/11/1194 of 14 October 2011 and the best practices document is available at ec.europa.eu/competition/international/bilateral/eu_us.pdf and. An earlier version of the best practices was published in 2002 but the revision in 2011 provides more details on issues regarding timing, collection of evidence and definition of remedies.

[86] By way of illustration, *Glencore/Xstrata* (M.6541 I 2012) was filed in eg the EU, China and South Africa; *Universal Music Group/EMI Music* (M.6458 II 2012) in eg the EU, US, Australia, Japan and Canada; *UTC/Goodrich* (M.6410 II 2012) in eg EU, US, Canada, Mexico and Brazil; *Novartis/Alcon* (M.5778 I 2010) in the EU, US, Canada, Singapore and China; and *Pfizer/Wyeth* (M.5476 I 2009) in eg the EU, US, Canada, Australia, Mexico, New Zealand and South Africa.

[87] The Merger Regulation, Arts 6(2) and 8(2), second paragraphs, respectively.

[88] The only change to phase II remedies (apart from the SIEC test) occurred during the merger review in 1998 where the wording in Art 8(2), second paragraph, of the original Merger Regulation was changed from 'with a view to modifying the original concentration plan' to 'with a view to rendering the concentration compatible with the common market'. The amended wording was appropriate as some remedies do not strictly speaking involve a modification of the original concentration plan.

ance of proportionality, transparency and effective consultation of the Member States and interested third parties.[89] Article 10 of the Merger Regulation contains procedural provisions relating to the deadlines for adopting inter alia remedies decisions whereas Articles 14 and 15 specify enforcement measures (fines and periodic penalty payments) if the parties fail to comply with conditions and/or obligations imposed by a remedies decision.[90]

Moreover, the Commission enjoys powers to lay down procedure and time limits for the submission and implementation of remedies.[91] Accordingly, Article 19 of the Implementing Regulation specifies the deadlines for the parties' submission of commitments in phase I and II, whereas the procedures for such submissions as well as certain trustee provisions are contained in Article 20. Finally, Annex IV of the Implementing Regulation contains a so-called Form RM specifying the information and documents to be submitted by the parties when offering commitments.[92]

### *1.3.2 Remedies Notice*

It was with pride that the Commission announced in March 2001 that it was the first competition authority in the world to publish guidance specifically on merger remedies, in the so-called old Remedies Notice.[93] The notice was an attempt to set out general substantial and procedural considerations based on the first 10 years of experience under the Merger Regulation with the aim of providing support and predictability for companies involved in remedies cases. The notice was well received by all stakeholders as it provided much-needed guidance. It also inspired other jurisdictions to adopt similar notices.[94] The notice remained unchanged for nearly eight years.[95] However, in April 2007 the Commission initiated a public consultation on a revised version of the notice,[96] resulting in the publication of a new Remedies Notice in October 2008, forming part of the so-called '2008 remedies package' as introduced above.[97]

[89] Recital 30 was introduced in 2004 but none of the listed requirements were newly invented policies or principles; they merely codified the Commission's long-standing practice. Previously, similar statements were stipulated in Recital 8 of Council Regulation 1310/97.

[90] The provisions will be explained in detail wherever appropriate throughout the book.

[91] Merger Regulation, Art 23(1)(c). Such procedures are introduced in the 2004 Implementing Regulation.

[92] Annex IV was added to the 2004 Implementing Regulation in 2008.

[93] For reference, see n 44 above. The notice was heavily influenced by the work and experience of the FTC in its 1999 Divestiture Study, see Speech by Monti (2001): 'I have no hesitation in acknowledging that the new EU approach to remedies has been strongly influenced by the FTC [Divestiture Study]' (p 8).

[94] For a description of similar US initiatives in 2003 and 2004, see section 1.3.4 below. For other jurisdictions, in December 2004 the UK Competition Commission published its first remedies guidelines 'Application of Divestiture Remedies in Merger Inquiries' (CC8) (revised in 2008); and in September 2006 Canada's Competition Bureau issued an 'Information Bulletin on Merger Remedies'.

[95] For literature on the old notice, see De Souka in Drauz and Jones (2012) (and previous edition from 2006), Holmes and Turnbull (2002), Baylis (2001), De Matteis (2001), Ersbøll (2001), Ysewyn (2001), and Speech by Mederer (2001).

[96] On 24 April 2007 the Commission published a draft revised Commission Notice on remedies acceptable under Council Regulation (EEC) No 139/2004 and under Commission Regulation (EC) No 802/2004 (the draft new Remedies Notice), available at: ec.europa.eu/competition/mergers/legislation/draft_remedies_notice.pdf. See also IP/07/544 of 24 April 2007. The Commission held a public consultation and 23 replies were submitted which are available at ec.europa.eu/comm/competition/mergers/legislation/merger_remedies.html. Some of these replies will be referred to throughout this book.

[97] The new draft notice and accompanying changes to the 2004 Implementing Regulation were discussed and adopted at the Commission's meeting on 8 July 2008 (PV (2008) 1838 final) but not formally published before 22 October 2008. For literature on the new notice, see De Souza and Brockhoff in Drauz and Jones (2012), De Valois Turk (2009), Snel and De Valois Turk (2009), Sorinas and Jorns (2009), Luebking (2007) and Competition Report 2008, paras 58–62.

The new notice contains no major surprises or revolutionary change of direction in the Commission's thinking but is primarily a comprehensive update and consolidation of the Commission's evolving past practice, taking into account all the above-mentioned developments. The document sets out the Commission's policy and practice under the following headings: (i) general principles applicable to remedies; (ii) main types of remedies; (iii) procedural requirements for submission of remedies in phase I and II; and (iv) main requirements for the implementation of remedies. The notice continues to focus on divestitures as being the preferred remedy.

In summary, the notice is particularly detailed in its guidance on the design and implementation of remedies and draws heavily on the (sometimes unfortunate) lessons learnt by the Commission in its Remedies Study (see below), in particular as to the nature and scope of remedies. The Commission has clearly tightened the requirements to the scope, viability and preservation of the assets to be divested. Many more safeguards are put in place in order to prevent deterioration of the assets, both pending divestiture and post-divestiture. Also, the Commission's continued reluctance to accept non-structural remedies is reinforced by stressing that such remedies must be *at least* equivalent in their effects to divestitures. More attention is paid to the purchaser's chances of survival in the respective market post-divestiture and the Commission is adamant to follow the implementation to the very last step in order not to close the case prematurely.[98] Finally, the role of trustees is clarified in accordance with the changes made to the Implementing Regulation.

### *1.3.3 Best Practice Remedies Guidelines*

As supplement to the old Remedies Notice, the Commission services issued in April 2003 its Best Practice Remedies Guidelines, consisting of a Model Text for Divestiture Commitments (MTDC) and a Model Text for Trustee Mandates (MTTM) together with an explanatory note.[99] Similarly to when the old Remedies Notice was published, the Commission was the first competition authority to introduce standard model texts in merger proceedings.[100]

The overall aim of publishing the model texts was to further increase efficiency, consistency and transparency in the negotiation and implementation of remedies, especially given the tight deadlines. In particular, the model texts prevent the parties from 'reinventing the wheel' in every case so they can instead focus on the substance and implementation of the remedies.[101] While the model texts are based on divestitures, they are meant to be adapted on a case-by-case basis to other forms of remedies.

98 In the Remedies Study the Commission observed on several occasions that cases had been closed too early, see p 86 (points 20–21).

99 See also n 14 above.

100 Other jurisdictions have subsequently introduced similar model texts. eg in February 2008 the German Bundeskartellamt published three model texts covering different types of divestitures as well as a model mandate form for monitoring trustees, see press release of 18 February 2008 www.bundeskartellamt.de. In May 2007 Canada's Competition Bureau issued a so-called 'Outline Consent Agreement' which is a remedies model text, see competitionbureau.gc.ca/eic/site/cb-bc.nsf/eng/02310.html.

101 Prior to the publication, practitioners had for several years urged the Commission to publish some kind of standard wording on the most important remedies aspects, see eg Rodriguez in IBA (2000) 267. Specifically in relation to the trustee mandate, the Commission had also experienced some unfortunate cases where the role of the monitoring trustee was unsatisfying with the result that remedy encountered problems in the implementation phase in terms of inadequate protection of the assets to be divested and delayed sale. To this effect, see *Carrefour/ Promodès* (M.1684 I 2000) where the sale of Carrefour's stake in Cora was not achieved on time and the trustee had encountered problems in ensuring that no competitive harm was caused to Cora during the implementation. The Commission later submitted that this experience had contributed significantly to its work in preparing the standard model text for trustees, see Competition Report 2001, para 313.

Although the model texts are neither intended to provide an exhaustive coverage for all issues that may become relevant in all cases, nor legally binding upon parties in a merger procedure,[102] it is now required in Form RM that the parties identify any deviations of the commitments from the model texts and explain the reasons for such deviations.[103] This obligation enables the Commission to immediately detect 'abnormalities' in proposals and is therefore timesaving for the Commission but equally time-consuming for the parties.

The main contents of each standard model text are the following:

- The Model Text for Divestiture Commitments (MTDC) sets out all requirements for achieving full and effective compliance with divestiture remedies. More specifically, the model describes key definitions in remedies cases (section A); the divestiture procedure and the obligations of the parties pending the sale as well as a framework for a detailed identification of the divested assets to be set out in an attached schedule (section B); any related remedies in order to ensure effective implementation, including various responsibilities of the parties vis-à-vis the Commission, the Trustee and the divested business (section C); purchaser standards designed to ensure viability and competitiveness of the new entity (section D); and appointment, functions and duties of a Trustee, whether its tasks are to monitor or divest the assets.
- The Model Text for Trustee Mandates (MTTM) sets out the role and functions of the Trustee, as provided in the MTDC. The model text describes key definitions (section A); appointment of Monitoring Trustee and/or Divestiture Trustee, including identification of the Trustee Team (section B); general duties and obligations of the Trustee (section C); specific tasks of the Monitoring Trustee and Divestiture Trustee, respectively (section D and E); reporting obligations (section F); duties and obligations of the parties vis-à-vis the Trustee (section G); Trustee related provisions such as conflict of interests, remuneration, indemnity and confidentiality (section H); termination of the mandate (section I); and additional provisions on amendments to the mandate and dispute resolutions (section J).

It is worth noting that the Best Practice Remedies Guidelines, including the standard model texts, introduced in 2003 a number of new important aspects to the Commission's remedies policy, which were not contained in the old Remedies Notice. For example, a re-acquisition prohibition of ten years was specified; the concept of hold-separate managers was introduced; deadlines for appointments of trustees were listed; and the possibility of trustees to appoint advisors at the expense of the parties was launched. Accordingly, these new aspects were only to be found in the non-binding standard model texts between 2003 and 2008 until they were finally incorporated in the new Remedies Notice.

Furthermore, when the guidelines were introduced, it was foreseen that the standard model texts would be regularly updated taking into account new developments in the Commission's remedies practice.[104] To date, this has never been done. Consequently, on a number of points the standard model texts are currently not up-to-date and even inadequate or incorrect in some places.[105]

[102] See Best Practice Remedies Guidelines, Explanatory Note, point 2, and Remedies Notice, para 21.

[103] See Implementing Regulation, Annex IV (Form RM), s 3. Prior to the introduction of Form RM in 2008, it had gradually become practice for the Commission to ask the parties to highlight deviations from the standard model texts in their commitment proposals.

[104] Best Practice Remedies Guidelines, point 4; and Remedies Notice, para 21, fn 1.

[105] See section 5.6 below.

### *1.3.4 US Remedies Guidance*

It is considered beneficial to briefly outline the main features of the US remedies guidelines as they have served as an inspiration for the Commission's guidance and decisional practice.[106] In 2002 the FTC held a number of public workshops on its future merger remedies policy.[107] In order to facilitate these discussions the FTC published a document entitled 'Frequently Asked Questions about Merger Consent Order Provisions' (the FTC's FAQ on Remedies).[108] Although this was a staff document, it formed the basis for the first US guidance on remedies briefly explaining the position of the FTC staff on very specific matters relating to, for example, purchaser requirements, up-front solutions, crown jewels, trustee provisions and so forth. The document was subsequently developed into formal and more comprehensive guidelines issued by the FTC in April 2003, called 'Statement of the Federal Trade Commission's Bureau of Competition on Negotiating Merger Remedies' and they served as the FTC's merger remedies guidelines for nine years.[109] These guidelines were revised in 2012 (the FTC Guidelines for Negotiating Merger Remedies)[110] and they address issues arising in the remedies negotiation process and cover the following areas: the assets to be divested; an acceptable purchaser; the divestiture agreement; additional order provisions; orders to hold separate and/or maintain assets; divestiture applications; and timing.

In October 2004 the DoJ issued its first merger remedies guidelines, called 'Antitrust Division Policy Guide to Merger Remedies' (the old DoJ Merger Remedies Guide).[111] This document was later revised in June 2011 in the recognition that the merger landscape had changed and therefore the DoJ published a new version (the DoJ Merger Remedies Guide).[112] Whereas the above-mentioned FTC documents take the form of practical guides to remedies negotiations and compliance with consent orders, the DoJ document is a more elaborate policy document providing more details into the DoJ's thinking and reasoning behind remedies. Compared to the 2004 document, the revision of 2011 contains two main changes in policy: greater acceptance of behavioural remedies and closer alignment with the FTC in terms of allowing up-front buyers and crown jewel provisions as well as the introduction of a Compliance Office.

[106] For literature on US mergers remedies and of relevance from the EU perspective, see in particular Weiser (2008); Speech by Kovacic (2008); Feinstein, van Kerckhove and Wootton (2008), Davidson (2006); Speech by Platt Majoras (2006); Baer et al (2004), Halverson and Ewing (2004); Speech by Platt Majoras (2002b); Halverson and Telpner (2002), Foer (2001b), Parker and Balto (2000); and Speech by Pitofsky (2000).

[107] The workshops were held as a follow-up to the FTC's Divestiture Study from 1999 (see section 1.3.4 below). For details on the remedies workshops, see the FTC's press releases of 21 May ('FTC Announces first Workshop on Merger Remedies', www.ftc.gov/opa/2002/05/bpr1.shtm) and of 18 October 2002 ('FTC Announces Second Workshop on Merger Remedies', www.ftc.gov/opa/2002/10/remidies.shtm as well as transcripts from the workshops at www.ftc.gov/bc/bestpractices/020618trans.pdf). The workshop discussions included fundamental issues, such as the basic purpose of any merger remedy; what needs to be divested; what the staff is seeking when evaluating a proposed purchaser and the divestiture agreements; the staff's concerns about continuing entanglements between parties and purchasers; the use of an up-front-buyer; and other provisions such as crown jewels, orders to hold separate, and monitor trustees.

[108] See www.ftc.gov/bc/mergerfaq.shtm.

[109] See www.ftc.gov/bc/bestpractices/bestpractices030401.htm.

[110] See www.ftc.gov/bc/bestpractices/bestpractices.shtm. The new guidelines follow the structure of the 2003 guidelines and are essentially an update taking into account recent decisional practice and it is therefore considered that the 2003 guidelines are no longer of relevance. Hence, all references throughout this book to the FTC Guidelines for Negotiating Merger Remedies are made to the new document from 2012.

[111] See www.usdoj.gov/atr/public/guidelines/205108.htm.

[112] See www.justice.gov/atr/public/guidelines/272350.pdf.

All in all, the formal guidelines from the FTC and DoJ, respectively, deal with similar issues as the Commission does in its Remedies Notice and their approaches are remarkably convergent, both in terms of designing and implementing remedies. The main difference is the methodology as the US authorities, contrary to the Commission, chose to first undertake an ex-post review of its past practice (in 1999) and then issue guidelines based on these experiences.

## 1.4 Remedies Reviews

### *1.4.1 The DG Competition Remedies Study*

The Commission published its first – and so far only – major in-house Remedies Study in October 2005.[113] The Commission carried out a comprehensive ex-post assessment of 96 remedies imposed in 40 cases under the Merger Regulation from 1996 to 2000. The study was a demanding exercise for the DG Competition as it involved a detailed stocktaking of selected cases, interviews with more than 300 persons and companies involved in the transactions at the time as well as quantitative questionnaires.[114]

The main part of the study is devoted to an assessment of the design and implementation of past remedies. It examines main aspects of remedies such as the scope of the business, third-party implications, alternative remedies, interim preservation and hold-separate provisions, the trustees involved and approval of purchasers. In the second (less detailed) part the Commission considers some measurable indicators that provide a broad picture of the impact of a remedy in a given market and thus the effectiveness of that remedy. However, as the Commission refrains from conducting a detailed ex-post assessment of the evolution of all of the markets concerned, the findings in this respect are broad and merely indicative.

The main conclusions of the study are that, although the overall approach of the Commission's remedies practice in the reference period is satisfactory and harmonise with remedies initiatives introduced after 2000 (notably the old Remedies Notice and standard model texts), a number of serious issues regarding the design and implementation of remedies are identified which would need to be addressed in future policy. The failure to adequately define the scope of the divested business was the most frequently occurring problem, followed by the approval of an unsuitable purchaser, incorrect carve-out of the assets and the incomplete transfer of the divested business to a new owner. Monitoring issues like the role and work of trustees and hold-separate managers were also identified as an area for improvement. Thus, a broad range of implementation issues proved inadequate. However, the study also contained some positive surprises, for example that joint venture remedies were most effective (despite the obvious risk caused by third party involvement).

[113] Remedies Study, n 15 above. For articles describing the main contents of the study, see in particular Ward (2006), Papandropoulos and Tajana (2006), Van Kerckhove (2006), Tajana (2006b) and Köpke (2005).

[114] Although it was a novel exercise for the DG Competition, the staff drew heavily on the experience and expertise of the 1999 FTC remedies study, see section 1.4.3 below. For a knowledgeable analysis of the differences between the two studies, see Davidson (2006).

### *1.4.2 DG Enterprise Econometric Remedies Study*

In parallel to the Remedies Study, the Commission (DG Industry and Enterprise) commissioned a study entitled 'Assessing the Consequences for Competition of EC Merger Remedies' (the Econometric Remedies Study).[115] The comprehensive study contains an ex-post economic analysis of merger remedies with the aim of assessing the economic effectiveness of a smaller number of remedies with simple econometric simulation models. The authors had access to the Commission's databases and confidential information on individual cases. They undertook a detailed investigation of seven merger cases in two industry sectors, paper and pharmaceuticals.[116]

An interesting conclusion from the study is that the authors' simulations did not always predict the same adverse consequences of a merger as those found by a simple market share analysis usually adopted by the Commission. Thus, the authors found that their proposed methodology, if adopted, would have led to different decisions (and outcomes) by the Commission.[117] Another interesting aspect is that the authors challenge the Commission's preference for structural remedies in some cases where they argue that behavioural remedies would have been more flexible and efficient.[118]

Many of the findings in the study are clearly critical of the Commission's methodology and economic assessments and practice in remedies cases and it is therefore rather surprising that the study received little attention among competition commentators. However, it has to be said that following the study the Commission significantly improved its economic analysis in merger cases through the involvement of the Chief Competition Economist and therefore some of the critique no longer applies to current practice.

### *1.4.3 The FTC Divestiture Study*

The FTC's report entitled 'A Study of the Commission's Divestiture Process' (the FTC Divestiture Study) from 1999 contains a detailed analysis of divestiture orders between 1990 and 1994 with the aim of investigating whether there were systematic reasons why some of the divestitures failed to achieve the FTC's remedial objectives in the 1990s.[119] The study looked at 35 divestiture orders and was interview-based with the main focus on the purchasers of the divested assets.

The study deserves mentioning for a number of reasons. Not only was it the first comprehensive review ever undertaken on the efficacy of remedies by any competition authority, but it also proved to be very influential on the DG Competition's Remedies

[115] Both authors are industrial economists from the Centre for Competition Policy, School of Economics, University of East Anglia, Norwich. In conducting their analysis the authors had access to confidential information from the DG Competition relating to specific cases and ex-post studies. Upon completion, the study remained confidential for nearly two years but a public version was finally published under the title *Mergers and Merger Remedies in the EU: Assessing the Consequences for Competition* (Davies and Lyons (2007)). For a summary of the study, see Davies and Lyons (2005). For a review of the study, see in particular Christiansen (2008).

[116] Rather surprisingly and contrary to the Remedies Study, the identity of the companies subject to analysis is made public and thus involves, for the paper industry, *SCA Packaging/Metsa Corrugated* (M.2032 I 2000) and *Kimberly-Clark/Scott* (M.623 II 1996), and for pharmaceuticals, *Glaxo Wellcome/SmithKline Beecham* (M.1846 I 2000), *Monsanto/Pharmacia & Upjohn* (M.1835 I 2000), *Sanofi/Synthélabo* (M.1397 I 1999), *Astra/Zeneca* (M.1403 I 1999), and *Hoffmann-La Roche/Boehringer Mannheim* (M.950 II 1998). All cases are explained in detail in the study, see Davies and Lyons (2007) 93–133 and 179–237, respectively.

[117] See eg Davies and Lyons (2007) 243.

[118] ibid, 247–48.

[119] See www.ftc.gov/os/1999/08/divestiture.pdf.

Study, both in terms of methodology, structure and conclusions.[120] Also, the study raised important new remedies issues that had not been recognised elsewhere and that proved vital in later formulations of remedies policies and practices in many jurisdictions.

The main focus of the study was on the purchasers of divested assets in order to determine how well they had fared operating the assets they acquired as a result of a divestiture order. As a novelty, the study suggested an informational and bargaining imbalance between the merging parties on the one hand and the FTC staff and the purchaser of the divested assets on the other hand. To this effect, the FTC suggested strengthening the emphasis on the identity of the purchaser and highlighted the importance of tight control of the transfer process.[121] At that point in time, many other authorities (including the Commission) were not aware of these pitfalls in their own remedies practice.

The study produced three general findings: (i) most divestitures had been successful in creating viable competitors in the concerned market; (ii) the merging parties tend to look for marginally acceptable purchasers and sometimes engage in strategic conduct to impede the success of the purchaser; and (iii) most purchasers of divested assets lacked access to vital information in order to prevent mistakes in the course of their acquisitions.[122] As it was found that these aspects diminished the effectiveness of divestitures, the FTC set out a number of specific recommendations for future practice, including reduced time to implement the remedy; additional assets to be divested to ensure viability; and limited scope and duration of any on-going relationships with the purchaser and the merging parties.[123] These recommendations inspired other authorities (including the Commission) to adopt similar provisions.

### *1.4.4 Other Reviews*

#### 1.4.4.1 The OECD Remedies Studies

In July 2012 the OECD published its latest merger remedies study, based on discussions held by the Competition Committee in June 2011 (the 2011 OECD Remedies Study).[124] The purpose of the meeting was to review current merger remedies policies of the OECD member and non-member countries and to discuss a number of specific policy questions, including the advantages and disadvantages of structural and behavioural remedies, the need for a different approach to remedies in horizontal and vertical mergers, ex-post review of remedies' effectiveness and international cooperation in the design, enforcement and monitoring of remedies.

[120] See n 114 above.

[121] Suggested measures included already then enhanced provisions on the use of trustees, hold-separate arrangements, up-front purchaser criteria, proposed rejection of inappropriate purchasers and the introduction of crown jewels and provisions on additional assets.

[122] FTC Divestiture Study, pp 8–15.

[123] Other recommendations included (i) acceptable business plans to be submitted by the purchaser; (ii) the merging parties to facilitate the transfer of knowledgeable staff to the purchaser; (iii) appointment of auditor trustees to monitor transfers of technology to the purchaser; (iv) provisions for the re-divestiture of certain types of assets where the purchaser would fail to exploit them; and (v) provisions for the divestiture of additional assets by a divestiture trustee where the merging parties would fail to fully divest assets within the required time, see FTC Divestiture Study, ss IV and V.

[124] See DAF/COMP (2011) 13, available at www.oecd.org/daf/competition/RemediesinMergerCases2011.pdf. The merger remedies discussions were held as a roundtable by the OECD's Competition Committee, Working Party 3, on 28 June 2011.

The discussions materialised in a comprehensive publication, consisting of an issues paper by the OECD Secretariat, numerous country contributions submitted in preparations of the meeting and addressing specific questions posed by the Secretariat and a summary of the discussions.[125] From the issues paper and the discussions, the Secretariat listed the following main policy points:[126] (i) structural and behavioural remedies have different benefits and drawbacks, which must be carefully considered when deciding which type of remedy to best employ; (ii) while generally competition concerns in horizontal mergers can be resolved through structural remedies and vertical mergers through behavioural remedies, each transaction should be evaluated based on its own merits; (iii) once a remedy is designed, competition authorities must determine the best means of monitoring its implementation and to this effect trustees and third party stakeholders are often employed; and (iv) competition authorities are exploring the best means of cooperation in cross-border mergers and in this respect effective communication has been used to assist in the negotiation, design and enforcement of remedies to the benefit of all parties involved.

While most of these general points do not add new aspects to the existing policy of the Commission,[127] other issues emerging during the roundtable discussions may serve as inspiration when reflecting on future policy. For example, an exchange of views between the OECD countries on case-specific experiences relating to non-compliance measures, the justification of behavioural provisions in certain situations as well as the use and further development of arbitration clauses are issues which may be further explored.[128] However, judging from the discussions, the need for enhanced communication and cooperation in cross-border mergers stands out as one aspect that deserves particular attention by the OECD countries in the future.[129]

In addition to the 2011 study, in 2004 the same OECD Committee carried out a similar and equally comprehensive merger remedies evaluation (the 2004 OECD Remedies Study), which was the first of its kind in that forum.[130] The differences between the two studies obviously relate to new developments in decisional practice of the member countries from 2004 to 2011 and, based on this experience, the discussions revolve around newer topics. However, several recommendations and findings in the 2004 study remain valid and are not necessarily dealt with in the same way in the 2011 study and will therefore be referred to where relevant throughout the book.

Finally, the OECD has published a number of other initiatives, which are of interest in merger remedies discussions. Most recently, in 2010 the Competition Committee held and

[125] See in particular the summary of the main findings of the study by the OECD Secretariat (pp 11–13); the Secretariat's issues paper (pp 19–26); contribution by the US (pp 221–31); contribution by the EU (pp 233–42) and summary of the discussions (pp 289–302).

[126] See the 2011 OECD Remedies Study, n 124 above, pp 11–13. Compared to the texts in the study, the listed points are shortened.

[127] Thus, many of the general observations in the study seem more relevant for less developed competition regimes.

[128] For the main issues raised during the discussions at the roundtable, see the 2011 OECD Remedies Study, n 124 above, pp 289–302.

[129] ibid, pp 300–302.

[130] See DAF/COMP (2004) 21, available at www.oecd.org/dataoecd/61/45/34305995.pdf. Similarly to the 2011 study, the publication includes a background note from the OECD Secretariat setting out certain questions to be discussed by the member countries, national contributions as well as a summary of the discussions. Of particular interest are the conclusions from the discussions drawn up by the OECD Secretariat (pp 7–10); the Secretariat's background note (pp 17–45); contribution by the US (pp 237–46); and contribution by the Commission (pp 253–61).

published a hearing on arbitration and competition (the OECD Arbitration and Competition review),[131] and in 2011 the OECD Global Forum on Competition debated 'Cross-Border Merger Control: Challenges for Developing and Emerging Economies' (the OECD Cross-Border Merger Review) which was published the following year and included an expert analytical account of the topic and an assessment of the main challenges ahead as well as written submissions from a number of OECD member countries, including the Commission and the US.[132]

1.4.4.2 The ICN Remedies Review Project

The ICN published in 2005 a Merger Remedies Review Project (the ICN Remedies Review Project).[133] Similarly to the OECD merger remedies studies, this review is a policy paper and outlines key principles and range of tools in the use of merger remedies, based on and illustrated by remedies practices in several jurisdictions. The document describes: (i) principles of remedial action (proportionality, effectiveness, potential remedies burdens and costs as well as transparency and consistency); (ii) choice and design of remedies (definitions of structural and behavioural remedies, factors affecting the design of divestitures and specific considerations on intellectual property rights); and (iii) implementation and monitoring remedies (effectiveness, trustees, monitoring, arbitration and dispute resolution and post-implementation modification).[134]

The project resulted in the adoption of a Recommended Remedies Practice,[135] containing four main points: (A) remedies should address the competitive harm arising from the proposed concentration; (B) the merger review system should provide a transparent framework for the proposal, discussion and adoption of remedies; (C) procedures and practices should be established to ensure that remedies are effective and easily administrable; and (D) appropriate means should be provided to ensure implementation, monitoring of compliance and enforcement of the remedy.

Among other initiatives, the ICN's Merger Notification and Procedures Implementation Handbook from 2006 contains a compilation of remedies wording or language from

[131] See DAF/COMP (2010) 40, published on 13 December 2011, available at www.oecd.org/daf/competition/abuseofdominanceandmonopolisation/49294392.pdf. This hearing inspired the Committee to look further into the use of arbitration clauses as a monitoring and enforcement tool in merger remedies in its 2011 Merger Remedies Study, see p 19.

[132] See DAF/COMP/GF (2011) 13, available at www.oecd.org/daf/competition/mergers/50114086.pdf. Similar discussions had been held in 2005 where the OECD hosted a round table on 'Cross-border Remedies in Merger Cases' (mainly on developed jurisdictions). These discussions were never published and the only source of information was the summary made in the Commission's Competition Report 2005, paras 712, 713 and 721. The discussions had focused on the monitoring and enforcement of cross-border remedies and it had been acknowledged that certain types of international cooperation in remedies cases were difficult due to different legal frameworks in the respective jurisdictions. Similar conclusions had previously been reached in the Final Report (2000) of the International Competition Policy Advisory Committee to the Attorney General and Assistant Attorney General for Antitrust of the DoJ (the 2000 DoJ ICPAC Report), see www.justice.gov/atr/icpac/finalreport.htm.

[133] The report was prepared for the ICN's annual conference in Bonn, June 2005, see www.internationalcompetitionnetwork.org/uploads/library/doc323.pdf.

[134] The review disregards procedural issues as much as possible as they tend to be dependent on the legislative frameworks of individual jurisdictions.

[135] The remedies aspect forms part of the ICN's Recommended Practices for Merger Notification and Review Procedures (section XI is on Remedies originating from discussions in 2005 – hereinafter referred to as the ICN Recommended Remedies Practice), available at www.internationalcompetitionnetwork.org/uploads/library/doc588.pdf. The format consists of a short statement of the practice followed by explanatory comments. The recommended practices are merely guiding and it is left to the ICN's members to implement them as appropriately.

different jurisdictions (including the EU) where member countries can seek inspiration when revising and drafting their remedies policy.[136] One of the latest general remedies initiatives was a workshop in 2008 where delegates discussed a wide range of remedies issues ranging from negotiations to designing, implementing and monitoring compliance with remedies.[137] According to the ICN's long-term planning (2011–2016) renewed reviews into merger remedies issues will be on the agenda at some point although no details are yet available.[138]

#### 1.4.4.3 Other studies

Little publicised, the Commission did commission a number of remedies case studies in the past, albeit far more limited in scope than the Remedies Study. In 1995 it commissioned two statistical and qualitative studies with the aim of analysing the impact of two remedies cases in the European nylon carpet fibre market and in the French mineral water market,[139] and in 1998 it commissioned a comprehensive ex-post study covering both antitrust and merger remedies.[140] None of the studies were published and it is generally considered that their impact was limited.

In 2006 the Commission commissioned another study with the aim of developing a general methodology for ex-post reviews in merger cases, focusing on one particular merger between the power cable producers Pirelli and BICC.[141] Although the merger was cleared unconditionally the study remains relevant in remedies discussions as some of the counterfactual situations analysed in the study involve possible remedies.[142] The study proposes methods for evaluation of merger cases and concludes that the Commission's evaluation of the *Pirelli/BICC* merger was appropriate.

Also, in the wake of the DG Enterprise Econometric Remedies Study, a large number of econometric working papers and studies measuring ex-post effects and efficiencies of merger remedies emerged from several institutes and universities.[143] In these empirical studies various econometric variables and models are developed,[144] and they are interesting as they quantify and highlight issues that are not discussed in traditional legal papers on

[136] Remedies are dealt with in ch 7 of the Handbook, www.internationalcompetitionnetwork.org/uploads/library/doc325.pdf.

[137] See the ICN Merger Notification and Procedures Workshop in March 2008, Brno, the Czech Republic.

[138] For the long-term planning goals of the ICN Merger Working Group, see www.internationalcompetitionnetwork.org/uploads/library/doc754.pdf

[139] The cases were *DuPont/ICI* (M.214 II 1992) and *Nestlé/Perrier* (M.190 II 1992), see Competition Report 1995, p 325.

[140] See Competition Report 1998, p 371. The study had the following conclusions for merger cases: remedies should address barriers to entry and seek entry of new firms; the focus should be on creating genuine competition and not just a new competitor; structural remedies are to be advocated; a matrix of competition problems and appropriate remedies is set out; and the Commission's policy is in line with current economic reasoning.

[141] The study was undertaken by Lear (Laboratorio di economia, antitrust, regolamentazione), analysing *Pirelli/BICC* (M.1882 II 2000). The 200-page study received little press coverage but continues to be available at ec.europa.eu/competition/mergers/studies_reports/lear.pdf.

[142] The case was controversial at the time of the adoption as a minority in the Advisory Committee disagreed with the Commission and found that the merger did raise competition concerns, see Opinion of the Advisory Committee [2003] OJ C59/25. The Final Report of the Hearing Officer is not available.

[143] See in particular Papers by Lyons and Medvedev (2007), Bougette and Turolla (2006), Cosnita and Tropeano (2005) and (2006), and Duso, Gugler and Yurtoglu (2005) and (2006). Other studies are listed in the bibliography.

[144] Some studies take into consideration stock prices and balance sheet data (see eg Study by Duso, Gugler and Yurtoglu (2006)) whereas others focus on efficiency gains (see Study by Cosnita and Tropeano (2005)).

merger remedies.[145] The weakness of these studies is that they are primarily based on publicly available information and thus relatively limited in scope. However, the studies have introduced some interesting new ways of quantifying certain aspects of merger remedies and, as the Commission is increasing basing its competitive assessments on comprehensive econometric analyses, it is expected that econometric methods will be further explored in the future.

Finally, practitioners have funded research into national merger remedies legislation and practice. To date, the most important on-going project of this kind is the so-called Merger Remedies Matrix.[146] In 2008 a Synthesis Report entitled 'A European Cross-country Comparison of Merger Remedies: Experience and Practice' (the Merger Remedies Matrix Report) was published. The research programme is a novelty as it involves the creation of a searchable database containing comprehensive case summaries of national merger remedies cases with links to the original merger decision and supporting documents.[147] The Synthesis Report includes:[148] (i) an overview of national remedies procedures (with comparisons to the EU); (ii) comparative studies concentrating on a group of six 'European peers';[149] and (iii) an analysis of merger remedies at an industry sector level, focusing on information and communication as the innovative and diverse sector, and wholesale and retail as the traditional sector.

As with reports of this kind, the assessments and conclusions tend to be of a quantitative nature and lack in-depth analysis. One of the limitations of the project is that it provides a descriptive overview of the design and implementation of merger remedies but excludes ex-post research into effectiveness issues due to resource and information difficulties.[150] However, the research is interesting as it has the potential to develop into a comprehensive source of information on specific merger remedies cases. It also provides a quick reference on general national merger remedies legislation and practice, especially in view of the large database. Thus the project serves as a handbook rather than a policy or reflective document.[151]

[145] By way of illustration, for the purposes of one study the authors built an impressive database consisting of 217 phase I and II merger cases between 1990 and 2005 (thus the reference period was significantly longer than the ones used in the Remedies Study and the Econometric Study) and they were able to statistically prove that the probability of a structural remedy in phase I significantly increases if the acquired company is French or Dutch, see Study by Bougette and Turolla (2006) 10–14.

[146] The research programme is funded by Clifford Chance and PricewaterhouseCoopers and led by the Institute of Competition Law, involving contributions from 480 authors in 30 European countries, from 12 law firms and 14 universities. On 28 November 2008 the first Synthesis Report was published and made available at www.concurrences.com/rubrique.php3?id_rubrique=669&lang=en. While the case summaries are available by subscription, the national reports are accessible for free.

[147] While the research currently focuses on mergers examined by national competition authorities, the aim is to expand it to merger remedies cases from the EU and the US, see Synthesis Report, p 9. Currently the review covers around 470 national cases from around 30 countries.

[148] ibid, pp 9–10.

[149] The so-called 'Big 6' are France, Germany, Italy, the Netherlands, Spain and the UK.

[150] However, according to the authors it is a goal of future research to include an investigation into the effectiveness of merger remedies in the database and the Merger Remedies Matrix will provide a first step towards this objective, see Synthesis Report, p 9.

[151] It is the hope of the authors that by making information of this kind more readily available, it will become easier for involved jurisdictions to steer towards natural harmonisation in merger remedies cases, Synthesis Report, p 7.

## 1.5 Reflections on Remedies Enforcement Objectives

Before embarking in the remaining chapters of this book on a thorough analysis of the procedural and substantive provisions governing merger remedies within the framework of the Merger Regulation, it would be beneficial to highlight the overall objectives and enforcement considerations with regard to merger remedies. An understanding of the dynamics of remedies enforcement is important in order to later establish and explain certain developments in the Commission's policy and practice.

European companies are free to search for the most productive and competitive organisational structures reflecting their current and strategic business needs, to the benefit of consumers. The commercial driving force behind such commercial restructurings is generally the desire to protect or enhance shareholder value by maintaining or increasing profitability. This can be achieved in several ways through, for example, reduced costs, increased revenues and/or enhanced market power. While corporate restructurings in the form of concentrations are generally welcomed by the EU and indeed considered important in achieving future growth and competitiveness as well as completing the internal market, it must be ensured that the restructuring process does not result in lasting damage to competition and therefore the Commission has been granted certain intervention powers.[152]

The remedies regulatory exercise is a delicate balance between, on the one hand, recognising and allowing the pro-competitive and welfare-enhancing effects of a merger which can be highly beneficial to the consumer[153] while, on the other hand, identifying, addressing and safeguarding against any competitive harms without unnecessarily or disproportionately reducing the overall anticipated synergies and efficiency gains of the transaction. Thus, the overall aim of the remedies policy may be summarised as allowing concentrations that protect or enhance shareholder value whilst ensuring that (parts of) transactions which deprive consumers of value through the exercise of significant market power are remedied by maintaining or restoring the conditions of competition subsisting pre-merger. This is achieved through reducing the merged entity's control over its post-merger combined assets to the extent required to reduce market powers to a level which will remove the projected competitive effects on competition, notably on consumer welfare, identified by the Commission. In doing so, the remedies must fulfil certain formal criteria, such as being proportionate, effective and timely executed, and in its administrative proceedings the Commission applies certain specific strategic objectives, such as adopting speedy decisions, safeguarding rights of all parties concerned and so forth.

It is important to stress that the main beneficiary of regulatory intervention by means of merger remedies should be the consumer who, all other things being equal, must be protected against any competitive harm resulting in reduced choices, increased prices and/or stifled innovation.[154] Consumer welfare is therefore considered the cornerstone in the

[152] Merger Regulation, Recitals 3–5 and Art 2(3).

[153] It is generally recognised that mergers will not be attractive to consumers and welfare if they do not achieve at least some level of efficiency and, moreover, that the change in consumer surplus increases as the level of efficiency achieved by the merger increases, see further Paper by Neven and Röller (2002) referring to relevant economic theory in this respect.

[154] Needless to say, by pursuing the objectives of protecting consumers the Commission also promotes those market players that can offer competitive and innovative products or services to the consumers, at all levels of the value chain. However, the Commission does not apply any producer welfare standards as such.

Commission's merger regulation.[155] As a novelty, the Commission has recently been able to estimate that the observable customer benefits derived from the Commission's intervention in the form of conditionally clearing (or prohibiting) a horizontal merger was in the range of 4 to 5.8 billion EUR for 2011.[156]

As merger control is based on an ex-ante analysis, it is inevitable that the identification and assessment of foreseen competitive harm as well as the effects of corresponding remedies entail risks and uncertainties. It is the responsibility of the merging parties to endeavour addressing such issues in an adequate way during the negotiations of remedies and for the Commission to verify in its competitive assessment whether the proposed measures contain sufficient safeguards and are indeed realistic and probable to materialise in the manner foreseen in the proposals.

Thus, a prospective analysis always carries the risk that the envisaged competitive effects of the accepted and imposed remedies develop differently than foreseen and/or are misjudged with the result that the identified competition concerns may be 'over-fixed' or 'under-fixed'.[157] Such decisional outcomes are generally referred to as 'type 1' errors (excessive or over-fixing remedies) or 'type 2' errors (insufficient or under-fixing remedies).[158] They may ultimately result in the remedies being less effective or even wholly ineffective at which point in time there are no possibilities of reversing the outcomes. The traditional benchmark for such decisional errors is a comparison between the actual market developments induced by the Commission's decision with the developments that would have taken place otherwise.[159]

Put in simple terms, excessive remedies eliminate not only the identified competition concerns but also reduce anticipated efficiency gains and thus pro-competitive effects stemming from the merger. While it is beyond the scope of the present book to pursue an analysis of economic theory in this respect, the following implications of over-fixing should

[155] See in particular paras 8 and 79 of the guidelines on the assessment of horizontal mergers under the Council Regulation on the control of concentrations between undertakings (the Horizontal Merger Guidelines) [2004] OJ C31/5, as well as Speech by Almunia (2011a). Throughout the years economists have debated whether it is relevant to look at total welfare standards or consumer welfare standards, see eg Motta (2004) 18–22. However, following the publication of the Horizontal Merger Guidelines there appears to be consensus that the consumer welfare standard is indeed the appropriate standard to apply in this context, see eg Working Papers by Garrod and Lyons (2011), Duso, Gugler and Yurtoglu (2005) and Medvedev (2004). See also Bishop and Walker (2010) 29–32, and Nazzini in Ezrachi and Bernitz (2009) ch 17.

[156] See the DG Competition Management Plan 2012, pp 29–30. In this context the term 'customer' relates to direct purchasers, whether final consumers or intermediary users. It should be noted that the estimate excludes eg customer benefits in terms of better quality or wider choice as these cannot be quantified in monetary terms.

[157] Occasionally the Commission may adopt a clearance decision, which intentionally from the outset risks over-fixing or under-fixing the issues at hand due to certain political or other enforcement considerations, see further section 5.9.2.

[158] More generally in merger control, 'type 1' errors occur when mergers that do not harm consumers (meaning that the market had anticipated as pro-competitive) are prevented from going ahead, and 'type 2' errors occur when mergers that do harm consumers (meaning that the market has anticipated as anti-competitive) are cleared, see eg Paper by Lévêque (2007a). The current reflections do not explicitly refer to situations where concentrations are wrongly prohibited (type 1 error) or wrongly unconditionally cleared (type 2 error). For these situations, see in particular Paper by Neven and Röller (2002) where the authors found a low frequency of 'type 1' errors and a high frequency of 'type 2' errors (based on the first 10 years of the Merger Regulation).

[159] Given that this exercise is difficult – if not impossible – for commentators not having access to market information possessed by the Commission, alternative ex-ante benchmarks have been suggested, namely the anticipation by the stock market of the anti-competitive consequences of particular mergers, see originally Paper by Neven and Röller (2002) which has been followed up and further expanded in later econometric analyses.

be highlighted.[160] First and most obviously, the parties are likely to subsequently abandon their merger if, overall, the costs associated with the remedies outweigh the envisaged synergies and efficiency gains.[161] Along the same lines, a policy of consistently over-fixing may discourage companies from even seeking out and pursuing efficiency-oriented mergers which, on the whole, would have benefited consumers. Secondly, when competition concerns are over-fixed the ultimate consumer may lose out on pro-competitive effects of the merger which it would otherwise have benefitted from and hence such solutions are at risk of leaving the market less competitive and, for example, less innovative than originally foreseen. Third, over-fixing remedies may be difficult for the Commission to properly evaluate inasmuch as they involve assets outside the appraised markets.

At the other end of the spectrum, insufficient remedies may result in the competition concerns not being adequately addressed with the obvious effect that the market and consequently the consumers may be deprived of the anticipated competitive benefits in the form of lower prices, higher-quality products, wider selection of goods and services and so forth. It is also considered that under-fixing (more precisely 'mis-fixing') exists when the accepted remedies later turn out to in fact increase the risk of collusion in a given industry.[162] This may be the case where, for example, the Commission has sought to ensure viability issues by requiring the parties to divest to an existing competitor instead of a newcomer.[163] Inadequate remedies may also come about if they do not address the issues in the correct manner and/or lack enforcement,[164] or if the approved purchaser turns out to be less adequate and competitive than originally anticipated by the Commission.

While the Commission is likely to try to avoid both types of decisional errors as they may be detrimental to competition and in particular the consumers, generate public criticism and result in subsequent appeals procedures, various – and often diverging – interests, incentives and cost considerations of all parties involved in remedies process may result in certain enforcement outcomes being more likely and more appealing to the parties involved than others. In this context it is of relevance to briefly highlight the various interests of the stakeholders in merger remedies proceedings.

**The Commission:** firstly, while strictly speaking the overall aim of the Commission is to resolve the identified competition concerns and no more than that, there may be situations where it is inclined to seek the broadest and most comprehensive structural solution that the parties are prepared to offer in order to ensure and maximise viability of the assets to be

[160] An analysis of the nature, frequency and implications of such decisional errors would presuppose access to detailed market information. For econometric studies seeking to investigate the implications of such regulatory errors in merger remedies, see eg Working Papers by Garrod and Lyons (2011), Lévêque (2007a), Vasconcelos (2006), Duso, Gugler and Yurtoglu (2005) and Medvedev (2004) as well as Motta, Polo and Vasconcelos in Lévêque and Shelanski (2003) 106–28.

[161] Indeed, in the past a number of transactions have been cancelled due to excessive remedies, see n 7 above. Furthermore, the Commission's prohibition in *UPS/TNT Express* (M.6570 II 2013) is one of the most recent examples where the merging parties declared during the advanced remedies negotiations that they were not prepared to submit any further remedies and therefore their only option was to accept a prohibition decision and abandon their transaction and pay TNT Express a termination fee amounting to EUR 200 million, see UPS press release of 14 January 2013, available from pressroom.ups.com.

[162] This issue has been raised by eg Motta who refers to the Commission's decision in *Nestlé/Perrier* (M.190 II 1992) as an example of a remedy facilitating collusion as the re-sale of the brand Volvic to the main competitor BSN helped Nestlé and BSN to restore the symmetry in the industry which would have been lost, had Volvic not been transferred to BSN, see Motta in Lévêque and Shelanski (2003) 113.

[163] ibid 114.

[164] See section 2.5.2 below on so-called 'take note commitments'.

divested.[165] This preference can be explained by, for example, the following facts and incentives: (i) the existence of information asymmetry between the Commission and the parties in the sense that the latter possesses significantly more information about the transaction and the markets involved, especially in phase I where the Commission has limited time to obtain detailed market data;[166] (ii) the knowledge that the parties have no natural incentives to strengthen their immediate competitors and may possibly engage in strategic behaviour in order to weaken the effects of the remedies post-decision;[167] (iii) the fact that the Commission cannot subsequently and unilaterally correct any past decisional errors even if they prove detrimental to competition unless circumvention can be established; and (iv) a conditional clearance decision containing excessive remedies are unlikely to be challenged before the EU Court and hence the Commission may not necessarily feel constrained by the 'threat' of subsequent judicial review.[168]

Secondly, the Commission has an obligation to keep the costs of enforcement to the public purse to a minimum. As the administrative resources available to the Commission are finite, the more resources the Commission spends on remedies compliance, the less are available to carry out its core competence.[169] This objective may materialise in the Commission keeping the administrative proceedings as short as possible as well as being less directly involved in the implementation phase as such policy priorities inevitably minimise the use of staff resources.[170] The Commission's preference for structural solutions – being relatively self-executing compared to behavioural remedies – and the considerable use of and reliance upon trustees is in line with the objective of keeping the Commission's administrative costs to a minimum.[171]

At the same time, the Commission is also – in accordance with the principle of proportionality – obliged to keep the costs of the merging parties to a minimum and adopt speedy decisions wherever possible.[172] Thus, the nature, scope, modalities and implementation of the remedies should be the least burdensome for the parties if several options exist.[173] Furthermore, it should be noted that EU merger control is based on a system whereby the parties do not pay a merger fee upon notification of their transaction which is in keeping with the obligation of minimising the costs for the parties but it also means that there is

[165] This so-called 'clear sweep' approach then allows for a possible 'scaling back' later during the implementation stage under the standard review clause, see section 4.4.4.2.

[166] Thus, in practical terms the Commission must ask itself whether, based on the information available at the time, the merging parties are likely to bluff and eg possibly downplay certain harmful issues that the Commission may not be fully aware of based on its initial investigation.

[167] For examples of past strategic behaviour, see section 4.6.4.

[168] One of the few decisions being challenged on the grounds of excessive remedies was *Omya v Commission II* (T-275/06 withdrawn 2008), see section 4.6.5.1.

[169] This is relevant as merger remedies are a means by which private mergers are authorised on the parties' promise that they will not reduce consumer welfare and thus the promise must be capable of implementation with minimal or without unreasonable public compliance costs, see further de Souza and Brockhoff in Drauz and Jones (2012) para 7.140.

[170] To this effect, it has been pointed out that a very high case load may bring about an administrative 'desk clearing' effect in order to limit the phase II burden, see further Paper by Garrod and Lyons (2011) 16 and 23.

[171] However, structural remedies may also by nature be more intrusive and not always proportionate to the competition concerns and thus conferring additional costs on the merging parties in that respect, see section 2.3.1 below.

[172] The Commission's obligation to adopt speedy decisions in in-depth investigations is set out in Art 10(2) of the Merger Regulation.

[173] In respect of the costs of trustees, see section 4.2.1.5 below.

no corresponding direct income to cover the expenses of the Commission in individual remedies cases.[174]

Thirdly, a remedies policy incurs various indirect regulatory costs for the Commission as it must provide legal certainty, transparency and predictability by, for example, issuing guidance and preferably also ex-post studies in order to convey to all parties involved that its policy is justifiable, appropriate and indeed necessary. However, on balance such regulatory measures also provide substantial benefits for the Commission itself as they do not only result in an improved quality of the competition regime as such but they also have preventive effects and hence making enforcement more efficient and possibly less costly in the long run.

Similarly, the Commission has a duty to ensure that the merging parties and other involved parties enjoy the optimal procedural safeguards in term of adequate hearing and consultation during the administrative proceedings wherever appropriate. Thus, although it may at times be tempting to settle cases earlier from a cost point of view, it may be deemed necessary to invoke additional procedural safeguards in prolonged proceedings in order to safeguards particular interests and rights of the parties involved. Furthermore, studies have suggested that a prolonged investigation period may significantly reduce the risk of decisional errors being made.[175]

Finally, there is an important overall political issue to consider in the Commission's remedies policy and objectives. In accordance with the principle of subsidiarity the Member States have granted the Commission exclusive powers to deal with certain mergers, including settling with remedies, and therefore they rely upon the Commission not only to intervene where appropriate but also to be informed of and consulted on intended enforcement measures in this respect. At the end of the day, the Commission is held responsible vis-à-vis the Member States for its policy and it must ensure and justify that the delegation of powers in this respect continues to constitute an effective control of all concentrations from the point of view of their effect on competition in the European Union.

**The merging parties:** inevitably the overall strategic goal is to give the Commission 'as little as possible' in order to maintain and optimise the envisaged synergies and efficiencies expected from the merger. These incentives are based on several considerations of which only a few will be highlighted in the present context. First, it goes without saying that the parties have no natural interest in strengthening the competitive positions of their closest competitors and commercially the most attractive solution for them is to ensure that future competition is as weak as possible. To this effect, the parties may have commercial incentives to divest less attractive assets or inadequate packages or, more extremely, try to sabotage the transfer of assets or even to collude with the purchaser.[176] They may also prefer to sell the assets at a lower price to a weaker competitor than at a higher price to a strong competitor.

Secondly, the parties are faced with numerous costs in the remedies procedure. There are the obvious direct costs when preserving and selling the respective assets, especially if

[174] The possible introduction of a merger fee is discussed by eg Cosnita and Tropeano (2009).

[175] See eg Paper by Neven and Röller (2002) 13. However, at the same time it should be pointed out that in the Remedies Study the Commission found that divestiture remedies were more effective in phase II than in phase I. As commentators have pointed out this finding is not necessarily counterintuitive because phase I remedies are more likely to be disproportionate to the anticompetitive effects, see Paper by Lévêque (2007b) 5.

[176] Indeed, the Remedies Study provides numerous examples of such strategic behaviour in past cases, see further sections 4.6.4 and 5.5 below as well as Paper by Lévêque (2007b) 6.

the assets are subject to a fire sale. The parties have strong interests in not only limiting their implementation costs to a minimum but also being in control of such costs.[177] Furthermore, studies show that, in the event the Commission opens an in-depth investigation, the merging parties' share prices when publicly listed are likely to fall immediately in the wake of the news of a prolonged approval procedure, which will have a significant impact on their profitability.[178] In addition, a prolonged administrative procedure incurs increased administration costs (legal fees) for the parties but, more importantly, the risk of information leakages, misinterpretations and speculations is obviously higher the longer the process lasts which can also prove costly for the parties.[179] For the sake of completeness, it should also be mentioned that, in the event the parties do not succeed in their remedies negotiations with the Commission and accordingly must abandon their transaction, the acquirer is faced with additional costs as an acquisition agreement usually stipulates that the acquirer must pay the target company a cancellation or termination fee in the event that the transaction does not materialise.[180] Moreover, in some cases a termination fee or other contractual obligations are triggered if a phase I conditional clearance decision is not obtained, which obviously strongly enhances the parties' incentives to settle with phase I remedies as quickly and convincingly as possible in order to exclude the risk of entering an in-depth investigation.[181]

Thirdly, in evaluating their strategic options in terms of the length of the administrative proceedings, the merging parties will be aware that possible third-party complainants (competitors in particular) have longer time to voice and argue their concerns vis-à-vis the Commission[182], the Member States and the hearing officer in phase II proceedings. This may give the parties additional incentives to settle their case in phase I, albeit at a higher cost in the form of possibly more substantial and even excessive remedies as well as loss of the possibility to invoke additional procedural safeguards applying solely to in-depth investigations.

**Other market participants:** generally the primary concern of third parties is that of transparency in the sense that they wish to be consulted and heard on possible remedies before

[177] As will be highlighted later, there are a number of features built into the Merger Regulation which allow the parties to manage their costs, such as (i) only they have the power to submit remedies; (ii) they propose trustees and negotiate their mandates; and (iii) they largely control the divestiture process during the first divestiture period. On the other hand, there are also a number of direct costs that the parties cannot influence, such as the administrative expenses of the trustees, see section 4.2.1.5 below.

[178] Studies have shown that the largest drop in the merging parties' share prices are likely to occur when phase II proceedings are initiated rather than when a final decision is adopted, see Duso, Gugler and Yurtoglu (2005) 38.

[179] ibid, p 43. Commentators have submitted that information leakage problems may play a crucial role during a phase II investigation with the result that stock prices of the merging parties as well as competitors are negatively affected.

[180] See n 161 above. See also *Unilever/Sara Lee Body Care* (M.5658 II 2010) where Unilever was obliged to pay Sara Lee EUR 25 million if the conditions for the transaction would not be met, including a conditional clearance decision from the Commission, see the parties' filing to the US Securities and Exchange Commission (the US SEC), Acquisition Agreement, para 4.2, available at www.faqs.org/sec-filings/101209/Sara-Lee-Corp_8-K/dex102.htm#b.

[181] In *IAG/BMI* (M.6447 I 2012) IAG was obliged to pay a termination fee of £10 million to BMI if the transaction did not obtain a phase I clearance, see IAG press release of 22 December 2011, available at www.iairgroup.com/phoenix.zhtml?c=240949&p=irol-newsArticle&id=1642163. In *Unilever/Sara Lee Body Care* (M.5658 II 2010) it was stipulated in the acquisition agreement that the assets to be acquired would change scope (ie the European Detergent Business would be excluded from the acquisition) if the Commission would enter phase II proceedings, see the parties' filing to the US SEC, Acquisition Agreement, para 3.10, see n 180 above.

[182] Practice shows that the Commission attaches great importance to the views of third parties (particularly competitors) during its market test of the remedies, see 2.4.1 below.

the Commission forms a final view. The incentives and interests of third parties (mainly competitors) to intervene in a merger notification obviously depend on their own agendas.[183] The most likely scenario is that third parties are sceptical to a merger and submit disapproving comments if the transaction has a negative impact on their own position or if they (competitors) wish to acquire certain assets from the merging parties.[184] Furthermore, they usually have an interest in the Commission opening an in-depth investigation in order to enjoy enhanced procedural rights and strategically it may also be in their advantage that the merging parties are subjected to longer proceedings.

When it comes to potentially purchasing any assets in a remedies package, competitors and other market participants are of course interested in acquiring such assets as cheaply as possible. To this effect, they may try to encourage the Commission to accept or impose a fire-sale or the addition of supplementary assets at no (or little) extra costs. In the past, unsuccessful acquirers of remedies packages have also brought actions before the Court claiming that the main transaction should be annulled (implicitly with the agenda that an annulment would provide them with a second opportunity to purchase the assets in question).[185]

**All in all**, it is evident from the above-described interests and incentives that remedies come at various costs for all parties involved in the process and that expectations on anticipated benefits and optimal solutions depend on the beneficiary in question. Whether the parties have submitted – and the Commission has accepted – the optimal remedy for the sake of competition and in particular the consumer can only be established through ex-post evaluations of the relevant markets several years after the respective transactions have been executed. While this book does not include ex-post assessments of the competitive impact of past remedies decisions, it does provide an opportunity to verify and evaluate whether the Commission's priorities and choices in its past and present remedies policy and practice are coherent with the overall objectives of remedies enforcement and whether the administrative procedures and enforcement outcomes adequately acknowledge and respect the different (and sometimes diverging) interests of all stakeholders.

[183] It goes without saying that there are instances where competitors have different interests in the outcome of remedies proceedings than the parties and/or the Commission, which may in some instances lead to enforcement errors, unless the Commission has carefully examined the underlying incentives of the respondents, see further Maier-Rigaud and Parplies (2009) 573–75.

[184] However, studies have shown that some mergers may generate positive profits for both the merging parties and its main competitors, see in particular Papers by Duso, Gugler and Yurtoglu (2005) 17–18, and Neven and Röller (2002) 6–12. In such cases the competitors may have an interest in remaining neutral or even positive during the administrative proceeding and in such scenarios the Commission must obviously clarify the interests of such third parties before relying on their input in the market test. Otherwise, wrong reliance on the input from competitors may lead to 'type 2' errors which Neven and Röller submit has indeed been the case in the past.

[185] See eg *Éditions Odile Jacob SAS v Commission, Lagardère SCA* (C-551/10 P 2012) and *Éditions Odile Jacob SAS v Commission* (T-279/04 2010) as well as older appeals like *easyJet v Commission* (T-177/04 2006), *ARD v Commission* (T-158/00 2003) and *Kaysersberg v Commission* (T-290/94 1997).

# 2

# Negotiating, Submitting, Assessing and Adopting Remedies

## 2.1 General Principles

### *2.1.1 Step One: Identifying Competition Concerns*

There is broad consensus amongst competition authorities that they should consider remedies only if a threat to competition can be identified.[1] The Commission undertakes its competitive analysis in conditional clearance cases based on this two-steps approach: first the verification of a potential competition concerns and secondly the elimination of the concerns through adequate remedies. The EU Court has confirmed the importance of this way of analysis as it is only once the competition concerns have been clearly identified and communicated to the parties that they can address them by considering remedies.[2] The Commission identifies potential competition concerns in accordance with the compatibility test; whether or not a concentration would significantly impede effective competition in the internal market or a substantial part of it, in particular as a result of the creation of a dominant position (the SIEC test).[3]

In its assessment the Commission takes into account certain appraisal criteria, including the need to maintain and develop effective competition and the interests of the intermediate and ultimate consumers.[4] Under current practice the assessment of compatibility is often a comprehensive and complex exercise (with the involvement of the Chief Economist's office), including advanced economic analysis of data as well as the application of economic methodology and theory.[5] Also the Commission is increasingly benchmarking its examination of the competition concerns and their possible solutions with alternative (counterfactual) scenarios, making its assessments more sound and sophisticated than previously.[6]

[1] See the 2004 OECD Remedies Study, pp 17–18.

[2] See eg *Schneider v Commission* (T-310/01 2002) paras 442–44.

[3] Merger Regulation, Arts 2(2) and 2(3).

[4] The appraisal criteria are listed in Arts 2(1)(a) and 2(1)(b) of the Merger Regulation.

[5] In certain cases the Commission has also commissioned expert studies undertaking econometric simulations of the respective mergers in affected markets, see *Lagardère/Natexis/VUP* (M.2978 II 2004) and *Volvo/Scania* (M.1672 II 2000), both explained in Bishop and Walker (2010) 646–48.

[6] In Davies and Lyons (2007) the authors recommend that the Commission abandons its market share calculations in favour of basic simulation models in order to compare the outcome of a merger cleared with remedies with a counterfactual of what would have happened, had the merger been allowed without remedies, see pp 44–73. In recent practice the Commission has undertaken extensive counterfactual analysis in particular in cases where the respective merger has strengthened already-existing links (cooperation) between parties, see eg *SNCF/LCR/Eurostar* (M.5655 I 2010) paras 36–60; *Lufthansa/Austrian Airlines* (M.5440 II 2009) paras 57–104; and *Delta/Northwest* (M.5181 I 2008) paras 22–37. For a description of the Commission's use of counterfactual analysis in mergers, see also Niels, Jenkins and Kavanagh (2011) 338–41.

The Commission has a considerable margin of discretion when assessing a transaction in accordance with the compatibility test. This discretion has been confirmed by the EU Court, especially with respect to assessments of an economic nature, and it has been stressed that review by the Court must therefore 'take account of the discretionary margin implicit in the provisions of an economic nature which form part of the rules on concentration'.[7]

In phase I (and before the issuance of the Statement of Objections (the SO) in phase II)[8] the Commission needs only to establish 'serious doubts' as to the compatibility of the concentration before it may accept remedies.[9] This criterion is a broad concept, which should be seen against the background that, given the tight deadlines in phase I, the Commission will not have had sufficient time to undertake a detailed investigation of the transaction and can therefore not be expected to go into great details about its competition concerns. However, this does not change the fact that the burden of proof rests on the Commission and that it must submit thorough arguments going through the traditional appraisal criteria (horizontal overlaps, vertical issues, potential competition and so forth) in order to establish serious doubts.[10]

In the past there have been remedies cases where the Commission failed to clearly identify and substantiate competition concerns to the requisite standard. These situations were often sparked by remedies being proposed (and accepted) very early in the proceedings and consequently the Commission did not fully complete its competitive assessment of the competition concerns.[11] Such incidences are regrettable as an improper and/or premature identification of the competition concerns could mean that subsequent remedies fail to address the 'real' competition problems or they are excessive and go beyond what is necessary or even superfluous. Fortunately, recent practice shows that the Commission has become significantly more thorough and generally adheres to the two-step analysis in remedies cases.

In phase II cases the Commission has consistently been more detailed in its analysis of the potential competition problems before resorting to a discussion of possible remedies.[12] While it is beyond the scope of this book to go into details about the compatibility test[13] – unless relevant for the corresponding remedies – it should be noted that the Commission's guidelines on horizontal and non-horizontal mergers, in particular, provide useful insight into the

[7] See *Cementbouw Handel & Industrie v Commission* (C-202/06 P 2007) para 53, referring to *France and Others v Commission* (C-68/94 and C-30/95 1998) paras 223–24, and *Commission v Tetra Laval* (C-12/03 P 2005) para 38.

[8] For examples of phase II conditional clearance decisions where no SO was issued and hence the objective of the remedies remained mitigating serious doubts, see *UTC/Goodrich* (M.6410 II 2012); *Syngenta/Monsanto's Sunflower Seed Business* (M.5675 II 2010); *StatoilHydro/ConocoPhillips* (M.4919 II 2008); *ABF/GBI Business* (M.4980 II 2008); *Kronospan/Constantia* (M.4525 II 2007); *Universal/BMG Music Publishing* (M.4404 II 2007); *Metso/Aker Kvaerner* (M.4187 II 2006); *Sonoco/Ahlstrom* (M.3431 II 2004); and *DSM/Roche Vitamins* (M.2972 II 2003).

[9] Merger Regulation, Arts 6(1)(c) and 6(2).

[10] In *Royal Philips Electronics v Commission* (T-119/02 2003) the General Court stressed that '[e]ven if the notion of "serious doubts" is an objective one, the identification of such doubts necessarily requires the Commission to carry out complex economic assessments, in particular where it must assess whether the commitments proposed by the parties to the concentration are sufficient to dispel those serious doubts', see para 77.

[11] By way of illustration, in *Orkla/Chips* (M.3658 I 2005) the Commission left the 'existence of the serious doubts open' in view of the submission of commitments in phase I, see para 25.

[12] In the past there have however been examples of less precise and insufficient competitive assessment, see eg *Mitsui/CVRD/CAEMI* (M.2420 II 2001) para 250.

[13] For literature on the compatibility test in EU merger control, see in particular Drauz and Jones (2012) Part 4; Whish and Bailey (2012) Ch 21(5); Jones and Sufrin (2011) Ch 12(5); Bishop and Walker (2010) Ch 7 and 8; Cook and Kerse (2009) Ch 7; Bellamy and Child (2008) paras 8.192, Faull and Nikpay (2007) Ch 5(c).

Commission's compatibility assessment under the Merger Regulation.[14] Also it should be mentioned that it is generally perceived among commentators that the Commission's shift from the so-called dominance test to the SIEC test in 2004 has not changed the Commission's basic approach to the compatibility analysis in any material way.[15]

As for statistics on the main types of identified competition concerns in remedies cases, the following breakdown was made in the Remedies Study of past cases: 80 per cent horizontal concerns, 14 per cent horizontal and vertical concerns and six per cent pure vertical concerns.[16] The study also found that 84 per cent of the remedies analysed were aimed at preventing single dominance (non-coordinated effects) and only 12 per cent of the remedies sought to address collective dominance (co-ordinated effects).[17] The vast majority of competition concerns were identified in the manufacturing segment.[18]

Finally, in terms of how the identified competition concerns are communicated to the parties, there are different procedures for phase I and II, respectively. In phase I the competition concerns are presented orally to the parties during a state-of-play meeting or a telephone conference.[19] While an oral presentation is considered an administrative necessity due to the tight deadlines, it may put the parties in an adverse situation of not having the concerns in writing, especially in complicated cases. Conversely, in phase II the competition concerns are set out in writing, often several times: first in the decision opening an in-depth investigation[20] and later in the SO if the initial concerns are upheld.[21] Also if the Commission identifies additional concerns at a later stage, they must be submitted to the parties in an additional written communication.[22]

[14] See the Horizontal Merger Guidelines (ch 1 n 155 above) and the guidelines on the assessment of non-horizontal mergers under the Council Regulation on the control of concentrations between undertakings (the Non-Horizontal Merger Guidelines) [2008] OJ C 265/ 6.

[15] See eg Maier-Rigaud and Parplies (2009); Cook and Kerse (2009) 204; Carles Esteva Mosso in Marsden, Hutchings and Whelan (2007) 384–88; and Faull and Nikpay (2007) 474. To this effect, the Horizontal Merger Guidelines stipulates: 'most cases of incompatibility [. . .] will continue to be based upon a finding of dominance' (para 4). This view is in line with a statement in 2004 of the then-Competition Commissioner Monti that the change in the substantive test should not be seen as a 'shift in enforcement policy or a revolution' and that, personally, he felt that the discussion on the test was largely semantic, see Speech by Monti (2004).

[16] Remedies Study, Chart 7, p 20. Going a step further, horizontal competition problems were addressed mainly by transfer of a market position but also by exit from a joint venture. Combined horizontal and vertical concerns were often mitigated by transfer of a market position whereas vertical concerns were mainly solved through access remedies, see Remedies Study, Table 4, p 20

[17] ibid, Chart 8, p 21 (the remaining 4% related to cooperation effects). The cases were decided under the original Merger Regulation and hence the dominance test. It should be noted that recent decisional practice indicates a significant drop in co-ordinated effects remedies cases, see further Petit (2010) 3, and Maier-Rigaud and Parplies (2009).

[18] Remedies Study, Table 3, p 14. A staggering 67% of all remedies in the period 1996–2000 related to the manufacturing industry. This result is likely to be very different today with more innovative and financial sectors involved in remedies cases.

[19] The meeting normally takes place around the fifteenth working day following notification, see Best Practice Guidelines on Merger Proceedings, para 33 a) and Remedies Notice, para 78. See also von Koppenfels in Drauz and Jones (2012) para 6.114.

[20] Merger Regulation, Art 6(1)(c).

[21] Implementing Regulation, Art 13(2).

[22] Along the same lines, if new significant facts arise or the Commission significantly modifies its concerns, any such changes must be communicated in writing to the parties, combined with an additional access to the file, in order to ensure their rights of defence, see eg *Unilever/Sara Lee Body Care* (M.5658 II 2010) where the Commission set out additional facts emerging after the SO in a so-called 'Letter of Facts', see Final Report of the Hearing Officer, [2012] OJ C23/28; and *Arsenal/DSP* (M.5153 II 2009) where the Commission issued a similar 'Letter of Facts' explaining the modified objection, see Final Report of the Hearing Officer, [2009] OJ C227/22.

### *2.1.2 Step Two: Remedying Competition Concerns*

#### 2.1.2.1 Initiatives, Onus and Responsibilities

Once the Commission has identified and communicated its competition concerns to the parties, it is entirely up to them to decide whether they wish to address the concerns by proposing commitments.[23] In phase II proceedings the parties will practically always propose commitments – even if they disagree with the finding of competition concerns – as this is the only way of avoiding a prohibition decision.[24] In phase I proceedings the parties may strategically submit commitments as soon as possible in order to avoid the initiation of a lengthy phase II proceeding (if they are confident that the Commission will not withdraw its initial concerns),[25] or they may wait for the Commission to substantiate its initial concerns in phase II before discussing or proposing possible commitments.[26] The overall important issue is that, contrary to some jurisdictions, the submission of commitments is voluntary and the Commission has no powers to unilaterally impose any conditions to a conditional clearance decision but only on the basis of the parties' commitments.[27] This also means that it is the responsibility of the parties to put forward commitments, which are comprehensive and effective from all points of view in order for the Commission to accept them.[28]

However, some critics have claimed that the Commission often heavily influences the contents of the parties' commitments.[29] The argument is that a commitment is, by its very nature, a response to a competition concern identified by the Commission and therefore it inevitably has a certain influence over the type, scale and scope of the commitment proposed by the parties.[30] Also, the EU Court has recognised that occasionally the Commission may have exercised a certain influence on the commitments proposals presented by the parties.[31] Along the same lines, it is evident from certain decisions that the Commission

[23] Remedies Notice, para 6.

[24] *Aerospatiale-Alenia/de Havilland* (M.53 II 1991) is the only prohibition in accordance with Art 8(3) of the Merger Regulation where proposed commitments were not discussed in the decision.

[25] See eg *Telefónica/O2* (M.4035 I 2006) and in particular IP/06/16 of 10 January 2006.

[26] See *Oracle/Sun Microsystems* (M.5529 II 2010) where the parties refrained from proposing commitments in response to competition concerns identified in phase I. This strategy paid off as the Commission subsequently withdrew its competition concerns in phase II and cleared the transaction unconditionally (albeit taking note of certain reassurances, see section 2.5.2 below).

[27] Remedies Notice, para 6. For a distinction between conditions and obligations in this respect, see section 2.5.1 below. Contrary to the EU policy, the UK Competition Commission may impose an order to implement remedies if an agreement with the parties on remedies cannot be reached timely, see 2008 Merger Remedies Guidelines (CC8), 1.26 and 1.27.

[28] In *General Electric v Commission* (T-210/01 2005) the General Court added that the Commission cannot be held responsible for technical or commercial gaps in the commitments, see para 52.

[29] See eg Ersbøll (2001) who claims that, in reality, the Commission imposes remedies and they are a powerful policy weapon for the Commission which can be used to engage in 'market engineering' while at the same time running a relatively small risk of being over-ruled by the EU Court if the imposed remedies are disproportionate or unnecessary (p 364).

[30] In the draft version of the old Remedies Notice (published for consultation on the DG Competition's website in September 1999 but no longer available online) the Commission recognised this causality by stating that 'it is the Commission's assessment of the competition problem to be resolved that is decisive in determining what the parameters of the remedy should be', see para 17. This wording was omitted in the final version of the old Remedies Notice.

[31] In *Cementbouw Handel & Industrie v Commission* (T-282/02 2006) the General Court observed that ' it must be acknowledged that the Commission may have exercised a certain influence on the terms of the commitments proposed by the parties' (para 314). While it should be noted that the given transaction already had been implemented and on that basis the Commission had indicated to the parties in the SO that it was prepared to issue an Art 8(4) divestment order if the parties did not propose commitments, it appears from the Court's summary of the administrative proceedings that the Commission did attempt to put pressure on the parties in this respect, see para 314.

requested certain provisions that the parties then submitted as their own proposals.[32] However, it should be remembered that, as remedies negotiations form part of a hopefully constructive dialogue between the Commission and the parties,[33] the latter usually expect the former to be pro-active in its advice and response to the adequacy of the proposals at hand in order to achieve an acceptable solution for all parties concerned.[34] While the Commission is prepared to submit observations in response to commitment proposals, it must be considered unlikely that it will take on a dedicated advisory role in formulating commitment proposals as previously suggested by some commentators and international organisations.[35]

In terms of assessing proposed commitments, it is once and for all clarified in the new Remedies Notice that it is the sole responsibility of the Commission to establish whether or not a concentration, as modified by commitments validly submitted, must be declared incompatible with the internal market.[36] This responsibility applies also to any modifications (submitted in due time) to previously submitted commitments.[37] Thus, as far as the burden of proof is concerned, a prohibition or a modified concentration is subject to the same criteria as an unmodified concentration.[38] In all scenarios the Commission has a duty to reason and substantiate its conclusions in a comprehensive and satisfactory way.[39] Thus, if the Commission considers the commitments insufficient, it must base its assessment on objective and verifiable criteria (and not on the mere fact that the parties have failed to provide sufficient evidence to carry out a substantive assessment).

**Commentary:** while the responsibilities when proposing, submitting and accepting remedies have become significantly more clear-cut, formalised and consistent in recent years, the fact remains that the negotiation process and the tactics involved are of such a nature that, in reality, the Commission informally indicates to the parties what is broadly needed in order to secure a conditional clearance

[32] Rather exceptionally, in *Sanofi-Avantis/Zentiva* (M.5253 I 2009) the Commission spelled out in its decision that, in view of negative comments during the market test, it had requested the parties to (i) extend the duration of a transitional supply agreement from two to three years; and (ii) insert specific purchaser requirements in order to ensure a smooth transfer of certain assets, see para 553. These provisions were then submitted as proposals from the parties, see Remedies Text, paras 4(f) and 13(b).

[33] As pointed out by several commentators, merger discussions are, generally speaking, conducted in an open and constructive way, see eg Van Bael (2011) 491 (rather unusually, the author reproduces photos of cartoons, which used to hang in the conference room of the old Merger Task Force, illustrating the alleged politically sensitive negotiations in *Boeing/McDonnell Douglas* (M.877 II 1997) and it is alleged that the drawings witness that the negotiations were conducted in a less than friendly atmosphere).

[34] Indeed the Best Practice Remedies Guidelines stipulate that 'although it is for the notifying parties to formulate suitable remedies proposals, the DG Competition will provide guidance to the parties as to the general appropriateness of their draft proposal in advance of submission' (para 41).

[35] In past merger reviews it has been suggested that the Commission should assume a more pro-active role in remedies negotiations by way of advising the parties what kind of commitments could be feasible in order to advance the negotiations, see the 2001 Green Paper, para 221. For similar internationals calls, see the ICN Recommended Remedies Practice, Comment 2 (*in fine*): 'the agency may take the initiative to propose alternative resolutions [in order to avoid an outright prohibition]'. For an opposite view, see Monti in IBA (2000) 432.

[36] Remedies Notice, para 8. In the old Remedies Notice the Commission suggested that the burden of proof rested on the parties, see para 6. The General Court dismissed this interpretation in *EDP v Commission* (T-87/05 2005), see para 64 of the judgment.

[37] *EDP v Commission*, para 67.

[38] Remedies Notice, para 8 *in fine*, and *EDP v Commission*, paras 61–65.

[39] Under current practice the Commission usually substantiates its compatibility assessments in a detailed and satisfactory way. However, in the past there have been examples of remarkably short and insufficient assessments of the adequacy of the proposed commitments, see eg *Teijin/Zeon/JV* (M.3235 I 2003), para 31 (the compatibility assessment was limited to one phrase: 'this undertaking will remove the horizontal overlap brought about by the notified transaction'). Although less extreme, see also *Teva/Barr* (M.5295 I 2008) where the assessment of remedies covering 17 affected markets is accomplished on less than one page in the decision, see paras 208–10.

> decision and then it is up to the parties to consider whether they wish to propose remedies along those lines. The Commission's bargaining powers are particularly prominent in phase I proceedings where competition concerns are identified more broadly and communicated less formally and the parties are under immense time constraints to consider and formulate any remedies proposals. In addition, it is a well-known fact for anyone involved in remedies negotiations that provisions such as additional assets, up-front solutions and fix-it-first clauses are usually explicitly (albeit informally) required by the Commission during remedies discussions although they are subsequently (formally) submitted by the parties as part of their proposals.[40]

In terms of timing and procedure, competition problems can be remedied in one of the following two ways: (i) the parties modify their concentration plan *prior* to the adoption of a Commission clearance decision; or (ii) the parties commit to modify their concentration *after* the Commission has adopted a conditional clearance decision.

### 2.1.2.2 Pre-clearance Modifications

In response to the identified competition concerns, the parties may voluntarily propose and implement changes to their concentration *prior* to the adoption of a clearance decision.[41] Such modifications generally refer to the transaction itself by, for example, not buying a particular business of a company, which was included in the original merger plan,[42] or by one of the acquirers withdrawing from the merger agreement.[43] In its competitive analysis the Commission will treat the modifications as facts and an integral part of the transaction and will not condition its approval on such modifications.

While from the regulator's point of view, pre-clearance modifications are evidently preferable as they minimise the alleged harmful effects of the original merger structure, the tight deadlines for clearances under the Merger Regulation automatically make pre-clearance modifications rare and confined to a handful of cases where potential remedies have been discussed at an early stage and/or where the amendments are limited and straightforward in terms of design and implementation.[44] Given their rarity the description of past and present practice will be confined to the following observations.

[40] One of the latest illustrations of these negotiation dynamics is found in *UPS/TNT Express* (M.6570 II 2013) where the Commission reasoned its prohibition of the transaction by inter alia referring to the fact that 'UPS would have needed to sign a binding agreement with a suitable purchaser before the concentration was implemented' which it was not prepared to do, see Commission press release IP13/68 of 30 January 2013 (public decision not yet available). Thus, it is evident from the statement that the Commission had explicitly requested an up-front buyer provision, see also the Commission's explanations of this case in MEMO/13/48 of 30 January 2013, pp 4–5.

[41] Remedies Notice, para 5.

[42] In *Kronospan/Constantia* (M.4525 II 2007) the notified original Framework Agreement was modified so Kronospan would acquire only two of the originally agreed three plants from Constantia, see para 3. The modification was supplemented with a commitment that Kronospan would not acquire control of the third plant for a certain period of time post-clearance, see para 91.

[43] In *Framatome/Siemens/Cogéma/JV* (M.1940 II 2000) the notified merger agreement provided that the three parent companies would acquire joint control of a joint venture, see para 8. However, in response to competition concerns relating to Cogéma's involvement in the joint venture, the parties modified their merger agreement so only Framatome and Siemens would acquire control of the joint venture, para 98.

[44] In *Ericsson/Nortel Group (MSS & Global Services)* (M.6095 I 2011) Ericsson extended an existing supply agreement with a competitor during the administrative proceedings in order to alleviate the Commission's initial concerns, see para 94. In *Interbrew/Beck's* (M.2569 I 2001) the parties modified a distribution agreement (which was originally submitted as a commitment) during the administrative proceedings and thus changed character from a commitment to a fact in the Commission's competitive assessment, see paras 2 and 29. In *Eurostar* (M.1305 I 1998) the parties to a consortium signed a supplementary shareholders agreement during the administrative proceedings limiting the exchange of sensitive information, see para 54.

Despite the Commission's general view that pre-clearance modifications must be fully implemented prior to the adoption date of the decision,[45] there have been (few) cases in the past where, although the modifications could not be fully implemented prior to the adoption of the clearance decision, the Commission nonetheless considered them an integral part of the transaction based on certain assurances or measures submitted by the parties.[46] There have also been examples of cases where the Commission has considered remedies submitted to other jurisdictions as facts in its assessment of the respective transactions, although strictly speaking the remedies had not yet been implemented in the other jurisdiction.[47]

While the number of accepted pre-clearance modifications has been low throughout the years, there are suggestions that such modifications may be subject to renewed discussions in the future. First, as discussed in detail below the Commission recently accepted so-called 'public pledges' as facts in a case, which is now subject to a pending appeal and where it is expected that the EU Court will rule on the appropriateness and use of such pledges (most of which were not fully implemented prior to the adoption of the unconditional clearance decision).[48] Secondly, in view of the growing number of multi-jurisdictional remedies cases and an increased openness from a number of regulators to consider enhanced cooperation on remedies enforcement, it is likely that a recognition – in one form or the other – of remedies given in the course of proceedings in another jurisdiction may start featuring more frequently in future decisions and could potentially be considered facts rather than remedies.[49] Thirdly, the Commission's increased acceptance in recent years of so-called fix-it-first and up-front buyer solutions encourages the parties to consider pre-decision or pre-closure measures, where possible.[50]

Finally, one last point on pre-clearance modifications deserves mentioning as it has received little, if any, attention in competition commentary so far. From the merging parties' point of view, pre-clearance solutions may be commercially attractive as the modalities of the modifications may not be subject to the Commission's scrutiny and acceptance in the same way as 'traditional' remedies are.[51] This could mean that particularly in cases

[45] Remedies Notice, para 5.

[46] In *Framatome/Siemens/Cogéma/JV* (M.1940 II 2000) the Commission found it sufficient that the French state issued a declaration setting out its support for future changes to a procurement policy and a future withdrawal of one of its companies (EdF) from Framatome, see paras 90–97. In *Procter & Gamble/VP Schickedanz (II)* (M.430 II 1994) the notification contained a modification whereby VP Schickedanz's baby nappy business would be separated from its other businesses and held in a separate company monitored by a trustee prior to completion of the transaction, see para 5. The Commission found that the business was an integral part of the transaction and thus it would not, despite any possible objections it would have, address this market, see para 7. On appeal, the General Court confirmed this approach by stressing that, since there was no lasting and actual transfer of control of the nappy business to P&G, the business was not covered by the concentration plan submitted to the Commission for its examination and hence beyond the powers of the Commission, see *Kaysersberg v Commission* (T-290/94 1997) para 192.

[47] In *Halliburton/Dresser* (M.1140 I 1998) a commitment to the DoJ was considered a 'fact' in the Commission's assessment, see paras 6–7.

[48] See the analysis of *Oracle/Sun Microsystems* (M.5529 II 2010) and related appeal *Monty Program v Commission* (T-292/10 pending) in section 2.5.2 below.

[49] In eg the DoJ's investigation of Cisco's acquisition of Tandberg in 2010 the DoJ took into account commitments made by Cisco to the Commission in *Cisco/Tandberg* (M.5669 I 2010), and on that basis decided not to challenge the transaction, see further n 241 below.

[50] See section 3.4.2 and section 3.4.3 below.

[51] In *Kaysersberg v Commission* (T-290/94 1997) the applicant (a competitor) unsuccessfully argued that the Commission, despite not looking into potential competition concerns relating to the excluded baby nappy business, should have adopted a position in regard to the choice of the third party designated to acquire the business. The General Court stressed that such an intervention would be impossible as the Commission would have no power to do so under the Merger Regulation, see para 192.

where the Commission does not insist on the pre-clearance modification being fully implemented prior to the adoption of the clearance decision, there may be scope for the parties to negotiate certain conditions with the acquiring party without the interference of the Commission. Although it could be argued that such a 'loophole' encourages circumvention, decisional practice shows that this has so far not been the case, based on publicly available reports.[52]

### 2.1.2.3 Commitments to Modify Post Clearance

The vast majority of modifications are drafted and executed as 'commitments to modify' certain aspects of a transaction, taking effect upon the date of adoption of the conditional clearance decision, so-called ex-ante commitments. Commitments become binding and enforceable when they are attached to the Commission's conditional clearance decision as conditions and obligations and they expire when the parties have fully complied with these measures. The mechanism of post-clearance implementation of commitments is necessary in a merger regime with strict timetables during the administrative proceedings.

Whereas pre-clearance modifications are analysed by the Commission as an integral part of the notified transaction, commitments to modify are analysed under a step-by-step approach whereby the Commission first assesses the competition concerns and then the implications of the proposed remedies *without* recommencing its competitive analysis in view of the commitments being offered. The EU Court has endorsed this methodology, referring to the requirement of speed under the Merger Regulation.[53] This approach also applies to cases where successive commitments are proposed as each proposal shall be assessed separately.[54] Along the same lines, the EU Court has confirmed that the submission of extensive commitments during the administrative proceedings whereby the notified transaction is (proposed) changed in a substantial way, but without being abandoned, has no bearing on the Commission's already-acquired competence to assess the merger.[55] Thus, the Commission is not required to conduct a fresh examination of its jurisdiction in situations where the parties propose commitments that change the transaction in such a way that it would not strictly speaking qualify for notification if the commitments were taken into account.[56]

[52] However, this could be an aspect that the Commission may want to consider for future adjustments, especially depending on the ruling of the General Court in *Monty Program v Commission* (T-292/10 pending).

[53] In *EDP v Commission* (T-87/05 2005) the General Court confirmed that it would be unrealistic to imagine that the Commission could, within the time constraints imposed by the Merger Regulation, recommence entirely its analysis of a merger, in the lights of the submission of commitments, as though that transaction had been notified anew in the form modified by the commitments, see para 80. Such an approach would conflict with the requirement of speed that characterizes the general structure of the Merger Regulation, see *Endemol v Commission* (T-221/95 1999) para 68.

[54] This approach is the same whether the successive commitments are merely modifications of earlier submitted commitments or new commitments, see *EDP v Commission*, para 80 *in fine*.

[55] See *Cementbouw Handel & Industrie* (C-202/06 P 2007) paras 41–47, as well as Opinion of Advocate General Kokott (delivered on 26 April 2007) points 47–56.

[56] As correctly pointed out by Advocate General Kokott in her Opinion in *Cementbouw Handel & Industrie* such a situation could otherwise lead to scenarios where the parties would deliberately make modifications to their concentration in the course of the administrative proceedings in order to exclude it from the jurisdiction of one competition authority and bring it within the jurisdiction of another, presumably more lenient, authority which could ultimately result in 'forum shopping', see Opinion of Advocate General Kokott, point 55.

Finally it should be noted that, although the Merger Regulation phrases the possibility of offering commitments as 'modification' of a notified concentration,[57] practice shows that the Commission has considerable discretion to accept not only commitments modifying the transaction itself but also altering the market conditions against which it is to be assessed.[58] These alterations are typically offered as commitments to modify post-clearance, as they require monitoring and an implementation period. Moreover, it is paramount that the remedies are merger specific in the sense that they are imposed in order to resolve particular competition problems and not for example to generally 'fix competition in a market'.[59]

The remainder of this chapter is devoted to commitments to modify a transaction post-clearance, as this type of modification is by far the most prevalent in the Commission's decisional practice. Given that the criteria for submitting and accepting remedies in phase I and phase II are slightly different, they will be explained separately. However before embarking on a description of these requirements, it would be helpful to briefly outline the various classifications of remedies used by the Commission in its past and current practice.

#### 2.1.2.4 Classifications of Remedies

The Commission is empowered to accept only remedies that are deemed capable of rendering the merged entity compatible with the internal market so that they will prevent a significant impediment of effective competition.[60] The question whether a remedy and, more specifically, which type of remedy is suitable to eliminate the competition concerns identified has to be examined on a case-by-case basis.[61] However, throughout the years the Commission has used different typologies when referring to and assessing remedies. To provide an overview, the following past and current classifications will be briefly mentioned.

First, the distinction between structural and behavioural remedies has been the most prevalent classification used throughout the Commission's practice.[62] Simplified, structural remedies are characterised by their lasting on-going effects on the structure of the relevant market through a one-off contract of sale and, once implemented, they result in a clean break or the

[57] Merger Regulation, Arts 6(2) and 8(2).

[58] Access remedies are typical examples of such alterations of market conditions, see eg *Newscorp/Telepiu* (M.2876 II 2003) paras 230–32. The General Court has endorsed the Commission's wide discretion in this respect, see eg *easyJet v Commission* (T-177/04 2006) where the Commission in the administrative proceedings in *Air France/KLM* (M.3280 I 2004) had accepted remedies (releasing airport slots) which did not alter the notified transaction but would lower the entry barriers facing potential competitors (para 175).

[59] The OECD and ICN have repeatedly stressed that competition authorities should not use their merger review for so-called 'industrial planning' purposes, see the 2004 OECD Remedies Study, p 18, and the ICN Recommended Remedies Practice, Comment A.1. Commissioner Almunia continuously reiterates that merger rules are enforced on competition principles only, see eg Speech by Almunia (2011e). For an opposite view on the Commission's policy objectives in certain cases, see Niels, Jenkins and Kavanagh (2011) who claim that the Commission used the remedies negotiations in *Fortis/ABN AMRO Assets* (M.4844 I 2007) as an opportunity to promote cross-border integration of European banking markets by requiring that the purchaser had to be a bank that was able to serve international corporate customers (p 447). It should be noted that the authors advised the merging parties during these proceedings.

[60] Recital 30 of the Merger Regulation, and Remedies Notice, para 9. The specific requirements in this context are described in section 2.3 below.

[61] Remedies Notice, para 16.

[62] Many commentators have offered their definitions and explanations of the structural/behavioural dichotomy, see eg Paper by Lianos (2013); De Souza and Brockhoff in Drauz and Jones (2012) paras 7.121–7.124, Blanke and Landolt (2011) paras 46-004–46-009,Van Bael (2011) 494–98, Cook and Kerse (2009) para 8-016, Faull and Nikpay (2007) paras 5.362–5.364; Davies and Lyons (2007) 39–43, Went (2006) 455, Paas (2006) 209; Motta (2004) 265–70; Ersbøll (2001) 360; and Drauz (1996) 223–26.

severance of any material links between the merged entity and the purchaser as well as the Commission.[63] The principal structural remedy is a divestiture, in one form or another, entailing a change in property rights[64] and they often address competition concerns raised by horizontal overlaps.[65] Behavioural remedies are characterised by an obligation on the new merged entity to behave in a particular manner and they typically result in on-going contractual relationships between the merged entity and the beneficiary and/or the Commission.[66] They are mainly put in place to solve foreclosure concerns and they are often used in particular sectors, such as air transport, telecoms, media, pharmaceuticals and hi-tech industries.

The Commission has consistently favoured structural remedies inasmuch as they prevent, durably, the competition concerns which would be raised by the merger, and do not, moreover, require medium or long-term monitoring measures.[67] Nevertheless, it does not automatically rule out the possibility that other types of remedies may be capable of preventing the significant impediment of effective competition.[68] This policy should be seen as a result of the position taken by the General Court in a landmark judgment in 1999 when it clarified that the decisive point is not whether a remedy is behavioural or structural in nature but whether it ensures competitive market structures.[69] Moreover, as practice has shown that many remedies are not necessarily clear-cut in the sense that they may be hybrid, consisting of structural as well as behavioural elements,[70] or some behavioural remedies may have specific features making them quasi-structural,[71] the Commission has been reluctant to use the structural/behavioural dichotomy in official documents in recent years. However, other organisations continue to use this dichotomy and hence the distinction remains relevant in at least international discussions.[72]

Secondly, in the Remedies Study the Commission introduced a wider classification based on the intended competitive effects of the remedies, being divided into four categories: transfer of a market position, exit from a joint venture, access granting and other remedies.[73] This categorisation surprised some commentators at the time, arguing that not only did the

[63] Davies and Lyons (2007) elaborates on the use of the 'clean break' principle as a determining factor, see pp 41–43.

[64] Motta (2004) argues that the key distinguishing feature is property rights, see pp 265–66.

[65] Examples include divestiture of assets or shareholdings, dissolution of a joint venture with a competitor, removal of structural links, including minority shareholdings and licence agreements, removal of personal links to competitors or refraining from exercising controlling rights or veto powers over strategic business decisions.

[66] Examples include not using a trademark for a certain period, granting licences or distribution rights to third parties, making part of a party's production capacity available to third parties, granting access to infrastructure or essential facilities on non-discriminatory terms.

[67] Remedies Notice, para 15.

[68] ibid.

[69] See Case T-102/96 *Gencor v Commission* (T-102/96 1999), in particular paras 314–20, explained in detail in Elliott (1999). Based on the applicable rules then, the Court referred to whether a remedy prevents the creation or strengthening of a dominant position. Similarly, see *easyJet v Commission* (T-177/04 2006) para 182; and *Tetra Laval v Commission* (T-5/02 2002) para 161, confirmed in *Commission v Tetra Pak* (C-12/03 2005) para 86 (for useful description of latter court proceedings in this respect, see Faull and Nikpay (2007) paras 5.363–5.364).

[70] See eg Drauz (1996) 224–25.

[71] See eg Paper by Lianos (2013) 50; De Souza and Brockhoff in Drauz and Jones (2012) para 7.124; and Cook and Kerse (2009) para 8-016.

[72] See eg the 2011 and 2004 OECD Remedies Studies.

[73] Remedies Study, pp 17–19 and 138–39. Some categories are sub-divided, such as the transfer of a market position (essentially divestiture remedies) which is further divided into (i) divestiture of a controlling stake in a company; (ii) divestiture of a business unit; (iii) divestiture of mix-and-match assets; and (iv) divestiture or grant of a long-term licence. Remedies intended to grant access are sub-divided into (i) access to infrastructure or technical platforms; (ii) access to technology via licences of IPRs; and (iii) termination of exclusive vertical agreements, see pp 18–19 (points 32 and 36).

approach seem somewhat unusual as it did not fit with the structure of the (old) Remedies Notice[74] but it was also not in line with the usual economic classification of remedies.[75] However, the classification seems to be linked to the methodology used by the Commission in the study of counting one remedy for each competition concern to be solved[76] and it served the specific purpose of assessing the effectiveness of remedies analysed in the study.[77] In any event, while the classification may have served a specific purpose in the Remedies Study, it is worth noting that it has not been repeated or further developed in other studies and the Commission has not used it in subsequent guidance.

Thirdly, in the Remedies Notice from 2008 the Commission introduced another classification with roots in the more traditional structural approach, distinguishing between the following three categories: divestiture of a business, removal of links with competitors, and other remedies (comprising access remedies, change of long-term exclusive contracts and other non-divestiture remedies).[78] At the same time, other distinctions are used: divestitures, other structural remedies like granting access to key infrastructure or inputs on non-discriminatory terms, and remedies relating to the future behaviour of the merged entity.[79] Reference is also occasionally made to the simplified and broad distinction between divestitures and other remedies.[80] All in all, it is fair to say that the classifications employed in the Remedies Notice signal a less formal or rigid way of labelling remedies with emphasis on the importance of examining the remedial solutions at hand on a case-by-case basis.[81] Furthermore, recent decisional practice implies that the Commission is increasingly willing to consider acceptance of less traditional solutions, where appropriate.[82]

## 2.2 Submitting Remedies

### *2.2.1 Requirements*

Although the parties are under no obligation to submit their commitment proposals before the last day of the legal deadlines for submissions in phase I and phase II, they are encouraged

[74] In the old Remedies Notice the Commission distinguished between structural commitments and 'other types of commitments', see para 9.

[75] See Papandropoulos and Tajana (2006) 444. The authors stressed that economists usually distinguish remedies on the basis of their impact on property rights: remedies can either reallocate or constrain the exercise of property rights.

[76] Remedies Study, Annex 8 'Methodology Used to Count Remedies'. Thus, the Commission explains that, if both a divestiture and a non-divestiture remedy were ordered to solve one competition concern in the same product market, these were counted as one remedy, see p 229 (point 4).

[77] ibid, p 139 (point 1).

[78] Remedies Notice, paras 22–69. Under the heading 'Different Types of Remedies' the Commission also lists a fourth category of remedies called Review Clauses, see paras 71–76. This category seems somewhat misplaced in the context of *types* of remedies, as review clauses are considered standard provisions contained in each remedies package, see also the Commission's explanation in para 71.

[79] ibid, para 17.

[80] ibid, paras 13 and 129.

[81] For a simplified approach in this book, structural remedies are generally synonymous with divestitures (of assets or stakes) and in some cases licences if accepted in lieu of divestitures, and behavioural remedies are generally synonymous with non-divestitures.

[82] Recent examples include *Glencore/Xstrata* (M.6541 I 2012), *ARM/Giesecke & Devrient/Gemalto/JV* (M.6564 I 2012) and *Intel/McAfee* (M.5984 I 2011).

to submit proposals earlier and on an informal basis, even before notification.[83] If time allows, the parties are encouraged to submit several drafts for informal advice and guidance, especially in phase II.[84] This practice seeks to avoid situations where the parties submit wholly unacceptable commitments on the last day of valid submission with the risk of running out of negotiation time.[85]

Once the parties decide to formally propose commitments in phase I or phase II, they must submit one original and ten copies of their commitments as well as the so-called Form RM.[86] The latter obliges the parties to provide detailed information on the contents of their commitment proposals, the conditions for their implementation and show their suitability to remove any significant impediment of effective competition. For commitments consisting in the divestiture of a business, the parties must describe in detail in particular how the business to be divested is currently operated as this information enables the Commission to assess the viability, competitiveness and marketability of the business by comparing its current operation to its proposed scope under the commitments.[87] While criticism has been voiced that the information required in Form RM is disproportionately burdensome on the parties,[88] the Commission considers this form necessary in order to properly assess any proposals, as it is only the parties who have full access to the required information.[89] To possibly ease the burden, the Commission may adapt the precise requirements to the information necessary in the individual case at hand and will be available to discuss the scope of the information with the parties in advance of the submission of Form RM.[90]

In addition, the parties shall identify confidential information and submit a separate non-confidential version of their commitments for the purposes of market testing them with third parties.[91] It is established practice that in the (likely) event that modified com-

[83] Remedies Notice, para 78. Practice shows that many phase I remedies cases involve extensive pre-notification discussions, both on potential competition concerns as well as possible remedies, see Competition Report 2002, para 256. While such discussions may generally benefit both the parties and the Commission, it should be noted that interested third parties are at a disadvantage due to the lack of transparency and publicity at this stage. For an example of a case where remedies were discussed extensively during pre-notification, see *Shell/BASF – Project Nicole* (M.1751 I 2000), Commission press release IP/00/313 of 29 March 2000 where this aspect is mentioned.

[84] Remedies Notice, para 90, and Best Practice Guidelines on Merger Proceedings, para 41.

[85] One of the latest examples in this respect is *UPS/TNT Express* (M.6570 II 2013) where one (of many) contributing factors leading to a prohibition was that the parties submitted their first remedies proposal on the very last day of the legal deadline for submission and this lead to scarce time for further negotiations and adjustments, see MLex, 'Comment: EC's Veto of UPS, TNT Reveals Pressure on Up-front Buyer Solution' (30 January 2013), www.mlex.com/EU/Content.aspx?ID=314061.

[86] Implementing Regulation, Arts 20(1) and 20(1a) as well as Annex IV. The paper copies of the commitments and Form RM go to the associated services within the Commission while electronic copies are immediately forwarded to the competition authorities of the Member States.

[87] See also Remedies Notice, para 7.

[88] See eg Speech by Rowe (2007). This issue was also raised by respondents during the public consultation in 2007 of the draft new Remedies Notice, see replies from eg Cromwel and Moring, p 3; IBA, point 26; Linklaters, p 4; and Slaughter and May, pp 2–3.

[89] The requested information in Form RM shall thus be seen in the context of the parties' general obligation to provide the Commission with all information necessary to facility an assessment of commitment proposals, see Remedies Notice, para 7.

[90] ibid.

[91] Implementing Regulation, Art 20(2); Remedies Notice, paras 79(d) and 91(d) as well as the Commission's Notice on the rules for access to the Commission file in cases pursuant to Arts 81 and 82 of the EC Treaty, Arts 53, 54 and 57 of the EEA Agreement and Council Regulation (EC) No 139/2004, [2005] OJ C325/7 (the Notice on Access to the File) paras 35–38. It should be noted that a 'non-confidential' version of the commitments does not imply that the document is publicly available. It is practice that third parties sign a so-called Confidentiality Declaration stating that the document is to be treated as confidential see further section 2.4.1 below. Thus, 'non-confidential' means that business secrets (deadlines and other sensitive information) have been omitted.

mitments are submitted, the parties shall re-submit one original and ten copies of their amended proposal. As a general rule, the Commission only requests the parties to submit a revised non-confidential version of the commitments, if it considers that the commitments have changed in a substantial way that necessitates a new market test. In both scenarios, the contents of the non-confidential version of the commitments must be such as to allow third parties to fully assess the workability and the effectiveness of the proposed commitments to remove the identified competition concerns.[92]

Finally, it is worth noting that while the parties are encouraged to use the standard model texts when submitting their commitment proposals, there are no legal obligations to do so.[93] However, with the introduction of Form RM in 2008 the parties are now explicitly required to identify any deviations of the commitments offered from the model texts and explain the reasons for any deviations.[94] It is therefore considered that the Commission has in effect made the standard model texts mandatory.[95] Furthermore, once the parties have formally submitted their commitment proposal, properly signed by a duly authorised officer or legal representative,[96] the commitments are binding upon the parties.

### *2.2.2 Phase I*

In phase I the notifying parties must submit commitments within not more than 20 working days from the date of the Commission's receipt of the notification.[97] Where commitments are validly offered, the deadline for the Commission's decision is extended from 25 working days to 35 working days from the date of notification.[98] The commitments may be offered together with or after the submission of the notification.[99]

[92] Remedies Notice, para 79(d) *in fine*, and see further section 2.4.1 below. The hearing officer has occasionally been asked to verify the contents of the version of the commitments sent out to third parties, see eg *Tetra Laval/Sidel* (M.2416 II 2001), Final Report of the Hearing Officer, [2004] OJ C39/2.

[93] See also Remedies Notice, para 21: '[The] model texts are neither intended to provide an exhaustive coverage of all issues that may become relevant in all cases, *nor are they legally binding* upon parties [...]. They complement the present Notice as they outline the typical arrangements for divestiture commitments in a format which *can* be used by the parties' (emphasis added).

[94] Implementing Regulation, Annex IV, section 3.

[95] It is therefore unfortunate that the model texts exist only in English.

[96] Remedies Notice, paras 79(b) and 91(b). The importance of commitment proposals being submitted in a final and properly signed version was highlighted in the prohibition decision in *Ryanair/Aer Lingus* (M.4439 II 2007) where the Commission dismissed revised commitments inter alia on the grounds that they were still in draft format and lacked a signature, see para 1237, see also the General Court's reiteration of this aspect on appeal in *Ryanair v Commission* (T-342/07 2010) para 503.

[97] Implementing Regulation, Art 19(1); and Remedies Notice, para 78.

[98] Merger Regulation, Art 10(1), second sub-para; and Remedies Notice, para 78. It should be noted that the Commission can exceptionally suspend the 25-days and 35-days periods (as well as the phase II periods) pursuant to Art 10(4) of the Merger Regulation if it has requested information by decision pursuant to Art 11 or ordered an investigation by decision pursuant to Art 13. On rare occasions, the Commission has dropped its initial competition concerns and, despite the submission of commitments, adopted an unconditional clearance decision following a prolonged phase I investigation, see eg *Ericsson/Nortel Group (MSS & Global Services)* (M.6095 I 2011), *Raytheon/Thales/JV* (M.2079 I 2001), *Cendant/Galileo* (M.2510 I 2001), *Interbrew/Beck's* (M.2569 I 2001) and *Tyco/Mallinckrodt* (M.2074 I 2000). In all cases the parties withdrew their commitments prior to the adoption of the Commission's decision. In *Shell/Enterprise Oil* (M.2745 I 2002) the submission of commitments and subsequent unconditional clearance were done within the original phase I timetable (the case is mentioned by the Commission as an example of its efforts to minimise over-regulation in the 2004 OECD Remedies Study, p 254).

[99] Under the old Merger Regulation the wording of Art 10(1), second sub-para, limited an extension of phase I proceedings to commitments offered after notification. This created a discrepancy whereby commitments offered together with the notification did not trigger an extension of the deadline. During the 2004 merger review the Commission deleted the wording 'after notification' in Art 10(1), second sub-para. For criticism of the old practice, see Josten (2000) 81–88.

Contrary to phase II proceedings (see below), the Commission has no powers to formally extend the legal deadline for submission of remedies in phase I. If the parties submit commitment proposals, or indeed modifications to such proposals, after the expiry of the deadline, the Commission must therefore in principle initiate an in-depth investigation prior to the expiry of the 25 days deadline. Whereas the Commission adhered rather rigidly to this deadline when the provision was introduced in 1998,[100] it gradually became evident – in particular in view of the increased complexity of many phase I remedies cases – that occasionally it would be desirable for all parties involved to be able to at least modify and improve the commitments after the expiry of the deadline. To this effect, the old Remedies Notice introduced a provision whereby limited modifications submitted beyond the deadline were acceptable if presented as an immediate response to the results of the Commission's consultations[101] and it was emphasised that such modifications would typically take the form of 'clarifications, refinements and/or other improvements' with the purpose of ensuring that the commitments were workable and effective.[102] The Commission explained that such modifications could only be limited in scope as phase I remedies are generally designed to provide a straightforward answer to a readily identifiable competition concern.[103]

The EU Court was subsequently required to interpret this provision in detail and in particular clarify whether the Commission was entitled and/or had a duty to accept limited modifications after the expiry of the legal deadline for the submission of phase I commitments.[104] It found that, whilst the parties to a concentration cannot oblige the Commission to take account of commitments and modifications submitted after the expiry of the legal deadline, the Commission must nevertheless be able, where it considers that it has the time necessary to examine them, to authorise a concentration in light of those commitments even if modifications are made after the expiry of the deadline.[105] The Court went a step further and undertook a detailed examination of the late modifications accepted by the Commission in the respective cases in order to verify whether they indeed qualified as 'improvements' of the initial version of the commitments and could be considered as 'limited modifications' within the meaning of the notice.[106]

Needless to say, the acceptance of limited modifications after the expiry of the legal deadline for the submission of phase I commitments puts additional pressure on the Commission to reach a conclusion as to the acceptability of such commitments within a short space of time. Indeed, under the old Remedies Notice there were a number of cases

[100] The deadline had been introduced precisely to give the Commission ample time to carry out a proper assessment of commitments and ensure due consultation of third parties and the Member States. The relevant provision was set out in the 1998 Implementing Regulation, Art 18(1).

[101] 'Consultations' would normally be understood as market testing of third parties. However, in *BaByliss v Commission* (T-114/02 2003) the General Court found that certain improvements could be regarded as an 'immediate response' although third parties had not been expressly consulted on the initial version of the commitments, as the improvements had addressed issues raised in responses to questionnaires sent to competitors, see para 148.

[102] Old Remedies Notice, para 37.

[103] ibid. In the equivalent provision in the new Remedies Notice 'straightforward' is replaced with 'clear-cut', see para 83. It is considered that the new wording is a matter of semantics.

[104] See in particular *ARD v Commission* (T-158/00 2003) paras 382–407.

[105] ibid, para 386. See also *BaByliss v Commission* (T-114/02 2003) para 140; and *Royal Philips Electronics v Commission* (T-119/02 2003) para 239.

[106] In *ARD v Commission* (T-158/00 2003) the General Court examined in detail 11 late modifications in order to verify that they were 'limited', as opposed to 'substantial', modifications, see paras 394–405. The Court's analysis implies that 'substantial modifications' would be considered new commitments and should therefore not be accepted beyond the legal deadline for submission of phase I commitments.

where modifications were submitted so close to the expiry of the deadline for adoption of a decision that, prima facie, it seemed questionable whether the Commission would have had sufficient time to adequately assess such modifications.[107] To this effect, while the corresponding provision in the new Remedies Notice largely reiterates the criteria in the old notice for submitting limited modifications in phase I after the expiry of the legal deadline, it is now explicitly provided that such modifications may only be accepted in circumstances 'where it is ensured that the Commission can carry out a proper assessment of those commitments'.[108] However, despite the Commission's efforts to leave adequate time for proper assessment of any subsequent modifications of proposed commitments, there continues to be cases where amendments (primarily in view of a negative market test) are submitted so late that prima facie it would have seemed more appropriate for the Commission to initiate an in-depth investigation.[109]

**Commentary:** the Commission's continuing acceptance of remedies amendments extremely close to – and even on – the deadline for adoption of a phase I conditional clearance decision in transactions that are also complicated and comprehensive is a matter of concern as there is a genuine risk that such a decisional practice is to the detriment of a thorough and timely assessment (let alone possible consultations) and may encourage 'quick fixes' for the merging parties as well as the Commission.

It needs to be born in mind that the actual time that the DG Competition has at its disposal to assess the last version of the parties' commitment proposal and incorporate any changes into the conditional clearance decision is further shortened by numerous internal administrative requirements in terms of obtaining the necessary approvals from the Commission's legal service and associated services, preparing press release, possibly briefing spokesman and the responsible Commissioner and finally submitting the case file to the Secretariat-General for delegation procedures and signatures before the final decision can be formally adopted within the legal deadline.[110] Thus, if the parties submit their last modifications a few days before the expiry of the legal deadline for adoption of a conditional clearance decision, the actual time allocated to the substantive assessment of the final version of the commitment proposals (and possible consultations) is less than those stated days.

While it of course cannot be excluded that some of the last amendments may relate to very minor modifications that do not require renewed assessments or additional consultations, the practice nevertheless raises the question whether the Commission puts itself under too much pressure to close cases in phase I instead of allowing more time to finalise the details by opening an in-depth investigation which does not necessarily have to go the full length (see below).

[107] In *Schering-Plough/Organon Biosciences* (M.4691 I 2007), a highly complicated case with serious doubts in 17 markets, and in *Deutsche Bahn/EWS* (M.4746 I 2007) the modified versions of the commitments were submitted one day prior to the adoption of the decisions. In *Apollo/Bakelite* (M.3593 I 2005) modified commitments were submitted three days prior to the adoption of the decision.

[108] See Remedies Notice, para 83, which also refers to recital 17 of the Implementing Regulation and *Royal Philips Electronics v Commission* (T-119/02 2003) para 237.

[109] For cases after the publication of the new Remedies Notice, see eg *IAG/BMI* (M.6447 I 2012) where improved commitments were submitted two days before the adoption of the decision; *Novartis/Alcon* (M.5778 I 2010) and *SNCF/LCR/Eurostar* (M.5655 I 2010) where amended versions (in view of a negative market test) were submitted on the very day of the adoption of the decisions; *Abbott/Solvay Pharmaceuticals* (M.5661 I 2010) and *DFDS/Norfolk* (M.5756 I 2010) where modified commitments were submitted one day prior to the adoption of the conditional clearance decisions; and *Agilent/Varian* (M.5611 I 2010) and *Sony/Mubadala Development/EMI Music Publishing* (M.6459 I 2012) where (substantial) modified commitments were submitted two days prior to the adoption of the conditional clearance decisions.

[110] See further section 2.5.3 below.

### 2.2.3 *Phase II*

#### 2.2.3.1 Deadlines

In cases where the identified serious doubts cannot be addressed in phase I, the Commission opens phase II proceedings.[111] Phase II decisions shall be taken as soon as it appears that the serious doubts referred to in Article 6(1)(c) of the Merger Regulation has been removed by modifications made by the parties.[112] This provision gives the parties an opportunity to propose commitments early and pre-empt an SO being issued if the Commission finds that the commitments mitigate its serious doubts.[113]

All deadlines for submission of commitments and adoption of decisions in phase II are calculated from the day the Commission initiates phase II proceedings in accordance with Article 6(1)(c) of the Merger Regulation. Commitments shall be submitted to the Commission within not more than 65 working days from the day proceedings were initiated.[114] This gives the Commission around 40 working days to consider and decide upon the commitments. If the parties submit commitments less than 55 working days after initiation of proceedings, the general deadline for adoption of all phase II decisions applies whereby a decision shall be taken within not more than 90 working days from the initiation of phase II proceedings.[115] The deadline will be extended to 105 working days if the parties submit commitments on or after 55 working days following the initiation of proceedings. In the event that the parties submit commitments within less than 55 working days, but submit a modified version on day 55 or thereafter, the period to take a final decision will also be extended to 105 working days.[116]

An added flexibility to the timetable was introduced in 2004 whereby the above working-day periods may be extended by another period not exceeding 20 working days, either

[111] On rare occasions, the Commission has referred (part of) a transaction to the national competition authority where the identified competition concerns could not be addressed through adequate remedies, see latest *CVC/Univar Europe/Eurochem* (M.5814 I 2010) where the review of the French aspects of the deal was referred to the French competition authority for further examination. As it happened, the French authority initiated an in-depth probe and, allegedly, in response to third parties demanding far-reaching remedies, the parties withdrew their filing to the French authority in October 2010, raising uncertainty as to the survival of the overall deal (the Commission had unconditionally cleared the transaction in other national markets), see reports by MLex, 'Univar Withdraws Eurochem Notification in France' (6 October 2010), www.mlex.com/EU/Content.aspx?ID=115841.

[112] Merger Regulation, Art 10(2).

[113] Numerous phase II conditional clearance decisions without an SO have been adopted in the past: see eg *Hutchinson 3G Austria/Orange Austria* (M.6497 II 2012); *UTC/Goodrich* (M.6410 II 2012); *Syngenta/Monsanto's Sunflower Seed Business* (M.5675 II 2010), *Thomson Corporation/Reuters Group* (M.4726 II 2008), *StatoilHydro/ConocoPhillips* (M.4919 II 2008), *ABF/GBI Business* (M.4980 II 2008), *Kronospan/Constatia* (M.4525 II 2007), *Metso/Aker Kvaerner* (M.4187 II 2006), *Sonoco/Alstrom* (M.3431 II 2004), *Areva/Urenco/ETC JV* (M.3099 II 2004), *DMS/Roche Vitamins* (M.2972 II 2003), *ENBW/ENI/GVS* (M.2698 II 2002), *BP Amoco/Atlantic Richfield* (M.1532 II 1999) and *BT/AT&T* (JV.15 II 1999). It should be noted that in some of these cases, the fact that the commitments were submitted prior to the issuance of SO did not result in a final decisions being adopted significantly prior to the expiry of the legal deadline (see in particular *BP Amoco/Atlantic Richfield, Metso/Aker Kvaerner* and all mentioned 2008 and 2010 decisions).

[114] Implementing Regulation, Art 19(2); and Remedies Notice, para 88. Where the phase II period has been extended, in accordance with Art 10(3), second sub-para, of the Merger Regulation, the period in which commitments must be submitted is automatically extended by the same number of days, see Implementing Regulation, Art 19(2), second sub-para.

[115] Merger Regulation, Art 10(3), first sub-para. The 55-days deadline was inserted in 2004 in order to encourage the submission of remedies at an early stage. In the Remedies Notice the Commission also encourages the parties to discuss suitable commitments well in advance of the end of the 65-days period and submit draft proposals in advance of the final version, see para 90.

[116] Remedies Notice, para 89 *in fine*.

at the request of the parties or by the Commission with the agreement of the parties.[117] Judging from decisional practice this extension is often triggered by the wish of the parties for further time to consider commitment proposals,[118] rather than the Commission requesting more time to carry out its analysis and market testing.[119] Furthermore, whereas previously the extension of the time period was often limited to a few days,[120] the parties have in more recent cases requested an extension to the full 20 days.[121]

### 2.2.3.2 'Exceptional Circumstances'

Contrary to phase I proceedings, the Commission has express legal powers to accept, in exceptional circumstances, commitments submitted for the first time (that is to say new commitments as opposed to modifications of existing commitments) after the expiry of the 65-days deadline.[122] Certain cumulative conditions must be fulfilled in order to benefit from this provision: (i) the request for an extension must be received within the 65-days period; (ii) the parties shall set forth the exceptional circumstances; and (iii) the Commission must have sufficient time to make a proper assessment of the proposal and allow for adequate consultation of the Member States and third parties.[123]

The Commission has never defined 'exceptional circumstances'. However, decisional practice gives a few indications. In *Telia/Telenor* the Commission accepted the existence of exceptional circumstances as the Swedish and Norwegian Parliaments had to be consulted prior to the submission of the proposed commitments and the business activities of the parties, and indeed those affected by the 'late' commitments, had an impact on wider policy issues of national concern requiring political consultation.[124] The Commission clearly wished to narrow down the criteria for accepting exceptional circumstances as much as possible in order to limit precedence for future cases.[125] Conversely, in *Airtours/First Choice*

[117] Merger Regulation, Art 10(3), second sub-para. The request from the parties shall be submitted not later than 15 working days after the initiation of proceedings. The Commission's decision to extend the deadline can be submitted any time after the initiation of proceedings.

[118] See eg *Syngenta/Monsanto's Sunflower Seed Business* (M.5675 II 2010) paras 12 and 14; *Friesland/Campina* (M.5046 II 2008), Final Report of the Hearing Officer, [2009] OJ C75/19; and *Omya/Huber PCC* (M.3796 II 2006) para 9.

[119] Thus, practice seems not to fully reflect the explanation by the Commission in its Remedies Notice that the purpose of the extension in Art 10(3), second sub-para, is to allow for sufficient time for the analysis and market testing of the proposed commitments, see para 90, fn 1.

[120] In *Friesland/Campina* (M.5046 II 2008) the period was extended by one working day; in *Gaz de France/Suez* (M.4180 II 2006) by five working days; in *Omya/Huber PCC* (M.3796 II 2006) by two working days; and in *E.ON/MOL* (M.3696 II 2005) by 11 working days.

[121] See eg *Universal Music Group/EMI Music* (M.6458 II 2012), *Outokumpu/Inoxum* (M.6471 II 2012), *Südzucker/ED&F MAN* (M.6286 II 2012), *Syngenta/Monsanto's Sunflower Seed Business* (M.5675 II 2010), and *Unilever/Sara Lee Body Care* (M.5658 II 2010).

[122] Implementing Regulation, Art 19(2), third sub-para; and Remedies Notice, para 88. The provision on 'exceptional circumstances' was introduced in the 1994 Implementing Regulation but its scope was not really tested or challenged before 1999 in two cases, *Telia/Telenor* (M.1439 II 1999) (exceptional circumstances accepted) and *Airtours/First Choice* (M.1524 II 1999) (exceptional circumstances rejected), see further Competition Report 1999, box 8, p 71.

[123] Remedies Notice, para 88.

[124] See *Telia/Telenor* (M.1439 II 1999), in particular paras 378–80. The Commission emphasised that the exceptional circumstances were not related to the state ownership of the companies.

[125] A case rarely mentioned in this context is *TotalFina/Elf* (M.1628 II 2000) where the Commission accepted a new commitment (divestiture of Elf Antargaz) submitted one week prior to the adoption of the decision. The commitment was submitted in response to a negative market test of an earlier proposal that was considered prima facie by the services of the Commission as sufficient. Due to its late submission, the new commitment could not be market tested but the Member States were consulted. The Commission concluded that the new proposal would

and *Volvo/Scania* the Commission dismissed the existence of 'exceptional circumstances', arguing that there was nothing in the revised commitments (in both cases submitted one week prior to the adoption of the final decisions) that the parties could not have included in their commitment proposals submitted within the legal time limit.[126]

All in all, decisional practice confirms a narrow interpretation of 'exceptional circumstances' leaving little room for submission of new commitments after the expiry of the legal deadline. However, in view of the introduction of more flexible timetables in 2004 as well as increased possibilities of submitting modified commitments (see below), the importance of – and need for – this provision has declined. However, it would nevertheless be desirable if the Commission were to clarify the acceptable nature and scope of 'exceptional circumstances' in order to make this provision more transparent and predictable, should it remain part of the Commission's future remedies policy.

#### 2.2.3.3 Post-Deadline Modifications

Save for 'exceptional circumstances', the provisions in the Merger Regulation impose no obligations on the Commission to accept commitments submitted after the expiry of the legal deadline in phase II.[127] However, it is established practice that, provided the parties have submitted a firm commitment proposal within the legal deadline, the Commission may accept post-deadline clarifications or modifications in specific circumstances. In this respect two cumulative conditions must be met: (i) the Commission must be able to clearly determine – on the basis of its assessment of information already received in the course of the investigation, including the results of prior market testing, and without the need for any other market test – that such commitments, once implemented, fully and unambiguously resolve the competition problems identified, and (ii) there shall be sufficient time to allow for an adequate assessment by the Commission and proper consultation with the Member States.[128]

Compared to previous practice the Commission has tightened its requirements to modifications submitted out of time in its new Remedies Notice. First, the (modified) commitments must 'fully and unambiguously' resolve the competition problems identified.[129] Thus no doubts can remain as to (even minor) unsolved issues. This practice is in line with

remove all competition concerns identified in that market and it therefore accepted the proposal although submitted after expiry of the deadline, see paras 319 and 345. It is unclear from the public version of the decision which circumstances qualified as exceptional.

[126] See *Airtours/First Choice* (M.1524 II 1999) para 193; and *Volvo/Scania* (M.1672 II 2000) para 359. Along the same lines, see also *EDP/ENI/GDP* (M.3440 II 2004) para 857.

[127] This follows from Art 8 of the Merger Regulation read in conjunction with Art 19 of the Implementing Regulation. See also *EDP v Commission* (T-87/05 2005) para 161.

[128] Remedies Notice, para 94. See also the old Remedies Notice, para 43, which was subject to scrutiny by the General Court in *EDP v Commission* (T-87/05 2005), in particular paras 159–70.

[129] The Commission used this term in *EDP/ENI/GDP* (M.3440 II 2004) where it set out to examine in view of para 43 of the old Remedies Notice 'whether, without the need of further market test, it can be concluded that the late remedies [. . .] address fully and unambiguously – that is, in a straightforward manner – the competition concerns identified during the investigation', see para 859. In the subsequent appeal in *EDP v Commission* (T-87/05 2005) the General Court noted the discrepancy between the wording of para 43 of the old Remedies Notice and its translation in the contested decision but, given that the applicant had not drawn any consequences from this discrepancy in its appeal, the Court refrained from considering the matter further, see para 169. It is noted that the Commission has not incorporated the wording 'in a straightforward manner' in the new notice, which seems logical as phase II remedies are often not straightforward although they may fully address the competition concerns.

the requirement that there should be no need for the Commission to undertake further market tests or gather new information in order to assess the modifications.

Secondly, the Commission is increasingly aware of allowing sufficient time for proper consultation of the Member States.[130] This requirement is one that has caused procedural difficulties and contributed to late modifications being dismissed in the past. Practice in this respect has changed over the years. In the early days of the Merger Regulation modifications were sometimes submitted extremely late in the proceedings, even after the official meeting of the Advisory Committee and so close to the legal deadline for the adoption of the final decision, that there would be little (or no) time for additional consultations of the Member States.[131] Needless to say, the Advisory Committee was discontent with this practice and did in fact question the legality of the provision in the old Remedies Notice allowing for acceptance of post-deadline modifications.[132] Although the practice of allowing late modifications has continued after the adoption of the new Remedies Notice, the Commission is more attentive to ensure that the formal requirements when consulting the Advisory Committee are adhered to as much as possible, in particular the deadline for sending a draft decision, including the assessment of the modified commitments, to the Member States in advance of their meeting.[133] In any event, in line with the sharp decline of phase II remedies cases in recent years the issue of timely consultation of the Advisory Committee has been less occurring and controversial in recent years.

Finally, in order to emphasise the limited use of the provision allowing for post-deadline modifications the Commission now stresses in its Remedies Notice that it will normally reject modified commitments, which do not fulfil the above criteria.[134] It may thus be expected that the Commission will be more rigorous when assessing a possible acceptance of post-deadline modifications – both in terms of procedure and substance – in future cases.

[130] While this requirement was already introduced in para 43 of the old Remedies Notice, the Commission further stresses the importance of timely consultation of the Member States in its new notice by referring to established jurisprudence by the EU Court and stressing that the 10-days-notice period for sending draft decisions, including an assessment of the modified commitments, to the Member States in advance of their meeting may be shortened in only exceptional circumstances, see Remedies Notice, para 94, fn 5 and fn 6. It should be noted that the fact that the Commission refers to its decision in *TotalFina/Elf* (M.1628 II 2000, para 345) is surprising given that the Commission accepted 'exceptional circumstances' in this case and thus allowed a new (and not modified) commitment proposal to be taken into consideration after the expiry of the legal deadline in the then Art 18(2) of the 1998 Implementing Regulation, see para 319 of the decision.

[131] By way of illustration, in *Air Liquide/BOC* (M.1630 II 2000) the Advisory Committee met on 5 January (see [2004] OJ C79/8) and amendments to the originally submitted commitments were made on 7 January 2000 (see Commission decision, para 307); and in *Danish Crown/Vestjyske Slagterier* (M.1313 II 1999) the Advisory Committee met on 25 February 1999 (see [2000] OJ C21/2) and clarifications were made on 4 March 1999 (see Commission decision, para 199). In these cases there would be no time to convene the Advisory Committee for a second time and it would therefore the likely that the members would merely be informed of the clarifications.

[132] In *Schneider/Legrand*, (M.2283 II 2001) a minority in the Advisory Committee found that para 43 in the old Remedies Notice did not comply with the then Art 18(2) of the 1998 Implementing Regulation (Art 19(2) of the current Implementing Regulation setting out the deadline for the submission of remedies). This minority also submitted that (i) late remedies can consist of only clarifications and not substantial changes, and (ii) substantial modifications are only possible if they qualify as 'exceptional circumstances' within the meaning of (the current) Art 19(2) of the Implementing Regulation, see para 9 of the Opinion of the Advisory Committee, [2004] OJ C86/13.

[133] In *EDP v Commission* (T-87/05 2005) the General Court confirmed that the Commission had been right in rejecting certain commitments submitted in a complete and unconditional form seven days after the Advisory Committee and three working days before the final decision was adopted 'on the sole ground of their extreme lateness' (para 166). The General Court elaborated on this aspect by stating that 'even on the assumption that the commitments [. . .] consisted only of minor modifications by reference to the previous commitments, they were none the less not provided in time to be submitted to the Advisory Committee' (para 167).

[134] See Remedies Notice, para 94. This provision did not exist in the old Remedies Notice.

**Commentary:** while the Commission should be commended on its clarified and enhanced guidance and practice in relation to the conditions for the timely submission and acceptance of phase II remedies (including post-deadline modifications), the impact of such improvements has regrettable been limited in recent years as few cases have been settled in phase II. However, the latest statistics for 2012, where the Commission rather surprisingly adopted no less than six conditional clearance decisions in phase II, may indicate the beginning of a new practice whereby phase II remedies are more of a prominent feature. Although the merging parties will of course always favour the shorter phase I proceedings if they are given the choice, recent decisional practice seems to confirm that, when their transaction is subject to an in-depth investigation, they do take advantage of the flexibility introduced by the Commission in 2004 whereby the timetable can be further extended by additional days and hence these provisions have proven appropriate and justified.

## 2.3 Assessing Remedies

### *2.3.1 Proportionality and Elimination of Competition Concerns*

Remedies should be proportionate to the competition problem and entirely eliminate it.[135] The two conditions are complementary when assessing the adequacy of remedies.[136] Simplified, the two conditions imply that the Commission may not accept remedies which are less than what is required to eliminate entirely the competition problem (second condition), or require more than what is strictly necessary to achieve this goal (first condition). However, there are many considerable nuances to this simplification.

First, the requirement that the competition problem shall be entirely eliminated means that post-decision the remedy should not merely reduce the competition problem in the given market but restore the conditions of effective competition pertaining pre-decision. This can be done in several ways. In mergers where the competition concerns relate to horizontal overlaps, the parties may divest of the overlapping activities and thus re-establish the pre-existing market structure (status quo ante) in the problematic market. Some commentators refer to this scenario as 'a prohibition within the market'.[137] In mergers where the competition concerns relate to vertical or conglomerate problems, which may foreclose access of other market participants to the given market, the parties may grant access to the foreclosed facilities. The Commission may accept such access remedies if they conclude that competition will be restored in that particular market.

In assessing whether a proposed commitment is likely to entirely eliminate the competition concerns, the Commission considers all relevant factors relating to the commitment itself, including inter alia the type, scale and scope of the proposed commitment, judged by reference to the structure and particular characteristics of the market in which the competition concerns arise, including the position of the parties and other players on the market.[138] In doing so the Commission will generally predict how the market structure

[135] Recital 30 of the Merger Regulation and Remedies Notice, para 1, fn 3. See also Remedies Notice, para 9, which lists the basic requirements.

[136] See *Cementbouw Handel & Industrie v Commission* (T-282/02 2006) para 307; and *Cementbouw Handel & Industrie v Commission* (C-202/06 2007) para 54.

[137] See Davies and Lyons (2007) 243.

[138] Remedies Notice, para 12.

would develop in the absence of any remedies and compare this scenario to the effects of a conditional clearance decision (counterfactual scenarios).[139]

The remedy must also be comprehensive and effective from all points of view.[140] This requirement means that the remedies must be self-contained in the sense that they do not need to be supplemented by for example the Commission taking action under Articles 101 and 102 of the Treaty on the Functioning of the European Union (the TFEU). As another example, if the fulfilment of a remedy requires a resolution mechanism in the event of disputes the parties must provide for this in the form of for example an arbitration clause in their proposed commitments. It is thus entirely the parties' responsibility to ensure that their commitment proposal contains all necessary provisions addressing all possible contingencies and the Commission cannot be held responsible for any technical or commercial gaps.[141]

Remedies must also be capable of being implemented effectively within a short period of time, as the conditions of competition on the market will not be maintained until the remedies have been fulfilled.[142] As will be explained later the Commission has over the years continuously shortened the allowed implementation duration, which currently amounts to a first divestiture period of approximately six months, running from the date of the adoption of the conditional clearance decision.[143] Put very simply, it is evident from past practice that the shorter the divestiture period is, the more likely it is that the overall remedy will be successful.[144]

Secondly, the proportionality requirement implies that, when faced with several alternatives, the Commission must always favour the least restrictive or cumbersome remedy, provided it entirely resolves the identified competition concerns.[145] This applies to the remedy itself as well as the modalities for its implementation. The requirement means that in some cases where the competition concerns are narrow or limited in scope compared to the overall transaction and markets involved, the Commission may settle for less far-reaching remedies, which could be for example a licence agreement instead of a divestiture.[146] The

[139] See section 2.1.2.1 above.

[140] Remedies Notice, para 9. In *EDP v Commission* (T-87/05 2005) the General Court used the term 'full and effective from all aspects' (para 105), whereas *in General Electric v Commission* (T-210/01 2005) it introduced the term 'comprehensive and effective from all points of view' (para 52).

[141] In *EDP v Commission* (T-87/05 2005) the applicant submitted that the Commission had failed to take into account the possibility that the competent Portuguese authorities might carry out the necessary monitoring of certain proposed commitments although the parties had not provided for such a monitoring possibility in their commitments. The General Court found that the Commission would not have been in a position to entrust the monitoring to a national authority, as this would have meant that it would have modified the proposed commitment, which the Commission is not empowered to do. The Court stressed that it was for the parties to foresee that the intrinsic weaknesses of their proposed behavioural commitments may have justified ex-post monitoring, see para 105. See also *General Electric v Commission* (T-210/01 2005) para 52.

[142] Remedies Notice, para 9 *in fine.*

[143] See section 4.1 below.

[144] Remedies Study, p 109 (points 1–3).

[145] Although the remedies provisions and guidance rarely explicitly refer to the principle of proportionality, it is an important underlying notion in many aspects of the Commission's remedies policy. In *Cementbouw Handel & Industrie* (C-202/06 P 2007) the Court of Justice emphasised that 'decisions taken by the Commission in [merger control proceedings] must satisfy the requirements of the principle of proportionality, which is one of the general principles of Community law' (para 52). See also *easyJet v Commission* (T-177/04 2006) para 133.

[146] In *Alcatel/Finmeccanica/Alcatel Alenia Space & Telespazio* (M.3680 I 2005) the Commission acknowledged that a divestiture of a larger manufacturing unit (where the products raising competition concerns accounted for a negligible part of the turnover) would be 'patently disproportionate to the narrow competition issues identified' and instead a licensing remedy was accepted, see paras 121 and 124. Along the same lines, in *Apollo/Bakelite* (M.3593 I 2005) the Commission accepted a licence agreement instead of a divestiture inter alia because

Commission may also allow for divestiture of carve-outs instead of stand-alone businesses if it appears reasonable that some (integrated) assets should not – or cannot – be divested, provided that the viability of the sold assets is ensured.[147]

Specifically on remedies packages the question continuously arises whether a package including a divestiture of activities, which are related to markets where the Commission has not raised competition problems,[148] is contrary to the principle of proportionality. The Commission maintains that it is entitled to accept such packages provided that it can show that the added assets are the only possible way to create an effective competitor with a viable business in the respective markets.[149] The EU Court has confirmed this approach.[150] Another and more problematic question emerging in recent years is whether, in Article 22 referral cases, it would be disproportionate of the Commission to require the divestiture of assets outside the scope of the referring Member State in cases where the markets are considered national. While the issue currently remains unresolved,[151] it is expected that such findings depend on whether the additional assets can be justified by the need to ensure viability of the assets in question.

Along the same lines, the EU Court has confirmed that the Commission is entitled to accept commitments which go beyond what is strictly necessary to restore the pre-merger competitive position, based on the assumption that the parties are not required to confine themselves to proposing commitments aimed strictly at restoring the competitive situation existing before the concentration.[152] Thus, if the parties propose adequate (including broader) remedies, the Commission does not have the discretion to dismiss them and instead adopt (i) a prohibition decision; or (ii) a conditional clearance decision attaching conditions aimed at (strictly) restoring the pre-merger situation which it

the problematic products accounted for less than 10% of the parties joint phenolic resins turnover and less than 5% of the parties' joint turnover, see para 162. Based on similar considerations, in *Glaxo Wellcome/Smithkline Beecham* (M.1846 I 2000) the Commission accepted that a certain overlap remained post-divestiture due to the negligible sales in that market, see para 221.

[147] Remedies Notice, paras 35–36. Para 35 is one of the very few provisions in the Remedies Notice that explicitly refers to the principle of proportionality. One of the most recent examples of a carve-out being accepted instead of a full divestiture is *Kinnevik/Billerud/Korsnäs* (M.6682 I 2012) where the Commission considered that the divestiture of a whole paper mill would be disproportionate and therefore accepted a carve-out and divestiture of a single paper machine, which would remain in a mill owned by the merged entity, see Speech by Italianer (2012) 4 (public decision not yet available at the time of writing). For another example, see *Thomson Corporation/Reuters Group* (M.4726 II 2008) where the Commission settled for the transfer of copies of databases as a full divestiture was not possible (para 484).

[148] Remedies Notice, para 17.

[149] The practice of adding assets in order to ensure viability commenced with the Commission's decision in *Sanitec/Sphinx* (M.1578 II 1999), see section 3.4.1 below.

[150] The issue arose in *easyJet v Commission* (T-177/04 2006) where the applicant (a competitor claiming insufficient remedies) argued that the Commission should have added certain assets in non-overlapping markets to the respective remedies package. Referring to para 17 of the old Remedies Notice (para 23 of the new notice) and the fact that this provision should be read in light of the principle of proportionality, the General Court considered that 'commitments must be decided on in the light of the competition problems raised on the affected markets, because if competition can be maintained on those markets it is not necessary for the Commission to extend the scope of the commitments to markets not affected, in accordance with the principle of proportionality' (para 134). A similar issue was raised by the appellant in *Omya v Commission* (T-275/06) where it was argued that the Commission breached the principle of proportionality by effectively imposing inappropriate (far-reaching) remedies going beyond the identified competition problems. The appeal was later withdrawn, see [2008] OJ C327/41.

[151] The issue is thought to have been one of the core disagreements between the Commission and the parties in *SCJ/Sara Lee* (M.5969 II withdrawn in 2011), reported by MLex Comment, 'Territorial Scope of Remedies is Central to EC's SCJ/Sara Lee Insecticides Probe' (24 March 2011), www.mlex.com/EU/Content.aspx?ID=137129.

[152] See *Cementbouw Handel & Industrie v Commission* (T-282/02 2006) para 308.

would have imposed unilaterally and independently of the commitments given by the parties.[153]

Finally, it should be mentioned that the proportionality requirement also implies that the Commission may not accept remedies, which are entirely unnecessary,[154] or remedies that do not address the competition problem.[155] Also, it is established practice that the Commission will review whether proposed commitments are indeed proportionate to the competition problem when assessing whether to attach them as conditions or obligations to its final decision.[156] Lastly, the principle of proportionality should also be taken into consideration when evaluating the cost of implementing the remedy for the parties, the consumer and the Commission.[157]

### *2.3.2 Certainty*

Limiting uncertainty is the Commission's primary concern when negotiating divestiture remedies with the parties.[158] The Commission therefore emphasises that structural solutions, particularly divestitures, are acceptable only if it can be concluded, with the requisite degree of certainty, that it will be possible to implement them and that it will be likely that the new commercial structures resulting from the remedies will be sufficiently workable and lasting to ensure that the significant impediment to effective competition will not materialise.[159]

Through its practice the Commission has experienced that issues relating to the actual transfer of the business to be divested may impede the certainty of implementation.[160] To this effect, the Commission lists by way of example the following risks: (i) conditions attached by the parties to the divestiture; (ii) third party rights in relation to the business; (iii) difficulties in finding a suitable purchaser; and (iv) possible degradation of the assets until the divestiture has taken place.[161] If doubts remain as to any of these risks, the Commission will dismiss the commitment proposals.[162]

Also in relation to quasi-structural or access remedies the Commission has been reminded by the EU Court that it may use its wide discretion as to the form which the remedies may take in order to enhance certainty.[163] For example, it may in certain cases be necessary for the Commission to require the parties to identify a new entrant, in particular where no competitor shows any interest in entering an affected market.[164] This assessment

[153] ibid, paras 309 and 311. It should be noted that, on appeal in *Cementbouw Handel & Industrie v Commission* (C-202/06 P 2007), the Court of Justice did not directly address these issues.

[154] See section 2.5.2 below.

[155] Thus, the Commission may not accept a remedy whereby one of the overlapping businesses are simply closed down as this would merely take competition out of the relevant market without maintaining it.

[156] Remedies Notice, para 85. This provision was inserted after the public consultation in 2007 of the draft new Remedies Notice.

[157] See De Souza and Brockhoff in Drauz and Jones (2012) paras 7.137–7.140.

[158] See Rakovsky in IBA (2000) 139–40 and 144.

[159] See Remedies Notice, para 10, which is essentially a citation of the General Court's findings in *General Electric v Commission* (T-210/10 2005) paras 555 and 612.

[160] Remedies Study, p 80 (point 3).

[161] Remedies Notice, para 11.

[162] In the prohibition decision in *General Electric/Honeywell* (M.2220 II 2001) the Commission submitted that, while prima facie the proposed commitment (in relation to large regional jet engines) would appear to be sufficient to remove the identified competition concern, a number of significant uncertainties relating to the timetable of the development as well as to the sales prospects of the aircraft rendered the proposed commitment unacceptable, see paras 519–20. On appeal, this line of assessment was confirmed, see *General Electric v Commission* (T-210/01 2005) paras 558–60.

[163] See *easyJet v Commission* (T-177/04 2006) para 197.

[164] ibid.

relating to whether the remedy will, with the requisite degree of certainty, materialise should be undertaken during the administrative proceedings (typically during the market test of the proposed commitments).[165]

Lastly, it is interesting to note that occasionally the Commission has been able to base its 'certainty reflections' on experience in previous, similar cases. For example, an important argument for dismissing remedies in *MCI WorldCom/Sprint* was that the Commission had previously experienced practical implementation difficulties with similar remedies in *WorldCom/MCI* and therefore the Commission concluded that the degree of uncertainty was such that these commitments were unacceptable.[166]

### *2.3.3 Complexity and Monitoring*

Former Commissioner Monti was often quoted for saying that 'a remedy cannot be more complex than the competition problems it tries to address',[167] and during his tenure a number of transactions were prohibited on the grounds that the proposed commitments were so complex that it was impossible for the Commission to determine with the required degree of certainty that effective competition would be restored.[168] At that time the Commission also voiced concerns that complicated remedies would need careful monitoring on the Commission's part in months if not years post-decision and thus would demand considerable time and resources.[169] This policy made some commentators question whether the Commission was really entitled to reject a proposed commitment on the (sole) ground that it is unacceptably extensive and complex.[170]

In subsequent practice the Commission broadened the scope by explicitly linking the complexity of a rejected remedy to difficulties in effectively monitoring the implementation and thereby putting the effectiveness of the remedy at risk.[171] To this effect, the Commission now submits that it may reject extensive and complex commitment proposals in particular on the grounds that (i) the implementation of the remedies cannot be effectively monitored and (ii) the lack of effective monitoring diminishes, or even eliminates, the effect of the commitments proposed.[172] While the complexity reasoning plays a prominent role in rejecting the parties' commitment proposals in prohibition decisions in newer practice, it has also at times been used in phase I cases as a reason for initiating phase II proceedings.[173]

[165] *easyJet v Commission*, n 163 above, paras 199–206. The General Court confirmed that the Commission had undertaken an adequate assessment prior to the adoption of its decision as to whether new competitors were likely to enter the market post-decision.

[166] See *MCI WorldCom/Sprint* (M.1741 II 2000) para 339, and Competition Report 2000, Box 6, pp 76–78. It is generally recognised that the remedies in *WorldCom/MCI* (M.1069 II 1998) were highly unsuccessful as the acquirer of the assets, Cable & Wireless, was unable to maintain market position, see Rakovsky in IBA (2000) 138–39.

[167] Competition Report 2000, para 277.

[168] See the old Remedies Notice, para 32, fn, 38, referring to *Volvo/Scania* (M.1672 II 2000) and MCI *WorldCom/Sprint* (1741 II 2000). In both cases commitments were submitted on the last day before the expiry of the legal deadline for the submission of commitments. In fact, in *Volvo/Scania* the revised remedies package, which was deemed complex, was submitted two weeks after the expiry of the deadline. Hence, it is submitted that in both cases the lack of time for the Commission to thoroughly assess the commitments played an important role in the Commission's conclusions relating to the complexity and inadequacy of the commitments.

[169] Competition Report 1999, para 180.

[170] See eg Ysewyn (2001) 254.

[171] See eg *Deutsche Börse/NYSE Euronext* (M.6166 II 2012) paras 1467–73; and *EDP/ENI/GDP* (M.3440 II 2004) para 663, confirmed in *EDP v Commission* (T-87/05 2005) para 102.

[172] Remedies Notice, para 14.

[173] See eg *Newscorp/Telepiu* (M.2878 II 2003) where the parties submitted a complex set of commitments in phase I and the Commission decided to initiate phase II proceedings because 'the sheer complexity of the remedies

Monitoring difficulties are primarily a concern in non-divestitures and in recent years the Commission has tightened its monitoring requirements as it has recognised that without effective monitoring the remedies would be mere declarations of intention by the parties and thus lack enforcement.[174] For example, experience shows that the use of price caps involves a heavy degree of market intervention, which is considered to be outside the mission of a competition authority, and firewalls have proven virtually impossible to monitor.[175] In cases where non-divestitures are accepted, monitoring uncertainties are sometimes resolved through not only standard trustee and dispute settlement mechanisms but also the involvement of the respective national regulatory or competition authority as a potential arbitral or appeal body, if necessary.[176]

**Commentary:** a common characteristic for all the above requirements is that the Commission enjoys a wide discretion in its application and evaluation of these remedies principles and measures. The scope of this discretion has proven advantageous to the Commission in numerous subsequent judicial proceedings, as the respective appellants, pleading inadequate remedies, have had no success in lifting the burden of proof and showing that the Commission had committed an error of assessment to the extent that it would justify an annulment of the respective conditional clearance decision.[177]

## 2.4 Consulting on Remedies

### *2.4.1 Market Test*

When considered appropriate, the Commission consults third parties and recognised employee representatives whose positions are directly affected by the commitment proposals.[178] This kind of consultation is termed 'market testing' whereby typically suppliers, customers and competitors, who have been involved in earlier stages of the proceedings, are approached by the Commission.[179] Other interested third parties may also be consulted if the Commission considers them bona fide and possessing relevant information.

The market test serves two purposes. First the Commission benefits greatly from the input of third parties as they are generally in a better position, given their industrial insight, to foresee the adequacy and effectiveness of the proposed commitments and may point out

proposed and the limited time available to carry out a proper assessment have made it impossible to conclude, in the short time available in first phase, whether they would be sufficient to remove, in a clear-cut manner, all competition concerns', see IP/02/1782 of 29 November 2002 announcing the initiation of proceedings.

[174] Remedies Notice, para 13 *in fine*. In this context the Commission refers to *easyJet v Commission* (T-177/04 2006) paras 186ff; and *EDP v Commission* (T-87/05 2005) para 72, in which the General Court confirmed that the Commission was right in refusing non-binding commitments.

[175] See Speech by Italianer (2012) 6.

[176] See eg *SNCF/LCR/Eurostar* (M.5655 I 2010) where the national railway regulator was empowered to review appeals (para 80); and *T-Mobile Austria/Tele.ring* (M.3916 II 2006) where the Austrian telecoms regulator would conduct the arbitration procedure (para 164), see further Blanke in Blanke and Landolt (2011) 1668.

[177] See section 4.6.5.2 below.

[178] For market tests in phase I cases, see Remedies Notice, paras 79(d) and 80; and for market tests in phase II cases, see para 91(d) (the provisions for market tests in phase I and II are largely identical as the latter provision refers to the former).

[179] In Competition Report 1994 the Commission defined interesting third parties in remedies cases as 'parties who have expressed comments following publication of the notice pursuant to Article 4 of the [Merger] Regulation and those which the Commission believes are liable to be affected by such commitments and modifications', see para 315. In practice, the respondents are usually third parties who have previously replied to a request for information (Art 11 of the Merger Regulation) or those who have approached the Commission voicing concerns about the transaction.

important aspects where there is still room for improvements.[180] Also, the Commission uses the market test to verify factual information submitted by the merging parties as well as sounding out interest from third parties in potentially acquiring the assets.

Secondly, the market test ensures transparency and safeguards the rights of third parties to be heard.[181] Although interested third parties lack an explicit statutory right to be heard specifically on proposed commitments, it is generally considered that the Commission consults interested third parties on first commitment proposals, both in phase I and II.[182] The consultation should be seen in the context of the fact that the Commission shall inform third parties of the 'nature and subject matter of the procedure' in order to make known their views.[183] It may therefore be argued that in cases where a concentration is modified through proposed commitments, the 'nature and subject matter of the procedure' change to an extent that warrants an additional consultation of third parties. Hence the practice of consulting third parties generally relates to *new* commitments and thus not necessarily modified commitments. In the latter situation third parties cannot expect to be consulted again, if they have previously been consulted on the 'core' commitment.[184] Finally, the Commission will usually not market test proposed commitments altogether if the proposal is considered prima facie wholly inadequate and unacceptable.[185] However, in borderline remedies/prohibition decisions the Commission normally market tests the most significant proposals.[186]

[180] 'Market-testing allows us to anticipate problems that could arise in the implementation phase. This is why we need to hear directly from industry which options are viable and which are not and why we encourage interested parties to reply to our market tests. This is very useful in achieving effective and proportionate remedies', see Speech by Italianer (2012) 9.

[181] In accordance with Art 18(4) of the Merger Regulation natural or legal persons showing a sufficient interest and especially members of the administrative or management bodies of the undertakings concerned or the recognised representatives of the employees shall be entitled, upon application, to be heard.

[182] See the Final Report of the Hearing Officer in *Oracle/Sun Microsystems* (M.5529 II 2010) where the hearing officer reasoned in the context of non-binding public assurances submitted by Oracle: 'Since the Commission has arrived at the conclusion that the merger will not raise competition concerns and no formal remedies within the meaning of the Remedies Notice have been submitted in this case *there can be no requirement for the Commission to perform a market test*' ([2010] OJ C91/5; emphasis added). The hearing officer thereby implies that the Commission is required to market test proposed commitments submitted by the parties in response to identified competition concerns. This view runs counter to observations expressed by some commentators that '[c]onsultation of third parties may not be appropriate where the remedies offered are so straightforward and clearly remove the Commission's competition concerns, that consultation would be superfluous', see De Souza and Brockhoff in Drauz and Jones (2012) para 7.73. However, the Commission's decisional practice confirms the views submitted by the hearing officer in *Oracle/Sun Microsystems* to the effect that prima facie acceptable commitments are usually market tested. In fact, in recent years it appears to have become standard practice that the Commission market tests any firm commitment proposals.

[183] Implementing Regulation, Art 16(1).

[184] Consequently in its Remedies Notice the Commission refers only to consultation of third parties in the context of situations where commitments are proposed *for the first time* (paras 79(d), 80 and 91(d)) and the existence of exceptional circumstances in phase II where *new* commitments may be proposed (para 89 *in fine*). Thus, in situations where *modified* commitments are proposed, the Commission does not mention consultation of third parties (paras 83 and 94 *in fine*). This does not prevent the Commission from consulting third parties on several proposals if considered appropriate, see eg *Universal Music Group/BMG Music Publishing* (M.4404 II 2007) where the Commission consulted on a first and second proposal and then considered that a new market test on the third proposal was unnecessary, see para 412.

[185] See eg *Omya/Huber PCC* (M.3796 II 2006) para 456 (relating to the second alternative). Only occasionally has the Commission proceeded with a market test despite firmly believing that the commitments were insufficient. In *Tetra Laval/Sidel* (M.2416 II 2001 – prohibition) the Commission market tested some of the proposed commitments that it found inadequate as it wished to assess the viability and stand-alone nature of the assets, see para 425. As it happened, the market test confirmed the Commission's view on inadequacy. On appeal the General Court did not address this aspect, see *Tetra Laval/BV v Commission* (T-5/02 and T-80/02 2002).

[186] In eg *Deutsche Börse/NYSE Euronext* (M.6166 II 2012) the parties submitted four commitment proposals and the Commission market tested two of them, see paras 1352–53.

In brief, the market test is usually conducted in the following way. The Commission approaches third parties in writing with a 'remedies document' consisting of: (i) a non-confidential version of the proposed commitments, provided by the parties;[187] (ii) an explanation by the Commission as to the context in which the commitments have been proposed (that is to say the aim of the remedies); and (iii) a number of questions addressing various aspects of the adequacy of the commitments, which the Commission would like the third parties to reply to.[188] Simultaneously with or prior to the sending of the remedies document, the recipients are asked to sign and return to the Commission a so-called Confidentiality Declaration according to which they confirm that the documents received will not be released to any third party and will not be used for any purposes other than the respective merger proceedings.[189]

The market test is conducted as part of the Commission's investigation and therefore third parties have a duty to reply and they will usually do so willingly if they are genuinely interested in or affected by the merger.[190] Due to time constraints and the need for speed third parties are usually given two or three working days to submit their written reply to the first proposal.[191] Once received, the Commission forwards a non-confidential version of the replies (or a summary thereof)[192] to the merging parties.[193] Confidentiality is important and the Commission does not underestimate the risk of possible retaliation by the

[187] Remedies Notice, paras 79(d) and 91(d).

[188] The parties may approach the hearing officer if they consider the Commission's questionnaire misleading or inaccurate. In *Tetra Laval/Sidel* (M.2416 II 2001) the parties alleged that the questionnaire was incomplete in respect of the duration of a proposed licence to be given to third parties. While the hearing officer recognised that the Commission's description could have been more accurate, it was observed that any interested third party could be expected to take the care to read all the documents made available by the Commission before replying to the questionnaire. It was concluded that the Commission had not omitted any information in this respect and therefore the allegations were dismissed, see Final Report of the Hearing Officer, [2004] OJ C39/2.

[189] In early decisional practice the Commission used a short standard text along the lines: 'I hereby confirm that the [proposed commitments] in the [case] received by ourselves will not be disclosed to any third party and will not be used for any purposes other than the referenced proceedings'. However, during the administrative proceedings in *Ryanair/Aer Lingus* (M.4439 II 2007) Ryanair complained to the European Ombudsman that the declaration was inadequate to prevent leaks to the press about the contents of its commitment proposals as the text did not explicitly refer to all the remedies documents, see decision of the European Ombudsman of 27 April 2009 in case 1342/2007/FOR, available at www.ombudsman.europa.eu/en/cases/decision.faces/en/3972/html.bookmark. The Ombudsman concluded that the Commission had failed to word appropriately the Confidentiality Declaration which constituted an instance of maladministration but at the same time he noted that, during the proceeding in *Ryanair/Aer Lingus,* the Commission had subsequently changed the wording of the declaration to the satisfaction of the Ombudsman (the new (significantly longer) standard declaration text is reproduced in the Ombudsman's decision, see para 38).

[190] Art 11 of the Merger Regulation empowers the Commission to obtain all necessary information for the purposes of its investigation, including aspects relating to the market test of proposed commitments. Although the Commission has measures at its disposal in case of non-compliance, they have – at least publicly – not been used in the context of third parties' refusal to reply in remedies market tests (for an example of third party refusal to comply with a request for information in the fact finding stage of a merger proceeding, see *Mitsubishi Heavy Industries* (M.1634 II 2000), [2001] OJ L4/31).

[191] In *Kaysersberg v Commission* (T-290/94 1997) the General Court confirmed that two days consultation of third parties on a *first* commitment proposal was adequate, see para 115.

[192] In *Tetra Laval/Sidel* (M.2416 II 2001) the hearing officer was called upon to verify the objective nature of the summary of third party replies. The parties claimed that the DG Competition had left out one reply in its summary. Indeed, this turned out to be the case and the hearing officer asked the Commission services to supplement its summary with that reply, see Final Report of the Hearing Officer, [2004] OJ C39/2.

[193] The provisions on access to the file and the parties' rights to be heard and of defence shall also be observed at this stage of the proceedings, see Merger Regulation, Art 18(1) and (3); and Implementing Regulation, Art 17(1). As to third parties' duty to identify confidential information and provide a non-confidential version of their reply, see Implementing Regulation, Art 18(2).

merging parties and hence the identity of the respondents and their sensitive date are often omitted.[194]

If the parties submit revised commitments in response to a negative market test, the Commission decides whether it wishes to undertake a new market test.[195] If it does so, it is usually only the respondents to the first market test will be approached,[196] and they will often be given shorter time to reply than on the original proposal.[197] The Commission incorporates the findings in the draft decision and finalises the decision for further consultations. The results of the market test are usually communicated (by separate document or orally) to the Advisory Committee and the appropriate Commission services before opinions and consents are submitted.[198]

In the past, commentators have voiced concerns that the Commission puts too much emphasis on the comments received by third parties (in particular competitors) during the market test.[199] Some have pointed out that the Commission's heavy reliance on third party comments should be seen as a way of compensating for the lack of experience and expertise within the DG Competition itself as regards the realities of buying and selling businesses.[200] In particular, it has been alleged that the Commission ignores that competitors have their own agenda in merger proceedings: they may for example recommend more comprehensive commitments because they wish to acquire some of the assets to be divested or in

[194] In *Bayer/Aventis Crop Science* (M.2547 II 2002) Bayer requested the hearing officer that the identity of the respondents in the market test be revealed as it was considered essential for a proper assessment of the results of the market test that the respondents were identified because the replies were likely to depend on the nature of a given third party and could vary between eg competitors interested in acquiring the assets to be divested, and customers. The hearing officer dismissed Bayer's request referring to jurisprudence by the EU Court to recognise the need to preserve confidential treatment (eg Case T-229/95 *Endemol v Commission* (T-221/95 1999)) and the fact that the Commission was itself capable of detecting potential 'vested interests'. The hearing officer also stressed that confidentiality was particularly important in cases with highly concentrated markets, see Final Report of the Hearing Officer, [2004] OJ C91/5.

[195] The EU Court has on several occasions confirmed that the Commission is not required under Art 18(4) of the Merger Regulation to send qualified third parties, for their prior comment, the final terms of the proposed commitments, see *ARD v Commission* (T-158/00 2003) para 422 and *Kaysersberg v Commission*, (T-290/94 1997) para 122.

[196] In the second market test in *Universal Music Group/BMG Music Publishing* (M.4404 II 2007) the Commission approached third parties (44 out of 100) who had responded in the first market test, see para 406.

[197] In *Union Carbide v Commission* (T-322/94 R 1994) the applicant (a competitor) complained that it was given *less than 24 hours* to respond to a *revised* version of draft commitments submitted by the parties during the administrative proceedings in *Procter & Gamble/Schickedanz* (M.430 II 1994), see Order, para 18. However, the applicant withdrew its appeal in the main case following the General Court's dismissal of its application for interim measures and therefore the Court did not get to rule on the appropriateness of a deadline being less than 24 hours. In *Babyliss v Commission* (T-114/02 2003) the applicant (a competitor) submitted – rather embarrassingly – that it had been given less than one day to reply to the market test of *revised* commitments (para 160) but, upon verification by the General Court, it turned out that it had been given 12 working days to lodge its comments, see para 180.

[198] The Advisory Committee and Commission bodies (eg the College of Commissioners) attach importance to the results of the market test, see *VEBA/VIAG*, (M.1673 II 2000) where the Advisory Committee made its approval of the remedies subject to the results of the market test (Opinion of the Advisory Committee given at its meeting on 24 May 2000, [2001] OJ C192/2).

[199] See Gilchrist (2001), a former Commission hearing officer, who takes the view that market testing of remedies should be abandoned given competitors' own agendas and interests. Other commentators have noted that the lack of resources available to the Commission compared to eg the FTC/DoJ, has led to an over-reliance by the Commission on competitor opinion and has allowed investigations to be extended and even biased by such complainants, see Cook and Kerse (2009) paras 6-018 and 8-023; and along the same lines, Brandenburger in IBA (2000) 284. To this effect, see also the ICPAC's Report (2000) 49.

[200] See Cook and Kerse (2009) para 8-023.

order to weaken the position of the merging parties in the respective market.[201] The Commission has dismissed this criticism by emphasising the merging parties' possibilities of responding to claims by third parties.[202] In the Commission's defence, it should be noted that in recent years it has become more systematic in its evaluation of whether concerns raised by third parties regarding the adequacy of proposed commitments are truly merger-specific and this approach indicates that the Commission tries to be more selective as to the genuine intentions behind third party objections in market tests.[203]

Finally, as indicated above in several cases, over the years a number of complaints from the parties or third parties relating to the way in which the Commission has conducted its market test have been put forward to the Commission's hearing officers whose overall mission is to safeguard the effective exercise of procedural rights throughout competition proceedings.[204] While the current Terms of Reference of the Hearing Officer contain no specific provisions or powers in respect of the conduct of market testing in merger remedies proceedings,[205] it is considered that complaints relating to the market test may nevertheless continue to be brought to the attention of the hearing officer if they relate to the effective exercise of the procedural rights of the involved parties and if they have not been resolved in prior contacts with the DG Competition.[206] Furthermore, the hearing officer may present his observations on the matter to the Commissioner for Competition in his interim report and/or in the form of separate observations as well as to the Commissioner and the College in his final report.[207] [208]

[201] See Gilchrist (2001) and Brandenburger in IBA (2000) 284. Although a prohibition decision, in *Deutsche Börse/NYSE Euronext* (M.6166 II 2012) the merging parties criticised the Commission for the way it had carried out the market test of proposed commitments as they argued that the market test was based on responses from biased market participants and therefore the merging parties requested that responses from all competitors and customers should have been discounted. The Commission dismissed the parties' request by responding that it had made a critical, comprehensive and objective analysis of all responses, see fn 1162.

[202] See Speech by Monti (2002a):

> The Commission decision making process has been also sometimes criticised for being too prone to capture by the competitors of the merging parties, who, the critics say, are able to influence excessively the investigation. While I believe that this criticism is exaggerated, and that it is in the interest of the Commission to listen to all – merging parties, consumers and competitors – I also consider that the merging parties should be given ample opportunities to defend their points of view during the procedure and confront the concerns of third parties at the earliest stages of the investigation.

The introduction of so-called 'triangular meetings' should be seen as an attempt to improve procedures in this respect, see the Commission's Best Practice Guidelines on Merger Proceedings, para 39.

[203] See eg *Arsenal/DSP* (M.5153 II 2009) where the Commission dismissed a number of objections from third parties to the initial set of remedies as it considered them to be 'non-merger specific' (paras 321–25).

[204] The tasks and powers of the hearing officer are now stipulated in Decision 2011/695 of the President of the European Commission of 13 October 2011 on the function and terms of reference of the hearing officer in certain competition proceedings [2011] OJ L275/29 (the Terms of Reference of the Hearing Officer). The general mission of the hearing officer is set out in Art 1(2).

[205] In the previous hearing officer mandate from 2001 ([2001] OJ L162/21), which was replaced by the Terms of Reference of the Hearing Officer, it was specifically stipulated that he could report on the objectivity of the Commission's market tests of remedies, in particular the selection of respondents and the methodology used, see Art 14.

[206] See the Terms of Reference of the Hearing Officer, recital 8 and Art 1(2), read in conjunction with Art 3(7). At the time of writing, no final reports of the hearing officer in merger remedies cases have been published after the entry into force of the current Terms of Reference of the Hearing Officer.

[207] See the Terms of Reference of the Hearing Officer, Arts 14(1), 3(5), 16 and 17, respectively. However, it should be emphasised that the hearing officer is only required to submit an interim report if an oral hearing has taken place and he is only required to submit a final report in those cases in which the Advisory Committee is consulted and thus these reporting powers are relatively limited in merger remedies cases, see further Wils (2012a) 453; and section 5.4 below.

[208] While a general explanation of the role and functions of the hearing officer is beyond the scope of this book, elaborate descriptions can be found in Wils (2012a,b), Albert and Jourdan (2011) and Albers and Williams (2010).

**Commentary:** in view of the information asymmetry between the merging parties and the Commission, there is no doubt that market tests of remedies are a vital tool in the Commission's investigation. However, as a word of caution, if the Commission relies too much on input from third parties (particularly competitors) there is a risk of so-called 'complaisance remedies' whereby remedies are submitted by the parties and accepted by the Commission with the main objective of satisfying third parties and minimising the risk of subsequent appeals rather than strictly addressing the identified competition concerns. As such remedies would typically involve additional 'pleasing' assets the result could ultimately be that the Commission's decision would be based on excessive remedies.

### *2.4.2 Member States*

Throughout the administrative proceedings the competent authorities of the Member States must be fully informed about any commitment proposals submitted in phase I and phase II.[209] Such documents should therefore be sent to the Member States as soon as the Commission receives them from the parties. The purpose of the transmission of any proposals is to facilitate the possibility for the Member States to express their views in line with the principle of close and constant liaison between the Commission and the Member States.[210] Such liaison may take place through direct correspondence between the respective national authority and the Commission (typically in phase I cases), attendance at oral hearings (solely in phase II cases, if applicable)[211] and Advisory Committee meetings (solely in phase II cases).

In phase I the Commission consults the Member States in writing by forwarding a copy of the proposed commitments and then it is generally up to the competent authority whether it wishes to submit any views. Given the tight deadlines in phase I any comments from the Member States shall usually be submitted within a couple of days following receipt of the proposals from the parties and the Member States do not have an opportunity to meet in a forum to consult each other or hear each others' views. While the short deadline for consultation in phase I remedies is a necessity, it poses great constraints on the Member States as their formal positions are often subject to domestic consultation before any comments can be submitted to the Commission.

The involvement of the Member States is more comprehensive and formalised in Phase II proceedings, mainly because of the mandatory consultation of the Advisory Committee.[212] The Committee consists of representatives from the competent authorities of the Member States.[213] While the consultation is initiated by invitation from the Commission who also

[209] Merger Regulation, Art 19(1).

[210] ibid, Art 19(2).

[211] Although the role of Member States in oral hearings is mainly confined to observing and possibly asking clarifying questions, it may still be an important part of the liaison as oral hearings constitute an opportunity for the Member States to familiarise themselves further with the facts of the case in preparation of the subsequent meeting in the Advisory Committee meetings. Having said this, it should be noted that the parties are increasingly waiving their rights to ask for oral hearings in potential remedies cases as they prefer to spend the (scarce) time discussing and preparing possible remedies proposals and in this context state-of-play meetings have proven more suitable than oral hearings, see Wils (2012b) 430.

[212] Consultations of the Advisory Committee are confined to draft decisions in accordance with Arts 8(1)–(6), 14 and 15, see Merger Regulation, Art 19(3).

[213] Details on representation are set out in Art 19(4) of the Merger Regulation. For a description of the role and functions of the Committee, see von Koppenfels in Drauz and Jones (2012) paras 6.193–98 and Cook and Kerse (2009) paras 9.007–9.008.

chairs the meeting,[214] the forum 'belongs' to the Member States in the sense that they appoint a *rapporteur* who is responsible for setting the agenda and drafting the opinion.[215] As a general rule, the date of the meeting is not publicly available but as a result of the intensified competition focus and coverage through newsletters and daily newswires,[216] the scheduled date is sometimes reported in the press in advance of the meetings which has the downside that the Member States are usually further exposed to (at times heavy) lobbying from not only the parties but also from third parties having an interest in the outcome of the case.

As previously mentioned, one of the controversial procedural issues in respect of the Advisory Committee has been the (lack of) timely consultation by the Commission.[217] In general the Commission must send to the Member States the invitation, including all relevant documents, no less than 10 working days prior to the meeting.[218] The purpose of the deadline is to allow the Member States sufficient time to examine the case file and conduct their own national consultations before adopting a formal view and provide their national representatives with instructions and mandates prior to the meeting.[219] However, in exceptional cases the Commission may shorten that period in order to avoid serious harm to one or more of the undertakings concerned by the concentration.[220]

While the Member States are generally sympathetic to the tight deadlines that the Commission works under in merger cases, there was a period in past practice where the late transmission of documents became the rule rather than the exception and where the late submission was not explicitly linked to the risk of serious harm to the parties. This practice caused a few clashes between the members of the Committee and the Commission and some members, in protest, declined to give a formal view on the adequacy of proposed commitments if the consultation period had been too short.[221] Due to the fewer in-depth investigations in recent years consultation issues have obviously been less of an issue and, judging on the issued opinions, the Committee has raised no formal objections or concerns in this respect.

Furthermore, the risk of shortened consultation periods is most prominent in cases where the Commission accepts modifications to remedies proposals after the expiry of the

[214] Merger Regulation, Art 19(5). With the invitation, the Commission will send the Member States a summary of the case, together with an indication of the most important documents and a preliminary draft decision.

[215] There are no publicly available formal provisions on the use and function of rapporteurs in the Advisory Committee (which are likely to be found in the internal manual of procedures for mergers of the DG Competition). However, practice seems to be that in each case the Member States appoint a *rapporteur* who, in the meeting, summarises the main contents of the case and poses to the Committee questions to be answered and subsequently published as its opinion. The task of being a *rapporteur* is usually taken in turns by the Member States but, if a Member State has particular national interests in a given case, the country shall not act as *rapporteur* in that case.

[216] See eg *Hutchinson 3G Austria/Orange Austria* (M.6497 II 2012) where the newsletter MLex reported that the Advisory Committee was foreseen to meet on 27 November 2012 to discuss the case, see MLex, 'EC Set to Clear Hutchinson's Orange Austria buyout' (20 November 2012), www.mlex.com/EU/Content.aspx?ID=291405.

[217] See section 2.2.3.3 above describing post-deadline modifications that may in exceptional circumstances be transmitted to the Advisory Committee in less than 10 working days.

[218] Merger Regulation, Art 19(5).

[219] It is often forgotten that, similar to the Commission's internal procedures, national competition authorities are usually required to consult other departments and ministries, affected industries and other organisations having an interest in the given case.

[220] Merger Regulation, Art 19(5) *in fine*.

[221] See eg *CVC/Lenzing* (M.2187 II 2001) where a minority abstained from commenting on the commitments proposals as it considered that the Commission had breached its obligation of timely consultation under Art 19(5) of the Merger Relation, see opinion of the Advisory Committee, [2004] OJ C69/5.

deadline for submission[222] as they will usually have a significant impact on the remaining timetable of the case. Therefore, the practice of allowing the parties post-deadline modifications has on rare occasions led some Member States to question whether this provision (contained in the Remedies Notice) is in fact compatible with the procedural requirements under the Merger Regulation.[223] The Court has to some extent come to the Commission's rescue in this respect by previously ruling that the Advisory Committee consultation period constitutes a purely internal rule of procedure, a breach of which cannot render a Commission decision unlawful as such.[224] In any event, the issue has become dormant in recent years due to the low number of in-depth investigations and it remains to be seen whether the Commission will further clarify the provision next time it reviews the Remedies Notice. A pragmatic procedural solution to late (substantial) modifications has been to convene the Advisory Committee for a second time or consult the members through an expedited written procedure on substantial changes.[225] Furthermore, in cases where the Committee has had doubts or particular concerns about the adequacy of the remedies, it has sometimes added in its opinion that it wishes to be kept informed post-decision of the implementation of the remedies.[226]

Finally, it is important to stress that the opinion of the Committee is not binding upon the Commission,[227] and, indeed, the Commission has rarely changed its conclusions in the preliminary draft decision after consulting the Committee.[228] However, since the opinion is attached to the documents presented to the College of Commissioners and any disagreements are recorded, it may carry some weight if a draft decision becomes controversial in the discussions before the College. Furthermore, as a relatively new practice the opinion is now being communicated, together with the decision, to the addressees of the conditional clearance decision.[229] Although this procedure may seem of historical interest for the parties, it could constitute useful information for them if they consider a possible appeal of the Commission's decision.

**Commentary:** albeit controversial, it is submitted that the Advisory Committee has lost its 'teeth' as a consultative body in merger remedies proceedings. It has become less prominent and more vague for a number of reasons. First, in view of the very low numbers of remedies decisions being adopted in phase II in recent practice, it could be argued that the Advisory Committee on

[222] See section 2.2.3.3 above.

[223] See the opinion of the Advisory Committee in *Schneider/Legrand* (M.2283 II 2001), [2004] OJ C86/13.

[224] See *Kaysersberg v Commission* (T-290/94 1997) para 88. The Court referred to settled law that the failure to comply with such a deadline can render the Commission's final decision unlawful only if it is sufficiently substantial and it has a harmful effect on the legal and factual situation of the party alleging a procedural irregularity. Furthermore, in the given case the Court attached importance to the fact that the Committee had not objected to its meeting taking place on that particular day (the Committee was convened five days before its meeting), see paras 80 and 89. In respect of the importance of a timely consultation of the Advisory Committee, see also *EDP v Commission* (T-87/05 2005) para 167.

[225] In *Boeing/McDonnell Douglas* (M.877 II 1997) the Advisory held three meetings discussing various draft decisions on 4, 16 and 25 July 1997, see [1997] OJ C372/17.

[226] See *Hutchison/RCPM/ECT* (JV.55 II 2001), opinion of the Advisory Committee, [2003] OJ C 210/13, para 4; *Danish Crown/Vestjyske Slagterier* (M.1313 II 1999), opinion of the Advisory Committee, [2000] OJ C21/2, para 8); and *Boeing/McDonnell Douglas* (M.877 II 1997), opinion of the Advisory Committee (second supplementary session), [1997] OJ C372/18, para 4.

[227] According to Art 19(5) of the Merger Regulation the Commission 'shall take the utmost account of the opinion of the Committee'.

[228] The Commission did so in *BP Amoco/Arco* (M.1532 II 1999) where it dropped its initial competition concerns in the northern North Sea gas pipelines market following consultation of the Committee, compare opinion of the Advisory Committee, [2001] OJ C17/24, para 3(a) and para 59 of the decision.

[229] Merger Regulation, Art 19(7).

Concentrations was almost redundant for a while (notably in 2009–11).[230] The diminishing role has been an unfortunate development as the Committee is generally an effective way of ensuring close and constant liaison with the national competition authorities in remedies cases and in the past it has produced fruitful discussions and inputs to mutual benefit.[231] Contrary to oral hearings, the discussions in the Advisory Committee are held 'in private' amongst representatives of the Member States and the Commission's services (DG Competition and associated services) with the possibility of a more open and possibly constructive discussion than in larger public forums.

From the Commission's point of view, it can use the Advisory Committee meeting to sound out and discuss the adequacy of potentially controversial remedies and detect any particular national interests so it is better prepared before advancing the draft decision to the Cabinets of the Commissioners and ultimately the College where the given case may become more political. From the Member States' point of view, the Advisory Committee meeting gives the national representatives an opportunity to hear the views of the other authorities (especially the ones mostly affected by the given transaction), form alliances and possibly adopt a more nuanced position based on the input and views from the other Member States.[232]

Secondly, in newer practice the Member States have not shown a great support for the Advisory Committee by being present at the meetings. Indeed, it is evident from the opinions of the Advisory Committee in recent years that less than half of the Member States sent their representatives to the meetings.[233] While the national competition authorities are of course entitled to make their own priorities (it is assumed that the lack of presence is down to financial considerations), the lack of support and presence is highly unfortunate if the Committee wishes to be considered as a consultative body with a voice vis-à-vis the Commission and any involved parties. It is furthermore observed that in recent years the opinions of the Advisory Committee have been surprisingly 'standardised' with very little variation in the texts and they have generally shown unanimity within the Committee, with no deviations or minority opinions expressed.[234]

Thus, it is hoped that the preliminary indications for 2012/2013 that the Commission is starting to initiate more in-depth investigations (and consequently remedying more cases in phase II) may be the beginning of a new practice whereby the Advisory Committee once again will become

[230] In 2011 the Committee met merely once whereas in 2010 and 2009 the Committee met twice per year to discuss and issue opinions in remedies cases. Although the numbers of phase II remedies decisions were higher in preceding years (5 in 2008, 4 in 2007, 6 in 2006, 3 in 2005, 4 in 2004 and so forth), the proportion of phase II decisions was still low compared to the overall number of remedies decisions being adopted each year and thus the Advisory Committee was consulted in a minority of remedies cases.

[231] The Advisory Committee has not always agreed with the Commission on the adequacy of proposed commitments, see eg *Alcan/Alusuisse* (M.1663 II 2000) where the Committee called for substantial improvements of the proposed commitments in order to consider the transaction compatible (opinion of the Advisory Committee, [2002] OJ C82/2, para 7).

[232] During the meetings in the Advisory Committee the rapporteur usually poses a number of questions to be addressed by every Member State present at the meeting in the form of a *tour de table*. Thus, the views and positions of each Member State will be voiced and the Member States may form certain 'coalitions' in the form of majorities or minorities when the opinion of the Committee is to be drafted.

[233] By way of illustration, in recent phase II remedies cases being discussed in the Advisory Committee the attendance of Member States was the following: 8/27 in *Syngenta/Monsanto's Sunflower Seed Business* (M.5675 II 2010); 8/27 in *Unilever/Sara Lee Body Care* (M.5658 II 2010); 11/27 in *Lufthansa/Austrian Airlines* (M.5440 II 2009); 15/27 in *Lufthansa/SN Airholding* (M.5335 II 2009); 15/27 in *Arsenal/DSP* (M.5153 II 2009); 12/27 in *Friesland/Campina* (M.5046 II 2008); 12/27 in *StatoilHydro/ConocoPhillips* (M.4919 II 2008); 12/27 in *ABF/GBI Business* (M.4980 II 2008); 9/27 in *Arjowiggins/M-Real Zanders Reflex* (M.4513 II 2008); and 8/27 in *Thomson Corporation/Reuters Group* (M.4726 II 2008). As of 1 May 2013, none of the opinions of the Advisory Committee in phase II remedies cases in 2011 and 2012 have been made publicly available.

[234] By way of illustration, if comparing the opinions of the Advisory Committee in *Syngenta/Monsanto's Sunflower Seed Business* (M.5675 II 2010) and *Unilever/Sara Lee Body Care* (M.5658 II 2010) there are hardly any differences in the wordings, except the products in question.

a prominent feature in the administrative process leading up to the adoption of remedies decisions.[235] However, it also requires that the Member States increasingly back up around the work of the Committee so its opinions truly reflect the position of all or at least the majority of Member States. The consultation of the Advisory Committee takes place at a crucial time in the administrative proceedings where the draft decision is not yet irreversible and the Member States should not underestimate their 'voices' in this respect.

### *2.4.3 Involvement of Other Authorities*

The Commission may involve other authorities in the remedies proceedings. First in markets with national regulatory authorities the Commission may, if appropriate, consult the competent national regulatory authorities.[236] Typical examples of such authorities are energy, aviation and telecommunications regulators. The regulators can be involved in different ways: they may regulate the activities of one or more of the parties in a national market in question and can thus contribute with national sector-specific knowledge that the Commission does not possess;[237] and/or they may become involved in the oversight of the implementation of the remedies, for example through a dispute resolution mechanism.[238]

Secondly, in cases involving a geographic market that is wider than the EU or where, for reasons related to the viability of the business, the scope of the business to be divested is wider than the EU territory, a non-confidential version of the proposed commitments may be discussed with non-EU competition authorities within the framework of the EU's bilateral cooperation agreements with these countries.[239] To date, the Commission has signed dedicated competition cooperation agreements relevant for merger remedies cases with the US, Canada, Japan and the Republic of Korea.[240] While by far most important and exten-

[235] In 2012 the Commission adopted no less than six remedies decisions in phase II. Regrettably, as of 1 May 2013, none of these decisions are yet publicly available.

[236] Remedies Notice, para 80. While the provision is only mentioned in the context of phase I remedies proceedings, it is assumed that it also applies to phase II cases. The part of the provision relating to national regulatory authorities was inserted in 2008 in the new Remedies Notice.

[237] Cooperation with national regulators has been particularly prominent in the telecoms sector, see eg *Hutchinson 3G Austria/Orange Austria* (M.6497 II 2012), and *T-Mobile/Orange* (M.5650 I 2010). See also *RWE/Essent* (M.5467 I 2009).

[238] Remedies Notice, paras 66 and 80. The provision is new and was inserted after the public consultation in 2007 of the draft Remedies Notice. However, prior to the introduction of this provision, national regulators were involved in the implementation of the remedies, see eg *Verbund/Energie Allianz* (M.2947 II 2003) where the Austrian energy regulator, E-Control, supervised the implementation of the commitment package relating to balancing energy and energy auctions (para 154).

[239] Remedies Notice, para 80 *in fine*. Compared to the old Remedies Notice (para 35) it is stressed in the new notice that it is only a 'non-confidential version' of the remedies that may be discussed with such authorities. Also it is important to note that the provision uses the term 'discuss' rather than 'consult' and thus a less formal and non-binding dialogue.

[240] The cooperation agreement between the EU and the US is from 1991 ([1995] OJ L95/47) (the 1991 EU/US Cooperation Agreement) with a strengthening of the positive comity provisions in 1998 ([1998] OJ L173/26) and the conclusion of a so-called 'Administrative Arrangements on Attendance' (AAA) text in 1999 providing for the authorities to mutually attend certain key events and meetings during proceedings in individual cases, see COM(2000) 618, dated 4 October 2000, pp 5–6; the EU/Canada cooperation agreement is from 1999 ([1999] OJ L175/50); the EU/Japan cooperation agreement is from 2003 ([2003] OJ L183/12); and the EU/Republic of Korea cooperation agreement is from 2009 ([2009] OJ L 202/36). Furthermore, the Commission has signed Memoranda of Understanding on Cooperation with Brazil (IP/09/1500 of 9 October 2009), Russia (IP/11/278 of 10 March 2011) and latest with China (IP/12/993 of 20 September 2012).

sive cooperation is with the FTC/DoJ[241], the other cooperation agreements have also been applied in remedies cases on a number of occasions.[242]

Furthermore, in addition to the bilateral agreements the Commission has recently adopted new US–EU Best Practices on Cooperation in Merger Investigations with the FTC/DoJ, which are intended to further strengthen cooperation with the overall aim of intensifying the dialogue and avoiding diverging outcomes whenever possible.[243] Specifically, in respect of the submission and assessment of remedies the best practices emphasise the importance of early and frequent communication and cooperation in order to avoid inconsistent or conflicting remedies and the possibility of accepting common remedies or even the appointment of common trustees or monitors, in the interest of the parties as well as the authorities.[244]

In the past the Commission has successfully exchanged information with the above jurisdictions with a view to coordinating actions on the competitive analysis and remedies negotiations in a number of cases. The weakness of the agreements is that the Commission cannot exchange information of confidential nature without the parties' consent and hence the Commission is dependent on the cooperation of the parties in these cases.[245] However, practice shows that the parties are often in favour of and consent to such information sharing during the administrative proceedings if the exchange promotes their chances of obtaining conditional clearances in the respective jurisdictions. It is also presumed that the cooperation agreements are enacted during the implementation of the remedies if (some of) the respective assets are located outside the EU.[246]

**Commentary:** in a time where globalisation and international cooperation are on the agenda of many competition authorities, it is inevitable that the Commission will need to pay more attention to ways of further increasing coherence and coordinated actions in multi-jurisdictional remedies cases. However, given the strict timetables under the current framework it is difficult to envisage how such additional aspects should be provided for and hence any significant developments or improvements in this area presuppose radical procedural changes.

[241] The decision in *Cisco/Tandberg* (M.5669 I 2010) is an example of a very close cooperation between the Commission and the DoJ with the result that the transaction was conditionally cleared by the Commission and unconditionally cleared by the US on the same day. Unusually, the DoJ took into account the commitments made by Cisco to the Commission, along with various market factors, and on that basis decided not to challenge the transaction, see DoJ's press release 29 March 2010 (where the DoJ also described the investigation as 'a model of international cooperation between the [US] and the [EU]'), available at www.justice.gov/atr/public/press_releases/2010/257173.htm. Similarly, see also *Thomson/Reuters* (M.4726 II 2008). Although the successful cooperation cases clearly outnumber the less successful cases, there have been several examples of controversial cases in the past where the EU and the US have clashed in potential merger remedies cases (with different or similar outcomes to follow), see eg *Oracle/Sun Microsystems* (M.5529 II 2010), *GE/Honeywell* (M.2220 II 2001), and *Boeing/McDonnell Douglas* (M.877 II 1997).

[242] See eg *Panasonic/Sanyo* (M.5421 I 2009) where the Commission worked in close cooperation with the FTC and the Japanese Fair Trade Commission, and *Evraz/Highveld* (M.4494 I 2007) where the assets to be divested were located in South Africa and thus the Commission cooperated with the South African authorities despite the lack of a dedicated merger cooperation agreement between the two jurisdictions.

[243] See ch 1 n 85 above as well as section 5.8 below.

[244] See in particular the US–EU Best Practices on Cooperation in Merger Investigations, paras 16–20. In recent practice the representatives from the authorities have also attended eg oral hearings in potential remedies cases, see eg *Deutsche Börse/NYSE Euronext* (M.6166 II 2012), Final Report of the Hearing Officer (not yet published in the OJ), para 12.

[245] Hence the inserted reference to the 'non-confidential version' of the remedies in para 80 of the Remedies Notice.

[246] These situations are normally not made public and therefore it is difficult to speculate the frequency of such cases.

Having said this, past cooperation cases have proven fruitful for the Commission's remedies policy in a number of ways. It is worth noting that many of the 'non-standard provisions' (meaning provisions not found in the standard model texts) originate from cooperation cases with other competition authorities or national regulatory bodies. For example, the vast majority of fix-it-first, up-front buyer and crown jewel provisions stem from EU–US cooperation cases and tailor-made dispute resolution mechanisms are often found in cases where national regulatory bodies or competition authorities have been involved.[247]

## 2.5 Adopting Remedies

### 2.5.1 *Imposing Conditions and Obligations*

When declaring a concentration compatible the Commission may attach to its decision conditions and obligations intended to ensure that the merging parties comply with the commitments they have entered into vis-à-vis the Commission.[248] Contrary to modifications and commitments proposals where the initiative rests with the parties, the Commission alone can impose conditions and obligations. Although in principle the Commission is not legally obliged to impose such measures, it is the only way of ensuring that the remedies can be enforced post-clearance.

In recent years the way in which the Commission imposes conditions and obligations has generally been clear, transparent and consistent.[249] In simple terms, the fulfilment of the measure that gives rise to a structural change of the market (typically the divestiture of assets) is a condition, whereas the implementing steps, which are necessary in order to achieve this result, are obligations.[250] Examples of conditions are (i) the identification and specification of the assets to be divested; (ii) commitments to maintain the viability of the divested business; (iii) commitments to divest to a suitable purchaser;[251] (iv) the deadline within which the assets must be divested;[252] and (v) the 10-year re-acquisition prohibition.[253] Obligations are the implementing steps to meet the condition, for example (i) preservation

[247] For a recent example of an up-front buyer provision in EU–US cooperation cases, see *Western Digital Ireland/Viviti Technologies* (M.6203 II 2011). For a recent example of an up-front buyer provision in a case involving cooperation with a national regulatory body, see *Hutchinson 3G Austria/Orange Austria* (M.6497 II 2012).

[248] Merger Regulation, Arts 6(2), second sub-para, and 8(2), second sub-para.

[249] Remedies Notice, para 19. Prior to the publication of the old Remedies Notice (para 12) the Commission had never defined the two terms, nor thoroughly explained the legal consequences of breach of conditions and obligations.

[250] In recent years this explanation has developed into a standard phrase used by the Commission in its remedies decisions.

[251] The specific purchaser criteria are imposed as obligations.

[252] Remedies Notice, para 20. While MTDC section B refers to the parties' commitments to divest within a first divestiture period, followed by a trustee period, the individual deadlines are submitted in MTDC section A. In some unfortunate instances the Commission has explicitly – presumably by mistake – referred to section A as constituting 'obligations' and hence strictly speaking made divestiture deadlines obligations rather than conditions, see *Syngenta/Monsanto's Sunflower Seed Business* (M.5675 II 2010), Art 3 of the operative part of the decision.

[253] The re-acquisition prohibition is set out in MTDC, para 3, and is therefore generally considered as a condition for the Commission's clearance decision, which is logical as the purpose of the provision is to maintain the structural effects of the remedies. In most conditional clearance decisions this provision is therefore listed as a condition. However, it should be noted that – for unknown reasons and after the public consultation in 2007 on the new draft Remedies Notice – the Commission inserted a new phrase referring to the re-acquisition as an 'obligation' in para 43 of the Remedies Notice. On the other hand, in para 20 of the notice, the re-acquisition prohibition is listed as an example of a 'condition' being breached. Thus, the provisions are contradictory.

and hold-separate provisions relating to the assets; (ii) provisions relating to the appointment of the trustee; (iii) non-solicitation obligations; and (iv) reporting obligations.[254]

According to newer decisional practice the Commission will usually conclude in its clearance decision that the finding of compatibility is conditional upon full compliance with the conditions and obligations of the parties' commitments as set out in the attached annex which forms an integral part of the decision. The Commission specifies which provisions in the parties' commitments are considered conditions (usually by referring to the relevant section in the commitments text – often being section B) while pointing out that the remaining provisions constitute obligations. By doing so, the Commission enhances legal certainty as the legal consequences of a breach of an obligation are different from that of a breach of a condition.[255]

This way of referring to (instead of citing or rephrasing) the provisions in the parties' commitments text ensures uniformity and avoids discrepancies between the proposed commitments, on the one hand, and the imposed conditions and obligation, on the other hand.[256] The methodology is also in line with the policy confirmed by the EU Court that the Commission cannot impose unilaterally any conditions to an authorisation decision, but only on the basis of the parties' commitments.[257] However, the Commission will review whether the commitments submitted by the parties are proportionate to the competition problem when assessing whether to attach them as conditions or obligations to its final decision.[258] Thus, the Commission makes it clear in its guidance that the conditions and obligations are carefully assessed before they are referred – and attached – to the Commission's clearance decision. It is believed that the Commission, by this statement,

[254] With respect to non-structural cases and in particular access remedies, the policy is less consistent as in some cases the Commission has considered all requirements set out in the remedies as constituting obligations (see *Intel/McAfee* (M.5984 I 2011) para 353; *SNCF/LCR/Eurostar* (M.5655 I 2010) para 102; and *News Corp/Premiere* (M.5121 I 2008) para 133) whereas in other cases it has considered the 'core provisions' relating to the access as conditions (see *Lufthansa/Austrian Airlines* (M.5440 II 2009) para 404; *Lufthansa/SN Airholding* (M.5335 II 2009) para 479; and *Deutsche Bahn/EWS* (M.4746 I 2007) para 119). See also Blanke in Blanke and Landolt (2011) who points to inconsistencies in the Commission's policy as to whether arbitration provisions are considered conditions or obligations (the author rightly submits that, given the ancillary function of arbitration provisions in facilitating the implementation of the remedies, they should be considered conditions which is also supported by the majority of cases), see para 46-052.

[255] See Remedies Notice, para 20, and section 4.6.4 below.

[256] Throughout the Commission's practice, the way in which conditions and obligations have been imposed and commitment proposals referred to has varied substantially. During the early days the Commission would merely summarise the commitments (referred to them all as obligations) in its clearance decision, see eg *Alcatel/Telettra* (M.42 II 1991). As there was a risk that this practice could result in disagreement as to the exact contents, the Commission started to cite the full text of the commitments in its clearance decisions without specifying conditions and obligations, see eg *Kimberly-Clark/Scott* (M.623 II 1996). This practice had the unfortunate effect that the voluminous (phase II) decisions had to be translated into all official Union languages for OJ publication purposes. In order to reduce the translation backlogs the Commission started to annex the commitments to its decisions but still without specifying conditions and obligations, see eg *Dow Chemical/Union Carbide* (M.1671 II 2000). It was not until the publication of the old Remedies Notice that the Commission started the practice of systematically identifying in the operative part of its conditional clearance decisions which parts of the commitments constituted conditions and obligations, respectively. The first decision of this kind was *The Post Office/TPG/SPPL* (M.1915 II 2001), see further Speech by Mederer (2001).

[257] Remedies Notice, paras 6 and 85. Reference is made to two important judgments in this respect. In *General Electric v Commission* (T-210/01 2005) the General Court stressed that the Commission is not responsible for technical or commercial gaps in the commitments (para 52), and in *EDP v Commission* (T-87/05 2005) the General Court confirmed that the Commission is not in a position, without modifying the proposed commitments which it is not empowered to do, to trust the monitoring to the national authorities (para 105). See also *Cementbouw Handel & Industrie v Commission* (T-282/02 2006) para 311.

[258] Remedies Notice, para 85. In this context reference is made to *Cementbouw Handel & Industrie v Commission* (C-202/06 P 2007) para 54.

wishes to reinforce its policy that it does not uncritically 'cut and paste' the parties' proposed commitments into conditions and obligations but instead undertakes an individual assessment of the necessity and adequacy of the proposals. Albeit controversial, it is submitted that sometimes realities may be less clear-cut as the parties often submit their proposal in accordance to what the Commission during the negotiations has indicated as necessary in order to clear the transaction. This is somehow logical as negotiations are all about dialogue and exchanging views on the appropriateness of certain proposals as long as the Commission does not insist on the parties proposing certain solutions.[259]

The question remains whether the Commission can formally impose obligations, which the parties have not proposed as commitments. In principle, there is nothing in the wordings of Articles 6(2), second sub-paragraph, and 8(2), second sub-paragraph that prevents the Commission from imposing *additional* obligations in order to ensure that the implementation of the commitments will be effective.[260] As the purpose of an obligation is to ensure that the conditions are fully implemented, it could be argued that it would be appropriate and proportionate – and even beneficial to the parties – if the Commission could impose certain additional obligations, which are considered necessary in order for the overall remedy to be efficient as the alternative could be to dismiss the parties' commitments proposal altogether. An example of such obligations could be that certain additional reporting obligations or preservation measures are introduced.[261] However, such changes should only relate to modalities of remedies and not the nature or scope of the assets to be divested as such additions would clearly qualify as new commitments.

Indeed, in the past there have been examples of such additional obligations being formally imposed although they have received little attention.[262] However, it is submitted that

[259] In *OMYA v Commission* (T-275/06) the appellant claimed that the Commission had *imposed* inappropriate conditions (a plant) and obligations with which the applicant had to comply and it therefore sought annulment of the Commission's conditional clearance decision in *Omya/Huber PCC* (M.3796 II 2006), see summary of Omya's action brought on 4 October 2006 in [2006] OJ C294/59. However, the General Court never got to rule on this issue as the appeal was later withdrawn, see [2008] OJ C327/41. A similar plea was submitted in *Western Digital and Western Digital Ireland v Commission* (T-60/12 2012) where the parties claimed that the Commission's conditional clearance decision in *Western Digital Ireland/Viviti Technologies* (M *Western Digital and Western Digital Ireland v Commission*.6203 II 2011) had breached fundamental principles of EU law by imposing disproportionate remedies, see announcement of action in [2012] OJ C98/26. Similarly, in this case the Court did not get a chance to rule as the parties withdrew their action, see [2012] OJ C355/38.

[260] In line with this view, a careful reading of paras 6 and 85 of the Remedies Notice reveals that the Commission refers only to 'conditions' (not obligations) in the context of the lack of power to impose unilateral measures. See eg the wording of para 6 of the notice: 'the Commission is not in a position to impose unilaterally any *conditions* to an authorisation decision, but only on the basis of the parties' commitments'(emphasis added). To this effect, see also *Cementbouw Handel & Industrie v Commission* (T-282/02 2006) para 311, where the General Court merely referred to 'conditions' and not obligations.

[261] Albeit not exactly the same situation, the Commission inserted in 2008 a new (and highly controversial) provision in the Remedies Notice according to which the Commission suggests that the parties could include a clause in their commitment proposals allowing the Commission to trigger a limited modification to the commitments, see Remedies Notice, para 75; and further section 4.4.4.2 below. Compared to the current situation at hand, para 75 appears to differ in the sense that it allows the Commission to modify or insert certain clauses during the implementation phase and not at the time of adoption of the conditional clearance decision.

[262] In *Boeing/McDonnell Douglas* (M.877 II 1997) the Commission added an obligation for Boeing to submit to monitoring of its compliance with its commitments by allowing the Commission and its experts to access internal data relevant for the monitoring and be prepared to discuss its compliance, whenever requested by the Commission, see para 123 and Art 1 of the operative decision. In *Ciba-Geigy/Sandoz* (M.737 II 1996) the Commission specifically required the parties to submit three-monthly reports containing detailed information on received and granted licence requests and reasons for any possible refusals of such requests, see para 280 and Art 2 of the operative part of the decision. Similar reporting obligations were imposed in *Agfa-Gevaert/DuPont* (M.986 II 1998), see para 118 and Art 2 of the operative part of the decision; *Siemens/Elektrowatt* (M.913 II 1997), Art 2 of the operative part of the decision; and *ABB/Daimler-Benz* (M.580 II 1995) para 146 and Art 2 of the operative part of the decision.

this area needs careful reflection by the Commission as jurisprudence indicates that the Commission cannot impose for example certain monitoring provisions, as they would require a modification of the commitments.[263] In any event, in recent decisional practice the Commission has changed its policy by negotiating additional obligations (usually in view of negative comments during the market test), which the parties have then submitted as their *own* commitments and thus the additional obligations were not imposed, as such, by the Commission.[264] The drawback with this practice is that it is not transparent which provisions have been proposed and imposed, respectively.

**Commentary:** while it is clear from jurisprudence that the Commission cannot unilaterally impose conditions for its clearance, it would be desirable if the Commission initiated a more transparent and 'honest' policy as to whether certain obligations are explicitly required by it in order to consider the modalities of the remedies acceptable instead of the current 'artificial' procedure whereby the parties are required to submit (and often resubmit) all provisions governing obligations – irrespective of whether they are instigated by themselves or the Commission – as their own commitment proposals. Indeed, a more transparent practice would enhance legal certainty.

### *2.5.2 'Take Note Commitments'*

So-called 'take note commitments' are unilateral statements submitted by the parties upon which the Commission does not base its conditional clearance decision by imposing them as conditions or obligations. Such commitments are generally considered not to have legal binding effects in the sense that a breach would not cause the revocation of the clearance decision.[265] Nevertheless, the Commission has used such commitments in several situations and for different reasons with the main goal of creating publicity or transparency as to the parties' future behaviour. Thus, the overall purpose for the Commission has been to inform the public (in particular other market participants) of the existence of the commitments in order to enhance the likelihood that the parties would adhere to their assurances.

The Commission's handling of 'take note commitments' has changed significantly throughout decisional practice and in recent years they were thought to be a feature of the past. However, the Commission's recent decision in *Oracle/Sun Microsystems* spurred a revived discussion on the use and justification of such commitments as the Commission based its competitive assessment on certain 'public pledges' by the parties, which in effect

Furthermore, it is worth noting that during the Court proceedings in *Ryanair v Commission* (T-342/07 2010) Ryanair maintained that the Commission had 'demanded' an up-front buyer provision, which it had then agreed to include in its commitment proposal that was later rejected by the Commission, see paras 473 and 475.

[263] In *EDP v Commission* (T-87/05 2005) the applicant submitted that the Commission had failed to consider the possibility that the competent Portuguese authorities might carry out the necessary monitoring of certain proposed commitments although the parties had not provided for such monitoring possibility in their proposal. The General Court found that the Commission would not have been in a position to entrust the monitoring to a national authority as this would have meant that it would have modified the proposed commitment which the Commission is not empowered to do, see para 105.

[264] As mentioned above, in *Sanofi-Avantis/Zentiva* (M.5253 I 2009) the Commission *requested* the parties to (i) extend the duration of a transitional supply agreement from two to three years; and (ii) insert specific purchaser requirements in order to ensure a smooth transfer of certain assets, see para 553. These additional obligations were *submitted* as proposals from the parties (as opposed to being explicitly imposed by the Commission), see paras 4(f) and 13(b) of the Remedies Text.

[265] See the General Court's conclusions in *Coca-Cola v Commission* (T-125/97 and 127/97 2000) para 106. However, the Court indicated that there may be circumstances where such commitments could produce legally binding effects if upon analysis of their substance, it is clear that the Commission could revoke its decision for breach of its terms, see paras 96–97. The Court has not subsequently addressed this issue in other appeals although this may soon change with the pending appeal in *Monty Program v Commission* (T-292/10), see n 293 below.

amounted to 'take note commitments'.[266] Thus the issue continues to be relevant and justifies the following observations.

'Take note commitments' typically emerge in cases where the Commission withdraws its initial competition concerns after the parties have submitted commitments[267] or where third parties have voiced concerns which may not necessarily amount to unlawful competition concerns.[268] In the past such superfluous commitments have featured in pure clearance decisions as well as conditional clearance decisions, both in phase I and II, and they have been submitted either as stand-alone commitments or part of remedies packages. The majority of cases have been behavioural in nature but structural commitments have also been taken note of.

Briefly outlining past practice, 'take note commitments' were accepted for the first time in a phase II conditional clearance decision in 1993,[269] followed by two pure clearance decisions in 1995.[270] From 1997 to 2001 (thus prior to the adoption of the old Remedies Notice) the policy really took off with nearly 20 cases referring to take note commitments.[271] During this period the Commission would typically not inform the parties in advance of the adoption of its decision that certain commitments were superfluous and thus the parties were not given an opportunity to withdraw them. Such commitments would consequently be taken note of in the final decision and occasionally the full text would be published.[272]

As of 2001 the Commission changed its policy by announcing that the parties would be given an opportunity to withdraw their commitments if the original competition concerns proved unfounded.[273] In the majority of cases the parties would thus withdraw their commitment proposals and no details would be published about their contents.[274] If the parties chose not to withdraw their superfluous commitments,[275] the Commission would either take note of their proposals or ignore them. In cases where the Commission did take note of the commitments, it would normally clarify in its decision that they did not constitute a condition for

[266] See *Oracle/Sun Microsystems* (M.5529 II 2010). The public pledges are reproduced in the Commission's decision in fn 154.

[267] See eg *Enso/Stora* (M.1225 II 1998) where the parties submitted a substantial remedies package in response to the concerns raised in the SO, including divestitures and price protection mechanisms. The Commission subsequently abandoned its concerns but noted the commitments in its unconditional clearance decision, see para 101.

[268] In *Deutsche Post/DHL* (M.1168 I 1998) the Commission concluded that the operation would not cause the creation or strengthening of a dominant position but commitments were offered, taken note of and annexed to the decision, in response to concerns raised by a number of third parties.

[269] In *Kali-Salz/MDT/Treuhand* (M.308 II 1993) the Commission took note of certain best-effort negotiations with other joint venture partners on an adaptation of a Canadian joint venture (Potacan) whereby the partners would be able to distribute their products independently for a given period of time, see para 67. On appeal in *France and Others v Commission* (C-68/94 and C-30/95 1998) the applicant (being the other joint venture partner) sought annulment of inter alia the 'take note commitment'. In the context of admissibility the Court of Justice ruled that this commitment 'cannot produce binding legal effects of such a kind as to affect the interest of [the applicant/joint venture partner] by bringing about a distinct change in that entity's legal position' (para 67).

[270] In *Mercedes-Benz/Kässbohrer* (M.477 II 1995) the Commission took note of a supply obligation and the termination of an exclusivity clause, see paras 78, 90 and Annex V of the decision; and in *Siemens/Italtel* (M.468 II 1995) two provisions on non-interference in the purchasing policy of a vertically linked subsidiary of one of the parents and separation of the management of that subsidiary were taken note of, see para 62.

[271] The first decision in this period was *Coca-Cola/Amalgamated Beverages GB* (M.794 II 1997) and the last was *Boeing/Hughes* (M.1879 II 2000).

[272] In *Mercedes-Benz/Kässbohrer* (M.477 II 1995) two standard letters from Kässbohrer to garages in Germany announcing the termination of exclusivity were published in Annex V of the decision; and in *Aerospatiale/Matra* (M.1309 I 1999) the 'take note commitments' were annexed to the decision.

[273] Old Remedies Notice, para 12, fn 13.

[274] See eg *Posten AB/Post Danmark A/S* (M.5152 I 2009) para 174.

[275] It may be envisaged that the parties in some cases would have an interest in not withdrawing their commitments offers, typically for public relations reasons or to pacify complainants.

clearance.[276] This change in policy was introduced in order to clarify the enforcement issue and provide the parties with an opportunity to withdraw unnecessary commitments.[277]

The use of 'take note commitments' declined dramatically in the following years, partly because the parties would withdraw unnecessary commitments but also because the Commission became more stringent in its categorising of commitments as either conditions or obligations and thereby ignoring unnecessary commitments. In the few cases where the Commission did take note of certain commitments, it explained why it had done so and emphasised that the aim of those commitments was to 'support' the overall remedies package.[278] With the adoption of the new Remedies Notice it seemed that the Commission had finally 'closed the door' on its past practice as it emphasised that unnecessary commitments, which had not been withdrawn by the parties, would normally be ignored in the final decision.[279] This approach seemed plausible in terms of enhancing legal certainty, for both the parties and third parties.

However, with the decision in *Oracle/Sun Microsystems* in 2010 there are indications that the Commission's 'take note policy' may change once more.[280] In brief, the Commission's dilemma in this case was the following: the initial competition concerns arose in horizontal markets, more specifically the combination of the parties' worldwide competing database activities (in particular the impact of Sun's MySQL, the largest open source database). As a divestiture proved unrealistic,[281] the Commission was left with the options of either prohibiting the merger or accepting behavioural commitments. A prohibition was considered questionable,[282] and, as the competition concerns stemmed from horizontal overlaps, the Commission would go against its established practice of accepting behavioural promises only exceptionally in conglomerate cases.[283] Moreover it was evident that the behavioural solutions would be difficult, if not impossible, for the Commission to monitor.[284]

With this dilemma in mind, the Commission introduced a novel methodology for its analysis. Although Oracle's so-called 'public pledges' were in reality submitted in response to

[276] See eg *Newscorp/Telepiu* (M.2876 II 2003) para 324; and *Mitsui/CVRD/CAEMI* (M.2420 II 2001) para 255. Occasionally in cases where phase I remedies were submitted in response to competition concerns which were later dropped in phase II, the Commission would briefly describe the phase I remedies as a 'procedural fact' without explicitly taking note of them, see *Blackstone/Acetex* (M.3625 II 2005) para 2. Interestingly, the French local authority appealed the Commission's unconditional clearance decision in 2010, claiming damages of EUR 10 million on the basis that the Commission acted unlawfully and deficiently in light of Acetex's non-compliance of the (non-binding) commitment, see *Communauté de communes de Lacq v Commission* (T-132/10 2011). The General Court dismissed the appeal on the grounds that the Commission was under no obligation to pursue non-compliance as the clearance decision had not been based on those commitments, see para 33.

[277] It is also believed that while the Commission was in favour of transparency by publishing some 'take note commitments', there were concerns that the policy would raise false expectations with third parties who could wrongly assume that the published commitments would somehow be binding.

[278] See *Verbund/Energie Allianz* (M.2947 II 2003) paras 143(e) and 156.

[279] Remedies Notice, para 84.

[280] See *Oracle/Sun Microsystems* (M.5529 II 2010). The case is explained (by Commission officials) in detail in Buhr et al (2010) 20–27.

[281] It was widely expected that a full divestiture of MySQL was commercially unrealistic, see MLex Comment 'Options for Remedies in Oracle/Sun Deal Seem Undesirable, But Not Impossible' (16 November 2009), www.mlex.com/EU/Content.aspx?ID=78729.

[282] It should be remembered that the parties were American companies and had already received an unconditional clearance from the DoJ. The Commission's SO sparked tensions between the DoJ and the EU to which the then-Commissioner Neelie Kroes diplomatically replied that she was optimistic that the case would reach a satisfactory outcome, see MEMO/09/551 of 14 December 2009. Some commentators indicated that the DoJ was almost bullying the Commission in these proceedigns

[283] See Remedies Notice, para 69.

[284] To this effect, see Remedies Notice, para 13 *in fine*, to which the Commission refers in the *Oracle/Sun Microsystems* decision (para 179).

the Commission's initial competition concerns (after the SO and oral hearing), they were formally submitted to the general public (primarily MySQL's users, customers and developers) and *not* to the Commission.[285] In its analysis the Commission considered that the pledges constituted factual elements, forming part of the case file.[286] The Commission concluded that these factual elements, together with the specific characteristics of MySQL as an open source product, would remove the initially voiced competition concerns.[287] In terms of (lack of) enforcement, the Commission observed that the first three of Oracle's public pledges were considered legally binding as Oracle had immediately implemented them by sending letters to eight third parties, pledging to amend the existing contractual terms by reproducing the relevant content of its public announcement.[288] The Commission recognised that although the remaining public pledges were not legally binding on Oracle, they provided for a self-enforcing mechanism due to the particular characteristics of the market.[289]

The Commission's recognition and assessment of Oracle's public pledges is a highly unusual blend of 'take note commitments' and 'pre-clearance modifications' that prima facie seems risky. The 'take note element' arises from the fact that the public pledges are submitted in response to initial competition concerns[290] and that (most of) these pledges lack binding effect.[291] The 'modification element' arises from the fact that the Commission views the public pledges as factual elements, although they were submitted well into the phase II proceedings and could not be implemented pre-decision. Also the overall aim of the pledges seems to be the same as in 'take note commitments' cases, namely to create sufficient transparency in the market in the hope that Oracle feels compelled to respect its non-binding pledges. At the same time, the Commission gives the impression that because

[285] See press release from Oracle of 14 December 2009 announcing the 'commitments' to customers, developers and users of MySQL: 'Oracle has engaged in constructive discussions with the European Commission regarding the concerns expressed by the Commission about the [transaction], and in particular the maintenance of MySQL as a competitive force in the database market. In order further to reassure the Commission, Oracle hereby publicly commits to the following: [listing the ten commitments]', available at ww.oracle.com/us/corporate/press/042364. Furthermore the pledges were announced on the last possible day before the expiry of the deadline for the submission of commitment proposals, see MLex Comment 'Oracle/Sun merger Appeal may Target Procedural and Substantive Issues' (27 July 2010), www.mlex.com/EU/Content.aspx?ID=108299. The public pledges are reproduced by the Commission in fn 154 of its clearance decision.

[286] *Oracle/Sun Microsystems*, in particular paras 180–81, 626–29, 654 and 757.

[287] ibid, para 757.

[288] ibid, para 184. It is assumed that the Commission's reference to 'legally binding' in this context is primarily aimed at provisions under contract law. However, it should be remembered that in *Coca-Cola v Commission* (T-125/97 and 127/97 2000) the General Court opened up for the possibility that 'take note commitments' could in certain circumstances produce legally binding effects if upon analysis of their substance, it is clear that the Commission could revoke its decision for breach of its terms, see paras 96–97. Also the Commission referred to the possibility of revocation in accordance with Art 8(6)(a) of the Merger Regulation in the event Oracle would fail to respect its public announcement, see fn 156 in *Oracle/Sun Microsystems*. Thus, the Commission indicated that – as an alternative to breach of conditions and obligation – the public announcements could be revoked as 'misleading information' if they would later be changed by the parties. This approach appears to constitute a novel line of reasoning from the Commission.

[289] ibid, para 182. The Commission considered that the strong specificities of open source software and the vibrant ecosystem surrounding MySQL provide for a self-enforcing mechanism ensuring that Oracle would not have the ability and incentives to deviate from its announced future conduct, inter alia as reputation and trust are considered of utmost importance in this field and the public pledges will be subject to close scrutiny from the open source community

[290] It is therefore questionable whether the Commission is right in submitting that '. . . the facts of this case allow the Commission to conclude that the merger will not raise competition concerns', see para 180. In fact, the structure and reasoning in the decision are in many ways similar to a prohibition decision although the conclusion is different, see eg paras 639 and 644.

[291] This is recognised by the Commission in respect of the seven last pledges, see para 182.

the public pledges are considered factual elements (albeit most of them not yet being implemented), Oracle can be held accountable for any changes to such pledges should they not materialise.[292] Thus, all in all the Commission's analysis of Oracle's public pledges appears questionable and will surely be a source of controversy for future remedies policy discussions, including the appropriateness of taking note of non-binding commitments. Moreover, it is not surprising that the Commission's clearance decision – and in particular the nature and assessment of the pledges – has been appealed and it is expected that the outcome will have significant implications on the formulation of the Commission's future policy in this respect.[293]

**Commentary:** with the recognition and acceptance of the so-called 'public pledges' in the *Oracle/Sun Microsystems* decision the Commission is not only at risk of undermining its past (successful) endeavours to clarify and be more consistent in its enforcement and policy issues relating to 'take note commitments' but it may also open up for similar requests to be considered in future cases using *Oracle/Sun Microsystems* as benchmark. The full impact of the Commission's decision will not be known until the EU Court rules on the appealed aspects (including the nature of the public pledges, the absence of market testing and thus depriving third parties the opportunity to formally make their views on the pledges known and the required standard of proof imposed by the Commission under EU law).[294] Also, it remains to be seen how the Commission will formally react if the parties do not fully adhere to or change their public pledges in the coming years.

### *2.5.3 Adoption and Publication*

If the Commission concludes after the consultations and deliberations that the proposed remedies are sufficient, it clears the transaction, as modified, by issuing a conditional clearance decision. Phase I decisions are adopted by the Commissioner responsible for Competition (or, in his absence, another Commissioner) under delegated authority,[295] while phase II decisions are adopted by the full College of Commissioners, either by written or oral procedure.[296] Given that the vast majority of remedies cases are now resolved in phase I, it is worth noting that the full College is rarely consulted on conditional clearances. It will later be pointed out that this development may not necessarily be the best way of maintaining impartiality and objectivity.[297]

[292] In this context the Commission refers to its possibility of revoking the clearance decision pursuant to Art 8(6)(a) of the Merger Regulation, should Oracle fail to respect its pledges, see fn 156 of the decision. Thus, the Commission would regard a non-fulfilment or change of Oracle's pledges as misleading information.

[293] The Commission's clearance decision was appealed in July 2010 by the open-source database competitor Monty Program (owned by the MySQL creator Ulf Michael Widenius who subsequently set up a rival database), see *Monty Program v Commission* (T-292/10 pending).

[294] See summary of the pleas in [2010] OJ C260/15.

[295] See Rules of Procedure of the Commission ([2000] OJ L308/26), Arts 12–14.

[296] When a draft decision is presented to the College, it must be accompanied by several documents such as the approval of the Legal Service, the final report of the hearing officer on the respect for the effective exercise of procedural rights throughout the proceedings, a confirmation if other Directorates-Generals have been consulted as well as the opinion of the Advisory Committee. If consensus has already been reached at the 'special chefs' meeting, the College may adopt the decision without discussion and vote (point A on the agenda). It is believed that this procedure applies to the majority of phase II remedies cases. Only in cases where the 'special chefs' fail to reach agreement, the full College will discuss the given draft decision (point B on the agenda) which will typically be (controversial) prohibition decisions, see eg *Deutsche Börse/NYSE Euronext* (M.6166 II 2012), minutes of the 1988th meeting of the Commission on 1 February 2012, PV(2012)1988 final, available at ec.europa.eu/transparency/regdoc/rep/10061/2012/EN/10061-2012-1988-EN-F-0.Pdf.

[297] See section 5.4 below.

Once the conditional clearance decision is signed and adopted, the parties are informed thereof as soon as possible.[298] Other involved parties in the proceedings will be informed of the decision at the same time as the general public when the Commission issues its press release.[299] A non-confidential version of the decision, including the contents of the remedies, is often not ready within several weeks (and sometimes months) post-clearance as the parties are given time to identify business secrets before publishing the decision on the DG Competition's website.[300] Thus generally third parties, who may be affected by the remedies or interested in purchasing some of the assets to be divested, do not get access to the decision and the remedies text before the non-confidential version of the decision is published.[301] However, as a new and very welcomed initiative, the Commission has started to publish a preliminary version of the remedies text together with, or shortly after, the release of the press release announcing the clearance decision, which increases transparency and legal certainty.[302]

Finally, it should be mentioned that, for phase II cases, the subsequent publication of a summary of the decision in the OJ has lost its importance given that all remedies cases are now published earlier and in their full length on the DG Competition's website.[303] Under current practice the announcements in the OJ of the adoption of phase I decisions and the summary of phase II decisions are primarily relevant in any subsequent judicial review as the deadlines for bringing an action by, for example, a third party seeking annulment of the Commission's conditional clearance decision run from the publication of the decision in the OJ.[304]

[298] In parallel, a copy of the decision is sent to the Member States and the EFTA Surveillance Authority, where appropriate. Informing the Member States is important as the remedies may affect the structure of competition on one or several national markets and, moreover, the divestiture may be subject to approval by the competition authority in question.

[299] Press releases are usually issued at the Commission press conference on the day following the adoption of the decision. Given that the decision is addressed to the notifying party/parties, it means that other parties directly involved in the proceedings, in particular target companies, will in principle not be informed of the decision before the general public through the press release and announcement.

[300] The Commission is required to publish its final phase II merger decisions (or its main contexts) in the OJ, see Merger Regulation, Art 20. According to current practice a summary of phase II decisions are published in the OJ but given the late publication (due to translations into all official Union languages) it is considered that this summary is mainly important in respect of possible appeals (see below).

[301] Interested third parties may be directly approached by the trustee but it will take several weeks before he is accepted by the Commission and starts embarking on his tasks. Moreover, it should be mentioned that in some cases the Commission sends a non-confidential version of the decision directly to interested third parties who have acted as complainants during the administrative proceedings, see *DaimlerChrysler/Deutsche Telekom/JV* (M.2903 I 2003) where it was submitted in the subsequent appeal in *Qualcomm v Commission* (T-48/04 2009) that the Commission had sent by fax a non-confidential version of the decision to the appellant (but still nearly one month post-decision), see para 25.

[302] See section 5.3.2 below.

[303] The publication of phase II decisions has changed substantially over time. From 1990 to 2004 the full text of the non-confidential decision was published in the OJ (series L) in all Union languages. As of May 2004, only a summary of the final decisions – together with the final report of the hearing officer and the opinion of the Advisory Committee – are published in the OJ (series C) in all Union languages while the full text of the non-confidential decisions is published on the DG Competition's website in English, French and German (as well as in the authentic language if different). The OJ summaries of the decisions have no legal effect and are published for information purposes only. Phase I decisions are similarly published on the DG Competition's website in the authentic language of the case and only the announcements of the adoption of the decisions are published in the OJ (series C) in all Union languages.

[304] To this effect, in *Qualcomm v Commission* (T-48/04 2009) the General Court confirmed that the deadline for bringing an action for annulment of the Commission's decision runs from the date of publication in the OJ and not from the day on which third parties receive a copy of the non-confidential version of the Commission's decision (as argued by the Commission in favour of inadmissibility), see paras 46–53.

# 3

# Essential Features of Divestiture Remedies

## 3.1 Ensuring Viability

While the general principles when assessing remedies have been outlined above, this chapter examines ways of ensuring viability and competitiveness of the business to be divested. In recent years the Commission has increasingly recognised that, unless the viability of the business to be divested is fully ensured from the outset, the remedy is severely at risk of not fully succeeding. Thus, it is now established practice that the remedy must consist of a viable business that, if operated by a suitable purchaser, can compete effectively with the merged entity on a lasting basis and that is divested as a going concern.[1] The parties must address potential uncertainties and risks related to the transfer of the business at the design stage.[2]

Viability can be ensured in a number of ways. First, it is crucial that the scope of the business to be divested is defined correctly as experience shows that insufficient or inappropriate assets may lead to a severe ineffectiveness during implementation.[3] The Commission has thus put much effort into further defining and improving this aspect of its guidance.[4] In brief, the business must include all assets and personnel which contribute to its current operation or which is necessary to ensure its viability and competitiveness.[5] To this effect, the parties must provide a precise description of the business listing all relevant assets to be transferred.[6] If the parties' description at a later point appears incomplete and the parties fail to complement the business with the additional assets or personnel

[1] Remedies Notice, para 23.

[2] ibid, para 24.

[3] This was one of the main findings in the Remedies Study where the Commission found that

> one or more serious issues where identified in 79% of the 84 divestiture remedies. A high number of these issues remained unresolved during the implementation process (48 serious issues in 21 remedies) and led [...] to four remedies being 'ineffective' and 17 'partially effective'. Thus, all 'ineffective' and all 'partially' effective divestiture remedies suffered from problems related to the inadequate scope of the divested business (p 140).

See also Luebking (2007) 7.

[4] The new Remedies Notice contains significantly more detailed provisions on this aspect, see paras 25–31. These provisions are sufficiently clearly described in the notice and will therefore be confined to the present short overview.

[5] Remedies Notice, para 25.

[6] Remedies Notice, para 27. The Commission lists in detail all the elements that a description should contain. Shared personnel and assets, which contribute to the operation of the business or are essential to ensure its viability and competitiveness, must also be included, see further para 26. In addition, the parties must describe any ongoing supply arrangements, see para 27.

required, the Commission may consider revoking its conditional clearance decision.[7] The parties must also clearly indicate any relevant assets or personnel that, in their view, should not be transferred and the Commission will accept such exclusions only if they do not undermine the viability of the business.[8] These submission requirements aim at ensuring that the Commission is fully informed of the proposed scope of the business in order to undertake a viability assessment.

The business to be divested may take the form of a stand-alone entity, a carve-out, individual assets or certain licences.[9] The viability requirements apply to all divestiture types albeit under different conditions. As a general rule the business must be considered viable in its own right already at the design/assessment stage.[10] This means that, unless a fix-it-first remedy is proposed, resources of a possible or even presumed future purchaser cannot be taken into account at the time of assessment of the remedies. Only once the purchaser is proposed and assessed, can the Commission exclude any unnecessary or unwanted assets from the package and only if such omissions do not affect the viability of the respective assets.[11] Specifically in respect of carve-outs and/or individual assets the assets to be divested must be immediately viable in the hands of a suitable purchaser in order to reduce the risks for the viability and competitiveness to a minimum.[12]

Secondly, the viability will be ensured only if and when the business is transferred to a suitable purchaser in whose hands it becomes an active competitive force in the market.[13] While the scope of the business is vital for what kind of – and how many – potential purchasers it is likely to attract, the general requirements to suitable purchasers must be clarified already at the design stage in order for the Commission to be able to conclude with sufficient certainty that the transfer of the business may remove the identified competition concerns.

Thirdly, once the scope of the business and purchaser requirements have been defined, uncertainties may remain as to some aspects of the transfer of the business, which may risk undermining the viability. If this is the case, the Commission and the parties have a number of 'ancillary tools' at their disposal, depending on the circumstances in each case.[14] For example, the parties may include activities, which are related to markets where the Commission has not identified competition concerns in order to create an effective competitor in the affected markets. If concerns remain as to possible interim competitive harm, untimely sale and/or lack of potential purchasers, the parties may propose up-front buyer solutions, fix-it-first remedies or alternative proposals in the form of crown jewels, as appropriate. These measures shift the risk of implementation from the Commission to the parties in order to further ensure and enhance the viability of the business to be divested.[15]

[7] Remedies Notice, para 25, fn 4. Thus, the neglect stemming from an inadequate description of the business followed by the lack of transfer of the respective assets is considered a breach of an obligation in the Commission's clearance decision. The provision, which was introduced in 2008, shows that the Commission is adamant that it is the parties' responsibility to ensure that the scope of the divested business is as complete as possible.

[8] Remedies Notice, para 29. The burden of proof rests on the parties.

[9] Remedies Notice, paras 32–38.

[10] Remedies Notice, para 30. This provision is a tightening of past practice where eg within pharmaceuticals the Commission occasionally accepted at the design stage that the transfer of certain assets would be unnecessary as any potential purchaser would already possess them, see eg *J&J/Guidant* (M.3687 II 2005).

[11] Remedies Notice, para 31, and see further section 3.3. below.

[12] Remedies Notice, paras 36–37.

[13] Remedies Notice, para 47.

[14] See further section 3.4 below where these tools are examined in detail.

[15] Remedies Notice, paras 44–46 and 53–57; as well as the 2004 OECD Remedies Study, p 9.

**Commentary:** it is indisputable that the viability of the assets to be divested constitutes a key component to a successful remedy. However, as will be explained later there is a fine balance between ensuring viability and potentially over-fixing the competition concerns by for example adding and separating out such assets early in the proceedings before the resources and needs of potential purchasers are established. Also, as a new development in viability discussions, recent practice suggests that the Commission and the parties start to explore new ways of further ensuring the viability of the assets to be divested in markets or industries with few existing players and where the viability of potential new players prima facie seems difficult to secure.[16]

## 3.2 Types of Structural Remedies

### *3.2.1 Stand-alone Business*

The divestiture of stand-alone businesses is generally the most straightforward and low- risk remedy.[17] The Commission has a strong preference for an *existing* stand-alone business, which may take the form of (i) a pre-existing company or group of companies; or (ii) a business division which was not previously legally incorporated as such.[18]

The first option is sometimes referred to as a 'full divestiture' and typically takes the form of the sale of a controlling stake in a company,[19] or of a wholly owned subsidiary.[20] As the viability already exists (the entity has already demonstrated its ability to compete in the relevant market) the transaction mainly consists of the transfer of ownership.[21] While the divestiture of a subsidiary belonging to one of the parties is legally very straight-forward, the main obstacle in the implementation of divestitures of controlling stakes is the possible existence of pre-emption rights of the other shareholders or other shareholder provisions in the respective company as they, in worst case scenarios, could hamper the divestiture process and cause delays in the implementation which could ultimately affect the effectiveness of the remedy.[22]

[16] Such new measures could eg take the form of additional financial support such as up-front cash injections, see *Ryanair/Aer Lingus III* (M.6663 II 2013) where, although the transaction was prohibited, the Commission noted that the proposed cash injection in the new company that Ryanair tried to create for the purposes of the remedies had been considered an important element in the remedies discussions, see Commission MEMO/13/144 of 27 February 2013 (public decision not yet available at the time of writing). According to Ryanair the proposed up-front cash injection would have amounted to EUR 100 million, see Ryanair's press release of 27 February 2013, available at www.ryanair.com/en/news/ryanair-will-appeal-eu-decision-decision-to-prohibit-its-offer-for-aer-lingus. To the best of my knowledge, such a substantial cash injection has not been proposed in previous cases.

[17] A stand-alone business is defined in para 32 of the Remedies Notice. Contrary to the old Remedies Notice, the Commission is now very clear that the divestiture of a stand-alone business should be the first choice of remedy and that other types of divestitures are only to be considered as alternatives if the sale of a stand-alone business cannot be accomplished (to this effect, see also para 35).

[18] Remedies Notice, para 33.

[19] See eg *RWE/Essent* (M.5467 I 2009) para 449, (Essent's 51% stake in swb AG) paras 449–52.

[20] See eg *La Poste/Swiss Post/JV* (M.6503 I 2012) (public decision not yet available); *Bilfinger Berger/MCE* (M.5664 I 2009) para 54 (MCE Energietechnik); *Nestlé/Novartis (Medical nutrition business)* (M.4540 I 2007) para 113 (in respect of competition concerns on the French market: transfer of shares in the stand-alone NMN healthcare nutrition business, Novartis Nutrition S.A.); *TUI/First Choice* (M.4600 I 2007); and *Siemens/VA Tech* (M.3653 II 2005) para 490 (VA Tech Hydro GmbH & Co).

[21] It is noteworthy that although being the most favoured remedy by the Commission, stand-alone divestitures were ranked in the Remedies Study as being only the third most common remedy (accounting for 15% of all remedies from 1996–2000), see p 13 (Chart 3).

[22] Hence the Commission will usually carefully evaluate the possible impact of pre-emption rights on the effectiveness of the respective remedy, see eg *RWE/Essent* (M.5467 I 2009) para 463.

The second option is also to be considered a pre-existing stand-alone business in the form of a business division although it may involve some separation from the parties' remaining businesses.[23] In past cases the stand-alone nature of such businesses has been put into question if they were previously dependent on support or input from other companies within the group.[24] Thus, in order for the remedy to be successful the severance of relations with the merging parties must not only be relatively easy to execute, but past support and/or input may also have to be maintained and/or reinstated.[25]

Where a competition concern results from a horizontal overlap, the parties may, in principle, choose to divest a stand-alone business belonging to either the acquirer or the target company (or one of the parties in the case of a merger). In its guidance the Commission remains neutral as to whether it prefers the business of the acquirer or the target to be divested.[26] This approach is in line with the Commission's past practice suggesting that the viability of the business is more important than the pre-merger ownership. Thus, although it is stipulated that the parties 'may be able to choose between two businesses', the choice will often by determined by which business the Commission finds most viable.[27] In any event, statistics imply that divestitures involving the acquirer's businesses and the target's businesses, respectively, are fairly equally represented in the Commission's decisional practice.[28] Also, it is not uncommon that in cases where the Commission identifies competition concerns in several product markets, the parties divest one party's business in one product market and another party's business in another product market.[29] The same practice applies to competition concerns in different geographic markets.[30]

[23] See eg *Kraft Foods/Cadbury* (M.5644 I 2010) paras 171ff; *Amcor/Alcan* (M.5599 I 2009) paras 129ff; *Manitowoc/Enodis* (M.5180 I 2008) paras 172ff; *Johnson & Johnson/Guidant* (M.3687 II 2005) para 358; and *Unilever/Bestfoods* (M.1990 I 2000) para 176.

[24] In *TUI/First Choice* (M.4600 I 2007) the stand-alone nature of the business was put into question by some respondents in the course of the market test, alleging that the divested business (Budget Travel) would be dependent on financial support from the other Group companies but the Commission concluded that such dependency was not justified, see para 172.

[25] In *The Post Office/TPG/SPPL* (M.1915 II 2001) the Commission preferred the divestiture in the Netherlands of TNT's business over The Post Office, which enjoyed higher market shares but was almost entirely based on the infrastructure, the market position and the reputation of The Post Office in the United Kingdom and its Royal Mail brand, see paras 138–45.

[26] Remedies Notice, para 34. A preference for divestiture of the acquirer's assets is voiced only in respect of hostile takeovers. De Matteis (2001) implies that the Commission's remedies policy results in a preference for divestitures of the acquirer's business, see section 4.A.i. However, there are no clear indications in the Commission's decisional practice to this effect. In fact, in the Remedies Study the Commission found that in cases where divestitures required carve-out, serious implementation issues arose more frequently in cases where the business to be divested belonged to the acquirer rather than the target, see p 73. The Commission referred to the findings of the FTC Divestiture Study that divested businesses belonging to the target company may experience fewer problems during transfer as the committing parties do not already possess sensitive business information of the target and thus have few possibilities to alter or degrade the business during the interim period.

[27] In *Exxon/Mobil* (M.1383 II 1999) the Commission required the divestiture of Exxon's aviation lubricants business with its own R&D and blending facilities because it was considered more viable and stand-alone than Mobil's business, which the parties had previously offered to divest, see para 860.

[28] Remedies Study, pp 73–74 (points 2–7).

[29] In *Degussa/Laporte* (M.2277 I 2001) the parties divested of Degussa's persulfate business as well as Laporte's cationic reagents and hydroxy monomers business, see paras 50–54.

[30] In *Nestlé/Novartis (Medical Nutrition Business)* (M.4540 I 2007) the Commission identified competition concerns within the healthcare nutrition businesses in France and Spain. Nestlé divested Novartis' business in France and Nestlé's business in Spain, see para 113.

### 3.2.2 *Carve-outs*

As an alternative to the divestiture of an existing stand-alone business, the Commission accepts in certain cases the divestiture of businesses, which have existing strong links or are partially integrated with businesses retained by the parties and therefore need to be carved out.[31] Although the term 'carve-out' is relatively new in the Commission's remedies vocabulary,[32] the practice of separating certain assets from one or more of the parties' other businesses is well established.[33] Indeed, it could be argued that the sale of any business typically involves some elements of carve-out. However, when the Commission refers to carve-outs in its guidance it is generally understood as divestitures that involve a *considerable* separation of the assets from the parties' retained business, which may entail risks for the viability and competitiveness of the business.[34]

The new (tightened) policy issue in carve-out cases is that the Commission accepts carve-outs only if it can be certain that, at least at the time when the business is transferred to the purchaser, the assets constitute a viable business on a stand-alone basis.[35] It is therefore essential that the actual carve-out is initiated as soon as possible after the adoption of the clearance decision with the aim of minimising the risk of deterioration of the assets to be divested while they are in the hands of the parties.[36] During this phase it is also important to not only separate and allocate assets to be divested but also to duplicate any assets that have previously been shared.[37] If difficulties or uncertainties arise in respect of the timely separation and transfer of assets, the parties may propose an up-front buyer solution.[38] It should be noted that, following the publication of the new Remedies Notice, up-front buyer solutions have been used rarely in carve-out remedies.[39]

As another means of reducing the risks associated with carve-outs the Commission has introduced a so-called 'reverse carve-out' option for the parties according to which they may carve out those parts of an existing business, which are not divested.[40] It is difficult to evaluate the significance of this option as information on how a carve-out is technically undertaken may be considered a business secret. However, given that a reverse carve-out necessarily implies that a large proportion of assets is divested it could result in the scope of

[31] Remedies Notice, para 35. The Commission refers to the principle of proportionality and thus acknowledges that there may be situations where the nature or scope of the competition concerns or the markets involved justifies a less radical remedy than a stand-alone divestiture.

[32] The Commission used the term for the first time in its Remedies Study, see pp 73 and 173.

[33] An example of an earlier case is *Crown Cork & Seal/CarnaudMetalbox* (M.603 II 1995).

[34] In para 35 of the Remedies Notice the Commission refers to divestitures that have 'existing strong links or are partially integrated with businesses retained by the parties'. In the Remedies Study the Commission distinguishes between divestiture remedies that require extensive carve-out and those requiring limited carve-out and focuses its analysis on the former, see p 73 (point 2). Some very extensive carve-outs were carried out in *Fortis/ABN Amro Assets* (M.4844 I 2007) and *Bayer/Aventis Crop Science* (M.2547 II 2002).

[35] Remedies Notice, para 36. The provision on carve-outs is therefore rather challenging and risky for the Commission as it must project, before adopting a clearance decision, how the assets to be carved out will form and develop into a stand-alone business at the time of transfer to a purchaser.

[36] In this respect the powers of the monitoring trustees have been strengthened, see in particular para 119, second point, of the Remedies Notice.

[37] Remedies Notice, paras 113–15.

[38] Remedies Notice, para 36.

[39] See section 3.4.2 below.

[40] Remedies Notice, para 35. One of the first examples of extensive reverse carve-outs was *Lagardere/Natezis/VUP* (M.2978 II 2004) where the assets to be sold accounted for about 60–70% of the acquired assets, see paras 989 and 996 as well as Annex 1 of the decision.

such remedies being so extensive that it puts the realisation of the merger at risk.[41] Also a reverse carve-out may result in additional costs being placed on the prospective purchaser as he may have to uphold fixed costs for facilities from which the parties have removed the assets that they retain – ultimately this may limit the number of interested purchasers.[42] Thus, from the parties' point of view there may be some reservations about the use of reverse carve-outs and it is not surprising that, following the introduction of the new provision, this procedure has rarely been used.[43] Moreover, in past cases the Commission has rather surprisingly accepted that such a reverse carve-out procedure would be triggered only at the discretion of the divesting parties post-decision.[44]

Finally, it is worth noting that, despite the risks associated with carve-outs, in the past they have been – by far – the most frequently accepted remedy with the ratio of carve-outs to stand-alone divestitures being three to two.[45] Moreover, in past extensive carve-out cases nearly 60 per cent raised serious implementation concerns and nearly 20 per cent of these concerns remained unsolved.[46] It remains to be seen whether the Commission's tightening of the carve-out provisions in the new Remedies Notice will result in a higher success rate in such cases than the statistics revealed in the Remedies Study.

### *3.2.3 Selected Assets*

As an alternative to a divestiture of a viable stand-alone business, the Commission may occasionally accept the divestiture of individual assets or a combination of assets, which did not previously constitute a uniform and viable business.[47] Compared to carve-outs, these assets are far more limited in scope and since they do not constitute a viable business in their own right, they usually complement assets already in the prospective purchaser's

[41] In *Arjowiggins/M-Real Zanders Reflex* (M.4513 II 2008) there are indications in the Commission's decision that the assets to be divested (the carbonless paper business which constituted the main production at a mill to be acquired by Arjowiggins) would be transferred through a 'reverse carve-out', see in particular para 549. This merger was later abandoned due to alleged excessive remedies, see press release of 20 June 2009 from M-Real under investor relations, accessed in 2009 at www.m-real.com (link no longer available).

[42] This seems to have been the case in *Arjowiggins/M-Real Zanders Reflex* (M.4513 II 2008) where the Commission accepted in its assessment that it would probably be difficult to find a potential purchaser who could operate the divested assets as a viable business as it would need to sustain the plant-level fixed costs arising from the on-site power plant, logistics, warehousing and general facility operation after the removal of the other paper assets retained by Arjowiggins, see para 549.

[43] One of the few examples of recent reverse carve-out cases is *Vattenfall/Nuon* (M.5496 I 2009) where the parties had the option to carve-out a few retained assets (primarily customer contracts related to markets outside the 'serious doubts markets') prior to the sale of the business to be divested, Nuon Deutschland GmbH, see paras 64–66. The business was in March 2010 sold to the German operator, ENERVIE – Südwestfalen Energie und Wasser AG (formerly known as SEWAG) but no details were given as to the exact scope of the transferred business, see press release from Vattenfall of 19 March 2010 announcing the finalisation of the sale, accessed in 2010 at www.vattenfall.com (link no longer available).

[44] See *Vattenfall/Nuon* (M.5496 I 2009) para 64, and Remedies Text, paras 5 and 41.

[45] Remedies Study, p 73. For statistics in this respect, see also p 13 (showing that extensive carve-outs constitute 40% of analysed remedies from 1996–2000).

[46] Remedies Study, p 73. In these cases the (failed) remedies had: (i) required intervention by the Commission to mediate between the seller and the purchaser; (ii) created long-term dependence by the buyer on the seller; and (iii) reduced the competitiveness of the divested business.

[47] Remedies Notice, para 37. Examples of such divestitures could be the sale of production and/or distribution capacity, brands or intellectual property rights. A divestiture package where individual assets come from more than one party is often referred to as a 'mix-and-match' remedy. This term originates from US antitrust, see the FTC FAQ About Merger Consent Order Provisions, Questions 21–22, and *Nestlé/Dreyer* (File No 021017, Docket No C-4082). While the Commission used the term extensively in its Remedies Study (pp 18, 19, 37 and 138), it is not used in the Remedies Notice.

possession. The viability requirement should therefore be fulfilled at the point in time when the assets are in the hands of the approved purchaser and, to this effect, the Commission's competitive assessment focuses on how easily and quickly the assets will be integrated with those of the purchaser. Needless to say, this is a difficult and risky assessment, especially in cases where the identity of the purchaser is not known at the time of the adoption of the clearance decision.[48]

As the Commission has tightened its policy on viability, limited asset divestitures have been in decline in recent years although they still occur in particular circumstances.[49] They have been accepted primarily in cases where the overlapping activities are limited to easily identifiable assets, which appear unproblematic to separate from the parties' other activities and integrate into a purchaser's business with only minor adaptations.[50] Example of such assets would be the divestiture of: (i) a production machine, plant or capacity;[51] (ii) tangible assets essential to a particular sector, such as terminals, petrol stations or warehouses;[52] and (iii) brands.[53] While some of these assets may in themselves already be considered a viable business, it is more common that supplementary 'smaller' assets, customer contract, support or licences of intellectual property rights (IPRs) are added in order to ensure viability.[54] Furthermore, in order to enhance viability the Commission has occasionally allowed that a number of input supply agreements between the merged entity and the purchaser may be put in place at the option of the latter. However, such arrangements must be carefully assessed in order to prevent the establishment of any anticompetitive dependency between the parties.[55]

[48] It is therefore surprising that the Commission does not specifically mention the option of combining the provision in para 37 of the Remedies Notice with up-front solutions.

[49] The Commission's practice is in line with the FTC's reluctance to accept mix-and-match assets, see the FTC's FAQ About Merger Consent Order Provisions, Questions 21–22; and the FTC Guidelines for Negotiating Merger Remedies, pp 6–7 (it is emphasised that mix-and-match solutions tend to slow the negotiations down, requiring a more fact-specific, detailed and time-consuming evaluation of each asset).

[50] With respect to 'mix-and-match' assets the Commission found in its Remedies Study that 9% of the analysed remedies constituted such remedies, see p 19 (Chart 6).

[51] See *Kinnevik/Billerud/Korsnäs* (M.6682 I 2012) (public decision not yet available); *Yara/Kemira Growhow* (M.4730 I 2007) para 138; *Industri Kapital/Perstorp (II)* (M.2396 I 2001) para 84; *Alcan/Alusuisse* (M.1663 II 2000) para 140; *Alcoa/Reynolds* (M.1693 II 2000) para 137; *Shell/BASF (Project Nicole)* (M.1751 I 2000) para 55; *Usinor/Cockerill* (M.1329 I 1999) para 46; and *Repola/Kymmene*, (M.646 I 1995) para 65.

[52] See *Posten AB/Post Danmark A/S* (M.5152 I 2009) para 186 (postal terminals); and *TotalFina/Elf* (2000) para 334 (petrol stations).

[53] The Commission stresses that brand divestitures are acceptable only in exceptional circumstances. One of the largest brand portfolio divestitures was undertaken in *Unilever/Bestfoods* (M.1990 I 2000). Generally brand divestitures have been prominent in fast-moving consumer goods (FMCGs) and more recently also in a particular retail channel, namely home-shopping, see *Otto/Primondo Assets* (M.5721 I 2010) para 100. For other brand divestitures, see eg *Reckitt Benckiser/SSL* (M.5953 I 2010), *Masterfoods/Royal Canin* (M.2544 I 2002), and *Unilever/Amora-Maille* (M.1802 I 2000). Brand divestitures as 'core remedies' were particularly prominent in the late 1990s and early 2000s. However, in line with the tightened policy on scope of remedies as well as voiced criticism that it was unrealistic and disproportionate for the Commission to insist on splitting up worldwide brands (see eg Speech by Collins (2002)) the Commission became more reluctant to accept brand divestitures as core remedies without additional supporting assets, see eg *SCA/Georgia-Pacific Europe* (M.6455 I 2012) where brand divestitures were coupled with the divestiture of significant production facilities (for the UK and Irish markets), see para 310. To this effect, *Unilever/Sara Lee Body Care* (M.5658 II 2010) was also a large brand portfolio, which was divested but all supporting assets were included in the transfer, see para 1415.

[54] eg in *Posten AB/Post Danmark A/S* (M.5152 I 2009) the parties added IT production systems and IT support in order to make the assets fully operational, see para 187; and in *Alcan/Alusuisse* (M.1663 II 2000) customer contracts were added in order to enhance the commercial viability of the transferred assets (machines), see para 142.

[55] See eg *Kinnevik/Billerud/Korsnäs* (M.6682 I 2012) (public decision not yet available) where the purchaser could opt for a number of input supply agreements. These arrangements seem prima facie slightly risky as the divested assets in question (a paper machine with related assets and personnel) would continue to be operated by the purchaser at the premises of the merged entity, see Speech by Italianer (2012).

In order to further minimise the risks associated with the divestiture of limited assets the Commission may also require the prospective purchaser to possess additional resources or qualifications to ensure a smooth integration of the assets.[56] Moreover, in cases where it is not evident that the remedies may attract many potential purchasers, the Commission may insist on adding further assets to enhance the attractiveness of the remedies package,[57] or require an up-front solution to ensure certainty.[58]

### *3.2.4 Licence Arrangements*

#### 3.2.4.1 Technology

As an alternative to asset divestitures, the granting of licences to technology or to IPRs is the single most important stand-alone remedy.[59] The Commission's basic approach is that, while licences may be considered if a divestiture of a business is not feasible, they must enable the licensee to compete effectively with the parties in a similar way as if a divestiture had taken place.[60] More specifically, licences may be accepted where: (i) a divestiture would impede efficient, on-going research;[61] or (ii) a divestiture would be impossible due to the nature of the business and/or sector.[62] In addition, decisional practice shows that licences are often accepted in cases where: (iii) the Commission's competition concerns are confined to some markets in individual Member States; (iv) the main assets needed to remedy the competition concerns are IPRs; (v) the respective IPRs are essential to the parties' retained businesses elsewhere in the EU or even worldwide; and (vi) the concentration raises no significant competition concerns elsewhere.[63] Generally, such licences are pronounced in sectors like pharmaceuticals, medical devices, agrochemicals, telecommunication, media and consumer products sectors.[64]

There are obvious implementation risks and uncertainties associated with licence arrangements as they will not enable the licensee to compete immediately in the market and they require an on-going relationship with the parties, which may allow the licensor to influence the licensee in its competitive behaviour and may also give rise to disputes

[56] See *Masterfoods/Royal Canin* (M.2544 I 2002) para 102 (proven expertise in the branded pet food market) and section 3.3.3 below.

[57] In *Rexam/American National Can* (M.1939 I 2000) the Commission ensured that sufficient capacity reserves were added to the three beverage can manufacturing plants with the aim of providing the purchaser with critical mass to compete on the market and recoup investments, see para 35.

[58] See section 3.4.2 below.

[59] While patent, know-how and design rights are particularly prominent in manufacturing, trademarks and copyrights are central to retailing and services, see Remedies Study, page 116. One of the most comprehensive 'core' licence remedies in newer practice was accepted in the highly complicated *BASF/Ciba* (M.5355 I 2009) in relation to competition concerns raised in UV filters for skin care products, see paras 229–33.

[60] The conditions for accepting licensing arrangements are listed in para 38 of the Remedies Notice. Such licences are sometimes referred to as quasi-structural remedies due to their competitive impact being similar to those of divestitures under certain conditions.

[61] In *DSM/Roche Vitamins* (M.2972 II 2003) the parties agreed to transfer and license all feed enzymes technology and IPRs, see para 82; and in *Glaxo/Wellcome* (M.555 I 1995) the licence concerned one of two compounds in phase III clinical trials, see para 29.

[62] In *Universal Music Group/BMG Music Publishing* (M.4404 II 2007) the rights to certain American repertoire music catalogues covering the EU were licensed rather than divested in order for the parties to retain the worldwide rights to the catalogues outside the EU which was considered proportionate to the EU-wide competition concerns, see paras 465–66. See also *Metso/Aker Kvaerner* (M.4187 II 2006) para 172; *Apollo/Bakelite* (M.3593 I 2005) para 160; and *Alcatel/Finmeccanica/Alcatel Alenia Space & Telespazio* (M.3680 I 2005) para 120.

[63] See De Souza and Brockhoff in Drauz and Jones (2012) para 7.241.

[64] ibid, para 7.243.

between the parties to the licence agreement over the scope, terms and conditions.[65] Therefore, the Commission is adamant that in cases where uncertainties exist as regards the scope of the licence or its terms and conditions, the parties must divest the underlying IPRs but may then obtain a licence back.[66] Furthermore, if it is questionable whether the licence will in fact be granted to a suitable licensee, the parties may propose a so-called 'up-front licensee' or fix-it-first solution in order to enhance certainty as to the foreseen implementation.[67]

The Commission usually prefers that licences are exclusive and without any field-of-use or geographical restrictions on the licensee.[68] Exclusive licences are typically designed to transfer a market position to a competitor, at least for a given period of time and/or in a given territory, and are thus particularly suitable when remedying competition concerns arising from horizontal overlaps and seeking to restore pre-merger structures.[69] Where a licence is exclusive and its duration irrevocable, it can have the same competitive effect as an assignment of the underlying IPRs.[70] Exclusivity is considered crucial to (i) stimulate investment in such innovation; (ii) avoid devaluation of the asset post-merger when compared to its value to the parties' pre-merger, (ii) prevent the emergence of incentives to collude with the parties; and (iv) guard against dampening the incentives to compete with others.[71]

Nonetheless, the Commission does occasionally accept non-exclusive and/or restricted field of use licences with the purpose of allowing as many entrants as possible into the market.[72] These 'softened' licences are typically used to remedy vertical or conglomerate foreclosure effects and in cases where no restrictions on field of use would be disproportionate.[73] They come with a variety of different clauses depending on the individual circumstances of each case and it is thus difficult to generalise about their nature, scope and impact for the purposes of the general descriptions in this book. However, in the context of key technology or IPRs being essential inputs for activities in downstream markets, it should be highlighted

[65] Remedies Notice, para 38.

[66] ibid.

[67] This has rarely happened although there have been cases where an up-front solution would have seemed obvious as eg in *Danone/Numico* (M.4842 I 2007) where the Commission itself admitted that 'the details of the licensing agreements between Danone and the acquirer [. . .] would be critical', see para 91.

[68] Remedies Notice, para 38. During the public consultation in 2007 of the draft new Remedies Notice respondents voiced concerns that these requirements were disproportionate and unjustified, see eg reply by Freshfield Bruckhaus Deringer (paras 5.5 and 5.6) but the Commission disregarded such comments. For an example of exclusive licences, see *Glaxo Wellcome/Smithkline Beecham* (M.1846 I 2000) paras 218–20. However, in recent years the Commission has also accepted 'sole licences' whereby the licensee obtains a proprietary right to exploit the product alongside the merging parties without the latter being able to grant any further licences or sub-licences, see *BASF/Ciba* (M.5355 I 2009) para 233, fn 57.

[69] As submitted by commentators the Commission's approach is based on the assumption that pre-merger the owner of the asset was not subject to any field of use restrictions and hence its successor post-merger should have the same freedom in order to replicate the parties' incentives regarding not only the static exploitation of the asset at the time of the Commission's conditional clearance decision but also its dynamic development through future innovation, which would have been open to the parties pre-merger, see De Souza and Brockhoff in Drauz and Jones (2012) para 7.250.

[70] Remedies Study, p 117 (point 11).

[71] De Souza and Brockhoff in Drauz and Jones (2012) para 7.250.

[72] In *Metso/Aker Kvaerner* (M.4187 II 2006) the Commission carefully assessed the impact of exclusive versus non-exclusive licences and opted for the latter in order to avoid the emergence of a de facto monopoly in the respective market, see para 174. See also *Hoffmann La Roche/Boehringer Mannheim* (M.950 II 1998) para 148; and *Ciba-Geigy/Sandoz* (M.737 II 1996) para 275.

[73] In the past the Commission has occasionally used non-exclusive licence agreements to remedy horizontal concerns but by and large they proved inefficient, see Remedies Study, page 119 (point 17).

that remedies to grant competitors licences on a broad and non-exclusive basis have proven useful in sectors where market players commonly cooperate by licensing patents to each other.[74]

Whether licences are irrevocable exclusive or open non-exclusive, the costs of licences have proven the single most essential element affecting the effectiveness of licensing remedies as onerous financial terms can discourage, or hinder access, thereby deterring market entry and not achieving the purpose of the remedy.[75] Furthermore, certain payment schemes may convey commercially sensitive information to the licensor or contain in-built disincentives for licensees to compete.[76] In determining how to address the pricing issue, the Commission is faced with a dilemma as pre-determined prices may pose problems in attracting new licensees later in the enforcement period (as the date for the expiration of the patent draws closer) whereas more general framework provisions allowing subsequent price setting in accordance with going market rates or fair market values may give rise to disputes between the parties during the implementation.[77]

Therefore, in newer decisional practice licensing remedies often include appropriate dispute resolution mechanisms, allowing the parties to resort to a speedy, independent expert determination in the event of implementation disagreements.[78] Such mechanisms can take the form of arbitration proceedings together with trustees or involving national regulatory authorities.[79] It is the parties' responsibility to propose the most qualified experts for such tasks, as the Commission is not in a position to delegate monitoring powers to any experts without itself modifying the remedies.[80] In these cases the Commission will generally intervene only if/when the parties do not comply with the solutions found by the dispute resolution mechanisms,[81] but in order to accept such enforcement frameworks in the first place the Commission must be reassured that the monitoring devices really do ensure an effective and timely implementation.[82]

#### 3.2.4.2 Re-branding

While technology and IPRs licences are important in the Commission's decisional practice, the remainder of this section is devoted to the so-called 're-branding remedies' whereby the parties grant an exclusive, time-limited licence for a given brand with the purpose of

[74] Remedies Notice, para 65, referring to *Axalto/Gemplus* (M.3998 I 2006). See also eg *Intel/McAfee* (M.5984 I 2011) paras 307, 315–16 and 337–40, and Remedies Text, para 4(b).

[75] Remedies Study, p 118 (point 15).

[76] ibid.

[77] Alternatively, some remedies may rely on royalty-free licences, see Remedies Notice, para 65, and eg *Intel/McAfee* (M.5984 I 2011) para 298, and Remedies Text, para 4(b).

[78] The Commission formally introduced the concept of dispute resolution mechanisms in the Remedies Notice in 2008 (para 66) in response to calls for increased monitoring in this respect, see Remedies Study, p 118 (point 15). As a recent example of such mechanism, including a fast-track dispute settlement procedure and arbitration, see *ARM/Giesecke & Devrient/Gemalto/JV* (M.6564 I 2012) para 213; and *Intel/McAfee* (M.5984 I 2011) para 302.

[79] Remedies Notice, para 66. Needless to say, arbitration provisions are not limited to price aspects of the remedies but can also be used to resolve any other issues where a successful implementation depends on potential market fluctuations, which are largely unpredictable at the time of the adoption of the Commission's conditional clearance decision. For a detailed description of arbitration clauses in the context of EU Merger Remedies, see in particular Blanke in Blanke and Landolt (2011) ch 46; and Blanke (2006b).

[80] *EDP v Commission* (T-87/05 2005) para 105.

[81] An exception to this rule is *Intel/McAfee* (M.5984 I 2011) where the respondents in the market test requested that the Commission should explicitly be granted the possibility of getting involved in the arbitration procedure, see paras 326 and 346.

[82] Remedies Notice, para 66.

allowing the licensee to re-brand the product within a certain period foreseen.[83] The purpose of re-branding remedies is to allow the licensee to capture the licensor's market share and maintain it through the transfer of the customers from the licensed brand to its own brand in order to create a viable competitor, without the licensed brand being permanently divested. Contrary to the above-described technology licences, the duration of re-branding licences is limited to what is strictly necessary in order to facility the re-branding, taking into account the life cycle of the respective product. Re-branding remedies thus require considerable effort and investment on behalf of the licensee within a relatively short space of time in order for him to migrate from the licensed brand to the replacement brand. Accordingly, a typical re-branding remedy consists of two phases: (i) an exclusive licence period with the purpose of allowing the licensee to re-brand the product;[84] and (ii) a black-out period where the parties abstain from using the given brand.[85]

It is worth stressing that, given the inherent risks in a re-branding process,[86] such remedies are generally confined to exceptional circumstances where a divestiture of a brand would be disproportionate.[87] [88] Re-branding remedies have been endorsed by the EU Court as an adequate means of remedying competition concerns in markets where trademarks are the most relevant competitive factor between producers,[89] and they have proven particularly useful in retail cases where brands – in which the brand owner has invested substantially for years in order to make it a successful and recognisable brand with consumers – are used across the EU and potentially worldwide but where the respective competition concerns may be confined to a few national markets.[90] In such cases the Commission may thus accept re-branding provisions if: (i) the brand at stake is widely used; and (ii) a high proportion of its turnover is generated in markets outside those in which competition problems have been identified.[91]

[83] Remedies Notice, paras 39–42. For re-branding cases, see eg *SCA/Georgia-Pacific Europe* (M.6455 I 2012) (relating to the Netherlands) paras 283–97; *Nestlé/Novartis (Medical Nutrition Business)* (M.4540 I 2007) para 113; *Akzo Nobel/ICI* (M.4779 I 2007) para 34 (relating to the UK/Ireland); *Danone/Numico* (M.4842 I 2007) paras 86–89; *Masterfoods/Royal Canin* (M.2544 I 2002) para 89; *Nestlé/Ralston Purina* (M.2337 I 2001) para 62; and *SEB/Moulinex* (M.2621 I 2002) para 129, appealed in *Babyliss v Commission* (T-114/02 2003).

[84] This period may sometimes be extended by another period, at the request of the purchaser, see eg *SCA/Georgia-Pacific Europe* (M.6455 I 2012) para 283.

[85] Remedies Notice, para 39.

[86] The Commission found in the Remedies Study that out of nine re-branding remedies, five experienced problems, three of which remained unresolved and led to insufficient viability, see pp 31–33 (points 18–23).

[87] In *Babyliss v Commission* (T-114/02 2003) the General Court confirmed that a divestiture of the respective brands would have amounted in substance to partially prohibiting the concentration, which would have been contrary to the principle of proportionality if brand licences were likely to solve the identified competition concerns, see para 173.

[88] For examples of recent brand divestitures, see *SCA/Georgia-Pacific Europe* (M.6455 I 2012) (relating to UK and Ireland); *Unilever/Sara Lee Body Care* (M.5658 II 2010); *Reckitt Benckiser/SSL* (M.5953 I 2010); *BAT/Skandinavisk Tobakskompagni* (M.5086 I 2008); *Pernod Ricard/V&S* (M.5114 I 2008); and *Kraft/Danone Biscuits* (M.4824 I 2007).

[89] In *Babyliss v Commission* (T-114/02 2003) the applicant submitted that a measure involving a trade mark licence unaccompanied by other remedies is not by nature capable of remedying the competition concerns, see paras 186–89. The General Court dismissed this plea inter alia by highlighting that trademarks are the most important competitive factor in the market of small electrical household appliances and that many producers have chosen to outsource all or part of their production and to retain only the brands, sales forces and marketing teams and therefore brand licence remedies are adequate in such situations, see paras 192–95.

[90] In retail cases the geographic market is often defined as national, see eg *Nestlé/Novartis (Medical Nutrition Business)* (M.4540 I 2007) para 54; and *Nestlé/Ralston Purina* (M.2337 I 2001) para 31.

[91] Remedies Notice, para 40. Regarding the latter condition, see eg *SCA/Georgia-Pacific Europe* (M.6455 I 2012) where 90–100% of the turnover of the brand at stake was generated outside the Dutch market in which competition concerns had been identified, see para 290.

Furthermore, as the success of re-branding remedies is substantially linked to the viability of the licensed brand, a number of other conditions must be met for the acceptance of such remedies:[92] (iii) the brand to be transferred must be well known and one of considerable strength to guarantee both immediate viability of the licensed brand and its economic survival in the re-branding period;[93] (iv) part of the assets related to the production or the distribution of the products marketed under the licensed brand or the transfer of know-how may be necessary to ensure the viability of the remedy; (v) the licence must be exclusive and normally comprehensive, meaning not limited to a certain range of products within a specific market, and has to include the IPRs to ensure that customers will acknowledge the familiarity of the re-branded products (and therefore the parties are not allowed to use similar words or signs as this could undermine the effect of the re-branding exercise);[94] and (vi) both the licence and the black-out period must be sufficiently long, taking into account the particularities of the case, so that the re-branding remedy is in its effects similar to a divestiture.

Two of the above conditions deserve elaboration. First, with respect to the scope of the remedy the Commission has on a number of occasions required that the exclusive brand licence should be broadened to product markets where the Commission raised no competition concerns in order to ensure viability.[95] One of the advantages of broadening the scope is furthermore the avoidance of potential disputes arising between the licensee and the licensor if the latter continues to use the brand for other products.[96] With respect to the geographic scope the Commission has usually accepted that the brand licence would be confined to the geographic market in which the Commission has raised competition concerns.[97] The geographic limitation would be in keeping with the very reason for accepting brand licences (instead of divestitures) as the brands are usually important to the merging parties in many non-problematic geographic markets.[98] However, experience has also

[92] Remedies Notice, para 41.

[93] See eg *Nestlé/Novartis (Medical Nutrition Business)* (M.4540 I 2007) para 127. However, the Commission found in the Remedies Study that the strength of a brand can also backfire in a re-branding case in the sense that the stronger the brand is, the higher the inherent risk is to the effectiveness, see p 31 (point 19). Thus the licensee may find it difficult to convince consumers to shift their loyalty to a replacement brand, if the licensed brand has a history of being particularly strong.

[94] Commentators have suggested that re-branding remedies should contain a prohibition on the introduction or maintenance of confusingly similar brands by the licensor, see De Souza and Brockhoff in Drauz and Jones (2012) para 7.262. However, as the authors correctly point out the problem with such prohibitions is that the Commission is not well placed to decide with regard to their breach since an enquiry into what may be 'confusingly similar' is more of a matter for expert trade mark law and practice to be decided bearing in mind what might be 'generically customary' in a particular sector in a Member State.

[95] In *SEB/Moulinex* (M.2621 I 2002) the exclusive brand licence extended to all small electrical household products as the Commission argued that, if the licences had covered only a limited number of products, the licensee would have seen its room for manoeuvre to effect re-branding severely reduced since the brand Moulinex would have been used by two competing entities in the countries concerned (para 141). See also *Nestlé/Ralston Purina* (M.2337 I 2001) where the scope of the brand licences encompassed the whole Friskies product portfolio (Remedies Text, para 2).

[96] To this effect, see *Danone/Numico* (M.4842 I 2007) where the Commission pointed to potential disputes of such kind (para 91, fn 23).

[97] In *Nestlé/Novartis (Medical Nutrition Business)* (M.4540 I 2007) the licences were confined to national markets in France and Spain, see para 113; and in *Nestlé/Ralston Purina* (M.2337 I 2001) the licences were confined to national markets in Spain, Greece and Italy, see paras 61–65.

[98] On rare occasions the Commission has allowed one brand to be substituted with another in the remedies package if the swap did not undermine the viability of the assets, see *Nestlé/Novartis (Medical Nutrition Business)* (M.4540 I 2007) where Nestlé was allowed to substitute Novartis' 'Impact' brand with its own 'Crucial' brand in respect of the French market, see para 118. While the Commission failed to provide reasons for the swap other than referred to 'very specific circumstances' (paras 119 and 125), one may speculate that 'Impact' was of significant for Nestlé in related markets.

shown that brand splitting across geographic areas may create problems for the licensee as well as the licensor.[99] To this effect, the Commission has occasionally extended the geographic scope to geographic markets, which are closely related to the problematic market and where market players' sales organisations would typically cover several countries.[100]

Secondly, the duration of the licence and the corresponding black-out period is particularly important for the success of the remedy in order to allow the licensee sufficient time and opportunity to re-brand and establish or strengthen its own brand on the relevant market. Given the individual characteristics of products and consumer behaviour the Commission is generally reluctant to indicate acceptable framework periods. However, when observing decisional practice it seems appropriate to distinguish between the following types of branded products in order to predict the duration of the licences and of the black-out periods: consumer durables and FMCGs. With respect to consumer durables an exclusive licence period would normally run for *at least* one life cycle of the product and thereafter the licensor would be banned from re-entering the market for a period equivalent to one life cycle of the product.[101] This would give the licensee protection and time to migrate from the licensed brands and to its own brands.[102] With respect to FMCGs an acceptable licence period generally varies between 3 and 5 years, followed by a similar blackout period.[103] In these cases the Commission looks at how much the licensee would have to invest in education and marketing efforts in order to succeed with the re-branding.[104]

Finally, the identity of the potential licensee is a key factor for the success of a re-branding remedy. Similarly to divestitures, if there is uncertainty as to the number of suitable prospective licensees, being able and having strong incentives to carry out the re-branding

[99] See Remedies Study, pp 31–33.

[100] See *SCA/Georgia-Pacific Europe* (M.6455 I 2012) where respondents to the market test of the remedies submitted that, due to the relatively limited size of the Dutch market (where competition concerns were identified) the re-branding remedy should be extended to Luxembourg and Belgium as their sales organisations would typically cover the entire region (para 294).

[101] In *SEB/Moulinex* (M.2621 I 2002) the Commission estimated the average lifetime of small electrical household products to be approximately 3 years and therefore a licence period of 5 years and a black-out period of 3 years were accepted while previously in the proceedings the Commission had dismissed proposals for the respective time periods being 3 years and 1 year, see paras 135 and 140. Upon appeal in *Babyliss v Commission* (T-114/02 2003) the General Court confirmed these time periods as appropriate and stressed that the duration of the remedies covered a period equal to about three product life cycles, whilst the duration of the non-entry period was equivalent to at least one product life cycle, see para 216. By contrast, in *Schneider/Legrand* (M.2283 II 2001) the Commission rejected a proposal to use trademarks for 3 years as the market test showed that a purchaser would need about 7 years to complete the proposed trademark substitution, the lifetime of low-voltage electrical appliances being very long. The Commission also found that a purchaser would have needed to be protected by re-entry prohibitions on the parties for a period of more than 10 years, see para 800.

[102] By way of example, Whirlpool successfully migrated from the Philips brand to the Whirlpool brand in 3 years from 1990 to 1993, which is the equivalent to one product life cycle, Dyson became market leader for vacuum cleaners in Britain in less than 5 years, and Colgate gained significant market shares in the French market for electric toothbrushes in 1 year. The General Court referred to these examples in *Babyliss v Commission* (T-114/02 2003) and they were not denied by the applicant, see para 217.

[103] In *Nestlé/Novartis (Medical Nutrition Business)* (M.4540 I 2007) involving healthcare nutrition products the licence period was 5 years, followed by a 5-year black-out period, see para 113; in *Danone/Numico* (M.4842 I 2007) involving baby food and baby milk products the licence period was 5 years, followed by a 5-year black-out period, see para 91; in *Masterfoods/Royal Canin* (M.2544 I 2002) involving pet food the licence period was 3 years, followed by a black-out period of approximately 7 years, see para 89; and in *Nestlé/Ralston Purina* (M.2337 I 2001) involving pet food products the licence period was 3 years, followed by a black-out period of 4 years and 9 months, see Remedies Text, paras 2 and 13.

[104] See in particular *Danone/Numico* (M.4842 I 2007) para 91.

exercise, the parties may propose an up-front or fix-it-first solution.[105] So far this has not been the case,[106] but occasionally the Commission has insisted on one single licensee for several brands in a given market,[107] or particular purchaser experience[108] in order to further enhance the chances of viability of the licensed brands. The fact that the respective geographic markets are normally national in scope in re-branding cases has usually resulted in the Commission insisting on only one licensee for each geographic market although it has also occurred that licences for several national markets have been 'grouped together' for one licensee.[109]

**Commentary:** to round up the above-description of the different types of asset divestitures, in the ideal world the merging parties would always divest a fully stand-alone and operative business but, as business realities have shown, such solutions are rare, as most transactions require some kind of carve-out, partial divestiture or even licensing arrangements. Understandably, substantial carve-outs require additional assurances and safeguards in order to minimise the inherent risks and uncertainties. The obvious measure would seem to be the inclusion of an up-front buyer provision in a carve-out remedy but, for unclear reasons, this has rarely been accepted since the publication of the new Remedies Notice. Given that carve-outs are by far the most frequently used remedy structure in divestiture cases as well as the fact that carve-outs accounted for the majority of cases raising serious implementation concerns in the Remedies Study, it is expected that the Commission continues to ensure that viability issues are fully addressed in these cases.

Licensing arrangements represent an enforcement area where the Commission compromises with its preferred option (divestitures) and instead facilitates some kind of quasi-structural solutions in the recognition of the fact that divestitures may not always be possible or feasible for various reasons. In doing so, the Commission takes due account of the principle of proportionality and generally it should be commended for showing flexibility in this respect. In particular, re-branding remedies illustrate a successful – albeit highly complicated – remedies policy area where the Commission relatively early on in its practice realised that evolving business realities required it to reconsider and change its policy despite obvious, additional implementation risks. However, the findings in the Remedies Study suggested that, at least in re-branding cases in the 1990s, more than half of the remedies encountered serious implementation flaws, which in the majority of the cases led to insufficient viability. Therefore, given the fairly high risks entailed in the migration of a product to a different brand or trademark, it is considered vital that the Commission soon undertakes an ex-post examination of more recent re-branding cases in order to verify whether its

[105] Remedies Notice, para 42. The Remedies Study points to a particular problem of sub-licensing in re-branding cases, see p 32 (point 19). In essence, the Commission has to be sure that the licensee is interested in developing the acquired business through re-branding and not instead sub-licensing this aspect of the remedy to another licensee.

[106] In some cases an up-front solution would have seemed obvious as eg in *Danone/Numico* (M.4842 I 2007) where the Commission itself admitted that 'the details of the licensing agreements between Danone and the acquirer [. . .] would be critical', see para 91.

[107] In *Danone/Numico* (M.4842 I 2007) the Commission rejected the parties' proposal to split two brands between two different purchasers as it claimed that a separation could strike a fatal blow for one of the brands (Milupa) as the acquirer of that brand would not achieve enough sales to retain the interests of retailers, see para 92.

[108] In *SCA/Georgia-Pacific Europe* (M.6455 I 2012) the Commission considered that a suitable purchaser should be already active in the tissue sector and have prior experience of re-branding or demonstrate sufficiently to the Commission that it would be able to undertake such an exercise successfully, see para 296.

[109] eg in *SEB/Moulinex* (M.2621 I 2002) the licences for 9 national markets could in principle be granted to 9 different licensees but were instead grouped in a way so the licences for 8 countries went to 1 licensee (Saeco) while the licence for another country, Greece, went to another licensee (Benrubi), see Commission press release IP/03/491 of 3 April 2003. On appeal in *Babyliss v Commission* (T-114/02 2003), the General Court confirmed that, in view of the national dimension of the relevant markets, the Commission was entitled to consider that one and the same brand may have been used by different operators in different Member States, see para 249.

enforcement track record has improved before considering such remedies a viable option in future cases.

### 3.2.5 *Severance of Links with Competitors*

#### 3.2.5.1 Introductory Remarks

Structural remedies may extend to the severance of links between the merging parties and their competitors in cases where the latter is prevented from competing freely with the merging parties as a result of the transaction in question. In its Remedies Notice the Commission lists three different types of remedies aimed at removing anti-competitive links with competitors:[110] (i) divestiture of a minority shareholding in a joint venture (with a major competitor) or in a competitor; (ii) waiving of rights linked to a minority stake in a competitor; and (iii) termination of certain agreements with a competitor.[111] For the purpose of the following description such remedies will be referred to as 'severance remedies'.

By way of introduction, severance remedies have occasionally been used as the second-best solution when it has proven impossible, or at least very difficult, to divest assets.[112] However, in sectors like banking, insurance and energy where minority shareholdings and interlocking directorships between competitors are customary business practices,[113] severance remedies often prove to be the most obvious and efficient measure solving competition concerns.[114] In other sectors severance remedies may not be the principal remedy but supplementary to another structural main remedy.[115]

From a commercial perspective, a minority shareholding in a competitor may be a purely passive investment that stems from the acquiring company's desire to invest in a familiar industry, to spread risk or it may be a result from developing ties between companies as part of strategic alliances. While there is no presumption of per se illegality of structural links between competitors, minority shareholdings and interlocking directorates may have negative implications on competition depending on the circumstances, either by

[110] Remedies Notice, para 58. The Commission used a similar classification in its Remedies Study, see p 121 (point 1).

[111] For articles on this issue, see in particular Paper by OFT/DotEcon (2010), Paper by the OECD (2009); Ezrachi and Gilo (2006) and Moavero Milanesi and Winterstein (2002). See also Speech by Rosch (2009).

[112] In *Konica/Minolta* (M.3091 I 2003) the Commission identified competition problems in the market for photometers. As Minolta's photometer business was a fully integrated division in Minolta, a divestiture of assets proved impossible or at least very difficult. Therefore, the Commission accepted instead a remedy for Konica to divest of its stake in Sekonic, a manufacturer of photometers, see para 53.

[113] In *BNP Paribas/Fortis* (M.5384 I 2008) the Commission acknowledged that BNP Paribas had a 6.1% stake in its closest competitor AXA who in turn held 5.9% of the shares in BNP Paribas and that the parties also had common participation in joint ventures and certain limited cooperation agreements but concluded that these links were not of such a nature as to reduce the level of competition in the respective market, see paras 131–32.

[114] For examples of severance remedies in banking and insurance cases, see *Nordbanken/Postgirot* (M.2567 I 2001); *Allianz/Dresdner* (M.2431 I 2001); *EDF/ENBW* (M.1853 II 2001); *VEBA/VIAG* (M.1673 II 2000); *Generali/INA* (M.1712 I 2000); *AXA/GRE* (M.1453 I 1999); *Allianz/AGF* (M.1082 I 1998) and *Bank Austria/Creditanstalt* (M.873 I 1997). However, it should be noted that in recent years banking and insurance cases have also involved the divestiture of assets, see eg *Vienna Insurance Group/EBV* (M.5075 I 2008); *BNP Paribas/Fortis* (M.5384 I 2008); *Fortis/ABN Amro Assets* (M.4844 I 2007); and *Talanx/Gerling* (M.4055 I 2006).

[115] See eg *Glencore/Xstrata* (M.6541 I 2012) involving mining; *Südzucker/ED&F MAN* (M.6286 II 2012) involving sugar; *Galp Energia/Exxonmibil Iberia* (M.5005 I 2008) involving oil and petroleum; *Yara/Kemira Growhow* (M.4730 I 2007) involving fertilisers; *Evraz/Highveld* (M.4494 I 2007) involving steel; *Exxon/Mobil* (M.1383 II 1999) involving oil and gas; and *Danish Crown/Vestjyske Slagterier* involving slaughterhouses (M.1313 II 1999). In the Remedies Study the vast majority of severance remedies analysed were supplementary rather than principal remedies, see p 121 (points 2 and 3).

reducing the individual incentives to compete (unilateral effects) or by facilitating collusion (coordinated effects).[116] Such behaviour in the form of reduced incentives to compete stems from a number of factors, being structural (market concentration, entry conditions, nature of products and so on) or transaction specific (the companies' costs and margins, market shares, size of the minority interest).[117]

The Commission has found that severance remedies are particularly relevant in situations where the Commission has concerns of co-ordinated effects among a few strong competitors and where the influence that competitors have over each other or the information they exchange enables them to better co-ordinate their market behaviour or to better penalise deviations.[118] However, it should be stressed that in the past severance remedies have been applied to unilateral as well as co-ordinated effects.

In terms of implementation, severance remedies are comparatively straightforward as the main measure is to divest of shares or eliminate the influence through board representation and/or information flow. Once the links have been severed, viability and competitiveness is generally ensured immediately, as the now-independent competitor or joint venture would already have existed on the market concerned. Thus, the Commission's main efforts and concerns relate to control issues rather than securing the viability of the business whose shares are being sold. The relative simplicity of such severance remedies is illustrated by the fact that the majority of these cases are settled in phase I.[119]

Finally, within the category of severance remedies the Commission is very clear in its guidance that the divestiture of stakes is by far the preferred solution whereas the waiving of rights are acceptable only in exceptional circumstances, provided the rights are waived comprehensively and in a permanent way, and the termination of certain agreements and/or withdrawal from the market as the only remedy will be acceptable only in very specific circumstances and sectors.[120] Given that the Commission's guiding provisions are short and general, the following description of main features of the three types of severance remedies is primarily based on the Commission's decisional practice throughout the years.[121]

### 3.2.5.2 Divestiture of Minority Shareholdings

The Commission stresses in its guidance that the relevant provisions concern *minority* shareholdings in joint ventures and competitors, respectively.[122] While the Commission provides no details in remedies contexts as to the definition of a minority shareholding, it

[116] See further Moavero Milanesi and Winterstein (2002) 15. The authors explain the Commission's main competition concerns by grouping them into the following three categories, based on a simplified example of X holding a significant share in competitor Y: (i) the parties may start to take each other's business interests into account so they change the way they maximise their profits and thereby compete less vigorously and adopt behaviour more conducive to joint profit maximisation (called 'non-aggression understanding'); (ii) if X also holds a significant share in another competitor Z, X's interests may also reduce competition between Y and Z; and (iii) interlocking directorships may act as a conduits for anti-competitive transfer of price and strategic information. For similar explanations, see the Commission's contribution to Paper by the OECD (2008) 183–84.

[117] See Paper by the OECD (2008) 9–10.

[118] See Remedies Study, p 121 (point 3).

[119] See the decisions examined in the following.

[120] Remedies Notice, paras 59–60.

[121] Regrettably, the Commission decided not to assess in detail the majority of severance remedies identified in the reference period of its Remedies Study, see p 121, fn 316. Thus, few considerations and findings can be found in the study on this issue.

[122] Remedies Notice, para 58.

is generally considered to be a stake where the associated voting rights do not confer control over the company in question or enable the shareholder to exercise decisive influence within the meaning of the Merger Regulation.[123] Thus, typically the minority shareholder has a financial interest in the performance of the company through the return that may be earned on the shares but the stake is insufficient for it to exercise decisive influence over the conduct of the company in question.[124] In addition, the minority shareholding may afford certain informational benefits to the shareholder.[125]

There are common features for the divestiture of minority stakes in competitors and joint ventures, respectively, which can be deducted from the Commission's decisional practice. The following aspects are primarily focused on stakes in competitors but any significant deviations with respect to joint ventures will be mentioned.

First, the parties may either divest of the whole stake or reduce its stake to a certain level that would ease the Commission's concerns.[126] Comparing the cases in the two scenarios, it is difficult to point out specific features (for example in terms of industries, public listing, size of the stake, market structure and nature of competition concerns) that justify a divestiture of the whole stake as opposed to a reduction. In virtually all observed cases the markets were concentrated, the holding was relatively significant (often a stake larger than 25%) and it was often held in the largest competitor post-merger. With respect to joint ventures, it appears that the merging parties are usually required to eliminate, rather than merely reduce, their stake in the given joint venture.[127]

[123] See Art 3(2) of the Merger Regulation as well as the Commission's Consolidated Jurisdictional Notice under Council Regulation (EC) No 139/2004 on the control of concentrations between undertakings [2008] OJ C95/1. The issue of control under the Merger Regulation is relevant in matters relating to: (i) jurisdiction (whether the acquisition of a minority shareholding constitutes a 'concentration' and whether the turnover of such a stake should be attributed to the merging parties); and (ii) competitive assessment. The current description of control is strictly limited to what is necessary in order to assess minority shareholdings in the context of merger remedies.

[124] However, in respect of stakes in joint ventures it should be noted that the stake of the merging parties often confers joint control with one or two other joint venture partners.

[125] See Paper by OFT/DotEcon (2010) where the authors correctly point out that the informational benefits may not be so significant a feature in the case of listed companies where much information is already disclosed to the market (p 17). However, as considered later for non-listed companies the access to additional information may be significant.

[126] Examples of divestitures of the whole minority stake: in *IPIC/MAN Ferrostaal* (M.5406 I 2009) the parties agreed to divest MAN Ferrostaal's 30% stake in a third-party supplier, see para 66 and Remedies Text, para 3; in *Siemens/VA Tech* (M.3653 II 2005) Siemens proposed to divest of its 28% stake in the closest competitor, SMS Demag, in response to concerns in the highly concentrated market of metal plant building, see para 491; in *Vivendi/Canal+/Seagram* (M.2050 I 2000) Vivendi agreed to divest its 25% minority stake in BSkyB, being a film supplier and a potential competitor to the merging parties, see para 75; and in *Carrefour/Promodes* (M.1684 I 2000) Carrefour undertook to sell its 42% stake in its retail/supermarket competitor Cora, see para 94. Examples of a reduction of the minority stake: in *Nordbanken/Postgirot* (M.2567 I 2001) Nordbanken agreed to reduce its pre-merger 27% stake in Bankgirot (a competing company to Postgirot) to 10%, see para 59. In *Allianz/Dresdner* (M.2431 I 2001) the parties committed to reduce its post-merger combined 32.3% stake (24.9% and 7.4% respectively) in the major competitor Münchener Rück/Ergo group to 20.5%, see para 45; and in *AXA/GRE* (M.1453 I 1999) GRE's 34.8% in the competitor Le Foyer was significantly reduced (the exact level being a business secret), see para 34.

[127] One exemption appears to be *GDF Suez/International Power* (M.5978 I 2011) where the Commission had required the merging parties to sell all shares (a 33.3% stake) in a joint venture called T-Power (see para 121) but it later emerged that the parties retained a part of its stake while the remaining part was sold to a Japanese energy company Itochu, compare press release from International Power, GDF Suez (18 May 2011), 'International Power Agrees Sale of T-Power in Belgium, available at www.iprplc-gdfsuez.com, with the Commission's subsequent approval of the new joint venture (ie the fulfilment of the remedy) in *Tokyo Gas/Siemens/Tessenderlo Chemie/International Power/GDF Suez/T-Power JV* (M.6422 I 2012). Thus, during the implementation of the remedy it seems that the Commission has allowed for the merged entity to retain a share of its stake in T-Power.

Conversely, in cases where the parties were allowed to retain a portion of their original stake, the Commission did not provide any reasoning as to why the entire stake should not be divested. The obvious argument of the parties would naturally be that the remaining stake is a purely passive financial investment where the parties' rights are strictly limited to what is allowed by statutory provisions (company law) in order to safeguard the financial value of the stake.[128] However, in such cases it must be fully ensured that the remaining stake is indeed only for financial purposes and cannot for example be used to obtain advantageous information on its competitor(s). It is therefore paramount that the parties withdraw from all privileges possibly connected to such a stake.[129]

Secondly, given that some of the share divestitures may take some time to implement,[130] it is customary that, pending implementation, the merging parties commit not to exercise any votes or only the number of votes that corresponds to the retained stake in case of share reductions.[131] To this effect, the Commission introduced in its Best Practice Remedy Guidelines a standard 'hold-separate' obligation, which applies inter alia to the divestiture of a stake in a company in cases where a strict separation of the corporate structure is considered necessary.[132] In such situations a monitoring trustee will usually be given certain tasks and responsibilities, including exercising the voting rights, replacing board members or directors, reporting particular events to the Commission, administering ring-fencing provisions and so forth.[133] However in some cases the Commission has allowed that the merging parties would simply not exercise their votes instead of transferring them to a trustee.[134] As such a 'freeze' of the votes could affect the balance of overall voting ratio in the competitor it must be assumed that the Commission would verify possible implications of such a changed balance with the competitor in question prior to its

[128] See *Nordbanken/Postgirot* (M.2567 I 2001) para 59.

[129] In *VEBA/VIAG* (M.1673 II 2000) one remedy concerned VEBA's divestiture of its minority stake (15.4% of the shares equalling 14.2% of the voting rights) in the German electricity company Hamburgische Elektrizitäts-Werke AG (HEW). The latter was jointly controlled by the Swedish company Vattenfall and the city of Hamburg. The aim of the remedy was to sever links between the merged entity and HEW. VEBA was allowed to keep an indirect minority stake in HEW, which it owned through a minority interest in the Swedish company Sydkraft. The Commission reasoned that the indirect stake would not give any entitlement to representation on the boards of HEW and therefore the stake would not afford any privileged access to information or any leverage over HEW, see para 241.

[130] While the deadlines for divestiture are usually considered a business secret, details have been given in a few cases, such as *Yara/Kemira Growhow* (M.4730 I 2007) where the parties committed to divest a stake in a joint venture within 6 months, see para 63; *Abbott/Guidant* (M.4150 I 2006) where Abbott committed to divest its minority stake in competitor Boston Scientific within 30 months, see para 98; and *Allianz/Dresdner* (M.2431 I 2001) where the share reduction should be completed by the end of 2003 (ie nearly 18 months after the adoption of the clearance decision), see para 45.

[131] In *Allianz/Dresdner* (M.2431 I 2001) the parties would, pending divestiture, not exercise more than 20.5% of their voting rights at the upcoming general meetings, see para 45; in *Nordbanken/Postgirot* (M.2567 I 2001) the parties ceased to exercise any rights it derived from its participating, except the rights recognised under Swedish company law connected to a 10% minority holding, see para 60.

[132] See the explanatory note to the Best Practice Remedy Guidelines, point 22, and in particular MTDC, para 8. To this effect, the parties shall grant the Monitoring Trustee a comprehensive and duly executed proxy attached to the Trustee Mandate, see MTTM, para 6(d).

[133] See eg *IPIC/MAN Ferrostaal AG* (M.5406 I 2009), Remedies Text, para 8; and *Siemens/VA Tech* (M.3653 II 2005) para 491, and further section 4.2.2 below. Occasionally, the Commission has accepted that, pending divestiture, the parties are allowed to keep one representative on the board, see eg *VEBA/VIAG* (M.1673 II 2000), Remedies Text, point I.3. In such cases the parties will then typically agree to ring-fence the activities of the director meaning that he will not be a party to commercially sensitive information on certain issues.

[134] See eg *Nordbanken/Postgirot* (M.2567 I 2001) where the remedies stipulate that the trustee shall monitor that Nordbanken refrains from exercising its voting rights, see Remedies Text, provision 2.3.

approval.[135] Similarly, during implementation the merging parties are usually excluded from accessing sensitive information about the competitor or the other joint venture partners and for example not being able to access shared central information technology networks.[136]

Thirdly, as the Commission's main objective is to sever the links between the merging parties and their competitor in question, the most important purchaser criterion in these cases is that the purchaser be independent of and unconnected to the merging parties.[137] Looking at past practice there appears to be no consistent policy as to whether the Commission prefers the minority holding to be sold to one or more purchasers.[138] However, it must be assumed that, before making the choice between the two alternatives, the Commission carefully assesses whether an en bloc sale or splitting up the shareholding has an impact on the composition of the overall shareholder-ratio and thus the control of the company in question.[139]

Finally, if the stake in the competitor in question is substantial and publicly listed, questions arise whether the shares should be sold en bloc directly to one or several purchasers or floated on the stock exchange. The way in which the stake is sold obviously affects the value of the shares and thus the financial strength of company that the Commission is trying to ensure and preserve as a viable competitor to the merging parties. Potential complications can be severe and are best illustrated by describing one of the longest-running bitter takeover battles in newer European corporate history in *Volvo/Scania*.[140] [141]

Prior to the transaction Volvo already owned a stake in Scania and following the Commission's prohibition of the transaction Volvo therefore remained a significant shareholder in Scania, much to the discontent of the latter.[142] During the administrative

[135] Throughout practice the Commission has become more careful to ensure that the parties cannot exercise any kind of influence in the interim period, see eg *Konika/Minolta* (M.3091 I 2003) where the parties within a few weeks after the Commission clearance decision withdrew from all board membership and waived all voting rights attached to also the remaining 9.82% stake (para 52). Earlier on that was not always the case, see eg *Volvo/Renault V.I.* (M.1980 I 2000) where Volvo was not excluded from retaining its voting rights and thus in principle exercised control for another 4 years post-decision.

[136] See eg *RCA/MAN Cargo* (M.5096 I 2008), Remedies Text, para 9; and *GDF Suez/International Power* (M.5978 I 2011) paras 129 and 132.

[137] See eg *Nordbanken/Postgirot* (M.2567 I 2001), Remedies Text, provision 2.1.III.b).

[138] In a number of cases the remedies have left both options open and thus left the decision to the parties as to whether the stake should be sold en bloc or to several purchaser, see eg *Carrefour/Promodes* (M.1684 I 2000) where Carrefour undertook to sell its 42% stake in its retail/supermarket competitor Cora to one *or* several purchasers (Remedies Text, para 1).

[139] Such considerations are particularly important in cases where the minority shareholding amounts to a de facto controlling stake as a divestiture of the shares inevitably will fundamentally change the ownership of the company in question.

[140] See *Volvo/Scania* (M.1672 II 2000) in which the Commission prohibited the transaction.

[141] On a different note, it remains to be seen whether the pending proceedings in another long-running hostile takeover, namely Ryanair's attempt to acquire Aer Lingus, may exceed the *Volvo/Scania* saga in duration and complication, see *Ryanair/Aer Lingus III* (M.6663 II 2013), *Ryanair/Aer Lingus II* (M.5434 I withdrawn in 2009), and *Ryanair/Aer Lingus* (M.4439 II 2007). As Ryanair has announced its intention to appeal the Commission's last prohibition of its attempts to acquire Aer Lingus in 2013, it is assumed that the last word has not yet been said in this case, see Ryanair's press release of 27 February 2013 announcing its intention to appeal, available at www.ryanair.com/en/news/ryanair-will-appeal-eu-decision (the appeal has not yet been registered with the General Court as of 1 May 2013).

[142] More specifically, Volvo retained a stake consisting of 45% of the capital and just over 30% of the votes, see details in *Volvo/Renault V.I.* (M.1980 I 2000) para 4. Scania was of the opinion that Volvo's stake conferred sole or joint control with the other large shareholder Investor AB over Scania and it therefore later appealed the Commission's refusal to order immediate divestiture of that shareholding, see *Scania v Commission* (T-163/03 withdrawn).

proceedings in Volvo's subsequent acquisition of Renault's trucks division, Volvo submitted its Scania stake as one of the remedies in order to obtain clearance.[143] The subsequent sale of Volvo's stake was prolonged for several years due to unfavourable share prices,[144] financial implications for Scania as well as Volvo shareholders, intense media coverage and lawsuits.[145]

In 2004 Volvo finally sold its B-shares (31.8% of the shares, 5.8% of the votes) close to break-even but still below the original buying price to Deutsche Bank AG.[146] However, as Volvo failed to find a purchaser for all A-shares (13.7% of the shares, 24.8% of the votes) within the allowed time period, it transferred the shares to a separate, independent and newly formed company 'Ainax' with the sole purpose of managing Volvo's interests in Scania and, within a year, distributing the shares to Volvo's shareholders as dividend. The main reason for this particular measure was to retain the shares en bloc and thereby avoiding dispersed flotation of the shares with the likely result of causing more turmoil for Scania's share prices.[147] This example goes to show the extra precautions that the parties and the Commission need to take when the companies involved are publicly listed.[148]

Specifically with respect to the divestiture of a minority stake in a joint venture, the Commission's main competition concerns relate to the impact that such cooperation may have on the competitive behaviour between the merging parties on the one hand and their joint venture partners being major competitors to the merging parties on the other hand.[149] As already mentioned, while most of the above considerations relating to the divestiture of

[143] See *Volvo/Renault V.I.* (M.1980 I 2000) paras 29 and 44.

[144] A possible extension of the allowed time for the sale was linked to the risk of a negative share price, see *Volvo/Renault V.I.* (M.1980 I 2000), Annex A. Furthermore, as the sale had entered the 'second divestiture period' the shares had to be sold at no minimum price, see the Commission's Open letter to Volvo, dated 7 April 2004, which was the published on the DG Competition's website (link no longer available).

[145] In addition to the appeal mentioned above, Scania launched a second appeal relating to Volvo's implementation of its remedy, see below.

[146] See Nicholas George, 'Volvo Sells Scania Stake for SKr 15bn' *Financial Times* (5 March 2004). The sale had not been without drama as Deutsche Bank's attempt to conduct the Nordic region's largest-ever placement had been complicated by a significant slide in Scania's share price.

[147] A further slide in Scania's share price would have had a negative impact on not only Scania but also Volvo shareholders. Furthermore, Deutsche Bank had conditioned its purchase of B-shares that Volvo would refrain from divesting its A shares involving public market transactions within a period of 90 days (a so-called 'lock-up period'), see by Nicholas George, 'Volvo to Seek Buyer for Scania A shares' *Financial Times* (6/7 March 2004). Scania was unhappy with the Commission's approval of the Ainex structure and claimed that it infringed the remedies and therefore launched its second appeal *Scania v Commission* (T-248/04 which was later withdrawn). The remedy was finally completed in 2006 when the distribution of Scania A shares to shareholders in Ainax was effected and Ainax was liquidated. To complete the saga, Volkswagen (VW) acquired sole control of Scania in 2008, see *Volkswagen/Scania* (M.5157 I 2008).

[148] Another example of how a publicly listed substantial stake can be gradually reduced in order to prevent share turmoil is *Konica/Minolta* (M.3091 I 2003) where the parties committed to divest Konica's 37.97% stake in its supplier Sekonic. The stake was sold in a three-step transaction: (i) Konica would almost immediately divest 28.15% of the shares to Sekonic as well as six already-identified purchasers and waive its right to exercise voting rights attached to the remaining shareholding; (ii) the remaining 9.82% would be sold at a later stage to purchaser(s) approved by the Commission or to the public through the stock exchange; and (iii) a divestiture trustee would step in and divest of the 9.82% shares if the parties did not succeed in doing so within the agreed period, see para 52.

[149] See eg *Südzucker/ED&F MAN* (M.6286 II 2012) (public decision not yet available); *GDF Suez/International Power* (M.5978 I 2011) para 121; *RCA/MAN Cargo* (M.5096 I 2008) paras 112 and 115; *Akzo Nobel/ICI* (M.4779 I 2007) para 53; *Yara/Kemira Growhow* (M.4730 I 2007) paras 58 and 63; *Continental/Phoenix* (M.3436 I 2004) para 220; *Areva/Urenco/ETC JV* (M.3099 II 2004) paras 229–330; *Teijin/Zeon/JV* (M.3235 I 2003) para 31; *Konica/Minolta* (M.3091 I 2003) paras 51–55; *Verbund/Energie Allianz* (M.2947 II 2003) para 143(a); *France Telecom/Orange* (M.2016 I 2000) para 47; *VEBA/VIAG* (M.1673 II 2000) paras 215 and 217; and *Bank Austria/Creditanstalt* (M.873 I 1997) para 106.

stakes in competitors apply equally in joint venture cases, a few different features deserve separate mentioning.

First, as indicated above the merging parties are usually required to eliminate, rather than merely reduce, their stake in a joint venture. A divestiture of a joint venture stake can take various forms, including (i) the existing joint venture partner(s) buy out the stake of the merged entity;[150] (ii) the joint venture is dissolved;[151] and (iii) the merged entity sells its stake to another business partner (outsider).[152]

Secondly, the existing joint venture partner(s) may have pre-emption rights that limit the scope of the divestiture in the sense that the stake to be divested shall first be offered to those partner(s).[153] As the Commission's conditional clearance decision can merely take into account such pre-emption rights but not require the other joint venture partners to amend or disregard their rights, such clauses can sometimes create obstacles in terms of timing and fulfilment of the divestiture proceedings.[154] As the other joint venture partners would invariably have substantial financial or strategic interests in the outcome of such a remedy, they have an incentive to protect their own interests as much as possible. Indeed, the Remedies Study showed that the consent of joint venture partners had posed unforeseen problems in several cases.[155] Nevertheless, the overall finding in the study was that commitments to exit from a joint venture were in fact the most effective types of remedies.[156] Despite potential third-party obstacles, the Commission found that, once implemented, joint ventures would usually be in a good position to operate successfully. This would particularly be the case if the other partner(s) would purchase the merged entity's stake, as they would already know the business well, effectively preserve it in the interim period and be able to exert effective competitive constrains as soon as the transaction were completed.[157]

[150] Thus, if the joint venture has only two partners, the joint venture is in effect dissolved but the operations continue under one owner. In *VEBA/VIAG* (M.1673 II 2000) the Commission found inter alia that the parties held a dominant duopoly position together with RWE/VEW on the German market for the supply of electricity at the interconnected level. Pre-merger VEBA and RWE were partners (41% and 54%, respectively) in a joint venture, Rhenag. The remedies stipulated that one way of dissolving the cooperation was for the shares held by RWE to be acquired by VEBA/VIAG, see para 215.

[151] Occasionally, the merging parties have committed to procure that the joint venture will be dissolved altogether, even though it has several other partners than the merging parties, see eg *Yara/Kemira Growhow* (M.4730 I 2007) para 58 (in respect of concerns in the distribution of fertilisers in Denmark).

[152] By way of illustration, in *GDF Suez/International Power* (M.5978 I 2011) the parties sold their stake in the joint venture T-Power to the Japanese energy company Itochu, see n 127 above.

[153] See eg *RCA/MAN Cargo* (M.5096 I 2008), Remedies Text, para 13(a).

[154] The Commission's decision in *Linde/BOC* (M.4141 I 2006) is a good illustration: the parties had submitted two alternative commitment proposals (a) to divest stakes in two joint ventures with Sonatrach; or (b) to divest a number of supply contracts in the event option (a) proved difficult to implement due to Sonatrach's rights as a joint venture partner. On reflection, the Commission decided that option (a) should be dropped as it was considered too risky due to the uncertainty as to whether Sonatrach would indeed consent to the change in the joint venture shareholdings and the investments necessary to remove some technical problems with these joint ventures, see paras 244 and 255. For a knowledgeable explanation of the case, see Kijewski et al (2006) 54.

[155] See Remedies Study, pp 47–48 (points 1–4). Examples were highlighted where joint venture partners had used all efforts to exclude potential candidates from the divestiture procedure in order to reduce the price of the stake to be sold to their own advantage and other situations where the existing partners had sought to capitalise on the fact that they knew they had a high degree of leverage by demanding excessively generous settlement terms.

[156] Remedies Study, p 135 (point 37).

[157] ibid.

### 3.2.5.3 Waiving of Rights and Termination of Agreements

In cases where a minority stake cannot, in itself, give the merging parties influence in the competitor in question, the Commission has accepted that the remedial solution may be limited to waiving of rights, mainly board representation.[158] In those very rare situations the Commission must be reassured that the financial gains derived from the minority stake will not in themselves raise competition concerns.[159] Thus, in order to accept the waiving of rights as a stand-alone remedy, it must encompass all associated rights, such as representations on the board, veto rights and information rights, and they must be waived comprehensively and in a permanent manner.[160] All in all, the Commission rarely accepts the waiving of rights as the sole remedy but the severance of such links is far more common as part of a stake divestiture package.[161]

Furthermore, where competition concerns result from agreements with companies supplying the same products or services, the Commission may accept the termination of such agreements as the principal remedy.[162] The agreements in question typically concern distribution arrangements,[163] but may also relate to the coordination of certain commercial behaviour.[164] The Commission stresses that its acceptance of such remedies presupposes that the products of the competitor will be distributed in the future and thus exercise effective competitive pressure on the merging parties.[165] While guidance contains no indications who should provide evidence – and the nature and scope of such evidence – on the continuing distribution of competitors' products in the future,[166] it is assumed that the burden of proof rests entirely on the parties although in some cases it may be difficult for

[158] In *Thyssen/Krupp* (M.1080 I 1998) Krupp kept its pre-merger 10% stake in the competitor Kone (elevators) but it gave up its right to appoint a member of Kone's boards of directors and certain privileges regarding acquisition of further shares in Kone as well as annulling a non-compete clause, see para 35. Based on these remedies alone, the transaction was conditionally cleared.

[159] Remedies Notice, para 59. See eg *Siemens/VA Tech* (M.3653 II 2005) where effects from Siemens 28% minority stake in a competitor in financial respect could be excluded as a put option for the sale of that stake had already been exercised (paras 327–28). The particular circumstances of the case were the existence of on-going litigations between the parties over the sales price, which could not be finalised before the Commission's adoption of its conditional clearance decision (para 328).

[160] Remedies Notice, para 59. In the prohibition decision *ENI/EDP/GDP* (M.3440 II 2004) the Commission dismissed the parties' commitment proposal that EDP would suspend its voting rights in the market player Turbogás (in which it held a 20% minority stake) and replace board members with independent persons during a period of 3 years and within certain fields of operations (paras 648–49) on the grounds that the proposal was limited in scope and duration (para 672).

[161] eg in *Abbott/Guidant* (M.4150 I 2006) the parties committed to not have any representation on the board of directors of the competitor Boston Scientific, pending the divestiture of their minority stake in that competitor within 30 months, see para. 98.

[162] Remedies Notice, para 60. For one of the most recent examples of supply arrangements constituting the core remedy, see *FrieslandCampina/Zijerveld & Veldhuyzen and Den Hollander* (M.6722 I 2013), Commission press release IP/13/319 of 12 April 2013 (public decision not yet available).

[163] In *American Home Products/Monsanto* (M.1229 I 1998) the parties agreed to terminate two distribution agreements in France with its competitor Organon (Akzo Nobel) in order to mitigate the Commission's concerns in the field of the oral contraceptive market in France, see para 53. See also eg *Pernod Richard/Allied Domecq* (M.3779 I 2005); *Orkla/Chips* (M.3658 I 2005) para 32.

[164] The termination of agreements has been particularly prominent in sea transport cases where the merging parties have committed to withdraw from certain liner conferences and consortia, see eg *Maersk/PONL* (M.3829 I 2005) para 179; and *TUI/CP Ships* (M.3863 I 2005) para 62. However, such remedies have also been used in eg telecoms, see *Telefónica/O2* (M.4035 I 2006) para 68.

[165] Remedies Notice, para 60.

[166] During the public consultation in 2007 of the new draft Remedies Notice some respondents sought clarifications as to the submission of evidence in this respect (see eg reply by Freshfields Bruckhaus Deringer, para 5.19) but the Commission did not elaborate on this issue in its final version of the notice.

them to obtain sufficient evidence from the competitor in question if the latter does not wish to cooperate.[167] Also, the merging parties may need to pay penalties for early contractual termination if the notice period is longer than the envisaged implementation period.[168] In any event, if any doubts remain as to a proper and timely fulfilment of the remedy, it is assumed that the Commission will simply not accept the termination of a contract as the principal remedy and the merging parties would need to provide for alternative solutions.

**Commentary:** the Commission's guidance on severance remedies is very short and general with the result that many nuances and aspects are left out. While the lack of details may be explained by the fact that many of the cases turn on their own merits (inter alia with respect to the establishment of structural links) and thus their features are difficult to generalise, it is nevertheless regrettable that the Commission's guidance is kept so broad as many severance remedies involve relatively problematic aspects such as third-party dependency, independence of share purchasers, issues relating to publicly listed companies and so forth. These aspects could warrant further reflections by the Commission, in one form or the other (including ex-post reviews).

## 3.3 Purchaser Requirements

### *3.3.1. Introductory Remarks*

Former Commissioner Monti once noted that '[e]ven if suitable assets can be identified, the parties' commitment simply to divest those assets regardless of who buys them will not be adequate'.[169] Throughout the years the Commission has attached great importance to the requirements that prospective purchasers must fulfil and, as they are an integral part of the Commission's overall assessment of the attractiveness and suitability of the commitment proposals, the requirements must be set out in details at the design stage.[170] This section examines the purchaser standards with emphasis on particular aspects, which have caused reflections by the Commission and a change of policy and practice throughout the years.[171]

The current standard purchaser requirements are the following:[172] (i) the purchaser must be independent of and unconnected to the parties; (ii) the purchaser must possess the financial resources, proven relevant expertise and have the incentive and ability to maintain and develop the divested business as a viable and active competitive force in competition with the parties and other competitors; and (iii) the acquisition of the business by a proposed purchaser must neither be likely to create new competition problems nor give

[167] In *Orkla/Chips* (M.3658 I 2005) the remedy did contain a provision according to which the competitor (Dafgard) confirmed to the Commission its agreement to replace the merging parties (Chips) as its distributor in Finland, see para 32. Similarly, in *American Home Products/Monsanto* (M.1229 I 1998) the other contractual party (Akzo Nobel) indicated its agreement to the termination of the distribution agreements in question, see para 54

[168] Along the same lines, in *Orkla/Chips* (M.3658 I 2005) the merging parties committed to agree to a premature termination of the distribution contact, should the other contractual party wish so (thus implying that the merging parties would need to pay any additional costs in this respect), see Remedies Text, para 1.

[169] Monti in IBA (2000) 431.

[170] Remedies Notice, para 47.

[171] In sections 4.5.1 and 4.5.2 below the approval procedure relating to the purchaser and the sales and purchase agreement (the SPA) as well as past cases where proposed purchasers have been considered unsuitable are examined.

[172] Remedies Notice, para 48; and MTDC, para 14. Compared to the old Remedies Notice (para 49), the criteria have been only slightly rephrased throughout the years.

rise to a risk that the implementation of the commitments will be delayed.[173] The conditions deserve the following comments.

### *3.3.2 Independence*

Despite being one of the most long-standing requirements introduced in decisional practice in 1997,[174] the Commission has never defined the slightly odd phrase of the purchaser being 'independent of and unconnected to the parties'.[175] However, the two terms imply that no direct or indirect shareholder links ('unconnected') or any personal (directors or board members) or economic (distribution or supply) relations ('independent') are tolerated between the parties and the prospective purchaser, which could influence the competitive behaviour and/or commercial decision-makings of the latter.[176] The independence requirement is closely related to the incentive requirement (see below) as without independence the purchaser is unlikely or less likely to possess the incentive to compete.

Although the wording suggests a rigid criterion of total structural independence, newer decisional practice suggests otherwise as many industries are now far more concentrated than when the criterion was phrased in 1997 and hence it may in some sectors prove increasingly difficult to find suitable independent purchasers.[177] In order to accommodate such changing market structures, the Commission has used its discretion in the past to either require additional concessions from the parties should a particular not-fully-independent purchaser announce its interest in acquiring the business to be divested,[178] or consider certain minor or past relations between the parties and the purchaser insignificant and thus acceptable.[179] Also, business realities may in some cases require that some

[173] In respect of the latter requirement, the proposed purchaser must reasonably be expected to obtain all necessary approvals from the relevant regulatory authorities for the acquisition of the business to be divested, see also Remedies Notice, para 104 *in fine*.

[174] The phrase was introduced in 1997 in *Guinness/GrandMet* (M.938 II 1997), see para 183(ix). Previously the Commission had often merely required the purchaser to be 'unconnected', see eg *TCCC/Carlsberg* (M.938 II 1997) para 110(1). However, in *Anglo American Corporation/Lonrho* (M.754 II 1997) the Commission's acceptance of Johannesburg Consolidated Investment Limited ('JCI') as an unconnected purchaser initiated a discussion and revision of the purchaser criteria. The merits of the case were unusual as AAC submitted, due to a substantial stake in JCI, some 'purchaser commitments' before the Commission accepted JCI as purchaser of AAC's stake in Lonrho, see press release IP/97/1102 of 10 December 1997. However, despite such measures it seemed doubtful whether JCI could indeed be considered unconnected to AAC as AAC retained a stake of around 10% in JCI and the executive chairman of JCI was also non-executive director of AAC. For unclear reasons, the Commission approved JCI as purchaser but the case made the Commission aware of the need to revise its policy in future cases.

[175] The phrase was once briefly referred to by a senior Commission official who stressed that the 'independent of and unconnected to' requirement evidently goes beyond the mere capitalistic relations and includes, in principle, any sort of personal links or economic relations (eg distribution, supply), see Rakovsky in IBA (2000) 143.

[176] ibid, 143–44. By way of comparison, the requirement to trustees is limited to 'independent', see Remedies Notice, para 124.

[177] See ch 1 n 75 above.

[178] In eg *TotalFina/Elf* (M.1628 II 2000) the parties undertook to divest its minority stake (34%) in Vitogaz, should the majority holder in Vitogaz express an interest in purchasing Elf AntarGaz (one of the businesses to be divested by the parties in accordance with the remedies), see para 344, and Remedies Text, para 42(c). See also *Anglo American Corporation/Lonrho* (M.754 II 1997) explained in n 174 above.

[179] An illustration of personal relations can be found in *CVC/SLEC* (M.4066 I 2006) whereby CVC divested, in accordance with the remedies, its subsidiary Dorna to another private equity firm Bridgepoint (see *Bridgepoint/Dorna* (M.4357 I 2006)). While at first glance the remedy seems to have been implemented correctly, it was claimed in the press at the time of the transaction that Bridgepoint and CVC had 'strong links' since the chairman of Bridgepoint and a co-founder and managing partner of CVC worked together in another private equity firm 3i in the 1980s, see press release of 19 July 2006, www.grandprix.com, accessed in 2006 (link no longer available). Furthermore, the two companies were co-investors and business partners in Blagden Packaging Group from 1998 to until 2004 when they decided to sell their interests, see press release of 12 January 2004, www.bridgepoint-

on-going commercial links or dependencies, also more than transitionally, are maintained in order to ensure viability. Such links could relate to essential inputs or outputs, especially if the purchaser or the business is relatively small or operates on a small market.[180] Alternatively, the Commission has chosen occasionally to lessen its standards by for example requiring that the purchaser is independent (not unconnected) of the parties.[181]

### *3.3.3 Resources, Expertise and Incentives*

First, the access of the purchaser to adequate financial resources is critical in ensuring the uninterrupted development of the divested business, especially in investment intensive markets.[182] The financial strength of the purchaser will thus be scrutinised when the business plan is presented.[183] The financial requirement raises the question whether the Commission has a general preference for larger purchasers rather than smaller ones in order to avoid subsequent financial mishaps. While the Commission has never expressed such a preference and this would indeed be problematic in many sectors where new entrants or smaller competitors are valued and required in already-concentrated markets, there have in the past been examples of purchasers being too small with the result that they were unable to maintain and develop the assets as they lacked the financial means, despite purchasing the business for virtually nothing.[184]

Moreover, the requirement of financial resources extends in particular to the way the acquisition is financed by the prospective purchaser.[185] The Commission is adamant that it will normally not accept any financing of the divestiture by the seller and in particular any arrangement that gives the seller a share in the profits of the divested business in the future.[186] As this form of seller financing varies in scope and nature and is highly complex, depending on the circumstances of each case, it is difficult to generalise and outline such arrangements in the present context. However, essentially in a seller financed arrangement the settlement of final payment to the seller (the merging parties) is deferred to a later date where it is linked to the value of the underlying respective assets at that time. From a competition viewpoint, such financing raises concerns as the seller may retain partial control over the assets and his incentives to compete with the purchaser may be impeded as vigorous competition

capital.com, accessed in 2006 (link no longer available). Although in this case the personal relations did not exist at the time of the respective transaction and the Commission obviously considered such past relations insignificant, the case merely goes to show how some sectors or areas – and in this case acquisitions by private equity firms – may be personally intertwined with the result that the independence of the respective companies may be somewhat more complicated than first assumed.

180 However, as such dependencies would often be linked to the lack of sufficient scope of the business the Commission would usually opt for strengthening the viability in terms of enhancing the scope of the business as opposed to allowing post-implementation relations. To this effect, see Remedies Study, p 105 (point 27).

181 See *Industri Kapital/Dyno* (M.1813 II 2000) para 133, and Remedies Text, paras 11 and 18.

182 Remedies Study, p 102 (point 15).

183 Often financial investors may have immediate access to financial resources whilst industrial purchasers may need to raise the necessary resources on the financial markets. To this effect, the DoJ states that a purchaser's inability to obtain financing from banks or other lending institutions raises questions about the purchaser's viability, see DoJ Merger Remedies Guide, Part IV.C.3.

184 Remedies Study, p 102 (point 16). See also *Danish Crown/Vestjyske Slagterier* (M.1313 II 1999) where a small new entrant acquired a slaughterhouse for a very low price (around EUR 125,000), only to go bankrupt one year after the acquisition inter alia as it lacked the financial means, see mentioning of this aspect in the conditional clearance decision of 24 April 2002 by the Danish Competition Authority of the transaction *Danish Crown/Steff-Houlberg*, pp 11 and 26, available at www.kfst.dk.

185 Remedies Notice, para 103.

186 ibid. Such selling financing is also named 'earn-outs' or 'structured sales'.

may be considered to jeopardise the purchaser's ability to repay the financing, among other things.[187] In the present context it suffices to note that, while previously the Commission paid little attention to financing issues, it has now recognised possible implications of this aspect and views any seller financing schemes with extreme caution and accepts them in only exceptional circumstances.[188]

Secondly, the requirement of 'proven relevant expertise' is closely linked to the purchaser's ability to compete. Such qualifications may be evident from the purchaser's past track record in the given industry and they include all types of know-how and organisational and management capabilities as well as expertise in a specific market and experience with the prevailing business practices of the industry.[189] Sometimes the required expertise is narrowed down to very specific capabilities or characteristics of the purchaser, such as certain production expertise,[190] possession of certain quantities of resources,[191] particular brand knowledge,[192] no significant captive use,[193] or specific geographic presence.[194]

[187] Contrary to the Commission, the DoJ explains in detail its reluctance to accept such financing measures, see DoJ Merger Remedies Guide, Part IV.C.3. For a similar position, see also the FTC Guidelines for Negotiating Merger Remedies, p 11. Furthermore, for a description of possible pitfalls, see De Souza and Brockhoff in Drauz and Jones (2012) paras 7.392–7.403. For a contrasting view, one respondent in the public consultation in 2007 of the new Remedies Notice submitted that earn-outs could also create strong incentives for the merging parties to transfer a viable business while not burdening the purchaser with additional financing, see reply by the American Bar Association, p 16. However, this submission does not dispute the dependency between the seller and the purchaser in this respect.

[188] Some commentators submit that financed sales may be appropriate where in the course of implementation it emerges that the divested business is encumbered with such liabilities, that it cannot be sold to a purchaser that meets the standard requirements even at no minimum price, see De Souza and Brockhoff in Drauz and Jones (2012) para 401. Such liabilities may arise from crippling debts which, the authors submit, was the case in *Hoechst/Rhône-Poulenc* (M.1378 I 2004 – modified decision of 1999 clearance) where the Commission accepted a structured sale as an 'irrevocable mandate to sell' for part of Aventis' stake in Rhodia to Credit Lyonnais as the continued involvement of Aventis in Rhodia was considered essential for its future turnaround by the company's creditors.

[189] Remedies Study, p 99 (point 7). Under current practice it is not uncommon for the remedies to specify that the prospective purchaser must currently be – or was previously – active within the sector of the business to be divested, see eg *Universal Music Group/EMI Music* (M.6458 II 2012), Remedies Text, para 19(d) (public decision not yet available) (recorded music or music publishing business); *SCA/Georgia-Pacific Europe* (M.6455 I 2012) para 296 (tissue sector); *Sony/Mubadala Development/EMI Music Publishing* (M.6459 I 2012) para 376 (music publishing); and *Reckitt Benckiser/SSL* (M.5953 I 2010), Remedies Text, para 18(iii) (sales and marketing of pharmaceutical products in the UK and preferably also in Ireland). While these requirements are usually imposed to enhance the immediate viability of the purchaser, some are imposed in order to comply with national regulations. In *TotalFina/Elf* (M.1628 II 2000) (commitment to divest a number of petrol stations along the French motorway) the purchasers were required to show experience in the operation of a petrol station network as required by national law, see Remedies Text, Annex 1, para 37(e).

[190] In *Syngenta/Monsanto's Sunflower Seed Business* (M.5675 II 2010) the purchaser was required to 'be a seed company with sufficient breeding capabilities and activities in order to successfully operate the Divested Business and with a sales force in Spain and/or Hungary, respectively, or the possibility of establishing such a sales force in a short time', see para 429 and Remedies Text, para 12(d). The narrow requirements were inserted after a negative market test to ensure the immediate restoration of effective competition, see para 428.

[191] In *INCO/Falconbridge* (M.4000 II 2006) the purchaser had to be a company active in metals mining and/or processing with sufficient nickel resources at a level of 55,000 MT nickel supply per year (which the parties previously supplied to the refinery to be sold) as a benchmark, see para 677.

[192] In *Masterfoods/Royal Canin* (M.2544 I 2002) the purchaser was required to show expertise in the branded (so not just own label) pet food market and possess sufficient R&D facilities, see Remedies Text, para 20. Along the same lines, in *SCA/Georgia-Pacific Europe* (M.6455 I 2012) the purchaser needed to have previous experience in (or demonstrate that it would be capable of) re-branding as well as being active in the tissue sector, see para 296.

[193] In *Degussa/Laporte* (M.2277 I 2001) the Commission submitted that, in the event that a purchaser would have a significant captive use of any of the three products involved, such a purchaser would possibly not be acceptable as this would limit the quantities available for the free market and thus the competitive force of the purchaser, see para 57.

[194] To this effect, in the Remedies Study the Commission highlights an example where a US company not present in the EU acquired a European company only to sell it on three years later for less than 5% of the original

Moreover, the Commission has occasionally specifically excluded certain types of purchasers from being considered suitable.[195] Although additional purchaser requirements significantly reduce the number of potential purchasers, they have in some cases proven crucial for the ultimate success of the divested business.[196] Thus, occasionally additional specific requirements have justified an up-front or fix-it-first solution in order to minimise the risk of failing to find a purchasers (see below).

The requirements of proven relevant expertise and ability to compete entail that there are cases where new entrants are unacceptable unless they are able to acquire or obtain the necessary expertise with immediate effect. Such considerations particularly put financial investors at a disadvantage, as they may not already possess the immediate qualifications unless they have previously acquired other companies in the same sector.[197] However, in some cases the market test shows that respondents do not consider it essential or necessary for the prospective purchaser to already possess industry knowledge or experience, the Commission has accepted that the requirement of 'proven expertise' is omitted from the purchaser criteria. This has proven to be particularly relevant where the remedies comprise of the divestiture of a stake in an industrial player.[198]

Thirdly, while the assessment of financial resources and proven expertise relies mainly on evidence provided by the proposed purchaser, the Commission must analyse this information and conclude whether the purchaser has a genuine interest in competing with the parties and other market players. This is probably the most difficult purchaser requirement to assess.[199] As the incentives of the purchaser are often indicated in the business plans, the starting point for the Commission would be to examine the plan, hear the opinion of the trustee and invite the prospective purchaser to orally explain its strategies.[200] However, as rightly pointed out by Commission officials, there are no guarantees, in a moving market, that the purchaser will adhere to its initial business plan and it would be unpractical as well as unrealistic in normal circumstances to impose long-term obligations on the purchaser not to deviate from its plan.[201] Nevertheless, the Commission will be able to check the assumptions on which the business plan is based in order to better assess whether there is sufficient evidence to consider that the purchaser's incentives and strategies are genuine.[202]

price. One of the reasons for the dramatic loss in value was that the purchaser lacked the necessary market knowledge and was not familiar with the dynamics of the market and the regulatory environment in the EU, see p 100 (point 8)

[195] In *Omya/Huber PCC* (M.3796 II 2006) the Commission did not only specify that the purchaser had to be an industrial purchaser with proven experience in the supply of coating calcium carbonates but it explicitly excluded any paper producer, see paras 508–12.

[196] However, in such circumstances the Commission must ensure that there are sufficient interested potential purchasers, despite the additional requirements, see Remedies Notice, para 52. As an example, in *Alcan/Pechiney(II)* (M.3225 I 2003) the Commission emphasised that, despite the very strict purchaser criteria, it was confident that potential purchasers existed, see para 171.

[197] In some cases the Commission explicitly excludes financial purchasers in the remedies, see *Syngenta/Monsanto's Sunflower Seed Business* (M.5675 II 2010) para 431. It is submitted that the lack of immediate sector-specific expertise is one of the main reasons for the Commission's reluctance to accept financial investors as purchaser, especially when the assets are not stand-alone.

[198] See *GDF Suez/International Power* (M.5978 I 2011) para 130.

[199] Indeed, the two cases to date where the Commission has formally rejected a proposed purchaser were based on lack of incentive and/or ability to compete, see section 4.5.2 below.

[200] Remedies Notice, para 102, and Remedies Study, p 102 (point 17).

[201] See Rakovsky in IBA (2000) 144.

[202] Remedies Study, p 104 (point 22).

Furthermore, it is important to stress that the purchaser's incentives may not always be consistent with the Commission's objectives behind the remedies.[203] While the Commission's overall objective is to remedy the competition concerns at hand, the purchaser's incentive is to generate an adequate return on its investment. To this effect, the purchaser may wish to ensure supporting provisions, such as long-term supply arrangements. In these situations it is important for the Commission to critically assess whether such provision are not at risk of ultimately undermining the remedies at hand.

With the benefit of hindsight, there are certain indications that the purchaser's incentives may not have been genuine from the outset. This has particularly proven to be the case where the purchaser: (i) rapidly ceased operation of the divested brands shortly after the acquisition; (ii) quickly re-sold the assets; and/or (iii) acquired the assets for free or at a negative price.[204] In the current context it suffices to stress that, as these outcomes cannot always be foreseen at the time of the purchaser assessment, the Commission can merely look for indications in the business plan and through interviews and then make its own projections.[205]

### *3.3.4 No New Competition Concerns or Delays*

The acquisition of the purchaser must neither be likely to create new competition problems nor give rise to a risk that the implementation of the commitments will be delayed.[206] This two-fold requirement is quite evident and self-explanatory and thus deserves only the following comments. Needless to say, the Commission cannot, as a matter of principle, accept that the solution in one case creates new competition concerns in another.[207] Indeed most of the conditional clearance cases, where the fulfilment of the remedies has required new notifications to the Commission, have been unproblematic, some of which have been cleared under simplified procedure.[208] Only a few 'fulfilment cases' have created competition concerns with the result that they were solved through new remedies.[209] As this procedure results in additional delays in the implementation of the remedies, it is considered

[203] See FTC Guidelines for Negotiating Merger Remedies, pp 13–14.

[204] Remedies Study, p 103 (points 18–20).

[205] In the Remedies Study the Commission quotes a case where the business plan provided that the purchaser had an option of dropping some of the acquired brands, see p 103 (point 18). An acceptance of such a provision is clearly risky.

[206] Remedies Notice, para 48.

[207] In cases where the divestiture does not require notification to the Commission, the purchaser approval is without prejudice to the merger control jurisdiction of national authorities, see Remedies Notice, para 104.

[208] For unconditional clearance of such transactions, see eg *Colgate Palmolive/Sanex Business* (M.6221 I 2011) (fulfilment of a remedy in *Unilever/Sara Lee Body Care* (M.5658 II 2010)); *Ferrovie Dello Stato/Cube Transport/Arrive Deutschland* (M.6124 I 2011) (fulfilment of a remedy in *DB/Arriva* (M.5855 2010)); *Pfizer/SP Assets* (M.5195 I 2008) (fulfilment of a remedy in *Schering-Plough/Organon Business* (M.4691 I 2007)); *PAI+UGI/Elf Antargaz* (M.2375 I 2001) (fulfilment of a remedy in *Totalfina/Elf Aquitaine* (M.1628 II 2000)); *Schmalbach-Lubeca/Rexam* (M.2542 I 2001) (fulfilment of a remedy in *Rexam/American National Can* (M.1939 I 2000)); *Campbell/ECBB (Unilever)* (M.2350 I 2001) (fulfilment of a remedy in *Unilever/Bestfoods*, (M.1990 I 2000)); *BP/JV Dissolution* (M.1820 I 2000) and *Mobil/JV Dissolution*, (M.1822 I 2000) (both fulfilment of remedies in *Exxon/Mobil* (M.1383 II 1999)); and *Heidelberger Zement/Scancem* (M.1562 I 1999) (fulfilment of a remedy in *Skanska/Scancem* (M.1157 II 1998)).

[209] By way of illustration, in *Vodafone Airtouch/Mannesmann* (M.1795 I 2000) France Telecom acquired the divested business (Orange). However, this acquisition resulted in horizontal overlaps in the market for mobile telecommunication services in Belgium where France Telecom was already present via its subsidiary Mobistar and Orange had a joint venture with KPN (KPN Orange). France Telecom/Orange therefore offered to divest their interests in KPN Orange to an independent third party, see *France Telecom/Orange* (M.2016 I 2000).

that such solutions are only acceptable in markets where no other (serious) prospective purchaser has announced its interest in acquiring the remedies assets.

It is worth noting that the standard model text contains the formulation '*prima facie* competition concerns' which is not mentioned in the Remedies Notice.[210] The purpose of the *prima facie* criterion at the purchaser approval stage is to emphasise that, based on the information available to the Commission at that point in time and hence without undertaking a material investigation, no competition concerns are immediately visible but this preliminary finding is without prejudice to subsequent investigation.[211] Also, as the divestiture must not give rise to risk of delays in implementation, the proposed purchaser must reasonably be expected to obtain all necessary approvals from the relevant regulatory authorities for the acquisition.[212] Situations have occurred in the past where for example a national regulatory authority imposed additional requirements on the prospective purchaser with the result that the implementation time was further delayed, as there were fewer purchasers to negotiate with.[213]

**Commentary:** the Director General for Competition was recently quoted for saying that effectiveness is an important guiding principal in the Commission's approval of purchaser with the result that in oligopolistic markets significant competitors of the merging parties are unlikely to be accepted as suitable purchasers of the assets to be divested.[214] Indeed, in recent years an increasing number of markets or sectors have undergone consolidation with the result that the number of existing market players have been reduced quite significantly.[215] Furthermore, current practice shows that ensuring viability of the assets is paramount for the Commission and one way of doing this is to apply the purchaser criteria in a stringent way and in some cases impose additional purchaser requirements in order for the divested assets to become operational and successful as quickly as possible once they are in the hands of the respective purchaser.

This policy combined with the market consolidations is likely to make it increasingly challenging for the merging parties to identify suitable purchasers amongst existing market players.[216] All things being equal, this could be good news for new market entrants (including financial investors)

[210] MTDC, para 14(c).

[211] It is unclear what will happen if the Commission post-approval is made aware of new competition concerns (eg from national or regulatory authorities). However, if concerns are severe, it is assumed that the Commission can 'freeze' the implementation, pending further investigations, supposing the divested business has not yet been transferred. If a transfer has been made, it is assumed that the Commission can revoke its decision, provided that the specific purchaser criteria have been listed as obligations in the main proceedings. As the Commission does not publish such measures or decisions, it is impossible to evaluate the significance of these circumstances.

[212] Remedies Notice, paras 48 and 104. In *Hutchison 3G Austria/Orange Austria* (M.6497 II 2012) the parties managed to obtain approval from the Austrian Cartel Court on 27 November 2012 of their commitment proposal to sell some assets ('Yesss!') to the market player A1 prior to the Commission's conditional clearance decision of the main transaction on 12 December 2012, see H3G press release of 12 December 2012, available at www.drei.at/presse. As the Austrian Competition Authority and the Federal Cartel Prosecutor would still have a right to appeal the Cartel Court's decision until 27 December 2012, this is presumably the reason why this commitment proposal could not be considered a fix-it-first solution in the Commission's conditional clearance decision.

[213] In the Remedies Study the Commission identified a case where a national defence ministry required that it had to be a European purchaser who would acquire the divested business, see p 106 (point 30).

[214] See Speech by Italianer (2012) 3.

[215] Apart from the sectors often mentioned in recent years in the context of consolidation (pharmaceuticals, energy, airlines, postal service, chemicals, banking and so forth), the European food sector is now also consolidating at an increased pace with the result that eg the sugar market has become increasingly concentrated with high barriers to entry, see Competition Report 2011, p 15.

[216] The recent prohibition decision in *UPS/TNT Express* (M.6570 II 2013) illustrates very well this point where it was clear from the outset that only very few potentially suitable purchasers existed (Fed-Ex being the obvious – but not interested – candidate; La Poste/DPD being the second – but not fully viable – candidate; and finally DHL being excluded due to its very strong market position), see press release IP/13/68 and MEMO/13/48 of 30 January 2013 (as of 1 May 2013, public decision not yet available).

who may not always have been the Commission's preferred candidates in the past. However, as pointed out above such a development could mean that viability may be more difficult to ensure and the divested assets may not be operational as swiftly as in the hands of existing market players. Leaving these potential concerns aside, it seems appropriate to conclude that in the near future the Commission may be faced with a new policy challenge relating to the implications of a shrinking 'pool' of potential purchasers in several markets. To this end, the Commission may need to review its existing policy on purchaser requirements and also possibly increase the use of fix-it-first or up-front buyer provisions if the parties are prepared to offer such commitments (see below).

## 3.4 'Ancillary' Viability Tools

### *3.4.1 Additional Assets*

For the business to be viable, it may be necessary to include activities related to markets where the Commission has not identified competition concerns.[217] While such assets are often formally proposed by the parties as part of their remedies package, it is submitted that the addition of such assets are in reality requested by the Commission in order to alleviate viability concerns, typically in view of results from the market test.[218] As the parties formally offer such additional assets as part of their proposal, the Commission considers itself entitled to accept such additions as long as it can be concluded that the overall package resolves the identified competition problems.[219] However, at the same time the EU Court has stressed that additional assets should be decided in the light of the principle of proportionality in the sense that, if competition can be maintained on those markets where concerns have been raised, it is not necessary for the Commission to extend the scope of the commitments to 'non-problematic' markets.[220] Hence, in its assessment the Commission must show that the added assets are necessary in order to ensure viability.[221]

The policy of adding assets from non-problematic markets was initiated in the last 1990s and since then numerous decisions have followed.[222] In most cases the additional assets have represented a relatively small proportion of the overall value of the business to be divested[223] and they have concerned assets or businesses in other product markets as well as in other

[217] Remedies Notice, para 23. Thus, this situation should be distinguished from scenarios where the parties voluntarily add supplementary assets post-clearance in order to make the remedies package more attractive to potential purchaser, see further section 4.4.3 below.

[218] One of the few cases where it is evident from the wording in the decision that the addition of assets was specifically required by the Commission is *Linde/BOC* (M.4141 I 2006), see paras 255(b) and 258.

[219] Remedies Notice, para 6. In *Lagardère/Natexis/VUP* (M.2978 II 2004) the Commission explicitly justified its right to accept a remedies package that went further than the identified competition concerns (following a negative market test raising concerns about viability the parties proposed to divest of the VUP group as a whole instead of smaller assets), see paras 1004–1007.

[220] See *easyJet v Commission* (T-177/04 2006) where the applicant submitted that the Commission had failed to extend the commitments to non-overlapping markets (paras 132–39).

[221] This approach has been endorsed by international organisations, see eg the 2004 OECD Remedies Study, pp 8 and 23.

[222] The first decision of this kind was *Sanitec/Sphinx* (M.1579 II 1999), see para 255. For other decisions, see *BASF/Congis* (M.5927 I 2010) para 102; *Universal/BMG Music Publishing* (M.4404 II 2007) para 17 (OJ version); *Linde/BOC* (M.4141 I 2006) paras 246 and 258; *Omya/Huber PCC* (M.3796 II 2006) para 503; *Lagardère/Natexis/VUP* (M.2978 II 2004) para 1006; *SEB/Moulinex* (M.2621 I 2002) paras 135–38; *Buhrmann/Samas Office Supplies* (M.2286 I 2001) para 87; *Unilever/Amora-Maille* (M.1802 I 2000) para 103; *Rexam (PLM)/American National Can* (M.1939 I 2000) para 30; and *Unilever/Bestfoods*, (M.1990 I 2000) para 177.

[223] *BASF/Congis* (M.5927 I 2010) is one of the few recent decisions where it is explicitly stated that the additional assets account for 'substantial parts of the overall activities of the [divested assets]' (para 102).

geographic markets.[224] Moreover, it is worth noting that in the past the provision of additional assets would be triggered only if requested by the approved purchaser.[225] This practice involved an implementation risk, as the additional assets would not be held separate together with the 'main' assets of the remedy from day one of the implementation but only if and when the purchaser requested so. However, with the increased emphasis in the new Remedies Notice on securing viability already at the design stage of the remedy the policy seems to have been tightened in the sense that the additional assets should no longer be separated from the parties' retained businesses at the purchaser approval stage but as soon as possible after the adoption of the conditional clearance decision.[226]

Finally it should be noted that, although adding assets in no way guarantees that viability will be ensured, past practice shows that the vast majority of such remedies were successful in preserving viability.[227] This finding is in line with US practice where both the FTC and DoJ pursue a practice of imposing the inclusion of additional assets, where appropriate.[228]

### *3.4.2 Up-front Buyers*

In some cases the Commission will not clear the transaction unless the parties undertake not to complete their notified operation before having entered into a binding agreement with an approved purchaser for the divested business.[229] These so-called 'up-front buyer' provisions were introduced in decisional practice around 2000,[230] largely inspired by an established US practice.[231] The underlying rationale behind the provision is to transfer the risk of a failed remedy to the merging parties.

According to current practice the Commission considers up-front buyer provisions relevant where:[232] (i) there are considerable obstacles for the divestiture, such as third-party

224 By way of examples, in *Sanitec/Sphinx* (M.1579 II 1999) the added assets were other products consisting of taps and mixers in the context of bathroom products, see para 255; in *SCA/P&G (European Tissue Business)* (M.4533 I 2007) the added assets related to the divestiture of the respective brand (Softis handkerchief/facial brand) in all other countries than Austria and Germany where the competition concerns were identified, see paras 175, 177 and 186; and in *Masterfoods/Royal Canin* (M.2544 I 2002) the divested brands were EU-wide despite concerns confined to France and Germany, see para 91.

225 See eg *SCA/P&G European Tissue Business* (M.4533 I 2007), Remedies Text, para 4(b); *Linde/BOC* (M.4141 I 2006), Remedies Text, para 10; *Sanitec/Sphinx* (M.1579 II 1999) para 255. Moreover it is worth noting that provisions on additional assets are not contained in the MTDC and hence the parties enjoy more flexibility when drafting provisions in this respect.

226 See eg *BASF/Congis* (M.5927 I 2010) where the substantial additional assets automatically formed part of the divested business and hence were subject to the standard preservation and hold-separate provisions from day one, see Remedies Text, para 4.2.

227 The Commission found in its Remedies Study that out of 12 remedies involving additional assets 10 of them were non-problematic and in fact rather successful, see p 37 (point 2).

228 See FAQ About Merger Consent Order Provisions, Question 15; and the DoJ Merger Remedies Guide, II.A.2.

229 See Remedies Notice, paras 53–55, and MTDC, para 1 *in fine*. The principle of suspension of an operation was already introduced in the now-abandoned Article 7(1) of the original Merger Regulation.

230 The first case was *Bosch/Rexroth* (M.2060 II 2000) and shortly thereafter the new practice was introduced in the old Remedies Notice (para 20). Coming close to an up-front buyer provision, in *WorldCom/MCI* (M.1069 II 1998) the divestiture remedy was made subject to – or should at least be carried out simultaneously with – the closure of the main transaction, see para 136.II.6. As the conditional clearance was carried out in close cooperation with the DoJ it is assumed that the at that point in time unusual up-front provision was initiated by the DoJ. Indeed, one week after the Commission's clearance the DoJ announced the conclusion of an up-front solution whereby Cable & Wireless would acquire the respective assets, see DoJ press release of 15 July 1998.

231 For an overview of the use of 'up-front buyers' in the US, see FTC FAQ About Merger Consent Order Provisions, Questions 7–14; FTC Guidelines for Negotiating Merger Remedies, pp 7–8; the FTC Divestiture Study, p 39; and DoJ Merger Remedies Guide, part IV.A.2.a.

232 Remedies Notice, paras 54–55.

rights, or uncertainties as to finding a suitable purchaser;[233] and/or (ii) there are considerable risks of preserving the competitiveness and saleability of the business pending divestiture.[234] In both situations the overall purpose of the provision is to enhance the parties' incentives to implement the divestiture as soon as possible in order to be able to complete their own transaction. Experience shows that up-front buyer provisions are more likely to be required in cases where the parties divest assets, which are not stand-alone businesses[235] and possibly also involving substantial carve-outs.[236] Furthermore, in recent practice up-front provisions have been used in the context of access commitments.[237] All in all, any up-front buyer provision is acceptable only if it is formulated in a clear and precise way leaving no doubt that the implementation of the transaction is indeed conditional on the prior fulfilment of the remedy.[238]

It should be noted that the EU and US notions of 'up-front buyers' differ, mainly due to procedural discrepancies. While the Commission requires the parties not to complete their transaction prior to the approval of the purchaser post-decision, the FTC does not clear the transaction before the purchaser has been identified and approved.[239] [240] This difference

[233] See *Western Digital Ireland/Viviti Technologies* (M.6203 II 2011), IP/11/1395 of 23 November 2011 (public decision not yet available); *Agilent/Varian* (M.5611 I 2010) para 120; *BASF/CIBA* (M.5355 I 2009) para 258; *Arjowiggins/M-Real Zanders Reflex* (M.4513 II 2008) para 549; *Omya/Huber PCC* (M.3796 II 2006) para 514; *Sonoco/Ahlstrom/JV* (M.3431 II 2004) paras 106–12; *DSM/Roche Vitamins* (M.2972 II 2003) para 80; *Nestlé/Ralston Purina* (M.2337 I 2001), Remedies Text, para 15; *Verbund/Energie Allianz* (M.2947 II 2003) para 157; *Post Office/TPG/SPPL* (M.1915 II 2001) paras 135 and 161; and *Bosch/Rexroth* (M.2060 II 2000) para 92. In addition, in *Hutchinson 3G Austria/Orange Austria* (M.6497 II 2012) the Commission seems to have accepted an up-front solution, which is only linked to part of the remedies package (an access agreement), see press release IP/12/1361 of 12 December 2012 (public decision not yet available).

[234] See *Masterfoods/Royal Canin* (M.2544 I 2002) paras 90 and 102; and *Bosch/Rexroth* (M.2060 II 2000) para 94. Reference should also be made to a similar provision, albeit not a real up-front buyer clause, in *Fortis/ABN Amro Assets* (M.4844 I 2007) where Fortis would not acquire control over certain assets involved in the transaction prior to the closing of the sale of two business units being part of an overall remedies package, see para 233.

[235] In *DSM/Roche Vitamins* (M.2972 II 2003) the remedies did not include the divestment of any feed enzyme fermentation production assets and the up-front buyer provision was therefore necessary as the Commission had to ensure that the purchaser would have access to independent production capacity, see para 93. In *Masterfoods/Royal Canin* (M.2544 I 2002) the business consisted of assets from both Mars and Royal Canin, see para 101. See also *Agilent/Varian* (M.5611 I 2010) para 168. The importance of up-front buyer solutions in non-stand-alone cases is in line with US experience, see FTC FAQ about Merger Consent Order Provisions, Q 9.

[236] In *Agilent/Variant* (M.5611 I 2010) all four divested businesses had to be carved out and thus the remedies contained four separate up-front buyer provisions, see paras 134–68.

[237] See *Hutchinson 3G Austria/Orange Austria* (M.6497 II 2012), the Commission's press release IP/12/1361 of 12 December 2012 (public decision not yet available). H3G committed not to complete its acquisition of Orange before it had entered into a wholesale access agreement with one mobile virtual network operator. As it happened, H3G had already entered into an agreement with one operator, UPC, during the administrative proceedings, see press coverage of 10 October 2012, available at www.prepaidmvno.com/2012/10/10/hutchison-3g-austria-h3g-announces-mvno-agreement-with-upc.

[238] In *Ryanair/Aer Lingus* (M.4439 II 2007) the Commission reasoned its rejection of proposed commitments inter alia on the basis that the proposed up-front buyer provision was not sufficiently clear, see paras 1197–98. To this effect, see also the appeal in *Ryanair v Commission* (T-342/07 2010) para 494.

[239] The difference between the two jurisdictions is illustrated in *Western Digital Ireland/Viviti Technologies* (M.6203 II 2011) where the parties committed vis-à-vis the Commission that they would not close their transaction before concluding a binding agreement for the sale of the divestment business to a suitable purchaser approved by the Commission (see press release IP/11/1395 of 23 November 2011 – public decision not yet available) whereas the FTC's clearance (four months later) was conditioned on the parties committing to sell the respective business to an already identified purchaser being named as Toshiba Corporation, see FTC press release of 5 March 2012 *in the Matter of Western Digital Corporation*, Docket No C-4350.

[240] Specifically on the FTC's conditions for approving up-front buyers it is specified in its latest guidance that the parties must identify an acceptable purchaser and then negotiate, finalise and execute the purchase agreement and all ancillary agreements with that purchaser before the FTC staff forwards the proposed order to the FTC for approval, see FTC Guidelines for Negotiating Merger Remedies, p 7.

will be seen in the context of the fact that US scrutiny is not subject to pre-defined deadlines in the same way as the EU where it is highly difficult for the parties to identify a purchaser, agree on terms of the sale and obtain approval from the Commission prior to the deadline for adoption of a clearance decision, especially in phase I cases (see fix-it-first solutions below). Hence, it is submitted that the Commission's interpretation of up-front buyer provisions is more like a 'suspension measure' than an up-front solution as such.[241]

The obvious disadvantage with the EU approach is that the Commission is unable to take into consideration the actual *identity* of the purchaser in its competitive assessment of the viability of the remedy before clearing the main transaction.[242] For example, the Commission cannot discuss with the proposed purchaser its incentives for competing with the parties and other competitors, evaluate business plans, and so forth. The Commission's assessment will instead focus on certain general criteria that a prospective purchaser must fulfil after the Commission's adoption of a clearance decision but prior to the parties' implementation of the transaction.

From the parties' point of view, it has been submitted by commentators that the parties should not rush into submitting up-front buyer proposals, unless as a last resort, as there are significant risks associated with such provisions.[243] In particular, the parties will need to be reasonably confident that one or more potential purchasers can indeed be found as the condition for the Commission's clearance of the transaction is otherwise not met and thus the decision no longer stands.[244] In such cases the parties must either abandon their transaction altogether,[245] or re-negotiate their transaction, submit a notification of a revised version, and go through the administrative procedure once more. In order to avoid such uncertain, lengthy and potentially damaging and expensive procedures, the parties have sometimes accompanied an up-front buyer provision with a crown jewel or alternative commitment (see below) in case the former proves impossible.[246] Furthermore, although

[241] It could be argued that the term 'up-front buyer' in the EU is somewhat misleading given that the purchaser is usually identified and approved post-clearance.

[242] Extraordinarily, in *Bosch/Rexroth* (M.2060 II 2000) Commission was able to announce the identity of the purchaser when clearing the merger but its competitive assessment in the clearance decision lacked the identification and assessment of the approved purchaser, see the Commission's press release IP/00/1457 of 13 December 2000 announcing the conditional clearance and confirming that the US company Moog was the approved up-front buyer. It is assumed that Moog was proposed and approved at a very late stage during the administrative proceedings.

[243] See Stennek (2006) 6; Papandropoulos and Tajana (2006) 447; Baer, Feinstein and Meisner (2004) 51, and Speech by Platt Majoras (2002b).

[244] Up-front buyer provisions are usually considered a condition for approval, see *Verbund/Energie Allianz* (M.2947 II 2003) para 161. Thus, in terms of enforcement of the remedies differences sometimes exist between the (lack of) fulfilment of an up-front buyer requirement and a 'standard' purchaser requirement, respectively, when the latter in some decisions are considered an obligation, see eg *Reckitt Benckiser/SSL* (M.5953 I 2010), Remedies Text, para 18.

[245] In *Arjowiggins/M-Real Zanders Reflex* (M.4513 II 2008) the parties committed that, if the sale of the business failed within the divestiture period foreseen, Arjowiggins would abandon the transaction and return the entire business (a mill) of the notified transaction to Zanders Reflex, see para 549 *in fine*. This did in fact happen a few weeks after the conditional clearance decision inter alia on the basis that 'the rationale to complete the transaction under the condition [the remedy to divest the mill] was considerably weakened', see press release of 20 June 2009 from M-Real, www.m-real.com, accessed in 2009 (link no longer available).

[246] In *Nestlé/Ralston Purina* (M.2337 I 2001) the parties' preferred commitment in respect of concerns in the Spanish pet food market was an exclusive licence of certain brands. While the Commission did not mention the existence of the up-front buyer requirement in its competitive assessment of respective commitment (it is assumed that this information was considered a business secret), the provision is evident from the attached Remedies Text, see para 15. As it happened, Nestlé did not implement its preferred commitment with the result that a crown jewel provision came into play (see below). Also, the FTC considers that an up-front buyer solution does not necessarily eliminate the need for a crown jewel provision (see FTC FAQ About Merger Consent Order Provisions, Q 27) whereas the DoJ insists on the inclusion of an alternative proposal (see the DoJ Merger Remedies Guide, part IV.A.2.a).

an up-front buyer provision is not considered a fire-sale, potential purchasers may get unfair negotiating leverage as they will be aware of the constraints on the parties which may be reflected in the price that purchasers are willing to pay for the business. To this effect, demanding purchasers may delay the implementation and hence the consummation of the parties' transaction due to lengthy negotiations which may effectively be expensive for the parties.[247]

From the Commission's perspective, up-front solutions are attractive as they reduce the risk for interim competitive harm and expedite the divestiture procedure. This is particularly the case where the Commission is not convinced that the parties have defined the correct scope for the assets or the business is not stand-alone.[248] Thus, while up-front buyer provisions are in principle voluntarily offered by the parties as part of their remedies package, such provisions are in practice requested by the Commission in order to mitigate any uncertainties that the assets will be effectively divested to a suitable purchaser.[249] Some commentators have suggested that the Commission may also use up-front buyer provisions as an alternative to a phase II investigation.[250] However, as that the vast majority of up-front buyer solutions have been accepted in phase II proceedings this argument does not reflect past practice.[251]

Whether up-front buyer provisions have been successfully implemented in the past is difficult to say as this would only be evident if/when the Commission undertakes and publishes an ex-post examination of relevant past cases.[252] However, based on the intentions behind the provision – that is to say preventing interim harm and shortening implementation time by creating strong incentives to identify purchasers as soon as possible – the usual risks inherent in remedies with no up-front provisions (or fix-it-first) would obviously be diminished and hence the likelihood of the ultimate success of the remedies would be

[247] To this effect, BIAC (Business and Industry Advisory Committee, 'the voice of OECD business') stressed in its submission to the OECD Merger Remedies Study that up-front buyer provisions may be problematic as the longer it takes for the transaction to close, the longer period of time the 'non-offending' assets remain at bay which can be very costly, see 2004 Remedies Study, p 274.

[248] Indeed, the high frequency of problems affecting the divested business' viability and competitiveness due to insufficient scope was highlighted as one of the main concerns in the Commission's Remedies Study.

[249] During the proceedings in *Ryanair v Commission* (T-342/07 2010) the parties submitted that their (rejected) up-front buyer proposal had been 'demanded by the Commission', see para 473. The General Court did not address this issue. For another example, see *Bosch/Rexroth* (M.2060 II 2000) where the Commission's press release announcing the clearance of the merger stated that the up-front buyer solution had been imposed by the Commission (see press release IP/00/1457 of 13 December 2000) while the wordings in the decision were less clear stating that Bosch had accepted a ban not to put the transaction into effect and that the ban had been promised by the parties, see paras 92–93.

[250] See Holmes and Turnbull (2002): 'In effect, the Commission says to the parties – unless you now agree to take the risk of finding a really effective buyer for your proposed divestment package (before closing the deal), we will have to take a more detailed look at the proposed merger in an in-depth phase II investigation' (p 509). The authors claim this happened in *Masterfoods/Royal Canin* (M.2544 I 2002).

[251] It is worth noting that the majority of up-front buyer cases mentioned in this section were adopted in phase II.

[252] The provision was not yet introduced in the cases subject to analysis in the Remedies Study. However, in 2004 the Commission suggested that, so far, there had been indications that up-front buyer provisions had contributed to short divestiture deadlines, see the 2004 OECD Remedies Study, p 258. Eg in *The Post Office/TPG/SPPL* (M.1915 II 2001) the up-front buyer provision resulted in a purchaser (Swiss Post International) being identified and accepted by the Commission less than 3 months following the clearance decision, see Competition Report 2001, para 306. At that time, divestiture periods were generally longer than the achieved 3 months. Also with respect to US cases, the FTC Divestiture Study found that the use of up-front provisions had resulted in shorter divestiture periods, see p 39. For a diverging view, see Papandropoulos and Tajana (2006) who is not convinced that up-front buyer provisions do result in a shorter divestiture process, see pp 446–47.

equally enhanced. Nevertheless, contrary to the FTC's practice of requiring up-front buyer solutions in the vast majority of its cases,[253] the Commission has accepted such provisions in relatively few cases (roughly one case per year), which may be due to several circumstances. The most obvious explanation is that the parties are simply not prepared to offer such a commitment due to the commercial risks listed above (and the Commission cannot unilaterally impose such provisions), and also the parties may in some instances instead opt for a crown jewel provision (see below).[254] Thus, it is difficult to envisage that there will ever be a systematic use of up-front buyer provisions in the Commission's practice as proposed by some commentators.[255]

### 3.4.3 *Fix-it-first*

In cases where the identity of the purchaser is crucial for the effectiveness of the proposed commitments, the parties may also identify and enter into a legally binding agreement with a purchaser outlining the essentials of the purchase during the administrative proceedings, a so-called fix-it-first remedy.[256] According to current practice, such solutions are relevant in cases where (i) only very few potential purchasers can be considered suitable, in particular where the business to be divested is not viable in itself but its viability will only be ensured by specific assets of the purchaser; or (ii) the purchaser needs to have specific characteristics in order for the remedy to solve the competition concerns.[257] Past fix-it-first solutions have often concerned cases with extensive carve-outs of the respective assets and where an identified purchaser was decisive for ensuring viability.[258]

A fix-it-first solution enables the Commission to assess and decide in its conditional clearance decision whether the transfer of the business to the identified purchaser will remove the competition concerns and hence no additional purchaser approval decision is necessary and the closing of the sale may take place shortly after the adoption of the conditional clearance decision. Obviously these benefits make fix-it-first solutions very attractive for the Commission as well as the parties. The Commission is more or less certain that the remedy will be implemented (unless the parties and/or the purchaser breach

[253] In the past the FTC has required up-front buyers in 85% of its cases while the DoJ imposed similar requirements in less than 10% of cases, see Stennek (2006) 6. FTC senior officials once said that 'up-front buyers are probably the most vital tool in assuring a successful divestiture', see Parker and Balto (2000) 7.

[254] Indeed the new Remedies Notice stipulates that in some cases the parties may choose between proposing an up-front buyer and an alternative divestiture commitment as they are considered to address the same concerns, see para 54 *in fine*, referring to para 46.

[255] See eg Motta, Polo and Vasconselos in Lévêque and Shelanski (2003) 113.

[256] Remedies Notice, paras 56–57. Hence, compared to up-front buyer solutions, fix-it-first remedies go a step further in the sense that the identity of the purchaser is crucial for the Commission's finding of compatibility. Indeed, in the past the Commission has rejected an up-front buyer proposal but accepted a fix-it-first solution, see *INCO/Falconbridge* (M.4000 II 2006) paras 576 (up-front buyer) and 680 (fix-it-first).

[257] For past fix-it-first solutions, see primarily *Vienna Insurance Group/EBV* (M.5075 I 2008) para 170 (relating to the divestiture of BACAV); *INCO/Falconbridge* (M.4000 II 2006) para 680; *T-Mobile Austria/Tele.ring* (M.3916 II 2006) paras 130 and 139 (two fix-it-first remedies); *Metso/Aker Kvaerner* (M.4187 II 2006) paras126–30 (two fix-it-first remedies); *Reuters/Telerate* (M.3692 I 2005) para 21 (up-front licensee); *Continental/Phoenix* (M.3436 I 2004) para 220 (three fix-it-first remedies); *GE/AGFA NDT* (M.3136 I 2003) para 48; *Pfizer-Warner-Lambert* (M.1878 I 2000) para 89 (in relation to N7D market). See also *Dow Chemical/Union Carbide* (M.1671 II 2000) where Dow committed to sell to BP Amoco its gas-phase Metallocene PE Technology assets (para 173). However, this remedy was primarily given in view of the parties' past cooperation in that area rather than ensuring viability of the assets to be transferred and hence the purpose of the remedy was slightly different than the above-mentioned fix-it-first remedies. Similarly, see *Exxon/Mobil* (M.1383 II 1999) para 841.

[258] See eg *Metso/Aker Kvaerner* (M.4187 II 2006) para 134.

their contractual obligations)[259] and sold to an identified purchaser who can be fully assessed by the Commission before reaching a final view on the compatibility of the overall transaction. As the prospective purchaser can be involved in the administrative proceedings and for example assist in identifying the necessary assets to be transferred, it may be easier for the Commission to ensure viability.[260] The difficulty for the Commission is that it must undertake not only a competitive assessment of the transaction but also a purchaser assessment within the usual deadlines but, if it is possible to do so, the Commission also stands to benefit in terms of saved resources as the usual implementation phase is cut short. In some cases it may be a disadvantage for the Commission that it has less influence on the way in which the divestiture is implemented as the usual divestiture measures and safeguards may not apply.

From the parties' point of view, fix-it-first solutions are beneficial for a number of reasons. The parties can in effect self-select a proposed purchaser without necessarily going through the usual divestiture steps in order to approach a broad range of potential purchaser and they can instead immediately initiate negotiations with a chosen purchaser. Once a purchaser is identified, they can tailor their presentation to the Commission of that specific purchaser without going through all standard provisions if not applicable.[261] When they have received the conditional clearance decision they can close their transaction as well as the sale of required assets significantly quicker than in standard remedies procedures, which is obviously time- and cost-saving. Although the time constraints during the administrative procedure may give the prospective purchaser negotiation leverage which may ultimately result in a lower price for the assets, such additional costs for the parties may easily be compensated by the speedier approval by the Commission, depending on the circumstances of the case.

The main challenge for the parties is to negotiate (including conducting due diligence) and enter into a binding SPA with a purchaser as well as present the purchaser to the Commission with adequate information in order to facilitate the Commission's purchaser assessment well in advance of the expiry of the legal deadline for adoption of a clearance decision. In view of the Commission's consultation obligations, it is considered that a binding contract with a purchaser must be in place and presented to the Commission at the latest three to four weeks prior to the legal deadline for adoption of a conditional clear-

[259] The contractual requirement is that it has to be a 'legally binding agreement'. This does not necessarily mean that the parties must conclude a detailed SPA in final form and it can thus be a preliminary or framework agreement recorded by eg a notary, see *Continental/Phoenix* (M.3436 I 2004) para 224. The parties may also commit to enter into full contract by a certain date but a framework agreement must be in place before the decision is adopted, see *T-Mobile Austria/Tele.ring* (M.3916 II 2006) para 130. In contrast, in *WPP/TNS* (M.5232 I 2008) the parties had identified a purchaser (Nielsen data) but had not yet concluded an agreement and therefore the remedy instead contained a crown jewel (see para 157), and in *ABF/GBI Business* (M.4980 II 2008) the Commission had a specific purchaser in mind (identity considered a business secret, see para 374) but the negotiations were not sufficiently advanced and therefore the remedy contained a crown jewel instead (para 381).

[260] See *Metso/Aker Kvaerner* (M.4187 II 2006) para 144.

[261] It is unclear whether the parties must present the purchaser to the Commission using the standard models for submission of remedies in order to facilitate the competitive assessment of the given purchaser. Practice varies at this point. Some Remedies Texts contain standard purchaser provisions (see *T-Mobile Austria/Tele.ring* (M.3916 II 2006), Remedies Text, Annex II, Part C.2; and *Continental/Phoenix* (M.3436 I 2004), Remedies Text, para 23), whereas in other cases the Commission has accepted a significantly shorter submission model (see the Remedies Text in *GE/AGFA NDT* (M.3136 I 2003)). In the context of the latter situation it is worth noting that the Remedies Text in *Metso/Aker Kvaerner* (M.4187 II 2006) contained no detailed information on the proposed purchaser (GLV) but the Remedies Text stipulated that, if the Commission were to waive the commitment to divest the business to GLV, Metso would submit commitments substantially in the form of the Commission's standard commitments, see para 55.

ance decision. This leaves very little time for the parties to negotiate and sign with a purchaser, especially in phase I proceedings, unless they have initiated purchaser negotiations well in advance of the notification of the transaction.

Understandably, fix-it-first remedies are relatively uncommon under the Merger Regulation and since the introduction in early 2000s only a handful of cases have been solved in this manner.[262] The majority of fix-it-first remedies have been accepted in phase II in order to benefit from the longer deadlines,[263] some being US cooperation cases where it is believed that the earlier-initiated US proceedings enabled the parties to submit similar remedies in the EU proceedings.[264] With respect to the few past phase I fix-it-first remedies, they have concerned relatively straightforward cases in terms of separating and transferring the respective assets,[265] or US cooperation cases with similar benefits as stated in respect of phase II cases.[266] The limited number of fix-it-first remedies reinforces the view that such solutions are generally not feasible under strict deadlines and it is thus expected that the Commission's acceptance of fix-it-first solutions will continue to be offered and accepted on an infrequent basis under the present rules. Moreover, as the Commission now emphasises in its guidance that up-front buyer solutions containing specific purchaser requirements are considered equivalent to fix-it-first solutions,[267] it is assumed that the parties would normally opt for the former, if possible.

Finally, it should be mentioned that the Commission does not specify in its guidance whether fix-it-first solutions allow for any post-decision monitoring and/or commercial relations (such as supply arrangements) between the parties and the purchaser. While for example the DoJ makes it clear that fix-it-first solutions are unacceptable if the respective remedy requires monitoring, any supply arrangements and/or any behavioural provisions,[268] the Commission seems to require less of a 'clean-break' in such cases. For example, it has occasionally accepted the appointment of monitoring trustees and regulatory authorities acting as arbitrators as well as the conclusion of substantial supply agreements and other interim measures in order to ensure the viability of the transferred assets.[269] On the other hand, the Commission has in other fix-it-first cases considered that there was no need for any interim measures, or the appointment of a trustee.[270] Thus, the Commission appears to consider each case on its own merits and, if needed, it may accept post-decision measures.

[262] Contrary to up-front buyer provisions, fix-it-first remedies were not formally introduced in the old Remedies Notice but the practice developed gradually over the years inspired by a long-standing US practice. For US guidance on fix-it-first remedies, see eg DoJ Merger Remedies Guide, Part IV.A.1.

[263] See eg *Continental/Phoenix* (M.3436 I 2004) containing no less than three fix-it-first remedies (two to the same purchaser).

[264] See *INCO/Falconbridge* (M.4000 II 2006) which was cleared in parallel by the DoJ, see DoJ press release of 23 June 2006.

[265] See *Vienna Insurance Group/EBV* (M.5075 I 2008) para 176.

[266] See *GE/AGFA NDT* (M.3136 I 2003)

[267] Remedies Notice, para 57 *in fine.*

[268] See DoJ Merger Remedies Guide, Part IV.A.1.

[269] For arbitration provisions, see *T-Mobile Austria/Tele.ring* (M.3916 II 2006) para 140, and for monitoring trustee and numerous interim measures, see *Metso/Aker Kvaerner* (M.4187 II 2006) para 147. For monitoring trustee and the acceptance of an important 10-year supply arrangement to secure long-term source of raw materials, see *INCO/Falconbridge* (M.4000 II 2006) paras 564–68, 672 and 677 (re supply agreement), and Remedies Text, para 16 (monitoring trustee). It is worth noting that in the latter case, which was a cooperation case with the US, the DoJ did extraordinarily accept the long-term supply agreement, see *United States v Inco Limited and Falconbridge Limited,* DoJ Case No 1:06CV01151, Competitive Impact Statement of 23 June 2006, p 8. As it happened, the transaction was later cancelled due to a competing hostile bid for Falconbridge by Xstrata, which was cleared unconditionally by the Commission in *Xstrata/Falconbridge* (M.4256 I 2006).

[270] See *GE/AGFA NDT* (M.3136 I 20003) para 50.

### *3.4.4 Alternative Proposals: Crown Jewels*

In some cases the implementation of the parties' preferred divestiture option may be uncertain due to, for example, third parties' pre-emption rights, potential problems in relation to the transferability of key contracts or IPRs, or uncertainty as to whether a suitable purchaser exists. Accordingly, the Commission will only accept such commitments under the following conditions: (i) absent the uncertainty, the preferred option would consist of a viable business; and (ii) the parties must propose an alternative divestiture which they must implement if their preferred option is not implemented within the given deadline.[271] The alternative proposal must normally be a crown jewel, meaning that it should be at least as good as the first option in terms of creating a viable competitor once implemented, it should not involve any uncertainties as to its implementation, and it should be capable of being implemented quickly. A crown jewel can be an entirely different business,[272] or additional businesses and assets being added to the initial remedies package.[273]

The Commission is clear that both submitted proposals must each be accompanied by short durations so the overall implementation time does not exceed what is normally regarded as acceptable in the conditions of the market in question.[274] To this effect, the proposals must establish clear criteria and a strict timetable as to how and when the alternative divestiture will become effective. Occasionally the parties have proposed that also the crown jewel should be implemented within the first divestiture period.[275] Moreover, it is indispensable that interim preservation and holding separate measures apply to all assets included in both divestiture alternatives.[276]

[271] Remedies Notice, paras 44 and 45. This provision was formally introduced in the old Remedies Notice, paras 22–23. The possibility of proposing an alternative option where uncertainties exist was endorsed in *General Electric v Commission* (T-210/01 2005) where the General Court noted that, if the applicant was unable to guarantee that its proposed remedy would be implemented, it should have proposed an alternative commitment, see para 617.

[272] See *Novartis/Alcon* (M.5778 I 2010) para 294 (termination of a distribution arrangement or divestiture of a business); *WPP/TNS* (M.5232 I 2008) para 136 (divestiture of a stake or a business); *Johnson & Johnson/Guidant* (M.3687 II 2005) para 358 (divestiture of alternative businesses); *Nestlé/Ralston Purina* (M.2337 I 2001) para 61 (exclusive licence or divestiture of a stake); *Industri Kapital/Dyno* (M.1813 II 2000) para 132 (divestiture of alternative plants); *Astra/Zeneca/Novartis* (M.1806 II 2000) para 470 (termination of distribution arrangement or divestiture of assets); and *AXA/GRE* (M.1453 I 1999) para 35 (a stake or a business – while it is unclear from the public decision that the remedy was a crown jewel, the decision was quoted as an example of such in the old Remedies Notice, para 23, fn 26).

[273] See *Teva/Ratiopharm* (M.5865 I 2010) para 493 (certain medicines within Ratiopharm's activities in NL or the entire Ratiopharm business in NL); *ABF/GBI Business* (M.4980 II 2008) para 376, and Remedies Text, s B (a production plant would be added to sales and distribution assets during the second period); *J&J/Pfizer Consumer Healthcare* (M.4314 I 2006) para 141 (geographic scope of the divestiture would be extended to the US, Canada and South Korea during the second period); *VEBA/VIAG* (M.1673 II 2000), Remedies Text re Chemicals, II Sodium dicyanamide, para 2 (customer lists and orders would be added during the second period); and *Dow Chemical/Union Carbide* (M.1671 II 2000) para 175, and Remedies Text, s A (if a plant owned by Polimeri could not be sold, UCC's controlling stake in Polimeri would be sold during the second period). Along the same lines but slightly more unusual, in *New Holland/Case* (M.1571 I 1999) the remedies contained three alternatives relating to certain types of tractors in Austria; first a supply agreement, then a licence, and finally a divestiture of the respective tractors, see para 87, and Remedies Text, s 3.5.

[274] The Commission does not indicate specific time periods but it states in the Remedies Notice that the first option should be sold 'within a very short time period' (para 44) and the second option 'quickly' and within 'shorter periods' (para 45).

[275] In *Teva/Ratiopharm* (M.5865 I 2010) it was considered that the crown jewel, being a stand-alone business, was capable of being implemented so quickly, if need may be, that a second divestiture period was unnecessary, see para 493.

[276] Remedies Notice, para 45.

The Commission's past practice on crown jewels deserves the following comments. First, crown jewels must be distinguished from 'pure' alternative commitments. Occasionally the parties have been allowed to choose, at their own discretion, between two alternatives without the second option necessarily being dependant on failed implementation of the first option[277] and where the second option may not necessarily be equivalent to, or more extensive than, the first option. Generally alternative remedies have been accepted in cases where the acquirer in the main transaction lacked access to sufficient information about the target's assets when submitting the commitments,[278] or where third-party rights made the preferred option uncertain.[279] In past decisions the second proposal often contained different assets or measures (rather than building upon the first proposal) and hence one option would often relate to the target's assets whereas the other option would be the acquirer's assets or vice versa.[280] While the Commission appears to continue to accept 'pure' alternative remedies on rare occasion,[281] it is submitted that in recent years they have taken the form of crown jewels.[282]

Secondly, it is worth noting that the Commission's requirements seem slightly different from the longer-standing US practice of imposing crown jewels. According to the Commission's current practice crown jewels must be 'at least as good as' the first proposed divestiture in terms of creating a viable competitor,[283] whereas for example the FTC requires 'a more marketable package' in order to create incentives for the parties to do their utmost to implement their first proposal.[284] The FTC approach should be seen against the background that a crown jewel is typically sold by a trustee if the parties fail to divest their first option on time and therefore, in order to facilitate a faster and easier sale by the trustee, the

[277] In *Panasonic/Sanyo* (M.5421 I 2009) it was stressed in the remedies that the parties and the trustee would both have the option to switch between the alternatives during the divestiture periods, see Remedies Text, para 4(a); in *Alcan/Pechiney (II)* (M.3225 I 2003) the remedies stipulated that the choice between two different divestitures was subject to Alcan's 'absolute discretion', see Remedies Text, para 1.6.1.1; and similarly in *Glaxo Wellcome/SmithKline Beecham* (M.1846 I 2000) the parties could freely chose between out-licensing two different second generation drugs, see para 219; and the first part of the Remedies Text relating to Anti-Viral Commitments.

[278] This could be in hostile takeovers, such as in *Alcan/Pechiney (II)* (M.3225 I 2003), or in innovation intensive sectors where all contingencies for eg pipeline products cannot be foreseen or addressed when submitting the commitments, such as in pharmaceutical cases like *Pfizer/Pharmacia* (M.2922 I 2003), *Glaxo Wellcome/SmithKline Beecham* (M.1846 I 2000), *Pfizer-Warner-Lambert* (M.1878 I 2000) and *Glaxo/Wellcome* (M.555 I 1995).

[279] In *Bayer/Aventis Crop Science* (M.2547 II 2002) (in relation to concerns in professional pest control) the preferred option of a divestiture of a full business (ACS's Fipronil) was subject to any rights of a supplier Merial Limited and hence Bayer was allowed to replace the remedy with an exclusive licence of the respective products, see paras 1143–44, and Remedies Text, para 65. For other examples of alternative commitments due to third-party rights, see *Telia/Telenor* (M.1439 II 1999) paras 210 and 381(c); and *Anglo American Corporation/Lonrho* (M.754 II 1997) paras 127 and 131, as well as Remedies Study, pp 52–54.

[280] See eg *Glaxo Wellcome/SmithKline Beecham* (M.1846 I 2000) para 219; *Pfizer-Warner-Lambert* (M.1878 I 2000) para 91; and *Telia/Telenor* (M.1439 II 1999) para 381(c).

[281] See eg *Panasonic/Sanyo* (M.5421 I 2009) para 223; and Remedies Text, para 4(a).

[282] Indeed, in current guidance the Commission only mentions crown jewels (and not pure alternative commitments) in the Remedies Notice, see paras 44–46.

[283] Remedies Notice, para 45. In the old Remedies Notice the requirement was phrased slightly differently as the crown jewel had to be 'at least equal if not better suited to restore effective competition', see para 22. Similarly, in the Remedies Study the Commission defined a crown jewel as having 'a more extensive scope' than the first option (p 52 (point 3)), which is also in line with the interpretation in the 2004 OECD Remedies Study, p 29.

[284] See FTC FAQ About Merger Consent Order Provisions, Question 24; the FTC Guidelines for Negotiating Merger Remedies, p 21; and DoJ Merger Remedies Guide, Part IV.A.2.b (it should be noted that the DoJ recently has changed its policy in respect of crown jewels as it used to disfavour such provisions, see old DoJ Merger Remedies Guide, Part IV.H). Furthermore, in the FTC Divestiture Study it was emphasised that, although a crown jewel is not designed as a penalty clause or as punishment for failure to divest, it is clear that the parties may see its imposition as a threat to the value of their transaction and therefore they will do their utmost to ensure that there will be no occasion to activate the larger divestiture, see p 31.

crown jewel must be more attractive than the first option.[285] In contrast, the Commission's requirement of the second option being 'at least as good as' the first option implies that it is satisfied if the alternative is equivalent to and thus not necessarily better than the first option.[286] While the US approach may run the risk of the competition concerns being over-fixed if the second option is triggered (albeit rarely), it is submitted that the EU approach may not put as much pressure on the parties to divest their first option (and do so quickly) if their second option is not 'excessive'.[287] Also compared to the US, the Commission does not usually insist on a trustee selling the crown jewel, unless the parties have failed to do so in a first attempt.[288] Thus, the Commission currently seems more lenient in its approach to crown jewels in this respect.[289]

However, there is another difference in the approach to crown jewels that makes the Commission more demanding in one sense than its US counterparts. In its guidance the Commission now stresses that the first alternative must, absent the uncertainty, consist of a viable business and thus the wording suggests that both options must be viable from the

[285] See FTC FAQ About Merger Consent Order Provisions, Question 26. Consequently, as of 13 March 2002 only once had a party subject to a crown jewel provision failed to divest of the assets contained in its first proposal within the time required, see FTC About Merger Consent Order Provisions, Question 25, referring to *Aventis* (namely *Hoechst/Rhone-Poulenc*, Docket No C-3919), where a trustee was appointed to accomplish the alternative assets when the parties failed to divest the original assets on time. Also, it is emphasised in the FTC Guidelines for Negotiating Merger Remedies that a crown jewel 'may include assets in addition to the ones included in the original divestiture or it may be different assets such as the assets of the other party to the merger' with the overall purpose that the FTC can conclude that the remedies package will be more readily divested, see p 21.

[286] For an example of a so-called 'reverse crown jewel', see *VEBA/VIAG*, (M.1673 II 2000) where the parties offered in response to competition concerns in certain chemical markets several alternatives comprising of fewer and fewer assets to be divested. First the parties would offer to sell production plants for making cyanuric chloride (CC) but, if no purchaser was found within a certain time period, the parties would reduce the divested assets to the CC business and, if no purchaser was found within an extended time period, the parties would offer to sell the CC business minus the production facilities within a third deadline, see Remedies Text, VIII.I, paras 1–3. It is submitted that it is unlikely that the Commission would accept such a 'diminishing provision' under current practice.

[287] Moreover, in some early cases it is not evident from the Commission's assessment that the second option was indeed as good as the first option. Eg in *AXA/GRE* (M.1453 I 1999) (quoted in the old Remedies Notice as an example of a crown jewel) the parties committed, in response to competition concerns in several non-life insurance markets in Luxembourg, to reduce GRE's stake in a competitor, Le Foyer, or divest some of AXA's portfolios (para 22). The second proposal appears to have been offered due pre-emption clauses attached to the sale of GRE's stake in Le Foyer. However, judging from the Commission's competitive assessment of the main transaction it appears prima facie doubtful whether the second option would be equal to the first option (and indeed adequately solve the identified competition concerns) as an implementation of the second option would mean that the market leader AXA would, through the acquisition of GRE, retain structural links to (if not control over) Le Foyer, one of the largest market players in several non-life insurance markets in Luxembourg, see paras 28–32.

[288] *Industri Kapital/Dyno* (M.1813 II 2000) is one of the few cases where a trustee was appointed to sell the crown jewel from day one, see Remedies Text, para 10.

[289] Indeed, the FTC has a tradition for 'tough' crown jewels in the sense that the scope of the crown jewel provisions may be so broad that the parties will inevitably do their utmost to avoid them. Eg in connection with Roche Holding Ltd's acquisition of Corange Limited from Boehringer Mannheim (BM) in 1998 a remedy provided that, if Roche failed to license or divest of BM's US and Canadian Retavase business within 90 days, a trustee would divest the worldwide rights to Retavase. Another remedy provided that, if Roche failed to license or divest of BM's worldwide DAT reagents business and grant licences to certain patents within 60 days, a trustee would divest all of BM's CEDIA reagents, see FTC press release of 25 February 1998 *In the Matter of Roche Holding Ltd* (File No 971 0103, Docket No C-3809). Thus, the first crown jewel extended the geographic scope of the remedy and the second crown jewel extended the product scope of the remedy to such an extent that Roche had strong commercial incentives to ensure a speedy first divestment. As it happened, Roche managed to divest within the initial time frames and avoided the crown jewels, see FTC press releases of 27 May 1998 and 23 September 1998 (Docket No. C-3809). The parallel EU case (albeit different remedies) was *Hoffmann La Roche/Boehringer Mannheim* (M.950 II 1998) in which the decision did not provide for a crown jewel.

outset, irrespective of a potential purchaser's assets.[290] In contrast, crown jewels may allow the FTC/DoJ to accept less-than-a-viable-package from the outset with the fall-back measure of having a crown jewel if the former does not turn out to be viable once in the hands of the purchaser.[291] While the US policy allows for less intervention if the first option appears successful in the hands of the approved purchaser, this approach would be more risky in the EU proceedings as the Commission often will not know the identity (and thus the assets) of the purchaser when assessing and accepting the remedies.[292]

Thirdly, companies have voiced concerns about crown jewels being too burdensome, expensive and disproportionate, as the Commission requires that interim preservation and holding separate measures apply to both options from the outset.[293] The overall argument of the critics is that, as the second option is far less likely to occur, it is unnecessary and disproportionate to require immediate separation of those assets and delay their integration as this will not only be more costly for the parties but also create uncertainty among employees as to whether the alternative assets will stay with its current owner or be divested.[294] However, by insisting on interim measures applying from the outset to both options the Commission clearly considers such safeguarding appropriate and proportionate in order to prevent a possible (and likely non-reversible) deterioration of the respective assets prior to completed implementation. It is considered that this policy is in line with the increased emphasis on the importance of interim preservation of the assets in recent years.[295]

Fourthly, under current practice the Commission appears to publish the main contents of a crown jewel provision in its market test as well as clearance decision.[296] However, it has been argued that by making potential purchasers aware of a crown jewel, they may take advantage of the situation and intentionally delay negotiating for the agreed-upon divestiture assets so they may later purchase the crown jewels at an attractive price which could ultimately be very costly for the parties and compromise the achievement of some synergies from the transaction.[297] While the Commission often accommodated such 'purchaser manipulation concerns' in early cases and considered even the existence of a crown jewel or alternative remedy a business secret,[298] the current view appears to be that full confidentiality would jeopardise the

[290] Remedies Notice, para 45. This approach is in line with the Commission's increasingly rigorous policy relating to the scope of a remedy as set out in para 30 of the Remedies Notice.

[291] See DoJ Merger Remedies Guide, Part IV.A.2.b (note that DoJ has changed its policy in its new Merger Remedies Guide from 2011 as it previously strongly disfavoured crown jewels), FTC FAQ About Merger Consent Order Provisions, Question 24, and Shapiro and Sohn (1997).

[292] The US approach should be seen against the background that the FTC/DoJ often know the identity of the purchaser prior to the final approval of the remedies. However, in the past the Commission has occasionally taken risks in terms of allowing a first option of a narrower and seemingly not up-front viable remedy such as a supply agreement in *New Holland/Case* (M.1571 I 1999), see para 87.

[293] This aspect received many critical comments during the public consultation in 2007 of the draft new Remedies Notice, see eg replies from Bars and Law Societies of the UK (para 2.12), Grimaldi e Associati (p 4), IBA (p 14) and Lovells (para 8). It should be noted that the Commission's practice has not been entirely consistent on this point as eg in *Industri Kapital/Dyno* (M.1813 II 2000) the hold separate obligation for the crown jewel applied only for the additional period of time that was required for the second option, see Remedies Text, para 8.

[294] See also Baer and Redcay (2001) 1712, as well as criticism cited in the Remedies Study, p 55 (point 12).

[295] Compared to the old Remedies Notice, the Commission has tightened its preservation requirements in the new notice, see paras 108–12.

[296] Some decisions refer to the crown jewel being market tested, see eg *ABF/GBI Business* (M.4980 II 2008) para 383; and *WPP/TNS* (M.5232 I 2008) paras 158–60.

[297] See critical comments during the public consultation in 2007 of the draft new Remedies Notice in replies by ABA (p 14) and IBA (para 62). The Commission did not address this issue in the final version of the notice.

[298] eg in *Pfizer/Pharmacia* (M.2922 I 2003) several divestiture remedies contain 'fall back' provisions in the event the parties failed to implement their divestitures but the entire contents of such provisions were considered business secrets, see Remedies Text, Schedule III, s E, and Schedule V, s E. Similarly, see also *Astra/Zeneca/Novartis*

Commission's market test and thus ultimately weaken its competitive assessment if third parties would be excluded from commenting on the viability of the second option. It is thus considered that the Commission's current practice of publishing at least general information on crown jewels seems not only reasonable but also necessary in a practice where the results of the market tests play an important role in the Commission's overall assessment.

Fifth, while the exact reasons for accepting crown jewels are not always evident from the Commission's decisions, practice shows that they have been accepted mainly in cases where the fulfilment of the first option depended on third parties' pre-emption rights,[299] or there have been concerns about the existence of suitable purchasers.[300] However, it is important to stress that the acceptance of crown jewels has been confined to a limited number of cases.[301] However, that does not necessarily mean that the Commission would not have considered, let alone accepted, such provisions given that it submitted in the Remedies Study that the efficiency of eight remedies would be have benefited from alternatives being proposed and accepted.[302] Although speculative, the infrequent use of crown jewels may well be due to the parties' reluctance to submit such proposals due to the above-mentioned disadvantages rather than the Commission's reluctance to assess and possibly accept them. Furthermore, while it is difficult to evaluate how often crown jewels have been triggered as such information is not readily available, one of the few publicly known cases is *Nestlé/Ralston Purina*[303] and it must thus be assumed that crown jewels are rarely implemented, which would also be in line with US practice. Moreover, it is worth noting that the vast majority of crown jewels and alternative commitments have been accepted by the Commission in cooperation cases with the FTC or DoJ.[304]

Finally, a few comments on the interplay between crown jewels and up-front buyer provisions seem warranted. First, on rare occasions the Commission has considered it necessary to combine the two provisions in order to ensure that, in the event the up-front provision is not fulfilled, an alternative option was in place.[305] While the combined provisions would prevent the parties' concentration from being declared void if they fail in finding a pur-

(M.1806 II 2000) para 470 and Remedies Text, para 12; and *Imetal/English China Clays* (M.1381 I 1999) para 86, where it is presumed, based on the wordings, that the Commission accepted that all references to crown jewels were deleted from the public version. Also in the Remedies Study the Commission highlights a case where the parties committed to divest certain assets as an alternative option if they failed to negotiate a supply agreement for the respective products and in the interview the purchaser under the supply agreement confirmed that he had never been made aware of the possible wider scope of the remedy, see p 52 (point 3).

[299] See eg *Novartis/Alcon* (M.5778 I 2010) and *WPP/TNS* (M.5232 I 2008).

[300] See eg *ABF/GBI Business* (M.4980 II 2008).

[301] For some cases in recent years, see *WPP/TNS* (M.5232 I 2008) and *ABF/GBI Business* (M.4980 II 2008).

[302] See Remedies Study, p 54 (point 10). To this effect, see also Speech by Monti (2002b) 5: 'the Commission expects to see more of [crown jewels] in the future'.

[303] See Speech by Collins (2002) and Speech by Monti (2002b) 5. While it is generally considered that *Nestlé/Ralston Purina* (M.2337 I 2001) is a 'classic' crown jewel case it should be noted that it is slightly atypical as the parties explicitly stated in their commitments that the second alternative (divestiture of a joint venture (JV) stake) would be 'according to Nestlé's own free choice', see Remedies Text, A.2.a). However, the second alternative (divestiture) was clearly wider in scope than the first option (licensing). In the end, the JV stake was sold to the other joint venture partner (Agrolimen). For an unnamed case where the second alternative ('the most beautiful baby in the sector') was also implemented, see Remedies Study, p 53 (point 6).

[304] See eg *Novartis/Alcon* (M.5778 I 2010), *Pfizer/Pharmacia* (M.2922 I 2003), *Nestlé/Ralston Purina* (M.2337 I 2001), *Astra/Zeneca/Novartis* (M.1806 II 2000), *Glaxo Wellcome/SmithKline Beecham* (M.1846 I 2000), *Dow Chemical/Union Carbide* (M.1671 II 2000), *Imetal/English China Clays* (M.1381 I 1999), and *New Holland/Case* (M.1571 I 1999). Similarly, *WPP/TNS* (M.5232 I 2008) was also reviewed by the Canadian competition authority.

[305] One of the few cases to date where such a combination has been offered and accepted was in *Nestlé/Ralston Purina* (M.2337 I 2001).

chaser for the up-front buyer assets,[306] it could be argued that such a scenario would not necessarily be in accordance with the requirement that phase I remedies must be straightforward and clear-cut. Thus, if applicable, the combination of the provisions seems more appropriate in phase II proceedings. In any event, practice shows that the use of the combined provisions has been confined to extraordinary circumstances.[307] Secondly, in its guidance the Commission indicates that in situations where the implementation of the divestiture is uncertain due to third-party rights or the lack of suitable purchasers, crown jewels and up-front buyer provisions address the same concerns and thus the parties may choose between the two options.[308] However, it is considered that such a genuinely 'free choice' between the two provisions is unlikely to apply to situations where there is a risk of potentially interim harm to the assets. Indeed the Commission itself previously found in its Remedies Study that up-front buyer provisions are particularly suitable if there are serious threats to competition in the interim period or that assets could be degraded in the interim[309] and hence a free choice is not considered to apply in such situations.

**Commentary:** all the above-described 'ancillary' tools are inspired by US practice and, indeed, the use of particularly up-front and crown-jewel provisions have been confined to EU/US cooperation cases in the past. Since the underlying rationale behind the provisions is to transfer the risk of a failed remedy to the merging parties, it is unclear why the Commission has not promoted such measures more frequently. However, it has to be said that there are indications from the latest decisional practice that especially up-front buyer provisions are being increasingly favoured if the parties are prepared to offer them.

While it is obvious that fix-it-first solutions are difficult to achieve within the strict timetables of remedies cases, up-front buyer provisions are a way of compensating for such timetables and indeed easily compatible with the existing remedies framework, as the impact is post-decision and focuses on the suspension of the parties' main transaction. Given that the parties have no natural incentives to quickly and properly implement a remedy (and may even pose obstacles), up-front buyer provisions mitigate risks of strategic behaviour in this respect as the parties have all incentives to implement the remedy as speedily as possible in order to implement their main transaction. Thus, it is considered that great sympathy should be voiced for the argument that up-front solutions should be used frequently, if not systematically.

From the parties' point of view, up-front buyer provisions should not necessarily be viewed with great scepticism (compared to offering substantial additional assets, for example) if they are reasonably confident that their remedies are viable. If any doubts exist, they may add a crown jewel to ensure that the validity of their main transaction is not endangered if no purchaser is found. Admittedly, crown jewels may prove costly and burdensome with wider financial and organisational implications for the parties, as the Commission generally requires that interim preservation and hold-separate measures are applied to all assets in both options from the outset. However, crown jewels could still with benefit be considered an attractive fall-back position if unexpected complications arise with the up-front solution.

306 This is the main reason why the FTC assesses the need for an up-front buyer and for a crown jewel separately and on a case-by-case basis, see FTC FAQ About Merger Consent Order Provisions, Question 27.

307 With respect to US practice (which differs from EU practice as the purchaser will be identified earlier in the proceedings) commentators have submitted that, given the slim risk of the sale to an up-front buyer falling through, there is a sound basis for opposing the inclusion of crown jewels in up-front buyer cases, see Baer, Feinstein and Meisner (2004) 51; Baer and Redkay (2001), and Shapiro and Sohn (1997) 32. However, it has to be remembered that these views do not entirely apply to the EU situation where a purchaser has not yet been identified at the point in time of adopting the conditional clearance decision and hence the risks of an up-front buyer solutions failing under the Merger Regulation is higher than in the US.

308 Remedies Notice, para 46.

309 Remedies Study, p 55 (point 13). See also Remedies Notice, para 55.

One last observation on the choice between up-front buyer provisions and fix-it-first provisions relates to the recent *UPS/TNT Express* prohibition decision.[310] Going against the general assumption that fix-it-first solutions are normally less feasible than up-front buyer solutions, it was alleged during the (failed) negotiations between the merging parties and the Commission that, on the one hand, UPS was not prepared to submit an up-front buyer commitment but was instead hoping for a fix-it-first solution while, on the other hand, the Commission insisted on an up-front buyer provision, claiming that UPS had run out of time to submit a fix-it-first solution.[311] While UPS refrained from publicly explaining why it preferred a fix-it-first solution, it may have been due to the fact that an up-front buyer provision would have prevented UPS from closing the transaction for several months and this delay could have given the prospective purchaser (already identified as DPD, a French parcel provider) an advantageous bargaining position to the extent that the anticipated remedies costs would have exceeded what UPS was prepared to pay for a conditional clearance.[312] Also, the resistance to an up-front buyer solution could indicate that UPS may not have been sufficiently confident of the prospective purchaser's intentions or capabilities with the result that, if the Commission would not eventually approve the purchaser, the main transaction would be declared void and no longer stand.

The fatal downside with UPS's strategy was that it simply ran out of time to conclude a fix-it-first solution prior to the deadline for the adoption of a conditional clearance decision.[313] The failed remedies negotiations demonstrate that fix-it-first solutions are indeed difficult to achieve within the tight deadlines, even in phase II proceedings. Also, the case shows that the Commission will insist on obtaining additional assurances (in this case the up-front buyer provision) if it has any remaining doubts as to the quantity and/or quality of prospective purchasers, despite the parties having submitted a substantial remedies package.[314]

[310] See *UPS/TNT Express* (M.6570 II 2013). As the public version of the decision is not yet available at the time of writing, the following comments relating on the Commission's position are based on the its press release IP/13/68 and MEMO/13/48 of 30 January 2013.

[311] See in particular Commission MEMO/13/48, p 5; and Mlex Comment: 'EC's Veto of UPS, TNT Reveals Pressure on Up-front Buyer Solution' (30 January 2013), available at www.mlex.com/EU/Content.aspx?ID=314061.

[312] This view is based on the assumption that, all things being equal, the divestiture price for the assets would be higher under a fix-it-first solution (where both parties would be eager to close a remedies deal as quickly as possible prior to the Commission's adoption of the conditional clearance decision) whereas under an up-front buyer solution there would be significantly more at stake for UPS than the prospective purchaser as any delays or disagreements in the negotiations could mean that the main transaction would fall through.

[313] Judging from the case file all available extensions of deadlines had been used.

[314] It is not entirely clear form the Commission's press release and memo whether the Commission would have considered the remedies package complete if the parties would have added the required up-front buyer provision.

# 4

# Implementing and Enforcing Remedies

## 4.1 Divestiture Periods

It has proven paramount for the overall success of a divestiture remedy that the duration of the implementation period is as accurate and appropriate as possible.[1] If the divestiture period is too long, the viability and competitiveness of the assets to be divested are likely to diminish and, more specifically, it may be difficult to retain personnel, customers and business partners during the implementation period. Also long periods entail increased monitoring costs and resources, both for the parties and the Commission, and it becomes increasingly difficult to reverse the original transaction if the divestiture encounters complications or ultimately fails.

On the other hand, excessively short periods may result in difficulties for the parties in finding and negotiating with a suitable purchaser and/or the latter may pursue strategic bargaining, which could have negative effects on the achievable sales price and potentially amount to a fire-sale. Equally, very short time periods may disadvantage prospective purchasers when assessing the business and undertaking due diligence with the risk of paying an excessive value for the assets or unwittingly foregoing vital assets.

In order to emphasise the importance of deadlines being adhered to and implemented as quickly as possible the Commission has in newer practice consistently required that deadlines are considered conditions, not obligations.[2] In terms of enforcement this means that the consequences of not divesting within the legal deadline are severe as, in principle, the conditional clearance decision no longer stands and the parties are liable to significant fines, unless the parties have applied for and been granted an extension of the deadline. Thus, the parties have every incentive to adhere to the deadlines.

Contrary to US policy, the exact duration of the deadlines in divestiture remedies constitute confidential information between the Commission and the parties.[3] While in some cases the parties may choose to announce the deadlines themselves upon clearance of the

[1] Remedies Notice, para 98; and Remedies Study, p 109 (in particular points 1–3 where the Commission lists the downsides of very long and excessively short deadlines, respectively). See also the ICN Remedies Review Project, p 4.

[2] Remedies Notice, para 20; and Remedies Study p 109 (point 2). See also Speech by Mederer (2001) 3.

[3] The main aim of the confidentiality is to prevent opportunistic behaviour by prospective purchasers, see Remedies Study, p 71 (point 12). In order to safeguard confidentiality, the DG Competition usually omits the exact deadlines in its consultation of not only third parties but also of associated services within the Commission as well as the Member States. Contrary to this, in the US divestiture deadlines (if known) are made publicly available immediately after the formal approval of the respective transaction. In some EU/US cooperation cases the Commission's conditional clearance decision has therefore stated the divestiture deadline as it has already been published in the US proceedings, see eg *Cisco/Tandberg* (M.5669 I 2010) para 147, and Remedies Text, para 2.1 (Cisco committed to divest certain assets within 120 days).

transaction – for strategic reasons or because the divestiture period is already known in the industry or public domain – the Commission usually never confirms or refutes such information.[4] However, in newer practice the Commission has found it appropriate to be more transparent in its implementation policy and has thus provided general indications of acceptable deadlines for the actual divestiture, possible extensions and time allowed for subsequent closing (meaning the transfer of the legal title of the transaction).[5]

Accordingly, the total time period for implementation is generally divided into two phases: (i) a period for negotiating and entering into a final agreement; and (ii) a further period for the closing.[6] The first phase is sub-divided into (i-a) a period where the parties can divest the assets themselves to a suitable purchaser (the first divestiture period); and (i-b) a period where a trustee is mandated to divest on behalf of the parties the assets at no minimum price before the expiry of that period (the trustee divestiture period).

As a general rule, the Commission currently allows around 6 months for the parties to divest the assets themselves, an additional 3 months for the trustee to divest, and another 3 months for the parties or trustee (as appropriate) to close the transaction with the approved purchaser.[7] In the vast majority of cases the deadlines run from the day of the adoption of the Commission's conditional clearance decision although the Commission may exceptionally accept that the periods run from a later time, such as the date of closing.[8] On rare occasions, the Commission has allowed that certain commitments would be triggered only if certain circumstances did or did not emerge at a later stage.[9]

Throughout the years the Commission has significantly shortened the time period allowed for the parties to divest their assets and the current initial period of six months is considered short compared to earlier practice.[10] Moreover, in recent years the Commission

[4] In *Arjowiggens/M-real Zanders Reflex* (M.4513 II 2008) M-real announced on the day of the adoption of the Commission's conditional clearance decision that the respective business had to be divested within 180 days, see www.m-real.com, press release of 4 June 2008. The Commission published no information in this respect.

[5] By contrast, in the early days the Commission refrained from providing any details on deadlines and to this effect the old Remedies Notice contained no guidance on durations. The first time the Commission published general indications on acceptable divestiture periods was in its Best Practice Remedies Guidelines (2003) para 15, and MTDC, para 2. Subsequently the Commission elaborated further on the details of such periods in its Remedies Notice, see in particular paras 97–99.

[6] See Remedies Notice, para 97. In fix-it-first cases the deadlines will relate only to the closing of the transaction, see para 100.

[7] ibid, para 98.

[8] As examples of the latter, the Commission lists public bids and events beyond the control of the parties (eg if state approvals are involved), see Remedies Notice, para 99. A particular situation arose in *GDF Suez/International Power* (M.5978 I 2011) where the joint venture, in which the merging parties were required to divest of their stake, was not yet operational as the plant that was the core of the remedy was still under construction. The parties argued that the divestiture period should start from the date when the plant would be operational (ie around 6 months following the conditional clearance decision) but the Commission concluded in view of the results from the market test that the divestiture period should commence from the effective date, see paras 129 and 133.

[9] See *Glaxo Wellcome/Smith Kline Beecham* (M.1846 I 2000) where the Commission, rather surprisingly, accepted that the remedies (relating to the treatment of Chronic Obstructive Pulmonary Disease (COPD)) would enter into force only when/if all the following conditions were fulfilled: (i) phase III clinical trials for the product for the licensed use have been completed; (ii) all the competing pipeline products have failed phase III clinical trials and (iii) there is no other competing product which has completed or is about to complete and subsequently completes phase III clinical trials for the respective products, see Remedies Text, in particular para 46. According to Cook and Kerse (2009) the implementation was postponed 3 years (para 8-031) while Davies and Lyons (2007) submit that the remedy was never triggered (p 225). In any event, this 'wait-and-see' approach displayed by the Commission in this case is considered unlikely to be acceptable under current practice.

[10] In the earlier days of the Merger Regulation the Commission accepted relatively long divestiture periods, see eg *Guinness/Grand Metropolitan* (M.938 II 1997) a first divestiture period of 15 months was deemed acceptable (para 183). By the end of the 1990s the Commission became more aware of this issue and eg one senior DG Competition official admitted that 'we may have sometimes been too "generous" in the past in granting

has been able to keep the *actual* divestiture period relatively close to – and even shorter than – the *foreseen* period: in the remedies cases between 1996 and 2000 the actual implementation time was 6.2 months (against the average foreseen time being 7.6 months) and out of the analysed remedies where 6-month deadlines were foreseen, 68 per cent of these were achieved within the prescribed time.[11] Interestingly, the majority of divestitures were executed 2, 6 or 10 months after the conditional clearance of the transaction.[12] This statistics implies that assets are generally either sold relatively quickly or the parties need the full time available or even an extension.

With respect to the frequency and duration of extensions of deadlines in past cases from 1996 to 2000, the Commission's experience shows that around 30 per cent of the remedies were extended but most extensions were normally given for only one or two months in order to complete an already advanced sales process.[13] While the formal requirements for extensions are dealt with elsewhere,[14] it is noted that the Remedies Study did not generate sufficient evidence to judge the appropriateness of the granted extensions.[15] However, a proportion of 30 per cent of remedies being extended seems relatively high, especially in view of the fact that at the time of the study a review clause was not yet standard practice. As the reasons for granting extensions – and indeed the extensions themselves – are generally not published, it is difficult to contemplate whether the high proportion of extensions being granted reflects miscalculations/misjudgements of the original divestiture period and/or unpredictable changes in market conditions pending implementation.

Regarding the prescribed 3-month period applying to the closing of the transaction, the Commission did not investigate in its Remedies Study whether the parties generally adhered to this deadline.[16] However, this period needed for the actual transfer of the business after the conclusion of a binding SPA seems less problematic and is, according to newer practice, usually supervised by a monitoring trustee. It is generally considered that the current 3-month period appears adequate.

Lastly, it should be noted that the implementation time for remedies relating to the divestiture of/exit from joint ventures is generally longer than in remedies relating to the divestiture of assets. Accordingly, the Remedies Study revealed that the joint venture deadlines were on average 8.5 months (compared to 7.6 months for the transfer of assets) while the actual average implementation periods were 7.7 months (compared to 6.2 months for the transfer of assets).[17] Thus, similarly to divestitures, joint venture remedies were implemented quicker than foreseen in the remedies texts. Furthermore it is worth mentioning that only a few of the deadlines in the joint venture remedies were extended (4 out of 15 remedies), primarily due to unforeseen obstacles caused by third party rights.[18]

unnecessary long transitory periods', see Rakovsky in IBA (2000) 141. In the following years the Commission managed to significantly shorten the divestiture period in several cases, see eg *The Post Office/TPG/SPPL* (M.1915 II 2001) (3½ months), and *Industri Kapital/Dyno* (M.1813 II 2000) (re 'Kitee Business': 4 months), mentioned in Speech by Mederer (2001).

[11] Remedies Study, p 111 (points 9–10).

[12] ibid, p 111 (point 9, chart 18).

[13] ibid, p 112 (point 12).

[14] See section 4.4.4.1 below.

[15] Remedies Study, p 112 (point 14).

[16] ibid, p 111 (point 9, fn 294).

[17] ibid, p 112 (points 15–16).

[18] ibid, p 112 (point 17). It could be argued that it is rather surprising that only 4 out of 15 remedies were extended given the prominent role of third-party rights in joint venture remedies and hence the increased risk that they may create implementation obstacles.

**Commentary:** As the foreseen and actual time periods used by the parties to implement their remedies are not made publicly available by the Commission, it is difficult to generalise about the duration of divestiture periods. However, based on the data in the Commission's Remedies Study it must be assumed that divestitures are generally implemented within the standard duration of around 6 months, taking into account the sector in question and the modalities of the remedies. However, it is worth noting that, based on publicly available information from other sources in certain cases, some implementation periods have been significantly longer, also in newer practice.[19] In any event, only new ex-post reviews by the Commission would be able to shed light on the possible success rate in this context.

Regarding divestiture periods being well-guarded business secrets, the necessity of confidentiality may seem questionable when compared to US practice where divestiture deadlines are made publicly available speedily and with little controversy. Indeed, in the past there have been examples of EU–US cooperation cases where deadlines (sometimes relating to identical remedies) are kept confidential in the Commission's clearance decision but made publicly available in parallel US press information and decisions.[20] Thus, it appears appropriate for the Commission to further reflect whether there is a genuine need for systematically keeping *all* remedies deadlines confidential.

If the Commission were to introduce more transparency on accepted divestiture deadlines, the implementation process becomes not only more transparent for interested purchasers but the Commission also sustains the pressure on the parties to divest timely, which may contribute to the efficiency of the remedy. Naturally, the benefits of publishing the exact divestiture deadlines must be carefully weighted up against the risk of fire sales to the detriment of the parties. However, the parties must also be prepared to take certain costs in connection with the implementation of remedies in order to get the underlying merger cleared and US practice shows that increased transparency surrounding deadlines does not necessarily result in fatal fire-sales (otherwise it is presumed that such a practice would not be adhered to). Furthermore, given that the guidelines in the Remedies Notice currently indicate that the main divestiture deadlines are likely to be around 6 months, exact deadlines may be less market sensitive compared to earlier decisional practice where no such indications were given. To this effect, the parties sometimes chose to disclose the agreed divestiture periods when the conditional clearance decision is announced.[21]

[19] A rather striking example can be found in *EDF/Segebel* (M.5549 I 2009) where the Commission emphasised the importance of one of the remedies (the divestiture of an energy project) being implemented 'immediately' in order to replace the parties with a different market player, see para 235 of the decision. However, it is apparent from the subsequent Court proceedings that this particular divestiture was not implemented before July 2011, hence more than 18 months after the adoption of the Commission's conditional clearance decision, see *EDF v Commission* (T-389/12 pending), order by the President of the General Court of 11 October 2012, para 2. It is also evident from the Court papers that the second remedy (investing in or divesting of another energy project) had been given a deadline of 30 June 2012 (see para 3 of the Court order) which the parties failed to meet and therefore asked the Commission for an extension until 31 December 2014. The Commission refused an extension and hence the parties appealed the Commission's decision in this respect. The Court proceedings are currently pending.

[20] See eg *Thomson Corporation/Reuters Group* (M.4726 II 2008) which involved an extensive cooperation between the Commission and the DoJ which the result that the authorities cleared the transaction on the same day and subject to three identical remedies (plus an additional remedy in the EU). When the DoJ announced its clearance it specified that Thomson was required to sell the respective assets within 60 days whereas the Commission treated the same divestiture deadlines as confidential information (also in the subsequent public decision), see DoJ press release of 19 February 2008, Case No 1:08-cv-00262 and Commission press release IP/08/260 of 19 February 2008.

[21] For a recent example, see *Outokumpu/Inoxum* (M.6471 II 2012) where Outokumpu's chief executive officer confirmed to the press even prior to the official approval approval by the Commission that the parties would be granted 6 months to sell the respective plant before a divestiture trustee would be appointed, reported by Bloomberg, Aoife White and Kasper Viita, 'Outokumpu Bid for Inoxum Unit Set to Win EU Approval' (29 October 2012), available at www.bloomberg.com/news/2012-10-29/outokumpu-bid-for-inoxum-unit-set-to-win-eu-approval.html.

## 4.2 Role and Functions of Trustees

### *4.2.1 General Characteristics*

#### 4.2.1.1 Approval Procedure and Mandate

Typically, the first step in the implementation of remedies is that the parties propose one or several trustees to the Commission, including the full terms of mandates and outline of work-plans.[22] Trusteeships in merger proceedings are somehow unique in the sense that the trustee acts on behalf – and under the supervision – of the Commission but is appointed and remunerated by the parties. Thus, while the contractual relationship governing the trustee mandate is purely between the parties and the trustee, the latter must act independently of the former and can accept instructions from the Commission only, which in effect makes the relationship a tripartite one among the Commission, the trustee and the parties. Moreover, the decision to appoint and set up a trustee as part of the respective remedies proceedings must be offered voluntarily by the parties and cannot be unilaterally imposed by the Commission.

Depending on the circumstances, the overall purpose of a trustee is to monitor the implementation of the remedies and/or execute any divestitures.[23] It is established practice that monitoring trustees are appointed in virtually all cases and their roles are considered vital for a timely and proper implementation of the remedies.[24] While divestiture trustees are normally provided for in the standard text of all divestiture remedies,[25] they are rarely appointed and active as the parties will have done their utmost to divest the assets themselves within the first divestiture period.[26]

As the proposal of trustees involves considerable work and costs for the parties (in terms of selecting and assessing potential trustees as well as drafting mandates and work-plans) the number of prospective trustees on the 'short-list' presented to the Commission is usually kept to a minimum.[27] According to standard provisions the parties shall propose (i) a

[22] For provisions relating to the approval of the trustee and mandate, see Remedies Notice, paras 123–27; MTDC, paras 16–21; and MTTM, paras 1–5.

[23] The monitoring trustee may or may not be the same person or institution as the divestiture trustee, see Remedies Notice, para 123. During the early days of the Merger Regulation one trustee would normally undertake both tasks. In newer practice the Commission has increasingly acknowledged that different tasks require different qualifications, see Remedies Study, p 90–92 (points 13–19).

[24] By way of illustration, from 2005 to 2010, 91 out of 99 conditional clearance decisions by the Commission contained a monitoring trustee provision, and in the last 2 years every conditional clearance decision contained such a provision, see Brueckner and Hoehn (2010). These statistics are similar to the ones found in the Remedies Study where virtually all remedies (66 out of 68) studied by the Commission from 1996 to 2000 required a monitoring trustee, see p 87 (point 3). Examples of cases where no monitoring trustee was provided for in the remedies include *Allianz/Dresdner* (M.2431 I 2001), *Vodafone/Vivendi/Canal Plus* (JV.48 I 2000), *Rohm+Haas/Morton* (M.1467 I 1999), *Fujitsu/Siemens* (JV.22 I 1999), *Thyssen/Krupp* (M.1080 I 1998), and *British Telecom/MCI (II)* (M.856 II 1997). Upon examination of these cases, there appear to be no common features or particular reasons why monitoring was deemed unnecessary.

[25] To the best of my knowledge, the first divestiture trustee was appointed in *Unilever France/Ortiz Miko* (M.422 I 1994), see Competition Report 1994, para 319.

[26] See section 4.2.3 below.

[27] In EU–US cooperation cases with identical remedies, the authorities have occasionally agreed to the appointment of a single trustee, see eg *Manitowoc/Enodis* (M.5180 I 2008) where the DoJ would, if needed, appoint the divestiture trustee, in consultation with the Commission, see *United States v The Manitowoc Company, Inc., Enodis plc, and Enocis Corporation*, Case No 1:2008CV01704, Final Judgment of 17 February 2009, section V.A. The same trustees were also appointed by the Commission in *Western Digital Ireland/Viviti Technologies* (M.6203 II 2011)

monitoring trustee within 1 week of the adoption of the clearance decision;[28] and (ii) a divestiture trustee within 1 month prior to the expiry of the first divestiture period.[29] Once the Commission has received and decided upon the proposal(s),[30] it informs the parties of its decision by sending an administrative letter either approving or rejecting the proposed trustee(s).[31] Under the Commission's current practice, trustee approvals or rejection letters are considered procedural and thus not made publicly available. However, a new practice seems to be emerging whereby the Commission, once the trustee is appointed and has commenced its activities, publishes the identity and details of the trustee on its website in order to provide a contact point.[32] While such publications are welcomed in order to enhance transparency in the implementation process, they are not followed up by for example any press announcements and thus interested parties will need to check the respective case file on the DG Competition's website in order to access such information. By contrast, the FTC announces the identity of appointed trustees when approving the transaction, if possible.[33] Also, it varies from case to case as to when the trustee information is made available on the

and by the FTC *In the Matter of Western Digital Corporation* (File No 111 0122, Docket No C-4350), see Ratliff and Louis in Knable Gotts (2012) 475.

[28] MTDC, para 18; and Remedies Notice, para 123 (as a technical comment, it is considered an unfortunate mistake that the new Remedies Notice prescribes a 2-week deadline in this respect, see para 123, fn 1). Before the publication of the Best Practice Remedies Guidelines in 2003 this deadline was typically 2 weeks, see eg *Danish Crown/Vestjyske Slagterier* (M.1313 II 1999) para 228, or even 4 weeks, see *Guinness/GrandMet* (M.938 II 1997) para 183(vi). In even earlier cases the remedies would sometimes contain no deadlines for the appointment of a monitoring trustee, see *Orkla/Volvo* (M.582 II 1995) para 123(2). At the other end of the spectrum, the parties agreed to start the approval procedure for a trustee on the date of the adoption of a decision in *Fortis/ABN Amro Assets* (M.4844 I 2007) in view of the important functions of the trustee and to ensure that sufficient safeguards were in place in the event of disputes which could affect the viability of the assets in question in a difficult carve-out case, see para 235. In *Metso/Aker Kvaerner* (M.4187 II 2006) the parties committed not to close the main transaction before a monitoring trustee had been appointed after approval by the Commission, see para 147.

[29] MTDC, para 16, and Remedies Notice, para 123.

[30] Remedies Notice, para 124. There is no deadline for the Commission's decision in this respect. In the early days of the Merger Regulation, a trustee would typically be approved under a so-called 'non-opposition procedure' where the trustee was automatically deemed approved if the Commission had not reacted within 2 weeks, see eg *Hoffmann La Roche/Boehringer Mannheim* (M.950 II 1998) para 162. This practice was later abolished due to the risk of the Commission not reacting promptly to a trustee proposal within the deadline and thus silently approving an unacceptable candidate.

[31] An approval is usually kept brief, merely referring to the various submissions made by the parties and the proposed trustee without explaining why the proposed candidate, mandate and outline of work plan is considered acceptable, whereas a rejection letter normally explains why the proposed candidate, mandate and/or outline work plan is unacceptable, see De Souza and Brockhoff in Drauz and Jones (2012) para 7.331.

[32] Para 126 of the Remedies Notice provides that the Commission may, in appropriate cases, publish the identity of the trustee and a summary of its tasks. While such publications were rare during the first few years after the provision was inserted in 2008, the practice has increased in recent years. For recent examples of such publications, see case files of *Glencore/Xstrata* (M.6541 I 2012), *IAG/BMI* (M.6447 I 2012), *UTC/Goodrich* (M.6410 II 2012), *Südzucker/ED&F MAN* (M.6286 II 2012), and *Western Digital Ireland/Viviti Technologies* (M.6203 II 2011). Extraordinarily, remedies have provided that the parties will publish the trustee's name and contact details on their website, see *Cisco/Tandberg* (M.5669 I 2010), Remedies Text, para 5.1.1.

[33] eg in *Procter & Gamble/Gillette* the identity of the interim trustee (Edward Gold of PricewaterhouseCoopers) was already revealed in the press release announcing the conditional clearance, see FTC press release of 30 September 2005 (File No 051 0115, Docket No C-4151) whereas in *BP Amoco/Atlantic Richfield Company* the trustee (Peter Denn, a partner at Deloitte/Touche LLP) was approved at a later stage and his identity announced by separate press release of 19 September 2000 and publication of the approval letter (File No 991-0192, Docket No C-3938).

DG Competition's website, typically ranging from 1 week to 1 month after the adoption of the Commission's conditional clearance decision.[34]

When the proposed trustees are approved, the parties must formally appoint them within 1 week of the Commission's approval.[35] In the event that none of the proposed candidates are acceptable to the Commission, the parties have 1 week after being informed of the Commission's rejection to make a new proposal, and if the new proposal is rejected, the Commission may nominate a trustee.[36] To date, there have been no official reports or discussions of the Commission having to nominate a trustee of its own choosing and this scenario is considered rare.

Thus in a straightforward trustee approval procedure, the lapse of time between the Commission's conditional clearance decision and the appointment of the trustee could be as short as a few weeks.[37] However, experience in the Remedies Study showed that the actual time needed to appoint trustees was often significantly longer.[38] Typical reasons for delays were failure by the parties to provide adequate information, failure to submit an adequate trustee mandate or rejection of the parties' initially proposed trustee.[39]

The Commission has therefore in recent years become more rigorous and stresses in its current guidance that the monitoring trustee must be in place *immediately* after the Commission's conditional clearance decision,[40] and that the remedies should normally foresee that the notified transaction can be implemented only once the monitoring trustee is appointed.[41] As mentioned above, judging from the information recently put on the case registers on the DG Competition's website in cases where the contact details of the appointed trustees have been published, it has proven possible in some instances to have a trustee appointed and active within a few weeks while in other cases it has taken considerably longer.[42] However, given the fact that it is not uncommon for the Commission to

[34] Obviously, such publications depend on how quickly the respective trustees are approved and appointed. In eg *BASF/INEOS/Styrene/JV* (M.6093 I 2011) the identity of the trustee was published 1 week after the adoption of the conditional clearance decision, and in *Western Digital Ireland/Viviti Technologies* (M.6203 II 2011) it took 7 weeks and in *ARM/Giesecke & Devrient/Gemalto/JV* (M.6564 I 2012) 8 weeks before the details of the trustees were published.

[35] MTDC, para 19. If more trustees than needed are approved, the parties are free to choose between them. Failure to appoint a trustee may amount to a breach of an obligation, see Remedies Notice, para 19 *in fine*. Accordingly, the Commission may revoke its decision, fine and/or impose periodic penalty payments in accordance with Article 14(2)(d) and 15(1)(c) of the Merger Regulation. To the best of my knowledge, the Commission has never pursued enforcement actions in this respect.

[36] MTDC, paras 20–21.

[37] See eg *T-Mobile/Orange* (M.5650 I 2010) where the conditional clearance decision was adopted on 1 March 2010 and the trustee appointed on 25 March 2010.

[38] The Remedies Study showed that the time that elapsed until the appointment of the trustee varied considerable from 2 days after the adoption of the Commission's clearance decision in only one case to (sometimes much) more than 1 month in most cases from 1996 to 2000, see p 88 (point 7). During the reference period of the study the deadline for appointment of a trustee was typically 2 weeks.

[39] Remedies Study, p 89 (point 9).

[40] Remedies Notice, para 123. As pointed out by several respondents in the public consultation in 2007 of the new draft Remedies Notice, the provision is poorly drafted and contradictory in the sense that the phrases 'it is of the essence that the monitoring trustee is *in place immediately after* the Commission decision' (emphasis added) and 'the parties shall *propose* a suitable trustee *immediately after* the Commission decision' (emphasis added) are inconsistent and, on top of that, the same provision refers to a deadline of 2 weeks to propose a trustee while the standard model text provides for a 1 week deadline in this respect, compare Remedies Notice, para 123, fn 1, with MTDC, para 18.

[41] See Remedies Notice, para 123; and eg *Cisco/Tandberg* (M.5669 I 2010) para 149, and Remedies Text, para 5.1.3.

[42] See n 34 above.

reject initial proposals of trustees,[43] it can be expected that a thorough selection procedure inevitably results in appointment delays.[44] The Commission is therefore placed in a dilemma: while it must ensure that the trustee is being carefully selected in order to satisfactorily pursue his tasks in the spirit of the remedy (see below), it is also paramount for the preservation of the assets to be divested that the trustee is in place as soon as possible in order to limit the parties' influence over and possible damage to the assets.[45] To this end, it has been suggested that the trustee approval procedure could start earlier, at least informally, so that the trustee would be ready to assume his duties when the clearance decision is adopted.[46] However, at least in phase I cases this option seems challenging given the tight deadlines.

Specifically on the draft trustee mandate and outline work plan accompanying the trustee proposal, these documents are usually prepared by the parties in agreement with their proposed trustee and presented to the Commission for approval.[47] The Commission is entitled to modify these drafts if deemed necessary.[48] To expedite matters, the parties are advised to use the trustee mandate template – and they usually do so – but there are also aspects where the parties and the trustee may agree their own terms, such as provisions on conflict of interest with potential purchasers, remuneration, confidentiality and severability.[49] The Commission must ensure that such non-standard provisions are in accordance with the commitments and do not hamper the trustee's independence and effectiveness in carrying out its mandate.

#### 4.2.1.2 Independence

The general trustee requirements – whether for monitoring or divestiture purposes – are that the trustee must be 'independent of the parties, possess all the necessary qualifications to carry out its mandate [. . .] and shall neither have nor become exposed to a conflict of interest'.[50] The onus is on the parties to supply adequate information for the Commission to assess whether the proposed trustee fulfils the listed criteria.

The Commission considers the independence of the trustee crucial in order to enable the trustee to properly fulfil its role of monitoring the parties' compliance for the Commission and to ensure its credibility vis-à-vis third parties.[51] The necessity of independence is particularly important because the trustee is selected and remunerated by the par-

[43] Brueckner and Hoehn (2010) 74.

[44] During the consultations in 2007 on the new draft Remedies Notice respondents pointed out that the Commission was being unrealistic in expecting trustees to be appointed and operating within such a short time span, especially in view of the strict trustee requirements and the difficulties of finding trustees that the parties have had no previous/recent dealings with, see eg reply by Lovells, para 19.

[45] There have been unfortunate examples in the past where the parties caused damage to the assets to be divested before the trustee was in place and where a lately appointed trustee had difficulties in reversing the effects of the parties' conduct, see Remedies Study, pp 89–90.

[46] For details on so-called 'up-front monitoring trustees', see Papandropoulos and Tajana (2006) 451.

[47] Provisions on trustee mandates and outline of a work plan can be found in the Remedies Notice, paras 124 and 126; MTDC, paras 18; and obviously MTTM.

[48] MTDC, para 19.

[49] MTTM, paras 22, 24, 26 and 35.

[50] MTDC, para 17, and Remedies Notice, para 124. These trustee requirements have remained unchanged since their introduction in the old Remedies Notice, para 55.

[51] Remedies Notice, para 125. While the independence criterion does not apply to competitors of the merging parties, such links may create broader issues of conflict of interest and the Commission is therefore likely to avoid such trustees, if possible.

ties and those parties are therefore strictly speaking in a contractual relationship. The Commission therefore has to ensure that – despite these relations – the prospective trustee does indeed have the capability and intention to act independently and challenge the parties, if needed. To this effect, the trustee, his team and partner firms must disclose all current relationships with the parties and affiliated undertakings.[52]

While the independence criterion may prima facie seem objective, it is one of the most difficult issues in the trustee appointment process and, besides the obvious lack of competence, is a common reason for the Commission to hesitate in approving proposed trustees.[53] As a general rule the Commission does not accept persons or institutions as trustees that at the same time are the parties' auditors or their investment advisors in the divestiture.[54] This dual-role ban should be seen in the context of past unfortunate experiences where links between the trustee and the parties' advisors put the monitoring process (carving-out, interim preservation and hold-separate) at risk as well as the interests of prospective purchasers.[55]

Experience suggests that independence or conflict issues are most likely to arise where the trustee is from larger investment, banking, consulting or auditing firms and particularly if long-term monitoring issues are involved.[56] Smaller advisory boutiques seem to have benefited from these potential conflicts as the number of such advisors has grown steadily in recent years.[57] Moreover, it is believed that the Commission does not generally accept trustee candidates who have had any material business dealings with the parties for the past 3 years prior to their appointment.[58] Clearly this practice limits the choice of potential advisors, especially in small markets where specific knowledge is required.

However, the Commission recognises that no conflicts of interest arise if the relations between the parties and the trustee do not impair the trustee's objectivity and independence

[52] MTTM, para 20.

[53] See Vassileff (2010) 54.

[54] Remedies Notice, para 125.

[55] Remedies Study, pp 92 (point 20) and 157–58. The study found that a conflict of interest had arisen in cases where (i) the parties' M&A advisors acted as monitoring trustee; (ii) the parties' M&A advisors acted as divestiture process monitor during the first divestiture period; (iii) the parties' auditors acted as monitoring or divestiture trustee; and (iv) the trustee had a dual role as monitoring trustee and replacement of a board member.

[56] See Brueckner and Hoehn (2010) 75. The authors have experienced that (i) companies may change auditors or want to appoint new consultants for major projects which in the eyes of the Commission may create a conflict of interest; or (ii) companies may be subject to a subsequent merger which combines firms that have a relationship with a trustee. However, in the past large auditing firms have also successfully offered trustee monitoring services and continue to do so, such as PriceWaterhouseCoopers and KPMG.

[57] Examples of such specialised advisors are CompetitionRx, Advolis, Baker Tilly, Grant Thornton UK LLP, Duff & Phelps, AlixPartners Ltd and Zolfo Cooper LLP – relevant references are www.competitionrx.com, www.advolis.com, www.bakertilly.co.uk, www.grant-thornton.co.uk, www.duffandphelps.com, www.alixpartners.com and www.zolfocooper.eu, respectively. These advisors have been identified by a simple search on the Internet for trustees in EU merger proceedings. During the public consultation in 2007 of the new draft Remedies Notice respondents suggested that the Commission should publish a list of the most frequently used advisors. It seems understandable that the Commission has refrained from identifying the most used trustees as this would imply preferential treatment of these advisors but it could be an idea to publish a complete list of all trustees used in recent years. However, given that the Commission since 2011 has published the identity and contact details of monitoring trustees in the vast majority of cases, it is straightforward to identify frequently used trustees. Based on the information available on case registers from 2011 and 2012, trustee like CompetitionRx, Corbel Conseil, ING Belgium and Advolis are mostly used.

[58] See De Souza and Brockhoff in Drauz and Jones (2012) para 7.307. In *Lufthansa/Austrian Airlines* (M.5440 II 2009) it was explicitly provided in the remedies that the monitoring trustee would have had no direct or indirect employment, consultancy or other relationships with the parties during the past 2 years, see Remedies Text, para 8.1.1.

in discharging its tasks.[59] It is believed the Commission has had to adopt this pragmatic approach as it may sometimes prove difficult to find trustees with no links to the parties, especially in cases where the trustee must be an industry expert as such advisors are likely to work – or recently have worked – for a number of players in the given market. Furthermore, there are a number of measures in place to maintain independence and ensure that no conflict of interest is created during and immediately after the implementation period.[60]

Whereas it is generally difficult to obtain further details on the Commission's assessment of independence as its trustee decisions are not publicly available, some recent and significant rulings by the EU Courts give a rare insight into trustee-related matters and particularly the assessment of the independence criterion. The rather ground breaking judgments relate to the Commission's conditional clearance of Lagardère's acquisition of the publishing business of Editis (formerly known as Vivendi Universal Publishing or VUP) in 2004 where Lagardère committed to sell the majority of the assets in Editis.[61]

First some facts are necessary in order to fully appreciate the reasoning and judgments of the EU Courts. During the administrative proceedings the Commission's standard trustee requirements applied – that is to say that the remedies prescribed that the trustee should be independent of Lagardère and Editis and not be exposed to any conflict of interests.[62] Once the conditional clearance decision was adopted, Largardère proposed – and the Commission accepted – the appointment of auditing firm S, represented by its director B, as trustee.[63] During the divestiture process a number of prospective purchasers voiced their interest in acquiring the respective assets, including a competing publisher Éditions Odile Jacob (Odile Jacob). On conclusion of the process, Lagardère decided to sell the assets to another undertaking, Wendel Investissement SA (Wendel). The Commission approved Wendel as a purchaser by decision on 30 July 2004 (the purchaser approval decision) inter alia on the basis of the trustee's report, which concluded that the proposed purchaser fulfilled the criteria set out in the remedies.[64]

Odile Jacob brought actions before the General Court seeking annulment of the Commission's conditional clearance decision of the main transaction and also the Commission's purchaser approval decision.[65] In respect of the latter action the applicant claimed among other things that the Commission's purchaser approval decision was adopted on the basis of a report from a trustee who was not independent and thus did not fulfil the conditions laid down in the Commission's conditional clearance decision.[66] During the Court

[59] Remedies Notice, para 125. It is the parties' responsibility to provide the Commission with adequate information to this effect.

[60] See MTTM, paras 21–23. Assignments or other business relationships with or financial interests in the parties require prior approval by the Commission, for example. Should a conflict of interest arise, the trustee must promptly inform the parties and the Commission and resolve it. Furthermore, the trustee undertakes not only during the term of the mandate but also for a period of 1 year thereafter that his team shall not provide services to the parties and their affiliates without the Commission's prior approval.

[61] See *Lagardère/Natexis/VUP* (M.2978 II 2004), in particular para 989. See also *Éditions Odile Jacob v Commission* (T-452/04 2010); *Commission v Éditions Odile Jacob* (C-553/10 2012) and *Lagardère v Éditions Odile Jacob* (C-554/10 2012).

[62] See *Lagardère/Natexis/VUP*, Remedies Text, para 15.

[63] See *Éditions Jacob v Commission* (T-452/04 2010) paras 34–35.

[64] The Commission's purchaser approval decision is not publicly available. For the Commission's announcement of Wendel as the approved purchaser, see press release IP/04/1013 of 3 August 2004.

[65] Relating to the action for annulment of *Lagardère/Natexis/VUP* (M.2978 II 2004), see *Éditions Jacob v Commission* (T-279/04 2010) where the Court confirmed the lawfulness of the Commission's conditional clearance decision. Éditions Odile Jacob brought an appeal against this judgment before the Court of Justice but the appeal was dismissed, see *Éditions Odile Jacob SAS v European Commission, Lagardère SCA* (C-551/10 P 2012).

[66] See *Éditions Jacob v Commission* (T-452/04 2010) para 64.

proceedings it became apparent that the trustee/director B had already been employed as 'independent' member of the board of directors at Editis (when it was called Investima 10) in 2002 with the specific responsibility of dealing with potential competition issues raised by authorities, including the Commission.[67] The dual roles of the trustee lasted approximately 1½ month until Editis on 25 March 2004 converted into a new company structure with a new board of directors.

The General Court carefully examined the trustee's tasks and responsibilities as set out in the remedies and compared them to those of B being a member of the board of directors of Editis (governed by French company law rules) and concluded that the trustee could not be considered as acting independently during the period of dual roles.[68] The Court observed that, as a member of the board of Editis, B had to act (by law) in the interest of Editis in protecting the viability, economic value and competitive position of that company and this responsibility was inconsistent with the tasks of an independent monitoring trustee.[69].

The General Court went on to assess to what extent the trustee's evaluation report of Wendel as a prospective purchaser had an impact on the Commission's final decision to approve Wendel. While the Court recognised that the trustee's report was merely one of several contributions, it was considered to influence the Commission's decision in a substantial way.[70] On that basis, the General Court concluded that the lack of independence of the trustee resulted in the annulment of the Commission's approval decision of Wendel as the purchaser of Editis.[71]

Not surprisingly, the Commission and Lagardère appealed the judgment of the General Court.[72] The Commission raised three grounds of appeal, namely that the Court: (i) failed to examine what effect the possible lack of independence of the trustee had on his duties in relation to Wendel; (ii) stated contradictory reasons for concluding that the trustee's report had a decisive influence on the Commission's purchaser approval decision; and (iii) infringed its duty to indicate the reasons as to why the Commission's purchaser approval decision might have been different if the trustee's lack of independence had not been a factor.[73]

The Court of Justice dismissed the grounds of appeals brought by the Commission and Lagardère.[74] Relating to the independence issue the Court of Justice found that the General

[67] ibid, paras 16 and 86. The ownership structures are complicated but, simplified, the respective activities of Editis had already in December 2002 been transferred to an interim company (named Investima 10 and owned by Natexis Banques Populaires SA, NBP) with the purpose of holding the assets of Editis until clearance had been obtained from the Commission and then the assets would be transferred to Lagardère. When Investima 10 was set up on 20 December 2002, auditor B was appointed to the board of directors. In October 2003 Investima 10 was renamed Editis SA.

[68] *Éditions Jacob v Commission* (T-279/04 2010), paras 88–104.

[69] ibid, para 104. The Court thus dismissed the Commission's arguments that the tasks and responsibilities of B as a director of Editis and as a monitoring trustee were compatible as their overall objectives were identical, paras 74, 76 and 105

[70] ibid, paras 109–17. In reaching this conclusion the Court cited many views and passages in the trustee's evaluation report that were identical to the ones in the Commission's final decision.

[71] ibid, paras 118–19.

[72] See joined cases *Commission v Éditions Odile Jacob* (C-553/10 P 2012) and *Lagardère v Éditions Odile Jacob* (C-554/10 P 2012).

[73] ibid, para 22. The Commission's stated grounds for appeal have been simplified for the present purpose of giving an overview of the main issues in the judgment of the Court of Justice. Lagardère relied on similar grounds of appeal, see para 23.

[74] It is worth noting that the Court of Justice did not follow the Opinion of Advocate General Mazák, delivered on 27 March 2012, proposing that the judgment of the General Court should be set aside inter alia as the General Court had erred in law by concluding (i) in an automatic and abstract fashion that the trustee's lack of independence was such as to vitiate the lawfulness of the approval decision; and (ii) that the trustee's report had a decisive influence on the approval decision, see in particular paras 52 and 64.

Court had not erred in concluding that the trustee did not satisfy the condition of independence required by Lagardère's commitments, which was sufficient ground for the annulment of the Commission's purchaser approval decision.[75] Regarding the claim that the General Court had erred in failing to examine whether the lack of independence actually had an effect on the Commission's purchaser approval decision or whether, without that irregularity, the content of that decision might have been different, the Court of Justice found that the lack of independence is itself sufficient ground for the annulment of the Commission's purchaser approval decision.[76] Thus, given that the General Court found that the trustee was not independent of the parties, it was under no obligation to examine whether that trustee actually acted in a way, which was evidence of his lack of independence.[77]

In conclusion of the two judgments in relation to the independence criterion, the following considerations are worth highlighting. First, the Courts are not reluctant to undertake a detailed examination of actual as well as potential tasks and responsibilities of the trustee in order to verify if he is indeed independent or gives rise to a conflict of interests. Second, despite the General Court's methodology of first assessing the independence criterion and then moving on to assessing whether the lack of independence had a significant impact on the trustee's input on the Commission's final purchaser approval decision, the Court of Justice is very clear that the lack of independence is in itself sufficient to warrant annulment. Third, both judgments serve as a reminder that a past procedural error (wrongfully approving a trustee), that may prima facie seem insignificant in the broader picture of successfully implementing a remedy, can have substantial implications on the outcome (namely the annulment of a purchaser), even many years down the line, and could leave the Commission (or the parties) susceptible to claims for damages by third parties.[78]

It is currently difficult to foresee the exact implications of the judgments. Rather unnoticeably, following the General Court's annulment in 2010 of the Commission's purchaser approval decision the Commission did in fact re-adopt its approval decision of Wendel in May 2011 but this decision was subsequently appealed by Éditions Odile Jacob in September 2011 and is still pending.[79] The Commission has not yet made any public announcements as to any possible further actions or measures in view of the judgment of the Court of Justice in November 2012, confirming the annulment of the General Court of the Commission's purchaser approval decision of Wendel.[80] After more than 8 years of proceedings – during which time the assets have even been re-sold – the last word has not yet been said in this epic case and thus it is still not clear what the final outcome will be for the business and the purchaser(s).

[75] See joined cases *Commission v Éditions Odile Jacob* (C-553/10 P 2012) and *Lagardère v Éditions Odile Jacob* (C-554/10 P 2012) para 44.

[76] ibid, para 51.

[77] ibid, para 52.

[78] The implications of the judgment may be wider than originally envisaged in the sense that not only are the consequences of the annulment felt at Wendel but also for the Spanish publisher Grupo Planeta who bought Editis from Wendel in May 2008 for EUR 1.026 billion, see www.wendelgroup.com/fr/communiques-de-presse-wendel-2008_93_278.html.

[79] To the best of my knowledge, the Commission's re-adopted decision of 13 May 2011 has not been made public but is only mentioned in *Éditions Odile Jacob v Commission* (T-471/11 pending), action was brought on 5 September 2011, see [2011] OJ C305/9. Éditions Odile Jacob applied for suspension of operation of the Commission's re-adopted purchaser approval decision but the Court dismissed the application, see Order of the President of the General Court of 24 November 2011, [2012] OJ C25/52.

[80] To the best of my knowledge, Lagardère, Wendel and the new owner of Editis, Grupo Planeta, have so far made no public announcements either.

#### 4.2.1.3 Qualifications and Specialist Advisors

The trustee must obviously possess the necessary qualifications in light of the requirements of the specific case, including the geographic area and the sector concerned.[81] In view of the findings in the Remedies Study, the Commission has made a policy statement that auditing firms and other consulting firms are particularly well placed to fulfil the tasks of a monitoring trustee while investment banks are particularly suitable for the role of a divestiture trustee.[82] The preferences reflect the nature of the specific tasks carried out by the trustees, respectively.[83]

In some cases the trustee may be required to possess additional qualifications or professional experience within a certain industry.[84] In such cases so-called industry experts may be appointed as trustees and experience shows that their knowledge and input is particularly beneficial in cases involving complex business transfers of substantial carve-outs or a high degree of monitoring.[85] In line with US practice, the Commission seems to increasingly use such experts. Also in cases where a particular expertise relating to a certain geographic area (eg national employment law) or a highly specialised area (eg IT skills) is required, the trustee may appoint one or several advisors if deemed appropriate and necessary.[86] Such advisors are instructed by and solely work for the trustee but they are approved and remunerated by the parties. Experience shows that trustees are generally reluctant to sub-contract specialised tasks to specialist advisors.[87] Albeit speculative, the reasons could be that trustees wish to protect their professional reputation by providing a 'one shop solution' and not impose additional costs on the parties.[88]

Specific qualifications aside, trustees may also be required to have previous experience with trusteeship.[89] While this requirement would have significantly limited the number of

[81] Remedies Notice, para 125.

[82] ibid, para 125, and Remedies Study, pp 90–92. Prior to the publication of the study, the Commission was reluctant to give any indication of the kind of advisor best suited to carry out certain tasks and the old Remedies Notice did not address this issue. However, in very early practice monitoring trustees were sometimes required to delegate the selling tasks to investment banks (see eg *Proctor & Gamble/VP Schickedanz* (II) (M.430 II 1994) para 186(1), where the trustee appointed Goldman Sachs to act on its behalf in negotiating and selling the business) but this practice was less prominent in subsequent years until the Remedies Study renewed the focus on this issue.

[83] Thus in recent years the Commission has been in favour of the parties employing different trustees for monitoring and divestiture purposes although it does not exclude that they can be the same person/institution. Contrary, the parties' preferred solution is often that the trustees are the same in order to reduce costs and avoid duplication, see De Souza and Brockhoff in Drauz and Jones (2012) para 7.336. To this effect, many commitment proposals in recent practice contain a standard provision whereby the parties will indicate to the Commission when the monitoring trustee is proposed whether it is the intention that this trustee is also to act at a later stage as the divestiture trustee, see eg *Outokumpu/Inoxum* (M.6471 II 2012), Remedies Text, para 20(c).

[84] The practice of requiring particular industry knowledge or experience started in the late 1990s, one of the first cases being within the slaughterhouse industry in *Danish Crown/Vestjyske Slagterier* (M.1313 II 1999) para 228. Subsequently there have been numerous cases requiring particular industry knowledge or experience in pharmaceuticals, media, airlines, energy and so forth.

[85] See Remedies Study where it was however recognised that the monitoring in some complex carve-outs was even a challenge for industry experts, see p 65 (point 32).

[86] See MTDC, para 30; MTTM, para 19; and Remedies Notice, para 120.

[87] Remedies Study, p 91 (point 17).

[88] The Remedies Study highlights a complicated separation case where a trustee employed 70 consultants to split the IT systems, see pp 62 (point 25) and 75 (point 9). The parties reported that the trustee had exaggerated its role and was consequently, in their view, unnecessarily costly. The Commission had to intervene and agree on a compromise work plan.

[89] The Remedies Study indicated that previous trusteeship experience contributed substantially to the success of the trustee, see p 91 (point 18). See eg *SCA Packaging/Metsä Corrugated* (M.2032 I 2000), Remedies Text, para 7; and *Alcoa/Reynolds* (M.1693 II 2000), Remedies Text, para 18.

potential trustees in the early days of the Merger Regulation, the recent emergence of more specialised trustee boutiques and hence the increased professionalism and experience makes this requirement easier to fulfil. However, in the event that the trustee is less experienced it has been suggested that some form of guidance (in a form similar to Best Practice Remedies Guidelines) could be a useful tool.[90] As another example of additional trustee specifications, occasionally it is provided in the remedies that a (national) regulatory body may perform the tasks of the trustee, typically in cases where such bodies have already been involved in the administrative proceedings.[91]

#### 4.2.1.4 Liaison between the Commission and the Trustee

While the specific tasks and responsibilities of the monitoring and divestiture trustees are described below, it should be stressed that the Commission attaches great importance to constant liaison between the Commission and the trustee throughout the duration of the trustee's mandate. In recent years the Commission has emphasised that, although the trustee is relatively autonomous in its daily work, it nevertheless carries out its tasks under the supervision of the Commission and, to this effect, the Commission is entitled to 'give any orders or instructions' to the trustee.[92]

It is considered that the increased emphasis on the supervision aspect should be seen in the context of the General Court's ruling in (the antitrust case) *Microsoft v Commission* where the Commission was overruled in its decision to grant a trustee powers to monitor compliance with certain obligations imposed on Microsoft in antitrust proceedings pursuant to Article 102 TFEU.[93] While Commission officials have downplayed the impact of the judgment on the trustee framework in merger proceedings,[94] it is obvious (through the changes in 2008 to the Implementing Regulation and the revised phrases in the new Remedies Notice) that the Commission has become more attentive to its supervisory role in relation to trustees and therefore the liaison between those two parties has become very important. Moreover, the Commission considers it essential that it has direct and immediate access to the trustee without the interference of the parties.[95]

In terms of procedural measures, the first post-appointment contact is usually a kick-off meeting with the trustee and usually without the presence of the parties.[96] At this meeting the Commission briefs the trustee (and his team) on key issues in the decision relevant for

[90] Remedies Study, p 92 (point 18).

[91] See eg *T-Mobile/Orange* (M.5650 I 2010), Remedies Text, para 22.

[92] See in particular the Implementing Regulation, Art 20a (inserted in 2008): 'the trustee shall carry out its tasks under the supervision of the Commission'. Also some of the main changes that the Commission made to the draft new Remedies Notice between the consultation in 2007 and its final publication in 2008 were the insertion of the phrases 'under the supervision of the Commission' in paras 118–21. See also Remedies Notice, para 118; MTDC, para 22; and MTTM, para 4.

[93] See *Microsoft v Commission* (T-201/04 2007), appeal of Commission decision in *Microsoft* (COMP/C-3/37.792 2004). It was the first time the Commission required the appointment of a monitoring trustee in an Art 102 (then 82) proceeding. In accordance with the terms of the Commission's decision, the Commission appointed Professor Neil Barrett, a computer scientist, as a trustee (see press release IP/05/1215 of 5 October 2005) who was later assisted by two technical advisors (see MEMO/06/119 of 10 March 2006).

[94] See interview with senior Commission official Claude Rakovsky in Blanc and Brueckner (2009).

[95] The current practice is very different from earlier cases where the contacts between the Commission and the trustee were often limited to formal written reports and the trustee was often seen as much as the parties' man as the Commission's representative.

[96] The importance of kick-off meetings was highlighted in the Remedies Study where several trustees indicated the desire for such meetings in order to clarify their role, see p 95 (point 31).

the compliance monitoring and it makes sure that the trustee understands the remedies issues in question. In the past commentators have pointed out that some trustees are weak on their interest in, and understanding of, how to preserve long-run competition and that they do not see themselves as being responsible to the Commission, other than to provide the required written reports.[97] It is considered that in recent years the Commission has been more proactive and attentive in briefing trustees in order to mitigate such shortcomings and, moreover, the trustees have generally become more experienced. Furthermore, at the first meeting with the Commission the trustee will also present and discuss in detail its work plan.

Finally, the most obvious means of ensuring constant liaison throughout the trustee period is the requirement that the trustee must report periodically (usually monthly) to the Commission and shall also, upon request, submit additional reports.[98] The reporting obligations cover inter alia the operation and management of the business to be divested, its holding separate, the progress of the divestiture process and any failure by the parties to comply with the remedies.[99] Experience shows that the Commission attaches great value to the opinion of the trustee, including its evaluation of proposed purchasers.[100]

#### 4.2.1.5 Remuneration

The parties are responsible for remuneration of the trustee under the mandate and, while in principle it is up to those parties to agree on a suitable fee structure, the remuneration must be such as to not impede the trustee's independence and effectiveness in fulfilling the mandate.[101] The fee structure must be provided for in the trustee mandate and it is therefore subject to the Commission's approval.

Although the Commission does not state any preferences for certain fee structures, experience shows that an agreed fixed fee tends to limit the amount of time and attention devoted by the trustee to the monitoring activities.[102] Therefore, the Commission is in favour of remuneration based on an hourly rate as it gives the trustee the flexibility to perform all activities deemed necessary in order to properly fulfil its monitoring tasks.[103] The obvious downside for the parties with hourly payment is the open-ended nature of the costs, which in effect amounts to signing a 'blank cheque'.[104] However, in the past the Commission has occasionally intervened and reduced the amount of the total fee if

[97] See Davies and Lyons (2007), in particular pp 197, 230 and 249. The authors mention *Monsanto/Pharmacia & Upjohn* (M.1835 I 2000) and *Glaxo Wellcome/Smithkline Beecham* (M.1846 I 2000) as examples of cases where the trustees failed to represent the Commission in an adequate way but they also submit that the shortcomings were partly due to the Commission's errors as it had not even briefed the trustees on the competition issues in question.

[98] Remedies Notice, para 119, MTDC, para 23(vi); and MTTM, paras 14–16.

[99] See in particular MTDC, section F.

[100] As mentioned above, in *Éditions Jacob v Commission* (T-452/04 2010) the General Court identified several views and even passages in the trustee's evaluation report that were identical to the ones in the Commission's final decision, see paras 109–17.

[101] Remedies Notice, paras 120 and 126; MTDC, para 17; and MTTM, para 24.

[102] Remedies Study, p 93 (point 21).

[103] This approach coincides with the FTC's policy, see Remedies Study, p 93, fn 253.

[104] During the public consultation in 2007 of the draft new Remedies Notice, several respondents raised concerns that the parties are given no control over the expenditures of monitoring trustees, which they claimed goes beyond what is necessary, see eg reply from Crowell and Moring, p 5; and reply from IBA, para 99.

considered excessive and disproportionate.[105] A way of avoiding unpleasant surprises of disproportionate fees would be for the parties and the trustee to agree upon provisions in the mandate providing for an up-front budget (covering for example a 3-month period) and possibly a reasonable fee cap.[106]

Specifically for divestiture trustees, it is business practice that such trustees – often being investment banks – are remunerated through an incentive payment scheme according to which the fee is tied to the sales price of the assets to be divested. While the Commission does not prohibit such schemes per se, it has expressed concerns that such arrangements could create a conflict between the Commission's preference for a swift sale and the trustee's desire to take the time to find the highest paying bidder in order to maximise its own income.[107] To this effect, the Commission's guidance provides that where a remuneration package of the divestiture trustee includes a success premium linked to the final sale value of the assets to be divested, the fee shall also be linked to a divestiture within the trustee divestiture period.[108] Whether such a provision provides adequate incentives for the trustee to act in a timely manner is difficult to assess.[109]

#### 4.2.1.6 Replacement, Discharge and Reappointment

The appointment of the trustee is irrevocable unless the trustee is replaced with the approval of or upon request by the Commission.[110] Thus, the parties or the trustee itself may request the Commission for a replacement or the Commission may at its own initiative request the replacement of the trustee, in which case the trustee must be heard.[111] A likely scenario where replacement could be required is if the trustee post-appointment is exposed to a conflict of interest that diminishes his impartiality. It is difficult to say how often a trustee is replaced as the Commission does not publish or announce such decisions. To date no Commission press releases or statements have been issued in this respect.

When the remedies have been fully implemented, the trustee may request the Commission for a discharge from further responsibilities.[112] A discharge can be requested when (i) legal title for the business to be divested has passed; (ii) the assets have been actually transferred to the purchaser; and (iii) specific arrangements which may continue post-divestiture have been fulfilled.[113] Specifically for monitoring trustees, the Commission stresses that their tasks are fulfilled only when the legal and actual transfer of the business to the approved purchaser is completed and they have issued a report to the Commission confirming such transfer.[114]

105 See example in Remedies Study, p 93 (point 23) where the Commission cites a past phase II case where the parties complained to the Commission that a trustee's fee amounting to EUR 1 million at the end of the trustee period could have been carried out more cheaply.

106 Whether the parties and the trustee normally agree such provisions is hard to say, as all such details are confidential. However, it is indicated in the Remedies Study that such provisions have at least occasionally been used, see p 94 (point 23).

107 Remedies Study, p 93 (point 22). It also has to be remembered that the divestiture trustee is usually required to sell the assets by the end of the period 'at no minimum price'. This requirement inherently goes against the trustee's interests in maximising the value of the assets if his fee is purely linked to such value.

108 MTDC, para 17.

109 Only a new ex-post study by the Commission would be able to reveal such details.

110 Remedies Notice, para 125 *in fine*.

111 MTDC, para 31.

112 Remedies Notice, para 127; MTDC, para 33; and MTTM, para 28.

113 Remedies Notice, para 127.

114 ibid, para 119.

These requirements are a tightening of past practice where trustees would normally be discharged after the closing of the sale of the divested business and would thus not necessarily monitor the actual transfer of the assets.[115] The current practice of ensuring the trustee's continued monitoring of post-closing matters appears appropriate and necessary in order to preserve the value of the assets. Also, it could be argued that the fact that the trustee's responsibility is extended to the actual transfer of the assets may have positive effects on the tasks carried out during the monitoring period pre-closure as the trustee is unlikely to take undue measures, which would complicate or delay the subsequent transfer of the assets.

Once the trustee has been discharged, it may occasionally be necessary for the Commission to reappoint the trustee if it subsequently appears that the remedies have not been fully and properly implemented.[116] However, the efficiency of this provision presupposes that the Commission is being made aware of inappropriate implementation issues, which may not always be the case.[117] Similarly as above, it is difficult to say how often trustees are reappointed due to the lack of public announcements in this respect.

**Commentary:** to sum up the trustee requirements, the consequences of the Courts' rulings in the numerous appeals relating to the original transaction *Lagardère/Natexis/VUP* may have taken many observers and involved parties by surprise. In very clear terms from the Courts it has now been confirmed that a seemingly minor procedural error relating to the assessment and approval of a trustee can have large implications on the lawfulness of the approval of the purchaser of the assets in question. The defeat for the Commission must clearly serve as a reminder to its staff how important it is to show vigilance in all stages of the administrative proceeding, including the assessment and approval of the trustee, although these administrative tasks may seem trivial and are executed after the conditional clearance decision has been adopted and thus at a time when the respective case handlers have usually moved on to new pressing notifications with tight deadlines.

### *4.2.2 Monitoring Trustee's Tasks*

In the Remedies Notice the Commission lists five main, non-exhaustive tasks that the monitoring trustee should carry out under the supervision of the Commission:[118] (i) overseeing the safeguards for the business to be divested in the interim period; (ii) monitoring, in carve-out cases, the splitting of assets and allocation of personnel between the divested business and retained businesses by the parties as well as the replication of assets and functions in the business previously provided by the parties;[119] (iii) overseeing the parties'

[115] The Commission found no remedy in the Remedies Study where the systematic monitoring of the actual transfer of the business was carried out post-closing, nor was such monitoring explicitly provided for in the commitments or the trustee mandates in the Study sample, see p 86 (point 21). The Commission considered that this practice was unsatisfactory. To this effect, see also Remedies Study, p 94 (point 27). Furthermore, the old Remedies Notice mentioned only the transfer of the legal title (thus not the *actual* transfer of assets) in the context of discharge, see para 57.

[116] Remedies Notice, para 127 *in fine*.

[117] The Remedies Study highlights an unfortunate case involving a re-branding remedy where an early termination of the trustee's mandate contributed to the ultimate failure of the remedy, see Remedies Study, p 32 (point 19).

[118] Remedies Notice, para 119. The formulation of these main tasks is based on the detailed provisions introduced and contained in the MTDC (para 23) and MTTM (para 6), respectively. Details on these tasks are provided in the respective sections dealing with various implementation steps.

[119] In past cases the trustee's tasks in carve-out remedies have proven challenging. For example, trustees have been overwhelmed by the scale and difficulty in monitoring carve-outs; have faced obstacles in gaining direct access to the premises; or have lacked specialised experience and/or knowledge in verifying the sufficiency of assets, see Remedies Study, p 78 (points 25 and 26).

efforts to find a potential purchaser and to transfer the business; (iv) acting as a contact point for any requests by third parties, in particular potential purchasers; and (v) reporting to the Commission.[120]

Using a cliché, the trustee serves as the Commission's 'eyes and ears' during the implementation phase as the Commission cannot be involved in all aspects relating to the divestiture.[121] The mandate of the trustee therefore embraces a wide variety of supervisory functions, such as guarding the assets and monitoring the parties' sales efforts. The Commission thereby views the trustee as an 'all-rounder' or 'multi-tasker' rather than a specialist possessing specific expertise targeted at a particular aspect of the implementation.[122] As the remedies provide for the appointment of a monitoring trustee in virtually all cases, the Commission does not undertake a systematic and individual assessment of the actual need for a trustee in each case.[123]

It is evident from the above list that the Commission currently puts emphasis on the trustee's *monitoring* tasks, as opposed to any decision-making tasks. This is contrary to previous practice where the trustee acted far more autonomously with powers to even *impose* any measures deemed necessary.[124] The switch to monitoring functions came about when the concept of hold-separate managers, operating under the supervision of the monitoring trustee, was introduced.[125] The monitoring trustee was thereby released from day-to-day implementation measures, although it can still make any proposals to the hold-separate manager but without being able to impose any measures as such. While these changes were first and foremost introduced in 2003 through the introduction of the standard model texts, the monitoring aspect (and conversely the downplaying of the decision-making aspect) is reinforced in the new Remedies Notice. As indicated above, this reinforcement of the monitoring tasks was most likely made in view of the General Court's ruling in *Microsoft v Commission*[126] and the Commission now appears reluctant to emphasise any autonomous duties of a monitoring trustee in order not to create potential conflicts with the ruling.[127]

[120] In order to facilitate the trustee´s tasks, the parties are obliged to support and cooperate with him, see Remedies Notice, para 120.

[121] ibid, para 118. The FTC has also taken a liking to this expression, see FTC Guidelines for Negotiating Merger Remedies, p 16.

[122] The DoJ reserves the use of monitoring trustees to relatively rare situations where a trustee with technical expertise unavailable to the DoJ staff could perform a valuable role, see DoJ Merger Remedies Guide, Part IV.I.3. While the FTC uses monitoring trustees more frequently than the DoJ, the tasks of the trustees may be confined to specific tasks such as monitoring continuing relationships between the parties and the purchaser, see FTC Guidelines for Negotiating Merger Remedies, p 16.

[123] It has been questioned whether this policy of systematically nominating monitoring trustees is correct, in particular in non-divestiture cases if eg an efficient dispute resolution mechanism is already in place, see Papandropoulos and Tajana (2006) 451.

[124] In the old Remedies Notice the mandate of the so-called hold-separate trustee (equivalent to today's monitoring trustee) could 'include for example, responsibilities for supervision, which include the right to *propose*, and, if deemed necessary, *impose*, all measures which the trustee considers necessary to ensure compliance' with the remedies (emphasis added), see para 52 *in fine* of the old notice. In the new Remedies Notice, the trustee may merely '*propose* to the parties any measures it considers necessary for carrying out its tasks' (emphasis added), see para 118.

[125] Formal provisions on hold-separate managers were introduced in the Best Practice Remedies Guidelines in 2003, see Explanatory Note, point 21, and MTDC, para 7. The US operates a similar distinction between 'operating trustees' and 'monitoring trustees', see DoJ Merger Remedies Guide, Part IV.I. However, contrary to EU practice, operating trustees are rarely used by the DoJ.

[126] See n 93 above.

[127] An example of the Commission's retreat is found in the Commission's rephrasing of the monitoring trustee's role in case of disagreements between the parties and third parties: in the draft Remedies Notice published for consultation in 2007 the trustee shall 'discuss those matters with both sides *and try to find a suitable solution*'

However, situations remain where the monitoring trustee is called upon to exercise certain rights and thereby to execute certain business decisions. Regrettably, the Remedies Notice provides little guidance on these not uncommon situations.[128] Most importantly, in cases where the parties commit to divest a stake in a company and where a strict separation of the corporate structure is necessary, it is established practice that the trustee is empowered to exercise the parties' shareholder rights, pending divestiture.[129] In such cases the parties transfer their voting rights to the trustee immediately after the adoption of the Commission's decision. In exercising the transferred voting rights, the trustee is usually obliged to act in the best interest of the company in question and without influence from the parties.[130] With the transfer of such rights to the trustee it is therefore crucial that the trustee has a thorough understanding of the business, as its tasks may involve taking some commercially important decisions pending the divestiture. The Commission may occasionally allow that where measures are involved which would result in a substantial financial burden being placed on the parties, such as for example in the event of a capital increase, the trustee exercises the voting rights only in agreement with the parties.[131] Moreover, in cases where the parties sell a stake in a joint venture, the remedies may exceptionally empower the other joint venture partner(s) to exercise the parties' votes in accordance with the best interest of the joint venture during a first divestiture period before the trustee possibly takes over the parties' voting rights.[132]

Finally, in share transfer cases where the trustee is authorised to exercise the parties' shareholder rights, the trustee is usually further empowered to replace members of the supervisory board and/or non-executive directors of the board of directors, who have been appointed on behalf of the parties.[133] Also the trustee can usually request that the parties resign as member of the boards or must cause such members of the board to resign.[134] Such provisions confer significant decision-making powers upon the trustee, as he is required to assess and select board replacements with suitable qualifications and experience. Needless to say, such tasks require commercial insight and knowledge on the trustee's behalf.

**Commentary:** the systematic appointment of monitoring trustees should be seen as a result of a policy decision by the Commission not to spend time and resources on being involved in the

(emphasis added) whereas the final version in the 2008 Remedies Notice uses the phrase 'discuss those matters with both sides *and report to the Commission*' (emphasis added), see para 119, fourth indent.

[128] The situation is briefly mentioned in the context of interim preservation in para 111 of the Remedies Notice.

[129] MTDC, para 8; and MTTM, para 6(d). For examples of past cases, see *Kraft Foods/Cadbury* (M.5644 I 2010); *IPIC/MAN Ferrostaal AG* (M.5406 I 2009), *BNP Paribas/Fortis* (M.5384 I 2008), *Galp Energia/Exxonmobil Iberia* (M.5005 I 2008), *Nestlé/Novartis (Medical Nutrition Business)* (M.4540 I 2007), and *VEBA/VIAG* (M.1673 II 2000). Regrettably, sometimes such provisions are left out of the public version, see *RWE/Essent* (M.5467 I 2009), Remedies Text, para 8. In some cases the shares may also be deposited with the trustee (then often named 'security trustee' or 'share trustee'), pending divestiture, see eg *Industri Kapital/Dyno* (M.1813 II 2000), Remedies Text, paras 13 and 14.

[130] The text of the mandate instructing the trustee to vote must usually be approved by the Commission, see eg *Teijin/Zeon/JV* (M.3235 I 2003), Remedies Text, para 6.

[131] For cases where the Commission has allowed the parties to instruct the trustee to vote, the Commission must give its prior consent, see *VEBA/VIAG*, (M.1673 II 2000), point I.3, and *Anglo American Corporation/Lonrho*, (M.754 II 1997) para 126.

[132] See *Teijin/Zeon/JV* (M.3235 I 2003), Remedies Text, para 6.

[133] MTDC, para 8. For decisional practice, see eg *Kraft Foods/Cadbury* (M.5644 I 2010), Remedies Text, para 8; and *IPIC/MAN Ferrostaal AG* (M.5406 I 2009), Remedies Text, para 8.

[134] MTDC, para 8. In the past the Commission has occasionally accepted that, pending divestiture, the parties were allowed to keep one director or board member, see *VEBA/VIAG* (M.1673 II 2000), Remedies Text, para I.3; and *Anglo American Corporation/Lonrho*, (M.754 II 1997).

day-to-day monitoring during the implementation stage. As will be submitted later, such a 'hands-off' policy has its pros and cons as, on the one hand, the Commission minimises its implementation costs in the form of dedicated staff to procedural essentials but, on the other hand, it takes a gamble as an efficient implementation to a large extent depends on the involvement, dedication and abilities of the appointed trustee.

### *4.2.3 Divestiture Trustee's Tasks*

From the parties' point of view, divestiture trustees are an unattractive option.

First, the trustee divestiture period is usually significantly shorter than the first divestiture period as the Commission puts emphasis on a quick sale.[135] The trustee will be under pressure to negotiate fast and effectively with prospective purchasers and for example quickly end negotiations and search for another candidate if the Commission considers that the first candidate appears unacceptable.[136]

Second (and more controversially), the trustee is given an irrevocable and exclusive mandate to dispose of the business 'at no minimum price' by the end of the trustee divestiture period.[137] The prospects of a fire-sale naturally have an impact on the negotiation powers of prospective purchasers who have all the incentives to bargain as much as possible, occasionally with the result that the sales price has been as little as EUR 1.[138] The only comfort for the parties is that the trustee is, after all, under an obligation to protect their legitimate financial interests.[139] This means that in the event of a multiplicity of offers from equally suitable purchasers, the trustee must favour the offer that nets the highest sales price.

Third, the trustee is given a certain room for manoeuvre as he may include in the SPA such terms and conditions, as he considers appropriate for an expedient sale, in particular customary representations, warranties and indemnities.[140] Fourth, for the divestiture to run as smoothly as possible the parties must grant the divestiture trustee comprehensive powers of attorney, covering all stages of the divestiture.[141]

While there seems to be a general consensus that the use of divestiture trustees may be appropriate in certain situations where the parties encounter problems divesting of the assets themselves, critics have voiced concerns that in the past divestiture trustees have been weak on their interest in, and understanding of, how to preserve long-run competition when evaluating and selecting prospective purchasers.[142] It has been submitted that the trustee's attitude has broadly been that of an independent auditor paid by the parties to ensure a fair sale, rather than seeing itself as responsible vis-à-vis the Commission.

135 As mentioned above, the duration is around 3 months, see Remedies Notice, para 98.

136 MTTM, para 13.

137 Remedies Notice, para 121; MTDC, para 24; and MTTM, para 11. The length of the trustee divestiture periods and the conditions of the sales have changed substantially throughout the years. In *Unilever/Bestfoods* (M.1990 I 2000), for example, if the parties failed to divest within the first 6 months, the divestiture trustee was given two periods for divestiture: an *initial period* (of 3 months) where the assets should be sold at 'a fair market price' and a *second and non-extendable period* (of 3 months) where the assets should be sold at 'no minimum price', see Remedies Text, points 11.4 and 11.5 (it is possible to state the exact deadlines as the confidential version of the remedies was made available on the DG Competition's website – it has now been deleted).

138 For details on the fire-sale provision, see section 4.4.2 below.

139 MTDC, para 24; and MTTM, para 11. In the past there have been variations as to how the trustee should pursue the sale, see eg *VEBA/VIAG* (M.1673 II 2000) where the trustee should effect the sale according to 'sound commercial principles' (Remedies Text, para I.1(b)).

140 Remedies Notice, para 121; MTDC, para 24; and MTTM, para 11.

141 Remedies Notice, para 122 *in fine*. The parties shall also support and inform the divestiture trustee and cooperate with the trustee in the same way as foreseen for the monitoring trustee.

142 See n 97 above.

However, as considered above the Commission seems to have addressed this issued by briefing trustees more thoroughly from the outset.

Whereas it is current practice that virtually *all* divestiture remedies contain divestiture trustee provisions, there have been cases in the past where the Commission has accepted that a business was sold without the involvement of a divestiture trustee in a second divestiture period. This has been the case where (i) the divestiture was relatively uncomplicated, such as the sale of a stake;[143] (ii) the parties agreed to an up-front buyer solution;[144] or (iii) the parties have already entered into agreement with an identified purchaser (a fix-it-first solution) and thus making a divestiture trustee redundant.[145] At the other end of the spectrum, the Commission has on rare occasions insisted on the immediate transfer of the assets to a divestiture trustee and thus given the parties no opportunity to divest the assets themselves,[146] or reserved the right to shorten the first divestiture period in order to transfer the assets earlier to the divestiture trustee.[147] These situations have been confined to cases where the Commission has had real concerns that the assets would quickly deteriorate if left in the hands of the parties post-decision.

Finally it should be stressed that over the years surprisingly few divestiture trustees have actually been operational, as the parties have had every incentive to execute the remedies prior to the deadline triggering the appointment of a divestiture trustee.[148] However, as it so far has been standard practice that the Commission does not make public announcements about the appointment of divestiture trustees, it is impossible to provide data or speculate about the frequency of their use.[149] [150] Contrary to the Commission's reluctance

[143] See *Allianz/Dresdner* (M.2431 I 2001).

[144] In *Arjowiggins/M-Real Zanders Reflex* (M.4513 II 2008) the parties rather exceptionally committed that they would abandon their transaction if they had not succeeded in divesting the assets within the divestiture period to an up-front buyer, see para 547 (as it happened the transaction was abandoned). For other up-front buyer cases with no provisions on divestiture trustees, see *Masterfoods/Royal Canin* (M.2544 I 2002) and *Nestlé/Ralston Purina* (M.2337 I 2001).

[145] See *Metso/Aker Kvaerner* (M.4187 II 2006) where the parties had already entered into a binding SPA with the Canadian competitor GL&V for Kvaerner's WOB business and Metso's digester business, see paras 140–46.

[146] See *YLE/TDF/DIGITA/JV* (M.2300 I 2001), Remedies Text, para 18; and *Proctor & Gamble/VP Schickedanz* (II) (M.430 II 1994) para 186(2) (however, in the latter case P&G was free to accept the offer it considered best in case of several offers being submitted to the trustee). The DoJ has also recognised that it may on rare occasions use 'selling trustees' (equivalent to EU divestiture trustees) from the outset, see DoJ 2004 Merger Remedies Guide, Part IV.I, caveat 1.

[147] See *VEBA/VIAG* (M.1673 I 2000), Remedies Text, point I.1(b).

[148] Brueckner and Hoehn (2010) submit that in their experience the appointment of a divestiture trustee has only happened once in 15 cases, see p 79.

[149] One of the few public statements from the Commission on the use of divestiture trustees can be found in the 2004 OECD Remedies Study where the Commission acknowledges that it has 'limited experience' with divestiture trustees, see p 257. Most recently, in *BASF/CIBA* (M.5355 I 2009) BASF submitted in its 2009 annual report that it had been unable to sell Ciba's dry strength agents for the paper industry within the first divestiture period and therefore the sale had been handed over to a trustee, see www.bericht.basf.com/2009/en/notes/scopeofconsolidation/acquisitionsdivestitures.html (10 February 2011). In Davies and Lyons (2007) the authors indicate in their remedies study that a divestiture trustee was used in one of their case studies, namely *Monsanto/Pharmacia & Upjohn* (M.1835 I 2000), see p 197 of the study.

[150] However, a very recent initiative by the Commission suggests that it may change its policy in the future. In *Südzucker/ED&F MAN* (M.6286 II 2012) the Commission posted on 26 February 2013 on the case register a short announcement that a divestiture trustee had been appointed in this case (including the relevant contact details). The announcement came around 9 months after the adoption of the conditional clearance decision. As of 1 May 2013 the non-confidential version of the clearance decision and/or the remedies text are regrettably not yet available and therefore no details can be provided as to the relevant remedies provisions but, presuming that the remedies contain standard provisions, the divestiture trustee would need to sell the stake (the remedy) at no minimum price within a relatively short space of time. Furthermore, it can be noted that the divestiture trustee is the same as the monitoring trustee (CompetitionRx) in this case.

to submit publicly available data, its US counterparts are more transparent in this respect.[151]

> **Commentary:** as a strategic measure to maintain the pressure on the parties to implement the remedies as quickly as possible there appears to be no arguments against the Commission publishing the appointment and identity of a divestiture trustee once it becomes relevant. It is considered that this is an example of an area where the Commission has too easily accepted the arguments of the merging parties to keep as many of the procedural steps confidential as possible under the excuse that they may have an impact on share prices, risk of fire-sale and so forth. Having said this, decisional practice indicates that divestiture trustees rarely come into action and thus they are not a significant feature in the divestiture process.

## 4.3 Interim Preservation

### *4.3.1 The Parties' Obligations*

Pending divestiture, it is the parties' responsibility to reduce to the minimum any possible risk of loss of competitive potential of the business to be divested and to this effect the Commission requires the parties to commit to maintain the independence, economic viability, marketability and competitiveness of the business.[152] The most important way of doing so is to hold the business separate from the parties' retained activities and ensure that it is managed as a distinct and saleable entity.

The monitoring trustee oversees the interim preservation process but it is the parties (or a delegated person) who must execute the hold-separate and preservation measures responsibly and appropriately. However, in view of past experience that the parties have no natural incentives to help or promote the business pending divestiture and in worst cases may weaken the business in order to ensure their own competitive advantage post-divestiture,[153] a number of safeguards must be put in place in order to protect the business from any degradation that may reduce its competitive potential. While these safeguards are agreed upon and submitted as commitments during the administrative proceedings, they take effect on the day of the adoption of the decision and they do not expire until the business has been transferred to the purchaser.

The interim preservation safeguards are usually considered obligations in the Commission's conditional clearance decision, and their scope and intensity vary according to the specific circumstances of each case.[154] As the Commission's guidance and practice have become increasingly consistent and transparent in recent years, the present description is limited to the following main features with emphasis on past critical issues.[155]

[151] eg in the FTC FAQ About Merger Consent Order Provisions 12 past cases are listed in which the agency had appointed divestiture trustees, including *Hoechst and Rhone-Poulent (Aventis)* (File No 991 0071, Docket No C-3919), see Q 38. Thus although the FTC submitted in the 2004 OECD Remedies Study that divestiture trustees have been used infrequently in the past (p 241), it seems to have used them more frequently than the Commission.

[152] Remedies Notice, para 108.

[153] These findings were first made in the FTC's Divestiture Study (pp 18–19) and subsequently confirmed in the Remedies Study (in particular p 57 (point 6) and pp 70–71). Whereas the FTC did not find conclusive evidence that they had formally violated any of the remedies in the study (p 18), the Commission detected several examples of the parties degrading tangible and intangible assets by active conduct or disregard (pp 70–71).

[154] Remedies Study, p 56 (point 4).

[155] Compared to the old Remedies Notice (paras 50–52) the Commission elaborates significantly on its guidance on interim preservation in the new notice, see paras 108–12. Preservation provisions are also found in

### *4.3.2 Preservation of Assets*

The parties must ensure that all assets of the business are maintained, pursuant to good business practice and in the ordinary course of business, and that no acts which might have a significant adverse impact on the business are carried out.[156] This relates in particular to the maintenance of fixed assets, know-how or commercial information of a confidential or proprietary nature, the customer base and the technical and commercial competence of the employees.

Experience shows that preservation measures become increasingly complex when the business to be divested is not a stand-alone business and problems arise in particular when the assets concern brands.[157] Some of the obstacles may be difficult to avoid as illustrated by one case where customers – presumably due to the uncertainties inherent in the announced sale of a business – overstocked the branded goods in question during the interim period with the result that post-closing the purchaser faced diminished turnover and the viability of the divested business was negatively affected.[158] More intentionally, the parties may sometimes encourage and carry out so-called 'front-loading' of the products in question, meaning that they offer exceptional pricing promotions on the products in the interim period with the result that the purchaser's new customers do not need supplies from the divested business immediately for a while after closing.[159] Hence the references to 'good business practice' and 'ordinary course of business' aim at preventing undermining behaviour from the parties.[160]

Furthermore, the parties must maintain the business in the same conditions as before the concentration, in particular provide sufficient resources, such as capital or a line of credit, on the basis and continuation of existing business plans, the same administrative and management functions, or other factors relevant for maintaining competition in the specific sector.[161] These requirements should be seen in the context of past cases where the parties neglected the normal needs of the business to be divested by discontinuing promotions of brands or failing to support investment programmes or customer relationship management as a result of which the business was economically harmed or hampered.[162] The existing business plan is therefore an important tool in the continuing preservation of the day-to-day business. In cases where brands are of essence the parties may specifically commit to maintain the marketing and sales efforts devoted to the business to be divested at their current levels; that is pre-clearance.[163]

MTDC, para 5, and hold-separate provisions in MDTC, paras 6–8. Unless otherwise stated, the present description refers to those standard provisions. In terms of references to past practice, the main source is the Remedies Study, as the Commission never publishes information on specific cases in this respect.

[156] Remedies Notice, para 110.

[157] Remedies Study, p 56 (point 4).

[158] ibid, p 57 (point 6).

[159] ibid, p 58 (point 7). The Commission submits that this delay may also enable the parties to further promote their own products to those customers, to the detriment of the purchaser who had legally acquired the commercial rights to these customers.

[160] Unfortunately, the standard provision in MTDC, para 5, refers only to 'good business practice' and therefore the commitments generally do not refer to the 'ordinary course of business' requirement. As a technical comment, the latter phrase ought to be inserted in the standard texts once revised by the Commission.

[161] Remedies Notice, para 110; and MTDC, para 5(b).

[162] Remedies Study, p 58 (point 8).

[163] See eg *Reckitt Benckiser/SSL* (M.5953 I 2010), Remedies Text, para 10(ii), which concerned the divestiture of well-known brands for mouth pain relief products in the UK and Ireland.

Finally, the parties must also take all reasonable steps, including appropriate incentive schemes,[164] to encourage all key personnel to remain with the business, and they must not solicit or move any personnel to their remaining business.[165] While retention programmes for key personnel (in the form of financial incentives or other motivational measures) are generally considered important in the interim preservation phase, the Commission has found it difficult to assess the effectiveness of such schemes in practice.[166] Logically, the longer the interim period is, the more uncertain the personnel become with the risk that they seek employment elsewhere.

### *4.3.3 Hold-separate Measures*

Hold-separate safeguards are relatively straightforward in cases where the business to be divested is already an autonomous entity, whereas it may be an entirely different and complex scenario when the assets need to be carved out. In the latter situation assets and personnel may not only need to be separated and allocated but also, if necessary, replicated and the Commission must ensure that the parties do not take advantage of this process by off-loading less attractive assets or personnel whilst retaining the more productive ones. While the most common specific separation measures will be described below, the role and significance of a hold-separate manager in the implementation process is first explained.

#### 4.3.3.1 Hold-separate Manager

According to current practice the parties are usually required to appoint a hold-separate manager who, with the necessary expertise, will be responsible for the day-to-day running and management of the business to be divested and the implementation of the hold-separate and ring-fencing obligations.[167] He shall manage the business independently and in the best interest of the business with a view to ensuring its continued economic viability, marketability and competitiveness and its independence from the businesses retained by the parties.[168] Hold-separate managers are a relatively new phenomenon,[169] but experience shows that they are very important – and even crucial – in particular in carve-out remedies

[164] In some cases it is specified that such schemes must be based on industry practice, see eg *GDF Suez/International Power* (M.5978 I 2011), Remedies Text, para 5(c), and *Friesland/Campina* (M.5046 II 2008), Remedies Text, para 5(c).

[165] Remedies Notice, para 110; and MTDC, para 5(c). Obviously this provision is left out in cases where the transfer of the business is limited to certain assets and rights, see eg *Syngenta/Monsanto's Sunflower Seed Business* (M.5675 II 2010), Remedies Text, para 5; or where the business has no dedicated personnel which can be transferred together with the business, see *Pernod Richard/V&S* (M.5114 I 2008), Remedies Text, para 24 *in fine.*

[166] Remedies Study, p 58 (point 10).

[167] Remedies Notice, para 112. For the standard provision on the appointment of a hold-separate manager, see MTDC, para 7. In recent practice most divestiture remedies provide for the appointment of a hold-separate manager. For exceptions, see *Kraft Foods/Cadbury* (M.5644 I 2010), where the standard hold-separate manager provision was omitted from the Remedies Text, para 7.

[168] MTDC, para 7 *in fine.* If the remedies consist of the divestiture of several separate businesses, the parties may be obliged to appoint one hold-separate manager for each business to be divested, see *Fortis/ABN AMRO Assets* (M.4844 I 2007), Remedies Text, para 10.

[169] The concept of hold-separate managers was formally introduced in the Best Practice Remedies Guidelines in 2003, see Explanatory Note, point 21, and MTDC, para 7. It partly replaced the notion of hold-separate trustees as defined in the old Remedies Notice, para 52, and whose functions were split up between the monitoring trustee and hold-separate manager. The equivalent in the US is an 'operating trustee', see DoJ Merger Remedies Guide, Part IV.I.

as a means of ensuring that the interests of the business is protected in the best possible way in the interim period.[170]

It is the parties who appoint the hold-separate manager and the appointment should take place immediately after the adoption of the Commission's conditional clearance decision and even before the parties may close the notified transaction.[171] In order to fulfil his tasks in the best possible way, the hold-separate manager is ideally (i) a senior member of the existing management with the necessary authority and decision-making powers to manage the business accordingly; (ii) a 'key personnel' of the business who is earmarked for transfer to the purchaser and to whom the parties' non-solicitation obligations apply;[172] or (iii) appointed from outside the parties' retained business (possibly from the monitoring trustee's team) if no suitable person is found from within the business to be divested.[173]

In either case the hold-separate manager acts at all times under the supervision of the trustee, who is able to remove him if he does not act in accordance with the remedies or endangers their timely and proper implementation.[174] Past cases show that it is important for the success of a hold-separate scenario that the manager cooperates extensively with the trustee and is answerable to the latter, not the parties.[175] It therefore seems surprising that trustees are not – as a standard provision – involved in the appointment of hold-separate managers.[176] In particularly complex (carve-out) cases the trustee has occasionally been empowered to influence the parties' appointment of the hold-separate manager but this is still the exception.[177] In any event, it is current practice that hold-separate managers are appointed in virtually all divestiture remedies.[178]

#### 4.3.3.2 Ring-fencing

In relation to confidential information, the parties must ring-fence the business to be divested and take all necessary measures to ensure that they do not obtain any business

[170] Remedies Study, p 79 (point 29).

[171] Remedies Notice, para 112. During the public consultation in 2007 of the draft new Remedies Notice it was pointed out that in cases where an acquiring firm is to appoint a hold-separate manager over the target assets, an appointment may be impossible prior to the closure of the transaction, see reply by Freshfields Bruckhaus Deringer, point 7.4.

[172] 'Key personnel' is defined in MTDC, section A.

[173] See Remedies Study, p 67 (point 42). It should be noted that at the time of the Remedies Study hold-separate managers were just starting to emerge as a standard in remedies decisions and thus the sample in the study was limited.

[174] Remedies Notice, para 112. In such cases a new appointment of a hold-separate manager will be subject to the approval of the monitoring trustee. It should be noted that the MTDC contains no express provision on the removal of the hold-separate manager and it was not until the publication of the new Remedies Notice in 2008 that this issue was clarified.

[175] Remedies Study, p 67 (point 41).

[176] This issue was identified as a potential shortcoming in the Remedies Study as it was suggested by several trustees that the work of the hold-separate manager would have been more effective, had the trustee been consulted on the appointment and supervised its work, see p 97 (point 37).

[177] In *Maersk/PONL* (M.3829 I 2005) involving a substantial carve-out the appointment of the hold-separate manager was subject to the agreement of the monitoring trustee, see Remedies Text, para 8. See also *Bayer/Aventis Crop Science* (M.2547 II 2002) where the remedies provided that not only was the appointment of the hold-separate manager subject to confirmation by the monitoring trustee, but in the event the trustee would veto the parties' suggested candidate, it had powers to appoint another manager, in consultation with the Commission, see Remedies Text, para 220.

[178] Contrary to the Commission's practice, the appointment of an operating trustee in the US is confined to very rare instances where the DoJ believes that the parties are likely to mismanage the assets to be divested (eg if the nature of the assets is such that their competitive value could quickly deteriorate), see DoJ Merger Remedies Guide, Part IV.I.

secrets or other confidential information relating to the business.[179] In particular, the participation of the business to be divested in a central IT network shall be severed to the extent possible, without compromising the viability of the business.[180]

However, there is an inherent conflict between the parties' obligation not to access commercially sensitive information of the business to be divested and at the same time negotiate the divestiture where they necessarily require access to commercially sensitive information of the business. It has been suggested that this issue may be solved in one of two ways.[181] First the parties may commit to limit access to such information to personnel of the retained business who is involved in conducting the sale.[182] Such persons must agree not to use the information in other contexts and keep its contents confidential from the remainder of the parties' retained business. Secondly, the parties may appoint a divestiture trustee to carry out the divestiture process on their behalf from the outset so the parties do not need to access confidential information.[183] Needless to say, the first option is by far preferable from the parties' point of view and indeed the most frequently used.[184] However, practice suggests that there is an alternative option whereby the parties transfer their so-called 'information rights' to the monitoring trustee and/or the hold-separate manager who then acts on the parties' behalf.[185] Such a 'compromise' provision appears reasonable and justifiable in situations where, due to the sensitivity of the information, there is a need for the trustee/manager to 'filter' the information.[186]

In any event, standard provisions usually provide the parties with the possibility of obtaining confidential information relating to the business to the extent that it is reasonably necessary for the divestiture of the business or whose disclosure to the parties is required by law.[187] Necessary information in this respect would typically relate to valuations of the business to be divested and purchase price negotiations. Finally, the Commission stresses that any confidential documents or information about the business obtained by the parties *prior* to the adoption of the conditional clearance decision must generally be returned to the business or destroyed.[188]

**Commentary:** as standard preservation and hold-separate measures have been significantly improved in recent years, this is an area where the Commission would benefit from undertaking a new ex-post review in order to evaluate the efficiency of the current provisions as they did not exist during the reference period of the Remedies Study (for example hold-separate managers).

[179] Remedies Notice, para 111; and MTDC, para 9. The latter provision specifies that the information at stake is 'any business secrets, know-how, commercial information, or any other information of a confidential or proprietary nature'. Thus, such information is defined very broadly.

[180] MTDC, para 9.

[181] See De Souza and Brockhoff in Drauz and Jones (2012) para 7.222.

[182] ibid, para 7.223. The author submits that this option is best suited to cases where the divested business is from the acquirer in the notified concentration and where the degree of access needed by the personnel is likely to be relatively limited.

[183] ibid, para 7.224. The author submits that this option is best suited to cases where the divested business is from the target company, particularly where the acquisition occurs through a hostile takeover. For examples of cases where a divestiture trustee has been appointed from the outset, see *YLE/TDF/DIGITA/JV* (M.2300 I 2001), Remedies Text, para 18; and *Proctor & Gamble/VP Schickedanz* (II) (M.430 II 1994) para 186.

[184] A recent example is *Reckitt Benckiser/SSL* (M.5953 I 2010), see Remedies Text, para 13.

[185] See *GDF Suez/International Power* (M.5978 I 2011), Remedies Text, para 9.

[186] Thus, the Commission may consider adding this provision to the standard model texts

[187] MTDC, para 9 *in fine*. For recent examples, see *GDF Suez/International Power* (M.5978 I 2011), Remedies Text, para 9; *Syngenta/Monsanto's Sunflower Seed Business* (M.5675 II 2010), Remedies Text, para 8; and *DB/Arriva* (M.5855 I 2010), Remedies Text, para 11. See also *VEBA/VIAG* (M.1673 II 2000), Remedies Text, para VIII.1.

[188] Remedies Notice, para 111. This provision is currently not contained in the standard model texts and therefore does not appear as a clause in the parties' commitment proposals.

## 4.4 Divestiture Process

### *4.4.1 Putting the Business up for Sale*

During the first divestiture period the parties are in charge of the sales process and the Commission has, in principle, no preference as to the method they use to select an acceptable purchaser as long as they meet the objective of the divestiture, namely to maintain or restore competition.[189] The main reason for leaving the sales process in the hands of the parties is that they are, after all, most knowledgeable about the business and the relevant market as well as the overall objective that the sales process should be as market-driven as possible. The Commission therefore intervenes as little as possible in the sales process.[190]

Nevertheless, there are certain minimum requirements that the parties must fulfil in order to ensure that the sales process is conducted in a transparent and non-discriminatory way. The sales process is often kicked off by the preparation of an information memorandum or prospectus.[191] The parties may put the business out for competitive bids by publishing the information documents in appropriate media,[192] or they may approach individual firms that they believe are interested and would be considered acceptable purchasers.[193] In either case the Commission will not interfere in the way the parties approach prospective purchasers as long as this is done in a manner consistent with the remedies.

The next step is that prospective purchasers must be able to access adequate information about the business to be divested to allow them to fully assess the value, scope and commercial potential of the business.[194] Such information is obtained through a due diligence procedure, including direct access to the personnel of the business to be divested.[195] Experience shows that at this stage of the sales process conflicting interests may arise between the parties and prospective purchasers as to the disclosure of confidential information contained in the Commission's conditional clearance decision, including all remedies details.[196] The core issue is whether the *precise* scope of the remedies must be made known to the prospective purchasers in this process.

While it prima facie seems obvious that purchasers should know all details relating to a potential acquisition in order for them to make an informed decision (and thus avoid finding 'skeletons in the closet' post-closure), it has been successfully argued by the parties in past cases that the disclosure of alternative remedies or the identification of specific plants to be divested would give potential purchasers an undue advantage and promote strategic

[189] See Best Practice Remedies Guidelines (2003), point 25.

[190] The Remedies Study identified only one case where it had objected to the parties' proposal to make an Initial Public Offering (IPO) of the shares on the stock exchange as this would have weakened the competitive position of the business to be divested, see p 68 (point 1).

[191] The parties shall submit a copy of the information memorandum to the Commission and the monitoring trustee before sending the memorandum to potential purchasers, see MTDC, para 13.

[192] eg in *Danish Crown/Vestjyske Slagterier* (M.1313 II 1999) the parties advertised the sale of slaughter capacity and a slaughter house in the newspaper Børsen (on 28 May 1999), the Danish equivalent to the Financial Times.

[193] Another possibility is an auction process which has the advantage of excluding the parties from the selection of the proposed bidders or purchasers but, on the downside, there is no guarantee that that the winning bidder in the auction will be an acceptable purchaser, see FTC Guidelines for Negotiating Merger Remedies, p 10.

[194] Remedies Notice, para 116.

[195] ibid and MTDC, paras 11 and 13.

[196] These issues are dealt with in the Remedies Study, pp 68–72 (points 1–15).

behaviour.[197] The Commission has thus accepted that specific details relating to the exact scope have been veiled at this stage in the sales process but it has also acknowledged that such omissions may result in slowing down the sales procedure, which in turn may have a negative impact on the overall effectiveness of the remedies.[198] It can therefore be assumed that the Commission currently is cautious about allowing omissions unless strictly necessary.

Also the Commission must not lose sight of the fact that the divesting parties may have a competitive interest in influencing – and even obstructing – the due diligence process with the aim of discouraging certain purchasers or optimising the sales price.[199] Indeed, it has emerged that in the past the parties sometimes organised very short due diligence procedures and deadlines or provided incomplete or inaccurate data regarding the business or the sales process.[200] More seriously, past cases also revealed the use of numerous 'dirty tricks' (as phrased by the Commission), which the parties hoped would escape the Commission's and/or the trustee's monitoring efforts. Such tricks ranged from the business being inoperative at the time of being offered for sale to incomplete transfer of assets and even the proposal of clearly unsuitable purchasers.[201]

As the Commission in its Remedies Study was able to establish a correlation between the parties' strategic behaviour and the ineffectiveness of a remedy,[202] it is expected that the Commission is particularly aware of such pitfalls and seeks to prevent them in its present practice. Indeed, an obstructed or less transparent sales process may not only slow down the sales process but may also attract less suitable potential purchasers that may not have the means or the intention to develop the business in the best possible way.[203] Adequate on-going monitoring of the sales process is therefore essential and, to this effect, in its latest guidance the Commission highlights the trustee's monitoring obligations, in particular reviewing the information memorandum (if available), the data room and the due

[197] See in particular the description of a phase I remedy where the seller successfully argued that the veiling of the specific plants to be divested was necessary for a fair sales process and was also beneficial in terms of interim operation and preservation (as the knowledge of divestment could have de-motivated the work force). The seller argued that otherwise the few suitable purchasers would have had an undue advantage which could have had a negative impact on the sales price and could have encouraged the purchasers to just sit and wait to make a bargain, see Remedies Study, p 68 (point 3).

[198] Remedies Study, p 68 (point 3).

[199] To this effect, some commentators have criticised the Commission for adopting a 'laissez faire approach' allowing the parties to steer the divestiture process strategically to present a weak competitor by excluding or discriminating against stronger competitors, see De Souza and Brockhoff in Drauz and Jones (2012) para 7.412.

[200] Remedies Study, p 69 (points 6–7). The Commission quotes one phase II case where the purchaser was given only 2 days to undertake due diligence and was restricted to gain access to vital data, including information on key employees. The purchaser was thus unable to fully understand the business and discovered later that it lacked key employees, customer documentation and other essential assets. The divested business went bankrupt after a few years.

[201] No less than 13 examples of past strategic behaviour by the parties are listed in the Remedies Study, see pp 70–71 (point 10). Along the same lines, during the Court proceedings in *Éditions Odile Jacob v Commission* (T-452/04 2010) it was alleged that potential bidders of the assets in question had to sign a confidentiality agreement preventing the bidders from bringing a Court action over the proceedings, see summary of this plea in [2005] OJ C45/25. While the Court did not address this issue in its judgment, this seems to be an area that requires more attention.

[202] Remedies Study, p 71 (point 11). Almost half of all remedies having unresolved design and/or implementation issues appeared to suffer from strategic behaviour by the seller.

[203] If the sales process has not been transparent and the parties have taken advantage of this by eg proposing a weak purchaser, it is difficult for the Commission to be pro-active and establish by own means whether other potential purchasers could have been more suitable candidates.

diligence process.[204] However, it is difficult to assess how successful the Commission has been in further ensuring compliance in the sales process since it rarely publishes information on non-compliance by the parties in this respect.[205]

### *4.4.2 Price Setting*

In remedies discussions the issue sometimes arises as to what role, if any, a competition authority should play in the pricing of the assets/business to be divested.[206] The Commission – in line with most other competition authorities – is generally reluctant to interfere as the price setting is considered a negotiation matter between the parties and the prospective purchaser.[207] Price evaluations are also complicated and require specific corporate finance and/or business expertise, which the Commission may not necessarily possess.[208] Furthermore, in many cases the final price agreed between the parties and the preferred purchaser consists of several interconnected elements which are particular for the respective case and/or industry and which may be difficult for the Commission to properly assess in terms of correct valuation.[209]

However, in recent years the Commission has become more aware of the possible post-divestiture implications that an incorrect sales price may have on the incentives and competitiveness of the purchaser.[210] Simplified, if the price for the assets is too low, the purchaser could have an incentive to discontinue the business as a going concern and instead liquidate or split up the assets post-divestiture as a way of making the transaction profitable.[211] On the other hand, if the price is too high the purchaser may give up competing actively as it cannot afford making the necessary investments. In both scenarios the Commission's dilemma is that, while it is not keen to interfere in pricing, once the assets have been transferred to the approved purchaser, it is difficult to 'turn back the clock' and oppose an incorrect sales price.

Therefore, in newer practice the Commission views the sales price as constituting a part of the SPA and should therefore be assessed, against the criteria laid out in the remedies, as a part of the divestiture procedure and approval of the purchaser.[212] To what extent the

[204] Remedies Notice, para 119, third indent. Also the parties must submit periodic reports on potential purchasers and developments in the negotiations, see Remedies Notice, para 116.

[205] For a description of the few cases where information relating to non-compliance was published, see section 4.6.4 below.

[206] See the 2004 OECD Remedies Study, p 33.

[207] See also FTC Guidelines for Negotiating Merger Remedies, p 11; and DoJ Merger Remedies Guide, part IV.C.1.

[208] If needed, the Commission could ask trustees and/or independent consultants for advice in such matters but it would still be very time and resource consuming.

[209] eg in *Nestlé/Novartis (Medical nutrition business)* (M.4540 I 2007) the purchaser's future use of licences were included in the purchase price for the French business to be divested, see Schedule to Remedies Text, p 41. Also in relation to specific situations of divestiture of brands belonging to a so-called 'category captain' in consumer product cases the sales/purchase price may be adjusted in order to reflect the disadvantage facing the brand once it is stripped of the category captain's support, see Klein and Wright (2004) and Foer (2001a).

[210] Remedies Study, p 104 (point 21).

[211] As a benchmark for what constitutes a 'too low' price the DoJ considers the assets' liquidation value, defined as the highest value of the assets when redeployed to some use outside the relevant market, see DoJ Merger Remedies Guide, Part IV.E. To this effect, see also FTC Guidelines for Negotiating Merger Remedies, p 11. The Commission has not published guidance on this issue and therefore it is unclear how the price is assessed in this respect.

[212] For the Commission approval of the SPA, see Remedies Notice, para 105; MTDC, para 15 (sale by the parties); and MTTM, para 10 (sale by the trustee). As to how the transaction is financed and the financial means of the purchaser, see Remedies Notice, para 103; and section 3.3.3 above.

Commission objects to the sales price when assessing the SPA is difficult to say, as such information is kept confidential. However, it must be assumed that the Commission will intervene only in cases where the agreed price is of such a nature that it may put the implementation and effectiveness of the remedy in danger. On the other hand, it can also be assumed that the mere fact that the Commission now attaches importance to the pricing aspect and reserves its right to intervene has a preventive effect on the parties when setting and negotiating a price.

Whereas the remedies are usually silent as to any price indications during the first divestiture period, the trustee has an exclusive mandate to dispose of the business at 'no minimum price' in a so-called 'fire-sale' by the end of the trustee period.[213] Some commentators have argued that this long-standing standard provision is irrelevant, as long as there are multiple possible purchasers.[214] This view may be plausible but it has to be borne in mind that the 'at no minimum price' provision was introduced with the aim of ensuring that in those (albeit possibly few) cases where there is little interest in the assets to be sold, the parties must commit up-front that they (or rather the trustee on their behalf) are prepared to reduce the sales price until a potential purchaser comes forward and an SPA can be concluded. Furthermore, given that many markets have become increasingly concentrated and specialised, the parties (trustee) may more frequently than previously encounter difficulties in attracting several prospective purchasers and in these situations the 'at no minimum price' provision is vital in order to guarantee divestiture.

Indeed the Commission has in the past experienced cases where the parties were unable to find a single suitable purchaser and had to offer the assets for free or agree to no up-front price being payable in order to attract interest.[215] However, in these cases the remedies turned out to be highly unsuccessful as one purchaser filed for bankruptcy after 1 year and in the other case the business performed very poorly post-closure.[216] Along the same lines, occasionally the price has even been negative.[217] In any event, it is difficult to provide details on how often assets are sold at 'no minimum price' or how often the Commission intervenes in the price setting for the assets as such information is not made publicly available. Also, the Commission rarely publishes the finally agreed sales/purchasing price[218] and so the circumstances surrounding the price setting are not very transparent.[219]

[213] See Remedies Notice, para 121; MTDC, para 24; and MTTM, para 11. Occasionally the Commission has accepted that the trustee period is divided into two phases: one period where the trustee must try to sell the business at 'a fair market price' and, if he fails to do so, he must ultimately sell at 'no minimum price', see *Unilever/Bestfoods* (M.1990 I 2000), Remedies Text, paras 11.4 and 11.5.

[214] See Davidson (2006) 6.

[215] See Remedies Study, pp 103–104 (point 20).

[216] ibid.

[217] Lufthansa paid a negative price for Austrian Airlines in *Lufthansa/Austrian Airlines* (M.5440 II 2009) where parallel state aid proceedings were initiated (see press release IP/09/1256 of 28 August 2009 and decision published in [2010] OJ L59/1) in order to assess whether the negative price amounted to illegal state aid (this was not the case). The state aid case was appealed by a competitor and is pending, see *Niki Luftfahrt v Commission* (T-511/09 pending) ([2010] OJ C80/27). It remains to be seen whether the appeal will involve the negative sales price issue.

[218] One of the few exceptions is *Campbell/ECDD (Unilever)* (M.2350 I 2001) where the acquisition was a fulfilment of some of the remedies in *Unilever/Bestfoods* (M.1990 I 2000). In its announcement of its unconditional approval of the transaction the Commission stated that the sale of ECBB to Campbell amounted to EUR 1 billion, see press release IP/01/494 of 3 April 2001.

[219] In the emerging econometric literature on merger remedies it has been suggested that, in order to assess efficiency gains, the Commission should introduce a so-called 'revelation mechanism' whereby two new tools are introduced: the regulation of the divestiture sales price and a merger fee. The authors propose that in less efficient mergers a trustee should enjoy full authority in the divestiture process and only sell the assets at the highest possible price, see Cosnita and Tropeano (2009) 192.

### *4.4.3 Voluntary Addition of Assets*

When putting the business up for sale or later in the sales process, the parties have sometimes added, on their own initiative, supplementary assets that go beyond the initial scope of the remedies package.[220] In earlier practice the Commission uncritically allowed such additions on the assumption that, as it is a matter for the parties to find a purchaser, they should be free to add other assets to make the remedies package more attractive to prospective purchasers.[221]

More specifically, assets have been voluntarily added in the following situations:[222] (i) the parties quickly recognise the initial lack of interest from prospective purchasers and thus broaden the remedies package in order to expedite the sales process; or (ii) the parties conclude that the original remedies package is not sufficiently viable and stand-alone to attract a purchaser who would qualify as a 'suitable purchaser' under the Commission's purchaser requirements. The supplementary assets have mainly involved issues of upstream/downstream dependence and insufficient critical size and the addition of the assets generally promoted the remedy's effectiveness and therefore the Commission saw no reason to intervene.

Unfortunately, the Commission found in its Remedies Study that some assets may also have been added for the wrong reasons and thereby obstructing the effective implementation of the remedies:[223] (i) the parties added less viable assets thereby burdening the purchaser with additional costs and liabilities, thus weakening the purchaser's competitive potential (for example, additional personnel that were unnecessary for the business, or older, obsolete facilities and assets); or (ii) the parties created a divestiture package that went far beyond the scope of the divested business primarily for the purpose of expediting the sales process and thereby attracting purchasers who were, in fact, more interested in the peripheral assets than in the 'main' assets to be divested.[224] The problem with such cases of clear circumvention is often that they are difficult for the Commission (or the trustee) to detect and prove until the time when the remedy has been fully implemented.

While the Commission has not categorically dismissed the possibility of the parties adding assets post-clearance in view of the findings in the Remedies Study, it no longer promotes in its guidance that the parties are free to add such assets.[225] It must therefore be assumed that the Commission takes a more cautious and restrictive approach in its current practice by carefully checking – possibly with the help of the trustee – likely implications of

[220] This addition of assets is done voluntarily by the parties post-decision and thus differs from the pre-decision situation where the parties add assets from non-problematic markets in order to enhance the viability of the remedies package (as described in the Remedies Notice, para 23 *in fine*).

[221] See the old Remedies Notice, para 21. In *Kraft Foods/Cadbury* (M.5644 I 2010) the Commission raised competition concerns with respect to chocolate confectionery in Romania and Kraft undertook to divest Cadbury's chocolate confectionery business as well as Cadbury's soft cake business in order to ensure viability. Post-clearance Kraft voluntarily added Cadbury's sugar confectionery business in Romania to the remedies package when it sold the assets to Oryxa Capital, see *Confectionery News*, Jane Byrne, 'Kraft Sells Romanian Business to Investment Fund Oryxa' (7 July 2010) available at www.confectionerynews.com. In *BP Amoco/Arco* (M.1532 II 1999) the parties were required to divest the interests in certain gas pipelines and processing facilities in the North Sea and they choose to divest also the interests in the related gas fields (quoted in the old Remedies Notice, para 21, fn 25).

[222] Remedies Study, p 29 (point 14).

[223] ibid, p 30 (point 15).

[224] In the latter case the outcome could thus be that the purchaser would keep the peripheral assets and sell the 'main' assets as soon as possible, see section 4.6.1 below on 'on-sales'.

[225] The wording of para 21 of the old Remedies Notice 'The parties may [. . .] add, on their own initiative, other assets to make the package more attractive to buyers' has been omitted in the new notice.

assets being added post-decision and opposing them, if necessary.[226] In the event that the Commission can prove that the added assets constitute a violation of the remedy, it may claim breach of a condition with appropriate legal repercussions to follow.[227] However, such a procedure will not be straightforward as it may take several years post-implementation and will require substantial Commission resources (in terms of staff) to establish the effects and existence of an unlawful addition of assets. To date, this issue has not been the subject of any formal infringements proceedings.

**Commentary:** a review of the divestiture process – including the execution of the sale, price setting and voluntary addition of assets – in the Remedies Study is considered to have been an eye-opener for the Commission as this was the first time that examples of past strategic behaviour of the parties were gathered across cases with the result that the frequency and scope of such behaviour when considered over several years of decisional practice appeared more severe than originally assumed. The findings were a clear message that the Commission had been far too hands-off or 'laissez-faire' in its enforcement. Although the execution of the sale is indeed a part of the process that should be as market-driven as possible, the findings demonstrated that some kind of regulatory monitoring is warranted and/or the trustees must monitor and report on the process in a more professional way than previously. Indeed, all detailed drafting during the remedies process pre-decision seems redundant if the merging parties are given ample room for manoeuvre during the essential phase of executing the sale.

### *4.4.4 Modification of Remedies*

Throughout the implementation stage the parties can, upon showing good cause, and accompanied by a report from the monitoring trustee, request the Commission to: (i) grant an extension of the time periods foreseen in the commitments; or (ii) waive, modify or substitute, in exceptional circumstances, one or more of the commitments.[228] While it is difficult to assess the impact and relevance of this provision as such amendments are rarely made publicly available, the fact that the Commission is very elaborate in its guidance on such provisions in the new Remedies Notice indicates that they are of significance.[229] While the Commission stipulates that review provisions are particularly important in non-divestitures (access remedies),[230] it will be submitted below that decisional practice suggests that such clauses are also relevant in divestiture remedies.

Before embarking on a description of the contents of the review provisions, it should be noted that the introduction of a standard review clause in 2003 solved some important procedural problems. In past cases where a conditional clearance decision did not contain a review clause, any subsequent changes – whether large or small – to the remedies would strictly speaking require the adoption of a new decision in order for the parties not to be

[226] As the Commission has never published information on the addition of assets to the remedies package post-clearance, it is impossible to submit any data in this respect.

[227] It considered that such circumvention would qualify as a breach of a condition (as opposed to an obligation) given that the addition of assets would have an impact on the scope of the assets to be divested and thus the 'core' of the remedy.

[228] The practice was introduced in 2003 with the publication of the Best Practice Remedies Guidelines, see MTDC, para 34.

[229] See Remedies Notice, paras 71–76 where the category 'Review Clauses' is listed as one of the four main types of remedies. In the old notice the concept of review clauses did not exist.

[230] ibid, paras 71 and 74.

considered in breach of their original remedies.[231] Needless to say, this would in many cases have been disproportionate to the potentially limited nature of the required amendments, and therefore such situations were avoided if possible.

#### 4.4.4.1 Extending Divestiture Deadlines

A request to extend the time periods is the most commonly used of the two review provisions and particularly important in divestiture remedies.[232] As the provisions governing such extensions solely refer to situations where the parties have the responsibility of divesting the assets themselves in the first divestiture period, it is assumed that the Commission is reluctant to grant such an extension in the second divestiture period where the trustee must sell the assets.[233] Moreover, to obtain an extension the parties must show good cause; that is to say they must provide evidence that they have been unable to meet the deadline for reasons outside their responsibility, and that it can be expected that they subsequently will succeed in divesting the assets within a short time-frame.[234] In assessing the request the Commission balances the effects of the extension on the economic viability, marketability and competitiveness of the divested business against the harm caused to the parties, the divested business or the process if no extension is granted. In doing so, the Commission carefully considers the input from the monitoring trustee before reaching a conclusion. Procedurally, the request must generally be submitted no later than 1 month prior to expiry of the given divestiture deadline.[235]

As the Commission is reluctant to publish information about requests for and granting of extensions, it is difficult to properly assess the frequency as well as the success rate of such requests.[236] However, in the Remedies Study it was revealed that around 30 per cent of the deadlines in the analysed divestiture cases (transfer of market position) had been extended one or several times, although the majority of extensions had been for only 1 or 2 months in order to complete an already advanced sales process.[237] It is submitted that this percentage is high and, although speculative, this could be due to several circumstances; the original deadline was too short, unforeseen events occurred and complicated the divestiture process, or the Commission was simply too lenient in granting such extensions. Moreover, the percentage may be even higher in subsequent practice as the analysed cases in the Remedies Study did not yet have a standard review provision which was introduced

[231] For phase II cases this would mean that a new decision would have to be approved by the College of Commissioners unless the original clearance decision contained appropriate delegation powers to the Commissioner for Competition, see recently Commission decision of 3 May 2011 waiving certain commitments in *Hoffman-La Roche/Boeringer Mannheim* (M.950 II 1998) (the original remedies did not contain a review clause).

[232] See Cook and Kerse (2009) para 8-035.

[233] Remedies Notice, para 72. This seems to be a tightening of past practice where the provision would apply to the parties' as well as the trustee divestiture periods, see De Souza and Brockhoff in Drauz and Jones (2012) para 7.429.

[234] Remedies Notice, para 72.

[235] See MTDC, para 34 *in fine*. Only in exceptional circumstances may the parties request an extension closer to the expiry of the deadline and in such situations it is expected that the parties submit their request immediately after the occurrence of the unforeseeable event, see De Souza and Brockhoff in Drauz and Jones (2012) para 7.429.

[236] In early practice the Commission would occasionally publish such information in its annual reports but given the significant time span between the granting of the extension and the publication thereof, such announcements were primarily of academic interest, see eg Competition Report 2001, para 313, where it was announced that an extension of the divestiture deadline had been granted in *Carrefour/Promodes* (M.1684 I 2000).

[237] Remedies Study, p 112 (point 12). In four cases the extension exceeded 6 months.

in the Best Practice Remedies Guidelines in 2003,[238] and those few cases with review clauses contained stricter requirements than those in the subsequent standard provisions.[239]

Furthermore, the Commission provides no details as to what constitutes 'a good cause', save that it has to be for reasons outside the parties' responsibility and that the parties must show that a divestiture can be expected within a short time frame.[240] Although speculative, circumstances like an unexpected shortage of potential purchasers,[241] obstacles caused by third parties,[242] delayed approvals from other competition authorities, or extraordinary circumstances like a change in ownership[243] or an unforeseeable and radical new development in market conditions could warrant an extension. Judging from the few public announcements on acceptance or rejection of requests for extensions the Commission appears to interpret the provision of good cause relatively narrowly especially in cases where (i) the first divestiture period is already longer than the standard duration; and/or (ii) the share/sales price is affected by cyclical evolutions in the market but still at a reasonable level.[244]

[238] Indeed in the study the Commission submitted that several of the analysed remedies lacked a review clause, see the Remedies Study, p 112 (point 13). Furthermore, the study did not generate enough evidence to evaluate the appropriateness of the granted extension, see p 112 (point 14).

[239] In *VEBA/VIAG* (M.1673 II 2000) the Commission would consider an extension only if the parties could prove *exceptional circumstances* beyond their control, see Remedies Text, point I.1(b).

[240] Regrettably the Commission provided no examples of 'a good cause' in its Remedies Study. During the consultations in 2007 on the new draft Remedies Notice several respondents commented on the condition 'outside their responsibility' as being too strict as there may be situations where the parties conduct the sale process in the best way possible but they are simply unable to reach an agreement with a purchaser in the time allowed based on a whole range of reasons that may not *all* be 'outside their responsibility'. It was therefore suggested that the Commission should have due regard to the overall way in which the sale process was run, compliance with the obligations and the satisfaction (or otherwise) of the monitoring trustee in this respect, see eg reply by Lovells, para 14. The Commission maintained the proposed wording in the final version of the notice.

[241] It is assumed that in such cases the parties must be able to show that they did not – or could not be expected to – know that the assets would attract few interested purchasers. If such difficulties were predictable at the time of the negotiating the remedies, the parties should instead have proposed alternative commitments or a 'crown jewel'.

[242] In *Carrefour/Promodes* (M.1684 I 2000) the Commission announced that Carrefour, despite genuine efforts, had been unable to sell its stake in Cora within the agreed deadline due to 'actions of third parties' (providing no further details) and it granted an extension of the deadline, with the sale being subsequently completed with a financial investor, see Competition Report 2001, para 313.

[243] In *Fortis/ABN Amro Assets* (M.4844 I 2007) the divestiture deadline was extended no less than three times: on 2 October 2009 for 17 days (press release IP/09/433), on 19 October for 24 hours (press release IP/09/464), and on 20 October for another period which was not made public (MEMO/09/471). The case was exceptional in many respects as the seller (Fortis) changed ownership during the implementation stage (it was taken over by the Dutch State) and there were complicated parallel state aid proceedings. However, during the divestiture period the CEO of Fortis fiercely criticised the then-Commissioner for Competition Neelie Kroes for not being willing to grant extensions in a satisfactory way and thereby prompting a fire-sale to Deutsche Bank, see *MLex Comment* 'Fortis Boss Slams EC over Forced Asset Sales in ABN Amro Purchase' (19 August 2008) available at www.mlex.com/EU/Content.aspx?ID=37948. The Commission refrained from issuing any public comments in this respect.

[244] By way of illustration, in *Volvo/Renault V.I.* (M.1980 I 2000) the Commission refused to extend the deadline for the divestiture of Volvo's stake in Scania. Volvo had divested its B-shares in Scania in March 2004 but in June 2003 it had requested the Commission to extend the deadline for divestiture of its shares. As a matter of principle, Volvo maintained that the Commission should decide on its request (due to related Court proceedings) although the sequence of events had overplayed the request. The Commission confirmed by letter of 7 April 2004 (published on the DG Competition's website – link is no longer available but the letter is summarised in press release IP/04/484 of 15 April 2004) that Volvo had failed to show good cause for the extension of the deadline in respect of the B-shares. The rejection was mainly based on the fact that the sale of the shares took place at a price level close to breakeven and therefore the disposal of Volvo's stake would not have had a noticeable impact on Volvo's ability to borrow and invest nor would it threaten its independence. The same conclusions were reached in respect of the sale of Volvo's A-shares which were sold at a later stage, see press release IP/04/484 of 15 April 2004.

The requirement that the parties must show that a divestiture (or another way of implementing the remedy) is expected within a short time frame is reasonable as the Commission cannot give an open-ended extension and it forces the parties to submit details as to an expected completion date. Normally the Commission expects the parties to implement within an additional few months.[245] Furthermore, in such cases the trustee normally plays a decisive role in ensuring that no further competition harm is added in the extended period.[246]

All in all, the Commission seems to take a reasonable and 'holistic' approach to a request for an extension of a deadline in the sense that it will carefully assess all relevant factors influencing the divestiture process and not unreasonably reject a request. However, in cases where the Commission does decide to reject a request for an extension of a divestiture deadline, the parties may wish not only to appeal the refusal decision but also ask the Court for interim measures in order to put the implementation on hold. Jurisprudence in this area is limited but in a recent application to the Court the parties failed to demonstrate that the alleged financial harm was sufficiently serious to justify interim measures and in this context the Court stressed that such measures are granted strictly by way of exception and may be granted only where such assertions produce a 'faithful overall picture' of the applicant's financial situation and are based on evidence'.[247]

### 4.4.4.2 Request for Waivers

Compared to extensions of deadlines, a request to waive, modify or substitute one or more of the commitments is viewed by the Commission far more carefully as the parties must show not only good cause but also the existence of exceptional circumstances. Interestingly, the Commission has indicated that this general review provision will very rarely be relevant for divestiture remedies as market conditions are unlikely to change within the short space of time of a divestiture remedy.[248] Instead, the Commission finds the review clause more relevant for non-divestiture remedies, such as access remedies, which may be on-going for several years and for which not all contingencies can be predicted at the time of the adoption of the Commission decision.[249] However, given that decisional practice suggests that these clauses are also relevant for some divestitures the following description will look at the requirements for such waivers.

Exceptional circumstances justifying a waiver, modification or substitution of commitments may exist if the parties can show that: (i) market circumstances have changed significantly and on a permanent basis (viewed over 'at least several years' following the conditional

[245] It is evident from the pending Court proceedings in *EDF v Commission* (T-389/12 pending) that in *EDF/Segebel* (M.5549 I 2009) the Commission had granted the parties another 3½ months to complete the divestiture of a project, which they had been unable to complete more than 2½ years after the conditional clearance decision. However, in the parties' view, this extension was insufficient and therefore they appealed, as they wanted an additional 2 years for implementing that remedy.

[246] See Monti in Lévêque and Shelanski (2003) 8.

[247] See *EDF v Commission* (T-389/12 pending) where the Court rejected the parties' application for interim measures, see Order of the President of the General Court, 11 October 2012, para 23. As the application was dismissed for lack of urgency, it was not necessary for the Court to consider whether the other conditions for granting interim measures were fulfilled.

[248] The Commission explains in para 73 of the Remedies Notice that modifications of divestiture remedies will normally take place under more targeted review clauses, such as the provision that the Commission may approve a purchaser without some of the assets or personnel foreseen as provided for in para 30 of the notice.

[249] The following description of such review clauses is based on the requirements listed by the Commission in para 74 of the Remedies Notice.

clearance decision); or (ii) the experience gained in the application of the remedy demonstrates that the objective pursued with the remedy will be better achieved if modalities of the remedy are changed. Exceptional circumstances may also arise and justify modifications if it becomes evident post-decision that there is an inadvertent and/or unintentional shortcoming in the remedies.[250] In any event, in its assessment the Commission will take into account the views of third parties and the impact a modification may have on the position of such parties, including rights already acquired,[251] and thereby on the overall effectiveness of the remedy.

While it is generally considered to be extremely difficult for the parties to alter core aspects (that is conditions) of the remedies post-decision, there have nonetheless been cases in the past where the Commission has acknowledged certain significant changes of circumstances, which warranted a review – even possibly a release – of the original remedies. For example, in *Gaz de France/Suez* the Commission adopted a formal decision 5 years post-transaction amending one remedy and waiving another.[252] The first remedy related to the development of gas storage capacity in France where the Commission recognised that there were legitimate grounds for delaying the sale of storage capacity and accepting modifications in respect of the sale of multiannual capacity, reserve price ceiling and timing for reserving gas transmission capacity.[253] The second remedy related to the installation of a gas deodorisation plant on the French/Belgian border where the Commission accepted that the construction of the plant had been seriously jeopardised by factors beyond the control of the merging parties and it no longer corresponded to real market demand and, on that basis, the remedy was withdrawn.[254] Another example is *Hoffmann–La Roche/Boehringer Mannheim* where the Commission by decision some 13 years post-transaction waived an open-ended commitment to grant certain licences dating back to 1998.[255] In essence, the Commission found that a waiver releasing the parties from their licence commitments were justified given that market conditions had changed significantly and third parties had not opposed to the waiver.

A last example worth mentioning in this context is *Newscorp/Telepiu* where Sky Italia (the Italian subsidiary of Newscorp) had been prevented from participating in public tenders for the allocation of nationwide digital terrestrial television (DTT) frequencies in Italy

[250] This situation is not explicitly mentioned in the Remedies Notice but nevertheless sometimes certain aspects are unavoidably overlooked by the Commission and/or the parties when drafting and accepting the remedies, and naturally such mistakes should be restored through appropriate amendments, see eg *Vodafone Airtouch/Mannesmann* (M.1795 I 2000) where the Commission through the adoption of a decision of 26 July 2002 (not publicly available) corrected an inadvertent shortcoming in the fast track dispute resolution mechanism, reported by De Souza and Brockhoff in Drauz and Jones (2012) para 7.430, fn 2836.

[251] As an example of such rights, the Commission refers in its Remedies Notice (para 74, fn 1) to the judgment in *Royal Phillips Electronics v Commission* (T-119/02 2003) para 184. In these proceedings the applicant (a competitor) claimed that a review clause (albeit not a standard clause but a 'renegotiation clause' according to which the parties could apply for a review of the remedies if the French competition authorities in the related referral case imposed remedies that would run counter to those accepted by the Commission) could have undermined the rights acquired by the licensees in question on the basis of the original remedies. The General Court refrained from ruling on this issue as it had become devoid of purpose at the time of the ruling, see para 188.

[252] See Commission decision of 28 October 2011 amending Commitments Nos 73 and 84 in *Gaz de France/Suez* (M.4180 II 2006), published in [2013] OJ C51/5 (it is unclear why the publication of the new decision was delayed some 16 months).

[253] ibid, para 4. Furthermore, it appears that the parties had previously been allowed to substitute the Alsace site (as originally foreseen in the remedies) with another site, see para 3. To the best of my knowledge, the substitution of the site was never made public although it appears to concern an important modification of a condition in the original conditional clearance decision.

[254] ibid, para 5.

[255] See Commission decision of 3 May 2011 waiving certain commitments in *Hoffmann–La Roche/Boehringer Mannheim* (M.950 II 1998), published in [2011] OJ C189/31.

since 2003.[256] The ban would have expired in 2011 but the Commission released, upon application, Sky Italia from this remedy in 2010 due to significant and permanent changes in the Italian TV market.[257] However, as the market investigation in connection with the review revealed concerns about Sky Italia's re-entry into the satellite pay TV market, Newscorp offered another two remedies aiming at limiting Sky Italia's market power in that market for another 5 years.[258] The cases illustrate not only the Commission's willingness (albeit still confined to exceptional cases) to reassess markets and remedies if market circumstances change significantly but, in the case of *Newscorp/Telepiu*, it also shows that new remedies are required if any competition doubts remain, even if this means that the remedies are stretched over a considerable number of years, in this case a total of 12 years.

While the above examples concern the review of non-divestiture remedies, including access remedies (mentioned in the Remedies Notice as being the most likely scenario for a review), there have been cases in the past where the Commission has reviewed request for waivers relating to divestiture remedies. As these cases are rare and have received little publicity, it is considered beneficial to briefly highlight the involved remedies, which were subject to review.

First the Commission has reviewed remedies in cases where subsequent decisions in other jurisdictions have had an impact on the Commission's original conditional clearance. Most notably, in *Shell/Montecatini* the parties had committed to keep Montedison's technology separate from the parties' notified joint venture as Shell had competing activities.[259] Following the Commission's decision, the FTC required Shell to divest itself of all its assets and interests in this particular technology and therefore the Commission's remedy became superfluous. Following a request by the parties, the Commission amended its original decision by formally revoking the respective conditions and obligations.[260] While it is unlikely that such a situation would occur in current practice due to international cooperation and the fact that the filing deadlines are now more flexible, review clauses taking into account possible implications of parallel proceedings in other jurisdictions may be still relevant.[261] Review clauses have also been considered important in cases of partial referral of a transaction to a Member State in accordance with Article 9 of the Merger Regulation.[262]

[256] See *Newscorp/Telepiù* (M.2876 II 2003) where Newscorp acquired control of Telepiù Spa and Stream Spa and therefore created a new digital satellite television company named Sky Italia. As part of the conditional clearance the Commission imposed a number of strict conditions, under which Sky Italia was not allowed to (i) offer pay-TV other than on satellite or (ii) keep or acquire digital terrestrial television (DTT) frequencies, see further press release IP/03/478 of 2 April 2003. Although the remedies in this case are non-divestitures they are worth mentioning in the context of review clauses as an example of an extraordinarily long implementation period.

[257] See press release IP/10/983 of 20 July 2010 where the Commission briefly explains why it considers that market circumstances have changed significantly to justify a revision. The Commission's review decision is regrettably not publicly available.

[258] Newscorp committed Sky Italia to (i) bid only for one of the five tenders coming up; and (ii) operate free-to-air channels for a period of 5 years after the public tender (in order to mitigate fears that Sky Italia would switch to pay TV as soon as the original remedies would have expired in December 2011).

[259] See *Shell/Montecatini (I)* (M.269 II 1994).

[260] ibid and press release IP/96/347 of 24 April 1996. The Commission's amended decision was formally adopted by the Commissioner responsible for Competition and published, see [1996] OJ L294/10. Commission officials later acknowledged that the facts of the case and the decision to release the parties from the remedy were exceptional as the parties had expressly reserved their rights to request a review of the remedy which was highly unusual at that point in time, see Drauz (1996) 229.

[261] In some multi-jurisdictional cases the remedies therefore explicitly refer to a possible request for a review as a result of the position of other competition authorities, see eg *Intel/McAfee* (M.5984 I 2011), Remedies Text, para 48; and *Procter & Gamble/Gillette* (M.3732 I 2005), Remedies Text, para 37.

[262] See particularly *Royal Philips Electronics v Commission* (T-119/02 2003) paras 176–95.

Secondly, the Commission has reviewed remedies where it proved difficult or impossible for the parties to divest the assets in accordance with the original divestiture requirements due to subsequent unforeseen changes in market behaviour or structures. In *Pirelli/Edizione/Olivetti/Telecom Italia* the remedies originally required Edizione to sell its shareholdings in the mobile phone operator Blu to a suitable purchaser.[263] Less than a year post-decision it became evident that no suitable purchaser had come forward and that Blu encountered serious financial difficulties and the Commission therefore agreed to modify the remedies to allow for a break-up of Blu's assets and separate sales of the assets to a number of Italian mobile phone operators.[264] As the Commission maintained that new potential competition concerns could arise in the wake of this break-up, it requested the Italian Minister for Communications to ensure that certain measures were put in place to ensure fair and non-discriminatory use of the assets.[265] Another example of changing circumstances can be found in *Bombardier/Adtranz* where the market structure changed during the implementation of the remedy with the result that the remedy (a purchase obligation), if unchanged, would paradoxically have established structural links between consolidated competitors.[266] To this effect, the obligation was repealed 4 years after the original condition clearance decision.

Furthermore, any description of review of remedies would be incomplete without mentioning the Commission's decision in *Hoechst/Rhône-Poulenc* (creating Aventis and later Sanofi-Aventis).[267] Whilst the remedies did not contain a review clause as such, Aventis nevertheless requested the Commission to substitute its original commitment to divest its stake in the chemical company Rhodia to one of divesting its stake in Wacker-Chemie. To this effect, the Commission adopted a formal decision in January 2004 (nearly 4 years after the conditional clearance decision) where it accepted the request, albeit under certain conditions.[268] The main justification for the substitution of remedies was Rhodia's declining financial health and the fact that the capital structure of Rhodia had to be sorted out in order to allow for a restructuring of the company.[269] The Commission received harsh criticism for its 'remedies swap' inter alia from a European Parliament member who claimed that the 2004 decision 'tarnishes the Commission's reputation for a rigorous approach to

[263] See *Pirelli/Edizione/Olivetti/Telecom Italia* (M.2574 I 2001). As the decision exists only in Italian, see also press release IP/01/1299 of 20 September 2001.

[264] See press release IP/02/1183 of 5 August 2002. During the proceedings there was disagreement between the Commission and the parties as to whether Edizione had indeed used its best efforts to find suitable purchasers, see MEMO/02/108 of 24 May 2002 and section 4.6.4 below.

[265] See press release IP/02/1183 of 5 August 2002. It is uncertain how such measures were imposed as the press release is the only public source. Some of the assets in the breakup were sold to Wind and subsequently cleared by the Commission, see *Wind/Blue* (M.2958 I 2002).

[266] See *Bombardier/Adtranz* (M.2139 II 2001) where Bombardier inter alia committed to sever its links with the train component supplier ETR, a subsidiary of VA Tech. In order to ensure the viability of ETR as a supplier, Bombardier was required to source certain components for an interim period until 2006. In the meantime, Siemens proposed to acquire VA Tech and consequently ETR would come under the ownership of a financially viable company and no longer need secured orders for its economic survival, see *Siemens/VA Tech* (M.3653 II 2005). In fact the interim purchase obligation would have created a structural link between the competitors Siemens and Bombardier, and the Commission therefore released Bombardier of its purchase obligations vis-à-vis ETR by a separate decision in 2005, see Commission decision of 13 July 2005 amending the original conditional clearance decision (not available on the DG Competition's website but published in [2005] OJ L329/35).

[267] See *Hoechst/Rhône-Poulenc* (M.1378 I 1999).

[268] On 30 January 2004 the Commission formally adopted a decision amending its original conditional clearance decision, see [2004] OJ C42/22 (decision published on the DG Competition's case file) and press release IP/04/135 of 30 January 20004. The case was dealt with in parallel by FTC, see *In the Matter of Hoechst AG and Rhone-Poulenc SA, to be renamed Aventis SA,* Docket No C-3919, File No 991 0071.

[269] See Competition Report 2004, para 228, as well as section 4.6.4 below.

mergers' and to this effect proposed, albeit unsuccessfully, an investigation into the Commission's handling of the case.[270]

Even more interestingly, another remedy seems to have been substituted during the implementation phase in *Hoechst/Rhône-Poulenc* as it transpired from the parallel US proceedings that the FTC in 2002 accepted that Aventis was released from its original commitment, submitted to both the Commission and the FTC, to divest of Rhône-Poulenc's rights in Revasc (an anti-coagulant drug) to Novartis or another independent third party.[271] As Aventis failed to divest Revasc within the imposed deadlines (presumably due to difficulties in finding suitable purchasers), the FTC required the divestiture of the competing product Refludan, which a divestiture trustee eventually sold to Schering AG (later Merck) in 2001.[272] Despite the lack of public announcements by the Commission, this substitution must also have been presented to, assessed and accepted by the Commission.[273] The alleged non-transparent handling of this remedy is peculiar and worrying, especially given that the Commission must have conducted an additional market investigation in order to verify not only the adequacy of the substituted remedy but also in order to evaluate and possibly contact potential purchasers for such new assets.[274]

The past cases of modifications and substitutions, described above, concern aspects relating to the core of the remedies and thus primarily conditions for clearance.[275] An example of another kind of condition that may be waived under the review clause is the so-called 're-acquisition prohibition' according to which the parties cannot re-acquire

[270] See the European Parliament's Report of 20 March 2006 on the Commission's Report on Competition Policy 2004, document No PE 362.754v02-00, p 8 (point 4). In the report the rapporteur Alain Lipietz from the French Green Party made some serious allegations that: (i) the Commission had made mistakes in the two original decisions from 1999 that had catastrophic consequences for both shareholders and workers; (ii) there is not retrospective analysis in the 2004 decision; and (iii) the case files on *Hoechst/Rhône-Poulenc* (M.1378 I 1999) and the related *Rhodia/Donau Chemie/Albright & Wilson* (M.1517 I 1999) had disappeared from the DG Competition's website while the draft Parliament report was being drafted and thus hampering parliamentary work. To this effect, the Rapporteur suggested that the Parliament should launch an inquiry but, to the best of my knowledge, no official documents confirm that such a procedure was initiated. Furthermore, in the end the European Parliament supported the Commission's Competition Report 2004 while the rapporteur withdrew his name from the report as he disagreed with the changes made to his original text at committee stage (implying that the allegations in connection with the *Hoechst/Rhône-Poulenc* and *Rhodia/Donau Chemie/Albright & Wilson* cases were dropped), see European Parliament (economic and monitory affairs) press release of 4 April 2006, available at www.europarl.europa.eu.

[271] The Revasc commitment to the Commission was stipulated in *Hoechst/Rhône-Poulenc* (M.1378 I 1999) para 121 and Annex 4 to the decision.

[272] See FTC press releases of 25 August 2000, 17 August 2001, and 28 September 2001.

[273] Indeed, in the FTC press releases reference is made to the fact that in connection with the transfer of the Refludan assets to Schering AG the divestiture contract was 'submitted to both the FTC and the European Commission', see FTC press release of 28 September 2001. Also several press reports confirmed that Schering's acquisition of Refludan had been accepted by both the FTC and the Commission, see eg report by newswire ChemEurope.com, 'Regulatory Agencies Approve Aventis Sale of Refludan to Schering AG', 10 February 2001, www.chemeurope.com/en/news/print/5089.

[274] The eventual purchaser accepted by the FTC was Schering, a German competitor. Moreover, it later emerged that not all required Refludan assets had been transferred to Schering and therefore the FTC reviewed once again the transaction and granted an additional modification accepting that Aventis would eg retain certain production facilities in France, see FTC press release of 15 March 2002. Thus, the US proceedings were very much focused on implications on European markets.

[275] As previously suggested, the Commission is not always transparent about subsequent changes to remedies, so some accepted amendments are evident only when comparing different publicly available sources post-merger. A recent example is *GDF Suez/International Power* (M.5978 I 2011) where the Commission had required the merging parties to sell all shares (a 33.3% stake) in a joint venture called T-Power (see para 121) but where it later emerged – by comparing press releases from the parties and other Commission documents – that the Commission had allowed the merged entity to retain a stake in the given joint venture, see further ch 3 n 127 above.

direct or indirect influence over the whole or part of the divested business, for a period of generally 10 years.[276] The Commission stresses that the remedies may provide for a waiver allowing it to relieve the parties of the re-acquisition prohibition, provided the market structure has changed to an extent that the absence of influence over the divested business is no longer necessary.[277]

Based on publicly available information, it appears that review requests and acceptances are rare and few in numbers (considering a 20-year practice).[278] Nevertheless the cases described above highlight the justification of review clauses and the need for the Commission to be able to re-consider even core aspects of remedies in certain, albeit exceptional, circumstances. To this effect, the Commission has taken the standard review provision a step further and now suggests that it may be appropriate in some cases to include a clause in the remedies, allowing the Commission to trigger limited modifications if the original remedies do not achieve the envisaged results and thus do not effectively remove the competition concerns.[279] Procedurally, the parties may be obliged to propose a change to the remedies in order to achieve the result defined in those remedies, or the Commission may itself, after hearing the parties, modify the conditions and obligations to this end. Although the Commission stresses that this type of clause will typically be limited to cases where specific modalities risk jeopardising effective implementation of the remedies,[280] the response to such a specific review clause has not surprisingly been sceptical and negative.[281]

Finally it should be mentioned that while the above description of past cases mainly concerns amendments to core elements of remedies (hence conditions), requests for waiver of minor implementation modalities – such as reporting obligations, one or more trustee requirements and/or purchaser requirements, non-compete, non-solicitation or ring-fencing provisions – are more common.[282] These are all obligations and it seems less problematic for the Commission to grant waivers for such provisions, as they do not require a new market investigation or changes the overall purpose and/or impact of the remedy.

[276] MTDC, para 3; and Remedies Notice, paras 43 and 73 fn 4 *in fine*.

[277] See Remedies Notice, para 43, and section 4.6.2 below.

[278] As the Commission does not normally publish review requests and acceptances it is difficult to estimate the frequencies of such incidences. Indeed, occasionally information appears in other contexts indicating that the parties did in fact request review of their commitments in past cases. In *BASF v Commission* (T-105/10 withdrawn 2010) the appellant (BASF) submitted that the Commission had rejected to modify certain commitments in accordance with the review clause set out in the Commission's conditional clearance decision in *BASF/Ciba* (M.5355 I 2009), see summary of pleas published in [2010] OJ C113/71. The pleas did not reveal any further details on the review request and as BASF withdrew its appeal, no further information is available. However, it is clear from the summary of the pleas that BASF had requested a review, which was dismissed by the Commission at the time of the proceedings (whether BASF withdrew its appeal due to the Commission's possible subsequent acceptance of the review request remains unknown).

[279] Remedies Notice, para 75.

[280] As an example the Commission refers to *DONG/Elsam/Energi E2* (M.3868 II 2006) where a provision in respect of a Gas Release Programme remedy stipulated that 'the Commission may *order* DONG to propose modifications and/or improvements in the [auction rules] on the basis of the experience gained from previous auctions'(emphasis added), see Remedies Text, para 24.

[281] Judging from the response during the public consultation in 2007 of the new draft Remedies Notice, the provision is considered one of the most controversial during the remedies review, see eg reply from Allen & Overy, para 10; reply from the American Bar Association, p 13; LIDC (Ligue Internationale du Droit de la Concurrence), p 9. It was inter alia suggested that the Commission should use such powers very rarely and only in the most exceptional circumstances eg where it would otherwise be necessary to prohibit the merger.

[282] See De Souza and Brockhoff in Drauz and Jones (2012) para 7.431.

#### 4.4.4.3 Means of Communication

As shown above, in the past the Commission has been inconsistent as to how it has communicated its review decisions to the parties; whether in the form of an administrative letter or a formal decision. The Commission now clarifies that, in response to review requests, it may either adopt a formal decision or simply take note of satisfactory amendments of the remedy by the parties where such amendments improve the effectiveness of the remedy and result in legally binding obligations of the parties, for example by contractual arrangements.[283] It appears that the Commission thereby distinguishes between reviewed conditions and obligations in the sense that an amended obligation can be taken note of more informally whereas a condition may require a formal ancillary decision. This distinction seems proportionate to the significance and impact of obligations and conditions, respectively, and is also in line with recent decisional practice.[284] All in all, the choice of communication seems to be within the discretion of the Commission.[285]

If the Commission does opt for a formal decision, it will be adopted by the College of Commissioners or an individual Commissioner to whom powers have been delegated,[286] whereas it will usually be the Head of Service or the Director-General responsible who signs an administrative letter.[287] In both scenarios the appropriate delegations of powers are provided for in the Commission's internal procedural paperwork attached to the original conditional approval decision.[288]

Finally, the Commission stresses that a modification of a condition or an obligation will normally only be effective *ex nunc* and it may therefore pursue a possible breach of remedies prior to the accepted modification and accordingly impose fines and/or periodic penalty payments.[289] It is believed that this provision is aimed at past situations where the Commission was not convinced that the parties had used their best efforts to fulfil the original remedies before requesting a review of the remedies.[290] However, to date the Commission has not publicly fined any parties for such breaches.

[283] Remedies Notice, para 76.

[284] See most recently Commission's decision of 28 October 2011 amending Commitments Nos 73 and 84 in *Gaz de France/Suez* (M.4180 II 2006), published in [2013] OJ C51/5; and Commission decision of 3 May 2011 waiving certain commitments (conditions) in *Hoffman–La Roche/Boeringer Mannheim* (M.950 II 1998), published in [2011] OJ C189/31.

[285] See Remedies Notice, para 76, referring to the fact that 'the Commission *may* [. . .] adopt a formal decision' (emphasis added).

[286] See Arts 1 and 3 of the Rules of Procedure of the Commission, [2000] OJ L308/26, as amended by Commission decision of 15 November 2005, [2005] OJ L347/83.

[287] An administrative letter is issued in accordance with the relevant delegation ('habilitation') provisions of the Commission, see Rules of Procedure of the Commission, Art 14. For an example of a case where the Commission issued an administrative letter (refusing to extend deadlines), see *Volvo/Renault V.I.* (M.1980 I 2000) where the letter of 7 April 2004 was signed by the director of the Merger Task Force (the letter was at the time published on the DG Competition's website – the link is no longer available but the letter is summarised in IP/04/484 of 15 April 2004).

[288] In the appeal *E.ON Ruhrgas and E.ON Földgáz Trade v Commission* (T-57/07 2009) relating to disagreement between the Commission and E.ON on the interpretation of an obligation set out in *E.ON/MOL* (M.3696 II 2005) E.ON argued that proper delegation rules had not been followed when the Commission issued two administrative letters (signed by the Director-General for Competition) setting out its understanding of the obligation, see pleas summarised in [2007] OJ C95/47. However, the General Court did not address this issue as the substance of the letters was not found to hold legal value.

[289] The Commission explicitly refers to its powers in accordance with Arts 14 and 15 of the Merger Regulation, see Remedies Notice, para 76 *in fine*.

[290] eg in *Pirelli/Edizione/Olivetti/Telecom Italia* (M.2574 I 2001) there was post-decision disagreement between the Commission and the parties as to whether Edizione had indeed used its best efforts to find suitable purchasers, see MEMO/02/108 of 24 May 2002 which is further explained below in the context of breach of remedies.

**Commentary:** the Commission's use of review clauses should be seen as an efficient tool to adapt the remedies to dynamic market conditions. Albeit speculative, it is considered that in past practice a 'review stigma' existed amongst Commission officials in the sense that a request for a review would imply that the remedies had been poorly negotiated and drafted in the first place and thus there was a reluctance to consider reviews. However, it is inevitable that not all contingencies can be foreseen at the design stage of the remedies and/or that markets develop differently than originally envisaged. Thus, statistically it is to be expected that a certain number of remedies require adjustments and reviews, especially in cases where the duration of the implementation is relatively long. Based on available information, such reviews have rarely happened in the past or alternatively they have not been published. In either case, it is hoped that the Commission initiates a more dynamic and transparent policy in this respect.

## 4.5 Completion of the Sale

### *4.5.1 Approval of Purchasers*

When the parties have reached a final agreement with the purchaser, they must submit a reasoned and documented proposal to the Commission.[291] The burden of proof is entirely on the parties, as they must demonstrate to the satisfaction of the Commission that the proposed purchaser meets the requirements,[292] and that the business is divested in a manner consistent with the Commission's decision.[293] The Commission interprets the purchaser requirements in the light of the purpose of the remedies (to immediately maintain effective competition in the market where competition concerns had been found) and of the market circumstances as set out in the decision.[294]

The Commission's assessment of the suitability of the purchaser is typically based on: (i) the submission of the parties, including the draft sale contract; (ii) the reasoned opinion of the monitoring trustee;[295] and (iii) further correspondence between the Commission, the parties and the prospective purchaser in the form of replies to requests for information, discussions with the proposed purchaser and an evaluation of a draft business plan. The latter aspect has become more prominent in recent years as it is now standard practice for the Commission to engage in a dialogue with the prospective purchaser and carefully review its business plan in order to get an insight into the purchaser's real intensions and incentives to compete.[296] While the Commission does not carry out a full-blown 'market

[291] Remedies Notice, para 101. The provision equally applies to situations where the divestiture trustee sells the business.

[292] For a description of the relevant provisions on purchaser requirements, see section 3.3 above.

[293] Where remedies provide for several purchasers being proposed for different parts of the remedies package, the Commission will assess whether each individual proposed candidate is acceptable and whether the total package solves the competition concern, see Remedies Notice, para 101 *in fine.*

[294] Remedies Notice, para 102.

[295] The trustee must submit a reasoned opinion in accordance with the Remedies Notice, para 119, third indent, and MTDC, para 23(vii). It was evident in *Éditions Jacob v Commission* (T-452/04 2010) that, in the view of the General Court, the Commission attaches great importance to the input of the trustee in its final evaluation of the purchaser, see paras 109–17. On appeal, the Commission submitted that it does not rely only on the trustee's report but collects information on its own initiative, see joined cases *Commission v Éditions Odile Jacob* (C-553/10 P 2012) and *Lagardère v Éditions Odile Jacob* (C-554/10 2012) para 26. The Court of Justice did not address this aspect.

[296] The practice of requiring the submission of a business plan was introduced in *Sanitec/Sphinx* (M.1578 II 1999) para 252, point 11.

test' of the proposed purchaser (as it does on proposed commitments), it may ask the opinion of interested third parties and employee representatives before reaching a final decision on the suitability of the proposed purchaser.[297] This consultation is not made publicly available.

Over the years the approval and selection procedures have changed slightly. First, during the early days of the Merger Regulation, the parties often proposed a shortlist of potential purchasers and, once the Commission had given its evaluations on those purchasers the parties would continue negotiations and eventually select the purchaser of their choice.[298] Under current practice the Commission is not formally asked to assess the proposed purchaser until a final agreement has been reached which is resource-saving for the Commission as its evaluation is often limited to one candidate per remedy but it also means that the Commission may not necessarily be aware of any other possible candidates.[299]

Secondly, in early cases purchasers were approved through a non-opposition procedure whereby the parties could execute the sale to the respective purchaser if the Commission had not formally objected in writing prior to the expiry of an agreed period (normally 2 weeks).[300] However, in view of some unfortunate incidences where the Commission – due to administrative errors – did not react promptly to the parties' proposed candidates within the stated period,[301] the policy was changed and now requires that the purchaser must be explicitly approved by the Commission without any specific time constraints other than 'as expeditiously as possible'.[302]

Third, according to current practice the Commission's approval includes the SPA and any other related agreements.[303] It is also at this stage that the Commission may, upon request by the parties, approve the divestiture of the business without one or more assets or

[297] In *Éditions Jacob v Commission* (T-452/04 2010) the Court listed the correspondence on which the Commission based its purchaser approval, see para 44. See also the subsequent appeal in joined cases *Commission v Éditions Odile Jacob* (C-553/10 P 2012) and *Lagardère v Éditions Odile Jacob* (C-554/10 P 2012) para 44.

[298] See eg *Guinness/GrandMet* (M.938 II 1997) para 184 (xiii).

[299] However, as the parties have an obligation to inform the trustee of possible purchasers (MTDC, para 27) and the trustee is obliged to inform the Commission of the progress of the divestiture process (MTDC, para 23), it may be assumed that the Commission is informed continuously.

[300] See eg *Industri Kapital/Dyno* (M.1813 II 2000), Remedies Text, para 23; *Hoffmann–La Roche/Boehringer Mannheim* (M.950 II 1998) para 162; *Anglo American Corporation/Lonrho* (M.754 II 1997) para 136; *Procter & Gamble/VP Schickedanz* (II) (M.430 II 1994) para 186(3).

[301] In *TotalFina/Elf* (M.1628 II 2000) the Commission nearly ran into trouble when missing the approval deadline. According to the remedies the Commission was obliged to inform the parties of its approval or rejection of proposed purchaser candidates within 10 days. The parties submitted their request for approval on 12 August 2000 and not before 13 September 2000 did the Commission adopt a decision (rejecting two candidates). In the rejected candidates' appeal before the General Court they claimed inter alia that the remedies were breached, as the Commission should have reached a decision before 28 August 2000, see *Petrolessence and SG2R v Commission* (T-342/00 2003) para 44. The Commission was saved by a rather unusual provision in the remedies (allowing an extension of the deadline in exceptional circumstances, see Remedies Text, paras 4 and 6) which the General Court accepted as valid, although remarking that the 'extension provision' was probably intended to cover other situations than the absence of a response from the Commission, see para 51 of the judgment. For what it is worth, the ruling serves as a reminder to the Commission that it was unnecessary to put undue constraints on it by inserting strict deadlines for purchaser approvals.

[302] Remedies Notice, para 106 *in fine*; and MTDC, para 15. In the new Remedies Notice the Commission decided to add the following phrase after the public consultation of the draft notice in 2007: 'The Commission will issue the necessary approvals as expeditiously as possible'.

[303] Remedies Notice, para 105; and MTDC, para 15. The practice of including the SPA in the purchaser approval was introduced in 2001, see old Remedies Notice (para 58). Compared to the old notice, the new notice is broader as it explicitly refers to 'any other agreement entered into between the parties and the proposed purchaser, including transitory agreements,' see Remedies Notice, para 105. The inclusion of all such ancillary agreements enables the Commission (and trustee) to review the substance and impact of the overall remedy.

parts of the personnel if not needed by the proposed purchaser, provided this does not affect the viability and competitiveness of the business after the sale, taking account of the own resources of the proposed purchaser.[304] The provision on exclusion of assets should be seen in context of the relatively new and stringent requirement that, at the design and assessment stage, the business to be divested must be viable as such and therefore the resources of a prospective purchaser cannot be taken into account at that stage.[305] Therefore, it is only when a purchaser is being formally approved that the Commission provides for the possibility of excluding assets.[306] It is also at this stage that the Commission assesses and approves any required supporting arrangements (relating typically to supply or services) between the merging parties and the purchaser for a transitional period.[307]

In any event, once a conclusion has been reached as to the suitability of the proposed purchaser, the Commission communicates its finding to the parties in the following ways:[308] (i) if the purchaser is unacceptable, the Commission adopts a rejection decision;[309] (ii) if the SPA (or any other agreement) is unacceptable, the Commission communicates this finding without necessarily rejecting the purchaser at this stage;[310] and (iii) if the purchaser and the SPA are suitable, the Commission approves the divestiture. In the latter situation the parties receives an administrative letter signed by either the Commissioner responsible for Competition or the Director of the DG Competition.[311] A specific situation should be mentioned in relation to EU–US cooperation cases with identical remedies covering assets in the EU as well as the US. If the remedies require that the assets should go to one single purchaser, the Commission formally approves the purchaser in respect of the European assets and the US formally approves of the same purchaser for the US assets.[312]

[304] Remedies Notice, paras 31 and 105, fn 3, as well as MTDC, para 15 *in fine*.

[305] Remedies Notice, para 30. See also section 3.1 above.

[306] It is difficult to evaluate the relevance of this provision, as such exclusions would normally be found in the SPA. However, with the introduction of the rigid requirement that assets of prospective purchasers cannot be taken into account at earlier stages of the remedies proceedings, the provision seems necessary in order not to force the purchaser to acquire superfluous assets which could burden financially and potentially weakening competitive position of the divested assets in the given market.

[307] The merging parties must provide for such possible arrangements already at the design stage of the remedies, see Remedies Notice, para 28. However, as these arrangements are usually triggered by an explicit request from the purchaser, the Commission concludes on the adequacy and necessity of such arrangements when approving the purchaser and the SPA, see Remedies Notice, para 105.

[308] Remedies Notice, para 106.

[309] See section 4.5.2 below.

[310] In its guidance the Commission is vague on how it communicates its findings to the parties but it is thought that the Commission may do so informally by sending an administrative letter signed by a senior staff member of the DG Competition (the Director or Head of Unit), assuring that once the SPA has been amended and acceptable, the Commission can proceed with its approval procedure of the proposed purchaser.

[311] The delegation rules are contained in the confidential Manual of Procedures for the DG Competition but in the few publicly available letters, an approval has been signed by either of the two mentioned (and thus not the full College of Commissioners). The decision is also sent to the trustee and the Member States. The latter is informed about the purchaser as it may trigger national proceedings.

[312] See in particular *Manitowoc/Enodis* (M.5180 I 2008) where the Commission's decision contained the standard purchaser requirements in relation to the assets in the EU, see Remedies Text, paras 12–13. With respect to the US assets, the DoJ emphasised that it had sole discretion in relation to the US assets but would consult the Commission before taking a formal decision, see *United States v The Manitowoc Company, Inc., Enodis plc, and Enocis Corporation*, Case No 1:2008CV01704, Final Judgment of 17 February 2009, section IV.A. While this case had a happy outcome as Warburg Pincus, a private equity company, was approved by both authorities as the sole acquirer of all assets in both jurisdictions as well as in China (see press release of 18 May 2009 from Warburg Pincus, accessed in 2009 at www.iceomatic.com (link no longer available)) this procedure may result in major time delays and frictions between the competent authorities if they cannot agree on one joint purchaser.

Under current practice the Commission's purchaser approval decisions are deemed procedural in nature and are not published and in most cases the Commission refrains from issuing a press release or any other information about the identity of the approved purchaser.[313] In the few cases where the Commission has published the identity of the purchaser, it has done so because of particular circumstances of the individual case, such as the divested company being publicly listed;[314] a high media interest in the purchaser approval;[315] or that the conditional clearance decision or the purchaser approval may be subject to complaints or even Court appeals.[316] Furthermore, in some cases the Commission may individually inform third parties if they are directly affected by the purchaser approval, for example joint venture partners.

### *4.5.2 Rejection of Purchasers*

As mentioned above, if the Commission considers that a proposed purchaser fails to meet the purchaser requirements, it will adopt a decision (under delegation) to this effect.[317] Such decisions are rare;[318] or at least they are rarely published. The few publicly known cases have involved Court proceedings.

[313] The lack of publicity is in sharp contrast to the FTC where the identity of the proposed purchasers is routinely published for public consultation and final approval. In Pernod Richard and Diageo's acquisition of the spirits and wine business of Seagram was notified and conditionally cleared by both the Commission and the FTC. The latter required the divestiture of Diageo's 'Malibu Rum Assets' by decision of 19 December 2001. On 15 March 2002 the FTC published a notice requesting comments (within 30 days) to a proposal that Diageo would sell its assets to Allied Domecq plc, and on May 10 2002 FTC's final vote and approval of Allied Domecq was published, see File No 011 0057, Docket No C-4032. By comparison, in the EU the parties were also required to divest a number of assets (different from ones in the US) but the Commission issued no press releases with respect to the implementation of the remedies, see *Pernod Richard/Diageo/Seagram* (M.2268 I 2001).

[314] In *Volvo/Renault* (M.1980 I 2000) the Commission issued a press release confirming the sale of AB Scania B-shares to Deutsche Bank, see press release IP/04/484 of 14 April 2004. Given the market sensitivity of the information the Commission chose furthermore – rather extraordinarily – to publish its approval letter (signed by the Director of the DG Competition) on its website on the same day (link no longer available).

[315] This was presumably the reason for the Commission's announcement of JCI as purchaser of the divested shareholding in *Anglo American Corporation/Lonrho* (M.754 II 1997), see press release IP/97/1102 of 10 December 1997.

[316] By way of illustration, in *Lagardère/Natexis/VUP* (M.2978 II 2004) the Commission issued a press release confirming the approval of Wendel Investissement as the purchaser on 30 July 2004 (press release IP/04/1013 of 3 August 2004) and on 8 July 2004 Éditions Odile Jacob brought an appeal against the Commission's conditional clearance decision before the General Court, see *Éditions Odile Jacob v Commission* (T-279/04 2010). In *TotalFina/Elf* (M.1628 II 2000) the Commission announced its approval of Carrefour, Agip, Avia and other companies as purchasers of 70 motorway service stations while at the same time acknowledging that during the process it had rejected a number of unsuitable purchasers (press release IP/00/1260 of 7 November 2000) and 6 days later the rejected purchasers brought an action for annulment of the Commission's rejection decision, see *Petrolessence and SG2R v Commission* (T-342/00).

[317] Remedies Notice, paras 101 and 106. However this does not prevent the parties from informally approaching the Commission earlier in the proceedings if they have any purchaser issues that they would like to discuss. The parties and the trustee will also inform the Commission about potential purchasers in accordance with the Remedies Notice, paras 116 and 119. It should be mentioned that during the early days of the Merger Regulation where the parties would submit a shortlist of potential purchasers to which the Commission would give an initial approval, it would often informally inform the parties that one (or more) of the shortlisted proposed purchasers would not fulfil the purchaser requirements, see eg *Nestlé/Perrier* (M.190 II 1992) where the Commission first informally rejected the proposed Castel group until the parties concluded a new agreement expanding the transferred assets, see press release IP/93/153 of 3 March 1993. The Commission did not publish its first rejection of Castel and this aspect was only mentioned in the subsequent Court proceedings, see Order of the President of 6 July 1993 in *CCE Vittel v Commission* (T-12/93 1993) para 4.

[318] In the Remedies Study the Commission confirmed that only once in the reference period had it formally rejected a purchaser, namely in *TotalFina/Elf* (M.1628 II 2000), see p 98 (point 4).

The most publicised 'purchaser rejection decision' was adopted in *TotalFina/Elf* where the Commission had conditionally cleared the transaction inter alia on the condition that TotalFina would divest around 70 petrol stations in France.[319] The parties proposed to sell 6 of the petrol stations to Petrolessence and SG2R (operating jointly as Mirabellier) who were rejected, by formal decision, by the Commission on the grounds that they did not provide enough certainty as to their viability as potentially or actually present in the market for French motorway petrol sales and their ability to maintain and develop effective competition.[320] The rejected purchasers appealed the Commission's decision but the General Court ruled in favour of the Commission that it had been right in taking into account in its purchaser assessment the fact that the applicants were newcomers to the market and hence it would not be evident that they would be capable of ensuring effective and long-lasting competition.[321]

In another less publicised case *BASF/Ciba* the Commission rejected by formal decision a proposed purchaser, Roquette Frères, of Ciba's dry-strength-agents business.[322] In March 2010 BASF appealed the Commission's rejection, alleging inter alia that the Commission had committed a manifest error of assessment with regard to the incentive for Roquette Frères to maintain and develop the business to be divested.[323] The General Court did not get to rule on this issue as BASF later withdrew its appeal, presumably as it had proposed another purchaser who was deemed acceptable by the Commission.[324]

Both purchaser rejection decisions were thus based on concerns as to the proposed purchasers' incentives and/or abilities to maintain and develop the business to be divested as a viable and active competition force as set out in the Commission's standard purchaser criteria. However, the problematic requirement potentially leading to a rejection that the Commission highlights in its guidelines is the risk that the purchaser may threaten to create new competition problems.[325] In particular, a purchaser will be rejected if the Commission suspects that difficulties in obtaining merger control clearance or other approvals may unduly delay the timely implementation of the remedies.[326] Based on publicly available information, the Commission has to date not adopted a rejection decision on such grounds.

[319] See *TotalFina/Elf* (M.1628 II 2000). The case and the purchaser rejection are summarised in Competition Report 2000, para 258. The 'purchaser rejection decision' is not publicly available but is described in detail in the subsequent Court proceedings in *Petrolessence and SG2R v Commission* (T-342/00).

[320] Following the Commission's rejection, the parties proposed a new list of purchasers eventually approved by the Commission, see IP/00/1260 of 7 November 2000.

[321] See *Petrolessence and SG2R v Commission* (T-342/00) paras 61–66. It is particularly interesting to note that, although the remedies did not expressly require the prospective purchaser to be currently active in the relevant market, the General Court confirmed that the Commission could rightly take into account the fact that the applicant was a newcomer to the market, see para 65. See also Remedies Study, p 98 (point 4).

[322] The purchaser rejection decision in *BASF/Ciba* (M.5355 I 2009) was adopted on 18 December 2009 but not made publicly available.

[323] See *BASF v Commission* (T-105/10 withdrawn 2010) and the summary of the pleas in [2010] OJ C113/70.

[324] It follows from BASF's Annual Report 2010 (p 155) that the respective business was sold on 30 September 2010 but the identity of the purchaser was not disclosed, see www.report.basf.com/2010.

[325] Remedies Notice, para 104.

[326] ibid. This provision should be seen in the context of the finding in the Remedies Study that delays in implementation caused by interventions from other governmental authorities may often be longer than anticipated and that consequently an up-front assessment of potential regulatory problems is crucial, see study, p 106 (point 28).

### *4.5.3 Transfer and Closing*

Once the final SPA has been signed and the purchaser approved by the Commission, the parties usually have 3 months to close the transaction.[327] Closure is complete only once the legal title has been passed to the approved purchaser and the assets have been transferred.[328] The Commission found in past cases that the physical or actual transfer of tangible and intangible assets often occurred long after closing and involved serious issues which were not always resolved after 3 to 5 years post-decision.[329] In particular, the transfer of intangible assets in carve-out cases proved difficult with the result that the effectiveness of the remedy was reduced.[330] In current practice the Commission is thus more aware of the trustee's role and responsibilities in overseeing the transfer process in order to minimise unforeseen obstacles.

At the end of the process, the parties as well as the trustee are required to submit a final report to the Commission, confirming the closing and the transfer of the assets.[331] Only then can the trustee request the Commission to be discharged.[332] It is practice that the Commission does not formally certify that the parties have fulfilled the remedies in order not to pre-empt the possibility of re-opening the case should it subsequently transpire that the remedies were not properly implemented.[333]

**Commentary:** no one involved in purchaser approval proceedings will dispute that the Commission has come a very long way in its approval procedure compared to the early days under the Merger Regulation where it was not unusual that a purchaser would be approved merely on the basis of information submitted by the merging parties as to its suitability without the Commission investigating business plans, undertaking interviews, receiving input from a monitoring trustee and so forth.

If any possible weaknesses with the current practice should be highlighted, it would be that, as the Commission is not necessarily directly involved in the purchaser selection procedure until one final candidate remains, it needs to somehow ensure that the divestiture process has not been conducted in a way whereby more suitable or stronger competitors have been discouraged or excluded from the process. It goes without saying (and it was shown in the Remedies Study) that the merging parties do not have a natural interest in proposing the strongest competitor to the Commission if less strong competitors exist that would also formally fulfil the purchaser criteria as set out in the remedies.

Prima facie there seems to be no obvious solution to this potential concern as it would be unrealistic and disproportionate to suggest that the Commission should be presented with a short list of prospective purchasers (including a full assessment of each candidate),[334] but it goes to show that the professionalism and integrity of the trustee is vital in the divestiture process as the

[327] Remedies Notice, para 98; and MTDC, para 2.

[328] Remedies Notice, para 116 *in fine.*

[329] Remedies Study, p 80 (points 2–3). It should be noted that, at the time of the reference period in the Remedies Study, the Commission had not yet introduced the 3-month deadline for closure contained in MTDC, para 2.

[330] Examples of transfer difficulties are listed in the Remedies Study, pp 81–84.

[331] Remedies Notice, paras 116 and 119, third indent.

[332] For discharge and possible re-appointment of the trustee, see section 4.2.1.6 above.

[333] See De Souza and Brockhoff in Drauz and Jones (2012) para 7.407.

[334] In fact, during early decisional practice it was not uncommon that the Commission was presented with a shortlist of purchaser candidates and if more than one candidate were considered suitable by the Commission, the merging parties were free to select the purchaser of their choice, see eg *Guinness/GrandMet* (M.938 II 1997) para 183(xiii). However, it is submitted that in those days the purchaser selection was done through a non-opposition procedure and the information required for evaluating the candidates was limited compared to current practice.

Commission needs to fully rely on his capabilities in monitoring and ensuring that the selection process has indeed been conducted in the spirit of the remedies.

## 4.6 Post-closing/'Aftermath'

### *4.6.1 On-sales Bans*

As a general rule, once the sale of the assets has been completed, the destiny of the divested business is in the hands of the purchaser and the Commission will usually not interfere. However, in some cases the Commission may consider it appropriate or even necessary to impose certain restrictions on the purchaser's future behaviour with regard to the purchased business in order to ensure that the business is maintained as a competitive force in the market. More specifically, the purchaser may be required not to re-sell the purchased assets within a certain period of time.[335] Such so-called 'on-sales bans' may be imposed in cases where it appears likely that the business will be re-sold within a short period of time with the risk of rapidly defeating the intent of the original remedy.

On-sales restrictions are controversial for a number of reasons.[336] First, given that the Commission suggests that such clauses may be contained in the SPA,[337] this means that it will be the responsibility of the parties to negotiate such restrictions with the prospective purchaser. Needless to say, such a contractual obligation would have a significant impact on the sales/purchase price as well as reducing the attractiveness of the assets to be divested with the possible result that the prospective purchaser may withdraw from negotiations. Secondly, it raises the question as to the appropriate timeframe. The Commission provides no other details than indicating that the business should not be re-sold within 'a short time-span'. It is assumed that an appropriate time span depends heavily on the industry in question and thus cannot be generally defined. Thirdly, on-sales bans would require a degree of monitoring on the part of the Commission and, as a matter of contract law, if the clause is stipulated in the SPA, it is unclear what the implications would be in the event of a subsequent breach of the on-sales ban as the Commission is not a party to the agreement. Finally and from a business point of view, on-sales bans are harsh restrictions if it later appears that the companies are commercially incompatible and that the acquisition was simply a mistake and in that respect the ban can be considered as an interventionist measure.[338]

Although the Commission does not mention on-sales bans in the context of financial investors as suitable purchasers,[339] it is considered that the risk of an early re-sale may at times be particularly imminent in cases where the purchaser is a financial investor whose

[335] See Remedies Notice, para 106, fn 5.

[336] The provision was subject to many critical comments during the consultation in 2007 of the draft new Remedies Notice, see eg reply from JWP, point 2.21; reply from Freshfields Bruckhaus Deringer, point 7.3; reply from Linklaters, point 11; and reply from Lovells, point 18. Despite the criticism the Commission maintained the core provision and subsequently made few changes to the final wording, such as the insertion of 'depending on the circumstances of the divestiture'.

[337] See Remedies Notice, para 106, fn 5.

[338] The DoJ does not normally impose such bans and this policy is based on the assumption that any corporate mistakes (eg that the merged companies are incompatible) will be corrected by the market itself as long as the purchaser is free to re-sell the assets to a company capable of operating them most efficiently, see DoJ Merger Remedies Guide, part IV.C.2.

[339] See Remedies Notice, para 49.

main activities are buying and selling companies; a private equity firm. Thus it may be assumed that it could be such situations that the Commission has in mind when it refers to the risk of on-sales in its most recent guidance. Another situation that could call for increased awareness of on-sales risks is when the divested assets are not stand-alone and sold as part of a larger commercial package as the Commission then needs to be vigilant that the purchaser (especially if the purchaser is relatively small) does indeed have the capabilities and intentions to develop the 'remedies assets' within its overall portfolio.[340] In such situations the Commission may wish to compensate for the uncertainties by asking the parties to conclude an on-sales ban during a certain period of time. In any event, very little information is available on the possible frequency and implications of on-sales in the Commission's current practice.[341] However, given that the ban is explicitly mentioned in the new Remedies Notice it must be assumed that it is an issue in current decisional practice.

As there is very little information available about on-sales bans in the Commission's policy and practice, it is worthwhile briefly considering the US approach to this issue as the Commission may have been inspired by its US counterparts when inserting the on-sales provision in the new Remedies Notice. The FTC occasionally insists on a so-called 'prior approval provision' in its acceptance of a purchaser.[342] In such cases the purchaser is required to seek prior permission from the FTC before subsequent sales, hence in effect an on-sales ban. The provision has been applied mainly in cases where the purchaser's business plans indicated that there was a high probability that the acquired assets would be re-sold within 2 to 5 years.

By way of illustration, when the FTC conditionally approved *Nestlé/Ralston Purina* in 2001, it accepted a financial investor, JW Childs Equity Partners II, LP ('Childs') as an up-front buyer for the assets (two of Ralston's dry cat food brands) to be divested in the US.[343] The approval was accompanied by statements from three Commissioners expressing fears that Childs would re-sell the acquired business in the short term to an unsuitable buyer and therefore in order to maintain the integrity of the conditional clearance a prior approval provision for 5 years was included.[344] As it turned out, in 2003 (thus less than

[340] This observation is based on the findings of the ex-post analysis of *Monsanto/Pharmacia & Upjohn* (M.1835 I 2000) in the DG Enterprise Econometric Remedies Study where the authors found that the merging parties had sold one product (Pethidin) to a small local company called Recip, only for the latter to sell the product to another purchaser *the day after* it had bought it from the parties, see Davies and Lyons (2007) 195. It turned out that Recip had only bought Pethidin because it was part of a package of 13 other products sold by the merging parties as part of a Nordic rationalisation. The authors claim that the merging parties as well as the original purchaser did not appear to have any interest in the ultimate fate of the 'remedy product'. The authors also note that, even more worrying, no one had told Recip that the purpose of the sale of Pethidin was in fact to restore competition, let alone got any assurances of a vigorous business plan.

[341] The Remedies Study found that 7% of purchasers had re-sold the business to a new purchaser who was still operating 3 to 5 years after the sale, see p 128 (point 20).

[342] See FTC FAQ About Merger Consent Order Provisions, Q 45. As mentioned above, the DoJ does not normally impose on-sales restraints and if it does the restraint is limited to a particular entity or type of entity, see DoJ Merger Remedies Guide, part IV.C.2.

[343] See File No 011 0083, Docket No C-4028, and in particular FTC press release of 11 December 2001 at www.ftc.gov/opa/2001/12/nestleralston.htm.

[344] The statements from Commissioners SF Anthony, MW Thompson and O Swindle were made public on www.ftc.gov/opa/2001/12/nestleralston.htm. Pursuant to para VI of FTC's Decision and Order, 'J.W. Childs shall not, for a period of five (5) years from the date this Order becomes final, sell or otherwise convey, directly or indirectly, all or substantially all of the Ralston Assets [. . .] to any Person without the prior approval of the Commission'. One Commissioner questioned whether, in view of the provision's 5-year duration and the dynamics of the market, the FTC would indeed be able to determine with a 'high degree of confidence' whether the 'prospective buyer of the resold assets would compete as effectively as Ralston would have competed in the absence of the Ralston/Nestlé merger', see FTC press release of 11 December 2001.

2 years later) the FTC received an application from Childs requesting permission to re-sell the acquired business (now called The Meow Mix Company) to another private equity firm Cypress Group L.L.C[345] which then in 2006 approached the FTC for permission to re-sell the Meow Mix assets to the industrial purchaser and pet care competitor Del Monte Corporation.[346]

Although an isolated case, the FTC's handling of *Nestlé/Ralston Purina* confirms that (i) on-sales issues may indeed arise when the purchaser is a financial investor and that the re-sale cycles may be relatively short (around 2 years); (ii) on-sales bans may impose significant additional resources on the Commission in terms of subsequent clearances as it is assumed that new market investigations are required in order to assess the suitability of the new purchaser; and (iii) although the first and second purchaser in this case were financial investors with short-term gains in mind, the ultimate outcome had a 'happy ending' in that the business was ultimately re-sold to a significant industrial player, Nestlé Ralston Purina (now Nestlé Purina PetCare).

Compared to the (scarce) information on on-sales from the Commission, one important difference is that the FTC imposes on-sales restrictions as part of its purchaser assessment when conditionally clearing the transaction and they are therefore not the subject of a subsequent contractual arrangement between the parties and the purchaser of the re-sold assets, as suggested by the Commission. By doing this, the FTC not only creates more transparency around the restriction but it also maintains the enforcement powers and thus does not transfer the responsibility to the selling parties. It is considered that these may be relevant issues for the Commission to consider if it wishes to apply on-sales restrictions in future cases. In any event, if the Commission considers on-sale bans as part of its current practice, it should clarify its guidance and be far more specific as to cases that would call for the imposition of such restrictions, as the currently scarce information is vague and unclear.

**Commentary:** re-sale bans constitute significant interventionist measures as the free market forces relating to particular assets are suspended for a certain time period. While the overall purpose of an intervention of this kind is understandable and justifiable if the respective re-sales are at risk of undermining the remedies, it seems harsh, if not even disproportionate, if the purchaser is excluded from executing business decisions to re-sell (some of) the assets if market conditions or strategic objectives change. Furthermore, a 'short time-span' may be relatively long in some markets depending on the market conditions and dynamics.

[345] The FTC announced Childs' application for public comments on 19 August 2003 and on 10 October 2003 the FTC announced its final approval of the re-sale, see documents on the original Nestle/Ralston Purina case file. The announcement contained no details as to the competitive analysis of the new purchaser but it is assumed that such a new market assessment has been carried out. In passing it should be noted that, given the FTC's original reservations about Childs as a financial purchaser, it seems somewhat surprising that it approved yet another private equity firm as a suitable purchaser with the inevitable risk that the business will be subject to further re-sales. However, it must be assumed that the FTC considered the business strong enough to be a competitive force with financial owners. According to the publicly available version of Childs' application for the re-sale it was submitted that the two divested Ralston brands had been transformed into a competitive business with its own R&D expertise, state-of-the-art manufacturing, proven distribution, and demonstrable market and financial strength, see application of 19 August 2003 on the original Nestle/Ralston Purina case file.

[346] Cypress' application was announced by the FTC for public comments on 28 March 2006 and on 19 May 2006 the FTC announced its final approval of the re-sale to Del Monto, see press release on the original case file of Nestle/Ralston Purina, File No 011 0083, Docket No C-4028. The re-sale to Del Monto was still *within the original 5-year prior approval provision* and therefore the FTC's consent was required. In its petition, Cypress stated that the proposed sale would create a strong and more efficient competitor to Nestlé Purina in the cat food market.

Thus, while it is difficult to provide constructive solutions on how to address possible circumventions in this area, a re-sale ban does seem to dangerously limit market participants' freedom to act and take business decisions. Moreover, if such a ban is deemed necessary in certain cases it is unclear why the Commission would prefer the provision to be stipulated in the SPA as this would not give it the needed enforcement powers in case of breach. Thus, it is hoped that the Commission will further reflect upon and possibly clarify its policy in this respect.

### *4.6.2 Re-acquisition Prohibitions*

The Commission stipulates that, in order to maintain the structural effect of a remedy, the commitments must foresee that the merged entity cannot subsequently acquire material influence over the whole or parts of the divested business for a significant period, generally 10 years.[347] Even in the absence of an explicit clause, a re-acquisition of the divested business is considered a violation, as this would affect the effectiveness of the remedies. Under current practice the ban is a standard clause in virtually all remedies and the duration is usually 10 years.

The provision calls for the following observations. First, the fact that the re-acquisition prohibition applies 'even in the absence of an explicit clause' should be seen against the background that a Commission decision is in principle valid forever or until it is reviewed.[348] The validity is not challenged by the fact that, following the decision, the transaction may change character (for example by selling European activities and thus no longer reach the thresholds for notification). However, the parties may at any time ask the Commission to revoke or review its decision if the factual circumstances on which the decision is based change.[349]

Secondly, the ban relates to the re-acquisition of 'material influence'. Over the years the Commission has changed its interpretation of 'influence' several times before currently settling on the 'material influence' threshold, which is considered to be 'influence by the previous owner of the business in the competitive behaviour of the divested business risking to frustrate the objective of the remedy'.[350] It is thus assumed that re-acquisition prohibitions do not apply to the acquisition of minority stakes.[351]

[347] The relevant provisions governing re-acquisition prohibitions are found in paras 43, 20 (breach), and 73 (fn 4) of the Remedies Notice, as well as MTDC, para 3. While the Commission names such commitments 'non-reacquisition clauses', the term 're-acquisition prohibitions' is used in this book. While a re-acquisition ban was introduced in the old Remedies Notice (para 49), a standard duration of 10 years was not included until the publication of the standard model texts in 2003. Thus, before then the re-acquisition ban was in principle an indefinite measure, see eg *Nestlé/Ralston Purina* (M.2337 I 2001) para 18.

[348] To this effect, the Commission also stresses in the context of divestitures that they are considered 'lasting' or competing on a 'lasting basis', see Remedies Notice, paras 10 and 23. By contrast, the FTC applies a so-called 'sunset policy' whereby administrative orders ordinarily terminate after 20 years, see FTC press release of 20 November 1995 introducing this policy, www.ftc.gov/opa/1995/11/sun3.shtm.

[349] The Commission's decisions in *Shell/Montecatini* (M.260 II 1994 and 1996) is an early example of a revoked decision due to changed circumstances, see section 4.4.4.2 and nn 259, 260 above.

[350] Remedies Notice, para 43, fn 3. In the old Remedies Notice the Commission used the general term 'influence' without further specifications (para 49); in the MTDC it uses the phrase 'direct or indirect influence' (para 3 – this phrase is thus still used in decisional practice); and in the draft new Remedies Notice the Commission introduced the interpretation that 'such influence does not have to amount to control in the sense of Art 3 of the Merger Regulation' which was later abolished in the final version of the Remedies Notice.

[351] In the US the ban has been applied to 'any interest', see eg the FTC's conditional clearance of *BP Amoco/Atlantic Richfield Company*, File No 991 0192 and Docket No C-3938, and in particular press release of 13 April 2000 where a 10-year re-acquisition ban applies to any direct or indirect interests, www.ftc.gov/opa/2000/04/bpamoco1.shtm.

Thirdly, a standard time frame of 10 years generally applies to all re-acquisitions, irrespective of the industry in question. The Commission would probably argue that by inserting a fixed time period of 10 years for all transactions, it has made the procedure more standardised and transparent instead of negotiating the duration of such a ban individually in each case. However, it is submitted that some industries are characterised by such dynamic market developments that a fixed ten-year ban would be inappropriate in these cases.[352] While the Commission has softened up its phrasing in the new Remedies Notice by adding '*a significant period, generally* 10 years' (emphasis added), it appears that virtually all current remedies contain the standard provision of 10 years.[353] Furthermore, it is unclear why the Commission settled for 10 years instead of for example 7, 8 or 12 years. However, it is assumed that the Commission – in setting the standard time frame – was inspired by its US counterparts who had used such a standard for quite a few years.[354]

Fourthly, the re-acquisition prohibition may be reviewed under the general review clause.[355] To this effect, the burden of proof rests entirely on the parties and they must show that the market has changed to such an extent that the absence of influence over the divested business is no longer necessary. In reviewing such a request the Commission has a wide discretion and is likely to launch an enquiry with other market participants in order to verify the alleged changed market structure. Based on publicly available information, re-acquisition prohibitions have been waived rarely.[356]

Finally, it should be noted that in its guidance the Commission is inconsistent as to whether it considers a re-acquisition prohibition a condition or an obligation.[357] It is submitted that the Commission mistakenly defines this clause as an 'obligation' in its 'core reacquisition ban provision' (paragraph 43) in the Remedies Notice but in other contexts (in relation to breach situations) the ban is mentioned as an example of a condition.[358] As the purpose of the re-acquisition ban is to maintain market structures it seems logical that

[352] During the public consultation in 2007 of the draft Remedies Notice, the Commission received many critical comments as to a standard provision of 10 years, see eg reply from Crowell & Moring, p 5: 'Given the diversity of industries in the various markets and their unique characteristics, the uniform application of a fixed time term, be it 10 or seven years, is not advisable' as well as reply from Freshfields Bruckhaus Deringer, point 5.7; and reply from IBA, point 59.

[353] Of recent examples, see *GDF Suez/International Power* (M.5978 I 2011), Remedies Text, para 3; *DB/Arriva* (M.5855 I 2010), Remedies Text, para 3; and *Syngenta/Monsanto's Sunflower Seed Business* (M.5675 II 2010), Remedies Text, para 3.

[354] For an example from US practice see the FTC's conditional clearance of *BP Amoco/Atlantic Richfield Company*, File No 991 0192 and Docket No C-3938, and in particular press release of 13 April 2000 referring to a 10-year re-acquisition ban, www.ftc.gov/opa/2000/04/bpamoco1.shtm. In the corresponding EU proceedings in *BP Amoco/Arco* (M.1532 II 1999) a similar ban was not mentioned. Also, in EU practice the 10-year period has been a feature in some early anti-trust cases, see eg *BT/MCI* (34.857 1994) where BT undertook not to acquire more than 20% in MCI within 10 years.

[355] Remedies Notice, para 43; and MTDC, para 3. See also section 4.4.4.2 above.

[356] The Commission granted a waiver in *Rexam/American National Can* (M.1939 I 2000) by amended decision of 30 June 2003, quoted by De Souza and Brockhoff in Drauz and Jones (2012) para 7.433, fn 2841. Regrettably, the Commission published no information on the waiver, save a listing of a new Article 6(2) decision in Competition Report 2003, p 222. However, Rexam confirmed to the press in 2003 that it had re-acquired a German can-making plant, stating that 'subsequent structural changes in the German beverage packaging market and the turbulence created since the introduction of a deposit on all one way beverage packaging at the start of 2003' had changed the circumstances under which the Commission originally obliged Rexam to divest of the plant, see Rexam press release of 1 July 2003, accessed at www.rexam.com (link no longer available) . Thus in effect, Rexam was allowed to re-acquire a plant that it had divested less than 3 years earlier. See also *Neste/IVO* (M.931 I 1998) (forming Fortum) where the Commission by decision in 2004 allowed the parties to re-acquire (or rather increase) a non-controlling stake in Gasum, see press release IP/04/2004 of 1 December 2004.

[357] Compare MTDC, para 3; and Remedies Notice, paras 43 and 73, fn 4 *in fine.*

[358] Remedies Notice, para 20.

such a clause is considered a condition, which is also generally confirmed in current decisional practice.[359]

**Commentary:** re-acquisition prohibitions seem fully justified as long as the respective market conditions are similar to the ones upon which the conditional clearance decision was based. Otherwise the objective and effects of the remedy would be seriously frustrated or undermined. If anything, it may seem liberal of the Commission to allow 'non-material influence' as this would in principle permit the merging parties to acquire minority stakes and thus potentially obtain certain shareholder privileges in this context.

### *4.6.3 Information Obligations*

In principle the parties' (and trustees') information obligations as set out in the remedies expire when the transaction is closed. However, in 2008 the Commission introduced a provision in the Remedies Notice whereby the remedies must foresee that for a period of 10 years post-decision the Commission may request information from the parties.[360] The stated aim of the provision is to monitor the effective implementation of the remedies.

The new provision warrants several comments. First, it is worth noting that the clause does not oblige the parties to submit any information on their own initiative but it merely allows the Commission to request information from the parties. Thus the provision is different from past cases where occasionally the parties have been required to inform the Commission of future acquisitions above a certain *de minimis* threshold in specified product and geographic markets in order for the Commission to monitor the future market structure.[361]

Secondly, the potential scope of the provision appears very broad, as it is not specified whether information requests are strictly limited to markets related to the remedies. Although the Commission submits that the aim of the provision is to monitor the effectiveness of the remedy it is for example unclear whether the Commission may request information strictly related to the parties' transactions in the given market or whether the parties can also expect requests from the Commission relating to estimates on the other players on the relevant product or geographic markets of the remedy in order to assess the overall market structure relevant for the remedy. One area where a long-term information obligation may have relevance is in cases where the purchaser and the parties have agreed on-going links in order to ensure viability, for example through various supply or service arrangements. As the Commission would need to ensure that such contractual dependencies do not change character or scope over the years with the risk of degradations of the divested business, this may be an obvious area for the Commission to request further information.

[359] See eg *GDF Suez/International Power* (M.5978 I 2011) para 150, referring to the Remedies Text, s B (thus including the re-acquisition ban) being a condition for clearance; and *Syngenta/Monsanto's Sunflower Seed Business* (M.5675 II 2010), the operative part in Art 2, also referring to the Remedies Text s B (thus including the re-acquisition ban) being a condition for clearance. Also the fact that para 43 is listed (as a separate section 1.3) in the Remedies Notice alongside divestitures and crown jewels provisions suggests that the clause is considered a condition.

[360] Remedies Notice, para 128. This provision was introduced after the public consultation in 2007 of the draft new Remedies Notice and thus was not introduced in the original draft notice.

[361] eg in *Nestlé/Perrier* (M.190 II 1992) Nestlé was required to inform the Commission in writing of any acquisition of a bottled water entity in France with a market share of sales exceeding 5%, for a period of 5 years from the decision, see para 136. For another early case, see *KNP/Bührmann-Tetterode and VRG* (M.291 II 1993) para 66(5) (5 years information duty).

Finally, it should be noted that the provision is currently not contained in the standard model texts and thus, to the best of my knowledge, the provision has not been included in any commitment proposals after the publication of the provision in 2008. As the Commission submits that the commitments 'have to foresee' such information requests, it is therefore necessary for the Commission to amend the standard model texts if it wishes to uphold this policy.

**Commentary:** while a general information obligation or entitlement may be justified in certain follow-up aspects of a remedy, it is considered that the Commission needs to further reflect on: (i) the phrasing of the obligation; (ii) the intended aim of the obligation; and (iii) whether it should be included in the standard model texts. Until then, the impact of the current provision is limited.

### *4.6.4 Breach of Remedies*

The conditional nature of remedies decisions means that the Commission must strictly monitor compliance with the imposed conditions and obligations. Reporting obligations of the parties and trustees are an important part of the monitoring as well as the Commission's own involvement[362] but occasionally the Commission also receives complaints from third parties claiming that the parties do not comply with the remedies. If the parties do breach a condition or obligation, the Commission has wide-ranging measures at its disposal of which the most important features will be highlighted below.

Most gravely, if the parties do not fulfil a condition the clearance decision is automatically void and thus no longer stands.[363] As a consequence, if the concentration is implemented, it should be treated in the same way as a non-notified concentration implemented without authorisation.[364] The Commission may take interim measures appropriate to restore or maintain conditions of effective competition,[365] and in phase II cases where the Commission has already found that, in the absence of the condition, the concentration would be incompatible with the internal market, it may order any appropriate measures to ensure that the parties dissolve the concentration so as to restore the situation prevailing prior to the implementation, or it may order any other appropriate measures to this effect.[366] In phase I and II cases the Commission may also take a decision pursuant to Article 8(1) to (3) of the Merger Regulation without being bound by any time limits.[367]

On the other hand, if the parties breach an obligation the Commission may, but is not obliged to, revoke its phase I or phase II conditional clearance decision.[368] In such cases, the Commission may replace the revoked decision with a new decision under Article 6(1)[369] or Articles 8(1) to (3), respectively, without being bound by any time limits.[370]

[362] Surprisingly, the Commission decided to abandon its merger enforcement unit in 2001 and the monitoring is now the responsibility of the individual case-teams, supported by Directorate A.

[363] See recital 31of the Merger Regulation and para 20 of the Remedies Notice. In such cases the situation rendering the concentration compatible with the internal market does not materialise and the concentration, as implemented, is therefore not authorised by the Commission.

[364] Recital 31 of the Merger Regulation.

[365] Merger Regulation, Art 8(5)(b).

[366] ibid, Art 8(4)(b).

[367] ibid, Art 8(7).

[368] ibid, Arts 6(3)(b) and 8(6)(b); and Remedies Notice, para 20.

[369] Thus the Commission may open phase II proceedings or adopt a new phase I conditional clearance decision based on revised remedies.

[370] Merger Regulation, Arts 6(4) and 8(7)(b).

There are no requirements as to how a clearance decision is revoked but the procedure can be illustrated by *Sanofi/Synthélabo* which, to date, is the only (albeit unconditional) clearance decision formally revoked by the Commission.[371] In this case, once the Commission had been made aware (through complaints) that its clearance decision was based on incorrect information, it sent an administrative letter to the parties setting out the grounds on which it would base its revocation and gave the parties the opportunity to submit observations and then the following day it formally revoked the clearance decision.[372]

Furthermore, the Commission may impose 'appropriate financial sanctions' where conditions or obligations are not fulfilled.[373] Accordingly the Commission may impose fines not exceeding 10 per cent of the aggregate turnover of the 'undertakings concerned' where they intentionally or negligently fail to comply with a condition or an obligation in phase I and II remedies decisions or with any measure ordered by decision in accordance with Article 8(4) and (5).[374] Similarly, the Commission may also impose periodic penalty payments for the same offences.[375] In these cases the Commission is required to adopt a formal decision and thus it may be a very lengthy administrative procedure with no deadlines for adoption of a possible decision.[376]

To date, the Commission has neither declared a conditional clearance decision void, nor revoked a conditional clearance decision, and consequently it has also never imposed fines in this respect. In one case the Commission issued a warning reminding the parties that it had the powers to revoke a conditional clearance decision if the parties did not comply with their commitments,[377] and occasionally it has also explicitly reserved its right to impose fines in the event of a breach.[378] Specifically in the context of fast-track dispute resolution provisions, the General Court has confirmed that breach of such obligations

[371] See *Sanofi/Synthélabo* (M.1397 I 1999).

[372] On 15 March 1999 the Commission adopted an unconditional clearance decision which was revoked in accordance to Article 6(3)(a) (incorrect information) on 21 April 1999, see press release IP/99/255 of 22 April 1999 and notice in [1999] OJ C117/4. The Commission reopened its examination of the notification, which in the meantime had been completed by the parties and a conditional clearance decision in accordance with Article 6(2) was adopted on 17 May 1999, see press release IP/99/335 of 19 May 1999. The Commission later imposed fines of EUR 100,000 for supplying incorrect information in the original notification, see *Sanofi/Synthélabo* (M.1543 1999) and Competition Report 1999, box 9 (p 74) and para 199.

[373] Recital 31 of the Merger Regulation.

[374] Merger Regulation, Arts 14(2)(c) and 14(2)(d). It is worth noting that prior to 2004 the original Merger Regulation did not refer to phase I conditional clearance decisions and thus the Commission lacked the power to impose fines in such cases.

[375] ibid, Arts 15(1)(c) and 15(1)(d).

[376] The administrative procedure involves setting out the alleged infringements, giving the parties the opportunity to be heard (thus issuing SO and possibly an oral hearing) and consulting relevant Commission services and the Member States in accordance with Art 19(3) of the Merger Regulation.

[377] See *Pirelli/Edizione/Olivetti/Telecom Italia* (M.2574 I 2001) where the Commission, while the divestiture was still being implemented, implied in a public statement that the parties had not used their best efforts in giving sufficient consideration to the interest expressed by several potential bidders in relation to Edizione's required divestiture of its stake in Blu, see MEMO/02/108 of 24 May 2002 'State of Play on Blu'. It is worth noting that, judging from the MEMO, the Commission somewhat confused the concepts of conditions and obligations as it stressed in the general context of the required divestiture of the Blu stake that it may revoke a clearance decision pursuant to Art 8(5) if the parties concerned commit a breach of an obligation. At the same time the Commission stated elsewhere in its statement that the divestiture of the Blu stake is a condition for its clearance. As it happened, the case was subsequently solved by a modification of the original commitments whereby the parties were allowed to break up Blu, see press release IP/02/1183 of 5 August 2002 and section 4.4.4.2 above.

[378] See eg *Procter & Gamble/VP Schickedanz (II)* (M.430 II 1994) para 189.

would result in the revocation of the clearance decision, even in the absence of explicit provisions to this effect.[379]

Moreover, in recent practice conditional clearance decisions often contain a standard paragraph whereby the Commission stresses its powers to enforce its decisions in the event of non-fulfilment.[380] Interestingly, in the Remedies Notice it is now also pointed out that a subsequent modification of the remedies (under the review clause) will not heal retroactively any breach of remedies which were committed prior to the modification and in such cases the Commission may further purse a breach and impose fines.[381] While to date the Commission has not imposed fines for such breaches, it is assumed that this provision was introduced in view of past issues in this respect.[382] The provision is clearly an indication of a tightening of the Commission's enforcement policy although it has so far not taken any formal actions in this respect.[383]

Moreover, third parties have on several occasions raised concerns alleging that the parties to a concentration have been in breach of their remedies. Based on publicly available information, such complaints have not resulted in further actions being taken by the Commission although a few cases seem – from an outsider's point of view – to have justified possible intervention and enforcement. For example, in *WorldCom/MCI (II)* the parties committed to divest of MCI's Internet assets, which were subsequently acquired by Cable & Wireless.[384] Two years later during the proceedings in the prohibition of *MCI WorldCom/Sprint*, where a similar remedy was rejected, it became apparent that Cable & Wireless had encountered difficulties after acquiring MCI's Internet assets, allegedly due to MCI WorldCom's lack of proper implementation of the remedies.[385]

[379] In *easyJet v Commission* (T-177/04 2006) the applicant claimed that the Commission had failed to make the contested decision (*Air France/KLM* (M.3280 I 2004)) expressly subject to revocation should the commitments not be fulfilled, see para 178. The General Court observed that the clearance decision laid down a fast-track procedure for resolving disputes which constituted obligations, any breach of which would result in revocation of the contested decision in accordance with Art 6(3)(b) of the Merger Regulation although the Commission decision did not explicitly refer to such legal consequences of a possible breach, see paras 186 and 188. For an account of how to enforce arbitration provisions in merger remedies proceedings, see Blanke in Blanke and Landolt (2011) 1638–41.

[380] See eg *Deutsche Bahn/Arriva* (M.5855 I 2010) para 330; *Amcor/Alcan* (M.5599 I 2009) para 143; and *Friesland/Campina* (M.5046 II 2008) para 1896.

[381] See Remedies Notice, para 76 *in fine*, where the Commission refers to its powers under Arts 14 and 15 of the Merger Regulation in this context. This provision was introduced in 2008.

[382] While speculative, the Commission may have based this provision on its experience in the controversial *Hoechst/Rhône-Poulenc* (M.1378 I 1999) where it subsequently in 2004 adopted a decision amending one of the remedies but did not impose fines for any possible infringement of the original remedy prior to 2004.

[383] See further section 5.5 below.

[384] See *Worldcom/MCI (II)* (M.1069 II 1998) where trilateral remedies negotiations were conducted between the Commission, the DoJ and the parties with the result that commitments were offered to both authorities and jointly market tested, see Competition Report 1998, p 321. The Commission decision contained an unusual provision whereby the Commission formally requested the DoJ's cooperation regarding the mutually offered commitments to which the DoJ confirmed that it would take whatever steps were necessary and appropriate to evaluate and seek the effective implementation of the remedies, see para 164. The subsequent sale to Cable & Wireless was announced on 28 May 1998 (the transaction was mentioned in press release IP/00/668 of 28 June 2000).

[385] See *MCI Worldcom/Spring* (M.1741 II 2000) where previous complaints by Cable & Wireless are indicated in para 360, see also Competition Report 2000, p 77. Moreover, the issue is spelt out in the DoJ's parallel prohibition proceedings where it is submitted in the DoJ's Complaint that

> shortly after acquiring the iMCI assets, C&W initiated legal and arbitration proceedings regarding WorldCom's implementation of its divestiture agreement with C&W. WorldCom settled this litigation earlier this year by paying $200 million to C&W. In connection with the settlement, WorldCom required that C&W agree not to continue to publicly state that it was impossible to successfully divest an integrated Internet business without weakening the new entity's competitive strength and thereby harm competition in the market. (Complaint para 13, available at www.justice.gov/atr/cases/f5000/5051.htm)

Another example of a third-party complaint is the following. In 2003 a former CEO, Mr Lebard, of Albright & Wilson (later forming part of Rhodia) approached the Commission about alleged irregularities in the implementation of the 1999 conditional clearance decisions in *Hoechst/Rhône-Poulenc* (later Sanofi-Aventis) and *Rhodia/Donau Chemie/Albright & Wilson* (later Rhodia) and in this context he also questioned the integrity of the Commission staff and members.[386] In 2006 the Commission decided to closed the file but Mr Lebard brought an action before the General Court claiming inter alia that the Commission had failed to re-examine the file, that it should have withdrawn its clearance in *Rhodia/Donau Chemie/Albright & Wilson*, and that it misused its enforcement powers by not maintaining tight control over the concentrations in the course of their implementation.[387] While the General Court dismissed the appeal as inadmissible,[388] it seems evident that the lengthy, complicated and controversial implementation of the remedies in these two cases could have warranted possible further actions on behalf of the Commission. Although the Commission lacked explicit powers to impose fines for breach of conditions (only obligations) in phase I cases at the time of the proceedings, it may have been appropriate to consider revoking any obligations attached to the condition of selling the stake in Rhodia as this remedy was changed and substituted with another remedy in 2004 and thus prior to the initiation of the Court proceedings.[389]

Finally, it is worth noting that some remedies simply prove difficult to implement in the way foreseen at the design stage and that, although the objective of the remedy may not be achieved, the parties cannot be considered to have breached their remedy as they have done their utmost to achieve timely and effective implementation.[390] While in principle the responsibility of ensuring that all potential uncertainties are catered for at the design stage rests on the parties, the Commission shares this responsibility, as it must assess – when accepting the commitments – the likelihood of new entrants entering the respective market.[391]

**Commentary:** it is fair to say that, based on publicly available information and judging from past and present decisional practice, the sanctions for breach of remedies are confined to a theoretical possibility rather than a genuine policy. Despite blunt statements from senior DG Competition

[386] See *Hoechst/Rhône-Poulenc* (M.1378 I 1999) and *Rhodia/Donau Chemie/Albright & Wilson* (M.1517 I 1999). The two cases were interlinked as Rhône-Poulenc had a controlling stake in Rhodia which it was requested to divest during the *Hoechst/Rhône-Poulenc* proceedings. In 2003 Mr Lebard sent the Commission several letters informing it that the remedies entered into in *Hoechst/Rhône-Poulenc* had allegedly not been complied with and requested that the clearance decision in *Rhodia/Donau Chemie/Albright & Wilson* should be revoked. The contents of the letters and the allegation of misconduct by Commission staff are summarised in the subsequent Court proceedings in *Lebard v Commission* (T-89/06 2009), see notably paras 7–14.

[387] See *Lebard v Commission* (T-89/06 2009). The pleas are summarised in [2006] OJ C131/42. Similar allegations had also been made previously by a member of the European Parliament about the Commission's 'remedies swap' in 2004 in *Hoechst/Rhône-Poulenc* (M.1378 I 1999) and the Commission's handling of the implementation of the remedies in the two cases, see n 270 above. Some years later Mr Lebard published a book on the alleged irregularities of the two cases, see Lebard and Ottenheimer (2008).

[388] The Court concluded that Mr Lebard was not 'directly concerned', see paras 35–41.

[389] This aspect was mentioned by the Commission itself in *Lebard v Commission* (T-89/06 2009), see para 10.

[390] This has been the case in the aviation sector where a typical remedy would be that the parties make slots available to prospective entrants. Eg in *easyJet v Commission* (T-177/04 2006) it became evident during the Court proceedings that – more than 2 years following the Commission's conditional clearance decision in *Air France/KLM* (M.3280 I 2004) – no new entrant had been found for the respective slots, see paras 196.

[391] ibid, paras 198–207. The applicant maintained that the Commission had committed an error by not insisting on an up-front buyer. However, the General Court found that – at the time of the adoption of the clearance decision – a sufficient number of potential purchasers had voiced an interest in entering the relevant markets and thus the Commission had been entitled to assume that it was very likely that a new competitor would enter the affected markets.

officials that the Commission does not tolerate any breaches of remedies,[392] there are no indications from practice that parties displaying an opportunistic behaviour in relation to the implementation of merger remedies should fear for repercussions any time soon.

### *4.6.5 Challenging Remedies*

The parties or third parties may challenge remedies issues before the EU Courts in accordance with the applicable rules.[393] Throughout the years the General Court and the Court of Justice have contributed substantially to the interpretation and development of the Commission's remedies policy. While the Courts' rulings on specific remedies aspects are described elsewhere, this section sets out (third) parties' reasons for and chances of challenging various remedies aspects in the Commission's conditional clearance decisions with a view of determining the role and impact of judicial review in the Commission's remedies policy and practice.[394]

#### 4.6.5.1 The Merging Parties

Generally, remedies decisions constitute positive outcomes for the merging parties and are thus rarely challenged by them. In the few cases where the parties have done so,[395] it has been due to very specific circumstances. For example, in *Cementbouw v Commission* the applicant alleged that the Commission had required further commitments than was necessary as the remedies went beyond the reinstatement of the pre-merger structure.[396] The case was extraordinary in the sense that the concentration had been implemented several years prior to the notification and therefore the remedies were more similar to dissolution orders in accordance with Article 8(4) of the Merger Regulation.[397] While the applicant was unsuccessful in its appeal, the General Court set out important principles for subsequent guidance and cases, for example that the Commission cannot unilaterally impose conditions which the parties have not offered as commitments and that the Commission is authorised to accept all commitments proposed by the parties, even if they go beyond the pre-merger structure.[398] Along the same lines, on a number of occasions the merging parties have appealed conditional clearance decisions claiming that the Commission breached funda-

[392] Recently, the Director General for Competition said 'if companies enter into commitments, they must do what they have committed or face the consequences', see Speech by Italianer (2012). While the comment was made specifically in the context of an alleged breach by Microsoft of its commitments in cartel proceedings, the Director General spoke about common features for merger and cartel remedies cases.

[393] A description of the powers and procedures of the EU Courts is outside the scope of this book. For a list of remedies-related Court appeals, see Annex C.

[394] The following description is by no means a complete overview of all past appeals containing remedies issues as such appeals are instead referred to throughout the book in the relevant contexts.

[395] The parties to a merger are entitled to bring an action in accordance with Art 263 TFEU since the Commission's conditional clearance decision is addressed to them, even if they abandon the transaction, see *MCI v Commission* (T-310/00 2004) paras 48–56.

[396] See *Cementbouw v Commission* (T-282/02 2006). Along the same lines, in *Omya v Commission II* (T-275/06 withdrawn 2008) the applicant claimed that the Commission disproportionately required the divestiture of a plant in *Omya/JM Huber PCC* (M.3796 II 2006). However, the Court did not get to rule on this aspect as the applicant withdrew its application, see [2008] OJ C327/41.

[397] A similar case is *Skanska/Scancem* (M.1157 II 1998) where Skanska acquired control of Scancem several months prior to notification and, in the end, competition concerns were solved through Skanska divesting of more than its controlling stake in Scancem.

[398] The findings of the General Court were confirmed in the subsequent appeal to the Court of Justice in *Cementbouw v Commission* (C-202/06 P 2007).

mental EU principles by imposing disproportionate remedies but so far the Court has had no chance to rule on this issue as the respective appeals were withdrawn by the parties.[399]

Past practice shows that a more likely aspect of a remedies decision to be appealed by the parties to the concentration relates to subsequent disagreement between the parties and the Commission during the implementation of the remedies. First, the parties may appeal a Commission decision rejecting a request to modify a remedy (deadline or modification) or rejecting a proposed purchaser.[400] In such cases the parties may bring an action as a precautionary measure in the event they fail to fulfil the remedies (by for example not finding another suitable purchaser) as the next step for the Commission would be to consider its conditional clearance decision void or revoke it. The parties may also seek to apply for interim measures in order to put their implementation on hold although they have so far had little success in justifying that the Court should grant such measures.[401] In view of the Commission's tightened policy for modifying remedies and approving purchasers, it is considered that such appeals are likely to be brought more frequently in the future.

Secondly, the parties may appeal decisions setting out the Commission's interpretation of specific remedies clauses, which are subject to disagreement between the Commission and the parties during the implementation. Experience shows that such situations may arise where the remedies contain clauses that are drafted too generally and thus leaving scope for interpretation.[402] In such cases it has proven important whether the Commission has communicated its views in a formally adopted decision considered as ancillary to the original conditional clearance decision or in an administrative letter setting out its preliminary views constituting expressions of intent with respect to the interpretation.[403] From the parties' point of view, it may therefore not be in their best interest to receive Commission communications on an informal basis although this usually constitutes a faster procedure than a formal adoption of a decision.

Finally, it should be mentioned that, to date, the most pronounced situation where the Court has reviewed and contributed to the interpretation of remedies in appeals brought by the merging parties relate to prohibition decisions where commitments were proposed by the parties but rejected by the Commission during the administrative procedure.[404] In these proceedings the Court has ruled on a wide range of remedies issues, including the

[399] See latest *Western Digital and Western Digital Ireland v Commission* (T-60/12 withdrawn 2012) explained in ch 2 n 259 above.

[400] See eg *BASF v Commission* (T-105/10 withdrawn 2011) which contained both elements as the applicant sought annulment of the Commission's decision to reject a proposed purchaser as well as a request to modify the commitments in accordance with the review clause of the commitments, see [2010] OJ C113/70. The applicant subsequently withdrew its appeal. One of the latest examples of such appeals is *EDF v Commission* (T-389/12 pending) where the parties seek to annul a Commission decision refusing to grant an extension of a divestiture deadline, see summary of pleas in [2012] OJ C331/29.

[401] See latest *EDF v Commission* (T-389/12 pending) where the Court rejected an application for interim measures on the grounds that the parties had failed to demonstrate that the alleged financial harm was sufficiently serious (Order by the President of the General Court of 11 October 2012, paras 22 and 27).

[402] See *E.ON Ruhrgas and E.ON Földgáz Trade v Commission* (T-57/07 2009) relating to disagreement between the Commission and E.ON on the interpretation of an obligation set out in *E.ON/MOL* (M.3696 II 2005).

[403] ibid. See section 4.4.4.3 above.

[404] In the vast majority of prohibition cases, where the Commission rejected commitments proposals, the parties' appeals included pleas on the Commission's assessment of the proposed commitments, see latest *Deutsche Börse v Commission* (T-175/12 pending), [2012] OJ C174/25. Rather exceptionally, the parties' appeal in *Aeroporia Aigaiou Aeroporiki and Marfin Investment Group Symmetochon v Commission* (T-202/11 pending) (relating to *Olympic/Aegean Airlines* (M.5830 II 2011)) contains no pleas in this respect, [2011] OJ C160/25.

nature of remedies,[405] formal shortcomings in terms of late and/or inadequate submission of commitments,[406] the parties' right to refuse to propose commitments,[407] and the parties' obligations to ensure that any commitment proposals are comprehensive and effective from all points of view.[408]

### 4.6.5.2 Third Parties

In recent years the number of appeals brought by third parties against conditional clearance decisions has been on the increase. The vast majority of applicants have been competitors, some of whom failed to acquire the divested assets during the implementation of the remedies.[409] Disregarding their motives and the specific circumstances of each case, third parties have been unsuccessful in overturning a conditional clearance decision, let alone succeeding in securing interim measures.[410] However, although the appeals have not resulted in the contested remedies being reversed by the EU Court, they have nevertheless given rise to a number of detailed reviews of the circumstances under which the Commission assesses remedies during the administrative proceedings.

In terms of the admissibility of actions brought by third parties, competitors and customers who have participated in the administrative proceedings are generally able to show that the decision is of 'direct and individual concern'.[411] More specifically, the contested decision is considered of direct concern if the applicant can show that it can be certain of an immediate or imminent change in the state of the (relevant) market.[412] This aspect has been fairly straightforward to establish for competitors and generally the Court has spent little time assessing this condition. In the (few) cases where the Court has denied an application for intervention on that ground, the applicant had failed to show that it had a direct, existing interest in the outcome of the main proceedings as opposed to an interest in relation to the pleas in law or arguments put forward in those proceedings.[413]

[405] See particularly *Gencor v Commission* (T-102/96 1999) introducing the much-quoted phrase 'the categorisation of a proposed commitment as behavioural or structural is [. . .] immaterial' (para 319).

[406] See eg *Ryanair v Commission* (T-342/07 2010) para 503 (re draft commitments); *MyTravel* (T-212/03 2008) para 131; and *EDP v Commission* (T-87/05 2005) para 163.

[407] See *Ryanair v Commission* (T-342/07 2010) para 493.

[408] See *General Electric v Commission* (T-210/01 2005) para 52. A related issue in the context of prohibition decisions is the parties' potential damages claims for unlawful conduct of the Commission in merger proceedings although this issue has related to divestiture orders rather than remedies, see *Commission v Schneider Electric SA* (C-440/07 P 2009).

[409] Also a few appeals have been brought by employee representatives, see *CCE Grandes Sources and others v Commission* (T-96/92 1995) and *CCE Vittel and others v Commission* (T-12/93 1995).

[410] As third parties have had little success in applying for interim measures in accordance with Arts 278 and 279 TFEU in respect of remedies (save in *Kali & Salz* (T-88/94R 1994)), this aspect has little practical relevance (and the need for such measures diminished with the introduction of expedited procedures in 2001) and will not be described in the present context.

[411] See Art 263 TFEU. In some appeals brought by competitors, the Commission did not contest the admissibility of a competitor's standing to challenge the conditional clearance decision and the Court abstained from considering this issue at its own initiative, see *Kaysersberg v Commission* (T-290/94 1997) paras 70 and 77. In *Qualcomm v Commission* (T-48/04 2009) the inadmissibility arguments focused on the date on which the applicant was considered to be notified of the decision (in order to verify whether the appeal was out of time) and did not address any other admissibility criteria, see para 58.

[412] See *easyJet v Commission* (T-177/04 2006) para 32; *ARD v Commission* (T-158/00 2003) para 60; *Babyliss v Commission* (T-114/02 2003) para 89; and *Air France v Commission* (T-3/93 1994) para 80.

[413] See latest order by the President of the First Chamber of the General Court of 8 April 2011 in *Monty Program v Commission* (T-292/10 pending) para 12. In this case a third party, Canonical which is an open-source software developer, sought to intervene in support of the Commission's unconditional clearance in *Oracle/Sun Microsystems* (M.5529 II 2010) but the Court ruled that the applicant failed to establish that the outcome of the main proceedings could have an adverse effect on Canonical's business activity and its arguments were considered vague.

In order for the contested decision to be of individual concern it must affect the applicant by virtue of certain attributes which are peculiar to it or by reason of circumstances in which the applicant is differentiated from all other persons and thus distinguishes it individually just as in the case of the merging parties to whom the clearance decision is addressed. To this effect, the Court has considered two elements; (i) participation in the administrative proceedings; and (ii) competitive relation with the merging parties and thus the effect on the applicant's market position.[414] In respect of the first element the participation of the appellant is in itself not sufficient to establish individual concern but an active participation is usually an indication, together with other specific circumstances, of locus standi.[415] Thus, third parties may be active by for example replying to the Commission's request for information and/or submitting their views on the suitability of the proposed commitments during the market test. The participation of third parties is also evident where it has had an effect on the course of the procedure and, at least in part, on the content of the contested decision.[416] In respect of the second element both actual as well as potential competitors may be individually concerned,[417] and even companies operating on neighbouring upstream or downstream markets may, in certain circumstances, also have standing.[418]

Finally, as to a third party's interest in bringing the proceedings, it is established case law that an action for annulment is admissible only if the applicant has an interest in having the contested measure annulled.[419] That interest must be vested and present (at the date on which the action was brought) and it exists only when the action, if successful, is likely to procure an advantage for the appellant.[420] This will normally be the case if the merging parties are competitors to the appellant.[421]

With respect to the nature of pleas put forward by third parties in their actions for annulment of conditional clearance decisions, they have mainly concerned alleged inadequacies of remedies accepted by the Commission in the contested decisions,[422] or inadequate consultation of third parties in the Commission's market test of the proposed commitments.[423] However, in recent years a number of appeals have been brought before

[414] See *easyJet v Commission* (T-177/04 2006) para 35; *Babyliss v Commission* (T-114/02 2003) para 95; and *Air France v Commission*, para 44.

[415] In *ARD v Commission* (T-158/00 2003) the General Court showed itself ready to examine in detail not only the participation of the applicants in the administrative proceedings but also the extent to which they commented on key issues which the Commission dealt with in its decision in order to determine whether competitors were individually concerned, see paras 63–72. It was emphasised that the 'mere participation in the procedure is indeed not by itself sufficient to establish that the applicant is individually concerned', see para 76.

[416] See *ARD v Commission* (T-158/00 2003) para 76.

[417] In *Babyliss v Commission* (T-114/02 2003) the General Court found that potential competitors may also be affected and thus individually concerned, in particular in oligopolistic markets characterised by substantial barriers to entry arising from strong brand loyalty and by the difficulty of access to retail trading, see para 100.

[418] See *ARD v Commission* (T-158/00 2003) para 78.

[419] See *easyJet v Commission*, para 40; and *Gencor v Commission* (T-02/96) para 40.

[420] In *Socratec v Commission* (T-269/03 2009) the General Court found that a competitor which had gone into liquidation and hence was no longer active in the relevant market lacked standing, irrespective of the fact of the competitor's potential rights of action for damages against either of the merging parties or the Commission, see paras 47 and 48.

[421] See *easyJet v Commission* (T-177/04 2006) para 41.

[422] Recent judgments of this kind include *Éditions Jacob v Commission* (T-279/04 2010) (confirmed in *Éditions Jacob v Commission* (C-551/10 P 2012), *Qualcomm v Commission* (T-48/04 2009), and *easyJet v Commission* (T-177/04 2006). See also pending appeals *Niki Luftfahrt GmbH v Commission* (T-162/10) and *Virgin Atlantic Airways v Commission* (T-344/12).

[423] See eg *Kaysersberg v Commission* (T-290/94 1997) paras 105–23. More unusually, see also the pending appeal *Monty Program v Commission* (T-292/10) where the applicant claims inter alia failure of consultation of 'take note' commitments ('public pledges') in *Oracle/Sun Microsystems* (M.5529 II 2010) as explained in section 2.5.2 above.

the Court by third parties on more unconventional remedies-related issues, such as claims that (i) remedies were breached by the parties;[424] (ii) alleged breach of non-binding remedies would qualify for damage claims;[425] (iii) the Commission unfairly rejected a proposed purchasers for the assets to be divested;[426] (iv) a monitoring trustee lacked independence;[427] (v) third parties were not given appropriate access to certain documents, including documents relating to the appointment of a trustee;[428] (vi) the Commission wrongfully accepted 'take-note commitments/public pledges';[429] (vii) the Commission unfairly organised the divestment of certain landing slots;[430] and (viii) the Commission infringed essential formal procedural requirements in not forwarding to (and hearing) the Member States the last version of commitment proposals.[431]

To date, third parties have been unsuccessful in arguing before the Court that the Commission erred in its assessment of contested remedies in such a way that the compatibility of the transaction was called into question. However, the lack of intervention on behalf of the Court in this respect should not be seen as reluctance to review the contested remedies. While the Court recognises the Commission's wide discretion, especially with respect to assessments of an economic nature, jurisprudence shows that it is prepared to review the Commission's interpretation of information of an economic nature, including the assessment of remedies. Thus, on a number of occasions the Court has extensively reviewed not only whether the evidence relied upon by the Commission was factually accurate, reliable and consistent but also whether the Commission was capable of substantiating the conclusions drawn from the evidence.[432]

To the best of my knowledge, the only successful third-party appeal in respect of merger remedies can be found in the recent *Éditions Jacob v Commission* where a procedural mistake on the part of the Commission in its appointment of a trustee led to the annulment of the Commission's approval decision of the purchaser of the divested assets.[433] While the implications of the Court proceedings are not yet clear (and a related appeal is pending), it suffices to observe in the present context that the General Court's judgment (confirmed by the Court of Justice) may serve as a good illustration that, if the Commission is to be over-

[424] See *Lebard v Commission* (T-89/06 2009) described in section 4.6.4 above.

[425] See *Communauté de communes de Lacq v Commission* (T-132/10 2011), as explained in section 2.5.2 above.

[426] See *Petrolessence and SG2R v Commission* (T-342/00 2003) explained in section 4.5.2 above.

[427] See *Éditions Jacob v Commission* (T-452/04 2010), confirmed in joined cases *Commission v Éditions Jacob* (C-553/10 P 2012) and *Lagardère v Éditions Jacob* (C-554/10 P 2012). To this effect, see also *Éditions Jacob v Commission* (T-471/11 pending) relating to the Commission's re-adoption of the trustee approval decision, see n 79 above.

[428] See *Éditions Odile Jacob v Commission* (T-237/05 2010) and related appeal in *Commission v Éditions Odile Jacob* (C-404/10 P 2012).

[429] See *Monty Program v Commission* (T-292/10 pending), [2010] OJ C260/15, and n 413 above.

[430] See *Aer Lingus v Commission* (T-101/13 pending), [2013] OJ C101/31. Aer Lingus brought an appeal on 14 February 2013 in respect of the interpretation and implementation of the remedies in *IAG/BMI* (M.6447 I 2012). Aer Lingus claims that the Commission erred in its interpretation of the remedies by how it organised the divestment of slots at Heathrow where it gave preference to Virgin over Aer Lingus in the allocation of slots. Aer Lingus also claims that the Commission failed to take appropriate account of advice from the Monitoring Trustee in this respect.

[431] See *SPAR Österreichische Warenhandel v Commission* (T-405/08 pending), pleas are summarised in [2009] OJ C6/32. The appellant furthermore claims that the Commission wrongfully accepted inadequate remedies in phase I.

[432] For a recent example of an extensive review, see *Qualcomm v Commission* (T-48/04 2009) para 92. See also *Commission v Tetra Laval* (C-12/03 P 2005) where the Court of Justice confirmed the comprehensive powers of review by the General Court in this respect (para 39).

[433] For reference, see n 427 above, and for facts and details, see section 4.2.1.2 above.

ruled on remedies-related issues, it will most likely be on procedural grounds rather than substantive analysis as to the adequacy of contested remedies.

**Commentary:** to sum up the above considerations, while third parties and in particular competitors who have been actively involved in the administrative proceedings are likely to have standing to bring proceedings challenging the Commission's conditional clearance decisions, the prospects of them succeeding in an appeal for annulment of the contested decisions are slim. This finding is not surprising in view of the Commission's margin of discretion when assessing remedies and the fact that the assessment is based on a broad range of considerations, which are very case-specific. It is therefore considered difficult for third parties to provide sufficient and convincing evidence calling into question the Commission's substantive assessments and conclusions in the respective decisions. It seems that third parties are best advised to concentrate on arguing their case before the Commission during the market test in the administrative proceedings rather than in a subsequent judicial review.[434]

From the perspective of the merging parties and the purchasers of the divested assets (the remedies), the point should be made that the implications of possible annulments of conditional clearance decisions would be devastating for all parties and businesses concerned. The relatively lengthy Court proceedings – even under the expedited procedure – make it difficult, if not impossible, to unwind already implemented remedies as assets and personnel are likely to be fully integrated at the time of a Court ruling and, moreover, the market conditions may have changed.[435] Naturally these circumstances cannot justify any reluctance to annul past conditional clearance decisions if there are legal grounds for doing so, but it remains to be seen how implemented remedies would be undone.

[434] Moreover, as will be considered below a more feasible complaints alternative for third parties – at least in respect of procedural complaints – may be an increased involvement of the hearing officer during the administrative proceedings, see section 5.4 below.

[435] It is believed that the unsuccessful applicant in *Qualcomm v Commission* (T-48/04 2009) refrained from further pursuing the General Court's unfavourable ruling from 2009 as the markets and the relevant technologies had moved on since the Commission's conditional clearance in 2003 of *DaimlerChrysler/Deutsche Telekom/JV* (M.2903 I 2003), as reported by MLex, 'Qualcomm Drops Legal Battle against Deutsche Telekom, DaimlerChrysler Truck Toll Venture' (25 August 2009), www.mlex.com/EU/Content.aspx?ID=66035. Furthermore, the applicant's recent withdrawal in *vwd Vereinigte Wirtschaftsdienste v Commission* (T-353/08 withdrawn 2013) illustrates how third parties are likely to abandon their appeal if the Court proceedings are unresolved for many years and hence any subsequent intervention seems increasingly unrealistic, especially in dynamic markets. In this case the applicant had contested inter alia the remedies accepted in *Thomson Corporation/Reuters Group* (M.4726 II 2008) and which had been implemented in April 2008 when FactSet Research Systems Inc bought the assets in question, see report by MLex, 'FactSet Research Systems Completes its Acquisition of a Copy of Thomson Fundamentals Database and Related Assets from Thomson Reuters' (25 July 2008), www.mlex.com/EU/Content.aspx?ID=37708. The applicant withdrew its application in April 2013 (the notice in the OJ is not yet available) after the proceedings had been pending for nearly 5 years.

# 5

# Building on Successes and Learning from Mistakes

## 5.1 The Overall Success Story

Throughout the previous chapters many aspects of the Commission's past and current remedies policy and practice have been scrutinised, ranging from the negotiation, submission, assessment, adoption, implementation and enforcement of merger remedies. Numerous positive as well as negative aspects have emerged from the examination. Some issues relate to specific provisions or cases while others concern more general policy issues.

In terms of identifying the remedies success stories it is evident from the analysis of the evolution of the Commission's remedies enforcement since 1990 that, overall, the Commission has succeeded in developing a significantly more consistent, predictable, flexible and sophisticated policy. It has learnt from past mistakes, undertaken a comprehensive ex-post study, adjusted and improved the relevant procedures and assessment techniques in often very complex merger cases. The result is a detailed and comprehensive 'remedies toolbox' consisting of remedies guidance, standard model texts, an additional submission form, a vast decisional practice as well as jurisprudence from the EU Court.

Overall, the 'remedies toolbox' has been successful in creating a more efficient remedies procedure to the benefit of all involved parties. From the merging parties' point of view, the Remedies Notice has provided more support and predictability and is now so detailed that it almost serves as a 'check-list' for the main aspects in a commitment proposal. The introduction of the standard model texts has increased efficiency, consistency and transparency as the parties and their advisors no longer need to 'reinvent the wheel' when drafting many of the details in their proposals. From the Commission's perspective, the introduction of Form RM has provided a more efficient way of collecting and accessing data on the business to be divested and the use of the standard model texts have created consistency in the case-handlers' drafting and thereby reduced the scope for individual errors. During the remedies implementation phase, the Commission now benefits from the assistance of a number of specialists (trustees, hold-separate managers and other experts, if necessary) whose expertise saves the Commission resources and adds skills that the Commission may not necessarily possess in-house. From third parties' point of view, as it has become standard practice for the Commission to carry out market tests of principal commitment proposals and increasingly rely on the results of such tests, interested third parties usually have a (decisive) voice in the proceedings before any conclusions are reached on the adequacy and suitability of the parties' proposals. With the introduction of up-front and fix-it-first solutions in recent years, interested purchasers of the respective assets may also benefit from being involved earlier in the administrative proceedings with the result that they may acquire the respective assets quicker and cheaper than otherwise foreseen.

When considering regulatory quantitative output, the increased standardisation and efficiency of the administrative proceedings has clearly enabled the Commission not only to clear increasingly complex and comprehensive transactions and remedies packages but also within a considerably shorter duration compared to early practice. It is worth noting that throughout the years progressively more remedies decisions have been adopted in phase I than in phase II and, moreover, the relative share of phase I remedies decisions has increased at an unprecedented pace.

To sum up, some of the most significant 'remedies success stories' highlighted throughout this book include: (i) an increased quality and sophistication of the Commission's competitive analysis of the competition concerns as well as the corresponding remedies; (ii) the facilitation of a better remedies dialogue by setting up state-of-play meetings, being more pro-active in giving advice and issuing guidance in the form of not only the Remedies Notice and standard model texts but also through the publication of the Remedies Study; (iii) an increased awareness of the importance of the scope of the divested business and the introduction of additional measures to this effect (including additional assets and up-front solutions); (iv) the introduction of more requirements to the qualifications, intentions and capabilities of potential purchasers; (v) a shift in focus from merely 'fixing the overlap' to creating a viable business with competitive assets comparable to those of existing market players; (vi) the recognition and clarification of the standard and burden of proof required in remedies cases; (vii) significant clarifications of conditions and obligations and their legal consequences; (viii) the introduction of a more flexible and proportionate regulatory response to changing market circumstances, such as the acceptance of re-branding licences in lieu of divestitures when appropriate; (ix) a significant reduction in the agreed divestiture periods as well as the actual implementation durations; (x) a better liaison between the trustees and the Commission with the result that the former are more informed and qualified when undertaking their tasks; (xi) an increased awareness of the potential strategic behaviour by the merging parties during the implementation phase and the introduction of various measures to this effect; (xii) an increased involvement of the hearing officer in phase II proceedings; (xiii) numerous successful cooperation cases between the EU and especially the US, including simultaneous remedies negotiations; and (xiv) valuable jurisprudence from the EU Court clarifying many procedural issues relating to the remedies.

All in all, it is considered that the nature and extent of the achieved successes are admirable and impressive, especially considering the tight deadlines under which the Commission negotiates, analyses and enforces merger remedies. However, every success usually has its downsides. Given the different and often diverging interests in merger remedies proceedings, one provision or measure, which benefits one party, is likely to disadvantage another party.[1] The Commission's ultimate aim with its enforcement policy is to find the right balance between the different interests, goals and priorities.[2] The remainder of this chapter is devoted to highlighting a number of critical issues within the overall remedies success story. As many of the aspects have been examined in detail in previous chapters, cross-references will be provided wherever possible in order to avoid repetitions.

[1] See section 1.5 above,

[2] See section 5.9 below.

## 5.2 Viability Requirements: Is the Commission Realistic?

> The [Remedies] Study confirms the [Commission's] preference for stand alone business but it does actually lead one to believe that the business reality in a globalized world is that stand alone businesses are probably few and far between. (Nadia de Souza, DG Competition, 2005)[3]

One of the main findings in the Remedies Study was the existence and damaging effects of an inadequate scope of the business or assets to be divested.[4] The Commission introduced several additional requirements and measures to mitigate such inadequacies.[5] While it is acknowledged that this shift in policy represents one of the most important improvements in recent years, it is considered that the Commission must be careful that its endeavours of ensuring an optimal – and preferably stand-alone – business to be divested continue to be in tune with business realities. As acknowledged by a Commission official (see quote above) few businesses to be divested are indeed stand-alone.[6] While in carve-out cases the Commission must of course ensure that the business can be considered sufficiently viable when the assets are transferred to the purchaser, there is a fine line between ensuring adequate viability and 'over-divesting/over-fixing'.

Some of the current viability provisions beg the question whether the Commission is in danger of requiring far too many viability assurances with the ultimate risk that the main transaction may not materialise or that the remedies become unnecessarily cumbersome to implement. Indeed, in the past there have been examples where the merging parties withdrew their transaction due to alleged excessive remedies or the Commission prohibited transactions on the grounds that the parties would not or could not ensure the required viability criteria.[7] There have also been cases where it proved difficult to find interested let alone suitable purchasers to the assets to be divested.[8] While the validity and implications of such decisions will not be further explored or questioned in the present context, it is submitted that the current policy justifies future considerations as to the possible effects of rigorous viability requirements. One example should be highlighted.

In 2008 the Commission introduced the requirement that the business to be divested must be proven viable in its own right at the assessment stage and hence any possible resources of potential purchasers cannot be taken into account at this stage.[9] It is considered that this requirement is categorical and even artificial as it means that the parties must

[3] See speech by the then DG Competition official Nadia de Souza, published in Marsden, Hutchings and Whelan (2007) 103.

[4] See section 3.1 above. To recapitulate, out of all serious unresolved issues, the lack of scope was the most prominent category, following by the lack of suitable purchasers.

[5] See section 3.4 above.

[6] See section 3.2.1 above.

[7] For cases where the parties concluded that the remedies costs outweighed the originally envisaged synergies and financial benefits of the transaction and hence cancelled their transaction, see ch 1 n 7 above (and Annex A for statistics on cancelled transactions albeit not necessarily due to remedies issues). Furthermore, for recent prohibition decisions where the parties did not succeed in accommodating the Commission's viability concerns during advanced remedies negotiations, see *Ryanair/Aer Lingus III* (M.6663 II 2013), *UPS/TNT Express* (M.6570 II 2013) and *Deutsche Börse/NYSE Euronext* (M.6166 II 2012).

[8] Indeed, the lack of interest in taking over remedies assets seems to have been an issue in especially airline cases. During the hearing in *easyJet v Commission* (T-177/04 2006), for example, it became evident that the Commission had not yet (ie almost 2 years after the adoption of the conditional clearance decision) found a new entrant to operate the slots made available as remedies in *Air France/KLM* (M.3280 I 2004), despite several airlines showing an interest during the administrative proceedings, see paras 193, 196 and 203 of the judgment.

[9] See sections 3.1 and 4.5.1 above.

for example initiate measures to separate, allocate and possibly replicate the identified assets during the interim period and until a formal approval of a suitable purchaser, disregarding any general assumptions that potential purchasers are unlikely to acquire all separated assets. The approach thus disregards the fact that there may be industries where, although the exact purchaser may not be known at the time of assessing the commitments, it is widely recognised that any prospective industrial purchaser would already possess certain assets, such as own R&D, manufacturing or warehouse facilities.[10]

Furthermore, if the Commission firmly insists on a broad remedies package from the outset, this may not only make the implementation of the remedy disproportionately cumbersome and costly for the parties but it could also create unnecessary uncertainties among employees of the respective assets with the inadvertent result that the assets may be weakened. Thus, it is considered that in such situations the Commission could benefit from making its standard framework provisions more flexible and less detailed in order to accommodate the specifics of each industry.[11] Indeed, the current Director General of the DG Competition recently said that decisional practice has taught the directorate that if remedies are too specific, they are not practical and he emphasised that the directorate has been encouraging a simplification of remedies in recent years.[12]

A more pragmatic and proportionate approach could be to 'shift' some of the viability requirements to the purchaser criteria. Thus, if the scope of the business is somewhat reduced already at the assessment stage, then additional purchaser conditions or other risk-reducing measures could be put in place. There are indications from recent decisional practice that the Commission is increasingly requiring specific qualifications, expertise or even resources of potential purchasers when evaluating the overall viability of the proposed commitment package.[13] Prospective purchasers fulfilling these requirements would normally also possess a variety of basic assets – whether tangible or intangible – and in this way it may not be necessary to single out all possible assets from the outset. However, it goes without saying that any tailored purchaser requirements must at the same time not be so specific that they unduly limit the 'pool' of potential interested and suitable purchasers as such restrictions could also ultimately have adverse effects on the overall success of the remedy.

## 5.3 Are Remedies Procedures Sufficiently Transparent?

> Fifteen months after I took office as Commissioner for Competition, I can tell you that the services I found were already first-class in terms of efficiency, fairness and transparency. (Joaquín Almunia, Commissioner for Competition, 2011)[14]

[10] This has been the case in some pharmaceutical cases in the past, see section 3.1 above.

[11] See also comments below in section 5.6 on possible implications of too many standard provisions.

[12] See Speech by Italianer (2012) 3:

> I consider that the most important 'innovation' in our remedies these last years has been a simplification push on our side for both mergers and antitrust, leading to greater effectiveness. Our case experience had taught us that if remedies are too specific, they are not practical and the risk of circumvention is higher. So we are encouraging remedies that are simple, workable and easy to implement.

[13] See section 3.3.3 above.

[14] See Speech by Almunia (2011d).

Beyond doubt, the DG Competition has earned a reputation for being efficient, fair and transparent (see quote above) compared to many other directorates within the Commission. However, as already suggested throughout this book there is room for improvement, especially in relation to transparency.[15] Enhanced transparency is essential for providing legal certainty and predictability in remedies cases, not only for the merging parties but also for interested third parties. Given the importance of this issue and in order to assess the exact nature of the current shortcomings, it seems beneficial to consider the administrative proceedings in the following stages: pre-decision, decision and post-decision.

### *5.3.1 Pre-decision*

The pre-decision stage instigates few comments in relation to traditional transparency issues as it is considered reasonable and indeed necessary that, given the sensitive nature of merger and remedies negotiations, only the most essential information is made publicly available, such as the publication of a summary of the transaction post-notification in the OJ in order to facilitate comments from third parties. The most frequently occurring disagreement between the merging parties and the Commission in respect of transparency issues during the administrative proceedings relate to the nature and scope of proposed commitments that the Commission wishes to market test with third parties.[16] It goes without saying that the parties endeavour to keep as many details confidential as possible while the Commission must ensure that third parties are sufficiently informed about the facts in commitment proposals in order to submit meaningful and constructive responses to any inquiries. In the past the hearing officer has been consulted on possible disagreements in this respect.[17]

However, at this stage a related transparency issue deserves mentioning, namely the risk of leaks of confidential or sensitive information about the transaction, proposed commitments and/or any significant procedural issues to third parties and the press in particular. It is submitted that in line with increased and in recent years intense coverage of on-going competition cases in newsletters, blogs and other commentaries, the Commission is under pressure to finding ways of reassuring the merging parties and its critics that it does its utmost to prevent leaks.[18] To this effect, Commission officials in the DG Competition as well as in associated services are under general confidentiality obligations, third parties sign confidentiality declarations during market tests[19] and, as a matter of principle, the

[15] The need for enhanced transparency has also been acknowledged by the Commission itself in recent years, see eg the DG Competition Management Plan for 2011 where increased transparency and communication efforts were highlighted as an important overall objective (pp 5, 32, 39 and 46). This was repeated in the DG Competition Management Plan for 2012 with a specific objective of efficient publication on the Europa website of competition case information and documents and improved access to such data (p 39). Regrettably, the DG Competition Management Plan for 2013 has no particular mentioning of continuing or increasing transparency on case information. The respective annual management plans are available at ec.europa.eu/dgs/competition/index_en.htm.

[16] See section 2.4.1 above.

[17] ibid.

[18] Whether justified or not, over the years the Commission has been subject to critique from several commentators about alleged leaks to the press. One of the more amusing comments was voiced during the Commission's investigation of the cruise operators in *Carnival Corporation/P&O Princess* (M.2706 II 2002) where the contents of the SO had been leaked to the press which prompted the following witty comment: 'the [SO] is supposed to be confidential but – as with Carnival – parts of it always get into the public domain because Brussels is more leaky than the Titanic', see *Financial Times* (25/26 May 2002).

[19] See section 2.4.1 above.

Commission does not comment on pending cases during for example press conferences, in speeches and in other public forums.[20]

Despite these measures, case details have been – and continue to be – unduly revealed in the press. The potential sources are numerous and it would be too speculative to go into further details as to their origins. However, it should be noted that occasionally the parties – often through their lobby organisations – may also have vested interests in certain aspects of their pending case being communicated to the press and hence the sources may not necessarily be the Commission and/or third parties.[21] Nevertheless it is evident that, with the increasing number of third parties (sometimes up to several hundred) being approached by the Commission in its market tests, it is difficult to fully ensure that information relating to the contents of proposed commitments is not prematurely passed on to a wider audience.[22] While the parties have the option of approaching the hearing officer and/or the European Ombudsman with alleged leaks, it is submitted that, once the information is out in the press, possible restoring measures are immaterial. For the Commission's part, it should be noted that it has never been established in past cases that alleged leaks were attributed to its officials.[23]

### *5.3.2 Decision*

The publication process of the Commission's conditional clearance decision has already been described.[24] While the Commission strives to publish a non-confidential version of every decision as soon as possible, it is considered that there are still far too many cases where there is an unacceptably long delay until the decision is published on the DG Competition's website.[25] Ironically, in some (albeit rare) cases the remedies are implemented before the conditional clearance decision is available,[26] but even so the publicly available decision continues to be relevant as it serves as guidance in similar subsequent

[20] However, on a related matter and in order to enhance transparency with respect to the procedural aspects in merger cases, it is hoped that the DG Competition will publish a Manual of Procedures similar to the one published in March 2012 in relation to procedures for the application of Articles 101 and 102 TFEU, available at ec.europa.eu/competition/antitrust/antitrust_manproc_3_2012_en.pdf.

[21] Albeit not a remedies but a prohibition case, in *Deutsche Börse/NYSE Euronext* (M.6166 II 2012) the College of Commissioners expressed regret that an external debate had been launched pre-decision and that internal information had leaked out. In this context Commissioner Almunia highlighted that a very powerful lobbying campaign had been run by the merging parties, see the minutes of the 1988th meeting of the Commission on 1 February 2012, PV(2012)1988 final, available at ec.europa.eu/transparency/regdoc/rep/10061/2012/EN/10061-2012-1988-EN-F-0.Pdf.

[22] As previously described, third parties do sign a confidentiality declaration but it is also generally considered that any breaches of such declarations may be difficult to establish and prove and, moreover, the Commission has scarce time and resources to pursue such issues during the administrative proceedings, see further section 2.5.3 above.

[23] This was eg the finding of the European Ombudsman in *Ryanair/Aer Lingus* (M.4439 II 2007) in relation to an alleged leak of certain remedies documents, see ch 2 n 189 above for case reference.

[24] See section 2.5.3 above.

[25] By way of illustration, as of 1 May 2013 none of the six phase II conditional clearance decisions adopted in 2012 are yet made publicly available. Significant publication delays are/were also encountered in other recent cases, see eg *Western Digital Ireland/Viviti Technologies* (M.6203 II 2011) (17 months and still pending as of 1 May 2013); *Teva/Cephalon* (M.6258 I 2011) (18 months and still pending as of 1 May 2013); *Unilever/Sara Lee Body Care* (M.5658 II 2010) (14 months); *BASF/Congis* (M.5927 I 2010) (6 months); and *Arsenal/DSP* (M.5153 II 2009) (8 months).

[26] In *Unilever/Sara Lee Body Care* (M.5658 II 2010) Unilever's Sanex business (the remedy) was sold (and cleared) to the Colgate-Palmolive Group in June 2011 which was more than half a year before the Commission published its clearance decision of the main transaction, compare *Colgate Palmolive/Sanex Business* (M.6221 I 2011) and *Unilever/Sara Lee Body Care* (M.5658 II 2010).

cases and potentially in appeals.[27] As the parties do not have a natural interest in accelerating the publication procedure, it is the Commission's administrative duty to follow up on this issue and ensure speedy publications.[28]

The Commission is likely to defend delays by referring to the fact that timely publication depends on timely identification of business secrets by the parties but, as they are usually given around 2 weeks to submit such identifications, a public decision should be available within 3 to 4 weeks, at the most.[29] Furthermore, while particular circumstances may exist for withholding the publication of a decision when for example a transaction continues to be assessed in other jurisdictions, cases remain where the delays in publication seem unnecessary and unacceptably long.[30]

As a new and welcomed initiative, the Commission occasionally publishes a preliminary version of the remedies text together with, or shortly after, the release of the press release announcing the conditional clearance decision.[31] While such remedies publications continue to be relatively rare but on the rise, they are an important procedural step in the right direction of ensuring early and enhanced transparency in the implementation of the remedies. The Commission is strongly encouraged to make this practice a standard procedure wherever possible and thus publish the remedies texts as speedily as possible post-clearance.[32] [33]

[27] As it happened, during the month where the transaction was cleared a similar branding case was notified in the later-abolished *SCJ/Sara Lee* (M.5969 II 2011 withdrawn).

[28] To this effect, it was submitted in the DG Competition Stakeholder Study (2010) that in particular the Commission's final decisions were published too slowly, see study (pp 9 and 56) available at ec.europa.eu/competition/publications/reports/aggregate_report_en.pdf.

[29] As a technical suggestion, the Commission could consider initiating a publication policy embracing a so-called non-opposition procedure whereby the Commission may assume that its decision does not contain confidential information, unless the parties have indicated otherwise within a certain (reasonable) deadline, see the newly introduced provision in Art 18(4) of the Implementing Regulation. This would clearly give the parties an incentive to comply with the given deadline.

[30] By way of illustration, in *Western Digital Ireland/Viviti Technologies* (M.6203 II 2011) the Commission adopted its conditional clearance decision in November 2011 but has not yet published a public version of the decision as of 1 May 2013 and thus the only publicly available documents are the short press release announcing the clearance and a short announcement of the contact details of the monitoring trustee (no preliminary text of the remedies have been made available). By contrast, the FTC cleared the transaction in March 2012 and immediately published all relevant case documents, including details on the remedies, which were identical to the ones accepted by the Commission. For another similar recent example, see *UTC/Goodrich* (M.6410 II 2012) and the DoJ's clearance and publication in Case No 1:12-cv-01230-RC of the same transaction.

[31] See eg *Glencore/Xstrata* (M.6541 I 2012), *Outokumpu/Inoxum* (M.6471 II 2012), *Univerval Music Group/EMI Music* (M.6458 II 2012), *BASF/INEOS/Styrene/JV* (M.6093 I 2011), *Intel/McAfee* (M.5984 I 2011), *Teva/Ratiopharm* (M.5865 I 2010), *T-Mobile/Orange* (M.5650 I 2010), *Lufthansa/Austrian Airlines* (M.5440 II 2009), *Lufthansa/SN Airholding* (M.5335 II 2009). For earlier practice, see *Gaz de France/Suez* (M.4180 II 2006) and *GE/Instrumentarium* (M.3083 II 2003) (re the Interfacing Commitment).

[32] In some cases the public version of the remedies text is put on the DG Competition case register several months after the clearance, see eg *Universal Music Group/EMI Music* (M.6458 II 2012) (4 months). As a practical consideration, as the parties are obliged to submit a non-confidential version of their commitments together with the actual proposal during the administrative proceedings, the remedies text can in principle be published at the date of announcing the adoption of the conditional clearance decision or very soon thereafter.

[33] As an alternative to the publication of the remedies text or as an additional transparency measure, the Commission could consider issuing more detailed press releases when transactions are cleared. Currently the vast majority of press releases are extremely short in their description of the remedies. More elaborate press releases are particularly justified in phase I remedies cases where the authentic language of the case is not one of the main languages, see eg *Polestar/Prisa/Inversiones Ibersuizas/JV* (M.3322 I 2003) (in Spanish), and *Generali/INA* (M.1712 I 2000) (in Italian).

### *5.3.3 Post-decision*

For many years the Commission would rarely make any case-related public announcements following the adoption of the clearance decisions. Thus, no information was made available on trustees, extended deadlines, waivers, purchasers and any other circumstances relating to the implementation of the remedies. This policy was undesirable and even unacceptable. In fact, in the interest of legal certainty and transparency as well as in line with the Commission's legal obligation to publish its (phase II) decisions it could be argued that the Commission is obliged to publish information significant to its original clearance decision and that for example waivers relating to conditions and substantial obligations, upon which the clearance decision is based, would qualify as such information.[34]

After all, the overall purpose of post-decision transparency measures is to attract suitable purchasers in order to ensure that the divestiture process is executed in the most efficient way.[35] By not publishing significant modifications to the remedies, it is considered that the Commission fails to adequately inform the market participants, unless this is done so directly, with the effect that interested third parties may be excluded from launching bids for the respective assets.[36] Along the same lines, it should be remembered that transparency has a self-regulating effect in the sense that third parties are more likely to report subsequent irregularities in the implementation process if they are made sufficiently aware of the contents and modalities of the remedies.

To the Commission's credit, in recent years it has launched some transparency initiatives. Most recently it has become standard practice to publish the identity and contact details of appointed monitoring trustees on the respective case files or registers.[37] The initiative is welcome and in line with the recent business practice that the parties and/or the trustees sometimes chose to publish such information independently of the Commission.[38] However, the practice would benefit from further adjustments as many of the past publications on trustees were put on the case registers on the DG Competition's website with no accompanying announcements, which meant they often went unnoticed.[39] Another initiative is the publication (albeit still quite rare) of decisions granting waivers, especially in relation to modifications and/or substitutions of conditions.[40] Although the area continues to lack transparency compared to the FTC/DoJ for example, it may be assumed that with the newly introduced

[34] It should be noted that Art 20 of the Merger Regulation requiring the Commission to publish its decisions in the OJ relates to phase II decisions only but recital 42 of the Merger Regulation provides that 'for the sake of transparency, all decisions of the Commission which are not of a merely procedural nature should be widely published'.

[35] In the Remedies Study it was observed that in a few cases the purchasers were not aware or fully informed of the remedies, see p 69 (point 4), fn 150. 'It must be emphasized that the information was publicly available on the Commission's website but the purchasers were too unsophisticated to know that and the sellers omitted to mention it'. It is submitted that instead of blaming the purchasers of being unprofessional, the Commission should have reflected on why the purchasers were not adequately informed.

[36] See sections 4.4.4.1 and 4.4.4.2. By way of comparison, the FTC not only publishes the identity of trustees and extension of deadlines as and when relevant but it also publishes proposed purchasers and waivers for public consultation as well as its final findings in this respect.

[37] The Commission published such details in one case in 2010 but dramatically changed its policy in 2011 and 2012 with announcements of trustees in the vast majority of cases. While the trustee publications provide no details on the specific tasks of the trustee, they do provide any interested third parties with the contact details.

[38] See ch 4 n 32 above.

[39] However, most recently such announcement can often be found in the 'what's new' section under mergers on the DG Competition's website, see ec.europa.eu/competition/elojade/isef/index.cfm?fuseaction=dsp_merger_by_date.

[40] See section 4.4.4.2 above.

provision, whereby the Commission distinguishes between issuing formal decisions when conditions are revised and merely taking note of amended obligations,[41] a more consistent approach can be expected in future cases. Finally, while the Commission on very rare occasions has disclosed the divestiture deadlines in the publicly available decision,[42] it appears appropriate for the Commission to consider whether there continues to be a genuine reason for systematically keeping all such deadlines confidential.[43]

All in all, it is submitted that there continues to be scope for improvement in the Commission's publication of case-related information, in particular during the implementation phase. Based on the observations throughout this book, it appears that in past practice the Commission has withheld as much case-related information as it was entitled to and it continues to do so in certain cases.[44] With an overall view to enhancing the efficiency in implementation, it is suggested that the Commission should consider *routinely* publishing information where for example (i) new (substantial) assets are added to the remedies package, (ii) a crown jewel takes effect, (iii) waivers are granted (in relation to extension of deadlines as well as modifications); and (iv) the appointment of divestiture trustees (in situations where the parties have failed to divest the assets themselves within the first period).[45] Also, it should be noted that purchaser approvals continue to be considered procedural in nature although it is unclear why the Commission is reluctant to publish such information.[46] While the mentioned procedural steps may not necessarily warrant a press release, the Commission could take inspiration from the UK OFT and consider introducing easily accessible and transparent registers of on-going merger reviews and implementations.[47]

## 5.4 Are Phase I Proceedings Suitable for Today's Remedies?

> It would [. . .] be appropriate for the Commission [. . .] to consider the possibility of an accelerated procedure in the second phase in clear-cut cases where an adequate remedy has been proposed by the parties. (The Commission, 1993)[48]

The above quote serves as a reminder that the original Merger Regulation did not initially envisage that remedies could or should be cleared in phase I proceedings.[49] Thus, the rem-

[41] See section 4.4.4.3 above.

[42] To the best of my knowledge, this has been done only in cooperation cases with the FTC/DoJ where the latter have already published such information, see ch 4 n 3 above re *Cisco/Tandberg* case.

[43] As previously submitted, confidential deadlines can sometimes be found in decisions from other jurisdictions or the parties publish such information themselves and hence there is no reason for the Commission to withhold such vital information, see ch 4 nn 4 and 21 above.

[44] One of the most recent examples is the Commission's high-profile defeat before the General Court in *Éditions Jacob v Commission* (T-452/04 2010) – confirmed by the Court of Justice in joined cases *Commission v Éditions Odile Jacob* (C-553/10 P 2012) and *Lagardère v Éditions Odile Jacob* (C-554/10 P 2012) – where its approval decision of the trustee in *Lagardère/Natexis/VUP* (M.2978 II 2004) was annulled. The Commission re-adopted its trustee approval in May 2011 with no public announcements at all, see further section 4.2.1.2 above.

[45] As mentioned, the FTC does so routinely, see section 4.2.3 above.

[46] As a one-off exercise the Commission listed in one annual report all the purchasers approved in its conditional clearance decisions that year, see Competition Report 1994, paras 318 and 324.

[47] See www.oft.gov.uk/OFTwork/mergers/register. While the DG Competition has recently set up online case registers, they currently contain few details, if any, on post-decision measures.

[48] See the 1993 Report to the Council, p 23.

[49] Indeed, according to the notes accompanying the original Merger Regulation the possibility for the parties to make changes to their transaction was explicitly confined to phase II proceedings, see Notes on Council Regulation (EEC) 4064/89, re Art 2 (link no longer available on the DG Competition's website).

edies decisions adopted in phase I prior to the Commission being granted express legal powers in 1997 were pragmatically considered 'a regulatory response proportionate to the size of the competition problem and the remedy already at hand'.[50] While the main differences between phase I and phase II remedies are described elsewhere,[51] it is important to highlight in the current context that some of the procedural safeguards that the Commission highly values in order to ensure an impartial and a fair process do not apply to phase I remedies proceedings.[52]

Most notably, in phase I the Commission is under no obligation to submit its competition concerns in writing, the hearing officer does not issue a report and is generally less involved in the proceedings, there is no possibility of requesting an oral hearing, the Advisory Committee is not consulted, and the full College of Commissioners is not presented with and does not adopt the decision. Whereas the merging parties sometimes welcome the absence of some or all of these additional procedural measures and, in any event, consider them the price to be paid for a speedier phase I decision, it is considered that the 'phase I setup' is not fully geared to accommodate comprehensive remedies solutions.

The following implications of the absence of phase II procedural safeguards should be highlighted.

First, the Commission's oral presentation and communication of the alleged competition concerns in phase I, usually during a state-of-play meeting or a telephone conference, entails a risk that the issues are presented more generally and/or with less supporting evidence than if the concerns had to be substantiated in writing in the form of an SO.[53] Furthermore, the parties usually have very little time to reflect on the contents and implications of the alleged concerns if they wish to try and settle the case in phase I as any first commitment proposals must be launched at more or less the same time or very shortly after the communication of the competition concerns. The combination of these issues may result in the merging parties eventually proposing broader – or even unnecessary – commitments. Once proposed, it is difficult for the parties to backtrack.

Secondly, the hearing officer plays virtually no role in phase I remedies proceedings.[54] While the time constraints in phase I necessarily limit the degree of involvement of the hearing officer in these proceedings, the lack of an independent arbiter means that for example the market tests of the remedies are not subject to any of the significant procedural safeguards in terms of ensuring objectivity, accountability and due process at this stage, which the merging parties as well as third parties would otherwise benefit from in phase II.[55] This aspect is considered increasingly significant as the Commission continues to attach greater importance to the outcomes of the market tests and this procedural step is decisive for the DG Competition's assessment of the adequacy of the commitment proposals before it

[50] See the 1993 Report to the Council, para 17, and further explanation in ch 1 n 25 above.

[51] See section 2.3 above.

[52] The Commissioner for Competition Almunia has on several occasions stressed the importance of these fundamental principles in the current merger proceedings, see eg Speeches by Almunia (2011b), (2011d) and (2010b).

[53] See section 2.1.1 above.

[54] Prior to 2011, the role of the hearing officer was explicitly confined to phase II and specifically post-SO. However, it should be noted that according to the new Terms of Reference of the Hearing Officer from 2011 the hearing officer may for example present any observations on any matter arising out of any Commission competition proceeding to the Commissioner, see Art 3(5). It is assumed that this provision in principle enables the hearing officer to submit comments in phase I remedies cases if warranted. However, given that such observations would be of a purely internal nature, no public announcements would be made in this respect.

[55] See section 2.4.1 above and in particular ch 2 nn 205 and 207 above.

advances to a draft decision. On a related matter, it should be noted that the parties have no right of access to the Commission's case file during phase I.[56] While this is obviously related to the lack of involvement of the hearing officer in phase I, it means that for example in view of a negative market test (which frequently occurs in respect of the parties' first commitment offer) the merging parties must base their further negotiation strategies on the non-confidential versions of the replies from third parties forwarded to them by the Commission without being able to verify the information by having a closer look themselves at the entire merger file. In phase II the parties' access to the file is considered an important integral part of their right to be heard and ensure procedural fairness. If the parties wish to take phase I disagreements with the Commission any further, an option is of course to lodge a complaint with the European Ombudsman, alleging that the disagreements are instigated by maladministration on the Commission's behalf.[57] However, based on identified past cases, such complaints are likely to be pending for several years and hence do not constitute an alternative to the tasks of a hearing officer during the administrative proceedings.[58]

Thirdly, in phase I an exchange of views on the alleged competition concerns and possibly also on remedies is confined to bilateral meetings between the case-team and the merging parties in the form of state-of-play meetings, teleconferences and other meetings.[59] Thus, no larger forums are part of the standard procedure during phase I. From the parties' points of view, the benefit of having an oral hearing in phase II is that it is an effective way of conveying their potential disagreements with the DG Competition, not only vis-à-vis the Member States but also associated services, none of whom normally participates in state-of-play meetings.[60] Moreover, as interested third parties may request to attend an oral hearing (and generally will be admitted by the hearing officer if they have a genuine interest) this is a useful forum for them to voice possible concerns and counter-

[56] See Notice on Access to the File, para 26. Furthermore, although the Commission may forward certain key documents to the parties in accordance with the Best Practice Guidelines on Merger Proceedings (paras 45–46), it is considered that such transmissions are mainly carried out during phase II proceedings and, in any event, they are subject to the discretion of the Commission.

[57] To the best of my knowledge, the European Ombudsman has on two occasions in past merger cases, both in phase II, issued decisions. In *Ryanair/Aer Lingus* (M.4439 II 2007) Ryanair launched a complaint, alleging improper disclosure of highly sensitive information by the Commission during its market test of proposed commitments. While the Ombudsman found no evidence that the Commission had breached confidentiality rules, he criticised the Commission for inadequate confidentiality declarations, see ch 2 n 189 above for case reference. In *Skanska/Scancem* (M.1157 II 1998) an in-house lawyer at Scancem launched a complaint on a private basis, alleging unfair and irregular handling of the case by the Commission (mainly in respect of information requests). The Ombudsman concluded that there had been no maladministration, see Decision 353/99/ME of 26 October 2000. Furthermore, in the context of *Volvo/Scania* (M.1672 II 2000) and *Volve/Renault V.I.* (M.1980 I 2000) a private person on behalf of Scania lodged a complaint to the Ombudsman as to the Commission's lack of disclosure of the terms of divestiture of the Volvo shareholding in Scania but, due to a pending appeal by Scania before the General Court relating to the same issue, the Ombudsman closed the file, see Decision 1115/2003/BB of 17 October 2003.

[58] In *Ryanair/Aer Lingus* (M.4439 II 2007) the complaint was launched in May 2007 and the Ombudsman reached a decision in May 2009. In *Skanska/Scancem* (M.1157 II 1998) the complaint was launched in September 1998 and the Ombudsman reached a decision in October 2000.

[59] Having said this, the Commission may call for so-called 'triangular' meetings involving third parties as part of its fact-finding investigation, see the Best Practice Guidelines on Merger Proceedings, paras 38–39. Whether the Commission calls such meetings in phase I is hard to say but time constraints would make it difficult.

[60] While the opportunity of having an oral hearing is increasingly being declined by the parties in phase II proceedings in order to allow for more time to negotiate and to draft remedies, it is reassuring that the option exists in case of possible deadlocks. Moreover, as pointed out by some practitioners the presence of senior officials at oral hearings have sometimes resulted in competition concerns being dropped, see MacGregor (2010) quoting *Oracle/Sun Microsystems* (M.5529 II 2010) in this respect.

argue the parties vis-à-vis the Commission services and the Member States. In contrast, in phase I all parties with vested interests in the outcome of a potential remedies case must make individual contact (usually though lobbying channels) with other Commission services and the competition authorities in the Member States which is obviously time-consuming and thus not really a realistic option in phase I.

Fourthly, as there is no formal consultation of the Advisory Committee in the form of a joint meeting in phase I, any objections or comments from the Member States are usually limited to written submissions addressed to the case-team, which the other Member States are not necessarily made aware of (unless the respective Member State makes direct contact with them). Although the merging parties may prima facie consider it advantageous that their case is not subject to additional scrutiny or discussions by the Member States, it is submitted that the involvement of the Advisory Committee in phase II cases generally strengthens due process, also at times to the advantage of the parties.[61] Indeed, in this forum the Commission must explain and argue its case before the committee and disagreements among the Member States are noted and published as well as reported to the College of Commissioners.

Lastly, as all phase I decisions are adopted by the Commissioner for Competition under delegated powers, there are no internal Commission deliberations in the form of weekly meetings of the Heads of Cabinets and of course no formal adoption by the College of Commissioners.[62] Thus, in phase I remedies cases where the parties may not necessarily feel they have the full understanding or backing of the Commissioner (for example if the latter has pushed for extensive remedies) the parties do not benefit from the collegial ownership of the conditional clearance decision and thus the impartiality that the College should ensure, as well as the input on Commissioner level of other affected directorates (for example Trade or Enterprise and Industry).[63]

The lack of additional procedural safeguards set aside, the tight deadlines in phase I also raise the question whether the current framework is suitable for complex and comprehensive remedies packages. It is submitted that there have been past cases where it prima facie seems doubtful whether the accepted remedies were sufficiently straightforward and clear-cut to comfortably justify a clearance in phase I. While it is beyond the means of this book to undertake ex-post evaluations of individual cases, a few general observations may support such doubts.

It is noted that some of the past phase I transactions have not only been extensive and complex in nature but have also involved many affected markets as well as numerous

[61] In the past the merging parties have benefited from members of the Advisory Committee disagreeing with the DG Competition's initial finding of competition concerns with the result that the concerns were later dropped, see ch 2 n 228 above.

[62] Noting in passing, in phase II cases this would normally be the point in time where the merging parties as well as interested third parties would carry out intensive lobbying, trying to argue their case with the other members of the Commission and their cabinets.

[63] Admittedly, there are diverging opinions whether the College in some merger cases pursues politically influenced decision-making as eg submitted by Ryanair recently when the Commission prohibited for the second time its attempted acquisition of Aer Lingus in *Ryanair/Aer Lingus III* (M.6663 II 2013). In a press release of 27 February 2013 Ryanair announced that it would appeal the Commission's decision as the College had adopted a 'political' decision by taking into account the vested interests of the Irish Government in the outcome of the case, see www.ryanair.com/en/news/ryanair-will-appeal-eu-decision-decision-to-prohibit-its-offer-for-aer-lingus. As of 1 May 2013, no appeal is yet formally registered before the General Court. For an opposite view, Commissioner Almunia has in the past stressed that 'Commission competition decisions are adopted not by the DG Competition, nor by me, but by the College of Commissioners [. . .] who have sworn to be and are genuinely independent of national, political and business interests', see Speech by Almunia (2010b).

complicated (including carve-out) remedies.[64] In addition, other issues not directly related to the nature of the transaction and the remedies have sometimes added further complications to the Commission's assessment in phase I, such as national referral requests or international cooperation measures.[65]

Despite the possibility of having pre-notification discussions and thus prolonging the time for a dialogue (to the advantage of the parties but to the disadvantage of interested third parties), the Commission's practice raises the question whether it sometimes puts itself under too much pressure to clear transactions in phase I instead of initiating an in-depth investigation.[66] While in no way constituting conclusive evidence, it is noted that in the past there have been phase I decisions where the competitive analysis of the accepted commitments has been remarkably short and even confined to a few paragraphs which implies that the assessment time has been scarce.[67] Furthermore, it is currently not uncommon that (last) phase I modifications are submitted so close to the expiry of the legal deadline for adoption of phase I decision – even on the day of the adoption or one or two days prior to that – that it seems questionable whether the Commission has indeed had sufficient time to carry out a proper assessment as well as the required consultations.[68]

It is acknowledged that phase II investigations do impose additional costs on the parties in the form of extended proceedings and, in worst cases, possibly declining share prices and devaluations as well as on the Commission in terms of additional resources. Nevertheless, it is submitted that the Commission should reconsider whether the lack of procedural safeguards continues to make phase I proceedings suitable for certain particularly complex and comprehensive remedies cases and, by the same token, whether any remedies cases recently and currently being cleared in phase I could have benefited from additional time being allocated to assessment as well as consultations. If the Commission finds that more safeguards and/or more time in phase I would have been appropriate in some cases,[69] it is considered

[64] By way of illustration, in *Sanofi-Aventis/Zentiva* (M.5253 I 2009) the Commission's phase I investigation covered over 100 national pharmaceutical markets and competition concerns were raised in 15 markets, see para 549. The parties offered to divest different businesses of either party in different national territories. In a subsequent article Commission officials acknowledged that the case (together with another pharmaceutical transaction being reviewed simultaneously) had displayed a number of grey areas, and had departed from previous practice in several respects, and in order to ensure viability several additional measures were put in place as no production facilities were transferred and the business was not stand-alone, see Greenaway et al (2009) 64–67. For similarly complex phase I cases involving extensive carve-outs, see eg *Schering-Plough/Organon Biosciences* (M.4691 I 2007) and *Fortis/ABN Amro* (M.4844 I 2007).

[65] In *Linde/BOC* (M.4141 I 2006), while the individual remedies may have seemed reasonably clear-cut, the remedies package nevertheless consisted of five very different remedies addressing different products and geographic markets in a highly concentrated industry and, on top of that, the Commission had to deal with a referral request from the Polish competition authority as well as extensive cooperation with the FTC. With respect to cross-border transactions requiring international cooperation and/or exchanges of information between authorities, see section 5.8 below.

[66] In a recent case, *Glencore/Xstrata* (M.6541 I 2012), the Commission even acknowledged when announcing its phase I clearance, that the substantive assessment had indeed presented a number of challenging issues during the administrative proceedings, see press release IP/12/1252 of 22 November 2012. Indeed, the nature and complexity of the remedies package (including behavioural provisions) seemed prima facie to raise doubts whether the overall solution was really 'clear-cut' to an extent that would justify a phase I clearance.

[67] In *Sanofi-Aventis/Zentiva* (M.5253 I 2009) the Commission's assessment of the remedies was confined to four paragraphs addressing only minor issues of a transitional supply agreement and a right-of-first-refusal clause, see paras 553–56. See ch 2 n 39 above for similar examples.

[68] See ch 2 nn 107 and 109 above listing numerous – and also very recent – examples of modifications being submitted one, two or three days prior to the adoption of the decision.

[69] It is considered that such assessments can be undertaken only by the Commission given the data required to carry out an ex-post analysis of the respective cases.

that such reflections are sufficiently important to warrant a review of the existing framework in the near future.

The obvious policy change under current rules would be to simply refer more cases to an in-depth investigation. With respect to voiced concerns of additional costs being placed on the parties, it should stressed that, once opening an in-depth investigation, the Commission is under an obligation to adopt a decision as soon as the competition concerns have been removed and thus the procedure may not go its full length.[70] Another possibility, but requiring legislative changes, would be to introduce an accelerated procedure in phase II (as preliminary considered by the Commission in 1993). By doing so, some of the procedural safeguards could be maintained while possibly leaving out others in order to minimise the overall duration of the proceedings.[71] Finally, if the Commission wishes to continue its current practice of clearing the vast majority of its remedies decisions in phase I but under less time-constraints, an alternative proposal could be to introduce a more flexible timeframe, similar to the one introduced for phase II proceedings in 2004. However, such changes would obviously not entail the introduction of additional procedural safeguards.

## 5.5 Policing Remedies: Does the Commission Do Enough?

> From the regulator's perspective it seems as if some parties forget about their [remedies] as soon as the ink is dry on their merger. (Graeme Samuel, Chairman of the Australian Competition and Consumer Commission (ACCC), 2008)[72]

In international antitrust circles there is a growing awareness that remedies may risk being undermined or even circumvented by the merging parties post-decision.[73] The above quote is from the ACCC's then Chairman in 2008 who voiced strong frustration in respect of past cases of bad faith behaviour by the parties and their advisors in the post-clearance remedies process and threatened that the ACCC would consider refusing all remedies during its merger review process if companies did not change attitude and behaviour.[74] While the statement seems harsh and indeed not in line with international best practice on remedies, it triggers the following two questions in respect of the Commission's remedies policy and practice: are the current monitoring measures adequate and suitable in detecting possible breaches and, if so, is the Commission sufficiently active in pursuing such breaches.

Concerning the first question, the Commission's current delegation of monitoring tasks to a trustee should be seen as a result of a general policy decision for the DG Competition not to be directly and actively involved in the monitoring process.[75] Obviously, this set-up has pros and cons. The advantage is that the Commission saves resources and that its staff

[70] See section 2.2.3.1 above.

[71] One possibility could be to leave out the oral hearing but maintain the role of the hearing officer. The Commission listed a number of other possibilities in its 1993 Report to the Council, see p 23.

[72] See Speech by Samuel (2008). Rod Sims replaced Graeme Samuel as Chairman of ACCC in 2011.

[73] This view has been expressed in several remedies studies, see the ICN Remedies Review Project, para 4.5; the 2004 OECD Remedies Study, p 9; and the FTC Divestiture Study, p 18.

[74] See Speech by Samual (2008). The criticism was not only aimed at the companies but also at their advisors.

[75] This policy is in contrast to eg the DoJ that uses monitoring trustees less frequently and instead has resources devoted to compliance enforcement in its newly established General Counsel's Office, see DoJ Merger Remedies Guide, part V.

may not always possess the qualifications to monitor certain aspects of remedies and therefore outsourcing such tasks can be efficient.[76] The downside is that the Commission needs to put a lot of trust in the capabilities of a trustee that it may not necessarily know from the outset. Another disadvantage is that, as the trustee must be proposed, assessed and approved, it is often in place several weeks if not longer after the adoption of the clearance decision and hence there is room for strategic behaviour by the parties in the interim period with potentially irreparable consequences.[77] It is therefore paramount for the trustee to be in place as early as possible. To this end, the following solutions may be considered.

One possibility is to (increasingly) use 'up-front trustees' whereby the parties commit not to close their transaction and start implementing the remedies until a trustee is appointed.[78] Similar to 'up-front buyer' provisions, the parties will thereby have an additional incentive to finalise the trustee arrangements as soon as possible and, where the business to be divested originates from the target company, the acquirer is prevented from undertaking any measures that could adversely affect the competitive position of the business post-divestment. Understandably, this requirement may prove practically difficult in some cases as merger agreements occasionally provide that completion must take place immediately or shortly after receipt of the necessary regulatory clearances. However, in the cases where 'up-front trustee' provisions are contractually possible, it is suggested that they are introduced as standard provisions.

Another possibility would be for the trustee and the mandate to be proposed pre-decision and approved as part of the conditional clearance decision.[79] To draw an analogy to remedies, such a trustee provision would amount to a 'fix-it-first' solution. This procedure would not only facilitate that the trustee could be announced together with the clearance[80] and commence its tasks straight after the adoption of the decision but as the trustee would be known at an early stage of the proceedings, it could assist in formulating trustee-related provision and get familiar with the details of all relevant circumstances of the case in order to be 'operational' from day one. Admittedly, there are downsides with this option as the contents of some remedies are negotiated at the last minute and potentially not known till possibly the last day before adoption of the decision and in such circumstances it is of course impossible to conclude trustee mandate provisions pre-decision. However, it could be a possibility worth exploring in for example phase II remedies cases.

Concerning the second question, it is considered that the Commission would benefit from pursuing a more active enforcement policy post-decision. Indeed, when looking at past practice it is striking that, to the best of my knowledge, the Commission has never considered a decision void, never revoked a decision and never imposed any financial sanctions on the parties for being in breach of their remedies.[81] This track record is remarkable in view of a decisional practice exceeding 20 years and it begs the question whether the

[76] To this effect, see Joined Cases *Commission v Éditions Odile Jacob* (C-553/10 P 2012) and *Lagardère v Éditions Odile Jacob* (C-554/10 P 2012) where the Court of Justice reiterated that the Commission could, if it possessed sufficient personnel, have carried out the tasks of the monitoring trustee itself (para 48).

[77] See section 4.3.2 above.

[78] See section 4.2.1.1 above.

[79] It is submitted that, as trustee provisions are now set out in the Implementing Regulation (Art 20a introduced in 2004) and hence not only in guidance, it is possible for the Commission to approve trustees already in its clearance decision.

[80] This would bring the practice in line with the FTC that publishes, wherever possible, the identity of the trustee in its press release when announcing the conditional approval of the transaction, see ch 4 n 33.

[81] See section 4.6.4 above.

parties' compliance always has been impeccable or the Commission has been reluctant to pursue breaches. It goes without saying that this is a politically sensitive issue.

With regard to whether the parties have behaved impeccably in past cases, the obvious short answer is 'no'. As described above, the Commission itself has detected several incidences of strategic behaviour by the parties during the divestiture process.[82] Based on information in the public domain, only in one case from 2001 did the Commission make a public announcement reminding the parties of its powers to revoke a decision, should the parties not comply with the remedies in question.[83] Moreover, there have been cases in the past where it seemed apparent, at least from an outsider's perspective, that certain implementation difficulties and/or irregularities could have warranted formal actions from the Commission.[84]

It is my considered opinion that, based on publicly available information, the Commission has been reluctant to investigate and enforce possible compliance issues in past cases. While it is difficult to speculate about the reasons behind this policy as particular circumstances may have justified the lack of enforcement in the respective cases, it is noted that merger control is generally forward looking and in its merger policy the Commission has traditionally spent little time and few resources on sanctions.[85] This approach makes sense, as merger – contrary to antitrust proceedings – is a procedure of administrative authorisation, which is not of a criminal nature (except for fines proceedings).[86] Also, from a practical point of view, as merger cases are assessed and adopted under tight deadlines due to the need for speed, there are generally few resources available to pursue other enforcement issues, including breach of remedies, which would require substantial investigations, consultations and adoption of formal decisions. Although speculative, the closure of the DG Competition's otherwise successful Enforcement Unit may also have contributed to a lower priority to post-decision enforcement as it is assumed that such measures would now have to be carried out in the respective sector units rather than in a dedicated enforcement/remedies unit.

However, based on some of the latest policy statements from the DG Competition, the Commission may be about to tighten its monitoring and enforcement policy.[87] To this effect, it is worth noting that the Commission introduced the following provisions in the new Remedies Notice in 2008. First, it now reserves the right to request information from the parties for a period of up 10 years after the adoption of the clearance decision in order

[82] See examples listed in section 4.4.1 above (some of them phrased by the Commission as 'dirty tricks' as they were intentionally aimed at obstructing the divestiture process).

[83] See *Pirelli/Edizione/Olivetti/Telecom Italia* (M.2574 I 2001) explained in section 4.4.4.2 above and esp ch 4 nn 263–65.

[84] See in particular *Hoechst/Rhône-Poulenc* (M.1379 I 1999), *Rhodia/Donau Chemie/Albright & Wilson* (M.1517 I 1999), and *WorldCom/MCI (II)* (M.1069 II 1998) described in section 4.6.4 above.

[85] Over 20 years the Commission has imposed (small) fines (mainly for late notifications) in merely 9 cases, see statistics provided on the DG Competition's website, and one of the few merger cases where the Commission has undertaken a dawn-raid in order to verify the validity of submitted information was in *Skanska/Scancem* (M.1157 II 1998), see para 11.

[86] On the differences between antitrust and merger proceedings in this respect, see Wils (2012a) 440 and 450. As correctly pointed out, antitrust proceedings generally relate to the finding of violations of the law and the imposition of sanctions for such violations and are therefore of a (non hard-core) criminal nature.

[87] See in particular Speech by Italianer (2012) where the Director General put it rather bluntly that 'if companies enter into commitments, they must do what they have committed to do or face the consequences'. Although the comment was specifically made in the context of the then on-going Microsoft antitrust case, Mr Italianer's remedies policy observations were made in the general context of remedies applying in mergers as well as antitrust cases.

to monitor effective implementation of the remedies.[88] Secondly, the Commission now stresses that a modification of a condition or obligation will normally only be effective *ex nunc* and thus indicates that it may pursue possible breaches prior to the given modification being granted.[89] Thirdly, albeit speculatively, an expected future increase in international cooperation cases as a result of more cross-border transactions and a continuing international consolidation of markets could also have the effect that the Commission starts pursuing a more vigilant enforcement policy as for example its US counterparts in the event of untimely or inadequate implementation of remedies in such cases.[90]

Another way of addressing implementation irregularities or difficulties would be to increase transparency in the way the UK Takeover Panel did when it issued a 'public statement of criticism' in connection with Kraft's takeover of Cadbury in 2010.[91] The case illustrates how public criticism can generate substantial press coverage, which is expected to have a positive impact on the parties' incentives to do their utmost to comply with their remedies (especially publicly listed companies are their share prices may be sensitive to such news). The downside with such public statements is the lack of legal consequences but they could nevertheless serve as an efficient first attempt (as the Commission did in one case in the past). Also, the awareness of the possibility of issuing such statements may have a preventive effect.

### 5.6 Forms and Guidance: A Potential Straightjacket?

> Form RM – a risk of repetitive strain injury? Parties could not have keener incentives to provide the Commission with the information necessary to judge the suitability of the remedy. (Michael Rowe, Slaughter and May, 2007)[92]

Over the years the remedies procedure has become progressively formalised and standardised with the result that, within the current framework, the parties are not only required to observe the detailed provisions and principles set out in the Remedies Notice but must also submit a number of forms simultaneously when proposing commitments; that is, albeit not mandatory, MTDC and MTTM (including non-confidential versions) as well as the newly introduced mandatory Form RM. While it is indisputable that the enhanced guidance and the standard model texts have been large contributors to the Commission's overall remedies success, the amount of information required in the forms taken together is extensive. Moreover, while originally the standard model texts were intended as an optional

[88] See section 4.6.3 above. However, as pointed out previously no remedies text contains this provision under current practice as it is not contained in the MTDC and the Commission should therefore make the necessary changes in order for the provision to have any effect.

[89] See section 4.4.4.3 above.

[90] See eg the FTC's continuous follow-ups *In the Matter of Hoechst AG and Rhone-Poulenc SA, to be renamed Aventis SA* (Docket No C-3919, File No 991 0071, see ch 4 n 272 above.

[91] See the statement at www.thetakeoverpanel.org.uk/wp-content/uploads/2009/12/2010-14.pdf. The UK Takeover Panel publicly criticised Kraft Foods for wrongly having announced during its then-hostile bid of Cadbury that it would save Cadbury's UK Somerfield facility from closure. While the Panel refrained from fining Kraft Foods for its wrongdoing, the statement of public criticism generated substantial bad press for Kraft Foods and its advisers, see eg Elizabeth Rigby and Brooke Masters, 'Kraft Censured over Cadbury Deal' *Financial Times* (26 May 2010). The Panel also criticised Kraft's financial advisor Lazard for having failed to discharge fully its responsibilities although the bank's conduct was not sufficient to merit public criticism.

[92] See Speech by Rowe (2007).

tool for the parties to ease their submission if considered relevant,[93] the latest amendments to the Implementing Regulation in 2008 made in effect the model texts mandatory as the parties are now required to identify any deviations of the model texts and explain the reasons for such deviations.[94]

The Commission has justified the required information in Form RM by referring to the inherent information asymmetry between the parties and the Commission and that it is the parties' responsibility to provide all such information as to facilitate the Commission's assessment. While from the Commission's view this justification appears plausible as it is based on past experience where full and correct information about the business may not always have been available,[95] the current policy raises the following issues.

First, Form RM requires not only a substantial amount of factual data, forecasts and descriptions relating to the business covering 4 years but it also obliges the parties to undertake a competitive assessment of their own commitments.[96] It is submitted that it would seem more appropriate for the Commission to undertake such an assessment based on the factual information provided by the parties and not ask the parties to do the same. Indeed, jurisprudence is now clear that the burden of proof as to the compatibility rests on the Commission.[97] Also, when comparing the information required in the standard model texts with that in the Form RM some requirements are repetitive, especially in relation to the scope and nature of the business to be divested. Moreover, given that commitment proposals are often revised and/or substituted at the last minute the parties face practical difficulties in collecting the required information prior to submission of their final proposal and even having to file it in two different formats; the standard model texts and Form RM.

Secondly, while the Commission is available to discuss the scope of the information required upfront and possibly grant waivers, it must be borne in mind that waiver requests and evaluations take time, which automatically introduces further delays into the remedies proposal, especially in phase I cases. Thus, although the parties may consider some of the required information unnecessary, they may nevertheless decide not to request waivers simply in order not to lose valuable time.

All in all, it is considered that Form RM appears unduly burdensome on the parties. This is particularly the case in a regulatory environment where speed is of essence (as recognised by the EU Court) and where conditions and obligations are often agreed upon very close to the submission deadlines. It is therefore suggested that the Commission would benefit from reconsidering the need for a rigid and detailed Form RM as currently in force.[98] Indeed, as the above quote by a lawyer indicates the parties could not have keener incentives to provide

[93] When introducing the standard model texts the Commission noted in its Best Practice Remedies Guidelines that 'the standard models are neither intended to provide an exhaustive coverage of all issues that may become relevant in all cases, nor are they legally binding upon the parties', see para 2.

[94] As a technical comment, given the (in practice) changed status of the standard model texts, it is essential for the Commission not only to update the texts reflecting current practice (the existing – and only – versions dating back to 2003) but also to ensure that they are available in other official languages than the current version in English.

[95] See Speech by Luebking (2007).

[96] The parties are eg required to submit information on the envisaged suitability of their commitments to remove the raised concerns and they must also state reasons why, in their view, the business will be acquired by a suitable purchaser within the envisaged time frame, see Form RM, paras 2 and 5.13, respectively.

[97] See section 2.2.5 above.

[98] It is worth noting that in other areas of merger control the Commission is currently considering lessening its information requirements, see the on-going consultation on a Commission proposal to not only expand the scope of simplified procedures but also to reduce the net amount of information required to notify all mergers as set out in Commission press release of 27 March 2013, IP/13/288.

the Commission with the necessary information in order to reach a decision of compatibility as swiftly as possible.

Additionally and more generally, the Commission's reliance on a framework consisting of several detailed submission forms as well as a comprehensive Remedies Notice raises the question whether the current policy is in danger of making the remedies process too 'mechanical' (as also stated above in respect of the viability requirements) and thus losing the individuality of each case. From the regulator's point of view, it is reassuring to have a comprehensive set of rules that the (especially inexperienced) staff can lean against, as such a framework provides consistency and transparency, minimises 'room for individual errors', speeds up the administrative procedure and ultimately saves resources. However, it also creates the obvious risk that the individual case-handlers may take too much comfort in the application of standard provisions without sufficient regard to the individual circumstances of the respective transaction and markets involved.[99] From the parties' point of view, a high degree of standardisation and detailed provisions when submitting commitment proposals obviously means that the risk of having to request waivers at a later stage is higher and, as previously mentioned, such requests are usually resource intensive and the outcomes may be known not only months but years later.[100]

It is thus considered that the current framework may ultimately lead to risks that certain aspects of remedies are either not addressed or over-fixed on the basis of standard provisions. As the Commission has not yet undertaken any ex-post studies of cases under the current rules, it is difficult to provide examples from decisional practice to this effect. However, it is worth noting that the current Director General for Competition recently said that case experience had taught his services that, if remedies are too specific, they are not practical and the risk of circumvention is higher.[101] Thus, it seems that a push towards simplification may be favoured in future policy considerations and, based on the above reflections, such a move appears plausible.

## 5.7 With Guidance come Responsibilities: Has the Commission Delivered?

> [I]t is expected that the text of these models will evolve, based on on-going practice, and will be regularly up-dated by the Commission, taking into consideration both the developments of the Commission's remedies policy and the experience gained from working with the merging parties and trustees in future matters. (The Commission, 2003)[102]

[99] By way of comparison, it is worth noting that the DoJ and FTC have refrained from issuing specific submission forms and kept their guidance relatively general. As an example, the DoJ states that 'any remedy assessment is fact-intensive [. . .]. Basing remedies on the application of economic and legal analysis to the particular facts of each case avoids merely copying past relief proposals and is most likely to result in relief effectively protecting consumers', see DoJ Merger Remedies Guide, part I.A. Similarly, instead of issuing a model standard text for a trustee mandate, the FTC has made available on its website some previous monitoring agreements to aid the parties while stressing that each case turns on its own facts and therefore unique provisions in each agreement may be required, see FTC Guidelines for Negotiating Merger Remedies, p 16.

[100] On the point of the length of procedures, see *Hoffmann–La Roche/Boehringer Mannheim* (M.950 II 1998) where Roche launched a request for a waiver (concerning the cancellation of an open-ended licence) on 24 September 2008, the Commission conducted a renewed market investigation in the first quarter of 2009, followed by another investigation in the beginning of 2010, with the final result that the remedy in question was formally waived by decision on 3 May 2011. Thus, the procedure lasted more than 2½ years.

[101] See Speech by Italianer (2012).

[102] See Best Practice Remedies Guidelines, para 4. The provision refers to the standard model texts, thus MTDC and MTTM.

On a related matter, while the Commission has been proactive in publishing remedies guidance and standard model texts in the past, it has failed to update any of them. Thus, the old Remedies Notice from 2001 remained unchanged until the publication of the new notice in 2008, and the highly important standard model texts from 2003 continue to be in force in their original formats. This is considered highly unfortunate for several reasons. First, as the relevant remedies provisions in the Merger Regulation are general and confer a wide discretion of assessment on the Commission, updated guidance is essential in order to ensure predictability in the proceedings.[103]

Secondly, it seems evident that the dynamic nature of mergers and remedies warrants regular updates and the Commission itself has recognised and foreseen that continuous revisions should be a part of the enforcement framework (see the quote above) so it is puzzling that updates are never undertaken. Consequently, a number of inconsistencies currently exist between the standard model texts from 2003 and the Remedies Notice from 2008.[104] Furthermore, when new legislative measures are rarely adopted, new commercial and procedural issues emerging from practice remain unaddressed for a long time.[105] It would therefore be in the interest of all parties concerned if the Commission started to continuously update particularly the standard model texts and Remedies Notice in order to adequately reflect the current practice. Continuous revisions could be undertaken through addendums to existing texts rather than new texts in order to save time and resources.

Furthermore, as the findings in ex-post studies of past remedies cases have proven essential for evaluations and further improvements in the Commission's guidance, it is considered inadequate that the Commission has carried out only one comprehensive remedies study in more than 20 years of practice.[106] Moreover, while the Remedies Study highlighted some important issues in past practice when it was published in 2005, its main weakness was its reference period being 1996 to 2000. Although a reference period obviously needs to be several years prior to the time of the assessment in order to measure the competitive effects, one of the main drawbacks of the study was that the Commission had initiated some of its most important new remedies policies between the reference period and the publication of the study.[107] The result was that some of the analysed issues in the study were less relevant at the time of publication and, more importantly, subsequent 'hot remedies topics' were not addressed in the study.[108] Thus, given the late publication compared to the reference period the study was in some respects limited and less pioneering than originally hoped for.

With the drawbacks of the Remedies Study in mind, it is considered that the Commission would benefit from undertaking more limited ex-post studies in the future, narrowed

[103] Despite the Commission initially arguing otherwise, the General Court has confirmed the binding nature of the Remedies Notice upon the Commission, provided it does not depart from the rules of TFEU and the Merger Regulation, see *Babyliss v Commission* (T-114/02 2003) para 143; and *Royal Philip Electronics v Commission* (T-119/02 2003) para 242.

[104] Technical comments on inconsistences and out-dated provisions have been submitted throughout this book in the relevant contexts.

[105] See eg the lack of implementation of the information obligation described in section 4.6.3 above.

[106] For the sake of completeness, the DG Enterprise Econometric Remedies Study should also be mentioned albeit being significantly more limited in reference period, number of cases and sectors.

[107] Between 2000 and 2005 some of the most significant policy changes were made: the Commission adopted its (old) Remedies Notice in 2001, standard model texts in 2003 and the revised Merger Regulation in 2004.

[108] By way of illustration, crown jewels, fix-it-first solutions, up-front buyers and hold-separate managers did not feature in decisional practice during the study's reference period but were already considered established practice when the study was published.

down to for example specific cases or specific sectors[109] in order to be able to process and publish its findings sooner and thereby enhance the relevance and impact of the study.[110] Disregarding the exact format, it is considered that the time is ripe for the Commission to undertake further ex-post evaluations, as they are instrumental to the formulation of possible new initiatives and/or change of directions.[111] [112]

## 5.8 International Cooperation: How Much Further Can the Commission Go?

> EU–US cooperation in the field of competition policy has been a remarkable success story, which has benefited consumers on both sides of the Atlantic. I am looking forward to intensifying this important dialogue with our American colleagues in order to bring about a greater knowledge and understanding of each other's rules and standards to avoid divergence whenever possible. (Joaquín Almunia, Commissioner for Competition, 2011)[113]

As geographic markets become wider in scope, international market players continue to consolidate and an increasing number of jurisdictions adopt merger review provisions, there is a growing need for enhanced international cooperation and coordination amongst competition authorities in order to minimise the risks of diverging decisional outcomes. There are several multilateral platforms and ways of enhancing international convergence of remedies policy and enforcement issues, such as the OECD and the ICN.[114] However, it is mainly the numerous bilateral cooperation agreements or memoranda of understanding that have a direct impact on the Commission's day-to-day handling of remedies cases.[115]

In the previous chapters the aspect of international cooperation in cross-border transactions has been mainly confined to comments on the cooperation in individual cases and in particular in EU–US proceedings. The nature, scope and implications of bilateral cooperation in cross-border merger cases are complex issues and could easily warrant a comprehen-

[109] Recent sector inquiries undertaken by the DG Competition have focused on anti-trust issues, such as the 2009 pharmaceuticals report and the 2007 energy report.

[110] The FTC recently undertook this kind of assessment when officials in 2009 examined the impact of Johnson & Johnson's acquisition of Pfizer's consumer health division from 2006, see Paper by Tenn and Yun (2009). The case was also notified to the Commission, see *J&J/Pfizer Consumer Healthcare* (M.4314 I 2006). The limited scope of the study enabled the FTC to publish its findings 3 years after the clearance of the transaction. To the best of my knowledge, this was FTC's first published ex-post study since its comprehensive Divestiture Study in 1999.

[111] While the Commission announced in its latest management plan that a new internal pilot study of past merger cases would be launched in 2012, no further publications or announcements have been made to this effect and it is unclear if remedies cases would be a part of this study, see the Management Plan for 2013, p 56.

[112] Several commentators have emphasised the need for the Commission to undertake a new evaluation of more recent remedies cases, see eg Davidson (2006) who calls for new initiatives to be launched in both the EU and US: 'The FTC and EU Studies on divestiture are actually landmark events on the path to better enforcement. It is time, however, for second-generation studies to be undertaken' (p 11). See also Christiansen (2008): '[The Remedies Study] can only be the first step towards a systematic ex-post evaluation of the Commission's practice' (p 493). Senior FTC representatives have also stressed the need for more ex-post evaluations of past interventions in order to move forward, see eg Speech by Kovacic (2008). Finally, it should be mentioned that the DoJ's recently established enforcement unit, the General Counsel's Office, is expected to undertake ex-post studies, see DoJ Merger Remedies Guide, part V.A.

[113] There words were the introductory remarks by Commissioner Almunia when announcing an advanced cooperation with the DoJ and the FTC in the form of the US–EU Best Practices on Cooperation in Merger Investigations, see press release of 14 October 2011, IP/11/1194.

[114] See section 1.4.4 above. Publications like the OECD's remedies studies in 2004 and 2011 have clearly contributed to a better understanding and exchange of policy issues in this respect.

[115] For a listing of current agreements and memoranda, see ch 2 n 240 above.

sive examination in its own right. However, for the purposes of highlighting some of the main challenges in the Commission's future remedies policy from an international cooperation perspective, the present section is confined to the following observations (primarily in relation to EU–US merger cooperation cases).[116]

First, it is indisputable that the cooperation between the Commission and the FTC/DoJ has been successful in the past, as indicated by Commissioner Almunia (see above quote). The transatlantic cooperation is based on the Commission's longest running bilateral arrangements originating from 1991 and it has proven highly useful for all parties concerned in numerous cases in the past.[117] While the intensity of the cooperation has varied throughout the years in accordance with the political and administrative agendas and priorities on both sides of the Atlantic,[118] recent decisional practice has shown examples of continuing willingness from all parties concerned to try and take the cooperation to new levels, whenever possible, by for example coordinating the negotiation, drafting, submission and assessment of (sometimes even identical) remedies.[119] Such parallel investigations are generally hugely beneficial to the merging parties in terms of reduced burdens and costs, including potentially fewer implementation measures.[120] The authorities may benefit from administrative synergies in the form of shared information and joint assessments.

However, it needs to be remembered that the extent of the cooperation is entirely in the hands of the merging parties, as the authorities can share confidential information only if they receive a waiver of confidentiality from the parties.[121] While the parties usually have every interest in allowing such information sharing in order to obtain speedy clearances or to potentially achieve symmetrical remedies, there may be situations where they consider that it would be to their disadvantage to waive confidentiality and hence an extensive cooperation would be obstructed even if the authorities would have an interest in pursuing it.[122]

[116] For publications on international cooperation in merger cases, see eg the OECD Cross-Border Merger Review (albeit devoted to developing countries), Ratliff and Louis in Knable Gotts (2012), Van Bael (2011), Papadopoulos (2010) and Galloway (2009).

[117] Cases like *UTC/Goodrich* (M.6410 II 2012), *Western Digital Ireland/Viviti Technologies* (M.6203 II 2011), *Novartis/Alcon* (M.5778 I 2010) and *Cisco/Tandberg* (M.5669 I 2010) are just a few recent examples of successful cooperation cases between the Commission and the FTC/DoJ. For older cooperation cases, see eg *Sanofi-Synthélabo/Aventis* (M.3354 I 2004), *GE/Instrumentarium* (M.3083 II 2003), *Bayer/Aventis Crop Science* (M.2547 II 2002), *Astra/Zeneca* (M.1403 I 1999) and *Exxon/Shell* (M.1137 I 1998), just to mention a few.

[118] Eg under the tenures of Commissioner Monti various cooperation initiatives were initiated, such as the creation of a new EU–US working group whose purpose was to enhance transatlantic cooperation in the control of cross-border mergers, see COM(2000)618 final, p 6. The working group undertook important work on remedies (see Competition Report 2000, p 294) but none of its findings were made publicly available. Around the same time the ICPAC's report was issued, followed by calls for global initiatives, see ch 1 n 132 above and Klein in IBA (2000) 59–64. However, later in the 2000s formal EU–US initiatives on international coherence quietened down somewhat until the publication of the renewed US–EU Best Practices on Cooperation in Merger Investigations in 2011, see ch 1 n 85 above.

[119] See in particular *Cisco/Tandberg* (M.5669 I 2010) where the DoJ made the following comment upon clearance: 'This investigation was a model of international cooperation between the United States and the European Commission', see ch 2 n 241 above. For details on the cooperation aspect in this case, see also the 2011 OECD Remedies Study, p 230. Identical remedies have been accepted in a number of parallel proceedings before the Commission and the FTC/DoJ, see latest *Western Digital Ireland/Viviti Technologies* (M.6203 II 2011) and *In the Matter of Western Digital Corporation* (File No 111 0122, Docket No C-4350), respectively.

[120] Coordinated proceedings may eg facilitate the appointment of a common trustees and even one purchaser approval procedure.

[121] See the EU–US Cooperation Agreement, Art VIII. For details on this clause, see Papadopoulos (2010) 78–81.

[122] eg the parties may not wish to waive confidentiality if they have concerns over leakage of information or if they are unsure how the other authority (with potentially different assessment criteria and procedures) will treat the respective information.

Also, the success of any cooperation is highly dependent on the parties' possibilities of notifying the respective authorities more or less simultaneously as the Commission needs to adhere to its tight deadlines and it can therefore not postpone its assessment and findings if the notification to the FTC/DoJ (or any other cooperating authority) is significantly delayed.[123] Along the same lines, the length of the regulatory reviews can be essential for coordinated measures to take place.

Secondly, there have been (rare) examples in the past of an even more intense cooperation in the form of so-called 'work sharing' arrangements between the authorities whereby one jurisdiction in its assessment and conclusions simply refers to the remedies formally accepted and adopted by the other jurisdiction.[124] The purpose of work sharing is obviously to reduce the number of separate reviews of the same transaction and accordingly reduce the risk of inconsistent outcomes to the benefit of all parties concerned. While such cooperation may be suitable for jurisdictions which have discretionary prosecutorial powers in merger control (the US) it does not seem compatible with regulatory frameworks where the authority is obliged to take both positive and negative decisions (the Commission).[125] Thus, work sharing arrangements would not under the current rules allow the Commission to abstain from adopting a decision altogether. However, in cases where remedies already have been submitted to and implemented in another jurisdiction (or firm measures have been set up to this effect) the Commission may see itself entitled to consider such remedies as facts upon which it bases a positive decision.[126]

Thirdly, it is worth pointing out that, although the cooperating authorities may have agreed on the acceptance of identical remedies in the administrative proceedings, a number of uncertainties or obstacles may arise in the implementation phase. For example, in cases where the authorities accept identical remedies covering assets in several jurisdictions and where the remedies require that the assets should go to one single purchaser, the authorities will need to carefully coordinate purchaser approval procedures. In these situations in the past the Commission has formally approved the purchaser in respect of the European assets and the FTC/DoJ formally approved of the same purchaser for the US assets.[127] However, this procedure can result in major time delays and frictions between the

[123] While in no way conclusive, it is worth observing that in many of the most recent EU–US cooperation cases involving remedies the Commission entered into phase II proceedings, see eg *Universal Music Group/EMI Music* (M.6458 II 2012), *UTC/Goodrich* (M.6410 II 2012), *J&J/Synthes* (M.6266 II 2012) and *Western Digital Ireland/Viviti Technologies* (M.6203 II 2011). This development could indicate that the Commission needs more time in international cooperation cases.

[124] Two cases are worth mentioning. Most lately, in *Cisco/Tandberg* (M.5669 I 2010) the DoJ simply took the remedies accepted by the Commission 'into account, together with various other factors [. . .] in reaching its decision to close its investigation', see ch 2 nn 49 and 241 above. Much earlier, the reverse situation occurred in the unconditional clearance of *Halliburton/Dresser* (M.1140 I 1998) where the Commission decided to rely on the companies' divestiture commitment to the DoJ and considered the commitment as part of the parties' notification, see paras 6–7. Thus, in the latter case the Commission considered the US remedy a fact in its investigation, see ch 2 n 47 above.

[125] This finding was highlighted in OECD discussions back in 2005 on how to tackle cross-border remedies in various jurisdictions, see summary in Competition Report 2005, para 713.

[126] See *Halliburton/Dresser* (M.1140 I 1998). In terms of enforcement the Commission would thus rely on the powers of its regulatory counterparts. Such remedies are not to be confused with the so-called 'public pledges' which the Commission considered as 'facts' in *Oracle/Sun Microsystems* (M.5529 II 2010) as they were submitted to the public rather than an authority, see ch 2 n 280 above.

[127] See ch 4 n 312 above, in respect of the Commission's conditional clearance in *Manitowoc/Enodis* (M.5180 I 2008) and, by the same token, the DoJ's conditional clearance in *United States v The Manitowoc Company, Inc., Enodis plc, and Enocis Corporation*, Case No 1:2008CV01704, Final Judgment of 17 February 2009.

competent authorities if they cannot agree on one joint purchaser.[128] Albeit less severely, similar considerations may apply in the case of joint trustees being proposed and appointed.[129]

Fourthly, as a growing number of cross-border transactions are simultaneously reviewed by numerous jurisdictions around the world,[130] the existing bilateral cooperation agreements entered into by the Commission are by definition insufficient to effectively and extensively coordinate regulatory reviews of truly global transactions. From the regulator' perspective, this could lead to a fragmented review of the overall impact of such transactions or even to global enforcement gaps.[131] From the merging parties' perspective, notifications to numerous jurisdictions, some of which may have different regulatory frameworks, may cause unforeseen additional delays with the result that the parties are forced to repeatedly postpone the closing of their transaction, which can prove highly costly.[132]

Finally, the ultimate downside with a global enforcement setup consisting of a large number of jurisdictions with their own merger controls and national agendas and procedures is when the respective proceedings result in findings, which are diverging or even incompatible. While the risk of such decisional outcomes was greater in early practice when larger time gaps existed between the parallel proceedings before the respective authorities,[133] it is unavoidable that some decisional outcomes differ due to the multitude of competition regimes and market structures. Indeed, discrepancies in national interests,

[128] By way of illustration, although one single purchaser was agreed upon in Manitowoc's acquisition of Enodis, the DoJ rather extraordinarily not only accepted a 150 days divestiture period from the outset but this period was also extended twice (5 March 2009 and 3 April 2009), see DoJ's case file in *United States v The Manitowoc Company, Inc., Enodis plc, and Enocis Corporation*, Case No 1:2008CV01704. In accordance with standard practice, the Commission published no information in this respect.

[129] See ch 4 n 27 above.

[130] By way of illustration, *Glencore/Xstrata* (M.6541 I 2012) was filed in eg the EU, China and South Africa; *Universal Music Group/EMI Music* (M.6458 II 2012) in eg the EU, US, Austrialia, Japan and Canada; *UTC/Goodrich* (M.6410 II 2012) in eg EU, US, Canada, Mexico and Brazil; *Western Digital Ireland/Viviti Technologies* (M.6203 II 2011) in eg the EU, US, Australia, Canada, China, Japan, Korea, Mexico, New Zealand, Singapore and Turkey; *Novartis/Alcon* (M.5778 I 2010) in the EU, US, Canada, Singapore and China; and *Pfizer/Wyeth* (M.5476 I 2009) in eg the EU, US, Canada, Australia, Mexico, New Zealand and South Africa. In terms of statistics, in 2010–11 the Commission worked with competition agencies outside the EU in half of its major merger investigations involving remedies, see Speech by Almunia (2013).

[131] Some commentators suggested that this was the case in Glencore's acquisition of Xstrata in 2013. The transaction was subject to regulatory approval in several jurisdictions, including the EU, China and South Africa. The Commission conditionally cleared the transaction in phase I in November 2012, see *Glencore/Xstrata* (M.6541 I 2012). Some commentators voiced concerns and surprise that such a large worldwide mining and commodities transaction received a phase I conditional clearance by the Commission and seemed to face little resistance from other jurisdictions and it has argued that such global commodity mergers benefit inter alia from the lack of international oversight, see 'Cry Bloody Merger' *Financial Times* (21 November 2012). Subsequently, the competition authorities in South Africa unconditionally cleared the transaction in January 2013 and the authorities in China conditionally cleared the transaction in April 2013 (some commentators considered the remedies to be modest, see WilmerHale newsletter, 'China Clears Glencore's Acquisition of Xstrata Subject to Remedies' (26 April 2013), available at www.wilmerhale.com/pages/publicationsandnewsdetail.aspx?NewsPubID=10737421260).

[132] To continue with the above example, in *Glencore/Xstrata* (M.6541 I 2012) the parties were forced to push back the closing date several times due to prolonged merger investigations in several jurisdictions, including in China where the investigation lasted more than 1 year. Some commentators noted in respect of this case that the Chinese authorities are likely to be the last major jurisdiction to clear any large cross-border transaction, partly because of the agency's preference to wait to clear transactions until clearances have been obtained in other jurisdictions even it delays closing by months, see WilmerHale newsletter, op cit.

[133] See eg *Air Liquide/BOC* (M.1630 II 2000) which the Commission conditionally cleared in January 2000, only for the FTC to prohibit the transaction 4 months later.

rules and procedures have sometimes resulted in political and administrative clashes between the Commission and the FTC/DoJ which may not necessarily have been pleasant for the parties involved during the peak of the disagreements.[134] Yet, once the respective cases have been settled the authorities usually acknowledge their differences, try to place them in the context of the many other cases being resolved without any conflict whatsoever and use them as a platform for further improving their cooperation in future cases. To this effect, the Commission and the FTC/DoJ renewed their US–EU Best Practices on Cooperation in Merger Investigations in 2011.[135]

Radical possible solutions aimed at mitigating the downsides of multiple notifications and reviews of cross-border mergers are complicated and must be considered measures, which are several years if not decades down the line. Innovative initiatives could go along the lines of further exploring the possibilities of an international harmonisation of competition laws or even some kind of unifying competition forum.[136] Obviously, this would require substantial changes of national laws and therefore a possible realisation must be viewed long-term. In the short term and based on the existing framework, the most realistic way forward seems to be for the Commission to conclude more bilateral cooperation agreements with new trading partners and/or intensify existing cooperation.[137] Also, as it is inevitable under the current bilateral setup that diverging or incoherent parallel decisions will occur, it is important for the authorities to acknowledge this risk by for example allowing the merging parties to request a review or adjustment of their remedies.[138]

[134] The first high-profile case displaying substantial disagreement was *Boeing/McDonnell Douglas* (M.877 II 1997) where the FTC unconditionally cleared the transaction while the Commission conditionally cleared it. For a detailed analysis of the case in the context of EU–US cooperation, see in particular Karpel (1998). One of the latest near-clashes was the Commission's unconditional clearance in *Oracle/Sun Microsystems* (M.5529 II 2010) (but with the acceptance of so-called public pledges after the DG Competition had headed for a prohibition decision) in the wake of the DoJ's outright clearance of the transaction earlier. In this case the tensions between the authorities escalated when the DoJ, in response to the Commission issuing SO, took an unusual step by publishing a statement stressing that in its review of the transaction it saw no competition issues and that they remained hopeful that the Commission would reach a speedy resolution, see DoJ press release of 9 November 2009. The actions of the DoJ caused a number of public exchanges between senior officials on both sides and some commentators labelled the DoJ somewhat of a bully, see *MLex Comment*, 'US Makes show of EU co-Operation in Cisco-Tandberg Clearances' (6 April 2010), www.mlex.com/EU/Content.aspx?ID=95495.

[135] See ch 1 n 85 above.

[136] Commissioner Almunia recently indicated that further convergence could be achieved through stepping up multilateral efforts eg through the ICN, see Speech by Almunia (2013). In the past senior officials have advocated exploring the possibility of setting up a unifying forum in the form of a Global Competition Initiative, see eg Joel Klein in IBA (2000) 62–63.

[137] eg in respect of the Commission's current memorandum with China the parties may take the cooperation a step further by including information sharing, as recently suggested by a senior representative for the Chinese authority, see Mlex, 'Chinese Authorities to Strengthen info-Sharing with EU, US Partners in Merger Reviews' (11 April 2013), www.mlex.com/EU/Content.aspx?ID=364855. Also, with the aim of intensifying its current cooperation the Commission and the FTC/DoJ renewed their US–EU Best Practices on Cooperation in Merger Investigations in 2011, see ch 1 n 85 above. Commissioner Almunia also recently echoed the need for the Commission to multiply its bilateral (as well as multilateral) exchanges to carry out its control in the best possible conditions, see Speech by Almunia (2013).

[138] The Commission has occasionally accepted a clause whereby the parties may request a review or adjustment of their remedies if the approval by another governmental authority is made subject to requirements that are potentially inconsistent with the remedies accepted in the former proceedings, see latest *Intel/McAfee* (M.5984 I 2011), Remedies Text, para 48.

## 5.9 Concluding Remarks

> However beautiful the strategy, you should occasionally look at the results. (Sir Winston Churchill (1874–1965))

Whereas the overall success of the EU merger remedies policy and practice is universally recognised, the analysis of the main aspects of the remedies procedures in the previous chapters has revealed a number of concerns and shortcomings which should be further considered and addressed by the Commission in its future policy reflections. The most important issues have already been highlighted in the present chapter and, wherever possible, suggestions for improvements have been made. However, some concluding remarks seem warranted as to (i) the potential impact of the identified shortcomings on the existing remedies policy and practice, and (ii) the potential impact of the Commission's current policy on enforcement outcomes.

### *5.9.1 Impact of the Identified Shortcomings on the Remedies Policy*

The question remains whether the identified concerns and shortcomings are of such a nature and extent that they risk diminishing or even undermining some of the accomplished successes of the existing remedies policy and practice. When trying to address this issue it is worth bearing in mind some of the general and fundamental principles upon which the Commission's merger control is based. These principles include proportionality, impartiality, legal certainty, due process, transparency, timely consultation and the need for speedy decisions. It is evident that these requirements are challenging for the Commission's administration, especially in view of the scarce time provided for the assessment of remedies cases. To this effect, the Commission has understandably had to make compromises and priorities within the overall legal framework. While many of the analysed remedies issues have been benchmarked against these requirements throughout this book, it is worthwhile briefly reiterating a few of them in the overall context of the Commission's obligations and choice of priorities within the current policy.

One of the noticeable developments in recent decisional practice is how the Commission has given particular priority to the need for speedy decisions by clearing the vast majority of remedies cases in phase I at allegedly the expense of certain procedural safeguards, such as consultations and hearing officer involvement which are not applicable to the same extent in phase I as in phase II proceedings. Another prominent feature worth highlighting is how the Commission continues pursuing a policy of limited transparency in respect of additional measures and waivers during the implementation phase to the detriment of providing legal certainty and predictability. An additional observation concerns the Commission's established preference for early identification of all assets needed in order to ensure viability already at the design stage irrespective of any likely resources of prospective purchasers. In some cases this requirement may arguably conflict with the principle of proportionality and confer unnecessary measures and costs on the merging parties (including early separation of assets and personnel) if/when it later appears that not all assets are indeed required by the proposed purchasers.

Moreover, one overall common feature in respect of many of the concerns raised previously in this chapter seems to be how the Commission through evolved standardisation and streamlining of its remedies procedures (in the form of guidance, standard model texts and forms) has created a framework that attempts to embrace and address all possible contingencies that may arise in a 'standard' remedies case. Put very simply, the parties' commitment proposals are expected to contain all standard provisions from the outset and only through subsequent requests for waivers can any deviations from a 'standard' case be granted. Throughout this book numerous examples of a standardised approach have been highlighted; such as the submission of information to the Commission, the identification of the scope of the business as well as a number of post-decision enforcement obligations. Overall, this policy approach shifts the initiative and burden of proof from the Commission and on to the merging parties in the sense that the Commission no longer needs to actively and individually request for example certain information but, instead, the parties must ask for waivers in order *not* to submit the required information.

The so-called standardisation should be seen as a result of the Commission having to make priorities within the existing framework and it has thus chosen this approach in order to comply with the need for speedy decisions, predictability and to some degree transparency, albeit arguably at the cost of proportionality in particular. However, if the Commission takes the standardisation of the remedies procedure much further, it is considered that such a policy is in danger of hampering some of the good intentions behind its otherwise successful remedies enforcement. Indeed, the consequences of a very detailed and standardised approach are that the procedures may become mechanical and potentially unduly burdensome for the merging parties as they must apply for waivers for many individual aspects and the burden of proof continuously rests on them.

While probably unintentional, standardisation also puts constraints on the Commission, as it must devote additional resources when investigating, assessing and granting possible waivers. Furthermore, since the Commission continues to be not very transparent in its waiver procedures, this aspect creates less predictability for the parties. The obvious alternative to the current policy is that the Commission takes a more individual approach, as it did in earlier practice before the standard model texts and detailed guidance were adopted, and thus creates room for more flexibility for each case to turn on its own merits.[139] Such an approach does not mean that a standardised approach should be abandoned, merely that more flexibility and individualism should be built into the existing framework. After all and as confirmed repeatedly through decisional practice, no two cases are alike.

On balance, has the Commission made the right priorities in its remedies policy within the current framework? Based on the reflections throughout this chapter, it is considered that there are valid reasons for arguing that the Commission should be mindful of and possibly reconsider some of its existing priorities; for example whether the need for speed and standardisation comes at a (too) high cost and possibly to the detriment of other important considerations such as proportionality, due process and impartiality. It is submitted that the Commission would benefit from taking a step back to reconsider whether the evolution in merger transactions and accompanying remedies practice in recent years justifies a change of some of its existing priorities in order to safeguard and maintain the

[139] Indeed such an approach would be in line with the latest indications from the Director General for the DG Competition who recently said that experience has taught his services that a simplification push in remedies cases would lead to greater effectiveness, see Speech by Italianer (2012). It would also be in keeping with recent initiatives to simplify other merger procedures, see ch 1 n 71 above.

best possible remedies proceedings to the benefit of all parties involved.[140] To this effect, it is hoped that the Commission will carefully evaluate past events (in the form of more ex-post studies) before formulating new strategies and provisions for the future.[141]

### *5.9.2 Impact of the Remedies Policy on Enforcement Outcomes*

It is indisputable that optimal remedies are those that are effective in achieving the overall policy objectives of maintaining and restoring effective competition in the given market, in a manner that is proportionate to the severity of the competition concerns and at the same time least costly and time-consuming to implement, to the ultimate benefit of the consumer. However, as observed throughout this book the Commission's prospective merger analysis inherently involves certain risks and uncertainties, which may result in a conditional clearance decision ultimately not addressing the identified competition concerns in the projected and/or optimal way. The likelihood of such decisional outcomes are furthermore influenced by the various – diverging as well as common – interests, incentives and objectives of all parties involved in the administrative proceedings.

While the achieved competitive effects of remedies in a given transaction can be established and evaluated only by a detailed ex-post analysis several years post-decision, it is nevertheless possible, on the basis of the previously described enforcement considerations and findings in past decisional practice, to provide some concluding reflections on likely enforcement outcomes and their possible effects on competition.

As previously submitted, the merging parties have an overriding strategic and financial interest in settling competition concerns as promptly and inexpensively as possible[142]. When faced with a strategic decision whether to submit commitment proposals or not, the merging parties will undertake an evaluation of the likelihood of the Commission clearing their concentration with phase I remedies, phase II remedies, no remedies or even prohibiting their transaction. Their decision will partly depend on how confident they are that the Commission has correctly identified the competition concerns or, for example, whether undisclosed concerns are likely to be uncovered during an in-depth investigation. Remedies statistics confirm that the parties are likely to settle concerns in phase I, wherever possible.

There are indications from decisional practice that phase I remedies are likely to err on the broader side of what may be strictly necessary to mitigate the identified competition concerns.[143] The merging parties will nevertheless find such remedial solutions attractive if their calculations reveal that the costs of settling their transaction in phase I through possibly broader remedies outweigh the potential additional costs and risks of entering phase

[140] Albeit in no way conclusive, there are recent indications in the Commission's remedies statistics that it may be about to change its priorities, as the number of phase II conditionally clearance decisions rose to six in 2012 (out of a total of 15 conditional clearance decisions), see Annex A. As of 1 May 2013, the Commission has adopted only one (phase I) conditional clearance decision in 2013 and hence it is not possible to make any forecasts on likely statistical developments for this calendar year.

[141] As previously mentioned, the Commission stated in its Management Plan for 2013 that a new internal pilot study of past merger cases had been launched in 2012, see ch 5 n 111 above. However, as of 1 May 2013 the Commission has made no publications or further announcements in this respect and it remains unclear if remedies cases would be included in this study.

[142] See section 1.5 above.

[143] See in particular sections 2.1 and 5.4 above. Furthermore, it lies in the nature of phase I that the competition concerns have been identified broadly based on a preliminary analysis and the corresponding remedies are likely to be equally broad as they must be clear-cut.

II proceedings.[144] Despite the Commission's general obligation to accept remedies which are proportionate to the competition concerns, it will usually be content with this decisional outcome, provided that the identified concerns as a minimum are resolved, as such an outcome entails a number of substantial short-term benefits, such as being resource- and cost-saving, eliminating the competitive harm sooner rather than later, compensating for any information asymmetry and so forth[145].

However, in the long run broad or excessive remedies may not necessarily always benefit competition and ultimately the consumer, as the Commission may be at risk of making a so-called 'type 1' decisional error if the remedies are of such a scope that they will deprive the given market of achieving the efficiencies originally associated with the concentration.[146] In these situations excessive remedies may come at a cost of lost efficiency for the merging parties, which in turn may have long-term implications for competition when synergies and efficiencies, which would otherwise have been gained and passed on to the consumer, are diminished. Also, specifically in respect of phase I remedies in complex or comprehensive transactions the Commission may not have had the opportunity to properly identify the competition concerns in terms of delineating the exact competitive harm with the risk that the remedies may not fully and adequately address the 'core harm'.[147]

Lastly, reverting to the overall regulatory objective of a remedy, namely to maintain or restore effective competition in order to protect consumer welfare, it is submitted that this objective may be at risk of not being fully adhered to at all times, if the Commission and the merging parties are too tempted to settle remedies as quickly and comprehensively as possible. Furthermore, as conditional clearance decisions containing allegedly excessive remedies are rarely challenged before the EU Court, let alone overruled, any possible decisional errors remain irreversible as the Commission lacks powers to unilaterally amend or reverse remedies if later they are found not to yield the expected benefits or solve the competition concerns in the foreseen manner (unless the parties are blatantly in breach of their remedies). Thus, the lack of reversibility reinforces the importance of the Commission striving to achieve the optimal remedy in each case by carefully weighing the costs and benefits for all parties involved and the consumer in particular throughout the entire remedies process.

[144] See section 1.5 above. Furthermore, there may be contractual obligations in the acquisition or merger agreement that provide the parties with additional incentives to settle in phase I. For example, a termination fee may be triggered if the Commission enters phase II proceedings and thus if a phase I conditional clearance decision is not obtained, see Ch1 n 181 above.

[145] ibid. This outcome should also be seen against the fact that the Commission cannot impose remedies on its own initiative, nor unilaterally amend the parties' proposals.

[146] See section 1.5 above.

[147] ibid.

# Annex A

REMEDIES STATISTICS[1]

| | 1990 | 1991 | 1992 | 1993 | 1994 | 1995 | 1996 | 1997 | 1998 | 1999 | 2000 | 2001 |
|---|---|---|---|---|---|---|---|---|---|---|---|---|
| Total clearance and prohibition decisions[2] | 5 | 55 | 51 | 52 | 85 | 100 | 116 | 129 | 217 | 249 | 321 | 329 |
| Phase I conditional clearance decisions | | 3 | 4 | | 2 | 3 | | 2 | 12 | 16 | 26 | 11 |
| Phase II conditional clearance decisions | | 3 | 3 | 2 | 2 | 3 | 3 | 7 | 4 | 7 | 12 | 9 |
| Total conditional clearance decisions | | 6 | 7 | 2 | 4 | 6 | 3 | 9 | 16 | 23 | 38 | 20 |
| *– share of total decisions* | | *10.9%* | *13.7%* | *3.8%* | *4.7%* | *6.0%* | *2.6%* | *7.0%* | *7.4%* | *9.2%* | *11.8%* | *6.1%* |
| Prohibition decisions | | 1 | | | 1 | 2 | 3 | 1 | 2 | 1 | 2 | 5 |
| *– share of total decisions* | | *1.8%* | | | *1,2%* | *2.0%* | *2.6%* | *0.8%* | *0.9%* | *0.4%* | *6,2%* | *1.5%* |
| Withdrawn Notifications/cases | | | 3 | 2 | 6 | 4 | 6 | 9 | 9 | 12 | 13 | 12 |

| | 2002 | 2003 | 2004 | 2005 | 2006 | 2007 | 2008 | 2009 | 2010 | 2011 | 2012 | Total |
|---|---|---|---|---|---|---|---|---|---|---|---|---|
| Total clearance and prohibition decisions | 255 | 222 | 239 | 296 | 346 | 396 | 340 | 241 | 270 | 310 | 271 | 4895 |
| Phase I conditional clearance decisions | 10 | 11 | 12 | 15 | 13 | 18 | 19 | 13 | 14 | 5 | 9 | 218 |
| Phase II conditional clearance decisions | 5 | 6 | 4 | 3 | 6 | 4 | 5 | 3 | 2 | 1 | 6 | 100 |
| Total conditional clearance decisions | 15 | 17 | 16 | 18 | 19 | 22 | 24 | 16 | 16 | 6 | 15 | 318 |
| *– share of total decisions* | *5.9%* | *7.7%* | *6.7%* | *6.1%* | *5.5%* | *5.6%* | *7.1%* | *6.6%* | *5.9%* | *1.9%* | *5.5%* | *6.5%* |
| Prohibition decisions | | | 1 | | | 1 | | | | 1 | 1 | 22 |
| *– share of total decisions* | | | *0.4%* | | | *0.3%* | | | | *0.3%* | *0.4%* | *0.5%* |
| Withdrawn Notifications/cases | 4 | | 5 | 9 | 9 | 7 | 13 | 8 | 4 | 10 | 5 | 150 |

[1] As of 1 May 2013, the Commission had adopted merely one conditional clearance decision (in phase I) in 2013.

[2] This figure comprises all clearance decisions in phase I and II as well as prohibition decisions but excludes Art 9 referral decisions and Art 8(4) decisions.

# Annex B

TABLE OF THE COMMISSION'S REMEDIES DECISIONS UNDER THE MERGER REGULATION[1]

(in reverse chronological order)

Key

* Appealed to the EU Courts
# Cooperation cases with the US FTC/DoJ
\+ Unilateral arrangements by the parties, i.e. commitments not formal attached to the Commission decision

| Date | Case No and Name | Phase & Sector | Remedies[2] |
|---|---|---|---|
| **2013:** | | | |
| 12.04 | M.6722 – *FrieslandCampina/ Zijerveld&Veldhuyzen . . .* | I Dairy | Amend supply agreement and other contracts |
| **2012:** | | | |
| 12.12 | M.6497 – *Hutchinson 3G Austria/ Orange Austria* | II Mobile telecoms | Divest assets and IRPs, provide network access |
| 27.11 | M.6682 – *Kinnevik/Billerud/ Korsnäs* | I Paper | Divest assets, optional input supply agreements |
| 22.11 | M.6541 – *Glencore/Xstrata* | I Mining, metals | Divest stake, terminate off-take agreements, purchase ban, behavioural ban |
| 07.11 | M.6471 – *Outokumpu/Inoxum* | II Steel | Divest business |
| 07.11 | M.6564 – *ARM/Giesecke & Devrient/Gemalto/JV* | I Software components | Information obligation to competitors & component design restrictions |
| 27.09 | M.6611 – *Arla Foods/Milk Link* | I Dairy | Divest assets |
| 21.09# | M.6458 – *Universal Music Group/ EMI Music* | II Music | Divest assets |
| 26.07# | M.6410 – *UTC/Goodrich* | II Aviation | Divest businesses and projects |
| 05.07 | M.6455 – *SCA/Georgia-Pacific Europe* | I Sanitary goods | Divest assets and brands |

[1] As of 1 May 2013.
[2] As this table of remedies decisions merely serves as an overview, the indication of the type of remedy is general and does not necessarily reflect the nature of the entire remedies package.

Annex B (*cont.*)

| Date | Case No and Name | Phase & Sector | Remedies |
|---|---|---|---|
| **2012:** | | | |
| 04.07 | M.6503 – *La Poste/Swiss Post/JV* | I Postal services | Divest subsidiary |
| 25.05 | M.6512 – *DS Smith/SCA Packaging* | *I* Paper | Divest assets (plants) |
| 16.05 | M.6286 – *Südzucker/ED&F MAN* | II Sugar | Divest stake |
| 19.04 | M.6459 – *Sony/Mubadala Development/EMI . . .* | I Music | Divest assets |
| 18.04# | M.6266 – *J&J/Synthes* | II Medical devices | Divest business |
| 30.03** | M.6447 – *IAG/bmi* | I Airlines | Divest slots and other rights |
| **2011:** | | | |
| 23.11#* | M.6203 – *Western Digital Ireland/ Viviti Technologies* | II Hardware | Divest assets |
| 13.10 | M.6258 – *Teva/Cephalon* | I Pharmaceuticals | Divest assets |
| 01.06 | M.6093 – *BASF/INEOS/Styrene/JV* | I Chemicals | Divest business |
| 29.04 | M.5047 – *REWE/ADEG* | I Retail | (See 2008–decision) |
| 26.01# | M.5984 – *Intel/McAfee* | I IT Software | Provide access through inter-operability provisions such as licences and behavioural clauses |
| 26.01# | M.5978 – *GDF Suez/International Power* | I Energy | Divest stake, transfer agreement |
| **2010:** | | | |
| 30.11 | M.5927 – *BASF/Congis* | I Chemicals | Divest business and production agreements |
| 17.11 | M.5675 – *Syngenta/Monsanto's Sunflower Seed Business* | II Seeds | Divest hybrids |
| 17.11 | M.5658 – *Unilever/Sara Lee Body Care* | II Retail, FMCP | Divest brands and assets |
| 25.10 | M.5953 – *Reckitt Benckiser/SSL* | I Pharmaceuticals | Divest brands |
| 11.08 | M.5855 – *Deutsche Bahn/Arriva* | I Transportation | Divest business |
| 09.08# | M.5778 – *Novartis/Alcon* | I Pharmaceuticals | Divest business |
| 03.08 | M.5865 – *Teva/Ratiopharm* | I Pharmaceuticals | Divest assets |
| 17.06 | M.5655 – *SNCF/LCR/Eurostar* | I Rail services | Provide access, release pathways |
| 17.06 | M.5756 – *DFDS/Norfolk* | I Freight | Conclude agreement with competitor |
| 29.03# | M.5669 – *Cisco/Tandberg* | I Networking | Divest IPR and other assets |
| 01.03 | M.5650 – *T-Mobile/Orange* | I Telecoms | Divest assets, revise agreement |
| 16.02 | M.5721 – *Otto/Primondo Assets* | I Retail | Divest trademarks, access to data |
| 11.02 | M.5661 – *Abbott/Solvay Pharmaceuticals* | I Pharmaceuticals | Divest businesses |
| 22.01 | M.5579 – *TLP/Ermewa* | I Transportation | Divest assets |
| 21.01# | M.5611 – *Agilent/Varian* | I Instruments | Divest businesses |
| 06.01 | M.5644 – *Kraft Foods/Cadbury* | I Confectionary | Divest businesses |

| Date | Case No and Name | Phase & Sector | Remedies |
|---|---|---|---|
| **2009:** | | | |
| 18.12 | M.5664 – *Bilfinger Berger/MCE* | I Industrial services | Divest business (subsidiary) |
| 15.12 | M.5599 – *Amcor/Alcan* | I Packaging | Divest assets (plants) |
| 04.12 | M.5597 – *Towers Perrin/Watson Wyatt* | I Consulting | Divest business |
| 12.11* | M.5549 – *EDF/Segebel* | I Energy | Divest assets (projects) |
| 29.09# | M.5421 – *Panasonic/Sanyo* | I Batteries | Divest assets (plant) and business |
| 28.08 | M.5440 – *Lufthansa/Austrian Airlines* | II Airlines | Transfer slots and ancillary rights |
| 17.07# | M.5476 – *Pfizer/Wyeth* | I Pharmaceuticals | Divest assets (plant) and businesses |
| 23.06 | M.5467 – *RWE/Essent* | I Electricity, gas | Divest stake in competitor |
| 22.06 | M.5335 – *Lufthansa/SN Airholding* | II Airlines | Transfer slots |
| 22.06 | M.5496 – *Vattenfall/Nuon* | I Energy | Divest assets |
| 21.04 | M.5152 – *Posten AB/Post Danmark A/S* | I Postal services | Divest assets |
| 13.03 | M.5406 – *IPIC/MAN Ferrostaal AG* | I Chemicals | Divest stake in supplier |
| 12.03 | M.5355 – *BASF/CIBA* | I Pharmaceuticals | Divest assets, grant licences |
| 04.02 | M.5253 – *Sanofi-Avantis/Zentiva* | I Pharmaceuticals | Divest businesses |
| 09.01 | M.5153 – *Arsenal/DSP* | II Chemicals | Divest assets (plant) |
| 09.01 | M.5364 – *Iberia/Vueling/Clickair* | I Airlines | Transfer slots |
| **2008:** | | | |
| 22.12 | M.5224 – *EDF/British Energy* | I Energy | Divest assets, terminate agreement |
| 19.12 | M.5295 – *Teva/Barr* | I Pharmaceuticals | Divest businesses |
| 17.12 | M.5046 – *Friesland/Campina* | II Dairy | Divest businesses, provide access |
| 03.12 | M.5384 – *BNP Paribas/Fortis* | I Banking | Divest business and stake |
| 25.11 | M.5096 – *RCA/MAV Cargo* | I Freight | Severe links |
| 31.10 | M.5005 – *Galp Energia/Exxonmobil Iberia* | I Petrol products | Divest assets and stakes |
| 21.10 | M.4919 – *StatoilHydro/ConocoPhillips* | II Fuel | Divest assets |
| 23.09 | M.5232 – *WPP/TNS* | I Market research | Divest assets |
| 23.09 | M.4980 – *ABF/GBI Business* | II Yeast | Divest businesses |
| 19.09# | M.5180 – *Manitowoc/Enodis* | I Food equipment | Divest businesses |
| 17.07# | M.5114 – *Pernod Richard/V&S* | I Spirits | Divest assets, terminate agreements |
| 16.07 | M.5190 – *Nordic Capital/Convatec* | I Medical care | Divest businesses |
| 11.07 | M.5020 – *Lesaffre/GBI UK* | I Yeast | Divest assets (production) |
| 01.07 | M.4835 – *Hexion/Huntsman* | I Chemicals | Divest assets |
| 27.06 | M.5086 – *BAT/Skandinavisk Tobakskompani* | I Tobacco | Divest assets (brands) |

Annex B (*cont.*)

| Date | Case No and Name | Phase & Sector | Remedies |
|---|---|---|---|
| **2008:** | | | |
| 25.06 | M.5121 – *News Corp/Premiere* | I Media | Provide access to platforms |
| 23.06* | M.5047 – *REWE/ADEG* | I Retail | Divest assets, network exit |
| 17.06 | M.5075 – *Vienna Insurance Group/ EBV* | I Insurance | Divest assets |
| 04.06 | M.4513 – *Arjowiggins/M-Real Zanders Reflex* | II Paper | Divest assets |
| 17.04 | M.5009 – *Randstad/Vedior* | I Employ services | Divest assets, grant licence (brands) |
| 04.03 | M.4898 – *Compagnie de Saint-Gobain/Maxit* | I Building materials | Divest businesses (subsidiaries) |
| 04.03 | M.4961 – *Cookson/Foseco* | I Ceramic prod | Divest businesses |
| 22.02 | M.4963 – *Rexel/Hagemeyer* | I Electrical prod | Divest business |
| 19.02# | M.4726 – *Thomson Corporation/ Reuters Group* | II Software | Divest assets |
| **2007:** | | | |
| 14.12 | M.4779 – *Akzo Nobel/ICI* | I Chemicals | Divest assets & stakes, grant licences |
| 09.11 | M.4824 – *Kraft/Danone* | I Foods | Divest assets (including brands) |
| 07.11 | M.4746 – *Deutsche Bahn/EWS* | I Railways | Fulfil expansion plans, provide access |
| 31.10 | M.4842 – *Danone/Numico* | I Baby food | Divest assets (plants) |
| 26.10# | M.4828 – *Owens Corning/Saint Gobain* Vetrotex | I Glass fibres | Divest assets (mainly brands) |
| 24.10 | M.4753 – *Antalis/MAP* | I Paper | Divest business, provide logistic services |
| 18.10 | M.4581 – *Imperial Tobacco/Altadis* | I Tobacco | Divest assets (brands) |
| 15.10 | M.4611 – *Egmont/Bonnier* | I Publishing | Abstain from purchasing certain assets |
| 11.10# | M.4691 – *Schering-Plough/ Organon Biosciences* | I Pharmaceuticals | Divest assets |
| 03.10 | M.4844 – *Fortis/ABN Amro Assets* | I Banking | Divest assets |
| 19.09 | M.4525 – *Kronospan/Constantia* | II Furniture | Abstain from purchasing certain assets |
| 21.09 | M.4730 – *Yara/Kemira Growhow* | I Fertilisers | Exit from a JV, divest assets |
| 06.09 | M.4533 – *SCA/P&G (European Tissue Business)* | I Household goods | Divest assets (brands) |
| 03.08 | M.4750 – *Luvata/Eco* | I Heating | Divest assets |
| 18.07 | M.4504 – *SFR/Tele 2* | II Media | Access, abstain from purchasing rights |
| 29.06 | M.4540 – *Nestlé/Novartis (Medical Nutrition B)* | I Healthcare | Divest assets, stakes, grant licence (brands) |
| 04.06 | M.4600 – *TUI/First Choice* | I Travel | Divest assets |

| Date | Case No and Name | Phase & Sector | Remedies |
|---|---|---|---|
| 22.05* | M.4404 – *Universal/BMG Music Publishing* | II Music publish | Divest assets (mainly catalogues) |
| 10.05 | M.4381 – *JCI/FIAMM* | II Auto batteries | Divest assets (capacity and brands) |
| 16.03 | M.4367 – *APW/APSA/Nordic Capital/Capio* | I Healthcare | Divest assets |
| 20.02 | M.4494 – *Evraz/Highveld* | I Steel | Divest assets or stakes |
| 08.02 | M.4475 – *Schneider Electric/APC* | I Electricity | Divest assets |
| **2006:** | | | |
| 12.12 | M.4187 – *Metso/Aker Kvaerner* | II Paper | Divest assets |
| 11.12 | M.4314 – *J&J/Pfizer Consumer Healthcare* | I Healthcare | Divest assets |
| 14.11 | M.4180 – *Gaz de France/Suez* | II Energy | Divest assets/stake, no control, start project |
| 09.11 | M.4242 – *Thermo Electron/Fisher Scientific* | I Laboratory equipment | Divest assets |
| 21.09 | M.4318 – *Veolia/Cleanaway* | I Waste | Divest assets (mainly plant) |
| 19.07* | M.3796 – *OMYA/J.M. Huber PCC* | II PCC | Divest assets |
| 04.07 | M.4000 – *INCO/Falconbridge* | II Mining | Divest assets |
| 19.06 | M.4153 – *Toshiba/Westinghouse* | I Nuclear | Modify contractual arrange-ments |
| 06.06 | M.4141 – *Linde/BOC* | I Industrial gases | Divest businesses, dissolve links |
| 02.06 | M.4137 – *Mittal/Arcelor* | I Steel | Divest assets (mainly plants) |
| 23.05 | M.4151 – *Orica/Dyno* | I Explosives | Divest business |
| 19.05 | M.3998 – *Axalto/Gemplus* | I Info equipment | Grant Licence (IPR), disclose information |
| 26.04 | M.3916 – *T-Mobile Austria/ Tele.ring* | II Telecoms | Divest assets |
| 11.04# | M.4150 – *Abbott/Guidant* | I Pharmaceuticals | Amend supply arrangement and stake |
| 05.04 | M.4055 – *Talanx/Gerling* | I Insurance | Divest business |
| 21.03 | M.4066 – *CVC/SLEC* | I Motor sports | Divest business (subsidiary) |
| 14.03 | M.3868 – *DONG/Elsam/Energi E2* | II Energy | Divest assets, release capacity |
| 23.02 | M.3946 – *Renolit/Solvay* | I PVC films | Divest assets |
| 10.01 | M.4035 – *Telefonica/O2* | I Telecoms | Exit from alliance |
| **2005:** | | | |
| 22.12 | M.3940 – *Lufthansa/Eurowings* | I Airlines | Divest slots, access to program |
| 21.12 | M.3696 – *E.ON/MOL* | II Energy | Divest assets, release capacity |
| 10.11 | M.3935 – *Jefferson Smurfit/Kappa* | I Packaging | Divest businesses |
| 12.10 | M.3765 – *Amer/Salomon* | I Skiing equip | Alter cooperation agreement |
| 12.10 | M.3863 – *TUI/CP Ships* | I Shipping | Exit from conferences |

Annex B (*cont.*)

| Date | Case No and Name | Phase & Sector | Remedies |
|---|---|---|---|
| **2005:** | | | |
| 25.08# | M.3687 – *J&J/Guidant* | II Pharmaceuticals | Divest businesses |
| 29.07 | M.3829 – *Maersk/PONL* | I Shipping | Exit from conferences, divest asset |
| 15.07# | M.3732 – *Procter & Gamble/ Gillette* | I Retail, FMCG | Divest assets, license brands |
| 13.07 | M.3653 – *Siemens/VA Tech* | II Electricity | Divest assets and stake |
| 07.07 | M.3817 – *Wegener/PCM/JV* | I Media | Refrain from joint advertising |
| 05.07 | M.3770 – *Lufthansa/Swiss* | I Airlines | Divest slots, reassurances from bodies |
| 24.06 | M.3779 – *Pernod Richard/Allied Domecq* | I Retail, FGCG | Divest brands, termination of contracts |
| 27.05 | M.3751 – *Novartis/Hexal* | I Pharmaceuticals | Divest assets |
| 24.05 | M.3692 – *Reuters/Telerate* | I Media | Grant licences |
| 29.04 | M.3680 – *Alcatel/Finmeccanica/ AlcatelAlenia/Space . . .* | I Satellite systems | Grant licences and supply arrangement |
| 12.04 | M.3593 – *Apollo/Bakelite* | I Chemicals | Grant licences and supply arrangement |
| 31.03 | M.3686 – *Honeywell/Novar* | I Security systems | Divest business |
| 04.03 | M.3658 – *Orkla/Chips* | I Retail, FMCG | Terminate distribution arrangement |
| **2004:** | | | |
| 20.12 | M.3558 – *Cytec/UCB-Surface Specialities* | I Resins | Divest assets (mainly plant) |
| 26.10 | M.3436 – *Continental/Phoenix* | II Rubber prod | Divest assets and stake |
| 23.11 | M.3570 – *Piaggio/Aprilia* | I Scooters | Supply arrangement |
| 19.11 | M.3544 – *Bayer Healthcare/Roche (OTC B)* | I Pharmaceuticals | Divest assets |
| 08.10 | M.3410 – *Total/Gaz de France* | I Gas | Provide access |
| 06.10 | M.3431 – *Sonoco/Ahlstrom* | II Paper tubes | Divest assets |
| 06.10 | M.3099 – *Areva/Urenco/ETC JV* | II Nuclear power | Remove rights, increase monitoring |
| 17.08# | M.3465 – *Syngenta CP/Advanta* | I Seeds | Divest assets |
| 16.06 | M.3420 – *GIMD/Socpresse* | I Publications | Divest assets |
| 10.06 | M.3397 – *Owens-Illinois/BSN Glasspack* | I Glass container | Divest assets (mainly plants) |
| 28.05 | M.3396 – *Group 4 Falck/Securicor* | I Security services | Divest assets |
| 26.04# | M.3354 – *Sanofi-Synthelabo/ Aventis* | I Pharmaceuticals | Divest assets and grant licences |
| 15.03# | M.3314 – *Air Liquide/Messer Targets* | I Industrial gas | Divest assets and stake in JV |
| 11.02* | M.3280 – *Air France/KLM* | I Airlines | Release slots, assurances from bodies |
| 07.01 | M.2978 – *Lagardere/Natexis/VUP* | II Publishing | Divest business |

| Date | Case No and Name | Phase & Sector | Remedies |
|---|---|---|---|
| **2003:** | | | |
| 15.12 | M.3322 – *Polestar/Prisa/Inversiones Ibersuizas* | I Printing | Divest stake |
| 05.12# | M.3136 – *GE/AGFA NDT* | I Ultrasound devices | Divest business |
| 29.09# | M.3225 – *Alcan/Pechiney II* | I Aluminium | Divest stake and/or assets |
| 02.09# | M.3083 – *GE/Instrumentarium* | II Medical equip. | Divest business, provide interface services |
| 13.08 | M.3235 – *Teijin/Zeon/JV* | I Mouldings | Divest stake |
| 29.07 | M.3197 – *Candover/Cinven/ Bertelsmann-Springer* | I Publishing | Divest assets |
| 23.07# | M.2972 – *DSM/Roche Vitamins* | II Feed enzymes | Terminate cooperation, divest assets |
| 20.07 | M.3149 – *Procter & Gamble/Wella* | I Retail, hair care | Grant licence (brands) |
| 18.07 | M.3161 – *CVRD/CAEMI* | I Iron ore | Divest stake |
| 11.07 | M.3091 – *Konica/Minolta* | I Photo equip | Divest stake |
| 11.06 | M.2947 – *Verbund/Energie Allianz* | II Energy | Divest stake, freeze rights, price caps |
| 30.04# | M.2861 – *Siemens/Drägerwerk/JV* | II Hospital equip | Divest business, provide interface services |
| 30.04 | M.2903 – *Daimler Chrysler/ Deutsche Tele* | II Toll-collection | Setup independent services |
| 02.04* | M.2876 – *Newscorp/Telepiu* | II Pay-TV | Divest assets, provide access |
| 27.02# | M.2922 – *Pfizer/Pharmacia* | I Pharmaceuticals | Divest assets, grant licences |
| 13.01 | M.2416 – *Tetra Laval/Sidel* | I Packaging | Grant licence (technology) |
| **2002:** | | | |
| 17.12 | M.2822 – *ENBW/ENI/GVS* | II Gas distribution | Amend supply arrangements |
| 29.11 | M.2879 – *Wallenius Lines/ Wilhelmsen/Hyundai* | I Transport | Withdraw from JV |
| 18.11 | M.2854 – *RAG/Degussa* | I Concrete | Divest assets |
| 24.07 | M.2698 – *Promatech/Sulzer Textil* | II Weaving machines | Divest assets |
| 10.07 | M.2803 – *Telia/Sonera* | I Telecoms | Divest assets, separate business, access |
| 02.07 | M.2761 – *BP/VEBA OEL* | I Petroleum | Ensure remedy from previous case |
| 26.06* | M.2650 – *Haniel/Cementbouw/JV (CVK)* | II Building mat | Divest stake |
| 25.06 | M.2817 – *Barilla/BPL/Kamps* | I Bakery product | Divest assets |
| 08.05 | M.2779 – *Imperial Tobacco/ Reemtsma* | I Tobacco | Amend distribution arrangements |
| 17.04# | M.2547 – *Bayer/Aventis Crop Science* | II Insecticides | Divest businesses, grant licences |
| 09.04# | M.2690 – *Solvay/Montedison-Ausimont* | I Chemicals | Divest stakes in JVs and plant |

Annex B (*cont.*)

| Date | Case No and Name | Phase & Sector | Remedies |
|---|---|---|---|
| **2002:** | | | |
| 09.04# | M.2568 – *Haniel/Ytong* | II Building mat | Divest assets |
| 19.03 | M.2684 – *EnBW/EDP/Cajastur/ Hidrocantabrico* | I Electricity | Increase capacity |
| 15.01 | M.2544 – *Masterfoods/Royal Canin* | I Pet food | Divest assets (including brands) |
| 08.01*[3] | M.2621 – *SEB/Moulinex* | I Household app | Grant trademark licences, re-branding |
| **2001:** | | | |
| 20.12* | M.2533 – *BP/E.ON* | II Petrochemicals | Divest stake |
| 20.12# | M.2389 – *Shell/DEA* | II Petrochemicals | Provide access |
| 20.12 | M.2530 – *Südzucker/Saint Louis* | II Sugar | Divest stake, provide access |
| 12.12 | M.2602 – *Gerling/NCM* | I Insurance | Divest businesses (branches) |
| 08.11 | M.2567 – *Nordbanken/Postgirot* | I Postal services | Reduce stake, exit from competitor |
| 30.10 | M.2420 – *Mitsui/CVRD/CAEMI* | II Iron ore | Divest stake |
| 26.09 | M.2434 – *Group Villar Mir/. . .* | II Electricity | Increase capacity |
| 20.09 | M.2574 – *Pirelli/Edizione/Olivetti/ Telecom Italia* | I Telecoms | Divest stakes |
| 27.07# | M.2337 – *Nestlé/Ralston Purina* | I Pet food | Divest assets, grant licences (brands) |
| 19.07 | M.2431 – *Allianz/Dresdner* | I Banking | Reduce stake |
| 27.06 | M.2300 – *YLE/TDF/GIGITA/JV* | I Media | Divest business |
| 14.05 | M.2396 – *Industri Kapital/Perstorp (II)* | I Chemicals | Divest businesses |
| 08.05 | M.2268 – *Pernod Richard/Diageo/ Seagram* | I Spirits | Divest assets (brands), separate distribution |
| 11.04 | M.2286 – *Buhrmann/Samas Office Supplies* | I Office supplies | Divest assets |
| 03.04[4] | M.2139 – *Bombardier/Adtranz* | II Railway equip | Grant licence, divest stake, retain supplies |
| 13.03 | M.1915 – *The Post Office/TPG/ SPPL* | II Postal services | Divest assets |
| 12.03 | M.2277 – *Degussa/Laporte* | I Chemicals | Divest assets (plants) |
| 07.02 | M.1853 – *EDF/ENBW* | II Electricity | Divest assets, access, dissolve links |
| 24.01# | M.2033 – *Metso/Svedala* | II Rock equip | Divest assets |
| 15.01# | M.2041 – *United Airlines/US Airways* | I Airlines | Divest assets (mainly slots) |

[3] See also second clearance of 11 November 2003 in *SEB/Moulinex* (M.2621 II 2003).
[4] 13.07.2005: amendment of decision (waiving a condition).

| Date | Case No and Name | Phase & Sector | Remedies |
|---|---|---|---|
| **2000:** | | | |
| 13.12 | M.2060 – *Bosch/Rexroth* | II Piston pumps | Divest assets |
| 06.12 | M.1940 – *Framatome/Siemens/...* | II Nuclear | Exit from JV, divest stake |
| 13.10 | M.2050 – *Vivendi/Canal+/Seagram* | I Media | Divest stake, provide access |
| 11.10# | M.1845 – *AOL/Time Warner* | II Music online | Divest stakes |
| 29.09 | M.1990 – *Unilever/Bestfoods* | I Food products | Divest assets (including brands) |
| 01.09#* | M.1980 – *Volve/Renault V.I.* | I Busses | Divest stake |
| 29.08 | M.2059 – *Siemens/Dematic/VDO/Sachs* | I Postal automation | Divest assets |
| 28.08 | M.2032 – *SCA Packaging/Metsä Corrugated* | I Paper | Divest assets |
| 11.08 | M.2016 – *France Telecom/Orange* | I Mobile telecom | Divest stake in JV |
| 04.08 | M.2020 – *Metsä-Serla/Modo Paper* | I Paper | Divest assets |
| 26.07# | M.1806 – *Astra Zeneca/Novartis* | II Crop protection | Divest assets, grant licences, terminate dist |
| 26.07 | M.2002 – *Preussag/Thomson* | I Package hols | Divest stake |
| 19.07 | M.1939 – *Rexam/American National Can* | I Beverage cans | Divest assets |
| 12.07 | M.1813 – *Industri Kapital/Dyno* | II Chemicals | Divest assets and/or stakes |
| 30.06 | M.1932 – *BASF/American Cyanamid (AHP)* | I Crop protection | Divest assets, grant licences, supply |
| 13.06 | M.1673 – *VEBA/VIAG* | II Electricity | Divest stake, purchase obligations, fee |
| 22.05# | M.1878 – *Pfizer/Warner-Lambert* | I Pharmaceuticals | Divest assets, grant licences |
| 11.05 | M.1745 – *EADS* | I Space | Divest assets, terminate supplies |
| 08.05# | M.1846 – *Glaxo Welcome/Smithkline Beecham* | I Pharmaceuticals | Grant licences |
| 08.05 | M.1892 – *Sara Lee/Courtaulds* | I Retail | Divest assets (mainly brands) |
| 05.05# | M.1920 – *Nabisco/United Biscuits* | I Retail, biscuits | Divest assets |
| 03.05# | M.1671 – *Dow Chemical/Union Carbide* | II Chemicals | Divest assets, grant licence (technology) |
| 03.05# | M.1693 – *Alcoa/Reynolds* | II Aluminium | Divest assets and stakes |
| 12.04 | M.1795 – *Vodafone Airtouch/Mannesmann* | I Telecoms | Divest assets, provide access |
| 07.04 | M.1874 – *Lafarge/Blue Circle* | I Building mat | Divest assets |
| 30.03 | M.1835 – *Monsanto/Pharmacia & Upjohn* | I Pharmaceuticals | Grant a licence |
| 29.03 | M.1751 – *Shell/BASF (Project Nicole)* | I Polypropylene | Divest assets, grant licences (patents) |
| 27.03 | M.1838 – *BT/ESAT* | I Telecoms | Terminate or change distr. arrangements |

Annex B (*cont.*)

| Date | Case No and Name | Phase & Sector | Remedies |
|---|---|---|---|
| **2000:** | | | |
| 21.03# | M.1636 – *MMS/Dasa/Astrium* | II Satellites | Divest assets, grant licences |
| 14.03# | M.1663 – *Alcan/Alusuisse* | II Aluminium | Divest assets |
| 08.03 | M.1802 – *Unilever/Amora-Maille* | I Food products | Divest assets (mainly brands) |
| 28.02 | M.1747 – *Telecom Austria/Libro* | I Telecoms | Withdraw licence application |
| 09.02* | M.1628 – *TotalFina/Elf Aquitaine* | II Fuel retail | Divest assets |
| 09.02 | M.1641 – *Linde/AGA* | II Industrial gases | Divest assets |
| 07.02# | M.1683 – *Hellenic Bottling Company* | I Retail | Divest stake |
| 25.01 | M.1684 – *Carrefour/Promodes* | I Retail | Divest stake, no change in contracts |
| 18.01# | M.1630 – *Air Liquide/BOC* | II Industrial gases | Divest assets, provide access |
| 12.01 | M.1712 – *Generali/INA* | I Insurance | Divest stakes, terminate distribution |
| **1999:** | | | |
| 20.12 | M.1760 – *Mannesmann/Orange* | I Telecoms | Divest stake in competitor |
| 01.12# | M.1601 – *Allied Signal/Honeywell* | II Aircrafts | Divest assets, supply technology |
| 01.12 | M.1578 – *Sanitec/Sphinx* | II Bathroom prod | Divest business |
| 22.11 | M.1681 – *Akzo Nobel/Hoechst Roussel Vet* | I Animal health | Divest assets |
| 28.10# | M.1571 – *New Holland/Case* | I Agriculture | Divest assets, provide access to distribution |
| 13.10 | M.1439 – *Telia/Telenor* | II Telecoms | Divest assets, provide access |
| 29.09# | M.1383 – *Exxon/Mobil* | II Crude oil, gas | Divest assets and stakes |
| 29.09# | M.1532 – *BP Amoca/Arco* | II Oil, gas | Divest stakes |
| 28.09 | M.1557 – *EDF/Louis Dreyfus* | I Electricity | Separate JV from parents' activities |
| 10.09 | M.1621 – *Pakhoed/Van Ommeren* | I Tank storage | Divest assets and stake |
| 09.08*[5] | M.1378 – *Hoechst/Rhône-Poulenc* | I Pharmaceuticals | Divest assets and grant licences |
| 13.07# | M.1517 – *Rhodia/Donau Chemie/Albright & Wilson* | I Chemicals | Toll manufacturing, grant licence |
| 21.05 | M.1430 – *Vodafone/Airtouch* | I Mobile telecom | Divest stake |
| 17.05 | M.1397 – *Sanofi/Synthelabo* | I Pharmaceuticals | Divest assets |
| 26.04# | M.1381 – *Imetal/English China Clays* | I Minerals | Divest assets and stakes |
| 19.04# | M.1467 – *Rohm and Haas/Morton* | I Chemicals | Terminate stake in JV, distribution ban |
| 08.04 | M.1453 – *AXA/GRE* | I Insurance | Reduce stake or divest assets |
| 26.03# | M.1464 – *Total/PetroFina* | I Fuels | Divest assets |
| 09.03 | M.1313 – *Danish Crown/Vestjyske* | II Slaughterhouse | Divest business, assets, provide supply |

[5] 30.01.2004: amendment of decision (replacing a condition).

| Date | Case No and Name | Phase & Sector | Remedies |
|---|---|---|---|
| **1999:** | | | |
| 04.03 | M.1365 – *FCC/Vivendi* | I Waste | Divest assets |
| 26.02# | M.1403 – *Astra/Zeneca* | I Pharmaceuticals | Divest assets, grant licences |
| 04.02 | M.1329 – *Usinor/Cockerill* | I Steel products | Divest assets |
| 03.02 | M.1221 – *Rewe/Meiln* | II Supermarkets | Divest assets |
| **1998:** | | | |
| 16.12# | M.1339 – *ABB/Elsag Bailey* | I Automation | Divest stake and assets |
| 11.12 | M.1293 – *British Petroleum/Amoco* | I Petrochemicals | Divest assets |
| 03.12 | M.1327 – *NC/Canal+/CDPQ/Bank America* | I Pay TV | Non-discrimination provisions |
| 11.11 | M.1157 – *Skanska/Scancem* | II Cement | Divest assets and stake |
| 28.10 | M.1286 – *J & J/Depuy* | I Orthopaedics | Divest assets |
| 28.09 | M.1229 – *American Home Products* | I Pharmaceuticals | Terminate distribution |
| 08.07# | M.1137 – *Exxon/Shell* | I Lubricants | Divest assets |
| 08.07# | M.1069 – *Worldcom/MCI* | II Telecoms/ Internet | Divest assets |
| 30.06 | M.1182 – *Akzo Nobel/Courtaulds* | I Coatings | Divest assets or stake in JV |
| 04.06 | M.1185 – *Alcatel/Thomson CSF-SCS* | I Satellites | Create arbitration body, non-transfers |
| 02.06 | M.1080 – *Thyssen/Krupp* | I Steel products | Reduce influence in competitor |
| 02.06[6] | M.931 – *Neste/IVO* | I Electricity | Reduce stake |
| 08.05 | M.1082 – *Allianz/AGF* | I Insurance | Divest stake, terminate personal links |
| 21.04 | M.1109 – *Owens-Illinois/BTR Packaging* | I Glass container | Divest assets and stakes |
| 11.02 | M.986 – *Agfa-Gevaert/DuPont* | II Offset printing | Terminate supply and distribution |
| 04.02[7] | M.950 – *Hoffmann La Roche/ Boehringer Mannheim* | II Vitro diagnostics | Divest assets, grant licences (technology) |
| **1997:** | | | |
| 18.12+ | M.997 – *Swedish Match/KAV* | I Retail, matches | Supply obligations, non-refusal provision |
| 03.12 | M.942 – *Veba/Degussa* | II Chemicals | Divest stake in JV |
| 18.11 | M.913 – *Siemens/Elektrowatt* | II Payphones | Divest assets |
| 15.10 | M.938 – *Guinness/Grand Met* | II Retail, spirits | Divest assets, stakes, terminate distribution |
| 12.08# | M.833 – *TCCC/Carlsberg* | II Retail, drinks | Divest stakes |
| 30.07# | M.877 – *Boeing/McDonnell Douglas* | II Aircrafts | Separation of target, behavioural |
| 05.06 | M.916 – *Lyonnaise des Eaux/Suez* | I Waste man. | Divest businesses and assets |
| 14.05 | M.856 – *British Telecom/MCI* | II Telecoms | Divest business |

[6] 01.12.2004: amendment of decision (modifying a re-acquisition prohibition).
[7] 03.05.2011: amendment of decision (waiving a condition).

Annex B (*cont.*)

| Date | Case No and Name | Phase & Sector | Remedies |
|---|---|---|---|
| **1997:** | | | |
| 23.04 | M.754 – *Anglo American Corporation/Lonrho* | II Platinum | Divest stake |
| 11.03 | M.873 – *Bank Austria/Creditanstalt* | I Banking | Divest and reduce stakes |
| **1996:** | | | |
| 08.11 | M.843 – *PTT Post/TNT/DG Express* | I Postal services | Provide access, limit cross-subsidising |
| 17.07* | M.553 – *RTL/Veronica/Endemol* | II Media | Change contents of channel, provide access |
| 17.07 | M.737 – *Ciba-Geigy/Sandoz* | II Pharmaceuticals | Grant licence, supply obligations |
| 16.01 | M.623 – *Kimberly-Clark/Scott* | II Retail | Divest assets (including brands) |
| **1995:** | | | |
| 14.11 | M.603 – *Crown Cork & Seal/ CarnaudMetalbox* | II Packaging | Divest assets (mainly plants) |
| 30.10 | M.646 – *Repola/Kymmene* | I Paper | Divest assets |
| 18.10 | M.580 – *ABB/Daimler-Benz* | II Rail technology | Divest business (subsidiary) |
| 20.09 | M.582 – *Orkla/Volvo* | II Retail | Divest assets |
| 20.07 | M.616 – *Swissair/Sabena (II)* | I Airlines | Provide access, terminate cooperation |
| 28.02 | M.555 – *Glaxo/Wellcome* | I Pharmaceuticals | Grant licence (clinical trial products) |
| **1994:** | | | |
| 29.07 | M.442 – *Elf Atochem/Rütgers* | I Chemicals | Severe links to competitor |
| 21.06 | M.430 – *Procter & Gamble/ Schickedanz* | II Retail | Divest assets (mainly brands and plant) |
| 08.06* | M.269 – *Shell/Montecatini (and 24.04.1996)* | II Polyolefins, PP | Separate business, withdraw from JV |
| 15.03 | M.422 – *Unilever France/Ortiz Miko (II)* | I Retail | Divest assets, terminate distribution |
| **1993:** | | | |
| 14.12* | M.308 – *Kali+Salz/MDT/Treuhand* | II Minerals | Exit coop, set up own distribution |
| 04.05 | M.291 – *KNP/Bührmann . . ./VGR* | II Paper | Terminate distribution, divest assets |
| **1992:** | | | |
| 27.11* | M.259 – *British Airways/TAT* | I Airlines | Provide access |
| 05.10* | M.157 – *Air France/Sabena* | I Airlines | Withdraw from routes, provide access |
| 30.09 | M.214 – *DuPont/ICI* | II Nylon fibres | Divest assets |
| 04.09 | M.235 – *Elf Aquitaine Thyssen/ Minol* | I Petrochemicals | Provide access to depots |

| Date | Case No and Name | Phase & Sector | Remedies |
|---|---|---|---|
| 22.07* | M.190 – *Nestlé/Perrier* | II Mineral water | Divest assets |
| 28.04 | M.126 – *Accor/Wagon-Lits* | II Hotels | Divest assets |
| 07.02 + | M.184 – *Grand Metropolitan/ Cinzano* | I Retail, spirits | Terminate distribution |
| **1991:** | | | |
| 20.12 + | M.113 – *Courtaulds/SNIA* | I Fibres | Divest stake |
| 02.12 + | M.102 – *TNT/GD Net* | I Postal services | Reduce exclusive arrange- ments |
| 31.07 | M.12 – *Varta/Bosch* | II Accumulators | Grant licence, cease board representation |
| 29.05 | M.43 – *Magneti Marelli/CEAc* | II Accumulators | Reduce stake |
| 12.04 | M.42 – *Alcatel/Telettra* | II Telecom equip- ment | Acquire competitor's Telettra stake |
| 08.02 | M.9 – *Fiat Geotech/Ford New Holland* | I Tractors | Terminate purchasing arrangements |

# Annex C

TABLE OF THE EU COURT'S JUDGMENTS CONTAINING REMEDIES ASPECTS[1]

(in reverse chronological order)

| Date | Name | Case No | ECR |
|---|---|---|---|
| 06.11.2012 | *Éditions Odile Jacob v Commission*[2] | C-551/10 P | Not yet reported |
| 06.11.2012 | *Commission v Éditions Odile Jacob*[3] | C-553/10 P | Not yet reported |
| | *Commission v Éditions Odile Jacob* | C-554/10 P | Not yet reported |
| 28.06.2012 | *Commission v Éditions Odile Jacob*[4] | C-404/10 P | Not yet reported |
| 12.10.2011 | *Association belge des consommateurs test-achats v Commission* | T-24/10 | Not yet reported |
| 13.09.2010 | *Éditions Jacob v Commission*[5] | T-452/04 | [2010] II-04713 |
| 13.09.2010 | *Éditions Jacob v Commission*[6] | T-279/04 | [2010] II-00185 |
| 06.07.2010 | *Ryanair v Commission* | T-342/07 | [2010] II-03457 |
| 09.06.2010 | *Éditions Jacob v Commission*[7] | T-237/05 | [2010] II-2245 |
| 16.07.2009 | *Commission v Schneider Electric* | C-440/07 P | [2009] I-6413 |
| 19.06.2009 | *Qualcomm v Commission* | T-48/04 | [2009] II-2029 |
| 19.06.2009 | *Socratec v Commission* | T-269/03 | [2009] II-88 |
| 09.09.2008 | *MyTravel v Commission* | T-212/03 | [2008] II-1967 |
| 18.12.2007 | *Cementbouw Handel & Industri v Commission ('Cementbouw II')* | C-202/06 P | [2007] I-12129 |
| 11.07.2007 | *Schneider Electric v Commission* | T-351/03 | [2007] II-2237 |
| 04.07.2006 | *EasyJet v Commission* | T-177/04 | [2006] II-1931 |
| 23.02.2006 | *Cementbouw Handel & Industri v Commission ('Cementbouw I')* | T-282/02 | [2006] II-319 |
| 14.12.2005 | *General Electric v Commission* | T-210/01 | [2005] II-5575 |
| 14.12.2005 | *Honeywell v Commission* | T-209/01 | [2005] II-5527 |
| 21.09.2005 | *EDP v Commission* | T-87/05 | [2005] II-3745 |
| 15.02.2005 | *Commission v Tetra Pak* | C-12/03 P | [2005] I-987 |
| | | C-13/03 P | [2005] I-1113 |
| 28.09.2004 | *MCI v Commission* | T-310/00 | [2004] II-3253 |
| 30.04.2003 | *ARD v Commission* | T-158/00 | [2003] II-3825 |
| 03.04.2003 | *BaByliss v Commission* | T-114/02 | [2003] II-1279 |

[1] As of 1 May 2013.
[2] Appeal of T-279/04 (validity of the conditional clearance decision).
[3] Appeal of T-452/04 (independence of the monitoring trustee).
[4] Appeal of T-237/05 (confidentiality issues).
[5] This appeal related to the Commission's appointment of the monitoring trustee.
[6] This appeal related to the Commission's conditional clearance decision in *Lagardère/Natexis/VUP* (M.2978 II 2004).
[7] This appeal related to confidentiality issues.

Annex C (*cont.*)

| Date | Name | Case No | ECR |
|---|---|---|---|
| 03.04.2003 | *Royal Philips v Commission* | T-119/02 | [2003] II-1433 |
| 03.04.2003 | *Petrolessence and SG2R v Commission* | T-342/00 | [2003] II-1161 |
| 25.10.2002 | *Tetra Laval/Sidel v Commission* | T-5/02 | [2002] II-4381 |
| | | T-80/02 | [2002] II-4519 |
| 22.10.2002 | *Schneider Electric v Commission* | T-310/01 | [2002] II-4071 |
| | | T-77/02 | [2002] II-4201 |
| 06.06.2002 | *Airtours v Commission* | T-342/99 | [2002] II-2585 |
| 22.03.2000 | *Coca-Cola v Commission* | T-125/97 | [2000] II-1733 |
| | | T-127/97 | [2000] II-1733 |
| 15.12.1999 | *Kesko v Commission* | T-22/97 | [1999] II-3775 |
| 28.04.1999 | *Endemol v Commission* | T-221/95 | [1999] II-1299 |
| 25.03.1999 | *Gencor v Commission* | T-102/96 | [1999] II-753 |
| 31.03.1998 | *France and Others v Commission* | C-68/94 | [1998] I-1375 |
| | | C-30/95 | [1998] I-1375 |
| 27.11.1997 | *Kaysersberg v Commission* | T-290/94 | [1997] II-2137 |
| 27.04.1995 | *CCE Grandes Sources and Others v Commission* | T-96/92 | [1995] II-1213 |
| | *CCE Vittel and Others v Commission* | T-12/93 | [1995] II-1247 |
| 19.05.1994 | *Air France v Commission ('Air France I')* | T-3/92 | [1994] II-323 |
| 24.03.1994 | *Air France v Commission ('Air France II')* | T-3/93 | [1994] II-121 |

# *Bibliography*

**Bibliographical note:** The Bibliography is divided into three sections. First, books, chapters in books and journal articles which have been cited in the notes simply by author name and date, or author in author name and date, are listed in a single alphabetical sequence. References cited in the notes as 'Papers by . . .' or 'Study by . . .' or 'Report by . . .' are listed in a section headed Reports, Studies and Working Papers. References cited in notes as 'Speech by . . .' are listed in the final section of the Bibliography headed Speeches.

## BOOKS, CHAPTERS IN BOOKS AND JOURNAL ARTICLES


**Albers and Jourdan (2011):** Michael Albers and Jérémie Jourdan, 'The Role of Hearing Officers in EU Competition Proceedings: A Historical and Practical Perspective' (2011) 2(3) *Journal of European Competition Law and Practice* 185–200.

**Albers and Williams (2010):** Michael Albers and Karen Williams, 'Oral Hearings: Neither a Trial, Nor a State of Play Meeting' (March 2010) *Competition Policy International.*

**Baer and Redcay (2001):** WJ Baer and RC Redcay, 'Solving Competition Problems in Merger Control: The Requirements for an Effective Divestiture Remedy' (2001) 69 *George Washington Law Review* 1701–12.

**Baer, Feinstein and Meisner (2004):** William J. Baer, Deborah L. Feinstein and Matthew D. Meisner, 'Fixing the Problem: Recent Developments in US Merger Remedies' (2004) *The Antitrust Review of the Americas, Global Competition Review* 50–53.

**Baylis (2001):** Neil Baylis, 'The Commission's Notice on Remedies' (April/May 2001) *Global Competition Review,* 25.

**Bellamy and Child (2008):** Christopher Bellamy and Graham D. Child, *Bellamy and Child: European Community Law of Competition,* 6th edn, edited by Peter Roth and Vivien Rose, Oxford University Press, 2008.

**Bishop and Walker (2010):** Simon Bishop and Mike Walker, *The Economics of EC Competition Law: Concepts, Application and Measurement,* 3rd edn, Sweet & Maxwell, 2010.

**Blanc and Brueckner (2009):** Francois Blanc and Jonas S Brueckner, 'Claude Rakovsky: EC Merger Remedies' (2009) (1) *Concurrences* art No 23236, www.concurrences.com.

**Blanke (2007):** Gordon Blanke, 'The Use of Arbitration in EC Merger Control: Latest Developments' (2007) 28(12) *European Competition Law Review* 673–94.

**Blanke (2006a):** Gordon Blanke, 'International Arbitration in EC Merger Control: A "Supranational" Lesson to be Learnt' (2006) 27(6) *European Competition Law Review* 324–37.

**Blanke (2006b):** Gordon Blanke, *The Use and Utility of International Arbitration in EC Commission Merger Remedies,* Europa Law Publishing, 2006.

**Blanke and Landolt (2011):** Gordon Blanke and Phillip Landolt (eds), *EU and US Antitrust Arbitration,* Wolters Kluwer, 2011.

**Blessing (2003):** Marc Blessing, *Arbitrating Antitrust and Merger Control Issues,* Swiss Commercial Law Series (Nedim Peter Vogt, eds), volume 14, Helbing & Lichtenhahn, 2003.

**Broberg (1997):** Morten Broberg, 'Commitments in Phase One Merger Proceedings: the Commission's Power to Accept and Enforce Phase One Commitments' (1997) 34 *Common Market Law Review* 845.

**Brueckner and Hoehn (2010):** Jonas S Brueckner and Thomas Hoehn, 'Monitoring Compliance with Merger Remedies: The Role of the Monitoring Trustee' (September 2010) *Competition Law International* 73–80.

**Buhr et al (2010):** Carl-Christian Buhr, Sabine Crome, Adrian Lübbert, Vera Pozzato, Yvonne Simon and Robert Thomas, 'Oracle/Sun Microsystems: The Challenge of Reviewing a Merger Involving Open Source Software' (2010) 2 *Competition Policy Newsletter* 20–27.

**Christiansen (2008):** Arndt Christiansen, 'Publication Review – Mergers and Merger Remedies in the EU: Assessing the Consequences for Competition by Stephen Davies and Bruce Lyons' (2008) 29(8) *European Competition Law Review* 493–94.

**Cook and Kerse (2009):** John Cook and Christopher Kerse, *E.C. Merger Control*, 5th edn, Sweet & Maxwell, 2009.

**Cosnita and Tropeano (2009):** Andrea Cosnita and Jean-Phillippe Tropeano, 'Negotiating Remedies: Revealing the Merger Efficiency Gains' (2009) 27 *International Journal of Industrial Organization* 188–96.

**Davidson (2006):** Kenneth Davidson, 'The Report on Divestiture Remedies of the US FTC and EU DG Comp' *AAI Commentary* (15 February 2006), available at www.antitrustinstitute.org/files/482.pdf.

**Davidson (2005):** Kenneth Davidson, 'The FTC Monitor Trustee', *AAI Commentary* (19 December 2005), available at www.antitrustinstitute.org/files/473_020920071631.pdf.

**Davies and Lyons (2007):** Stephen Davies and Bruce Lyons, *Mergers and Merger Remedies in the EU: Assessing the Consequences for Competition*, Edward Elgar, 2007.

**Davies and Lyons (2005):** Steve Davies and Bruce Lyons, 'How Simple Simulations Would Improve EC Merger and Remedy Appraisal' (May 2005) 8 *CCP Newsletter* 2–3.

**De Matteis (2001):** Andrea De Matteis, 'The Commission Develops its Policy on Merger Cases: The New Notice on Remedies and its Recent Application' (2001) 4(3) *International Antitrust Bulletin* 21–33.

**De Rivery and Guerard (2005):** Eric Morgan De Rivery and Vincent Guerard, 'Case No COMP/M.3410 – TOTAL/GAZ DE FRANCE: Merger Control as a Tool to Greater Liberalisation in the Gas Sector' (2005) 26(11) *European Competition Law Review* 624–37.

**De Valois Turk (2009):** Maurice de Valois Turk, 'The EC's Revised Remedies Notice: The Trustee's Perspective' (2009) 30(7) *European Competition Law Review* 332–39.

**Dobson (2001):** Paul Dobson, 'Competition and Mergers in Consumer Goods Industries: The Case of Pet Foods' (2001) 22(10) *European Competition Law Review* 443–57.

**Drauz (1996):** Götz Drauz, 'Remedies under the Merger Regulation' (1996) *Fordham Corporation Law Institute* 219.

**Drauz and Jones (2012):** Götz Drauz and Christopher Jones (eds), *EU Competition Law*. Volume II: *Mergers and Acquisitions*, 2nd edn, Claeys & Casteels, 2012.

**Elliott (1999):** G Porter Elliott, 'The Gencor Judgment: Collective Dominance, Remedies and Extraterritoriality under the Merger Regulation' (1999) 24 *European Law Review* 638–52.

**Ersbøll (2001):** Niels Christian Ersbøll, 'Commitments under the Merger Regulation' (2001) 22 (9) *European Competition Law Review* 357–64.

**Ezrachi (2012):** Ariel Ezrachi, *EU Competition Law: An Analytical Guide to the Leading Cases*, 3rd edn, Hart Publishing, 2012.

**Ezrachi and Bernitz (2009):** Ariel Ezrachi and Ulf Bernitz (eds), *Private Labels, Brands, and Competition Policy, The Changing Landscape of Retail Competition*, Oxford University Press, 2009.

**Ezrachi and Gilo (2006):** Ariel Ezrachi and David Gilo, 'EC Competition Law and the Regulation of Passive Investments Among Competitors' (2006) 26(2) *Oxford Journal of Legal Studies* 327–49.

**Faull and Nikpay (2007):** Jonathan Faull and Ali Nikpay (eds), *The EC Law of Competition*, 2nd edn, Oxford University Press, 2007.

**Feinstein, van Kerckhove and Wootton (2008):** Deborah Feinstein, Marleen Van Kerckhove and Barbara Wootton, 'Merger Remedies in the EU and US' (2007/2008) *PLC Cross-border Competition Handbook*, volume 1, available at uk.practicallaw.com/3-378-7788.

**Foer (2001a):** Albert A. Foer, 'Divestiture and the Category Captain: New Considerations in Merger Remedies', *AAI Column* (19 November 2001), available at www.antitrustinstitute.org/node/10508.

**Foer (2001b):** Albert A Foer, 'Towards Guidelines for Merger Remedies' (2001) 52 *Case Western Reserve Law Review* 211–30.

**Galloway (2009):** Jonathan Galloway, 'Convergence in International Merger Control' (2009) 5(2) *The Competition Law Review* 179–92.

**Gilchrist (2001):** Joseph Gilchrist, 'Rights of Defence and the Role of the Hearing Officer in EU Merger Cases' (December 2000/January 2001) 19 *Global Competition Review* 23.

**Greenaway et al (2009):** Sean Greenaway, Erika Jakab, Dag Johansson and Jasmin Kundan, 'Recent Commission Merger Control Decisions in the Pharmaceutical Sector: Sanofi-Aventis/Zentiva and Teva/Barr' (2009) 2 *Commission Competition Policy Newsletter* 64–67.

**Halverson and Ewing (2004):** Hanes Halverson and Kenneth Ewing, 'Recent Developments in EU and US Merger Remedies' (2004) *Global Counsel Competition Law Handbook 2004/2005.*

**Halverson and Telpner (2002):** James T Halverson and Brian J Telpner, 'Divestiture, Disgorgement, and the Doughboy Dispute: Recent Developments in Merger Remedies', *Steptoe & Johnson LLP Newsletter* (10 June 2002), available at www.steptoe.com/assets/attachments/22.pdf.

**Holmes and Turnbull (2002):** Sarah Holmes and Simon Turnbull, 'Remedies in Merger Cases: Recent Developments' (2002) 23(10) *European Competition Law Review* 499–511.

**IBA (2000):** International Bar Association (IBA) in cooperation with the European Commission, *EC Merger Control: Ten Years On*, Papers from the EC Merger Control 10th Anniversary Conference, September 2000, Brussels, printed by IBA, 2000.

**Jones and Sufrin (2011):** Alison Jones and Brenda Sufrin, *EU Competition Law*, 4th edn, Oxford University Press, 2011.

**Josten (2000):** Yvonne Josten, 'Six-week Period in Case of Commitments?' (2000) 23(4) *World Competition* 81–88.

**Karpel (1998):** Amy Ann Karpel, 'The European Commission's Decision on the Boeing-McDonnell Douglas Merger and the Need for Greater US–EU Cooperation in the Merger Field' (1998) 47 *The American University Law Review*1029–69.

**Kijewski et al (2006):** Sandra Kijewski, Enrique Sepulveda Garcia, Kamila Kloc-Evison, Mariusz Hubski and Uli Wienrich (DG Competition), 'Linde/BOC: Concentration in the Industries of Industrial Gases, Specialty Gases and Helium' (2006) 3 *Competition Policy Newsletter* 50–55.

**Knable Gotts (2012):** Ilene Knable Gotts (ed), *The Merger Control Review*, 3rd edn, Law Business Research Ltd, 2012.

**Köpke (2005):** Alexander Köpke, 'Mergers Remedies Study' (2005) 3*Competition Policy Newsletter* 3–5.

**Lebard and Ottenheimer (2008):** Daniel Lebard and Ghislaine Ottenheimer, *L'Affaire: L'Histoire du plus grand scandale financier français*, Éditions du Seuil, 2008.

**Lévêque and Shelanski (2003):** F Lévêque and H Shelanski (eds), *Merger Remedies in American and European Union Competition Law*, Edward Elgar Publishing, 2003.

**Luebking (2007):** Johannes Luebking, 'Revision of the Notice on Merger Remedies' (2007) 2 *Competition Policy Newsletter.*

**MacGregor (2010):** Anne MacGregor, 'The Urge to Merger' (April–June 2010) *MLex Ab Extra* available at www.cadwalader.com.

**Maier-Rigaud and Parplies (2009):** Frank Maier-Rigaud and Kay Parplies, 'EU Merger Control Five Years after the Introduction of the SIEC Test: What Explains the Drop in Enforcement Activity?' (2009) 30(11) *European Competition Law Review* 565–79.

**Marsden (2006):** Philip Marsden (ed), *Handbook of Research in Trans-Atlantic Antitrust*, Edward Elgar Publishing, 2006.

**Marsden, Hutchings and Whelan (2007):** Philip Marsden, Michael Hutchings and Peter Whelan (eds), *Current Competition Law*, volume V, British Institute of International and Comparative Law, 2007.

**Moavero Milanesi and Winterstein (2002):** Enzo Moavero Milanesi and Alexander Winterstein, 'Minority Shareholdings, Interlocking Directorships and the EC Competition Rules: Recent Commission Practice' (2002) 1 *Commission's Competition Newsletter* 15–18.

**Morgan (2002):** Eleanor Morgan, 'Steering Mergers through the EU's Regulatory Rocks: Remedies under the EU Merger Control Regulation' (2002) 20(5) *European Management Journal* 549–61.

**Motta (2004):** Massimo Motta, *Competition Policy, Theory and Practice*, Cambridge University Press, 2004.

**Neven, Nuttall and Seabright (1993):** Damien J Neven, Robin Nuttall and Paul Seabright, *Merger in Daylight: The Economics and Politics of European Merger Control*, Centre for Economics Policy Research, 1993

**Niels, Jenkins and Kavanagh (2011):** Gunnar Niels, Helen Jenkins and James Kavanagh, *Economics for Competition Lawyers*, Oxford University Press, 2011.

**Paas (2006):** Katri Paas, 'Non-structural Remedies in EU Merger Control' (2006) 27(5) *European Competition Law Review* 209–16.

**Papadopoulos (2010):** Anestis S Papadopoulos, *The International Dimension of EU Competition Law and Policy*, Cambridge University Press, 2010.

**Papandropoulos and Tajana (2006):** Penelope Papandropoulos and Alessandro Tajana, 'The Merger Remedies Study: In Divestiture We Trust?' (2006) 27(8) *European Competition Law Review* 443–54.

**Parker and Balto (2000):** Richard G. Parker and David A. Balto, 'The Evolving Approach to Merger Remedies' (May 2000) *Antitrust Report*.

**Petit (2010):** Nicolas Petit, 'Remedies for Coordinated Effects under the EU Merger Regulation' (2010) 6(2) *Competition Law International*.

**Röller and Buigues (2005):** Lars-Hendrik Röller and Pierre A Buigues, 'The Office of the Chief Competition Economist at the European Commission' (May 2005), available at ec.europa.eu/dgs/competition.

**Russo et al (2010):** Francesco Russo, Maarten Pieter Schinkel, Andrea Günster and Martin Carree, *European Commission Decisions on Competition: Economic Perspectives on Landmark Antitrust and Merger Cases*, Cambridge University Press, 2010.

**Shapiro and Sohn (1997):** Carlos Shapiro and Michael Sohn, 'Crown-Jewel Provisions in Merger Consent Decrees' (1997: Fall) *Antitrust Magazine* 27–32.

**Snel and De Valois Turk (2009):** Jan Jaap Snel and Maurice de Valois Turk, 'EU Divestiture Remedies No Waiver for Merger Control' *Finance Week Newsletter* (21 January 2009), available at www.duffandphelps.com.

**Sorinas and Jorns (2009):** Sergio Sorinas and Christine Jorns, 'European Union: EU Merger Remedies', IFLR, 1 October 2009, available at www.iflr.com/Article/2324298/European-Union-EU-merger-remedies.html.

**Stennek (2006):** Johan Stennek, 'A New Perspective on Mergers and Acquisitions: Evidence Explained, Policies Prescribed' (2006) 1 *CESifo Forum* 3–8.

**Tajana (2006a):** Alessandro Tajana, 'EC Mergers: Wall Building Materials – Conditional Approval – Appeal' (2006) 27(9) *European Competition Law Review* 157–58.

**Tajana (2006b):** Alessandro Tajana, 'European Union: Merger Remedies Study Published by the European Commission' (2006) 12(3) *International Trade Law & Regulation* 26–27.

**Van Bael (2011):** Ivo Van Bael, *Due Process in EU Competition Proceedings*, Wolters Kluwer, 2011.

**Van Kerckhove (2006):** Marleen Van Kerckhove, 'The EU Remedies Study: Toward Further Transatlantic Convergence in Merger Remedies?' (2006) 21 *Antitrust* 66–73.

**Vassileff (2010):** Antoni Vassileff, 'A Question of Commitment' (2010) 2 *MLex Magazine* 52–55.

**Voigt and Schmidt (2010):** Stefan Voigt and André Schmidt, *Making European Merger Policy More Predictable*, Springer, 2010.

**Ward (2006):** Philippa Ward, 'Merger Remedies: An Interview with DG Comp' (April 2006) *Global Competition Review* 26–28.

**Went (2006):** David Went, 'The Acceptability of Remedies under the EC Merger Regulation: Structural versus Behavioural' (2006) 27(8) *European Competition Law Review* 455–75.

**Whish and Bailey (2012):** Richard Whish and David Bailey, *Competition Law*, 7th edn, Oxford University Press, 2012.

**Wils (2012a):** Wouter PJ Wils, 'The Role of the Hearing Officer in Competition Proceedings before the European Commission' (2012) 35(3) *World Competition* 431–56.

**Wils (2012b):** Wouter PJ Wils, 'The Oral Hearing in Competition Proceedings before the European Commission' (2012) 35(3) *World Competition* 397–430.

**Ysewyn (2002):** Johan Ysewyn, 'The New World of the Merger Task Force' (2002) 23(5) *European Competition Law Review* 207–9.

**Ysewyn (2001):** Johan Ysewyn, 'The Commission's Commitment' (2001) 22(7) *European Competition Law Review* 253–55.

## REPORTS, STUDIES AND WORKING PAPERS[1]

**Bougette and Turolla (2006):** Patrice Bougette and Stéphane Turolla, *Merger Remedies at the European Commission: A Multinomial Logit Analysis*, Working Paper (preliminary version for EARIE 2006, Amsterdam), University of Montpellier, France, DR No 2006-08, available at www.lameta.univ-montp1.fr/Documents/DR2006-08.pdf.

**Cosnita and Tropeano (2006):** Andreea Cosnita and Jean-Philippe Tropeano, *Negotiating Remedies: Revealing the Merger Efficiency Gains*, Working Paper GAEL 2008–05, Laboratoire d'Économie Appliquée de Grenoble, available at www.grenoble.inra.fr/Docs/pub/A2008/gael2008-05.pdf.

**Cosnita and Tropeano (2005):** Andreea Cosnita and Jean-Philippe Tropeano, *Screening Divestitures: Structural Merger Remedies with Asymmetric Information*, Working Paper, EUREQua-University Paris I, Maison des Sciences Économiques, February 2005, available at acle.uva.nl/events/competition--regulation-meetings/working-papers-cr-meeting-2005.html.

**Duso, Gugler and Yurtoglu (2006):** Tomaso Duso, Klaus Gugler and Burcin Yurtoglu, *How Effective is European Merger Control*, Discussion Paper No 153, GESY (Govervance and the Efficiency of Economic Systems), July 2006, available at epub.ub.uni-muenchen.de/13398/1/153.pdf.

**Duso, Gugler and Yurtoglu (2005):** Tomaso Duso, Klaus Gugler and Burcin Yurtoglu, *EU Merger Remedies: A Preliminary Empirical Assessment*, Discussion Paper SP II 2005–16, Wissenschaftszentrum Berlin (WZB), September 2005, available at www.cepr.org/meets/wkcn/6/6641/papers/Duso.pdf.

**Garrod and Lyons (2011):** Luke Garrod and Bruce Lyons, *Early Settlement and Errors in Merger Control*, CCP Working Paper 11-5, available at ssrn.com/abstract=1883394.

**Geradin and Petit (2010):** Damien Geradin and Nicolas Petit, *Judicial Review in European Union Competition Law: A Quantitative and Qualitative Assessment*, Preliminary draft published for GCLC's Annual Conference, Brussels, October 2010, available at ssrn.com/abstract=1698342.

**Klein and Wright (2004):** Benjamin Klein and Joshua D Wright, *The Antitrust Law and Economics of Category Management*, George Mason University Law and Economics Research Paper Series 06-38, originally from 2004 and reprinted in 2006, available at www.law.gmu.edu/assets/files/publications/working_papers/06-38.pdf.

**Lear (2006):** Lear (Laboratorio de economia, antitrust, regolamentazione), *Ex-post Review of Merger Control Decisions*, Study for the European Commission, December 2006, available at ec.europa.eu/comm/competition/mergers/studies_reports/lear.pdf.

**Lévêque (2007a):** Francois Lévêque, *Merger Control: More Stringent in Europe than in the United-States?* CERNA Working Paper, Paris, France, November 2007, available at www.cerna.ensmp.fr/Documents/FL-MergerEUvsUS.pdf.

[1] Quoted as 'Study or Paper by [Author] [year]'.

**Lévêque (2007b):** Francois Lévêque, *Are Merger Remedies Effective in the EU?* CERNA Working Paper, Paris, France, February 2007, available at www.microeconomix.eu/files/default/import/FL-WP-MergerRemediesEffectiveness.pdf.

**Lianos (2013):** Ioannis Lianos, *Competition Law Remedies in Europe – Which limits for remedial discretion?* CLES (Centre for Law, Economics and Society) Research Paper Series, January 2013, available at ssrn.com/abstract=2235817.

**Lyons and Medvedev (2007):** Bruce Lyons and Andrei Medvedev, *Bargaining over Remedies in Merger Regulation*, CCP Working Paper 07-3, February 2007, available at papers.ssrn.com/sol3/papers.cfm?abstract_id=970250.

**Medvedev (2004):** Andrei Medvedev, *Structural Remedies in Merger Regulation in a Cournot Framework*, CERGE-EI working paper No 229, Charles University, Prague, Czech Republic, July 2004, available at papers.ssrn.com/sol3/papers.cfm?abstract_id=841225.

**Neven and Röller (2002):** Damien J Neven and Lars-Hendrik Röller, *Discrepancies between Markets and Regulators: An Analysis of the First Ten Years of EU Merger Control*, HEI (Institut Universitaire de Hautes Études Internationales) Working Paper No 10/2002, August 2002, available at graduateinstitute.ch/webdav/site/international_economics/shared/international_economics/publications/working%20papers/2002/HEIWP10–2002.pdf

**OECD (2005):** OECD, Directorate for Financial and Enterprise Affairs, Competition Committee, DAF/COMP/WP3(2005)1, Working Party No 3 on Co-operation and Enforcement, *Cross-border Remedies in Merger Cases* (Issues Paper by the Secretariat).

**OECD (2009):** *Antitrust Issues Involving Minority Shareholding and Interlocking Directorates*, OECD, Directorate for Financial and Enterprise Affairs, Competition Committee, DAF/COMP (2008) 30 (23 June 2009).

**OFT/DotEcon (2010):** Office of Fair Trading (OFT), *Minority Interests in Competitors*, A research report prepared by DotEcon Ltd, OFT1218 (March 2010), available at www.oft.gov.uk/shared_oft/economic_research/oft1218.pdf.

**Ormosi (2011):** Peter L Ormosi, *The Determinants of Merger Litigation Strategies: An Empirical Analysis of EC Mergers*, May 2011, available at ssrn.com/abstract=1532758.

**Tenn and Yun (2009):** Steven Tenn and John M Yun, *The Success of Divestitures in Merger Enforcement: Evidence from the J&J – Pfizer Transaction*, FTC Working Paper No 296, April 2009, available at www.ftc.gov/be/workpapers/wp296.pdf.

**US DoJ ICPAC Report (2000):** US Department of Justice, Antitrust Division, International Competition Policy Advisory Committee (ICPAC), Final Report 2000, Washington.

**Vasconcelos (2006):** Helder Vasconcelos, *Efficiency Gains and Structural Remedies in Merger Control*, Working Paper, IGIER, Università Bocconi, Milan, March 2006.

## SPEECHES[2]

**Almunia (2013):** Joaquín Almunia, 'The Evolutionary Pressure of Globalisation on Competition Control' (ICN 12 Annual Conference, Warsaw, 24 April 2013).

**Almunia (2012a):** Joaquín Almunia, 'The Role of Competition Policy in Times of Crisis' (29th Annual AmCham EU Competition Policy Conference, Brussels, 6 December 2012).

**Almunia (2012b):** Joaquín Almunia, 'Merger Review: Past Evolution and Future Prospects' (Conference on Competition Policy, Law and Economics, Cernobbio, Italy, 2 November 2012).

**Almunia (2011a):** Joaquín Almunia, 'Competition – What's in it for Consumers?' (European Competition and Consumer Day, Poznan, 24 November 2011).

[2] Quoted as "Speech by [author] [year]".

**Almunia (2011b):** Joaquín Almunia, 'Policy Objectives in Merger Control' (Fordham Competition Conference, New York, 8 September 2011).

**Almunia (2011c):** Joaquín Almunia, 'Improving Europe's Competitiveness in the Global Economy' (Annual British/American Business Conference, London, 28 June 2011).

**Almunia (2011d):** Joaquín Almunia, 'Fair Process in EU Competition Enforcement' (European Competition Day, Budapest, 30 May 2011).

**Almunia (2011e):** Joaquín Almunia, 'EU Merger Control Has Come of Age' (Merger Regulation in the EU after 20 years, co-presented by the IBA Antitrust Committee and the European Commission, Brussels, 10 March 2011).

**Almunia (2010a):** Joaquín Almunia, 'Due Process and Competition Enforcement' (IBA – 14th Annual Competition Conference, Florence, 17 September 2010).

**Almunia (2010b):** Joaquín Almunia, 'EU Antitrust Policy: The Road Ahead' (International Forum on EU Competition Law, Brussels, 9 March 2010, IP/10/81).

**Collins (2002):** Philip G.H. Collins, 'Recent Developments and Innovations in the Commission's Approach to Remedies and Commitments' (British Institute of International and Comparative Law, Second Annual Conference on International and Comparative Law, London, May 2002)

**Italianer (2012):** Alexander Italianer, 'Legal Certainty, Proportionality, Effectiveness: The Commission's Practice ON Remedies' (Charles River Associates Annual Conference, Brussels, 5 December 2012).

**Italianer (2011):** Alexander Italianer, 'EU Priorities and Competition Enforcement' (Institute for European and International Affairs, Dublin, 25 March 2011).

**Italianer (2010):** Alexander Italianer, 'Safeguarding Due Process in Antitrust Proceedings' (Fordham Competition Law Institute, Annual Conference on International Antitrust Law and Policy, Session on 'Enforcers' Perspectives on International Antitrust', 23 September 2010).

**Kovacic (2008):** William E. Kovacic, FTC, 'Rating the Competition Agencies: What is Good Performance?' (CBA Competition Law Conference, Gatineau, 18 September 2008).

**Leibowitz (2009):** Jon Leibowitz, 'Introduction of Philip Lowe and Announcement of Joint FTC/DOJ Project to Modernise the Horizontal Merger Guidelines' (The Third Annual Georgetown Law Global Antitrust Enforcement Symposium, 22 September 2009).

**Lévêque (2002):** Francois Lévêque, 'A Merger Control Authority's Preference for Divestiture' (Guidelines for Merger Remedies: Prospects and Principles, Ecole des Mines de Paris, 17–18 January 2002).

**Luebking (2007):** Johannes Luebking (European Commission), 'The New EU Merger Remedies Policy' (BIICL Conference, London, 16 November 2007).

**Mederer (2001):** Wolfgang Mederer, 'Remedies in Merger Cases', (IBA's Fifth Annual Competition Conference, Florence, 21 September 2001).

**Monti (2004):** Mario Monti, 'Private Litigation as a Key Complement to Public Enforcement of Competition Rules and the First Conclusions on the Implementation of the New Merger Regulation' (IBA 8th Annual Competition Conference, Fiesole, 17 September 2004).

**Monti (2002a):** Mario Monti, 'Merger Control in the European Union: A Radical Reform' (European Commission/IBA Conference on EU Merger Control, Brussels, 7 November 2002).

**Monti (2002b):** Mario Monti, 'The Commission Notice on Merger Remedies: One Year After' (CERNE – Centre d'économie industrielle, Ecole Nationale Supérieure de mines – Paris, 18 January 2002).

**Monti (2001):** Mario Monti, 'Antitrust in the US and Europe: A History of Convergence' (General Counsel Roundtable – ABA, Washington DC, 14 November 2001).

**Pitofsky (2000):** Robert Pitofsky, 'The Nature and Limits of Restructuring in Merger Review' (The Cutting Edge Antitrust Conference, New York, 17 February 2000).

**Platt Majoras (2006):** Deborah Platt Majoras, 'Reforms to the Merger Review Process' (16 February 2006).

**Platt Majoras (2002a):** Deborah Platt Majoras, 'Antitrust remedies in the United States: adhering to sound principles in a multi-faceted scheme' (Canadian Bar Association, 2002 Annual Fall Conference on Competition Law, Canada, 4 October 2002).

**Platt Majoras (2002b):** Deborah Platt Majoras, 'Houston, We Have a Competition Problem: How Can We Remedy It?'(The Houston Bar Assocation, Antitrust and Trade Regulation Section, Houston, Texas, 17 April 2002).

**Rosch (2009):** J Thomas Rosch, 'Terra Incognita: Vertical and Conglomerate Merger and Interlocking Directorate Law Enforcement in the United States' (Remarks before the University of Hong Kong, 11 September 2009).

**Rowe (2007):** Michael Rowe (Slaughter and May), 'The New EU Merger Remedies Policy' (College of Europe, Global Competition Law Centre, Brussels, 29 June 2007).

**Samuel (2008):** Graeme Samuel (Chairman of the Australian Competition & Consumer Commission (ACCC)), 'Changing Regulatory Structures' (Australian M&A Forum, Sydney, 21 August 2008).

# Index

**accelerated procedure, proposal for** 199
**acceleration phase** 5, 9–11
**access to documents** 184, 196
**access remedies** 44–5, 57–8, 110, 153, 157
**accountability** 195
**ad hoc approach** 7–8
**additional assets** 108–9, 153–4, 194
**additional remedies provisions** 72–3
**adequacy of remedies** 2, 29–30, 35, 54, 56–63, 66, 72, 195–6
**administrative letters** 128, 163, 166, 177, 181
**adoption of remedies** 70–8
**Advisory Committee on Concentrations** 53, 64–8, 197
**aftermath** *see* **post-closing/aftermath**
**alternative commitments/crown jewel provisions** 20, 80, 111–13, 116–22, 194
**ancillary tools** 80, 108–22
**annulment decisions** 2–3, 59, 78, 132–3, 183–5
**appeals** 15, 180–4, 192
**approval**
  purchasers 164–7, 169–70
  regulatory approvals, obtaining 107
  trustees 13, 71, 127–31, 184–5, 200
**arbitration** 4, 14, 23–4
**Arbitration and Competition Review (OECD)** 23–4
**assessments** 54–9
  access remedies 57–8
  additional assets 108
  adequacy of remedies 54, 56–7
  adoption of remedies 71–2
  classification of remedies 43–4
  conditional clearance decisions 55, 56–7
  criteria 39–40
  crown jewels 120
  effective competition, restoration of 54
  elimination of competition concerns 54–7
  ex-post assessments 13
  fix-it-first solutions 114
  foreclosure 54
  implementation 55, 57–8
  individual/selected assets, divestiture of 85
  modification of remedies 39, 54–9
  phase I proceedings 48–9, 58, 198
  phase II proceedings 58
  post-clearance, commitments to modify 54–9
  price gaps 59
  Remedies Notice 39–40
  suitable purchasers 101, 164–5
  suitable trustees 130–6
  up-front buyer solutions 111
  viability 189
**Australian Competition and Consumer Commission (ACCC)** 199
**banking sector** 12–13
**behavioural remedies** 14, 20, 23–4, 43–5, 75–6
**benchmarking** 35, 211
**bilateral agreements** 206–7, 209–10
**Best Practice Remedies Guidelines (Commission)** 10, 14, 18–21, 96, 155–6, 208 *see also* **Model Texts**
**board of directors, replacement of** 141
**brands** *see* **re-branding licences**
**breach of remedies** 176–80, 200–1
**burden of proof** 36, 164, 174, 187, 203, 212
**business divisions** 81, 82
**business plans** 145, 164–5
**business secrets** 8, 78, 126, 147–8, 192

**carve-outs**
  assessments 56
  business secrets 83–4
  definition 83
  divestiture 80, 83–4, 110
  fix-it-first solutions 113
  hold-separate measures 146–7
  implementation 84
  number of cases 84
  reverse carve-out options 83–4
  stand-alone entities 83
  transfer and closing 169
  up-front buyer solutions 83, 110
  viability 80, 188
**certainty** 32, 57–8, 71, 75, 78, 87, 190, 193, 211
**challenging decisions** 180–5
**Chief Competition Economist, appointment of** 11, 22
**chronological overview of policy** 7–16
**citations** 5–6
**classification of remedies** 43–5
**closing sales** 169–70
**collective dominance (co-ordinated effects)** 37
**College of Commissioners** 77, 163, 197
**collusion (coordinated effects)** 94
**Commissioners** 77, 163, 197
**commitments, proposal of** 38–40
**communication**
  administrative letters 128, 163, 166, 177, 181
  College of Commissioners 77, 163, 197
  Commissioners 77, 163, 197
  delegation 163
  divestiture 163–4
  formal decisions 163
  identification of competition concerns 37
  interpretation 181
  modification of conditions or obligations 163
  oral presentations 37, 62, 64, 105, 195–6
  review decisions 163

**communication** (*cont*):
suitability of purchasers 164, 166
writing 37, 61, 64, 165, 195
**compatibility, assessment of** 35–7
**competition harm** 25, 28–9, 80, 112, 157, 214
**complaisance remedies** 64
**completion of the sale** 164–70
**complexity** 2, 4, 6, 9, 35, 48, 58–9, 145–7, 186–7, 198, 214
**conditional clearance decisions**
annulment actions 2–3, 59, 78, 132–3, 183–5
assessments 55, 56–7
breach of remedies 176–9
challenging decisions 180–5
divestiture periods 123–6
enforcement 31, 213–14
fix-it-first solutions 113–15
hold-separate measures 147
identification of competition concerns 35
independence of trustees 132–4
individual/selected assets, divestiture of 85
interim preservation 144
monitoring trustees 200
new competition concerns 106
publication 78
reviews 153–4
revocation 80
sale, putting the business up for 149
'take note commitments' 73–7
time limits 114–15
transparency 191–2
trustees, role and function of 129–30
**conditions** *see also* **conditional clearance decisions**
adoption of remedies 70–3
breach of remedies 176
clarification 187
Merger Regulation 16
modifications 163
monitoring 73, 202
policy 71–5
re-acquisition prohibitions 174–5
re-branding licences 90
**confidentiality**
business secrets 8, 78, 126, 147–8, 192
crown jewels 119–20
declarations 61–2, 190–1
divestiture periods 123–4, 126
international cooperation 69, 207
market test 61–2
non-confidential versions 46–7, 61, 68, 78, 191, 196, 202
preservation measures 145
price setting 152
retaliation 61–2
ring-fencing 147–8
submission of remedies 46–7
transparency 190–1, 194
trustees, role and function of 19, 130
**conflicts of interest** 19, 130–4, 138, 149
**consistency** 10, 18, 70, 186
**consolidation phase** 5, 11–13
**consultation on remedies** 17, 51, 59–70, 114–15, 197, 211
**consumer welfare** 28–9, 214
**cooperation** *see* **international cooperation**
**costs** 84, 88, 114, 127–8, 198–9, 211
**Court of Justice, table of judgments of** Annex C
**Cross-Border Merger Review (OECD)** 24
**crown jewel provisions/alternative commitments** 20, 80, 111–13, 116–22, 194

**damages** 134, 184
**deadlines** *see* **time limits**
**decentralisation** 10
**decisional errors** 31–2, 59, 134, 168, 214
type 1 errors (excessive or over-fixing remedies) 29–30, 214
type 2 errors (insufficient or under-fixing remedies) 29–30
**decision-making tasks of trustees** 140–1
**degradation of assets** 57, 83, 143
**delay**
crown jewels 119
fix-it-first solutions 122
Form RM 203
implementation 81, 101–2, 106–7, 111–12, 168
international cooperation 208–9
suitable purchasers 101–2, 106–7
transparency 191–2
trustees, role and function of 130, 139
**delegation** 163, 199–200
**Department of Justice (DoJ) (US)** 16, 20–1, 68–9, 109, 119–20, 193, 207–10
**deregulation** 9
**design of remedies** 7–8, 18, 22–7, 40, 79–80, 211
**DG Competition Remedies Study** *see* **Remedies Study (DG Competition)**
**direct and individual concern** 182–3
**directors, replacement of** 141
**dirty tricks** 150
**dispute resolution mechanisms** 88 *see also* **arbitration**
**divestiture** 79–122 *see also* **divestiture periods**
additional assets 108–9, 153–4
ancillary tools 80, 108–22
approval of purchasers 164–7, 169–70
assessments 54–7, 69
carve-outs 80, 83–4, 110
challenging decisions 184
classification of remedies 44–5
communication, means of 163–4
crown jewels/alternative remedies 80, 111–13, 116–22
degradation of assets 57, 143
enforcement 30, 32–3
extension of time limits 48, 51–4, 123, 125, 153, 155–7
fix-it-first solutions 80, 113–15, 121–2, 143
Form RM 13, 46
hold-separate measures 147
ICN Remedies Review Project 25
incentives 32–3, 110, 143–4
individual/selected assets 80, 84–6
learning phase 7–8

licence arrangements 80, 86–93
minority shareholdings 94–9, 121
Model Texts 3, 18–21, 202–3
modification of remedies 154–7
monitoring 139–41, 201
preservation 144–5
process 149–64
purchasers 23, 80, 101–8, 168
re-acquisition prohibitions 173–4
re-branding licences 88–93
Remedies Study 22–3
sale, putting the business up for 149–51, 153
severance of links with competitors 93–101
stand-alone entities 80, 81–3, 86
time limits 155–7
trustees, role of 19, 137–9, 142–4, 148, 194
types of structural remedies 81–101
United States 20, 22–3, 143–4
up-front buyer solutions 109–13, 121–2, 143
viability 18, 79–81, 85, 90, 92–4, 108–23, 188–9
waivers, requests for 157–62
**divestiture periods** 123–7, 187
commencement of period 124
confidentiality 123–4, 126, 194
duration 123–5, 142, 155
extension of period 123, 125, 155–7
implementation 123–7
joint ventures, exit from 125
long periods 123
Remedies Study 125–6
sale, putting the business up for 149
short periods 123–5, 142, 155
trustees, role and function of 124, 142–3
United States 123–4, 126
**DoJ (Department of Justice)** (US) 16, 20–1, 68–9, 109, 119–20, 193, 207–10
**dominance test** 37
**dual-roles** 131–3
**due diligence** 123, 149–51
**due process** 195, 211–12

**econometric working papers and studies** 13, 22, 26 7
**effectiveness**
classification of remedies 45
communication, means of 163
consultation 17
ICN Remedies Review Project 25
market test 59–60
Model Texts 19
OECD Remedies Study 23–4
price setting 152
re-acquisition prohibitions 173, 175
sale, putting the business up for 150
structural remedies 24
technology licensing 86
transfer and closing 169
trustees, role and function of 130
viability 79
waivers 158
**efficiency** 18, 186–7, 214
**employee representatives** 59, 165
**enforcement**
breach of remedies 178
conditional clearance decisions 31, 213–14
consolidation phase 11
consumer welfare 28–9
decisional errors 31–2, 214
divestiture 30, 32–3
Enforcement Unit 10, 201
excessive remedies 29–31, 214
ex-post analysis 15–16, 213
ICN Remedies Review Project 25
Merger Regulation 28–30
merging parties 32–3
monitoring 200–2
objectives 5, 28–9
policy 1, 4–5, 28–34, 74–5, 178, 200–1, 213–14
proportionality 31–2, 213–14
re-branding licences 92
re-evaluation phase 15–16
remedies toolbox 186
resources 31–2
restructuring 28
reversibility, lack of 31, 214
technology licensing 88
third parties 33–4
transparency 32–4
viability 30–1
**essential procedural requirements** 184
**European Ombudsman (EO)** 196
**exceptional circumstances** 51–2, 94, 153, 157–8, 162
**excessive remedies** 2, 15, 29–31, 188–9, 214
**exclusion of assets** 166
**exclusive licences** 87–9, 90
**expertise** 101, 104–5, 135–6, 151, 186
**ex-post reviews** 13, 15, 21–2, 26, 205–6, 213
**extension of divestiture deadlines** 48, 51–4, 123, 125, 153, 155–7

**Federal Trade Commission (FTC)** (US)
additional assets 109
consultation 68–9
crown jewels 117–20
Divestiture Study 22–3
DoJ 20
FAQ on Remedies 20
guidance 20–1
information, access to 23
international cooperation 16, 207–10
Divestiture Study 22–3
Statement of FTC on Negotiating Merger Remedies 20
transparency 193
trustees, role and function of 128–9
up-front buyer solutions 110–11, 113
waivers 160
**financial sanctions** 177–9, 200–1
**fire sales** 33–4, 112, 123, 126, 142, 144, 152
**fix-it-first solutions** 143, 186–7
carve-outs 113
conditional clearance decisions 113–15
consultation 114–15
delay 122

**fix-it-first solutions** (*cont*):
divestiture 80, 113–15, 121–2
expertise 105
identification of purchaser 113–15
implementation 113–14
incentives 121
interim measures 115
Merger Regulation 115
modification of remedies 41
monitoring trustees 115, 200
re-branding licences 92
resources 114
technology licensing 87
time limits 115, 122
up-front buyer solutions 121–2
viability 80, 113–15
**flexibility** 10, 50–2, 212
**foreclosure** 44, 54
**Form RM**
Best Practice Remedies Guidelines 19
burden of proof 203
divestiture 13, 46
efficiency 186
Implementing Regulation 17
incentives 203–4
Model Texts 19, 47, 203
phase I proceedings 46
phase II proceedings 50, 53
submission of remedies 46–7
time limits 203–4
**forms** 202–3 *see also* **Form RM**
**French mineral water market, study on** 26
**front loading of products** 145
FTC *see* **Federal Trade Commission (FTC) (US)**

**general principles** 18, 25, 211–12 *see also* **consistency; effectiveness; legal certainty; proportionality; transparency**
**geographic market** 68–9, 82, 90–2, 108–9, 175, 206
**global economic crisis** 12–15
**guidance**
Best Practice Remedies Guidelines 10, 14, 18–21, 96, 155–6, 208
dialogue 187
ex-post evaluations, need for 205–6
fix-it-first solutions 115
informal advice and guidance 45–6
interim preservation 144
Merger Regulation 16–17, 205
policy 16–21, 204
publication 205
re-acquisition prohibitions 174–5
Remedies Notice 17–18, 205
Remedies Study 205-6
remuneration of trustees 138
responsibilities 203–6
severance remedies 101
transparency 191–2
United States 20–1
updates 205
voluntary addition of assets 153–4

**harmonisation of laws** 210
**heard, right to be** 60
**hearing officers** 33, 63, 187, 190, 195–6, 211
**hold-separate measures**
Best Practice Remedies Guidelines 19, 96
carve-outs 146–7
conditions 71
interim preservation 144, 146–7, 148
managers 146–7, 148
minority shareholdings, divestiture of 96, 121
monitoring trustees 140

ICN *see* **International Competition Network (ICN)**
**identification**
competition concerns 35–7
purchasers 110–15, 119, 121, 139–40, 143, 153
specification of assets 19, 70
**impartiality** 211–12
**implementation**
ad hoc approach 7–8
additional assets 109
assessments 55, 57–8
breach of remedies 178–9
carve-outs 84
challenging decisions 180–1
classification of remedies 43–4
conditions and obligations 70
consultation 68
crown jewels 116–17
delay 81, 101–2, 106–7, 111–12, 168
divestiture periods 123–7, 157
efficiency 194
fix-it-first solutions 113–14
Form RM 17, 46
hold-separate measures 147
ICN Remedies Review Project 25–6
Implementing Regulation 13, 17–18, 136, 203
independence of trustees 132
international cooperation 69, 208–9
legal certainty 57–8
minority shareholdings, divestiture of 97
modification of remedies 40–2, 153
monitoring 139–42, 200, 202
post-clearance, commitments to modify 42
price setting 152
Remedies Study 22
severance remedies 94, 101
specialists 186
suitable purchasers 102
technology licensing 86–8
time limits 11, 17
transfer and closing 169
transparency 191–4, 202, 211
trustees, role of 18, 136
up-front buyer solutions 110–13
viability 189
voluntary addition of assets 153–4
waivers 160, 162
**incentives**
approval of purchasers 164–5
crown jewels 117
divestiture 123, 143–4

fix-it-first solutions 121
Form RM 203–4
genuineness 106
independence 102
interim preservation 144
monitoring trustees 200
preservation measures 146
price setting 151
rejection of purchasers 168
retention programmes for key personnel 146
suitable purchasers 101–2, 105–6, 164–5
trustees, role and function of 138, 142
unilateral effects (individual incentives to compete) 94
**indemnities** 19, 142
**independence** *see* **independence of purchasers; independence of trustees**
**independence of purchasers** 101, 102–3
**independence of trustees**
approval by parties 130–1
challenging decisions 184
conflicts of interest 130–4
contractual relationships 131
dual-roles 131–3
large firms, trustees from 131
monitoring role 130–3
remuneration by parties 130–1, 137
third parties, damages claims by 134
trustees, role and function of 127, 130–4, 137
**individual/selected assets, divestiture of** 80, 84–6
**individualism** 204, 212
**information**
asymmetry 31, 203, 214
crown jewels 119–20
effectiveness 175
enforcement 31, 214
Form RM 203
FTC Divestiture Study 23
geographic market 175
Implementing Regulation 17
international cooperation 69, 207–8
Model Texts 176
monitoring 175, 201–2
obligations 175–6
post-closing/aftermath 175–6
precise scope of remedies, information on 149–50
price setting 152
prospectuses or information memoranda 149
Remedies Notice 175
sale, putting the business up for 149–50
severance remedies 94
time limits 155–6, 201–2
viability, on-going links to maintain 175
**intellectual property** 85–7, 89–90, 92, 104, 145
**interim preservation** 144–8
**interim remedies** 115–16, 119, 157, 176, 182
**International Competition Network (ICN)**
international cooperation 206
Remedies Review Project 5, 25–6
**international cooperation**
bilateral agreements 68–70, 206–7, 209–10
confidentiality 69, 207
consultation 68–70
delay 208–9
enforcement 202
enhanced cooperation 15–16
harmonisation of laws 210
information sharing 69, 207–8
non-standard provisions 70
OECD 23–4, 206
parallel proceedings 207, 209–10
policy 206–10
re-evaluation phase 15–16
reviews 208–10
trustees, proposal for joint 209
United States 4, 15–16, 69, 115, 126, 206–10
work sharing arrangements 208

**joint ventures** 22, 44–5, 125
**judicial review** 31, 93–9, 185

**know-how** 90, 104, 145

**learning phase** 3–4, 5, 7–8
**legal certainty** 32, 57–8, 71, 75, 78, 87, 190, 193, 211
**licence arrangements** 86–93
intellectual property 85
re-branding 88–93, 187
technology 86–8
viability 80, 86–93
waivers 158
**limited assets, divestiture of** 80, 84–6
**links with competitors, removal of** 45, 93–101

**market test**
complaisance remedies 64
Confidentiality Declaration 61–2
consultation 59–64
crown jewels 119–20
effectiveness 59–60
employee representatives 59
hearing officers 63
phase I proceedings 60, 195–6
phase II proceedings 60
post-clearance, commitments to modify 59–64
suitability of purchasers 164–5
third parties 59–64, 183–4, 186
time limits 61–2
transparency 60, 190–1
**material influence, re-acquisition of** 173–5
**media**
leaks 190–1
meetings 65
press releases 49, 78, 128, 138, 192, 194
purchaser approval 167
sale, putting business up for 149
sector 13, 44, 86
'take note commitments' 73
transparency 78, 126, 128, 190–2, 194, 202
**meetings** 11, 37, 64–8, 136, 187, 195–7
**Merger Notification and Procedures Implementation Handbook (ICN)** 25–6

**Merger Regulation** *see also* **Remedies Notice**
breach of remedies 176–7
challenging decisions 180
compatibility, assessment of 37
conditions and obligations 16
enforcement 17, 28–30
entry into force 11
fix-it-first solutions 115
guidance 16–17, 205
Implementing Regulation 17
learning phase 7
old Merger Regulation 7
minority shareholdings, divestiture of 96
modification of remedies 40, 42–3, 66
nature of acceptable remedies 16–17
number of cases 11–12
phase I proceedings 16–17, 194–5
phase II proceedings 16–17
policy 1, 5, 16–17
post-clearance, commitments to modify 42–3
Remedies Study 22
review clause 159
suitability of purchasers 165
table of decisions Annex B
time limits 17, 176
trustees, role and function of 17, 136
**Merger Remedies Matrix** 27
**Merger Task Force, abandonment of** 10
**minority shareholdings, divestiture of**
definition of minority shareholding 94–5
hold-separate obligation 96, 121
illegality 93–4
Merger Regulation 95
monitoring trustees 96
pre-emption rights 99
purchaser criterion 97
re-acquisition prohibitions 173
reduction of stake 95, 99
severance remedies 93–9
voting 96–7
waiver 93–4, 100–1
whole stake 95–6, 99
**Model Texts**
acceleration phase 10
Best Practice Remedies Guidelines 14
consistency and efficiency 186
Divestiture Commitments, Model Text on (MTDC) 3, 18–21, 202–3
efficiency 186–7
Form RM 19, 46
guidance 205
information 176
monitoring trustees 140
policy 5, 176
reasons for deviation 47, 203
Remedies Notice 19
transparency 196
Trustee Mandates, Model Text on (MTTM) 3, 18–19, 140, 202–3
updating 19, 205
**modification of remedies**
assessments 39, 54–9
breach of remedies 178
challenging decisions 181
communication, means of 163
design 40
divestiture 154–7
extension of time limits 153
fix-it-first solutions 41
implementation 40–2, 153
Merger Regulation 40, 42–3, 66
monitoring 43, 153
obligations 163, 193–4
post-clearance, commitments to modify 40, 42–78
post-deadline 52–4
pre-clearance modifications 40–2, 75–5
standard review clause 153–4
step-by-step approach 42
submission of remedies 45–54
time limits 40, 65–6
up-front buyer solutions 41
waivers 153, 157–8, 161–2
**monitoring** 199–202 *see also* **monitoring trustees**
adequacy 199–202
breach of remedies 176, 200–1
complexity 58–9
conditions 83, 176, 202
divestiture 125, 201
enforcement 200–2
fix-it-first solutions 115
ICN Remedies Review Project 25–6
information 175, 201–2
international cooperation 202
modification of remedies 43
obligations 176, 202
OECD Remedies Study 23–4
policy 58, 135, 200–1
post-clearance, commitments to modify 43
post-clearance phase 199, 200–1
Remedies Study 22
resources 199–200
structural remedies 44
technology licensing 88
time limits 201–2
transparency 202
trustees, role and function of 127–8, 135–7, 139–42
**monitoring trustees** 127–8, 130–41
approval 200
board, replacing members of 141
challenging decisions 184
contact point, acting as a 140
delegation 199–200
directors, replacement of 141
discharge 139
divestiture 139–41
fix-it-first solutions 200
hold-separate managers 140, 147
identification of purchasers 139–40
implementation 139–42, 200
incentives 200
independence 130–3, 184
interim preservation 144
liaison with Commission 136–7, 187
minority shareholdings, divestiture of 96